READING ABBEY CARTULARIES II

In piam memoriam
F. M. STENTON

READING ABBEY CARTULARIES

British Library Manuscripts:
Egerton 3031, Harley 1708 and Cotton
Vespasian E xxv

edited by

B. R. KEMP

II
Berkshire Documents, Scottish Charters and Miscellaneous Documents

CAMDEN FOURTH SERIES
VOLUME 33

LONDON
OFFICES OF THE ROYAL HISTORICAL SOCIETY
UNIVERSITY COLLEGE LONDON
GOWER STREET WC1E 6BT
1987

© Royal Historical Society

British Library Cataloguing in Publication Data

Reading Abbey cartularies: British Library
   manuscripts—Egerton 3031, Harley 1708 and Cotton
   Vespasian E XXV.—Camden fourth series; v. 33)
2: Berkshire documents, Scottish charters and
   miscellaneous documents
1. Reading Abbey   2. Church lands—England—
   Reading (Berkshire)   3. Cartularies
I. Kemp, B.R.   II. Royal Historical Society
III. British Library. Manuscript. Egerton 3031
IV. British Library. Manuscript. Harley 1708
V. British Library. Manuscript. Cotton Vespasian
E XXV   VI. Series
333.3′22′0942293   BX2596.R/
ISBN 0–86193–112–2

Printed and bound in Great Britain by
Butler & Tanner Ltd, Frome and London

CONTENTS

CORRIGENDA AND ADDENDA TO VOLUME I

p. ix, line 4—for *asservatorium* read *asservatorum*

p. 3, line 30—*for* possibly dating March × May 1194 *read* dating Sept. 1198 × Mar. 1199

p. 4, n. 3, line 4—*for* 1239 *read* 1229 × 38

p. 66, no. 38—*amend date to* [Sept. 1198 × Mar. 1199]; *delete note and substitute:*

> After Roger de St Edmund became archdeacon of Richmond, Mar. × June 1198 (EYC, iv, p. xxv; Landon, *Itin.*, 129), and before the king's death, 6 Apr. 1199; in this period Hubert Walter was in Normandy from mid-Sept. 1198 and is last recorded with the king 11–12 Mar. at Chinon, returning thence to Normandy while Richard went to Limoges (Landon, 134, 144).

p. 73, line 8—for *amd* read *and*

p. 116, line 28—*for* Ricardio *read* Ricardo

p. 122, note to no. 132—*delete second sentence and add:*

> Although the text does not make it clear, the account in fact refers to two William of Englefields. The elder, who paid over the $13\frac{1}{2}$ marks, was still living when John of St Valery was sheriff, 1264–5 (*List of Sheriffs*, 107), but dead by Mar. 1271 (*Cat. Anc. Deeds*, iii. 441, D.306). The younger, his grandson, whose heir [Roger] is here in the bishop's wardship, succeeded by 1277 (BL, Add. Ch. 20253) and was dead by Mar. 1281 (*Cat. Anc. Deeds*, iii. 440, D.298). See also no. 768 n.

p. 138, no. 167, line 10—*for* C f 222r–v *read* C f 222v; F f 78r

p. 159, line 2—for *diocease* read *diocese*

p. 199, line 36—*for* Kirkby *read* Kirby

p. 202, no. 239, Latin text, line 3—*for* ima *read* proxima

p. 205, Latin text, line 6—for *Willielmus* read *Willelmus*

p. 223, no. 266, lines 10–11—*note that for* manifestius *A has* manefestius

pp. 232–3, no. 279—*amend date to* [14 Dec. 1175 × June 1177]; *delete note on p. 233 and substitute:*

> After the consecration of John of Oxford as bishop of Norwich and before the settlement over Cam church (see nos. 284–5); poss. Mar. or May 1176 or Mar. 1177 (Eyton, 200, 202, 211).

p. 250, line 1, and p. 254, line 1—*for* Ivetta *read* Juetta

p. 259, line 8—*for* Iohanne *read* Iohannes

p. 262, no. 325, witness list—*insert a comma after* Linc(olniensi)

p. 307, line 2—*for* 1184 *read* 1173
p. 308, no. 379, line 1—*delete* [?]
p. 311, note to no. 381—*add*:
> Nos. 381–3 may be earlier than Mar. 1207, by which time the abbey had acquired land and rent in Berkhamstead (see no. 165).

p. 344, line 5—*note that* Wanton' *is sic in Ms but rectius* Wauton'
p. 346, line 2—*for* temporo *read* tempore
p. 353, no. 459, Latin text, line 8—*note that* Cicestr' *is sic in Ms but rectius* Cestr'
p. 356, line 9—*for* presetibus *read* presentibus
p. 382, no. 503, line 24—*for* wter *read* water
p. 406, note to no. 536, lines 10–11—*delete* and the Empress *and* 537
p. 416, line 3—*for* Louvain *read* Lower Lorraine
p. 418, textual note *f*—*for* Sutton's *read* Sutton'
p. 456, no. 614, heading, line 1—for *Rivhard* read *Richard*
p. 459, no. 618, line 1, and note, line 1—*for* Ockley *read* Oakley
line 9—*for* Robert *read* Roger
p. 460, note to no. 619a, line 4—*for* 'of Pilerton' *read* 'of Pillerton'
p. 465, no. 627, heading, line 1—for *Huert* read *Hubert*
p. 477, no. 649, heading, line 2—for *her heir* read *his heir*

ABBREVIATIONS

Reading Abbey cartularies and registers are cited as follows:

A   BL, Egerton 3031
B   BL, Harley 1708
C   BL, Cotton Vespasian E xxv
D   BL, Cotton Vespasian E v
E   BL, Cotton Domitian A iii
F   Cambridge University Library, Dd. ix. 38
G   Trowbridge, Wiltshire Record Office, D1/19

NOTE: A complete list of abbreviated references is given in volume I, pp. ix–xvi.

BERKSHIRE DOCUMENTS

ALDWORTH

660 *Quitclaim by Halnoth de Sifrewast to Reading Abbey of the annual crop of two acres of his demesne in Aldworth over which there has been a dispute between them and which the abbey has received for more than forty years by gift of Samson, Halnoth's predecessor, namely, one acre of corn and one acre of maslin* [*c.* 1186 × *c.* 1217; ?*c.* 1193 × 1200]

A f91r; B f75r; C f39v

Sciant presentes et futuri quod ego Hanelath*ᵃ* de Sifrewast, cum controversia inter me et monachos de Rading(ia) verteretur super blado duarum acrarum de dominio meo in Aldewrþa quas prefati monachi de dono Samsonis predecessoris mei habuerunt et perceperunt*ᵇ* per .xl. annos et eo amplius tenuerunt, pro anima mea et patris mei et omnium parentum meorum clamavi eis illas .ii. acras quietas et concessi singulis annis in perpetuum percipiendas de dominio meo eiusdem manerii, scilicet unam acram de frumento et alteram de mestilun. Et ut hec concessio mea rata et firma permaneat, eam presenti carta mea et sigilli mei munimine roboravi.*ᶜ* His testibus.

ᵃ Halenath *B,C*   *ᵇ* Insert et *B,C*
ᶜ B ends with T', *C ends*

Halnoth de Sifrewast held 1 knight's fee of the king in chief in Hampstead Norris, Aldworth and Purley (all Berks.) and died in or before 1217, when he was succeeded . by his son William (*Rot. Lit. Claus.*, i. 347). He already held in the county in 1186–7 and was in possession of 1 knight's fee there in 1190–1 and 1194–5 (*Red Bk. Exch.*, i. 67, 73, 93), although his land was temporarily forfeit to the Crown in 1194 (*Rot. Cur. Reg.*, i. 80), and in 1201 (*Rot. de Ob. et Fin.*, 160). See also *VCH Berks.*, iv. 3, 74. This deed was not entered in the original part of A, but in a similar hand soon afterwards, perhaps *c.* 1193 × 1200. The following deed, no. 661, shows that Samson's original gift to the abbey took place in *c.* 1140.

661 Notification by Simon *de Suwelle*, farmer of the heir of Aldworth (*Aldewrþe*), that, since Reading Abbey has received for more than 100 years the crop of two acres annually, viz., one acre of corn and one acre of maslin, by gift of the lords of Aldworth, lest the abbey should suffer impediment during his farm he has voluntarily bound himself to pay the same or, if the abbey shall prefer, 3s annually to be paid at Reading at Michaelmas. Sealing. Witnesses [omitted]

15 Nov. 1242

B f 75r; C f 39v

Act(um) anno domini M.CC.xlii. apud Rading(iam) in crastino sancti Bricii episcopi [14 Nov.].[1]

In 1239 the then lord of Hampstead Norris and Aldworth, William de Sifrewast, leased the manor of Aldworth to Ralph de Astin and his assigns for 20 years, this being confirmed by the king in August (*Cal. Chart. R.*, i. 245). William died in 1244 (*Cal. Inq. P.M.*, i. 11), when wardship of his heir and land, excluding Aldworth, was granted to Bartholomew Peche (*Excerpta e rot. fin.*, i. 428). Simon de Suwelle's deed thus antedated William de Sifrewast's death, and the reference to 'the heir of Aldworth' was probably made in the belief that William would be dead before the lease expired in 1259, as was indeed the case. It also seems clear that by 1242 Ralph de Astin had passed on his lease of Aldworth to Simon de Suwelle.

1. This is according to the use of Salisbury, to which diocese Berkshire belonged, but the Black Book of the Exchequer dates the feast to 13 Nov.

ARDINGTON

662 *Gift in perpetual farm by Gilbert Basset to Reading Abbey of his demesne meadow at Ardington called* Lankedale *for an annual rent of 20s, for which the abbey shall also have pasture rights for 24 oxen or other beasts in his meadows and those where he has common pasture in the northern part of Ardington at a specified time of the year. For this the abbey has given him 15 marks of silver*
[1193 × 1205; ?c. 1205]

A f 95r; A f 107v; B f 74r–v; C f 39r
Pd. Kennett, *Parochial Antiquities*, i. 183

Sciant presentes et futuri quod ego Gilebertus*a* Basset*b* dedi et concessi pro amore dei et pro salute anime mee et anime patris mei et anime matris mee et Thome filii mei et omnium antecessorum meorum et successorum abbati et monachis de Rading(ia) totum dominicum pratum meum apud Herdetune*c* quod duobus locis continetur et appellatur Lankedale, tenendum de me et*d* heredibus meis ad firmam perpetuam reddendo annuatim mihi et heredibus meis .xx. solidos ad festum sancti Iohannis Baptiste pro omni servitio terreno. Concessi etiam prefato abbati et monachis ut habeant per prenominatum redditum .xxiiii. boves cum dominicis bobus meis in omnibus pratis meis et in omnibus pratis ubicumque communem pasturam habeo vel habere debeo in boreali plaga de Herdetune*c* a die quo totum fenum meum dominicum asportatum fuerit vel secundum oportunitatem temporis asportari poterit usque in diem quo prata ponantur in defensum. Ita ut in quacumque pratorum ex illa parte de Herdetune*e* communi pastura potero warantizare boves meos warantizabo boves abbatis et monachorum de Rading(ia). Quod si abbas et monachi de*f*

Rading(ia) .xxiiii. boves in prenominata pastura vel habere noluerint vel non potuerint, habeant in eadem totidem averia eadem libertate qua et boves eis habere concessi. Ut igitur de hac mea donatione et concessione de me et heredibus meis firmam et perpetuam habeant[g] securitatem et warantum, eam sigilli mei impressione confirmavi. Pro hac itaque concessione dederunt mihi[h] prefatus abbas et monachi .xv.[i] marchas[j] argenti.[k] Hiis testibus:[l] Roberto de Sanfort, Iohanne filio Hugonis, Galf(redo) de Turbevile, Ricardo clerico de Ledec(um)b', Osb(erto) Turpin, Andrea Basset, Reginaldo filio Helie de Ledec(um)b'. Ricardo Franceis de Henrede, Waltero de grava, Ilg(ero) de Chausi, Nicolao filio Petri, Huberto de Anreda, et multis aliis.

[a] Gillebertus *A f 107v*	[b] Basseth *B,C*
[c] Erdetun' *B*, Erdintun' *C*	[d] *Insert de A f 107v*
[e] Erdetune *B*, Erdintune *C*	[f] *Om. in A f 107v*
[g] *Interlined in A f 95r*	[h] michi *C*
[i] .xx. *C*	[j] marcas *B,C*
[k] *B ends with* T', *C ends*	[l] *A f 107v ends*

Gilbert Basset held Ardington from 1180, when his father Thomas died, until his own death in 1205 (*VCH Berks.*, iv. 269; *VCH Oxon.*, vi. 325). Since this deed was not entered in the original section of A, it probably dates not earlier than 1193, but, since the first four witnesses 'and many others' also witnessed no. 663 (q.v.), it may date from shortly before his death.

663 *Confirmation of the same by Richard de Camville and Eustachia his wife*
[prob. *c.* 1206]

A f 99r-v; B f 74r; C f 39r
Pd. (cal.) Kennett, *Parochial Antiquities*, i. 252

Sciant presentes et futuri quod ego Ricardus de Canvill(a)[a] et Eustach(ia) uxor mea concessimus et presenti carta nostra confirmavimus abbati et monachis de Rading(ia) concessionem quam eis fecit Gilbertus[b] Basseth in pratis, in[c] pascuis apud Herdintun(e)[d], videlicet totum dominicum pratum nostrum in eadem villa quod duobus locis continetur et appellatur Langedale, tenendum de nobis et heredibus nostris ad firmam perpetuam reddendo inde annuatim nobis et heredibus nostris viginti solidos ad festum sancti Iohannis Baptiste pro omni servitio terreno. Concessimus etiam prefatis abbati et monachis ut habeant per prenominatum redditum viginti .iiii. boves cum dominicis bobus nostris in omnibus pratis nostris et in omnibus pratis ubicumque communem pasturam habemus vel habere debemus in boreali plaga de Herditun(e)[d] a die quo totum fenum nostrum dominicum asportatum[e] fuerit vel secundum oportunitatem temporis asportari poterit usque in diem quo prata ponantur in defensum. Ita ut in quacumque pratorum ex illa parte de Herditun(e)[d] communi pastura poterimus warantizare boves nostros warantizabimus boves abbatis et monachorum de Rading(ia). Quod si abbas et monachi de Rading(ia) viginti quatuor boves [*f99v*] in prenominata pastura vel habere noluerint*ⁱ* vel non potuerint, habeant in eadem totidem averia eadem libertate qua et boves eis habere concessimus. Ut igitur de hac nostra concessione de nobis et heredibus nostris firmam et perpetuam habeant securitatem et warantum, eam sigillorum nostrorum impressione confirmavimus.*g* Hiis testibus: Roberto de Sanford, Iohanne filio Hugonis, Galfrido de Turberevile, Ricardo clerico de Ledecumbe, et multis aliis.

a Camvill' *B,C*   *b* Gilebertus *B,C*
c et *B,C*   *d* Erdintun' *B,C*
e apportatum *C*
f A has noverint; *correct reading supplied from B,C*
g B ends with T', *C ends*

Richard de Camville married Eustachia, Gilbert Basset's only surviving daughter and heir, to whose inheritance he succeeded in 1206 (*Rot. de Ob. et Fin.*, 348). In view of the similarity between the witness lists of this and no. 662, they cannot be far apart in date, suggesting that this deed was given shortly after Richard acquired possession of Ardington.

BEENHAM

664 Gift in free alms by Walter son of Robert of Padworth (*Pedewrþe*)*a* to Reading Abbey of ½ acre of meadow which he had in *Norþmed'ᵇ* extending in length from the bed of the [River] Kennet (*ab alveo Kenete*) to the arable land of the abbey in Beenham (*Bienham*). To be held free of all exaction, claim, demand and service. Warranty. The donor and his heirs will answer for all foreign service of the said land. Witnesses*c* [omitted]   [13th cent.; not later than 1258]

B f71r; C f36v

a Padewrthe *C*   *b* Northmed' *C*
c Om. in *C*

Dating very uncertain. The deed was not entered in A, but appears in the original section of B.

665 Final concord in the king's court at Reading in the octave of St Martin, 37 Henry III, before Gilbert of Preston (*Prestona*), master Simon of Walton (*Wauton'*), Henry de Colevill (*Colevile*) and Simon of Thrupp (*Trop*), justices-in-eyre, and others, between Robert of the Guildhall (*de la Gydyhall'*), Alviva his wife and Edith sister of Alviva, seeking, and Abbot Richard [I] of Reading, holding, concerning 1 hide of land in Beenham (*Bienham*). Assize of mort d'ancestor, in which the abbot recognized the said land, excluding 5 acres in the field called *Rokesham*, to be the right of Alviva and Edith and returned it to them, to be held by Robert, Alviva and Edith and the heirs of Alviva and Edith of the abbot and his successors and the abbey of Reading in perpetuity by rendering annually 1 mark of silver at Michaelmas and 3 quarters of oats at the Annunciation, by finding each autumn 5 men for 1 day to reap the abbot's and his successors' corn in the vill, at the feeding of the abbot and his successors, and by performing such foreign service as belongs to the land, for all service, custom and exaction. The 5 acres in *Rokesham* shall remain to the abbot and abbey to be held in perpetuity of the chief lord of the fee by the services belonging to them. For this Robert, Alviva and Edith gave the abbot one sore sparrowhawk (*spervarius sorus*)

18 Nov. 1252

B f167r; C ff97v–98r

The foot of this fine is PRO CP 25(1)/8/21/1.

666 Record of the proving of the age of Richard son of William *de la More* of Beenham (*Benham*),[a] taken on Monday the morrow of St Gregory, pope [12 Mar.], 35 Edward I, before Nicholas of Wood-mancote (*Wodemannecote*),[b] steward of Reading. The jurors, William Carter (*le Cartare*), Adam Hood, Richard Carpenter, Thomas *le Sutare*, Robert *Godwy* and Robert White (*le Whyte*), say that the said Richard was more than 22 years old at Christmas, 35 Edward I [25 Dec. 1306]. [Therefore] he had seisin of his land, which the abbot had in custody, and did fealty to the lord.

13 Mar. 1307

B f226v; C f138r

[a] Bienham *C* [b] Wodemancote *C*

BLEWBURY

667 Gift in free alms by Empress Matilda, daughter of King Henry and lady of the English, to Reading Abbey, for the souls of King Henry her father, Queen Matilda her mother and her ancestors, and for the love and lawful service shown to her by Brian fitz Count, of Blewbury, to be held as well and freely and with all liberties as her father held it

[1144 × 47; ?1144]

Original charters: BL Add. Chs. 19579 and 19577[1]
A f15r–v; B f19v
Pd. *Arch. Journ.*, xx. 290; Warner and Ellis, i. no. 22 (with facsimile); *Journ. B.A.A.*, xxxi. 394; *Regesta*, iii. 259 (no. 703); (cal.) Hurry, *Reading Abbey*, 162

Testibus:[a] Roberto comite Gloec(estrie), et Reginaldo comite Cornubie, et Rogero comite Heref(ordie), et Unfrido de Buh(un) dapifero, et Willelmo filio Alani, et Iosco[b] de Dinan, et Walkelino Maminot, et Willelmo Paganell(o), et Willelmo filio[c] Hamonis, Hugone filio Ricardi, et Riulf(o) de Sessun. Apud Divis(as).

Endorsed: 19579 M. imperatricis [*12th cent.*] de Bleberia [*early 13th cent.*]
 19577 Matillidis imperatricis de Bliebiria [*13th cent.*]
Size: 19579 170 × 112 mm
 19577 184 × 147 mm
Seal: 19579 missing; originally on tongue of which only the root survives
 19577 missing; white cords through hole in fold at bottom

[a] *B ends*   [b] *Ioscio Add. Ch. 19577 and A*
[c] *Om. in Add. Ch. 19577 and A*

If genuine (see note 1), after Roger became earl of Hereford, 24 Dec. 1143, and before the death of Robert earl of Gloucester, 31 Oct. 1147; the editors of *Regesta*, iii, suggest 'most probably 1144' in view of the similarity of the witness list to that of *ibid.*, no. 111.

1. 19579 may possibly be genuine, but 19577 is a pretended original probably copied from it (see *Regesta*, iii, no. 703, and cf., *ibid.*, no. 695, note on date). A and B have one text only, but each notes a second copy—*Item alia carta de eodem* (A); *Hec duplex est* (B).

668 Gift in free alms by Henry, son of the duke of Normandy and the count of Anjou, to Reading Abbey, for the souls of King Henry his grandfather, Queen Matilda his grandmother and his ancestors, and for the love and lawful service shown to his mother Empress Matilda and himself by Brian fitz Count, of Blewbury as his mother gave it, to be held as well and freely and with all liberties as his grandfather King Henry held it   [1147 or 1149]

A f 20r; B f 24r
Pd. *Regesta*, iii. 260 (no. 704)

Testibus:[a] avunculo meo Reginaldo comite Cornubie, Patricio comite Wiltescir(e), Iohanne filio Gisleberti, et multis aliis. Apud Divisas.

[a] *B ends*

In reality a confirmation of no. 667, this deed dates from one of Henry's visits to England while his father was still duke of Normandy (*Regesta*, iii, p. xlvi).

669 Gift by King Stephen to Reading Abbey, for the health of his soul and those of Queen Matilda his wife, Eustace his son and his other sons, and for the soul of King Henry his uncle, of his manor of Blewbury; and precept that the abbey shall hold it freely in perpetuity with all free customs with which King Henry and he held it and as the monks hold their other lands [Christmas 1146 × 1147]

Original charter: BL Add. Ch. 19581
Af 18r; Bf 30r–v; Cf 6r–v
Pd. *Arch. Journ.*, xx. 291–2; *Pal. Soc. Facs.*, i. pl. 192 (3) (with facsimile); *Trans. Royal Soc. Lit.*, 2nd ser., xi. 24–5; *Regesta*, iii. 256 (no. 694); (cal.) Hurry, *Reading Abbey*, 162–3

Testibus:*ᵃ* M(athilde) regina uxore mea, et H(enrico) Wint(oniensi) episcopo fratre meo, et Rogero episcopo Cestr(ensi), et H(enrico)*ᵇ* decano de Waltham, et comite E(ustachio) filio meo, et W(illelmo) de Ipra, et W(illelmo) Mart(el), et Ricardo de Luci. Apud Lond(oniam).

Endorsed: Stephani regis [*12th cent.*] de Bleberia [*late 12th × early 13th cent.*]
Size: 225 × 135 mm (left side torn away at bottom)
Seal: fine example of Stephen's second seal in white wax on tongue

ᵃ B,C end
ᵇ For expansion, see Holtzmann, Papsturkunden, i. 253

After Eustace became count of Boulogne and before Roger bishop of Chester left on crusade, to die at Antioch in 1148 (*Regesta*, iii. 256). I am grateful to Dr Rosalind Ransford for help in identifying Henry dean of Waltham. There were two copies of this charter—*Item alia carta de eodem* (A); *Hec duplex est* (B,C). The deed is almost certainly subsequent to the Empress's (no. 667) and, as *Regesta* points out, the two together provide an interesting case of a recipient of royal land obtaining charters from opposing sides in this confused period.

670 Confirmation by Eustace son of the king, count of Boulogne, of the gift by his father, King Stephen, to Reading Abbey of the manor of Blewbury [Christmas 1146 × 1147]

Af 18r; Bf 30v; Cf 6v
Pd. *Regesta*, iii. 256 (no. 694a)

Testibus:*ᵃ* W(illelmo) de Ipra, at Ricardo de Luci, et W(illelmo) Mart(el). Apud Lond(oniam).

ᵃ B,C end

No doubt contemporary with no. 669.

671 *Mandate and precept by King Henry II to the men of Reading Abbey of Blewbury to obey and serve the abbot and monks as do their men of Reading and their other lands* [1156 × 59]

Af 25v; Bf 24r

Henricus rex Anglie et dux Norm(annie) et Aquit(anie) et comes Andeg(avie) omnibus hominibus abbatis et monachorum Rading(ensium) *ᵃ*de Bleoberia,*ᵃ* salutem. Mando vobis et precipio quod in pace et libere et honorifice obediatis et serviatis et rectitudines vestras plenarie faciatis abbati et monachis meis de Rading(ia), sicut homines eorum de Rading(ia) et de aliis terris suis eis melius et plenius et honorificentius obediunt et serviunt. Quod nisi feceritis, precipio quod abbas et monachi vos iusticient per catalla vestra. Et si ipsi vos iusticiare non poterint,[b] iusticia mea vos iusticiet, ut eis obediatis et serviatis sicut dominis vestris. Testibus:[c] domina Imperatrice, et Roberto de Novo Burgo. Apud Rothomagum.

[a-a] *Om. in B, but included in B rubric:* de Bleobir'
[b] potuerint *B*   [c] *B ends*

Robert de Newburgh is no doubt the seneschal of Normandy, who became a monk at Bec shortly before his death in Aug. 1159 (Eyton, 47). The writ dates before this and after Henry's return from England to Normandy in Jan. 1156 (*ibid.*, 16); it may be contemporary with nos. 26-7 above. Van Caenegem notes the writ from B, which lacks witnesses (*Royal Writs*, 240 n. 2).

672   *Final concord in the king's court at Oxford by which Thomas of Sandford recognized that the service of 1 hide of land in Blewbury was the right of Abbot Hugh [II] and the convent of Reading, in return for which the abbot and convent leased the land to him and his heirs for an annual service of 10s, and the abbot took his homage*   5 Feb. 1191

B f167v; C f98r

Hec est finalis concordia facta in curia domini regis apud Oxon-(efordiam) die martis in festo sancte Agathe virginis, anno secundo regni regis Ricardi, coram Godefr(ido)[a] Winton(iensi) episcopo, et Henrico de Cornhill',[b] et Roberto de Witef(eld), et Michaele Belet,[c] et magistro Thoma de Husseburn', et Hugone Pipard', et coram aliis baronibus et fidelibus domini regis ibi tunc presentibus, inter Thomam de Samford'[d] et Hugonem abbatem Rading(ensem) et conventum eiusdem loci et Willelmum monachum predicti abbatis, quem idem abbas et conventus de Rading(ia) posuerunt loco suo in curia domini regis ad lucrandum vel perdendum, de servitio unius hyde terre in Bleobyr',[e] unde placitum fuit inter eos in curia domini regis, et quod servitium predictus abbas et conventus de Rading(ia) clamaverunt sicut ius ecclesie sue.[f] Scilicet quod predictus Thomas de Sanf(ord')[g] recognovit predictum servitium esse ius ecclesie de Rading(ia). Et pro hac recognitione predictus abbas et conventus de Rading(ia) concesserunt eidem Thome de Samf(ord')[g] et heredibus suis totam predictam hydam terre cum pertinentiis in Bleobyr'[h] tenendam de se et successoribus suis et de ecclesia de Rading(ia) per servitium .x. solidorum annuatim pro omni servitio ad duos terminos anni per-solvendorum, videlicet ad Pascha .v. sol' et ad festum sancti Michaelis

.v. sol'. Et inde cepit predictus abbas homagium prefati Thome *de Samford'.[i]

[a] Godfr' *C*	[b] Cornhull' *C*
[c] Bellet' *C*	[d] Stamford' *C*
[e] Bleobur' *C*	[f] *Insert* de Radyng' *C*
[g] Stamf' *C*	[h] Bleobury *C*
[i-i] *Om. in C*	

673 *Recognition by Thomas of Sandford that a tenement in Blewbury is to be held by him and his heirs of Reading Abbey for 10s annually. Accordingly the abbot's plea against him in the king's court has been stayed and Thomas has done homage to the abbot and fealty to the abbey*   [Feb. 1191]

A f39r; B f72v; C f38r

Sciant omnes tam presentes quam futuri quod ego Thomas de Sanford recognovi tenementum de Bleoberia[a] tenendum mihi et heredibus meis de abbatia[b] de Rading(ia) pro decem solidis annuatim reddendis pro omni servitio ad duos terminos, videlicet ad festum sancti Michaelis .v. solidos et ad Pasca[c] .v. solidos. Et per hanc concordiam remansit placitum quod abbas movit contra me in curia domini regis. Et pro predicto tenemento feci homagium meum abbati de Rading(ia) et fidelitatem domui predicte.[d] His testibus: Ricardo de Cardif, Thoma Baiocensi, Iordano Basset, et multis aliis.

[a] Bleoburi *B*, Bleobir' *C*	[b] abbathia *C*
[c] Pascha *B,C*	[d] *B ends with* T', *C ends*

No doubt contemporary with no. 672, although in B and C the text is preceded by a note of a lease by Abbot Hugh of ½ hide (no. 673a) and itself has a rubric implying that it is concerned with that lease.

673a Note of a lease (*concessio*) by Abbot H(ugh) to Thomas of Sandford (*Sanford'*) of half a hide of land in Blewbury (*Bleobir'*)   [?*c.* 1191]

B f72v; C f37v

This appears to relate to the concord in nos. 672–3 (see no. 673 n.), but, if so, 'half a hide' is an error for 'one hide'.

674 Final concord in the king's court at Reading, 3 Henry III on the vigil of the Purification, *coram Ricardo Sar(esburiensi) episcopo, Matheo filio Hereberti,[a] Rad(ulfo) Hareng, Waltero Foliot,[b] Jacobo de Poterna, Waltero de Ripar(iis), Mauricio de Turevill', Johanne de Wikenholt', justic(iariis) itinerantibus, et aliis domini regis fidelibus ibidem tunc presentibus,* between Robert son of Gilbert, seeking, and Abbot Simon and the convent of Reading, holding, concerning 68 acres of land in Grove (*Grave*) [in

Blewbury].[1] Assize of mort d'ancestor. Robert recognized the land to be the right of the abbot and convent and their successors in perpetuity, for which they gave him 10 marks of silver

1 Feb. 1219

B f 168r–v; C ff 98v–99r

[a] Herb' C   [b] Folyot' C

The foot of this fine is PRO CP 25(1)/7/7/31. For discussion, see no. 675 n.

1. See no. 679.

675   Final concord in the court of Simon, abbot of Reading, 3 Henry III on the vigil of the Purification, *coram Waltero Foliot,[a] Johanne de Wikenholt', justic(iariis) itinerantibus missis ad curiam dicti abbatis a domino Ricardo Sar(esburiensi) episcopo, Matheo filio Hereberti, Rad(ulfo) Hareng, Waltero Foliot,[a] Jacobo de Poterna, Waltero de Ripar(iis), Mauricio de Turevill', Johanne de Wikenholt' justic(iariis) itinerantibus in comitatu de Berk(e)syr' ut audirent et viderent quod curia illa unicuique exhiberet iustitiam quam per cartas regum Angl(ie) quas idem abbas porrexit et per libertates ecclesie Rading(ensis), quibus idem abbas et monachi tempore precedenti semper usi sunt, quas etiam abbas Rading(ensis) per iudicium [curie][b] domini regis Johannis et per iudicium baronum de Scaccario aliquando disrationavit, et ideo per iudicium militum de comitatu Berk(e)syr' et de aliis comitatibus ibidem tunc presentium coram eisdem justic(iariis) adiudicata fuit curia predicto abbati,* between Robert son of Gilbert, seeking, and Abbot Simon of Reading, holding, concerning 68 acres of land in Grove (*Grave*). Assize of mort d'ancestor. Robert recognized the land to be the right of the abbot and convent and their successors in perpetuity, remitted all right and claim in the same for himself and his heirs and resigned the land to the abbot and convent, confirming this with an oath in the same court for himself and his heirs. For this the abbot and convent gave him 10 marks of silver   1 Feb. 1219

B f 168v; C f 99r

[a] Folyot' C
[b] *Supplied, as in the full text of nos. 678, 1270 (q.v.)*

This and no. 674 are of great interest in the context of the abbey's liberties in Berkshire. They were levied in the Berkshire eyre of 1219, each on the same day in Reading and each concerned with the same settlement, although the present fine records fuller details. However, while no. 674 was made in the king's court before all itinerant justices and is conventional in every way, no. 675 was made in the abbot's court before only two of the justices, who had been sent by the full bench to supervise proceedings in the abbot's court particularly in respect of the liberties recently restored to the abbey by King John. Those liberties involved the foreign hundred of Reading, later called the hundred of Theale (see nos. 50–52), and were rehearsed and confirmed in the present eyre (no. 53). In the same eyre a similar duplication of fines was made for another case in Blewbury (nos. 677–8), while, for two further cases relating to Windsor, fines in the abbot's court only were levied (nos. 1270, 1272). To all these cases the abbey was itself a party, and, although the places concerned did not form parts of the foreign hundred of Reading, the intention behind the making of the unconventional fines was clearly to underline the abbey's judicial powers in its own lands in the manner in which they had been restored in the foreign hundred. See also Clanchy, *Berks. Eyre of 1248*, xxx–xxxi.

676 Quitclaim by Robert son of Gilbert to Abbot Simon and the convent of Reading of all his right in 68 acres of land in Grove (*Grava*),*ᵃ* *unde ego Robertus in curia domini regis assisam mortis antecessoris super ipsum abbatem aramiavi et de quibus cyrographum factum fuit in curia domini regis H(enrici) filii regis Johannis,* for which quitclaim the abbot and convent have given him 10 marks of silver. Sealing   [*c.* 1 Feb. 1219]

A f99v; B f72r; C f37r–v

*ᵇ*Hiis testibus: domino Ricardo tunc episcopo Sar(esburiensi), Matheo filio Herberti, Rad(ulfo) Hareng, Waltero Foliot, Jacobo de Poterna, Waltero de Ripar(iis), Johanne de Wikenholt, et multis aliis.

ᵃ Grave *B,C*   *ᵇ* *B ends with* T', *C ends*

Close in date to nos. 674–5, since the witnesses are the justices of the eyre less Maurice de Turville.

677 Final concord in the king's court at Reading, 3 Henry III in the quindene of St Hilary, before Richard [Poore] bishop of Salisbury, Matthew fitz Herbert, Ralph Hareng, Walter Foliot, James of Potterne (*Poterna*), Walter *de Ripariis*, Maurice de Turville (*Turevill'*), John *de Wikenholte*, justices-in-eyre in Berkshire, and others, between Robert son of William, seeking, and Abbot Simon and the convent of Reading, holding, concerning half a virgate of land in the vill of Blewbury (*Bleobyr'*).*ᵃ* Assize of mort d'ancestor. Robert recognized the land to be the right of the abbot and covent, for whch they conceded to Robert's son, Geoffrey, 14½ acres of arable land in the field of the said vill and two crofts, viz., the acres and crofts which Robert held on the day when the concord was made, to be held by Geoffrey and his heirs for an annual service of 8s at Michaelmas   27 Jan. 1219

B f167v; C f98r

ᵃ Bleobury *C*

The foot of this fine is PRO CP 25(1)/7/7/33. For discussion, see no. 678 n.

678 Final concord in the court of Simon, abbot of Reading, 3 Henry III on the morrow of St Scholastica [10 Feb.], *coram Waltero Foliot,*ᵃ *Johanne de Wikenholte, justic(iariis) itinerantibus, missis ad curiam* [etc., as verbatim the italicized passage in no. 675], between Robert son of William, seeking, and Abbot Simon and the convent of Reading, holding, concerning half a virgate of land in Blewbury (*Bleobyr*).[b] Assize of mort d'ancestor. Robert recognized the land to be the right of the abbot and convent in perpetuity, quitclaimed all right and claim in the same for himself and his heirs and resigned the land to the abbot and convent. For this they conceded to Robert's son, Geoffrey, 14½ acres of arable land in the field of the said vill and two crofts, viz., the acres and crofts which Robert held on the day when the concord was made, to be held by Geoffrey and his heirs for an annual service of 8s at Michaelmas   11 Feb. 1219

B f 168r; C f 98v

[a] Folyot *C*   [b] Bleobur' *C*

This and no. 677 are another pair of duplicated fines, one levied in the king's court, the other in the abbot's court (see no. 675 n.), but, unlike nos. 674–5, which were both made on the same day, the first of these was levied in the king's court a week or so before the second in the abbot's court. It looks as though in this case the second fine was made following the precedent set on 1 Feb. in nos. 674–5.

678a   Note of a final concord between Robert Basset and Ralph Basset concerning customs and services from a tenement in Blewbury (*Bleobyr'*)   [3 Nov. 1241]

B f 167v

The foot of this fine is PRO CP 25(1)/7/14/22, dated at Reading the morrow of All Souls, 26 Henry III. Ralph recognized that he owed Robert 12s annually for the tenement which he held of him in Blewbury.

679   Gift in free alms by Robert Basset (*Basset*)[a] of Blewbury (Blebir')[b] to Reading Abbey of all his land which he had or could have in The Grove (*La Grave*) in the manor of Blewbury, and also that part of land which Christina, widow of Ralph Basset, Robert's brother, held in dower from the same land after her death, with all pastures which Robert sometime had in Grove (*Grava*) and in the meadow called North Brook (*Northbrok'*) in common with the abbot, except the land which Andrew, Robert's father, gave to Andrew, Robert's brother, in the same Grove (*Grave*). To be held free of all secular service, exaction and demand. Warranty and sealing

[?c. 1250 × 1258]

A f 103v; B f 72r; C f 37r

'Hiis testibus: domino Roberto Dauvers, domino Willelmo de Wyndlesor', magistro Roberto de Lond(onia), Haunsero[d] de Saundrevile, Roberto de Saunford, Milone de Mortun', Ricardo de Hakeburne,

Johanne de Hakeburne, Roberto dispensatore de Blebir', Willelmo de Walingeford, Roberto de Geres, Johanne clerico, et aliis.

^a Bassath *B,C*
^c *B ends with* T', *C ends*
^b Bleobir' *B,C*
^d *Sic in Ms, prob. error for* Manasero (*see note*)

The deed was among the latest entries in A, along with no. 791, which dates 1255 × 59, and was entered in the original section of B. The donor was a member of a grand assize in Berkshire in 1248 and a juror for Eagle hundred (Clanchy, *Berks. Eyre of 1248*, 261, 293). Robert Danvers, William of Windsor, Manasser of Sanderville, Robert of Sandford, Miles of Moreton, Richard of Hagbourne and William of Wallingford all occur in the 1248 eyre (*ibid.,* index *sub nominibus*). Danvers acquired half the nearby manor of Aston Tirrold in 1241, Windsor held West Hagbourne and Sanderville held Sanderville (in South Moreton) from before 1242–3 (*VCH Berks.*, iii. 499, 453; iv. 478). The deed yields the following genealogy:

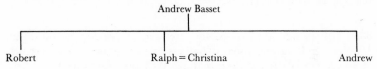

Robert was uncle of Miles Basset of North Moreton (see no. 680 n.).

680 Gift by Robert Basset (*Bassath*) to Reading Abbey of 12s worth of rent to be received annually from Andrew Basset (*Basseth*) and his heirs from the land which Andrew held of Henry Basset in the vill of Blewbury (*Bleobir'*), which rent the said Henry gave to Robert with homages, reliefs, wardships, escheats and all appurtenances and casual rights (*fortuita que accidere possunt*). To be held freely by rendering to him and his heirs 1 pair of gloves or 1d at Easter for all service, exaction and demand, saving the king's service. For this the abbey has given him 10 marks of silver as entry-fine. Warranty and sealing. Witnesses^a [omitted]   [before Nov. 1252]

B f 72v; C f 37v

^a *Om. in C*

The Henry Basset who gave this rent to Robert, and was probably a kinsman, held North Moreton before Sept. 1242, by which time he had been succeeded by his son John (*Cal. Inq. P.M.*, i. 3), who was in turn succeeded before June 1248 by Miles, Robert's nephew (*VCH Berks.*, iii. 493; Clanchy, *ibid.,* 108–9). In Nov. 1252 Robert, having been vouched to warranty by the abbot of Reading, recognized the 12s rent *inter alia* to be the right of Miles, who conceded it to him (PRO CP 25(1)/8/20/24). The present charter dates therefore before Nov. 1252. The 12s rent appears to be different from that which Ralph Basset owed Robert in 1241 (see no. 678a).

680a Note of a charter between Henry Basset (*Basseth*) and the same Robert concerning the same rent   [before Sept. 1242]

B f 72v; C f 37v

Henry Basset of North Moreton had been succeeded by his son by Sept. 1242 (see no. 680 n.).

681   Gift in free alms by John *With* of Blewbury (*Bleobir'*) to Reading Abbey of his whole land and tenement which he sometime held of the abbey in the vill of Blewbury. Warranty and sealing. Witnesses[a] [omitted]   [13th cent.; not later than 1258]

B f 72r-v; C f 37v

[a] *Om. in C*

Not in A, but in the original section of B.

682   Gift in free alms by Simon, steward (*dispensator*) of Blewbury (*Bleobir'*), to Reading Abbey of half his pasture on *Indune*, viz., pasture of 100 sheep. Warranty and sealing. Witnesses[a] [omitted]
[13th cent.; not later than 1258]

B f 72v; C f 37v

[a] *Om. in C*

Date as for no. 681.

683   *Mandate by Peter de la Beche, sheriff of Berkshire, to the bailiffs of the Liberty of the abbot of Reading to execute a writ from the king to the sheriff ordering him, if the manor of Blewbury was ancient demesne, to allow the abbot of Reading reasonable tallage from his tenants there*
[soon after 10 July 1279]

B f 144v; C f 85r

P(etrus) de la Beche[a] vicecomes Berk' ballivis libertatis abbatis Rading(ensis),[b] salutem. Mandatum domini regis rec(epimus)[c] in hec verba.

Edwardus dei gratia rex Angl(ie), dominus Hibern(ie) et dux Aquit(anie) vicecomiti Berk', salutem. Quia dominica nostra per Angliam fecimus talliari, tibi precipimus quod, si manerium de Blebur'[d] aliquando fuerit antiquum dominicum nostrum vel progenitorum nostrorum regum Angl(ie) et hucusque talliari consueverit, tunc dilecto nobis in Christo abbati de Redingg'[e] de tenentibus suis in eodem manerio racionabile tallagium habere facias sicut alias fieri consuevit. T(este) R(oberto)[f] Bathon(iensi) et Wellen(si) episcopo, apud Westm(onasterium) x. die Julii, anno regni nostri septimo.

Quare vobis mandamus quod mandatum istud exequam(ini).

^a Besche *C*   ^b Radyng' *C*
^c *Expanded in plural in view of* mandamus *in last sentence*
^d Bleobur' *C*   ^e Redyng' *C*
^f J' *in both texts, but witness was Robert Burnell, chancellor*

The date must be shortly after that of the royal writ quoted in the text (also entered in Ff123r). The text has been printed in full, since it is a rare example of part of the process involved in the privilege of return of writs, for which in general see M. T. Clanchy, 'The franchise of return of writs', *TRHS*, 5th ser., xvii (1967). An analogous example for 1253 relating to the liberty of St Albans is to be found in Matthew Paris, *Chronica Majora*, vi. 255. Reading Abbey claimed the franchise by virtue of the founder's grant of exemption from shires and hundreds, but it was not specified in royal charters to the abbey until the general confirmation by Edward III in 1338 (no. 109). However, the abbey was said to exercise it in the 1270s in Blewbury, Leominster, Rowington and Whitsbury (*Rot. Hund.*, i. 12, 186; ii. 226, 248).

684   Record of the action brought against Abbot Robert [of Burgate] of Reading by William *Sene*, Juliana *Plente,* Roger *Tovi*, Alice widow of William *Sturewowe*, Ralph *Sewine*, Richard *le Swon*, John Herbert, Alice widow *le Tache*, Robert *de Stedewill'*, Edith widow of Walter *Brodefot*, William *Gilemin*, John *Barun*, Richard of Grove (*la Grave*), Alice widow of John *Dame Eine,*^a Robert *Godrich*, Andrew Herbert, Ralph Gardener (*le Gardener*), Andrew of Hendred (*Henreth'*), John *del Angle*, Laurence Carter (*le Charetir*), Walter *Deyme*, Edith widow of John *Horri*, Agnes widow of Hervey King (*le King*), Matilda widow of Richard *Segar*, Elias of Bradfield (*Bradefeld'*), Helewise widow of Robert *le Viger'*, and Robert King, the abbot's men of the manor of Blewbury (*Blebir'*), which is ancient demesne. Whereas the king ordered the abbot not to demand from his men customs or services other than what they ought to do and used to do when the manor was in royal hands, the abbot has not ceased to distrain them to undue services and customs; namely, whereas their ancestors in the time of King Henry I had held their tenements for fixed services—viz., the holder of 1 virgate by the service of 5s annually and reaping the lord's corn for 3 days in autumn at the lord's feeding, on the first day by 4 men, on the second by 3 men and on the third by 2 men, and carting the corn in autumn by 1 cart if they had one and, if they had neither horse nor cart, they were to provide 1 man for 1 day's stacking, also at the lord's feeding, and by tallage when the king tallaged his demesnes— and these customs were maintained until the time of King John; and the said Robert^b and the other men of the said manor on the vigil of the Nativity of St Mary [8 Sept.], 7 Edward I, brought against the abbot a royal prohibition; the abbot has not ceased to distrain them to the said undue customs and services, and demands from one virgate 10s, from another 8s and so diversely from other virgates, and he tallages them at his will, demanding merchet and

redemption of blood, and ploughing and carting services of their
ploughs and carts, and he appoints them as reeves at his will, to their
total loss of £1000. The abbot, through his attorney, says that he
ought not to answer by this writ because it has been newly devised
and another writ is usually pleadable in such a case. This claim being
upheld by the court, since the writ *Summone* should have been used,
the said men can obtain nothing by their new writ and are in mercy
for false claim. The abbot is *sine die*, and the men are to seek by the
old writ pleadable in such a case   [after 7 Sept. 1279]

B f 244v

^a *Reading uncertain*
^b *Sic in Ms, but the first plaintiff was called William*

After the bringing of the king's prohibition. The case was finally brought to court in
1284 (see no. 686), when, however, only three of the present plaintiffs were named
among the abbot's men. In Michaelmas term 1279 the abbot was again impleaded by
his men and tenants of Blewbury in the same cause, but the case was dismissed because
they stated that Henry II had held the manor, whereas the abbot proffered the charter
of gift by the Empress Matilda (*Abbreviatio Placitorum*, 197).

685 Precept by King Edward I to the sheriff of Berkshire not to
hinder, nor permit the hindrance of, the abbot of Reading in dis-
training his men of his manor of Blewbury (*Bleobir'*) to do the due
and customary services, notwithstanding that the same men have a
plea pending *coram rege* against the abbot concerning his allegedly
excessive demands upon the men of the manor, which is ancient
demesne, and have withdrawn their services since the writ was
obtained to the great loss of the abbot   13 Nov. 1283

B f 13v

Teste me ipso apud Hereford(iam) xiii. die Novembris, anno regni
nostri undecimo.

Cf. *Abbreviato Placitorum*, 276.

686 *Record of the action brought against the abbot of Reading by his men of
Blewbury, which is ancient demesne, concerning the allegedly excessive customs
and services which the abbot is demanding from virgaters, half-virgaters and
cottars. The sheriff of Berkshire is ordered to assemble at Westminster 4 lawful
suitors and a keeper or serjeant¹ from each ancient demesne manor in the county
then in the king's hands to give evidence as to the services they owe, and 18
knights and freemen from the neighbourhood of² Blewbury through whom the
truth might be discovered. After adjournments of the case to Staines Bridge and
then to Caversham Bridge, the matter is settled. The services demanded by the
abbot are excessive, but the men owe more than they claim, and both parties are
therefore in mercy*   1284

B ff 227r–231r; (in part) C f 138r–v

Abbas de Rading' attachiatus fuit ad respondendum Thome le Kave, Edithe Orri, Roberto le Franceys*a* et Christiane uxori eius, Matildi que fuit uxor Ricardi Segar, Johanni Gomel, Simoni le Rede, Nicholao Dodde, Willelmo Osmund, Henrico Boton et Agnet(e)*b* uxori eius, Willelmo Witelok et Matildi uxori eius, Willelmo Sene, Waltero Thein, Willelmo Lok', Waltero Alwine, Johanni Alwine, Rad(ulfo) Weland et Eve Herebert, hominibus predicti abbatis de Rading' de manerio de Blebur'*c* quod est de antico*d* dominico regis, de placito quare idem abbas exigit a prefatis hominibus alias consuetudines et alia servitia quam facere debent et facere consueverunt temporibus quibus manerium illud fuit in manibus predecessorum regis regum Anglie. Et unde predicti Thomas le Kave et alii queruntur quod, ubi tenere debeant terras et tenementa sua per certa servicia tempore H(enrici) regis filii regis Willelmi conquestoris Anglie, qui manerium illud dedit abbati et monachis Rading' — videlicet quod quilibet virgat(arius) qui tenet unam virgatam terre debet de redditu in denar(iis) quinque solidos per annum, et ad plus plus, et ad minus minus; et metere in autumpno per tres dies ad cibum domini, videlicet primo die per quatuor homines, secundo die per tres homines, tercio die per duos homines; et cariare bladum in autumpno per unum diem cum una carecta, si habeat, et si non habeat carectam nec equum, inveniat unum hominem per unum diem ad tassandum, et omnia ista facere debent ad cibum domini; et hoc secundum quantitatem terrarum suarum; et similiter, cum incidissent in misericordiam, amerciari debuerunt et consueverunt per pares suos; et post mortem antecessorum suorum consueverunt heredes ingredi hereditatem suam per redditum duplicatum; et etiam tum pro pastura apud Kingesmede quam habere debuerunt post fena asportata, tantum dare debuerunt pro bestia unius anni unum denarium et obolum, et pro bestia maioris etatis duos denarios; ita quod antecessores sui fuerint*e* in seisina de tenementis suis tenend(is) per predicta servicia nichil aliud pro predictis tenementis suis faciendo tempore predicti regis et temporibus aliorum regum — quociens quidam Helyas, qui fuit abbas de Rading', ipsos distrinxit ad indebitas consuetudines et indebita servicia faciend(a). Videlicet, preter recta servicia que facere consueverunt et que cognoscunt, distrinxit quosdam tenentes unam virgatam terre dare per annum nomine redditus .vi. solidos et quosdam octo ad voluntatem. Et amerciavit eos ad voluntatem et non per taxationem parium suorum. Et cepit ab eis redemptionem carnis et sanguinis ad voluntatem suam. Et fecit eos cariare bladum et fenum de die in diem ad voluntatem suam. Et cepit de heredibus post mortem antecessorum suorum pro ingressu ad terram ad voluntatem suam. Et inparcari*f* fecit averia sua

infra curiam suam, ubi consueverunt habere parcum in media villa
in certo loco. Et deforciavit eis communiam pasture apud la Grave
cum averiis ipsius abbatis. Et etiam deforciavit eis communiam pasture apud Kingeswod'.[g] [f 227v] Et nichillominus cepit[h] ab eis denarios
secundum numerum averiorum que habent. Et etiam talliavit eos ad
voluntatem suam, cum non consueverunt talliari nisi quando rex
talliat dominica sua. Et etiam distrinxit eos ad dandum gallinas et
ova, ubi quieti esse consueverunt. Et etiam non permisit eos habere
ovilia sua in terris suis prout habere consueverunt. Et distrinxit eos
operari in crastino sancti Michaelis[i] ab ortu solis usque ad terciam
horam, et de gula Augusti [1 Aug.] usque ad festum sancti Mathei[j]
quolibet die ab hora meridiana usque ad occasum solis. Ad predicta
indebita servicia facienda primo distrinxit eos predictus Helias quondam abbas Rading' et predictas extorsiones eis fecit. Et abbas qui
modo est ad predictas indebitas consuetudines ipsos distringit et predictas iniurias et extorsiones eis de die in diem facit. Unde dicunt
quod deteriorati sunt et dampnum habent, et cetera, ad valenciam
trecentarum librarum, et cetera.

De virg(atariis) tenent(ibus) virgatam terre in Blebur'[c]
    Et abbas per attornatum suum venit. Vim et iniuriam quando, et
cetera. Et non dedicit quin predictum manerium sit de antiquo dominico corone regis et bene defendit quod nunquam exigebat a prefatis
hominibus alias consuetudines, et cetera, quam facere, et cetera,
temporibus quibus manerium illud fuit in man(u) domini H(enrici)
regis predecessoris regis nunc. Et dicit quod antecessores Thome le
Kave reddere solebant[k] pro una virgata terre ad festum [sancti][l]
Michaelis .x. solidos, et antecessores Edithe Orri pro una virgata terre
.x. solidos, et antecessores Roberti le Franceys[a] et Christiane uxoris
eius pro una virgata terre et dimidia .xi. solidos, et antecessores
Matildis que fuit uxor Ricardi Seger pro una virgata terre .x. solidos,
et antecessores J(ohannis) Gomel pro una virgata terre .vi. solidos .x.
denarios, et antecessores Nicholai Dodde pro una virgata terre .vii.
solidos .vi. denarios, et antecessores Simonis le Rede pro una virgata
terre .x. solidos, et antecessores Willelmi Osmund pro una virgata
terre .vii. solidos .vi. denarios, et antecessores Walteri Aywine[m] et
antecessores J(ohannis) Aylwine pro una virgata terre .xi. solidos et
.vi. denarios. Et quilibet istorum antecessorum debet pro una virgata
terre cariare cum una carecta tempore fenationis fenum domini qui
pro tempore fuerit de die in diem exceptis Sabbato et diebus festivis
donec totum introducatur. Et tempore Augusti debent cariare bladum
domini quolibet die ad sum(monitionem) domini predicti quando-
cumque sibi viderit expedire donec introducatur,[n] ita[o] scilicet quod
quilibet eorum inveniet[p] unam carectam ad cariandum bladum ipsius

domini ab ortu solis usque ad horam terciam, et tunc quilibet eorum habebit unam garbam rationabilem de carecta sua; et etiam cariare solebant quolibet die ab hora meridiana usque ad occasum solis, et tunc quilibet eorum habebit aliam garbam. Et quando solebant cariare per totum diem ad cibum abbatis, tunc non habebit garbam. [*f 228r*] Quando vero solebant cariare fenum domini, tunc habebunt pro cariagio tocius feni unum multonem et unum caseum et illud vas plenum salis,^{*q*} scilicet in quo sit caseus, et duos denarios. Et quilibet eorum tenens unam virgatam terre integram solebat invenire quatuor homines ad primam bedripam autumpni, et ad secundam tres homines, et ad terciam tres homines; et hoc totum ad cibum domini. Et quilibet eorum solebat operari cum uno homine in crastino sancti Michaelis usque ad horam terciam opus manuale. Et quilibet eorum antecessorum solebat talliari quando dominus rex talliavit dominica sua, et hoc secundum quantitatem vel portionem terrarum et bonorum suorum. Et quilibet eorum solebat dare merchettum pro sanguine suo secundum quod finem facere poterit cum domino. Et quilibet eorum solebat esse prepositus si eligeretur in curia et facere sectam ad curiam domini de tribus septimanis in tres septimanas. Et quilibet eorum dare solebat ova ad Pascha et dare relevium secundum quod finem facere posset cum domino. Et quilibet eorum solebat dare bis in anno pro quolibet bove et vacca duorum annorum .ii. denarios, et pro quolibet animali superannato .i. denarium, videlicet ad Nativitatem sancti Johannis Baptiste et die sancti Martini, et eodem die pro porco superannato^{*r*} unum denarium, et pro hogietto dimidii anni .i. obolum. Et quilibet eorum facere solebat .ii. precarias cum caruca sua in anno cum omnibus equis suis vel bobus euntibus in caruca sua.

Tenentes dimidiam virgatam terre ibidem

Dicit etiam predictus abbas quod antecessores Rad(ulfi) Weyland solebant reddere pro dimidia virgata terre .vi. solidos tempore predicti regis H(enrici) predecessoris regis nunc. Solebant etiam facere .iii. precarias in autumpno; ad primam precariam invenire solebant duos homines, ad secundam unum, ad terciam unum. Solebant etiam dare pannagium herbarum pro bobus et porcis suis. Solebant etiam operari^{*s*} in crastino sancti Michaelis cum uno homine usque ad horam terciam. Et talliari solebant quando dominus rex talliavit dominica sua secundum portionem bonorum suorum et terrarum. Et solebant dare merchettum pro filiabus suis maritandis ad voluntatem domini. Et quilibet eorum solebat facere finem pro terra sua post mortem antecessorum suorum ad voluntatem domini et facere sectam curie domini de tribus septimanis in tres septimanas. Et solebant dare tolcestrum, scilicet illi qui solebant facere cervisiam ad vend(endum), videlicet .vi. lagenas cervisie. Et quilibet eorum antcessorum solebat esse prepositus, carec-

tator, messor,[f] bercarius, porcator, fugator, carucator, et non solebat
habere ovile. Et solebant tondere omnes oves domini. Et solebant dare
chercetum, scilicet tres gallinas et unum gallum. Dicit etiam predictus
abbas quod antecessores Willelmi Witelok' et Matildis [*f 228v*] uxoris
eius solebant reddere pro dimidia virgata terre .v. solidos et .vi.
gallinas et facere omnia predicta servitia que Rad(ulfus) Weyland
facit. Et antecessores Willelmi Sene solebant reddere pro dimidia
virgata terre .iiii. solidos et facere, et cetera. Et antecessores Eve
Herbert facere solebant omnia predicta servicia que predictus
Rad(ulfus) Weylond facit.

Cotseth(li)[u]

Dicit etiam predictus abbas quod Henricus Boton et Agnet(a) uxor
eius, Walterus Theyn, Editha uxor eius, Willelmus Lock' sunt cotsetli
ex quibus antecessores eorum solebant operari quolibet die excepto
Sabbato et diebus festivis a festo sancti Michaelis usque ad tempus
falcationis pratorum ab ortu solis usque ad horam terciam omnimoda
opera manualia secundum quod ballivus eis voluerit iniungere. Et
incipiente tempore falcationis quilibet eorum solebat falcare cum uno
homine quolibet die donec totum falcaretur, et tunc solebat illud
levare donec totum levaretur. Et quilibet eorum solebat operari a
gula Augusti [1 Aug.] usque ad festum sancti Michaelis quolibet die
operabili ab ortu solis usque ad horam terciam cum uno homine. Et
quolibet[v] die per predictum tempus quilibet eorum solebat operari ab
hora meridiana usque ad occasum solis cum uno homine. Et quilibet
antecessorum eorum solebat invenire ad primam precariam duos
homines, ad secundam unum hominem et ad terciam unum hominem.
Et quilibet eorum, si sum(monitus) esset, solebat metere dimidiam
acram in autumpno que vocatur nedelve cotidie durante Augusto
et solebat[p] habere unam garbam. Et si quis eorum braciaverit ad
vendend(um), solebat[p] dare sex lagenas cervisie. Et quilibet eorum
solebat esse prepositus, bercarius, porcarius, messor, carucator,
fugator. Et quilibet eorum solebat talliari secundum portionem bonorum suorum et terrarum quando rex talliavit dominica sua. Et quilibet
eorum solebat[p] dare tres gallinas et unum gallum ad festum sancti
Martini pro chirchet et quinque ova ad Pascha. Et quilibet eorum
solebat dare merchettum pro filiabus sus maritandis ad voluntatem
domini. Et quilibet eorum post mortem antecessorum suorum solebat
facere finem pro terra sua ad voluntatem domini. Et solebat dare
melius averium cum obierit ad herietum. Et solebant facere sectam
ad curiam domini sui de tribus septimanis in tres septimanas. Et nullus
eorum solebat[w] habere ovile sine licentia abbatis.

Et quod tales consuetudines et talia servitia[x] facere solebant tempore
predicti regis H(enrici) predecessoris regis nunc, et etiam temporibus

omnium predecessorum istius abbatis a tempore illo usque nunc, petit
quod inquiratur per patriam, et predicti homines similiter.

Ideo preceptum est vicecomiti quod venire faciat coram J(ohanne)
de Kyrk(ebi), R(ogero) de Northwod' et J(ohanne) de Cobbeham
apud Westmonasterium in crastino sancti Johannis Baptiste de quolibet manerio quod est de antico dominico corone regis in manu regis
nunc existente in [*f 229r*]^y comitatu predicto .iiii. [de]^l legalioribus et
disc(retioribus) sokemannis una cum custode [seu]^l serviente predicti
manerii ad certificandum regem cuiusmodi serv(itia) et cuiusmodi
cons(uetudines) sokemanni^z regis ten(ementa) tenentes in dominico
regis in manu regis existente facere debent et consueverunt pro ten-
(ementis), et preter illos .xviii. tam mil(ites), et cetera, de viceneto^{aa}
de Blebur', per quos, et cetera, et qui non, et cetera, ad rec(og-
no)s(cendum), et cetera, que servitia^x et consuetudines antecessores
hominum de Blebur' facere debuerunt et consueverunt tempore
H(enrici) quondam regis Anglie filii Conquestoris, antecessoris domini
regis nunc, qui predictum manerium dedit abbati et monachis de
Radingiis; et si easdem consuetudines et eadem servicia facere
debuerunt et consueverunt tempore predicti regis que homines de
antiquis dominicis regis propinquioribus nunc in manu regis existentibus faciunt et facere consueverunt pro tenementis suis vel alia; et
si ad alias consuetudines vel alia servitia^x teneantur, ad que et ad quas
et qua ratione seu occasione; et ad certificandum de quibusdam aliis
transgressionibus et extorsionibus quas predicti homines questi fuerunt
sibi fuisse illatas per predictum abbatem, secundum quod ^{bb}compreri
[poterit] in recordo quod dilectus et fidelis regis R(adulfus) de
Hengham predictis J(ohanni), R(ogero) et J(ohanni) misit^{bb} sub sigillo
suo quia causa, et cetera. Et habeat ibi nomina sokemannorum,
servient(ium) et rec(ognitorum), et cetera.

J(ohannes) de Thedmers vicecomes Berck' ballivis Rading',
salutem. Mandatum domini regis in hec verba suscepimus.
Edwardus dei gratia, et cetera, vicecomiti Berck', salutem. Precipimus
tibi quod venire facias^{cc} coram dilectis et fidelibus nostris Johanne
de Kyrkebi, Rogero de Northwode et Johanne de Cobbeham apud
Westmonasterium in crastino sancti Johannis Baptiste de quolibet
manerio quod est in dominico antiquo corone nostre in manu nostra
modo existente in comitatu tuo quatuor de legalioribus et dis-
cretioribus sokemannis una cum custode seu serviente predicti manerii
ad certificandum nos cuiusmodi servicia et cuiusmodi consuetudines
sokemanni nostri ten(ementa) tenentes in dominicis nostris in ^{dd}manu
nostra^{dd} nunc existentibus facere debent et facere consueverunt pro
tenementis suis, et preter illos^{ee} octodecim tam milites quam alios
liberos et leg(ales) homines de vic' de Blebur', per quos rei veritas

melius sciri poterit, et qui nec abbatem de Rading' nec homines de Blebur' aliqua affinitate attingant, ad recognoscendum super sacramentum suum que servicia et quas consuetudines antecessores hominum de Blebur' facere debuerunt et consueverunt tempore H(enrici) quondam regis Anglie filii Conquestoris, antecessoris nostri, qui predictum manerium de Bleburi dedit abbati et monachis de Rading'; et si eadem servicia et consuetudines facere debuerunt et consueverunt tempore predicti regis que homines de antiquis dominicis nostris propinquioribus nunc in manu nostra existentibus[ff] nobis faciunt et facere consueverunt pro tenementis suis vel [*f 229v*] alia; et si ad alia [servitia][l] et alias consuetudines teneantur, ad que et ad quas [et][l] qua ratione seu occasione; et ad certificandum de quibusdam aliis transgressionibus et extorsionibus quas predicti homines questi fuerunt sibi fuisse[gg] illatas per predictum[hh] abbatem, secundum quod comperi poterit in recordo quod dilectus et fidelis noster R(adulfus) de Hengam predictis J(ohanni), Rog(ero) et Johanni misit sub sigillo suo, quia tam predictus abbas de Rading' quam predicti homines de Blebur', inter quos contentio inde est, posuerunt se in inquisitionem illam. Et habeas ibi nomina sokemannorum, servient(ium) [et][l] recogn(itorum) et hoc breve. Teste R(adulfo) de Hengham apud Karnarvan[ii] xi. die Maii, [jj]anno regni regis E(dwardi) xii.[jj] 11 May 1284

[kk]Tenentes unam virgatam terre[kk]

Et quia iur(atores) inquisitionis predicte et alii de[q] dominicis regis non dum venerunt apud Westm(onasterium) in crastino sancti Johannis Baptiste [24 June], partes adiornate fuerunt apud pontem de Stanes coram eisdem, ubi partes comparuerunt et Johannes de Kyrkeby, qui associavit sibi Walterum de Augmodesham et Galfridum de Picheford' propter absentiam predictorum Rogeri et Johannis, adiornavit partes ad requisitionem et de assensu earumdem apud pontem de Kaveresham die veneris proxima post festum sancti Jacobi apostoli[q] [25 July] coram R(adulfo) de Hengham et sociis suis, qui de consilio domini regis exist(entes) eodem die ibidem conventur(i) [fuerunt],[l] ad faciendum et recipiendum quod curia domini regis consideraverit in hac parte. Et eadem dies data est iurat(oribus) et aliis quod tunc sint ibidem sub periculo amissionis omnium bonorum suorum. Postea ad pontem de Kaveresham die veneris proxima post festum sancti Jacobi apostoli venit predictus abbas et similiter homines sui predicti et similiter iurat(ores), scilicet [ll]J(ohannes) de Sancta Helena, G(alfridus) de Wanci, G(alfridus)[ll] de Turbervile, Rolandus de Erleya, Ricardus de Pesye, Thomas Daunvers, Rogerus de Burgefeld', Rad(ulfu)s Chanduyt, Thomas Hurskarl, Almaricus de Vernay, Willelmus de Iverinton', Math(eus) de Grantcurt, Ricardus de Westwode, Johannes de Ildesleya, qui dicunt super sacramentum

suum quod quelibet*mm* virgata terre integra debet per annum septem
solidos de redditu assiso et debet metere bladum abbatis in autumpno
per tres dies, videlicet primo die per quatuor homines, secundo die
per tres homines et tercio die per tres homines, scilicet qualibet die ad
sustentationem predicti abbatis, videlicet ad duos repastus. Et debent
cariare bladum abbatis per tres dies ad custus abbatis, videlicet ad
duos repastus. Et sero quilibet eorum habebit unam garbam de blado
quod cariaverunt. Dicunt etiam quod quando debent amerciari pro
aliquibus transgressionibus debent taxari in plena curia per quatuor
sectatores curie predicte, et quod post mortem antecessorum suorum
debent redimere terram suam ad voluntatem abbatis, ita quod predictus abbas non sit eis tam durus quin possit ad terram suam evenire.
Dicunt etiam quod omnes [*f 230r*] debent cariare fenum abbatis
quousque totum fenum sit cariatum, et debent habere pro eodem
cariagio unum multonem et unum caseum de factura citra festum
sancti Johannis Baptiste et vas plenum salis in quo sit caseus et sex
denarios ad potationem. Et dicunt quod nullam habent communiam
pasture in Kingesmede nec in la Grave, sed super Aschesdone, et
dabunt pro eadem communia quolibet anno pro bovetto unius anni
unum denarium et obolum, et pro bove vel averio maioris etatis tres
denarios. Preterea dicunt quod debent redimere sanguinem suum, ita
quod maritagium non se defaciat propter duritiam predicti abbatis.
Dicunt etiam quod debent habere communem heywardum et communem parcum. Et debent habere emendationes transgressionum in
bladis propriis et pastur(a) secundum considerationem vicinorum
suorum. Et non debent talliari nisi quando dominus rex tall(iat)
dominica sua per Angliam, et tunc debent talliari secundum quantitatem terrarum suarum et catallorum. Et dicunt quod non debent
dare ova, set debent dare chereschet ad festum sancti Martini, scilicet
tres gallinas et unum gallum si vir sit superstes, et si sit vidua dabit
tres gallinas absque gallo. Et debent habere caulas cum ovibus propriis
super suas proprias terras. Et quilibet debet operari cum uno homine
omne opus manuale, exceptis equis et carectis, in crastino sancti
Michaelis ab ortu solis usque ad horam terciam. Et debent metere
bladum abbatis in autumpno ad voluntatem abbatis, ita quod habeant
pro qualibet dimidia acra unam garbam de mensura cuiusdam liga-
minis quod vocatur cingulum.*nn* Et non debent operari a tempore
meridiano usque ad occasum solis. Et debent esse prepositi si eligantur
in curia. Et facient sectam ad curiam predicti abbatis de tribus septimanis in tres septimanas. Preterea debent dare quolibet anno pannagium de porcis suis, scilicet pro porco superannato unum denarium,
et pro porco infra annum unum obolum. Et predictus abbas habebit
de eis duas precarias carucarum per annum que vocantur betierches
et cum qualibet caruca duos homines qualibet die ad prandium*oo*

predicti abbatis. Et quod vidua post mortem viri sui dabit domino
melius averium nomine herieti, et ipsa, si remaneat vidua, teneat
terram quam vir suus tenuit usque ad terminum vite sue. Et dominus
post mortem ipsius vidue habebit melius averium suum nomine
herieti. Et si se velit maritare, introitus viri sui super terram predictam
sit ad voluntatem predicti abbatis. Preterea si braciant ad ven-
dend(um), dabunt de cervisia sua predicto abbati quandam consuetudinem que vocatur tolsuster, scilicet de qualibet bracina quatuor
lagenas quocienscumque braciaverint.

*kk*Tenentes dimidiam virgatam terre*kk*

Dicunt etiam quod tenentes dimidiam virgatam terre debent pro
dimidia virgata terre per annum quatuor solidos de redditu assiso, et
quod debent [*f 230v*] tres precarias in autumpno, videlicet primo die
per duos homines, secundo die per unum hominem et tercio die per
unum hominem, ad prandium abbatis quolibet die ad duos repastus.
Et dabunt pannagium pro porcis et pro bobus suis, pro communia
super Aschesdone quolibet anno sub eadem forma qua predictum est.
Et operabuntur*pp* in crastino sancti Michaelis sicut prenominati. Et
debent talliari sicut alii secundum portionem terrarum suarum et
catallorum. Et debent redimere sanguinem suum sicut predicti. Et
debent redimere terram suam post mortem antecessorum sicut alii
secundum portionem terrarum suarum et catallorum. Et debent esse
prepositi sicut alii prenominati. Et debent sectam ad curiam predicti
abbatis de tribus septimanis in tres septimanas. Et quando debent
amerciari pro aliquibus transgressionibus debent amerciari eodem
modo quo predictum est. Preterea dicunt quod, si predictus abbas
velit habere aliquem eorum in carectarium, idem abbas dabit ei
liberationem suam et stipend(ium) sicut extraneo. Et idem carectarius
reddet pro terra sua servitia inde debita et consueta. Et si velit aliquem
eorum habere in messorem, bercarium aut porcarium, habebunt terram suam quietam a redditu et servicio. Et carucar(ius) qui tenet
carucam domini pro terra sua habebit comod(um) operis caruce per
diem sabbatum in qualibet alia septimana et terram suam quietam a
redditu et servicio. Et fugator caruce qui fugat carucam domini pro
terra sua habebit terram suam quietam a redditu et servitio. Et si
debeat custodire averia domini, predictus abbas dabit ei liberationem
et stipend(ium) sicut extraneo, sed faciet servicia et consuetudines pro
terra sua inde debita et consueta. Et dicunt quod dabunt tolsuster
sicut prenominati. Et habebunt caulas suas cum ovibus suis propriis
super terras suas proprias. Dicunt etiam quod debent lanare et tondere
oves predicti abbatis, et dabunt churschet sub eadem forma qua
predictum est.

[qq]De coterell(is)[qq]

Dicunt etiam quod tenentes coterellos nullum debent redditum assisum, set debent operari omne opus manuale, exceptis equis et carectis, a gula Augusti [1 Aug.] usque ad festum sancti Michaelis per tres dies in septimana, scilicet per diem lune, mercurii et per diem veneris, et quolibet die ad cibum suum proprium. Et si aliquod festum cadat in aliquo predictorum dierum, erit ad allevationem ipsorum. Et debent operari omne opus manuale, exceptis equis et carectis, per tres dies in septimana a festo sancti Michaelis usque ad quindenam ante festum Nativitatis sancti Johannis Baptiste. Et debent falcare et levare prata et fenum predicti abbatis tempore fenac(ionis)[rr] quolibet die cum uno homine. Et debent tres precarias in autumpno, et invenient primo die duos homines, secundo die unum [f231r] hominem et tercio die unum hominem, quolibet die ad custus abbatis ad duos repastus per diem. Et dabunt tolsester sicut prenominati. Et fiant prepositi, bercarii, messores, carectarii et carucarii sicut tenentes dimidiam virgatam terre. Et debent talliari sicut alii secundum portionem terrarum suarum et catallorum. Et dabunt churschet sicut predictum est. Et facient redemptionem sanguinis sui sicut alii secundum quantitatem terrarum suarum et catallorum, et finem terre sicut alii et heriet(um). Et facient sectam ad[ss] curiam predicti abbatis de tribus septimanis in tres septimanas. Et habebunt caulas suas sub eadem forma qua predictum est.

Et ideo consideratum est quod predictus abbas recuperet predictas consuetudines sibi dedictas versus predictos homines suos. Et predicti homines quieti sint de consuetudinibus sibi iniuste exactis. Et abbas in misericordia. Et predicti homines in misericordia pro falso clamore.

---

[a] Fraunceys C
[b] *For this expansion, rather than* Agneti, *see the later occurrence of her name, p 20, line 12*
[c] Bleobur' C [d] antiquo C
[e] fu'nt B, fu'int C [f] inparcare B, inparcar' C
[g] *Sic in* B, Kyngeswode C; ? *rectius* Kingesmede
[h] capit *in* Mss [i] Michah' B
[j] Michaelis C [k] solebat B
[l] *Supplied* [m] Aylwine C
[n] introducantur B [o] *C ends*
[p] *plural in* Ms [q] *Interlined*
[r] superanato *in* Ms [s] operare Ms
[t] mersor Ms
[u] *Heading added twice in margin in two later hands, the text running on without beginning separate paragraph*
[v] quilibet Ms [w] solid' Ms
[x] servisia/servis' Ms [y] *in repeated in* Ms
[z] sokemannor' Ms [aa] *Reading uncertain;* Ms *has* vicec'
[bb-bb] Ms *has* comperi in recordo quod dilecti et fidel' regis R. de Hengham predicti J., R. et J. misit, *which is clearly garbled; the corrected version is based on the text of the royal writ which follows immediately in the account*

cc faciatis *Ms*
ee illo *Ms*
gg fuissent *Ms*
ii Karvannan *Ms*
kk-kk Added in different, poss. later, hand
ll-ll For expansions, see VCH Berks., iv. 63, 16n., 297
mm qualibet *Ms*
oo pranduu(m) *Ms*
qq-qq Added in margin in later hand, the text running on without beginning separate paragraph
rr fanac' *Ms*

dd-dd manus nostras *Ms*
ff existentes *Ms*
hh Ms has here servic' deleted
ii-ii Added in later hand

nn cingl'm *Ms*
pp operabunt *Ms*

ss a *Ms*

This case began *coram rege* in Easter term 1284 (*Abbreviatio Placitorum*, 206), and was finally settled at Caversham Bridge on 28 July 1284. For the abrupt ending of the text in C, see vol. I, p. 10. The account has been printed here in full on account of its extremely interesting and detailed evidence on the services due from tenants of ancient demesne in Berkshire at this time. For discussion, see *VCH Berks.*, ii. 172–3; D. M. Stenton, *English Society in the Early Middle Ages*, 4th edn. (Harmondsworth 1965), 155–7.

1. Lady Stenton (*ibid.*) read 'keeper or serjeant' as 'serjeant keeper', but the writ of Edward I quoted in the record confirms the correct reading.
2. Lady Stenton (*ibid.*) read 'the vill of', but see above, textual note *aa*.

687   Agreement, indented, dated Monday the morrow of St Simon and St Jude, 4 Edward III, by which Abbot John [I, of Appleford] and the convent of Reading demised to John *le Foghelere*, junior, pasture for 100 sheep (*bidentes*) at Blewbury (*Blebury*) in a place called *le Houtwethereslese*, for 40 years or for John's life, whichever is shorter. For this John gave the abbot and convent a certain sum of money. Sealing *alternatim*   29 Oct. 1330

B f 73v; C f 38v

Hiis testibus: Willelmo Boton, Willelmo Barfot, Waltero Whatmot, Willelmo Phelip,*a* Ricardo le Chaumberleyn, Johanne Godrych, et Ricardo David et multis aliis. Dat' apud Radyngg' die et anno supradictis.

a Philipp' *C*

BUCKLEBURY

688   *Settlement, reached in the chapter of St Albans and ratified in the chapter of Reading, between the abbeys of Reading and St Albans, by which Reading renounces in perpetuity the claim of its church of Aston to the parish of Shephall [Herts.], whose church is to be regarded as an independent church, of the right of St Albans, which shall pay half a mark annually to Reading; and in return St Albans and [its] priory of Wallingford concede their church of Bucklebury to Reading in perpetuity for 2 marks annually payable to Wallingford*   [May 1151 × Dec. 1154]

Original charter: BL Add. Ch. 19590
Af47r–v; Bf203v; Cf124r

Pd. Warner and Ellis, i, no. 30 (with facsimile); (transl.) Humphreys, *Bucklebury*,
    152–3; (cal.) Hurry, *Reading Abbey*, 164–5

CYROGRAPHVM

Notum sit omnibus fidelibus sancte ecclesie tam presentibus quam
futuris hanc esse compositionem que inter ecclesiam de Radinges et
ecclesiam Sancti Albani de ecclesia de Sepehale*a* facta est. Ecclesia de
Rading(es) penitus renuntiavit calumnie*b* quam habebat adversus
ecclesiam Sancti Albani super parrochia de Sepehale,*a* quam ad ecclesiam de Estuna*c* pertinere et sui iuris esse asserebat, et concessit ut
apud Sepehale*a* habeatur mater ecclesia et ipsa iuris sit Sancti Albani
cum omnibus decimis et pertinentiis suis, eo tenore ut ecclesia Sancti
Albani annuatim persolvat ecclesie de Rading(es) ad octavas Pasche
dimidiam marcham*d* argenti, ecclesia de Sepehale*a* libera permanente
ab omni alia subiectione in perpetuum. Ecclesia vero Sancti Albani
et ecclesia de Walingef(ordia)*e* concesserunt ecclesie de Rading(es)
ecclesiam de Burchildeberia,*f* que sui iuris erat, perpetuo iure possidendam cum omnibus decimis et pertinentiis suis, liberam ab omni
calumnia*g* pro duabus marchis*h* argenti quas ecclesie de Walin-
gef(ordia)*i* annis singulis inde persolvet, unam quidem marcham*d* ad
octavas Pasche, aliam vero ad octavas sancti Michaelis. Hec compositio primo facta est in capitulo Sancti Albani presente Rodberto*j*
abbate et conventu eiusdem loci, assidente etiam Hugone priore de
Rading(es) et cum eo duobus fratribus eiusdem ecclesie; deinde in
capitulo de Rading(es) presente Edwardo abbate et conventu illius
loci recitata et unanimi omnium assensu confirmata est.

Endorsed: Carta Sancti Albani de ecclesiis de Schepehala et de Bur-
    childeburia [*12th cent.*]
Size: 263 × 168 mm
Seal: missing; slit for tag in fold at bottom

a Schepale/Schepehal'/Schepeh' *B,C*	*b* calumpnie *B,C*
c Estona *A*	*d* marcam *A,B,C*
e Walengef' *A*, Walingf' *B*	
f Burchildeburia *A*, Burgh' *B*, Burghilberi *C*	
g calumpnia *A,B,C*	*h* marcis *A,B,C*
i Walingf' *B*	*j* Roberto *A,C*

After 19 May 1151, when Abbot Robert of St Albans was blessed (*Heads of Relig.
Houses*, 67), and before 7 Dec. 1154, by which time Abbot Edward of Reading's
successor was in office (see no. 276).

689 *Confirmation by the abbeys of Reading and St Albans of the same
settlement, giving further details and stipulating that Reading shall pay Wall-*

ingford 20s annually for the church of Bucklebury for as long as Richard is parson, but that, if Reading cannot free the parish of Shephall from Amfrey [parson of Aston], it shall pay 30s and St Albans shall not pay the half mark to Reading until free from Amfrey   [1151 × 54]

Af47r; Bf203v; Cff123v–124r

Sciant omnes tam presentes quam futuri sancte ecclesie fideles quod compositio que super ecclesia de Sepehale*ᵃ* inter ecclesiam Sancti Albani et ecclesiam de Rading(ia) facta est, assensu utriusque ecclesie ita confirmata est quod rata et stabilis in perpetuum permanebit iuxta tenorem cyrographi quod inter easdem ecclesias conscriptum est. Hoc autem superadditum est compositioni: monachi ecclesie Sancti Albani saisiaverunt monachos de Rading(ia) de decimis de Sepehala,*ᵃ* qui et*ᵇ* ipsi in continenti resaisiaverunt monachos ecclesie Sancti Albani de eisdem decimis et clamaverunt eas liberas et quietas, preter quod persolvent singulis annis dimidiam marcam argenti ecclesie de Rading(ia). Monachi vero*ᶜ* Sancti Albani saisiaverunt monachos de Radingia de ecclesia de Burchildeburia*ᵈ* cum omnibus decimis et pertinentiis suis in capitulo de Warengef(ordia),*ᵉ ᶠ*de qua reddent singulis annis monachis de Warengeford(ia)*ᶠ* .xx. solidos quamdiu Ricardus presbiter persona extiterit. Quod si monachi de Rading(ia) non potuerint liberare et adquietare parrochiam*ᵍ* de Sepehale*ᵃ* de Ansfrido, facient monachi ecclesie*ʰ* Sancti Albani quam melius potuerint erga Ansfridum. Et tunc non persolvent dimidiam marcam argenti monachis de Rading(ia) donec liberentur de Ansfrido, et monachi de Rading(ia) persolvent ex integro .xxx. solidos monachis de Wareng(e)f(ordia).

ᵃ Schepehale/Schepehal' *B,C*   *ᵇ* etiam *C*
ᶜ *Insert* ecclesie *B,C*   *ᵈ* Burghildebir' *B,C*
ᵉ Waring'f' *B*, Waringef' *C*   *ᶠ ᶠ Om. in B,C (in error)*
ᵍ parochiam *C*   *ʰ Om. in B,C*

Date as for no. 688. For the identification of Amfrey as parson of Aston, see no. 691.

690 *Grant by Prior Nicholas and the convent of Wallingford to Reading Abbey of the church of Bucklebury in perpetuity for two marks of silver annually, with the assent of the abbot and convent of St Albans*   [1151 × 54]

Af47v; Bf197v; Cf116v
Pd. (transl.) Humphreys, *Bucklebury*, 153

Notum sit omnibus sancte ecclesie filiis presentibus et futuris quod ego Nicol(aus)*ᵃ* prior et conventus sancte Trinitatis de Warengef(ordia),*ᵇ* concessu domni abbatis et conventus Sancti Albani, concessimus ecclesie sancte Marie de Rading(ia) ecclesiam de Burchildeburia*ᶜ* liberam et quietam cum decimis et elemosinis cunctisque pertinentiis suis, ut habeant eam et possideant in perpetuum, reddendo annuatim ecclesie

Warengef(ordie)[b] duas marcas argenti, unam in oct(avis) Pasche, alteram in oct(avis) sancti Michaelis.

[a] Nich' *B*, Nich's *C* [b] Warengeford' *B*, Warengford' *C*
[c] Burchildebir' *B*, Burgthildebir' *C*

Clearly contemporary with nos. 688–9. Nicholas was prior of Wallingford from some time after 1149 until 1183, when he became abbot of Malmesbury (*Heads of Relig. Houses*, 97).

691 *Notification and confirmation by John [of Pagham], bishop of Worcester, acting as papal judge-delegate, of the settlement reached between Abbot Robert of St Albans and Amfrey, parson of Aston, over the church of Shephall, and of that between the same abbot and Gilbert, nephew of the same Amfrey, over the land of Henley.[1] Amfrey shall hold Shephall church of St Albans abbey for life and receive 12 marks of silver from that abbey for damages inflicted on him by the abbot, and Gilbert shall receive 5 marks from the abbey for the land of Henley, saving the right of Reading Abbey and any suit it may wish to move against St Albans* [1151 × 57]

A f 93r; B ff 203v–204r; C f 124r

I(ohannes) dei gratia Wigorn(iensis) ecclesie servus devotus universis sancte matris ecclesie filiis, salutem. Notum sit[a] tam presentibus quam futuris quod controversia que inter abbatem Sancti Albani Robertum[b] et Amfridum personam ecclesie de Eston(a) super ecclesia de Sepehale,[c] et alia que inter abbatem eundem et Gill'[d] prenominati Amfridi nepotem super terra de Henleia, diu vertebatur, cum a domino papa utraque canonice diffinienda nobis delegata fuisset, communi partium assensu hoc fine amicali terminata est. Videlicet, quamdiu vixerit ecclesiam de Sepehale[e] cum omnibus pertinentiis suis libere et quiete de monasterio Sancti Albani tenebit et insuper[f] .xii. marcas argenti pro recompensatione dampnorum suorum[g] que per abbatem sibi illata dicebat ab eodem monasterio percipiet. [h]Gill'[d] vero prenominatus pro terra de Hanleia .v. marcas a prenominato monasterio[i] percipiet.[h] Quapropter uterque prenominatorum omni querele sue prius mote tam super ecclesia de Sepehal(e)[j] quam super terra[k] de Hanleia quam et[l] super dampnis in perpetuum renuntiavit. Nos itaque vice domini pape qua in huius cause cognitione fungebamur et scripti nostri auctoritate compositionem istam corroboravimus, salvo in omnibus iure[m] Rading(ensis)[n] monasterii et querela si quam adversus monasterium Sancti Albani movere voluerit. Huius autem rei[o] testes sunt.[p]

[a] *Insert* omnibus *B,C* [b] Rodbertum *B*
[c] Shepehale *B*, Shepehal' *C* [d] G' *B,C*
[e] Shepeh' *B*, Shepehal' *C*
[f] *A has here* tene, *probably intended for deletion*

^g *Om. in B,C*
^{h-h} *A has this passage in the margin in the same hand and marked for insertion; in B,C in the text*

ⁱ *Insert* similiter *B,C*   ^j Shepeh' *B,* Schepehal' *C*
^k *A has* terram   ^l etiam *B,C*
^m *B,C have* iure *after* monasterii   ⁿ Radyngie *C*
^o compositionis *B,C*   ^p *Add* et cetera *B,C*

The bishop is identified in the rubric of A (*I. de Pageham*). After the blessing of Abbot Robert of St Albans and before the bishop's death on 31 Mar. 1157. It is not certain whether this act dates earlier or later than the agreement between the abbeys of St Albans and Reading recorded in nos. 688–9. Although it does not directly concern Bucklebury church, but rather the rights of Reading's church at Aston (Herts.), it has been given here in view of its close relationship to the preceding charters. Cf. also no. 374.

  1. Possibly Henley Hill, in Digswell, near Aston (*VCH Herts.*, iii. 82).

692 *Exhortation by Jocelin [de Bohun], bishop of Salisbury, to all faithful of the diocese to visit the holy place built in honour of St Mary Magdalen at Bucklebury, by the cross of St James, on her vigil and feast day [22 July], and grant of an indulgence of 40 days to all who do so and make an offering*
[prob. 1158 × 65]

  A f 60r

Ioc(elinus) dei gratia Sar(esburiensis) episcopus omnibus Christi fidelibus per Sar(esburiensem) episcopatum constitutis, salutem et dei benedictionem. Quoniam pastoralis cure et officii est gregem sibi commissum pietatis opera docere et ad ea caritatis officia que salutem conferunt invitare, universitatem vestram rogamus attentius et exhortamur in domino quatinus pro salute vestra venerabilem ac religiosum locum de Burghild(eburia) iuxta crucem sancti Iacobi apostoli in honore dei omnipotentis et beate Marie Magdalene constructum, cui quia multum dilexit veniam peccatorum suorum Christus donavit, in vigilia et festo eiusdem pia devotione visitetis. Nos autem, de dei misericordia confisi, omnibus qui eundem locum religiosum predictis diebus benigne visitaverint et de propriis facultatibus aliquam caritatis intuitu portionem erogaverint, de iniuncta sibi penitentia quadraginta dies relaxamus.

This and the following act date almost certainly from the abbacy of Abbot Roger of Reading, 1158–65, and are concerned with the site of a miraculous cure of plague wrought in his time at Bucklebury by the Hand of St James, the abbey's principal relic. To commemorate the miracle a wooden cross in honour of St James was erected (B. R. Kemp, 'The miracles of the Hand of St James', *Berks. Arch. Journ.*, lxv (1970), 11–12). Near the cross and on the place mentioned in the present act a chapel was soon erected in honour of St Mary Magdalen (see no. 693). This chapel, though now disappeared, is probably to be identified with the Magdalen Chapel in Chapel Row, whose ruins remained until 1770 (*VCH Berks.*, iii. 296).

693 *Grant by Jocelin [de Bohun], bishop of Salisbury, to all penitents who honour and reverence the chapel of St Mary Magdalen and its cemetery blessed by the bishop near Bucklebury, of part of the indulgence which he gave there and a share in the prayers and benefits of Salisbury Cathedral*

[prob. 1158 × 65]

A f 6or

Iocelinus dei gratia Sar(esburiensis) episcopus omnibus Christi fidelibus in episcopatu Sar(esburiensi) constitutis, salutem in vero salutari. Ut ea que a nobis rationabiliter facta sunt rata et inconvulsa valeant permanere, tam scripture testimonio quam nostre auctoritatis patrocinio volumus sicut et debemus communire. Inde est quod nos omnibus confessis et vere penitentibus qui capellam beate Marie Magdalene iuxta Burchildeburiam constructam et cimiterium ibidem a nobis benedictum honoraverint et reverentiam exhibuerint partem indulgentie quam ibidem dedimus benigne concedimus, et participes orationum et beneficiorum que in Sar(esburiensi) fiunt ecclesia esse concedimus. Si quis vero, quod absit, temeritatis ausu locum predictum violare seu adnichilare temptaverit, noverit nos in ipsum tanquam sacrilegum et episcopalis dignitatis contemptorem iustitie rigorem prolaturos. Valete in domino.

For the date and further comment, see no. 692 n.

694 *Notification and confirmation by Hugh abbot of Abingdon, William abbot of Thame and Ralph prior of Hurley, acting as papal judges-delegate, of the settlement in their presence of the dispute between Abbot Hugh [II] and the convent of Reading and Bartholomew, chaplain of Bucklebury, over the church of Bucklebury. Bartholomew resigned the church into the hands of the officials [of Salisbury], and Reading, at the request of the count of Mortain and because of Bartholomew's former education in the abbey, granted the church to him in free alms saving the ancient pension, but retained the chapel of G(ilbert) Martel with all its tithes and obventions and gave it in free alms to the poor hospital outside the abbey gate*

[1189 × 93; ?1191 × 93]

A ff 71v–72r; B ff 197v–198r; C ff 116v–117r
Pd. (transl.) Humphreys, *Bucklebury*, 155–6

Universis Christi fidelibus *a*ad quos presens scriptum pervenerit*a* H(ugo) de Abbend(onia) [*f 72r*] et W(illelmus) de Thame dei gratia abbates et R(adulfus) prior de Hurl(eia), *b*eternam in Christo*b* salutem. Noverit universitas vestra causam que vertebatur inter H(ugonem) abbatem Rading(ensem) et monachos eiusdem loci et Bartholomeum capellanum de Burkilleb(er)i*c* super ecclesia eiusdem ville, nobis a domino papa commissam, hoc fine quievisse. Quod videlicet*d* prefatus B(artholomeus) prefatam ecclesiam in manus officialium in presentia nostra ex toto resignavit. Prefatus autem abbas Rading(ensis)*e* consentiente conventu, ad petitionem nostram et domini comitis Moret(onii) et propter pristinam educationem prefati B(artholomei) in domo Rading(ensi), ei prenominatam ecclesiam salva antiqua pensione divini amoris intuitu in puram ac perpetuam concessit elemosinam, retenta sibi capella G(ilberti)*f* Martel cum omnibus decimationibus tam maioribus quam minoribus et omnibus obventionibus de dominio ipsius et de tota terra rusticorum quas prefatus B(artholomeus) in audientia nostra ex integro abiuravit. Dedit autem prefatus abbas de consensu totius capituli prefatam capellam cum omnibus predictis decimationibus et obventionibus hospitali pauperum extra portam abbatie in perpetuam elemosinam. Ut autem predicta compositio et preassignata predicte*g* capelle memorato hospitali a sepedicto abbate facta donatio perpetuam teneat*h* firmitatem, eas presentis scripti testimonio et sigillorum nostrorum appositione auctoritate qua functi sumus apostolica corroboravimus, in eos sententiam excommunicationis inferentes quicumque predictam compositionem vel prefatam donationem infringere presumpserint. Fauctoribus autem et protectoribus earum apostolicam largimur benedictionem.

a–a et cetera B,C
c Burchildebir' B, Burghilb'i C
e Radyngie C
g supradicte B,C

b b Om. in B,C
d C repeats quod here
f For expansion, see above no. 211 n. 2
h teneant B,C

After the election of Hugh abbot of Abingdon in 1189/90 (*Heads of Relig. Houses*, 25) and, since Gilbert Martel's chapel was granted to the hospital while Hubert Walter was bishop of Salisbury (see no. 224), not later than May 1193. The reference to the officials suggests the bishop's absence on crusade, Feb./Mar. 1190–20 Apr. 1193 (see nos. 203–4). The involvement of (John) count of Mortain fits nicely with other evidence of his interest in Reading's affairs (see nos. 40–44) and may indicate a date for this act of not earlier than 1191, when the first certain notice of his concern for the abbey occurs ('Ann. Rad. Post.', 401). The act was not included in the original composition of A, but was entered soon afterwards and listed as a later addition in the margin of the table of contents (A f 6v).

695 *Notification and confirmation of the same by the officials of Hubert [Walter], bishop of Salisbury*   [1189 × 93; ?1191 × 93]

A f 72r; B f 198r; C f 117r
Pd. (transl.) Humphreys, *Bucklebury*, 155

Universis Christi fidelibus *a* ad quos presens scriptum pervenerit*a* officiales domini H(uberti)*b* Sar(esburiensis) episcopi, *c* eternam in domino*c* salutem. Noverit universitas vestra causam que vertebatur inter H(ugonem) abbatem Rading(ensem) et monachos eiusdem loci et Bartholomeum capellanum de Burkilleber(ia)*d* super ecclesia eiusdem ville hoc fine quievisse. Quod videlicet prefatus B(artholomeus) prefatam ecclesiam in manus nostras coram iudicibus delegatis ex toto resignavit. Prefatus autem abbas Rading(ensis) consentiente conventu, ãd petitionem nostram et predictorum iudicum et domini comitis Moret(onii) et propter antiquam educationem prefati B(artholomei) in domo Rading(ensi), ei prenominatam ecclesiam salva antiqua pensione divine pietatis intuitu contulit, retenta sibi capella G(ilberti)^e Martel cum omnibus decimationibus^f tam maioribus quam minoribus et omnibus obventionibus de dominio predicti G(ilberti)^e et de tota terra rusticorum quas prefatus B(artholomeus) in presentia iudicum et nostra ex integro abiuravit. Dedit autem prefatus abbas de consensu totius capituli prefatam capellam cum omnibus predictis decimationibus^f et obventionibus hospitali pauperum extra portam in perpetuam elemosinam. Ut autem predicta compositio et preassignata eiusdem capelle memorato hospitali a sepedicto abbate facta donatio perpetuam teneat firmitatem, eas presentis scripti testimonio et sigilli domini H(uberti)^b Sar(esburiensis) episcopi appositione corroboravimus.^{g}

$^{a-a}$ Om. in B,C ^{b} For expansion, see no. 694 n.
$^{c-c}$ Om. in B,C ^{d} Burchill' B,C
^{e} For expansion, see no. 211 n. 2 ^{f} decimis C
^{g} Add Hiis testibus B

Contemporary with no. 694. The act was entered in A and listed in the margin of the table of contents exactly as for no. 694.

696 *Further notification of the same by the officials of Hubert [Walter], bishop of Salisbury, and admission and institution of Bartholomew as parson of Bucklebury at the presentation of the abbot and convent of Reading for an annual pension of 30s* [1189 × 93; ?1191 × 93]

B f198r; C f117r
Pd. (transl.) Humphreys, *Bucklebury*, 156–7

Universis sancte matris ecclesie filiis, et cetera, officiales domini H(uberti)^a Sar(esburiensis) episcopi, salutem. Noverit universitas vestra quod, cum controversia verteretur inter dominum abbatem et conventum Rading(enses) et B(artholomeum) capellanum de Burgh-(ildebiria) super ecclesia eiusdem ville, predictus B(artholomeus) omni iuri quod in predicta ecclesia habere videbatur renuntians eandem ecclesiam in manus nostras resignavit. Moti autem misericordia predictus abbas et conventus eandem ecclesiam predicto B(artholomeo) caritatis intuitu contulerunt, retenta capella G(ilberti)^b Martel cum omni iure suo, scilicet decimis dominii sui et hominum suorum^c et obventionibus, et eundem B(artholomeum) ad prefatam ecclesiam nobis presentaverunt. Nos autem ad eorum presentationem sepedictum B(artholomeum) ad prenominatam ecclesiam admisimus et personam instituimus, retenta predicta capella cum omni iure suo prenominato ad usus hospitalis Rading(ensis). Reddet autem prefatus B(artholomeus) prefato abbati et conventui annuatim .xxx. solidos nomine pensionis. Ne autem in posterum valeat hec donatio infringi, sigillo domini Sar(esburiensis) episcopi eam communimus. Hiis testibus.

a For expansion, see no. 694 n.   *b For expansion, see no. 211 n. 2*
c C repeats suorum

Contemporary with nos. 694–5. For the abbey's grant of the church to Bartholomew for an annual payment of 30s, see below, Appendix B, no. 1.

697 Mandate by Pope Honorius III to the abbots of St Albans, Evesham and Thame, on information from the abbot and convent of Reading that, whereas the church of Bucklebury *(Burghild(eburia))*[a] and other of their churches had been appropriated to the abbey by the local diocesans for the use of hospitality and the poor and for other pious uses, and confirmed by Popes Celestine [III] and Innocent [III], certain abbots of the house and others have converted the churches to other uses, that, if this is so, they are to procure the restoration of the said churches, when vacant, to the said pious uses and the induction of the abbot and convent into corporal possession of the same   16 July 1217

C f 223v; D ff 77v–78r
Pd. (transl.) Humphreys, *Bucklebury*, 159–60

Dat' Anagnie xvii. kl' Augusti, pontificatus nostri anno primo.

a Burkildeberi D

For the bulls of Celestine III and Innocent III to which this mandate refers, see nos. 158–61, 166.

698 *Licence by Robert [Bingham], bishop of Salisbury, to Abbot Richard [I, of Chichester] and the convent of Reading to appropriate the church of Bucklebury to the support of the abbey's hospitality, saving a vicarage to be assessed by the bishop's authority, which will be in the abbey's presentation*

17 Aug. 1239

A f 74r; B f 194r; C f 113v
Pd. (transl.) Humphreys, *Bucklebury*, 160–1

Robertus dei gratia Sar(esburiensis) episcopus dilectis in Christo filiis R(icardo) eadem gratia abbati Rading(ensi) et eiusdem loci conventui, salutem gratiam et benedictionem. Particeps mercedis efficitur qui bonorum operum se constituit adiutorem. Sane, cum facultates

monasterii vestri ad hospitalitatis*a* gratiam sectandam, a qua nullus
cuiuscumque ordinis, etatis, sexus vel conditionis pro vestris beneficiis
ad vos declinans se queritur alienum, noverimus minime sufficere,
nos, ut de mercede vestra participium reportemus, ecclesiam de
Burghildebur(ia)*b* cum omnibus pertinentiis suis, salva vicaria in
eadem auctoritate nostra taxata, cuius presentatio ad vos pertinebit,
ad hospitalitatis honera*c* supportanda de assensu capituli nostri Sar(esburiensis) in vestros usus proprios et perpetuos duximus concedendam,
auctoritate pontificali statuentes quod ecclesiam predictam cum pertinentiis salva vicaria predicta pacifice possideatis in posterum et
inconcusse, salvis in omnibus iure auctoritate et dignitate Sar(esburiensis) ecclesie et nostra et successorum nostrorum et loci archidiaconorum. In huius rei testimonium presens scriptum sigillo nostro
duximus*d* muniendum. Hiis testibus, et cetera.*e* Dat' apud Sar(es-
buriam) xvi. kl' Septembris, pontificatus nostri anno xi.

a hospitatis (*sic*) B,C   *b* Burghildebir' B, Burghilberi C
c onera B,C   *d* Om. in C
e B,C end

Cf. no. 215, which concerns the churches of Bucklebury and Thatcham. The bishop's
act which is there confirmed by the dean and chapter of Salisbury is of the same date
as the present act, and the witnesses were probably the same for both.

699   Inspeximus and confirmation of the same by R(obert), the dean,
and chapter of Salisbury. Sealing   17 Aug. 1239

A f74r; B f194r; C f113v
Pd. (abridged transl.) Humphreys, *Bucklebury*, 161

Hiis testibus, *a* et cetera.*a* Dat' *b* per manus A(de) cancellarii nostri, xvi.
kl' Septembris,*b* anno gratie M.CC.xxxix.

a-a Om. in B   *b-b* Om. in B,C

The copy in A quotes the bishop's act in full apart from the dating clause; the copies
in B and C give only its opening words.

700   *Notification by William, archdeacon of Berkshire, that, in execution of a
mandate to him from Robert [Bingham], bishop of Salisbury, he has inducted
the abbot and convent of Reading into corporal possession of the church of
Bucklebury*   [1229 × 38]

A f73v; B f194r-v; C ff113v-114r
Pd. (transl.) Humphreys, *Bucklebury*, 161

Universis sancte matris ecclesie filiis *a* has litteras inspecturis*a* W(illelmus) archidiaconus Berk(esire), salutem *b* eternam in domino.*b*
Mandatum domini Sar(esburiensis) episcopi in hec verba suscepi.

Robertus dei gratia Sar(esburiensis) episcopus dilecto filio archidiacono Berk(esire), salutem gratiam et benedictionem. Cum ecclesia
de Burghild(eburia)*c* dudum a venerabilibus patribus et predecessoribus nostris Huberto, Hereberto*d* et Ricardo quondam Sar(esburiensibus) episcopis dilectis filiis abbati et monachis Rad(in-
gensibus) in proprios usus concessa fuerit et nos postmodum
concessionem illam eis factam auctoritate pontificali duxerimus con-
firmandam, vobis mandamus quatinus prefatos abbatem et conventum in corporalem possessionem eiusdem ecclesie faciatis induci,
salva sufficienti et honesta vicaria a nobis in ipsa ecclesia ordinanda.
Valete.

Et quia mandatum predictum ea qua decet diligentia executus
prefatos abbatem et conventum in corporalem predicte ecclesie *'*induxi
possessionem,*'* ne super hoc in posterum a quoquam possit hesitari,
hoc presentibus litteris duxi testificandum. In cuius rei testimonium
f[presenti scripto sigillum meum apposui].*f*

a-a Om. in B,C	*b-b* Om. in B,C
c 'Burghildebir' B, Burghilberi C	*d* Herb' B,C
e-e possessionem induxi B,C	*f-f* Supplied from B,C; A has et cetera

The relationship of this act to nos. 698–9 is problematical since, although at first sight
it would appear to follow them, the naming of archdeacon W. in the two independent
texts in A and B (C being a copy of B) makes that impossible. Giles of Bridport had
become archdeacon of Berkshire by Feb. 1238 at the latest (*The Cartulary of Cirencester
Abbey*, ed. C. D. Ross (1964), ii. 486—dated about (*circa*) Purification 1237, i.e. in
modern dating 1238); hence, unless the W. in the Reading texts is an error for G., the
archdeacon was probably either William of Merton, who was already in office when
Robert Bingham was consecrated on 27 May 1229 and who became dean of Wells by
Mar. 1238 at the latest (*Reg. St Osmund*, ii. 108; *Sarum Charters and Documents*, 243), or
William of Raleigh, whom in 1249 Giles of Bridport referred to as his predecessor as
archdeacon of Berkshire (*Civil Pleas of the Wiltshire Eyre, 1249*, ed. M. T. Clanchy (Wilts.
Rec. Soc., xxvi, 1971), 83) and who may be the William of Raleigh who was elected
bishop of Norwich on 10 Apr. 1239 and translated to Winchester in 1243. Moreover,
since there was a 'vicar' at Bucklebury by 1238 at the latest (see Appendix B, no. 2)
and by Mar. 1243 Philip had been 'vicar' for at least 4 years (see no. 701), an
appropriation of some kind had clearly taken place before the date of nos. 698–9. It
seems likely, therefore, that what was intended by nos. 698–9 was the further specific
appropriation of the church to the abbey's hospitality. I am grateful to Dr Diana
Greenway for help in dating this act.

701 Acknowledgement by Philip, vicar of Bucklebury (*Burghildebyr'*),*a* that, since he is bound to pay 20s annually to Reading
Abbey for the greater tithes of Marlston (*Martelest(ona)*), he owes £4
in arrears, which he obliges himself to pay at the rate of 10s annually
along with the 20s. Thus, until the arrears are paid, he will pay
the abbey 30s annually, viz. 10s each at the Purification, Hockday

(*Hokedai*)[b] and the Nativity of St John Baptist, reverting to 20s annually thereafter. Sealing. Done A.D. 1242

25 Mar. 1242 × 24 Mar. 1243

B f 194v; C f 114r
Pd. (transl.) Humphreys, *Bucklebury*, 161–2

[a] Burghilberi *C* [b] Hokeday *C*

The interpretation of the date assumes the year to begin on 25 March. Marlston in the parish of Bucklebury was held by the Martel family (*VCH Berks.*, iii. 292). The greater tithes in question here are the same as those of Gilbert Martel's chapel retained by the abbey in the settlement in no. 694. As early as 1201, however, the tithes were leased to the incumbent of Bucklebury (see no. 211).

702 Quitclaim, in the full court of Bucklebury (*Burghildebir'*) and of Thatcham (*Tacheham*),[a] before the *villata* of Beenham (*Benham*) and of Crookham (*Crocham*),[b] by Humphrey *le Cunreur* of Winchester and Edith his wife, with the assent of Richard their heir, to Reading abbey of the whole land called *terra Kerebin*[1] [at Bucklebury] and all their right in the same. For this the abbey has given them in their great need 2½ marks of silver and 2s, and to Richard their heir 2s. Sealing with Humphrey's seal and, since Edith had no seal, that of Juliana formerly wife of Gilbert of Colthrop (*Colethrope*). Witnesses[c] [omitted]

[13th cent.; not later than 1258]

B f 70v; C f 36r
Pd. (transl.) Humphreys, *Bucklebury*, 119

[a] Tacheam *C* [b] Crokham *C*
[c] *Om. in C*

Dating very uncertain. The deed was not entered in A, but appears in the original section of B and is therefore not later than 1258. The rubrics of B and C locate the land at Bucklebury.

1. Possibly related to the modern Carbin's Wood (*Berks. Place-Names*, i. 156).

703 Final concord in the king's court at Reading in one month from St John Baptist, 32 Henry III, before Roger of Thirkleby (*Turkeby*), Gilbert of Preston, master Simon of Walton (*Wauton'*) and John of Cobham (*Cobbeham*), justices-in-eyre, and others, between John son of Alexander and Claricia his wife, seeking, and Abbot Richard [I, of Chichester] of Reading, holding, concerning 80 acres of land in Bucklebury (*Burghildebyr'*).[a] John and Claricia recognized the land to be the right of the abbot and his abbey of Reading and quitclaimed the same for themselves and the heirs of Claricia. For this the abbot gave them 1 mark of silver

22 July 1248

Bf17or; Cf100r–v
Pd. (transl.) Humphreys, *Bucklebury*, 118–9

ª Burghilberi *C*

The foot of this fine is PRO CP 25(1)/8/16/21

BURGHFIELD

In this section nos. 707–748c are given in the order in which they appear in B and C.
Those occurring in B ff146–55 are in the section of the cartulary devoted to the
almoner's charters.

704 *Last will and testament of Aumary son of Ralph, including gifts to
Reading Abbey of lands in Burghfield and Carswell* [*in Buckland*]
[prob. 1185 × 86]

Af38r–v; (in part) Bf59v; Cff26v–27r

In nomine patris et filii et spiritus sancti. Hoc est testamentum Amal-
rici filii Rad(ulfi) in quo extreme voluntatis sue*ª* conscribi voluit
testimonium. Hec ergo sunt que libera voluntate pro salute anime sue
donavit. Radingensi monasterio dedit terram Iacob*ᵇ* de Berchefeld*ᶜ*
cum pertinentiis suis, et in villa de Carsewelle*ᵈ* terram quam carta
sua confirmavit. Gileberto fratri suo [*f38v*] donavit unam marcam.*ᵉ*
Pueris suis ex concubina susceptis .x. marcas argenti delegavit. Hec
sunt que fide interposita debuit et solvi precepit. Bevero .vii. marcas,
Waldero .x. solidos, Agnete .x. marcas, Ricardo stabulario .viii. solidos
et .vii. denarios, Edwardo Gentil .xx. et .i. denarios, Radulfo de
Oxoneford .xx. et .i. denarios, Willelmo vinitori .iii. solidos et .ii.
denarios et obolum, Willelmo de Waltham .xviii. solidos, Gileberto
de Wicumbia .l. et .ix. solidos, Aluredo de Oxoneford .xx. solidos,
Roberto Huchet .xx. solidos, Willelmo Ruffo dimidiam marcam, Ade
unam marcam, Ricardo de Abbedonia*ᶠ* .ix. solidos et .vi. denarios,
Emme .viii. solidos, Rogero de Belesoure .xiiii. solidos. Hiis testibus:
Anselmo suppriore Rading(ie), Radulfo phisico, Philippo de Sae,
Helia de Catmere, Willemo capellano Sancte Marie, Roberto capellano Sancti Laurentii, Willelmo de Ticheham, Iohanne de Hida,
Oeno filio Restwoldi, Ricardo le Franceis, Willelmo de Bosevilla,
Ricardo aurifabro, Ricardo stabulario, et aliis multis. Horum ergo
debitorum et aliorum quorum tempore facti testamenti non est facta
mentio solutionem commisit faciendam de rebus suis Willelmo de
Ticheham, Oeno filio Restwoldi, Ricardo le Franceis. Et si qua sunt
alia debita que catalla sua excedunt et per istos solvi non possunt,
heredibus suis solvenda reliquit. Si autem ad predicta perficienda

cetera catalla non suffecerint, de bladis suis crescentibus ea perfici precepit.

^a*A has* sui
^cBerghefeld *B*, Bergh'feld' *C*
^e*B,C end with* Et cetera. Hiis testibus

^b*Sic in all texts*
^dCarswalle *B,C*
^f*Sic in Ms*

Aumary son of Ralph was dead by Michaelmas 1186 (*PR 32 Henry II*, 112). Henry II's confirmation of his gifts to Reading can be dated 1185 × 87 (see no. 33).

705 *Gift in free alms by Aumary son of Ralph to Reading Abbey of the land which James held of him in Burghfield* [prob. 1185 × 86]

A f38v; A f83v; B f59r-v; C f26v

Sciant presentes et futuri quod ego Amalricus filius Radulfi dedi et presenti carta confirmavi deo et sancte Marie de Rading(ia) et mon-achis ibidem deo servientibus totam terram quam Iacob et ante-cessores eius tenuerunt de me et antecessoribus meis in Berchefeld^a in perpetuam elemosinam et liberam et quietam de me et heredibus meis, cum homagio et eodem servitio quod predictus Iacob mihi facere consuevit quamdiu^b de me tenuit. His^c testibus:^d Willelmo de Tikeham, Oeno filio Restwaldi, Thoma de Berchefeld, et multis aliis.

^aBurgefeld *A f83v*, Berghefeld *B,C*
^cHiis *A f83v, B, C*

^bquandiu *A f83v*
^d*A f83v, B,C end*

Probably contemporary with no. 704. This gift appears to have been the origin of the abbey's later manor in Burghfield (*VCH Berks.*, iii. 401; *Aids*, i. 48).

706 *Confirmation of the same by William, Earl Ferrers* [*earl of Derby*] [prob. 1185 × 86]

A ff38v–39r; A f107r; B f59v; C f27r

Notum sit omnibus tam futuris quam presentibus quod ego Willelmus comes de Ferr(ariis)^a concedo et confirmo deo et sancte Marie et monachis de Rading(ia)^b totam terram quam Amalricus^c filius Rad(ulfi) eis dedit et confirmavit, scilicet^d terram quam Iacob tenet in Berchef(eld),^e et totum servitium quod mihi et heredibus meis pertinet de terra illa, salvo servitio Isolde sororis mee et heredum suorum.^f Hii [*f 39r*] sunt testes:^g R(obertus) de Ferr(ariis) frater comitis, Henricus de Ferr(ariis) avunculus comitis, et multi alii.

^a*Rubric of A ff 38v–39r has* Ferres, *of B* Ferreres
^bRadinges *A f 107r*
^d*Om. in A f 107r*
^eBerf' *A f 107r*, Bergf' *B*, Bergh'feld' *C*
^f*B,C end with* T'

^cAmauri *A f 107r, B*

^g*A f 107r ends*

Probably contemporary with, or soon after, no. 705. The Ferrers lordship had obtained since at least 1086, but is not mentioned after this confirmation (*VCH Berks.*, iii. 401).

707 Gift by Robert of Burghfield (*Burghf(eld)*)^a^ son of Robert of Burghfield^b^ to Reading Abbey of 12d rent which Simon *Merewin* used to pay him annually for the land which he held of him in Burghfield (*Burgef'*).^c^ To be held freely. The said Simon and his heirs shall pay the said 12d rent annually, viz., 6d each at Michaelmas and Easter. Warranty. For this the abbey has given him 10s sterling. Sealing. Witnesses [omitted]   [?*c.* 1220 × 1258]

B f 59v; C f 27r

^a^Bergh'feld' *C*   ^b^Burgh'feld' *C*

Not later than 1258, since it was entered in the original section of B. The donor may have been Robert grandson of Thomas of Burghfield (see no. 723), the latter of whom probably held a second manor in Burghfield in the later 12th century (see no. 721a n.). If so, his father Robert apparently succeeded to the estate in 1202 (*PR 4 John*, 7) and the donor was himself certainly in possession by 1227 (*Cur. Reg. R.*, xiii. 28) and possibly by *c.* 1220 (*PR 3 Henry III*, 162). He is probably to be identified also with the Robert of Burghfield who held half a knight's fee in Burghfield of Ralph de Mortimer in 1242–3 (*Fees*, ii. 854) and was a coroner of the abbot of Reading's liberty in 1248 (Clanchy, *Berks. Eyre of 1248*, 387).

708 Gift by Amis *de Pelethot*^a^ to Reading Abbey of 12d rent which Luke of Grazeley (*Greyshulle*)^b^ used to pay him annually for a certain moor which he held of him by charter in Burghfield (*Burgefeld*)^c^ lying next to (*subtus*) *Pusecrofte* to the north and next to (*iuxta*) a certain meadow called *la Moregarstune*^d^ to the west. To be held freely. Warranty. For this the abbey has given him in his great need 10s sterling as entry-fine. Sealing. Witnesses [omitted]   [?*c.* 1220 × 40]

A f 83r–v; B ff 59v–60r; C f 27r

^a^Peletoth *B,C*   ^b^Greysull' *B*
^c^Burgh'feld' *C*   ^d^Moregarstone *B,C*

The donor's main holdings were in Hartley, in Shinfield, Berks. (*VCH Berks.*, iii. 263). He appears to have been related to Matthew of Burghfield, who held Reading Abbey's Burghfield manor in the early years of Henry III (*ibid.*, 263, 401; *Cur. Reg. R.*, xiii. 28). This deed was entered in A in a section written in one hand preceding deeds of 1241 (below, nos. 1202–3) in another hand. It is in any case not later than 1258, since it appears in the original section of B. The donor was dead by Feb. 1261, having drowned in a ditch after falling from his horse (PRO JUST 1/40, m. 28d).

709 Grant in free alms by Amis *de Peletot*^a^ to Reading Abbey and its men of Grazeley (*Greysull'*)^b^ of common and easement in Pinge (*Punge*) [in Burghfield], and gift in free alms of 3s rent to be received annually at Michaelmas for the purpresture which he has occupied in Pinge.

Neither he nor his heirs shall be able to occupy or enclose more than was enclosed at Michaelmas, 25 Henry III. For this the abbey has remitted to him the purpresture which he has occupied in Pinge. Warranty and sealing [?Oct. 1241]

B f6or; C f27v; C f219r[1]

Hiis testibus:[c] [Richero Nernut, Roberto de Uffynton', Johanne de la Huse, Johanne Banastr(e), Roberto de Burffeld, Roberto Bencheff, Gilberto Kent, Henrico de la Stane, Thoma de Hanle, et multis aliis].

[a]Pelytot C f219r   [b]Greyshull' C f27v
[c]B and C f27v end here, the witnesses being supplied from C f219r

Certainly afer 29 Sept. 1241, the terminus specified in the text, and possibly during the main session of the 1241 Berkshire eyre, 6 Oct.–3 Nov. (Crook, General Eyre, 103), since the first five witnesses were jurors for Theale hundred and the sixth a juror for Reading hundred in that eyre (PRO JUST 1/37, m. 27). Pinge Wood is a hamlet in Burghfield parish (VCH Berks., iii. 399).

1. This copy was written in a later 14th-century hand, which added the note: Rog' Folk(us) tenet.

710 Gift by Adam de Mora, at the instance of Walter the almoner, to the almonry of Reading for the support of the poor living there, of 1 virgate of land which Richard Abboth sometime held in Burghfield (Burgefeld'),[a] except for a moor called Thrift Moor (la Frithmor'), lying between the land of Robert of Burghfield and the land called Thrift (Frith), and Berkemor', lying between Buricrofta and the land of Alard of Burghfield and extending in length from the king's way to new Garstona, which the donor has retained for his own use; except also for a meadow which William of Englefield (Englef') holds of him and his heirs for an annual rent of 4d, and a small moor which Matthew of Burghfield holds of him and his heirs by the service of $\frac{1}{2}$d, in exchange for which meadow and small moor Adam has given the said almonry 1 acre of meadow in his meadow lying next to (subtus) Pusecroft,[b] and the rest of this meadow he has given in free alms. To be held by the almonry freely by rendering annually to him and his heirs 2d at Michaelmas for all services, claims (querele) and secular exactions, saving the king's service. For this the said Walter has given him 60 marks of silver to pay off the great debt which he owed the Jews of Winchester. Warranty, with provision for reasonable exchange in his land of Mora, and acquittance of all suit of the court of Robert of Burghfield. Sealing. Witnesses[c] [omitted]

[not later than 5 Jan. 1231]

B f146r; C f 85v; D f24r-v

[a]Burgh'feld' C   [b]Puscroft D
[c]Om. in C

The date is derived from that of Henry III's confirmation (no. 713). The reference in
no. 711 to Robert of Chineham indicates that this virgate was the one which Adam
acquired from Adam of Chineham in 1203 (*Fines sive Pedes Finium*, i. 129–30). The two
moors of *Berkemor'* and Thrift Moor were later given to the almonry by Adam's son,
Gilbert (no. 741).

711 Receipt, in the form of 'letters patent', by Adam *de Mora* in
respect of 60 marks of silver received from Walter, almoner of Reading,
for 1 virgate of land which Richard *Abboth* sometime held of Robert
of Chineham (*Chinham*) in Burghfield (*Burgefeld'*),[a] except for Thrift
Moor (*la Frithmor'*) and *Berkemor'* [described as in no. 710], which
virgate excluding the said two moors he gave to the almonry of
Reading for the support of the poor living there. Neither Adam nor
his heirs in the name of inheritance, nor his wife in the name of dower,
shall be able to claim (*vendicare*) any right in the said virgate in
perpetuity apart from 2d annually payable to him and his heirs at
Michaelmas, saving the king's service. Sealing. Witnesses [omitted]
[not later than 5 Jan. 1231]

B f 146r–v; C ff 85v–86r

[a]Burgh'feld' *C*

Date as for no. 710.

712 Quitclaim by Adam *de Mora* to the almonry of Reading of 1
acre of meadow in *Landmed'*[a] belonging to the mill of Burghfield
(*Burgef(eld)*),[b] viz., that which Thomas of Englefield (*Englef(eld)*)
sometime held at farm of Nicholas *Sexy*,[c] miller of Burghfield. For this
Richard the almoner has given him 10s sterling. Sealing. Witnesses[d]
[omitted]   [? 1231 × 40]

B f 146v; C f 86r; D f 27r

[a]Lanmed' *C*, Landmede *D*   [b]Burghfeld' *C*
[c]Sexu *D*   [d]*Om. in C*

Richard was almoner later than Walter, who occurs *c*. 1231 (see no. 710), as is clear
from no. 717. He may have been followed by a Robert who occurs as almoner in
1239 × 40 (D f 22v). The acre quitclaimed in this deed is possibly that which William
of Englefield was now holding of William the miller (no. 735).

713 Confirmation by King Henry III to the almonry of Reading of
the gift which Adam *de Mora* made to it, for the support of the poor
living there, of 1 virgate of land in Burghfield (*Burgef(eld)*)[a] which
Richard *Abbot*[b] sometime held, except for two moors called Thrift
Moor (*la Frithmor'*) and *Berkemor'*. Witnesses [omitted]
[5 Jan. 1231]

B ff 146v-147r; C f86r; D f24v
Pd. (cal.) *Cal. Chart. R.*, i. 128 (from Charter Roll)

*ª*Burgh'feld' *C*   *ᵇ*Abboth *D*

The Charter Roll entry is dated 5 Jan. 1231 at Reading.

713a   Notes of the following:
   (i)   charter by Mary daughter of Richard to Adam *de Mora*
         concerning the same land
   (ii) charter between Adam *de Mora* and Isabel daughter of
         Mary concerning the land of Richard, her grandfather
                                                    [?early 13th cent.]

   B f 147r; C f86r

The first of these is entered in the Almoner's cartulary (D f 73v). Mary, daughter of
Richard Abbot, gives to Adam her part of her father's land, i.e. ½ virgate of the fee of
Thomas of Burghfield, and half the land called *Heimundesesse* and 1 acre of meadow,
and her part of the land which her father held of the fee of Amis de Peletot, i.e. a half.

714   Gift in free alms by Ralph *de Mora* to the almonry of Reading
of a certain part of his land in the field called *Westham*, viz., that part
which extends laterally alongside the land which the almoner has of
Amis *de Peletoth*,*ª* to make a ditch 7 feet in width and as long as the
said almoner's land, to enclose the said land, beginning at the ditch
of the meadow of *Pusecroft* which he sometime gave the same almonry
in a similar way, as his charter witnesses. Sealing. Witnesses*ᵇ* [omitted]
                                                    [?*c.* 1220 × 1258]

   B f 148r; C f87r-v

   *ª*Pelytoth' *C*   *ᵇ Om. in C*

Entered in the original section of B and clearly dating after one of the gifts to the
almonry by Amis de Peletot, on whom see no. 708 n. Ralph de Mora was a juror for
Theale hundred in 1241 and 1248 (PRO JUST 1/37, m. 27; Clanchy, *Berks. Eyre of
1248*, 296).

715   Gift by Ralph *de Mora* to the almonry of Reading of a certain
part of his land lying on the northern edge of the meadow called
Pusecroft (*que iacet ad septemtrionalem plagam prati quod vocatur Pusecroft*),
viz., all the land extending east–west alongside the said meadow
outside the hedge enclosing it as far as the ditches which have been
made in his presence and in that of other lawful men, in order to
make a ditch there to enclose that meadow on that side. To be held
in perpetuity as freely as any alms can be given. Sealing. Witnesses
[omitted]   [?*c.* 1220 × 1258]

B f 148r; C f 87v; D ff 30v–31r

Probably within the same dating limits as no. 714, but earlier than it, since this gift provided for the ditch already existing in no. 714

716 Gift by Ralph *þurebern*[a] [b]of Burghfield (*Burgef(eld)*)[cb] to the almonry of Reading, at the instance of Walter, almoner of Reading, of a certain acre of his land in *Burchefeldingefeld*[d] called *Sarpacra*, beginning at the king's way and extending to the east towards the court (*curia*) of Matthew of Burghfield (*Burgefeld*).[c] To be held freely by rendering annually to him and his heirs 1d at Michaelmas for all services, claims (*querele*), secular exactions and demands, saving the king's service belonging to 1 acre of land in the same vill. For this the said Walter has given him in his great need 4s sterling as entry-fine. Warranty, with provision for equal exchange elsewhere in his land in Burghfield, and sealing. Witnesses [omitted]   [?*c.* 1220 × 31]

B f 148v; C ff 87v–88r; D ff 28v–29r

[a]Thurebern *D*   [b-b]*Om. in D*
[c]'Burgh'feld'/Burghfeld *C*   [d]'Burghfeldingefeld' *C*

Dating very approximate and based on the occurrence of Walter as almoner in or before 1231 (see no. 710).

717 Gift by Ralph *þur(ebern)*[a] to the almonry of Reading, at the instance of Richard the almoner, of 1 acre of arable land in Burghfield (*Burgef(eld)*)[b] apart from the acre which he gave previously in the time of Walter the almoner. The almoner shall hold the two acres freely in perpetuity by rendering annually to him and his heirs 1 penny (*sterlingus*) at Michaelmas for all services, claims, secular exactions and demands, saving the king's service belonging to that amount of land. For this the said Richard has given him in his great need 4s sterling as entry-fine. Warranty, with provision for equal exchange elsewhere in his land in Burghfield, and sealing. Witnesses[c] [omitted]
[?1231 × 40]

B f 148v; C f 88r; D f 29r

[a]Thurebern *D*   [b]'Burgh'feld' *C*
[c]*Om. in C*

For Richard's time as almoner, see no. 712 n. The acre given here was called *Putacra* (see no. 719).

718 Gift by Robert *de la Broke*, son of W. *de la Broke*, of Burghfield (*Burgf(eld)*)[a] to the almonry of Reading, at the instance of Walter, almoner of Reading, of his entire croft in Burghfield (*Burgef(eld)*)[b] called *Estcrofta* as it is enclosed by a hedge on all sides. To be held freely by rendering annually to him and his heirs 2d on the feast of St Giles [1 Sept.] for all services, claims and secular exactions, saving the king's service belonging to such a tenement. For this Walter the almoner has given him 18s sterling as entry-fine. Warranty, with provision for equal exchange, and sealing. Witnesses[c] [omitted]

[?*c.* 1220 × 31]

B ff 148v–149r; C f 88r; D f 29r–v

[a]'Burgh'feld' *C*, Burgefeld *D*   [b]'Burgh'feld' *C*
[c]*Om. in C*

Date as for no. 716. W. de la Broke is possibly the William son of Ansketil of no. 721a.

719 Confirmation by Robert of Burghfield (*Burgef(eld)*)[a] to the almonry of Reading of the gift by Ralph *þurebern*[b] of 2 acres of land in Burghfield, one called *Sarpacra* and the other *Putacra*, to be held by the almoner freely by rendering annually to Ralph and his heirs 1 penny (*sterlingus*) at Michaelmas; and of a croft in the same vill called *Estcrofta*, to be held by the almoner freely by rendering annually to Robert *de la Brok*(*e*) and his heirs 2d (*sterlingi*) on the feast of St Giles, saving the king's service. For this Richard the almoner has given him ½ mark of silver. Warranty and sealing. Witnesses [omitted]

[?1231 × 40]

B f 149r; C f 88r–v; D f 29v

[a]'Burgh'feld' *C*   [b]'Thurebern *D*

For Richard's time as almoner, see no. 712 n. This deed confirms nos. 716–8.

720 Gift by Christina, daughter of the late Robert [a]*del Broc,*[a] to the almonry of Reading of 4 crofts of her land in the vill of Burghfield (*Burgefeld*),[b] which crofts are called *la Brok'londe*.[c] They lie together lengthwise between the land which the almoner of Reading holds of the same tenement and the land of Richard son of Miles, and breadthwise between the purpresture which Nicholas of Sherborne (*Syreburn'*)[d] holds of Robert of Burghfield and the purpresture of the same Robert. Also gift of 1 acre of meadow lying in *Istlandemed*[e] next to the meadow of Nicholas *del Heec* on the west. To be held freely by rendering annually to the chief lord of the fee 3s 8d, viz., 22d each at the Annunciation and the feast of St Giles, and to Christina and her heirs 2d as increment on the feast of St Giles, for all secular service, exaction, custom and demand, saving the king's service belonging to that amount of land in the same vill. For this Robert of Oxford (*Oxon'*), almoner of Reading, has given her 6 marks of silver as entry-fine. Warranty and sealing. Witnesses [omitted]   [?*c.* 1250 × 1256]

B f 149r–v; C f 88v

*a-a*de la Brok' *C*   *b*Burgh'feld' *C*
'Broklond' *C*   *d*Syrebourne *C*
'Estlandemed' *C*

In Nov. 1256 the same almoner, Robert of Oxford, conveyed part of this land to
Richard *de Brocland'* (D f 58r). When Robert took office is unknown, but for earlier
almoners, see no. 727 n.

721   Gift in free alms by Robert of Burghfield (*Burgef (eld)*)*a* to Reading Abbey, for the support of the almonry there, of all the land which
Robert *de la Brok*(*e*) sometime held of him in the vill of Burghfield,
along with 2 crofts of purpresture at *Hulla* which Gilbert *Deuh* sometime held in the same vill. To be held freely of Robert and his heirs
quit of all custom, demand, suit of court and secular service. Warranty
and sealing. Witnesses [omitted]   [?*c.* 1250 × 1256]

B f 149v; C ff 88v–89r

*a*Burgh'feld' *C*

According to the rubrics of B and C, this confirms no. 720. It is presumably therefore
of roughly the same date.

721a   Note of a charter by Thomas of Burghfield (*Burgef (eld)*) to
William son of Ansketil concerning the same land
                                                [late 12th cent. × 1202]

B f 149v

Thomas of Burghfield probably held the manor in Burghfield later known as Burghfield
Regis or Nethercourt (*VCH Berks.*, iii. 400). He occurs in 1176 and 1197 × 8 (*PR 22
Henry II*, 134; *Ancient Charters*, 107) and was dead in 1202, when his son Robert
succeeded (*PR 4 John*, 7; cf. *PR 9 Richard I*, 204; above, no. 707 n.).

722   Quitclaim by Alice, daughter of the late Gilbert *Kipping*, to the
almonry of Reading, at the instance of Walter the almoner, of all her
right in the whole land in Burghfield (*Burgef (eld)*)*a* which Gilbert
Kipping her father held by gift of Sir Thomas of Burghfield. For this
the said Walter has given her 1 mark of silver. She has handed over
to him the charter which her father had from Sir Thomas of Burghfield
concerning that land. Sealing. Witnesses*b* [omitted]   [?*c.* 1220 × 31]

B ff 149v–150r; C f 89r; D f 28r

*a*Burgh'f' *C*   *b*Om. in C

Date as for no. 716.

722a   Note of a charter by Thomas of Burghfield (*Burgf*(*eld*)) to G(ilbert) *Kipping* concerning the same land

[late 12th cent. × 1202]

B f 150r

Date as for no. 721a. This deed is entered in the Almoner's cartulary (D ff 27v–28r). Thomas of Burghfield gives to Gilbert son of Roger Kipping all his land at *Hulla* and 1 acre of meadow in North Mead (*Northmede*) which William Serle held, amounting to 1 cotland. Thomas was the grandfather of Robert of Burghfield, who confirmed no. 722 (see no. 723).

723   Gift by Robert of Burghfield (*Burgef*(*eld*))[a] to the almonry of Reading, at the instance of Walter the almoner, of all the land in Burghfield which G(ilbert) [b][son of Roger][b] *Kipping* held by gift of Thomas of Burghfield, Robert's grandfather. To be held freely by rendering annually to Robert and his heirs 4s, viz., 2s each at the Annunciation and the feast of St Giles, for all services, claims, exactions and secular demands, saving the king's service belonging to 1 cotland (*cothsethlande*). For this the said Walter has given him 2 marks of silver as entry-fine. Warranty and sealing. Witnesses [omitted]

[?*c.* 1220 × 31]

B f 150r; C f 89r–v; D f 28r–v

[a]'Burgh'feld' C   [b-b] *Om. in B,C; supplied from D*

Date as for no. 716. The rent retained by Robert in this deed is the same as that retained by Thomas of Burghfield in his deed to Gilbert Kipping (no. 722a).

724   Gift by Robert of Burghfield (*Burgef*(*eld*))[a] to the almonry of Reading of 4s annual rent which he used to receive from the land which G(ilbert) [b][son of Roger][b] *Kipping* sometime held by gift of Thomas of Burghfield (*Burgefeld*'),[a] Robert's grandfather. To be held by the almoner freely in perpetuity. For this Richard the almoner has given him 3 marks of silver. Warranty and sealing. Witnesses [omitted]

[?1231 × 40]

B f 150r; C f 89v; D f 28v

[a]'Burghfeld' C   [b-b] *Om. in B,C; supplied from D*

For Richard's time as almoner, see no. 712 n. In this deed Robert of Burghfield relinquishes the rent retained in no. 723.

725   Gift in free alms by John *Serle* to the almonry of Reading of 1 acre of his land in the field of Burghfield (*Burgef*(*eld*))[a] lying between the land of John *le Stive* and that of Uthred White (*le Wite*[b]). Warranty and sealing. Witnesses [omitted]   [c. mid-13th cent.]

  B f 150r–v; C f 89v

  ᵃBurgh'feld' C   ᵇWhite C

Entered in the original section of B and possibly of about the same date as no. 726.

726   Gift by John *Serle* of Burghfield *(Burgef(eld))*ᵃ to the almonry of
Reading of ½ acre of his land in Burghfield in the field called *Estfeld*,
one head facing north and the other south, lying between his land
and that of Nicholas *Serich*. To be held freely by rendering annually
to him and his heirs 1d at Michaelmas for all secular service, exaction
and demand. For this Robert of Oxford *(Oxon')* the almoner has given
him 6s sterling as entry-fine. Warranty and sealing
                                                  [?c. 1250 × 1258]

  B f 150v; C f 89v; D f 35v

Hiis testibus:ᵇ [Roberto de Burgefeld, Waltero Alard, Johanne Rumbald, Stephano de la Wile, Hervico Belet, Thoma Turg',ᶜ et multis
aliis].

  ᵃBurghfeld' C
  ᵇ B,C end, the witnesses being supplied from D
  ᶜ Reading doubtful, perhaps intended for Thomas Turnagain who occurs in ?c. 1240 (see nos.
757, 1096–7)

Date as for no. 720.

727   Gift by Adam son of Alard of Burghfield *(Bur'f(eld))*ᵃ to the
almonry of Reading of 2 acres of land in *Brocfurlong*ᵇ and 1 acre of
meadow lying in *Estelondemed(e)*.ᶜ To be held of him and his heirs freely
by rendering annually to Robert of Burghfield *(Burf(eld))*ᵈ and his
heirs 3d on the feast of St Giles for all services and exactions. For this
Robert the almoner has given him in his great need 26s sterling as
entry-fine. Warranty and sealing. Witnessesᵉ [omitted]   [?c. 1240]

  B f 150v; C ff 89v–90r; D ff 29v–30r

  ᵃBurgh'feld' C, Burgef' D   ᵇBrocforlong' C, Brochfurlong D
  ᶜEstlondemede C,D   ᵈBurgef' D
  ᵉOm. in C

The sequence of almoners of Reading in the 13th century is very uncertain. A Robert
occurs in 24 Henry III, 1239–40 (D f 22v), apparently following Richard (?1231–),
who followed Walter (?c. 1220–31)—see nos. 712, 716, notes. Stephen occurs as almoner
in 1244 × 45 (see no. 731 n.).

728   Confirmation by Robert of Burghfield *(Burg(e)f(eld))*ᵃ to the
almonry of Reading of the gift by Adam son of Alard of 2 acres of

land in *Brocfurlong*[b] and 1 acre of meadow lying in *Estlandmed*(e);[c] and of ½ acre of land which Roger *Fuzedam* held of him in Burghfield. For this confirmation the almoner of Reading shall render to him and his heirs annually 4d, viz., 2d each on the feast of St Giles and at the Annunciation. Warranty and sealing. Witnesses[d] [omitted]

[?c. 1240 × 1258]

B ff 150v–151r; C f 90r; D f 30r

[a] Burgh'feld' *C*   [b] Brocforlong' *C*
[c] Estlondemede *D*   [d] *Om. in C*

After no. 727 and, since entered in the original section of B, not later than 1258. The rent due from these lands was quitclaimed to the almonry in no. 732.

729 Gift in free alms by Robert of Burghfield (*Burg*(e)*f*(*eld*))[a] to the almonry of Reading, at the instance of Robert the almoner, of 2 acres of land in Burghfield[b] lying on the eastern side of the croft which belonged to Robert *de la Brok*(e). To be held freely by rendering annually to Robert and his heirs 4d for all service and secular exaction, viz., 2d each at the Annunciation and on the feast of St Giles. For this Robert the almoner has given him 10s sterling. Warranty, with provision for the return of the 10s if the land cannot be warranted, and sealing. Witnesses[c] [omitted]   [?c. 1240]

B f 151r; C f 90r; D f 30v

[a] Burefeld' *C*   [b] Burgfeld' *C*
[c] *Om. in C*

Date as for no. 727. Robert the almoner in the present deed was presumably later than Richard, in whose time Robert of Burghfield confirmed Robert de la Broke's croft to the almonry (see no. 719).

730 Gift in free alms by Robert of Burghfield (*Burg*(e)*f*(*eld*))[a] to the almonry of Reading of the acre of land called *Buthacre*[b] which Uthred White (*Albus*)[c] held. To be held freely and quit of all secular service, by rendering annually to him and his heirs 2d, viz., 1d each on the feast of St Giles and at the Annunciation. Warranty and sealing. Witnesses [omitted]   [?c. mid-13th cent.]

B f 151r; C f 90r–v; D f 30v

[a] Burefeld' *C*   [b] Burhacra *D*
[c] Abbas *D* (*in error*)

Not later than 1258, since it was entered in the original section of B, and possibly of about the same date as no. 725.

731 Gift in free alms by Robert of Burghfield (*Burg*(e)*f*(*eld*))[a] to the

almonry of Reading, at the instance of Stephen the almoner, of the
plot (*pars*) of land lying in the marsh (*mariscus*) next to the small hill
(*parva duna*). Warranty and sealing. [Witnesses]*ᵇ*　　[?*c.* 1240 × 50]

　Bf151r–v; Cf90v; Df30r–v; Df34r

　ᵃBurfeld' *C* (*interlined*)
　ᵇ*Om. in B,C; supplied from both texts in D*

Stephen the almoner is presumably identical with the Stephen of Burgundy, or of
Leominster, who occurs as almoner in 1244 × 45 (Df33v). A Robert was almoner in
1239 × 40 (Df22v) and an Alfred (or Andrew) at some time in the mid-13th century
(see no. 910). Neither copy of this deed in D gives the witnesses.

732　Quitclaim in free alms by Robert of Burghfield (*Burg(e)f(eld)*)ᵃ
to the almonry of Reading of 12d rent which the almoner of Reading
used to pay him, viz., from *la Brok(e)lande*ᵇ 6d, from *la Burthacre* 2d,
from certain land which belonged to Adam Small (*le Smale*) 3d, and
from certain land which belonged to Roger *Fucedame* 1d. To be held
quit of all custom, demand, suit of court and secular service. Warranty
and sealingᶜ　　　　　　　　　　　　　　　　[*c.* 1250 × 1258]

　Bf151v; Cf90v; Df74r

Hiis testibus:ᵈ [domino Willelmo de Englefeld', domino Roberto de
Uffynton', domino Rogero de Hyda, Henrico de la Stane clerico,
Gilberto de la Mora, Amisio de Peletoth, Johanne Rumbald', Waltero
Alard, et aliis].

　ᵃBurgh'feld' *C*, Burgefelde *D*　　　　　ᵇBroklonde *C*, Broclande *D*
　ᶜ*C ends*
　ᵈ*B ends, the witnesses being supplied from D*

After nos. 727–8 and 730, which retain the last three of the rents quitclaimed here,
and not later than 1258, since the deed was entered in the original section of B; cf. no.
736 n. Adam Small is clearly identical with Adam son of Alard in no. 727.

733　Gift by William the miller of Burghfield (*Burg(e)f(eld)*)ᵃ to the
almonry of Reading of all his land in the croft to the south of his
house, lying between the eastern hedge and the acre which belonged
to Adalardᵇ of Burghfield; also of 1½ acres on the eastern side of his
house next to the same hedge. The almoner will have these freely
by rendering annually to him and his heirs 1 penny (*sterlingus*) at
Michaelmas for all services and secular exactions, saving the king's
service belonging to that amount of land. Warranty. For this Richard
the almoner has given him in his great need 22s sterling as entry-fine.
Sealing. Witnesses [omitted]　　　　　　　　　　　[?1231 × 40]

Bf15Iv; Cf90v; Df27r–v

*Burgh'feld' C   *Apelard D

For Richard's time as almoner, see no. 712 n.

734 Gift by W(illiam) the miller to the almonry of Reading of 1
acre of arable land in Burghfield (*Burg(e)f(eld)*),[a] viz., that which
formerly belonged to Gocelin and lies on the eastern side of the donor's
house. To be held in perpetuity free of all secular service and exaction.
Warranty. For this Richard the almoner has given him in his great
need 5s sterling. Sealing. Witnesses [omitted]   [?1231 × 40]

Bf15Iv; Cf91r; Df27v

*Burghfeld' C

Date as for no. 733.

734a Note of a charter by Matilda, widow of the same W(illiam),
concerning her dower at Burghfield (*Burg(e)feld'*)[a]

[before June 1248]

Bf15Iv; Cf91r

*Burghfeld' C

This is entered in the Almoner's cartulary (Df34v). Matilda, widow of William the
miller son of Nicholas the miller of Burghfield, quitclaims to the almonry her right of
dower in the tenement of her late husband in Burghfield. Among the witnesses is Roger
of Whitchurch, who was dead by the time of the Berkshire eyre of 1248 (Clanchy,
Berks. Eyre of 1248, 175).

735 Gift by W(illiam) the miller to the almonry of Reading of the
whole of his part of the mill of Burghfield (*Burg(e)f(eld)*),[a] namely
half, with all appurtenances in lands, waters, fisheries, meadows and
pastures; with the exception of 1 acre of land with a small moor which
W(illiam)[b] of Englefield (*Englef(eld)*) holds of him and his heirs for
an annual rent of 1d, and of a garden which Emma the donor's sister
holds by the service of 1d, and of a weir (*gurges*) on the eastern side
of the great bridge which G(ilbert)[b] *de Mor(a)* holds of him and his
heirs by inheritance for 1d annual rent; these men and their heirs will
hold the said lands and weir in fee and inheritance of the almoner of
Reading by paying to him the same rent which they used to render
to the donor. To be held freely by the almoner by rendering annually
to the lord of the fee 13s sterling, viz., 6s 6d each on the feast of St
Giles and at the Annunciation, and 12 sticks of eels at Shrovetide
(*quaremme pernant*);[c] and to the donor and his heirs or assigns 1 penny
(*sterlingus*) annually on the feast of St Giles for all services and secular

exactions, saving the king's service belonging to 1 cotland. For this Richard the almoner has given him in his great need, viz., the prosecution of his pilgrimage to the Holy Land, $4\frac{1}{2}$ marks of silver as entry-fine. Warranty. For greater security he has handed over to the almoner the charter which Nicholas, his father, had from Thomas of Burghfield concerning the same mill. Sealing. Witnesses [omitted]

[?1231 × 40]

Bf152r; Cf91r; Df26r–v

*ᵃ*Burgh'feld' *C*   *ᵇExpansion from D*
*ᶜ*quarame pernaunt *D*

Date as for no. 733.

735a Note of a charter by Thomas of Burghfield (*Burgef(eld)*)*ᵃ* to Nicholas son of Sexus (*filius Sexi*), viz., the father of W(illiam) the miller, concerning the mill of Burghfield*ᵇ*   [late 12th cent. × 1202]

Bf152r; Cf91r

*ᵃ*Burghfeld' *C*   *ᵇ*Burfeld' *C*

Date as for no. 721a. This deed is entered in the Almoner's cartulary (Df26r). Thomas of Burghfield gives to Nicholas son of Sexus his half of the mill with the suit of his men, his fishery in the Kennet and 3 selions adjacent to Nicholas's messuage, held by Robert *Stiward*, Jocelin and Thomas *Halfald*'. The services are the same as those payable to the lord of the fee in William the miller's deed, no. 735.

736 Confirmation by Robert of Burghfield (*Burg(e)f(eld)*)*ᵃ* to the almonry of Reading of the gift| by W(illiam) the miller of Burghfield of half the mill of Burghfield,*ᵇ* for which the almoner shall render annually to him and his heirs 2s of silver, viz., 12d each at the Annunciation and on the feast of St Giles, for all custom, demand, suit of court and secular service, saving the king's service belonging to 1 cotland of the same fee, and saving to Robert and his heirs free multure of his demesne table as he and his ancestors have had it hitherto. Also gift in free alms of a fish-pond (*vivarium*) next to the mill to the east, free of all secular service and demand. For this Stephen of Leominster (*Leom'*) the almoner has given him 16 marks of silver. Warranty and sealing*ᶜ*   [?*c.* 1240 × 50]

Bf152r–v; Cf91v; Df55v

ᵈ[Hiis testibus: domino Willelmo de Englefeld, domino Roberto de Uffinton', domino Rogero de Hyda, Henrico de la Stane clerico, Gileberto de Mora, Amisio de Peletoth, Johanne Rumbald, Waltero Alard', et aliis].*ᵈ*

*ᵃ*Burghfeld' *C*   *ᵇ*Burgfeld' *C*

Date as for no. 731. This was Robert of Burghfield's second confirmation of William's gift, made after he had become a knight, as the rubrics of B and C indicate. It represents a significant reduction in the services payable to the lord of the fee. For the first confirmation, see no. 736a. The witnesses to this and no. 732 are the same and probably indicate a similar date for each, ?*c*. 1250.

736a Note of another charter by the same, before he became a knight, concerning the same mill. This is now void and superseded by the above charter   [?1231 × 40]

B f 152v; C f 91v

This confirmation is entered in the Almoner's cartulary (D ff 26v–27r) and was made in the time of Richard the almoner, for whom see no. 712 n. Robert confirms to the almonry half the mill for an annual rent of 1d to William the miller and an annual service to himself of 18s, made up of 13s rent and 5s for the 12 sticks of eels, payable in two instalments of 9s at the Annunciation and the feast of St Giles. He also gives in free alms the fish-pond.

737 Gift in free alms by William Grey (*Grey*), at the instance of Walter the almoner, to the almonry of Reading, for the support of the poor living there, of all the land at the moor of Burghfield (*Burgef(eld)*)*a* which he held of Amis *de Peletoth*.*b* To be held freely by rendering annually to him and his heirs 1d as recognition on the feast of St Martin for all service and secular exaction, and to Amis *de Peletoth*,*c* lord of the fee, or his heirs 2s, viz., 12d each on the feast of St Martin and at the Nativity of St John Baptist, for all secular service, saving the king's service. Warranty and sealing. Witnesses [omitted]
                                         [?*c*. 1220 × 31]

B f 152v; C ff 91v–92r; D f 25r

a Burghf(eld) *C*   *b* Pelytoth' *C*
c Pelytot' *C*

Date as for no. 716.

738 Confirmation by Amis *de Peletoth*ª to the almonry of Reading, at the instance of Walter the almoner, of all the land at the moor of Burghfield (*Burgef(eld)*)*b* which W(illiam) Grey sometime held of him and conveyed to the almonry. Sealing. Witnesses [omitted]
                                         [?*c*. 1220 × 31]

B ff 152v–153r; C f 92r; D f 25r

a Pelytot' *C*   *b* Burgh'feld' *C*

Date as for no. 716. For Amis, see no. 708 n.

739 Quitclaim in free alms by Amis *de Peletoth,*[a] at the instance of Walter the almoner, to the almonry of Reading for the support of the poor living there, of 2s rent which he used to receive annually from William Grey for a tenement which he held of him at the moor of Burghfield (*Burgef(eld)*).[b] Amis and his heirs shall be able to claim nothing in the rent and tenement apart from such royal service as belongs to such a tenement. For this Walter the almoner has given him 30s sterling. Warranty and sealing. Witnesses [omitted]

[?*c.* 1220 × 31]

B f 153r; C f 92r; D f 25r–v

[a] Pelytot' *C*   [b] Burefeld' *C*

Date as for no. 716.

740 Gift in free alms by G(ilbert)[a] *de Mora*, at the instance of Stephen of Burgundy (*Burgund'*)[b] the almoner, to the almonry of Reading for the support of the poor living there, of all the land in the moor of Burghfield (*Burgef(eld)*)[c] which W(illiam)[a] Grey sometime held of him, viz., all the land which he, Gilbert, acquired from Amis *de Peletot*[d] by a concord *de sub scuto*, saving a messuage which W(illiam)[a] *Hereward* holds. To be held freely by rendering annually to Gilbert and his heirs $\frac{1}{2}$ mark of silver, viz., 3s 4d each on the feasts of St John Baptist and St Martin, for all services, claims and exactions. For this the said Stephen has given him in his great need 6 marks of silver. Warranty, with provision for reasonable exchange in his land of *Mora*, and sealing. Witnesses [omitted]   [?*c.* 1240 × 50]

B f 153r; C f 92r–v; D ff 33v–34r

[a] *Expansion from D*
[b] *Expansion from D; the rubric of D calls him Stephen of Leominster*
[c] 'Burghfeld' *C*   [d] Pelytot' *C*

Date as for no. 731. The donor was the son of Adam de Mora of nos. 710–2 (see no. 748c n.).

741 Gift by G(ilbert) *de Mora* to the almonry of Reading of the whole two moors in Burghfield (*Burgef(eld)*)[a] called *Berk(e)mor'* and Thrift Moor (*Friþmore*).[b] To be held freely by rendering annually to him and his heirs, by the hand of the almoner, 1 pair of gloves, price 1d, at Easter for all custom, demand, suit of court and secular service. Warranty. For this the abbey has given him 12 acres of land in exchange and, for the harvest of the wood of the said moors, 22 marks of silver. Sealing. Witnesses [omitted]   [1238 × 58]

Bf153v; Cf92v

^a'Burghfeld' C   ^b'Frithmor' C

The Almoner's cartulary contains a deed by Abbot R. and the convent of Reading giving Gilbert 12 acres of land in exchange for the two moors (Df77r–v). The present deed dates therefore not earlier than 1238, when the first Abbot R. of the 13th century, Richard I, became abbot, and not later than 1258, since it was entered in the original section of B. It gives the two moors retained by Gilbert's father in no. 710.

742 Gift in free alms by G(ilbert) *de Mor(a)* to the almonry of Reading of the whole ditch (*fossatum*) between his moor of Pinge (*Punge*) [in Burghfield] and the moor of the almoner of Reading which W(illiam) Grey sometime held of him. The ditch extends from the king's road from Pinge round as far as (*per circuitum usque ad*) the moor called *Neugarston(e)* and is 7 feet in width. Warranty and sealing. Witnesses [omitted]   [?*c.* 1240 × 50]

Bf153v; Cf92v

The date is perhaps the same as that of no. 740, by which Gilbert gave the almonry the moor which William Grey sometime held of him. For Pinge, see no. 709 n.

743 Gift and quitclaim by G(ilbert) *de Mora* to the almonry of Reading of all his right in the fishery of a weir (*gurges*) near the bridge of the [River] Kennet on the eastern side in the lordship (*tenura*) of Burghfield (*Burgef(eld)*).^a To be held freely by the almoner in perpetuity. For this Richard the almoner has given him in his great need 30s sterling in the name of rent and entry-fine (*nomine redditus et gersume*). Warranty and sealing. Witnesses [omitted]   [?1231 × 40]

Bff153v–154r; Cf93r; Df27v

^a'Burgh'feld' C

For Richard's time as almoner, see no. 712 n. This weir was reserved by William the miller from his gift of half the mill of Burghfield to the almonry in the same years (see no. 735).

744 Gift in free alms by Amis *de Peletoth* to the almonry of Reading of the whole moor in Burghfield (*Burgef(eld)*),^a between the meadow called 'Almoner's meadow' and the land of W(alter)^b Vachell (*Fachel*) and extending eastward from the moor of Pinge (*Punge*) as far as the field called *Westham*, which moor ought to be 4 perches in width. Warranty and sealing   [?*c.* 1220 × 1258]

Bf154r; Cf93r; Df74v

Hiis testibus:[c] [domino Roberto de Offinton', Roberto de Burgefeud', Waltero Alard, Johanne Rembaud, Gilberto de Mora, Nicholao[d] de Syreb(urne),[e] Thoma de Hanle, Willelmo le Poer, et multis aliis].

[a]Burgh'feld' C, Burgefeud' D   [b]Expansion from D
[c]B,C end, the witnesses being supplied from D
[d]D has Nicholaus   [e]D has Syreb'r

For Amis, see no. 708 n. The deed was entered in the original section of B. The rubrics of B, C, D state that this concerns the meadow of *Pusecrofte*. Cf. above, nos. 714–15.

745 Agreement, in chirograph form, between Amis *de Peletoth*[a] and Abbot Richard [I] of Reading by which the abbot has conceded for himself and his successors that Amis and his heirs may enclose, purpresture and cultivate a certain part in the moor of Pinge (*Punge*) [in Burghfield], viz., that which is between the house of Stephen *Lefwine* and that of William *Sucle* and extends eastward as far as the land of Walter Vachell (*Fachel*), in return for which Amis has given to the almonry of Reading 3 acres of land in the said purpresture, viz., those nearest the land of G(ilbert) *de Mora* called *la Rudinge*, to be held freely in perpetuity. Sealing by both parties. Witnesses [omitted]   [1238 × 58]

Bf154r; Cf93r

[a]Pelytoth' C

During the abbacy of Richard I (1238–62) and, since it was entered in the original section of B, not later than 1258.

746 Gift in free alms by Gilbert *de Mora*, for the health of his soul and those of his wife, Emma, and all his ancestors and successors, to Reading Abbey, for the support of the poor living there, of all his land in the vill of Burghfield (*Burugfeld*)[a] which he held of Amis *de Peletot*,[b] with woods, moors, meadows, pastures, roads, paths, homages, reliefs, rents, escheats and other appurtenances. To be held freely by rendering annually to Amis or his heirs 1 lb of pepper and 2 pairs of gloves, price 1d, or 1d at the feast of St Martin for all service, custom, suit of court and demand, saving hidage due from the land. Warranty and sealing   [?c. mid-13th cent.]

Bf154r–v; Cf93r–v; Df52v; Df58v

Hiis testibus:[c] [domino Willelmo[d] Englefeld, domino Nicholao de Hanred', domino Roberto de Mapelderh(am), domino Roberto de Bur-(gefeld), domino Roberto Dauvers, domino Ricardo de Handred', et multis aliis].

^aBurghfeld' *C*, Bur' *D f 52v*, Burgfeld *D f 58v*
^bPelytoth *C*, Pelitot *D f 58v*
^c*All texts end here, except D f 52v, from which the witnesses are supplied*
^d*Omission of* de *sic*

Date as for no. 747, q.v. Nicholas of Hendred was already a knight in 1248 (Clanchy, *Berks. Eyre of 1248*, 155), was sheriff of Berks. 1250–9 (*List of Sheriffs*, 107) and occurs into the 1270s (see below, nos. 759, 792, 1194; *Cal. Inq. P.M.*, ii. 29). For Robert of Mapledurham, see no. 863 n.

747 Quitclaim in free alms by G(ilbert) *de Mora* to the almonry of Reading, for the use of the poor living there, of $\frac{1}{2}$ mark worth of annual rent in Burghfield (*Burgefeld*)^a which the almoner of Reading used to pay him from the moor which William Grey (*de Grey*) sometime held of him in the said vill. Sealing. Witnesses [omitted]
[?*c*. mid-13th cent.]

B f 154v; C f 93v; D f 58v

^aBurghfeld' *C*, Burgfeld *D*

According to the Almoner's cartulary (D f 58v), this deed and nos. 746 and 748–748c were acquired in the time of Robert of Reading, then almoner (*He sunt carte de terra de Mora, scilicet de terra Gileberti de Mora. Que quidem carte adquisite sunt tempore fratris Roberti de Radinges tunc elemosinarii*). This almoner clearly held office after Stephen of Burgundy (or Leominster), who was almoner when the rent quitclaimed by the present deed was retained by Gilbert de Mora (no. 740). He may be the same as Robert of Oxford, who occurs as almoner in 1256 (D f 58r; cf. above, no. 720). The present deed is in any case not later than 1258, since it appears in the original section of B.

748 Confirmation in free alms by Amis *de Peletot*^a to Reading Abbey of all gifts of lands, rents and all other things which it has by gift of Gilbert *de Mora* in Burghfield (*Burugfeld*);^b also of all the purprestures in Pinge (*Punge*) concerning which he, Amis, brought the king's writ *de rationabilibus divisis faciendis* in the hundred [court] of Theale (*la Thele*), as they are enclosed on all sides by hedges and ditches. To be held freely by rendering annually to Amis and his heirs 1 lb of pepper and 2 pairs of gloves, price 1d, or 1d at the feast of St Martin for all service, custom, suit of court and demand, saving the service of 9d in hidage. Sealing. Witnesses [omitted]   [?*c*. mid-13th cent.]

B ff 154v–155r; C ff 93v–94r; D ff 52v–53r; D ff 58v–59r

^aPelytoth' *C*
^bBurghfeld' *C*, Bur' *D ff 52v–53r*, Burgefeld *D ff 58v–59r*

Date as for no. 747.

748a Note of a charter by Amis *de Peletot* to Gilbert *de Mora* concerning certain lands in Burghfield (*Burgefeld'*)

[before *c*. mid-13th cent.]

Bf155r

This deed is entered in the Almoner's cartulary (Df59r). Amis gives to Gilbert a parcel of his land of Pinge and all his land in the western part of the field formerly belonging to Adam de Mora called *la Ruding'*, in Burghfield, for an annual rent of 1 pair of white gloves or ¼d at Martinmas; warranty *excepta vi brevis domini regis de nova diseisina*; entry-fine 2 marks. Before no. 746.

748b Note of another charter by the same to the same concerning certain lands in Burghfield (*Burgefeld*)   [before *c*. mid-13th cent.]

Bf155r

This deed is entered in Df59r-v. Amis gives to Gilbert half the tenement in Burghfield for which battle was waged between Gilbert and him for Isabel daughter of Mary (for whom see no. 713a); 4 acres of land in Pinge; 1 acre bf land in the western part of the field of Adam de Mora called *la Rudinge*; and 1 acre of land in the northern part of the croft formerly of Adam *de la Rudinge*; for an annual rent of 1 pair of white gloves, price ½d, at Martinmas; entry-fine 66s 8d. Before no. 746.

748c Note of a quitclaim by the same A(mis) to the same G(ilbert) concerning 10s worth of rent in Burghfield (*Burgefeld*)
                                                              [before *c*. mid-13th cent.]

Bf155r

This deed is entered in Df59r. Amis sells and quitclaims to Gilbert for 10 marks the 10s rent which Adam de Mora, Gilbert's father, used to pay him for all the land which he held of him in Burghfield; annual payment of 1 lb of pepper at Martinmas instead. Before no. 746. Nos. 748a–c were among those acquired by Reading Abbey in the time of Robert of Reading, almoner (see no. 747 n.).

748d Note of a final concord between Adam Noble (*le Noble*), William of Wallingford (*Walingford'*) and Richard *Spade*, seeking, and *Reimbald'* of Burghfield (*Burghef'*), holding, concerning 1 virgate of land in Burghfield (*Burghf'*)   [not later than 1258]

Bf170v

Not later than 1258, since the note was entered in the original section of B. No foot appears to survive in the PRO, suggesting either that the fine was made before 1195 or that it was not made in the king's court.

749 Grant, in a tripartite deed, by Peter of Burghfield (*Burgh'feld*) to Reading Abbey that the water-course[1] in Burghfield shall in perpetuity run from the main stream (*aqua*) of the [River] Kennet through the middle of the eastern part of his meadow called *Chalnemede* as far as *Dynbroke*; it shall be 10 feet wide at its entry and 8 feet wide throughout its length to *Dynbroke*;^a if the water-course shall be impeded in any way, the abbot and convent and their successors may enter it, flood and repair it at their will without contradiction or impediment of him and his heirs or assigns. For this the abbey has granted to him and his heirs in perpetuity a white monk's loaf (*unus panis albus monachilis*) to be received annually at Reading at the Annunciation from the granger. Both parties have granted also that John *de la Wik*'^b and his heirs shall have in perpetuity the fishery of the said water-course in exchange for that of *la Dynebroke*^c which is now blocked (*nunc obstruitur*), in return for which the said John has granted that the water-course shall be in perpetuity as aforesaid. The tripartite deed is sealed by the three parties *alternatim* [*c.* 1270 × 98]

Bf51r–v; Gf14r–v

Hiis testibus: dominis Rolando de Erle, Rogero de Burghfeld, Thoma de Anvers, militibus, Willelmo de Blebury, Gilberto Pynson', Johanne Fachel,^d Nicholao Shirburne,^e Willelmo de Colle, Gilberto clerico, et multis aliis.

Rubric (*B only*): Carta Petri de Burghfeld de cursu aque voc(ato) le Garenters broke

^aDyndbroke *G*   ^bWick' *G*
^cDynbroke *G*   ^dFachell' *G*
^eShirborne *G*

This is in effect an agreement between three parties. Peter of Burghfield was the tenant of the abbey's manor in Burghfield, being the grandson of Matthew of Burghfield (see no. 708 n.; *VCH Berks.*, iii. 401; *Cal. Pat. R. 1272–81*, 408), and was in possession by 1279 (*Cal. Misc. Inq.*, i. 350). Roger of Burghfield held the other Burghfield manor by the same time (*ibid.*). Roland of Earley occurs as early as 1261, perhaps in the household of Giles of Bridport, bishop of Salisbury, and was later one of the bishop's executors (BL Add. Ms. 28870 (cartulary of Vaux College, Salisbury), f9r, f42r); in 1269 he was steward of John Breton, bishop of Hereford, and apparently not yet a knight (*Charters and Records of Hereford Cathedral*, ed. W. W. Capes (Hereford, 1908), 125); he had become a knight by May 1270 and died 1297 × 1305 (see nos. 759, 1257). William of Coley is probably the one who was dead by Nov. 1298 (see no. 1044). For Thomas Danvers and William of Blewbury, see respectively *VCH Berks.*, iii. 424, and below no. 855 n.

1. The rubric of B names the water-course as *le Garenters broke*, i.e., Granger's or Granator's Brook, but, since the entry was made in a 15th-century hand, it is uncertain whether this was its name in the 13th century. It occurs as *Graneterisbrok*' in a Reading deed of 1444 (Df67v) and was an alternative name for Holy Brook, flowing into the Kennet in Reading by the abbey (*Berks. Place-Names*, i. 11).

750   Licence by King Edward III to John Oliver (*Olyver*), parson of Finchampstead (*Fynchamstede*), and Adam *atte Aumerye*, chaplain, by a fine made by them, to alienate in mortmain to Reading Abbey 1 messuage, 122 acres of land, 6 acres of meadow, 8 acres of wood, 18 acres of moor and 20s worth of rent in Burghfield (*Burghfeld*), to find a secular chaplain to celebrate daily in the church of St Laurence, Reading, in perpetuity for the souls of John and Adam, their ancestors and heirs and all the faithful dead. Licence also to the abbot and convent to receive and hold the same   4 Jan. 1344

C f 225r
Pd. (cal.) *Cal. Pat. R. 1343–5*, 157 (from Patent Roll)

Teste me ipso apud Wodestoke, iiii. die Januarii, anno regni nostri Anglie xvii, regni vero nostri Francie quarto.

The patent roll adds that the fine was £10 and the licence was granted at the instance of Queen Philippa (*ibid.*).

750a Note of a charter by King [Edward III] concerning lands and tenements formerly of Robert *Alard* in Burghfield (*Burghfeld'*), 4 Jan. 17 Edward III—John *Estbury*, escheator   4 Jan. 1344

C f 225v

This appears among notes mostly of royal licences of mortmain and almost certainly refers to the licence in no. 750.

SHEFFIELD (in Burghfield)

751 *Gift in free alms by Alan of Whitchurch to Reading Abbey of 1 virgate of land which Robert son of Hugh son of Toky holds in East Sheffield*
[late 12th × early 13th cent.]

B f 58r; C ff 25v–26r

Sciant presentes et futuri quod ego Alanus de Whitcherch' dedi concessi et hac presenti carta mea confirmavi deo et sancte Marie et beato Iacobo de Rading(ia) et monachis ibidem deo servientibus, pro salute anime mee et omnium antecessorum et successorum meorum,[a] unam virgatam terre in Estsufeld cum omnibus pertinentiis suis quam Robertus filius Hugonis filii Toky tenet in puram et perpetuam elemosinam. Hanc autem predictam terram cum omnibus ad eam pertinentibus tenebunt prefati monachi de me et heredibus meis libere et quiete, plene et integre et honorifice, quietam ab omni demanda et exactione et seculari servitio, cum communa ad predictam terram pertinente absque omni calumpnia. Ego autem et heredes mei warantizabimus predictam terram predictis monachis contra omnes homines et contra omnes feminas. Et acquietabimus eos de forinseco servitio si forte ab eis exactum fuerit. Hiis testibus.

*C has meorum *after* antecessorum

Alan was lord of the manor of Sheffield, in Burghfield parish, under the overlordship of the priory of Noion (Eure, Normandy) in the late 12th and early 13th centuries (*VCH Berks.*, iii. 402; *Ancient Charters*, 105–7).

751a Note of a charter by William son of Saer to Richard son of James of Burghfield (*Burgefeld*)* concerning half a virgate of land in Sheffield (*Schefeld*)* [?late 12th × early 13th cent.]

B f58r; C f25v

*Burghfeld *C*   *Shefeld' *C*

The recipient was presumably son of the James of Burghfield who held of Aumary son of Ralph in (probably) 1185–6 (see nos. 704–6).

752 Gift by Philip of Cowley (*Coveleye*) to Reading Abbey of all the lands which he sometime had in Sheffield (*Schefeld*) and Sulhamstead [Bannister] (*Silamsted'*),* both of the fee of Fulk de Cowdray (*Coudray*) and of the fee of John Bannister (*Banastre*). To be held freely by rendering annually to him and his heirs 1 pair of gloves, price 1d, at Easter, and to Fulk de Cowdray (*Codray*)* and his heirs 1 lb of pepper at the same time and what belongs to a fifth part of the serjeanty of Padworth (*Paddewrthe*),* viz., of holding a rope in the queen's ship (*nacta*) when crossing to Poitou (*Pictavia*), and to the monks of Valmont (*Walemunt*) [Seine-Maritime, Normandy] at Stratfield [Saye] (*Stratfeld*)[1] 5s 10d, viz., 2s 6d each at Michaelmas and the Annunciation and 1 lb of incense or 10d on the feast of St Leonard [6 Nov.], for all custom, demand, suit of court and secular service, saving to the monks of Valmont the foreign service of 1 virgate of land in Sulhamstead [Bannister] (*Silhamsted'*) of the fee of John Bannister, viz., 18d when scutage is at the rate of 40s. Warranty. For this the abbey has given him 100 marks of silver. Sealing. Witnesses [omitted] [1238 × 51]

B f57v; C f25r

*Silhamsted *C*   *Coudray *C*
*Padewrthe *C*

In a deed dating after 18 Apr. 1238 John Bannister relinquished to the abbey an annual rent of 5s which he used to receive from Philip of Cowley's land in Sulhamstead Bannister (below, no. 1106); since the present deed makes no mention of such rent, the two deeds were probably made at the same time. Philip's land of the fee of Fulk de Cowdray was confirmed to the abbey by Fulk (no. 753), who died in 1251 (*VCH Berks.*, iii. 413). In 1248 Philip was one of the heirs of the late Roger of Whitchurch (Clanchy, *Berks. Eyre of 1248*, 175).

1. The hermitage of St Leonard at Stratfield Saye, founded by William de Stuteville, *c.* 1175, and given by him to the abbey of Valmont (*VCH Hants.*, iv. 57–8; *Hist. MSS Comm.*, 9th report, i. appendix, 355b).

753 Confirmation by Fulk de Cowdray (*Kodray*) to Reading Abbey of the lands given by Philip of Cowley (*Covele*), and quitclaim in free alms of all service which Philip and his ancestors used to do him from the lands they held of him in Sheffield (*Sefeld*),[a] viz., 1 lb of pepper annually and a fifth part of the service of the serjeanty of Padworth (*Powrthe*),[b] viz., of holding a rope in the queen of England's ship (*nacka*) when crossing the sea, and suit of court and all demands and exactions. Fulk and his heirs will acquit the fee of Sheffield of all foreign service as their free alms. Warranty and sealing. Witnesses [omitted]   [1238 × 51]

B ff 57v–58r; C f 25v

[a] Shefeld C   [b] Podewrthe C

Date as for no. 752. Fulk was lord of Padworth (*VCH Berks.*, iii. 413).

754 Quitclaim by William *Henteluve* of Sheffield (*Sefeld*)[a] to Reading Abbey of all his right in a fishery between *Smitheshey* and *Langeney*.[b] Sealing. Witnesses [omitted]   [?*c.* 1250]

B f 58r; C f 25v

[a] Shefeld C   [b] Langeleye C

A William *Hentelove* was a tenant in Sheffield in 1270 (see no. 759), but, since the deed was entered in the original section of B, it is not later than 1258.

755 Gift by Ansketil son of Robert *Serle* to the almonry of Reading of a croft of arable land in Sheffield (*Sofeld*)[a] called *la Dune*, as defined by hedges on all sides. To be held freely by rendering annually to him and his heirs 4d (*sterlingi*) at Michaelmas for all services, claims and secular exactions. For this Richard the almoner has given him 33s 4d as entry-fine in his great need. Warranty and sealing. Witnesses [omitted]   [?1231 × 40]

B f 147r; C f 86v; D f 23v

[a] Sefeld' C

For Richard's time as almoner, see no. 712 n. The present deed and nos. 756–8 appear in the section of B devoted to the almoner's charters.

756 Confirmation by Roger of Whitchurch (*Witchirche*)[a] to the almonry of Reading of the gift by Ansketil son of Robert *Serle* of a croft of arable land in Sheffield (*Sofeld*)[b] called *la Dune*, as defined by hedges on all sides. To be held as freely as Ansketil's charter to the abbey witnesses, by rendering annually to Ansketil and his heirs 4d at Michaelmas. Sealing. Witnesses[c] [omitted]   [?1231 × 40]

B f 147r–v; C f86v; D ff 23v–24r

a Witechurch' *D*   *b* Shefeld' *C*
c Om. in C

Probably of the same date as no. 755. Roger was lord of the manor of Sheffield in succession to Alan of Whitchurch (*VCH Berks.*, iii. 402; *Ancient Charters*, 107). He was a juror for Theale hundred in 1241, but was dead in 1248 (PRO JUST 1/37, m. 27; Clanchy, *Berks. Eyre of 1248*, 175).

757 Gift in free alms by Nicholas *de Lindenisse* of Sheffield (*Suffeld*) to the almonry of Reading of $\frac{1}{2}$ acre of land lying between the land of the said almonry called *Anketill(es)dune*[a] and that of Gilbert Pincent (*Pinzun*)[b] called *Stonicroft*, and extending from north to south. To be held freely by rendering annually to him and his heirs 1d at Michaelmas for all secular service, exaction and demand. For this Robert the almoner has given him 6s 3d as entry-fine. Warranty and sealing[c]   [?*c.* 1240]

B f 147r; C f86v; D f 34v

Hiis testibus:[d] [Roberto de Burgefeld, Johanne Rumbald, Waltero Alard, Gileberto Pincun, Roberto Venatore, Thoma Turnegan, et aliis].

a Anchetillesdune *D*   *b* Pincun *D*
c C ends
d B ends, the witnesses being supplied from D

After no. 755. For Robert the almoner, see no. 727 n. Cf. below, no. 1097.

758 Gift in free alms by Robert *Leir* of Sheffield (*Sofeld*) to the almonry of Reading of a croft in Sheffield called *Wlurone Cothstoe* and of 12d rent which Emma *Pasturele* used to pay him annually for the land which she held of him in Sheffield called *la Russi Puddel*.[1] To be held as freely as any alms can be given. Sealing. Witnesses[a] [omitted]
              [13th cent.; before 1248]

B f 147v; C ff 86v–87r; D f 24r

a Om. in C

Dower rights in this croft and rent were quitclaimed to the almonry by Robert's wife, Haenilda, *post conversionem dicti Roberti viri mei ad religionem leprosorum* (D f 77r). Her charter is witnessed by Richer Neirenuit, who was a juror for Theale hundred in 1241 but had been succeeded as such in 1248 by John Neyrnuyt (PRO JUST 1/37, m. 27; Clanchy, *op. cit.*, 295). Richer is not mentioned in the 1248 Berkshire eyre roll and had presumably died by then.

 1. Possibly named after the Roger Russi who held $\frac{1}{2}$ virgate in Sheffield in 1198 (*Memoranda Roll 10 John ... [etc.]*, ed. R. Allen Brown, PRS, lxix (1955), 108; *Ancient Charters*, 106—reading *ruffi* for *Russi*).

759 Gift by William of Huntercombe (*Huntercumbe*) to Reading Abbey of £8 6s 10d worth of annual rent is Sheffield (*Scufeld*),[a] half at Michaelmas and half on Palm Sunday, which he used to receive from the following tenants: John of Englefield (*Englefeud*) for his part of Sheffield 21d, William *Serle* for ½ virgate of land ½ mark, the same for a parcel of land 9d, the same for 1 acre of new land 3d, Roger Carter (*le Kareter*) for 1 cotland (*cotscetla terre*) and 8 acres of new land [42d],[b] Ralph *Hentelove* for 11 acres of new land and a parcel of meadow 20s 4d, Asketil *Serle* for 1 virgate of land and for new (*et pro nova*) 6s, Robert *Reinald* for 1 cotland 4s 4d, Adam of the mill for several parcels of land 14s 8d, Bartholomew of the mill for 10 acres 10s, Ralph *le Chivaler* for a piece (*pecia*) of land 2d, Henry *Bernard* for several parcels of land and of moor 8s, Richard *Winegod* for 3 acres and land 40 perches long and 19 feet wide 2s 2d, *Haӡenilda*[c] *Hapewy* for a piece of land 1d, William *Balrich* for 7 acres of land 4s 10d, Nicholas *de*[d] *Lindenisse* for 5 acres of new land 3s, John *Brichward* for ½ virgate of land and several parcels of new land 12s, Matilda *Niweman* for 1 cotland and 2 feet of land 3s 2d, Thomas *le Red(e)* for a parcel of land 18d, William *Hentelove* for ½ virgate and several parcels of land 1 mark, John *Bernard* for 3 acres of new land 18d, Roger *atte Newegarston'*[e] for ½ virgate of land ½ mark, the same for 9 acres of new land 5s 6d, James *Apewy* for 4 acres of new land 2s, Christina Baldwin (*Baldewine*)[f] for a croft 18d, Ralph *de la Hide* for a meadow 6s, William *Page* for a parcel of land 2s, Sewal *le Verder* for 12 acres and a parcel of land 6s 8d, Richard *le Venur* for 1 virgate of land and certain new land and a meadow 19s 6d, and Robert *Asketil* for a parcel of land 2s 6d. To be held freely, with homages, fines, amercements, reliefs, escheats, wardships and suit of the same tenants to the court of Sheffield (*Scefeld*) as they are accustomed and ought to do, and with waters and fisheries, by rendering annually to the prior of Noion (*Nuygun*), chief lord of the fee, 40s, viz., half at Michaelmas and half on Palm Sunday; and to John of Englefield and his heirs, by a settlement reached between the donor and William of Englefield, John's father, over certain partial purprestures, 2s; and to Reading Abbey 8d, for all other services, suits and secular demands. Warranty and sealing   27 May 1270

B ff 209v–210v; C ff 126r–127r

Hiis testibus:[g] domino Waltero de Riparia, Willelmo Hurcale, Nicholao de Henred, Roberto de Bergefeud, Willelmo de Britinoll', Rolando de Erleya, militibus, Roberto de Offinton', Hervico Belet, Olivero de Asele, Nigello de Sandervilla, Ricardo filio Mathei, Johanne le Buteler, Waltero de Madehacche, Radulfo de Pelitot, Radulfo Banastre, Henrico Ylger, et aliis. Dat' apud Rading(iam)

sexto kl' Junii, anno ab incarnatione domini M.CC. septuagesimo, et
anno regni regis Henrici filii regis Johannis quinquagesimo quarto.

a Scefeld' *C*
b *Om. in B,C; supplied from rental in no. 761*
'Hatenilda (*sic*) *C*   *d* *Both texts have* le
'Nywegarston' *C*   *f* Baldewyn *C*
g *C continues*: domino Waltero de Riparia, Willelmo Huscarl', Thoma de Hendred',
Rolando de Erleia et aliis, sicut patet in alia carta simili precedenti; *but the reference is
unclear*

This deed conveyed to Reading Abbey the manor of Sheffield (see no. 760), which
William had acquired by June 1248 (Clanchy, *Berks. Eyre of 1248*, 175).

760 Notification by William of Huntercombe (*Huntercumbe*), knight,
that on the feast of the Nativity of St John Baptist [24 June], A.D.
1270, he received from Reading Abbey £121 17s 2d for the manor of
Sheffield (*Scefeud*) with appurtenances, and £26 16s 2d in clearance
of old debts (*in allocationibus veterum debitorum*). Letters patent
                                                        1 July 1270

B f 210v; C f 127r

Dat' apud Huntercumbe die martis proxima post festum apostolorum
Petri et Pauli [29 June], anno supradicto. Valete.

761 *List of tenants formerly of Sir William of Huntercombe in Sheffield, now
of Reading Abbey, from whom the subprior shall receive the rents to provide three
refections for the souls of Robert of Burgate, abbot of Reading, Nigel his father
and Felicia his mother*   [1270 × c. 1275]

B f 243v

Isti subscripti quondam tenuerunt de domino Willelmo de Huntercumbe in villa de Shefeld' qui modo effecti sunt tenentes abbatis
et conventus Radyng', de quibus supprior recipiet redditus ad tres
refecciones faciendas, videlicet pro anima Roberti de Burgate abbatis
Radyng' et pro anima Nigelli patris sui et pro anima Felicie matris
sue.

	De termino Michaelis	De termino Palmarum
Johannes de Englefeld	x.d' ob'	x.d' ob'
Willelmus Serle	iii.s' x.d'	iii.s' x.d'
Marginal note in different hand: Inde Cam' viii. d'		
Rogerus le Cartere	xxi.d'	xxi.d'
Radulphus Hentelove[1]	v.s'	v.s'
Asketillus Serle	iii.s'	iii.s'

Robertus Reynald	ii.s' ii.d'	ii.s' ii.d'
Adam de Molendino	vii.s' iiii.d'	vii.s' iiii.d'
*Christina Wynegod*ᵃ²	v.s'	v.s'
Radulphus le Chivaler	ii.d'	
Henricus Bernard	iiii.s'	iiii.s'

Marginal note in different hand: deficiunt ii.s' [per] annum

Ricardus Wynegod	xiii.d'	xiii.d'
Hagenilla Hadewey	i.d'	
Willelmus Balrych	ii.s' v.d'	ii.s' v.d'
Walterus Alard³	xviii.d'	xviii.d'
Johannes Brycward⁴	vi.s' vii.d'	vi.s' vii.d'
Ricardus Wynegod⁵	xix.d'	xix.d'
Thomas le Rede	ix.d'	ix.d'
Willelmus Hentelove	vi.s' viii.d'	vi.s' viii.d'
Johannes Bernard	ix.d'	ix.d'
Rogerus atte Newgarston'	vi.s' i.d'	vi.s' i.d'
Jacobus Haþewey	xii.d'	xii.d'
ᵇCristiana Baldewyne	ix.d'	ix.d'ᵇ
Radulphus de la Hyde	iii.s'	iii.s'
Willelmus Page	xii.d'	xii.d'
Ricardus Hory⁶	iii.s' iiii.d'	iii.s' iiii.d'
Ricardus le Venur⁷	xiii.s' iiii.d'	ix.s' ix.d'
		ꞌItem iiii.d'ᶜ

Marginal note in different hand: deficiunt iiii.s' i.d' per annum

Robertus Asketyl'	xv.d'	xv.d'

Summa de termino sancti Michaelis: iiii.li' i.d' ob'
Summa de Pascha: lxxix.s' x.d' ob'
Summa totalis: viii.li' cum redd' de Noiun

ᵃ⁻ᵃ *This name written in a later hand over an erasure (see note 2)*
ᵇ⁻ᵇ *This line deleted in different ink*
ᶜ⁻ᶜ *Added in different ink*

The entry is in brown ink with later amendments mostly in black ink. The original entry dates after no. 759 and before the death of John of Englefield in *c.* 1276 (*VCH Berks.*, iii. 406); he was still living at the beginning of August 1275 (see no. 765). Robert of Burgate was abbot of Reading 1269–90.

1. In William of Huntercombe's charter (no. 759) he owed 20s 4d.
2. In William's charter the rent was paid by Bartholomew of the mill, probably Christina's husband whom she survived (cf. Bartholomew *Wynegod* in no. 767).
3. Since William's charter he had replaced Nicholas *de Lindenisse*.
4. In William's charter he owed 12s.
5. Since William's charter he had replaced Matilda *Niweman*.
6. Since William's charter he had replaced Sewal *le Verder*.
7. In William's charter he owed 19s 6d.

762 Quitclaim by Margery, widow of William of Englefield (*Engle-*

feud²), knight, to John of Englefield, her son and the heir of William, of two mills, viz., a fulling mill and a corn mill, with all rents and services which she had and received from Thomas *le Rede*, Richard *Bernard*, Bartholomew *Wingod*, John *Maurici*,[a] Bartholomew *Morterel*,[b] Richard *Uterad*, Robert *Adelard*,[c] Robert *Baghot*,[d] John *Bernard*, Roger *de la Garstone*, William *Stevene* and Roger Carter (*le Caretere*[e]) by assignment of her dower in Sheffield (*Scefeude*) from the tenements of her late husband. Sealing [*c*. 8 Aug. 1275]

B f209r; C f126r

Hiis testibus: domino Roberto Fulconis, Andrea de Englefeld rectore ecclesie eiusdem loci, [f]Johanne Lil rectore ecclesie de Erbergefeud',[f] Roberto[g] de Uffinton', Petro fratre eiusdem, Nicholao de Dideham, Willelmo de Walton', Gilberto Pincun,[h] Bartholomeo de Hakeburne, Thoma de Morton' clerico, et aliis.

[a]Mauricii *C*	[b]Mortrel *C*
[c]'Adhelard' *C*	[d]Bagot *C*
[e]'Carter' *C*	[f-f]*Om. in C*
[g]Will'o *C* (*sic*)	[h]Pinzun *C*

The date must be close to that of no. 763. In 1198 the mill of Sheffield with certain plots of land had been given by Alan of Whitchurch to William of Englefield and his heirs for an annual rent of 4s (*Ancient Charters*, 105–7; *Memoranda Roll 10 John* ... [*etc.*], 108–9).

763 Power of attorney by Margery of Englefield (*Englefeud*) to Andrew of Englefield (*Englefeld*) to deliver to John of Englefield (*Englefeud*), her son, seisin of the mill of Sheffield (*Scefeud*).[a] Sealing
8 Aug. 1275

Original charter: PRO E210/4574 (Ancient Deed D 4574)
B f209r; C f126r

Dat' apud Englefeud[b] die jovis proxima ante festum sancti Laurencii [10 Aug.], anno regni regis E(dwardi) tercio.

Endorsed: none
Size: 173 × 43 mm
Seal: small, circular, in green wax on tongue; profile of ?lady's head and shoulders; legend lost

[a]Soef' *C*
[b]*Original has* Engleud; *B,C omit and leave blank space*

764 Gift in free alms by John of Englefield (*Englefeld'*) to Reading Abbey—for the souls of, among others, William of Willington (*Wyllynton'*)[a] his kinsman, monk of the abbey, and of the latter's father and mother—of two mills in Sheffield (*Scefeld'*),[b] viz., a corn mill and a fulling mill, and the homage, service and rent of Thomas *le Rede*, Richard *Bernard'*, Bartholomew *Wynegod'*, John *Moriz*, Bartholomew *Mortrel*, Richard *Uwtred'*, Robert *Athelard'*, John *Bernard'*, Roger *de la Niwegarston'*,[c] Thomas *Stevene* of Wokefield (*Wokfeld'*)[d] and Roger Carter (*le Careter'*[e]) from the tenements which they individually held of him. Warranty, against Jews and Christians, and sealing

[*c.* 8 Aug. 1275]

Original charter: PRO E210/6882 (Ancient Deed D 6882)
Bf208v; Cf125v

Hiis testibus: domino Roberto Fulcon(is) clerico, dominis Rowlando de Erle, Johanne de Chaus(eie), Johanne de Ted(e)mers(e),[f] Thoma de Auvers,[g] Rad(ulfo) de Chayndut, militibus, Willelmo de Blebyr',[h] Roberto de Uffenton',[i] Thoma Huscarl', Nigello de Saundrevill',[j] Hervic(o)[k] Belet, Gileberto Pynzon,[l] Gileberto de Molesham, Willelmo de Colle, Waltero de Madehach', [m]Johanne de Colle, Ricardo de Benham, Ricardo de la More, Thoma de Mortune[n] clerico,[m] et aliis.

Endorsed: Carta Johannis de Engelfeud de terra de Schofeld [*13th cent.*] Carta Johannis de Englefeld duplicata de Sefeud' [*13th cent.*] A gyfte to Reding' abbe [*16th × 17th cent.*]
Size: 312 × 227 mm
Seal: circular of green wax on tag; impression *c.* 25 mm in diameter—relief profile of man's head surrounded by oak sprays within quatrefoil; legend: + S. IOHANNIS DE. ENGLEFEVD

[a]Willenton' *B,C*	[b]Soefeld *B*, Soeffeld' *C*
[c]Newegarston' *C*	[d]Wogf' *C*
[e]Carect' *C*	[f]Thedmersh' *C*
[g]Danvers *C*	[h]Bleburi *B*, Bleoburi *C*
[i]Offenton' *B,C*	[j]Sandrevill' *C*
[k]Henr' *C*	[l]Pync(un) *B,C*
[m-m]*Om. in C*	[n]Morton' *B*

The date must be close to that of no. 765. The tenants named here are the same as those in Margery of Englefield's quitclaim to John (no. 762), except that Rober *Baghot* is here omitted and William *Stevene* is here Thomas *Stevene*. Very similar to this deed is PRO E210/8777 (Anc. Deed D 8777), being a gift by the same of the same, but omitting Thomas *Stevene* and Roger Carter; it is endorsed: Carta Johannis de Englefeld' de molend' de Schefeld'. triplicata. Also closely related is E210/3649, which is John's gift in free alms to the abbey of his mill of Sheffield, which his mother Margery sometime held in dower, to be assigned to the cellarer to provide an annual refection for the whole convent of three dishes with wine on the anniversary of his kinsman William of Willington, monk of the abbey, after his death. The witness-lists of all three deeds are similar, but no two are identical.

765 Power of attorney by John of Englefield (*Englefeud*) to Ralph of

Henley (*Henle*) to deliver to Reading Abbey seisin of his corn mill of
Sheffield (*Scefeud*). Letters patent   8 Aug. 1275

B f209r; C f126r

Dat' apud Englefeud die jovis proxima ante festum sancti Laurencii
[10 Aug.], anno regni regis E(dwardi) tercio.

766   Grant (*concessimus*) by Abbot Robert [of Burgate] and the convent of Reading to Lady Margery, widow of the late Sir William of
Englefield (*Englefeud*), that they have acquired no claim in the waters
of the [River] Kennet belonging to the manor of Englefield, by reason
of the sale to them by John of Englefield, son and heir of William, of
two mills, waters and rents with all appurtenances in the vill of
Sheffield (*Sefeud*). Sealing with the seals of the abbot and convent
                                                    12 Sept. 1275

C f230v

Dat' apud Rading' die jovis proxima ante festum Exaltacionis Sancte
Crucis [14 Sept.], anno regni regis Edwardi tercio. Hiis testibus:
domino Roberto Fulcon(is) clerico, Andrea*ᵃ* Englefeud' rectore, Willelmo de Bleoburi, et aliis.

*ᵃ*Andreo *Ms*

This is entered in a late 14th-century hand and is the last item on the last written folio
of the cartulary. The rubric describes it as a *syrografum* between Abbot R. and the lady
of Englefield.

767   *List of tenants formerly of Sir John of Englefield, now of the cellarer of
Reading, with their rents; and note concerning the rents from the mills of Sheffield*
                                                    [?*c.* 1280]

B f244r

Isti subscripti quondam tenuerunt de domino Johanne de Englefeud',
qui modo tenentes cellerarii Radyng' effecti sunt.

	De termino Michaelis	De termino Annunciacionis beate Marie
Thomas le Rede	xx.s'	viii.d'
Willelmus Bernard¹	viii.s'	viii.s'
Bartholomeus Wynegod	v.s'	v.s'
Johannes Moryz	iiii.s'	iiii.s'
Bartholomeus Moterel	ii.s'	ii.s'
Ricardus Wtred	vi.s'	

Walterus Athelard[2]	x.s'	
Hugo Bernard[3]	x.s'	
Rogerus de la Newgarston'	x.s'	
Thomas Stevene de Weufeld	ii.s'	ii.s'
Rogerus le Carter	ii.s'	

Summa de termino Michaelis: lxxix. s'
Summa ad Pascha: xxi.s' viii.d'

Bartholomeus Fullerat(or) reddet cellerario sex marcas, vii. solidos et viii. denarios de molendinis de Shefeld, videlicet de molendino aquatico v. marcas, de molendino fullet(ico) xxi.s', ad quatuor anni terminos, videlicet ad festum Annunciacionis beate Marie xxi.s' xi.d', ad festum sancti Johannis Baptiste xxi.s' xi.d', ad festum Michaelis xxi.s' xi.d', ad festum Nat(alis) domini xxi.s' xi.d'. Et sic est summa molendinorum iiii.li' vii.s' viii.d'.

[a]Summa tocius redditus et firme molendinorum: ix.li' viii.s' iiii.d'. Unde tercia pars eiusdem: lxii.s' ix.d' q[a].[a]

[a-a] Written at the foot of the folio after a large blank gap

Probably a few years after John of Englefield's charter (no. 764), since the rental has three changes of name among the tenants listed by John.

1. Since John's charter he had replaced Richard *Bernard'*.
2. Since John's charter he had replaced Robert *Athelard'*.
3. Since John's charter he had replaced John *Bernard'*.

768   Record of a plea of dower brought against the abbot of Reading by William de Balliol (*Baylol*) and Burga his wife, concerning a third part of two mills and 10 marks rent in Sheffield (*Shefeld'*). The abbot vouches to warranty Roger son of William of Englefield (*Englefeud*), then in the wardship of Roger [Longespee], bishop of Coventry and Lichfield. The bishop says through his attorney that, since he has the said tenements for life by demise of William, father of the said Roger, and not by custody, he is not bound to warrant as guardian. The abbot agrees that the bishop sometime had them by demise of the said William for a term of years, but says that after the said William's death Roger de Somery (*Sumeri*), chief lord of the fee, took possession of the said tenements as in his custody since the said Roger was under age, and that afterwards the said bishop gave Roger de Somery 200 marks to have custody, so that the bishop holds the tenements as guardian and not for the term of his life. Both parties put themselves on the country. The jury, chosen with the consent of both parties, declare entirely in favour of the abbot. Therefore the bishop is bound to warrant and is in mercy because he did not do so earlier. The said

William [de Balliol] and Burga are to recover dower against the bishop as guardian, because he has sufficiency [in his custody]*a* of the lands and tenements which belonged to John*b* [of Englefield], first husband of Burga, and the abbot shall hold in peace

[3 × 12 Nov. 1284]

B f 231r–v

Rubric (in margin):[1] Inrotulatio de Sefelde contra Borg' et episcopum de Lichefeld'

a Supplied from PRO JUST 1/48, m. 13d (see note)
b Ms has 'the said John', but see note

This case was heard in the Reading session of the Berks. eyre of 1284 (see Crook, *General Eyre*, 163), the text being a transcript from one of the plea rolls, e.g. PRO JUST 1/48, m. 13d, which is the fullest version. However, this and the other plea rolls concerned (1/43, m. 10d; 1/45, m. 9d; 1/47, m. 9) state near the end that Burga's first husband was 'the said William', but in fact he was John of Englefield, William's father, who was dead by 1277 (BL Add. Ch. 20253; PRO CP 40/21, m. 45d). The Reading text corrected the error, but anomalously retained 'the said' when no John was previously mentioned. William of Englefield conveyed the manor of Englefield and appurtenances to the bishop for life on 28 Sept. 1277 (BL Add. Ch. 20254) and was dead himself by Mar. 1281, being survived by his widow Alice (*Cat. Anc. Deeds*, iii. 440, D.298). Roger de Somery was lord of Bradfield (Berks.), upon which the manor of Englefield was dependent (*VCH Berks.*, iii. 396, 405), and died in 1291 (*Cal. Inq. P.M.*, ii. 492).

1. Incomplete owing to subsequent trimming of the folio.

CARSWELL (in Buckland)

769 *Gift in free alms by Aumary son of Ralph to Reading Abbey of all the land which named tenants held of him in Carswell*   [prob. 1185 × 86]

A f 38v

Sciant presentes et futuri quod ego Amalricus filius Rad(ulfi) dedi et presenti carta confirmavi deo et sancte Marie de Rading(ia) et monachis ibidem deo servientibus, pro salute anime mee et antecessorum meorum et successorum meorum, in elemosinam perpetuam, liberam et quietam de me et heredibus meis ab omni servitio terreno, totam terram quam tenuerunt de me in Karsewelle Rog(erus) prepositus, Ricardus vallet, Rod(bertus) de Buleflet, Edwardus de Heffedford, Alanus piscator, Sewalus, Edwinus, Frewinus, Godricus, cum omnibus pertinentiis suis. His testibus: Willelmo de Tikeham, Iohanne de Hida, Oeno filio Restwoldi, et multis aliis.

This land was bequeathed to Reading Abbey by Aumary in his last will and testament (no. 704) and the gift was confirmed by Henry II in 1185 × 87 (no. 33). In 1230 the abbey exchanged its land in Carswell, 8½ virgates, with Aumary son of Robert, the present donor's grandson, for a mill and land in Adwell, Oxon. (nos. 486–8), which explains why the present deed was not copied into the abbey's later cartularies. The place is certainly Carswell in Buckland and not a lost name in Burghfield, as stated in *Berks. Place-Names*, i. 205. Aumary son of Ralph granted the tithes of his demense of *Kersewelle* to Wallingford priory (BL Lansdowne MS 442, f 178v), to which they were confirmed by Jocelin, bishop of Salisbury (Oxford, Bodleian Library, Berkshire Charters, 3). In 1319 the tithes were leased to the rector of Buckland (Lansdowne 442, f 178v) and so came into the possession of Edington College, Wilts., when it acquired Buckland church in 1358 (*VHC Berks.*, iv. 460; B.R. Kemp, 'Monastic possession of parish churches in England in the twelfth century', *JEH*, xxxi (1980), 10 n.4).

CHOLSEY

770 Order by King Henry I to the bishop of Salisbury and Earl David that, if the sheriffs of Berkshire and the reeves of Cholsey have given any of the inland of Cholsey and put it out of the demesne, they are to cause it to return to the demesne of Reading Abbey by the oath of lawful men of the hundred. Witness(es) [omitted]

[prob. latter half of 1123]

B f 17v
Pd. *Regesta*, ii. 353 (no. clxxv); (cal.) *ibid.*, 191–2 (no. 1423)

The date is after the appointment of the first abbot, 15 Apr. 1123 (*Flor. Hist.*, ii. 49) and probably also after 19 June, the date of Pope Calixtus II's confirmation to Reading, which does not mention Cholsey (no. 139). The king's attempt to recover alienated demesne probably took place at the same time as his recovery of the church of Cholsey from the abbey of Mont St Michel in the latter half of 1123 (no. 3). Earl David is King David I of Scotland, earl of Huntingdon and Northampton 1113/14–36.

771 *Request by Abbot Roger and the convent of Mont St Michel to Roger, bishop of Salisbury and provisor of England, to give and confirm to Reading Abbey the churches of Cholsey and Wargrave, which they have given to the abbey, and to cause to be assigned to them the 12 librates of land in Budleigh [Devon] which King Henry has given them*   [prob. latter half of 1123]

A f 47r; B f 195r; C f 114v

Reverendo *a*domino et patri*a* R(ogerio) Saresb(uriensi) episcopo gratia dei strenuo regni Angl(ie) provisori frater Rog(erius) abbas Sancti Michaelis de periculo maris et conventus fratrum eiusdem loci, devotum cum oratione servitium. Ecclesias de Chealseia*b* et de Wellegrava,*c* quas in episcopatu vestro habuimus, pro salute domini nostri regis H(enrici) concedimus et donamus in elemosinam fratribus in monasterio Radingensi deo servientibus, et per vos tanquam per episcopum eas Radingensi ecclesie iure donari deposcimus. Ecclesias itaque supradictas cum decimis et terris et omnibus ad ipsas more antiquo pertinentibus date et confirmate Radingensi ecclesie, vobis a deo commisse. Precamur insuper ut .xii. libratas terre quas dominus noster rex Henricus in Buddeleia donavit nobis vestra liberalitate assignari nostre ecclesie citius faciatis. Valete.

a-a patri et domino *B,C*   *b* Chals' *B,C*
c Wellegrave *with* .i. Weregrave *written above, B,C*

For the date, see nos. 3, 175. The request is addressed to the bishop both as diocesan and as *provisor* of England, the latter rôle being that in which the bishop would assign the land in Budleigh to Mont St Michel. The text of the sentence beginning *Ecclesias itaque* appears odd and may be corrupt.

772 Precept by Pope Alexander III to the abbot of Reading not to convey to anyone the church of Cholsey or any other church or possession of the abbey without the counsel and assent of the chapter or of its greater and wiser part, nor to alienate the same churches or possessions from the uses to which they have been assigned; and faculty to the monks to revoke a grant if the abbot does otherwise

[1159 × 81]

A f 70r
Pd. Holtzmann, *Papsturkunden*, iii. 421 (no. 298)

The dating limits are those of Alexander III's pontificate.

773 Confirmation by Pope Alexander III to Reading Abbey of the appropriation of its church of Cholsey to the uses of the monastery with the assent of Jocelin [de Bohun], bishop of Salisbury

[1159 × 81]

A f 70r–v
Pd. Holtzmann, *Papsturkunden*, iii. 421 (no. 299)

Date as for no. 772.

773a Note of a charter by Abbot Hugh I [of Reading] concerning the land of Raimbald in Cholsey (*Chaus(eia)*)   [1123 × 30]

B f 71v

The dating limits are those of Hugh I's abbacy.

774 *Demise by William son of Gerold to Reading Abbey of the land in Cholsey from which he was paying the abbey 100s annually by order of King Henry, in return for which the abbey has remitted the said rent and will pay him 5s annually at Michaelmas*   [1158 × c. 1174]

A f42r; (noted) B f71v

Sciant presentes et futuri quod ego Willelmus filius Geroldi dimisi abbati et monachis Radingie terram illam in Chelseia unde eis redde- bam annuatim centum solidos per preceptum domini nostri regis Henrici et per testimonium carte ipsuis, ad tenendum in dominio suo. Et ipsi mihi remiserunt annuum redditum predictorum centum solidorum et insuper mihi reddent singulis annis ad festum sancti Michaelis .v. solidos. Et hoc factum ratum et stabile erit omni tempore quamdiu ipsos .v. solidos bene reddiderint. Huius rei testes sunt Turoldus presbiter, Petrus nepos Rogerii abbatis, Iurdanus filius Wil- lelmi, Ricardus filius Milonis, et multi alii.

The presence among the witnesses of Peter nephew of Abbot Roger dates this not earlier than the beginning of Roger's abbacy. William died in *c.* 1174 and was lord of Moulsford, near Cholsey, which had been given by Henry I to his father, Gerold son of Walter (*VHC Berks.*, iii. 505; *Rot. Chart.*, 186). Henry II's general confirmation to Reading in 1156 × 7 includes Cholsey with the farm of 100s which William son of Gerold used to pay to Henry I (no. 19), but William was already paying this sum to the abbey in the time of Roger, bishop of Salisbury, perhaps by late 1123 (no. 175); therefore the King Henry of the present deed was Henry I.

775 *Demise by Odo son of William to Reading Abbey of the same land in return for the same remission and annual payment of 5s* [*c.* 1174 × 1193]

A f42r; B f71r–v; C f36v

Sciant presentes et futuri quod ego Oddo filius Willelmi dimisi abbati et monachis de Rading(ia) illam terram in Chelseia unde eis debebam reddere annuatim .c. solidos per preceptum domini*ᵃ* regis H(enrici) et per testimonium carte ipsius, ad tenendum*ᵇ* de me et de heredibus meis in dominio suo. Et ipsi mihi remiserunt annuum redditum pre- dictorum .c. solidorum et insuper mihi reddent singulis annis ad festum sancti Michaelis .v. solidos. Et hoc factum ratum erit et stabile omni tempore quamdiu ipsos .v. solidos bene reddiderint.*ᶜ* Huius rei testes sunt Turoldus presbiter, Petrus nepos abbatis Rogerii, Robertus Pechie, Paganus de Molesford(ia), et multi alii.

ᵃ Insert nostri *B,C*   *ᵇ A has* tendu(m)
ᶜ B ends with T', *C ends*

After the death of William son of Gerold (see no. 774 n.) and, since the deed was entered in the original section of A, not later than 1193. However, William was succeeded first by his eldest son, Raymond, who died childless (*VCH Berks.*, iii. 505). This is in effect a confirmation of Odo's father's demise.

776 *Perpetual lease by Odo son of William son of Gerold to Reading Abbey of the land which Herbert the larderer held of Odo's father in Cholsey for 60s*

*annually and quitclaimed to Reading Abbey for 7 marks of silver with Odo's
father's consent; to be held by the abbey for the same 60s annual rent*

[*c.* 1174 × 1193]

Af42r–v; Bf71r; Cf36v

Notum sit omnibus fidelibus quod ego Oddo filius Willelmi filii Geroldi
concessi monachis sancte Marie de Rading(ia) tenere de me et de
heredibus meis perpetuo reddendo annuatim ad festum sancti
Michaelis .lx. solidos terram illam quam Herbertus lardinarius de
patre meo solebat tenere in Chelseia per idem servitium. Nam isdem
Herbertus*ᵃ* predictam terram clamavit quietam finaliter de se et de
heredibus suis ecclesie de Rading(ia), salvo servitio patris mei et meo
quod inde consuevit habere pater meus. Et hoc fecit Herbertus*ᵃ* pro
.vii. marcis argenti quas monachi Rading(enses) ei dederunt. Cui
conventioni pater meus interfuit et firmiter illam concessit. Et inten-
dentes sumus ego Oddo et heredes mei monachis Rading(ensibus)*ᵇ*
de predicto servitio ab ipsis recipiendo. Huius concessionis con-
firmatores et testes sumus*ᶜ* ego Oddo et Willelmus filius Geroldi pater
meus. Et ego Oddo filius Willelmi filii Geroldi predictis monachis
de Rading(ia) predictam terram concessi et presenti [*f42v*] carta
confirmavi pro .lx. solidis annuatim solvendis ad festum sancti
Michaelis pro omni servitio.*ᵈ* His testibus: Philippo de Barri, Roberto
filio Ricardi, Reimundo filio Hugonis, et multis aliis.

ᵃ Herebertus *B,C*   *ᵇ* de Radig' *B,C*
ᶜ fuimus *B,C*   *ᵈ* *B ends with* T', *C ends*

Date as for no. 775, since the references to Odo's father, though somewhat ambiguous,
suggest a date after his death (particularly if the *fuimus* of B and C in textual note *c* is
preferred to A's *sumus*). Odo was living as late as 1199, for as Odo de Carew (*de Cario*,
alias *de Karliun*, alias *le Cariun*) he was in dispute in 1198–9 with Sibil de Somery, widow
of William son of Gerold, over her dower in the latter's land in Cholsey (*Cur. Reg. R.*,
i. 36, 66, 88). In 1194 as Odo *de Karno* he appointed his son, William, as attorney
against Geoffrey of Cholsey in a plea of land in Moulsford (*Rot. Cur. Reg.*, i. 20; see
also no. 777 n.).

777   *Grant by William de Carew to William the cordwainer of Bristol and
Roger his brother of the 3 marks which Reading Abbey used to pay to Raymond,
the grantor's uncle, from the land which it held of the grantor's father and of
Raymond in Cholsey; and precept to Reading Abbey to pay the same accordingly*

[?late 12th cent.]

Af46v; (noted) Bf71v

Sciant presentes et futuri quod ego Willelmus de Carrio concessi et
hac mea carta confirmavi Willelmo Cordebanario de Bristoll(o) et
Rogerio fratri eius illas tres marcas argenti quas monachi de Rad-
ing(ia) solebant reddere Reimundo avunculo meo de terra quam prefati

monachi de patre meo et de illo tenuerunt in Chauseia. Quare volo
et firmiter precipio monachis de Rading(ia) ut annuatim ad festum
sancti Michaelis illas tres marcas prefatis Willelmo et Rogerio de
Bristoll(o) et heredibus eorum *post eos*[a] plenarie persolvatis,[b] sicut
carta patris mei Oddonis et Reimundi avunculi mei et mea testatur.

a-a Interlined   *b Sic*

Dating problematical. William was the son of Odo son of William, *alias* Odo de Carew
(see no. 776 n.; and a marginal note against A's copy of no. 775, describing William
de Karrio as Odo's son). He had certainly succeeded his father by 1207, when he made
fine with the king not to be impleaded concerning his land of Moulsford, which
Geoffrey of Cholsey claimed against him by writ of right (*Rot. de Ob. et Fin.*, 414–15;
Cur. Reg. R., v. 61), presumably a continuation of Geoffrey's claim against his father
(see no. 776 n.). However, although the present deed was not entered in the original
section of A, it was added very soon afterwards, apparently in the same hand, and was
included in the original table of contents (A f 4v), while on the other hand William's
father was still alive in 1199 (see no. 776 n.). From the evidence of nos. 774–7, and
from *VCH Berks.*, iii. 505, the following genealogy can be drawn:

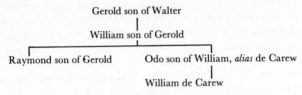

Gerold son of Walter
|
William son of Gerold
|
Raymond son of Gerold   Odo son of William, *alias* de Carew
|
William de Carew

778   *Lease by Abbot Simon of Reading to Andrew son of Gerold and Christiana,
his wife, for their lives in survivorship, of 13 acres of land and ½ acre of meadow
which were Edward the carpenter's and 1 messuage which was Siward the
palmer's, for an annual rent of 6s*   [July 1213 × Apr. 1215]

A f 99v

Hec est conventio facta in curia domini Simonis abbatis Rading(ensis)
apud Chauseiam inter ipsum abbatem et Andream filium Geroldi
super tresdecim acris terre et dimidia acra prati que fuerunt Edwardi
carpentarii et uno mesuagio in clausum quod fuit Siwardi palmarii.
Videlicet quod predictus Andreas tenebit predictam terram cum predicto mesuagio tantummodo in vita sua et in vita Christiane uxoris sue
quam diu alteruter eorum vixerit, reddendo inde annuatim predicto
abbati Rading(ensi) sex solidos ad festum sancti Michaelis. Hiis
testibus: Iohanne de Wichenholt tunc vicecomite, magistro Ricardo
clerico eius, Roberto de Sideham, et multis aliis.

After Simon became abbot (i.e., after 21 July 1213, when his predecessor died) and
before John de Wickenholt ceased to be sheriff of Berkshire at Easter 1215 (*List of
Sheriffs*, 6). Since the lease was made in the abbot's court at Cholsey, the land, etc.,
were presumably there. Andrew son of Gerold was probably related to those who figure
in nos. 774–7.

778a Note of two charters concerning the tenement formerly belonging to Richard of Brightwalton (*Brichtwaltone*) of the tenement in Winterbrook (*Wynterbrok*) [in Cholsey][1] [?later 13th cent.]

B f71v

Entered in a later 13th-century hand. A Richard of Brightwalton was mayor of Wallingford in 1273–5 (N.M. Herbert, 'The Borough of Wallingford 1155–1400' (Reading University Ph.D. thesis, 1971), appendix iii, p. xiii).

1. See *Berks. Place-Names*, i. 163–4.

779 Agreement and final concord, in chirograph form, between Abbot Simon and the convent of Reading and Geoffrey Marmion (*Marmiun*)[a] concerning the water of the Thames, regarding which there was a plea between them before Richard [Poore], bishop of Salisbury, Matthew fitz Herbert, Ralph Hareng, Walter Foliot, James of Potterne (*Poterna*), Walter *de Ripar(iis)*, Maurice de Turville (*Turevile*)[b] and John *de Wikenholte*, justices-in-eyre. Geoffrey recognized half the Thames between Cholsey (*Chauseia*), vill of the abbot and convent, and Checkendon (*Chakendene*) and Stoke Marmion (*Stoche*[c] *Marmiun*[a]), vills of Geoffrey, to be the right and demesne of the abbot and convent and quitclaimed all his right in the same to them, saving that Geoffrey and his heirs shall have their weir, mills, islands and improvements on their side, provided they be not to the harm of the abbot and convent, their tenement and men, and saving similarly to the abbot and convent and their successors their mills, islands, waters, fisheries and other improvements which they will be able to make without harm to Geoffrey and his heirs. Each party shall have its fish-traps (*burroce*) and other contrivances (*ingenia*) for catching fish on its side at will, and when they fish by net and boat what is caught in the middle shall be divided between them. Both parties granted in good faith that they will observe each other's profit and indemnity in the said waters and do nothing to the other's harm. Sealing by both parties[d] [Jan. × Feb. 1219]

A f98v; B f71v; C ff36v–37r; Aylesbury, Buckinghamshire Record Office, AR 38/62/1 (Boarstall Cartulary), f8v (not collated)

Pd. *The Boarstall Cartulary*, ed. H.E. Salter, Oxford Historical Society, lxxxviii (1930), 17 (from that cartulary)—with slight differences from the Reading texts and an abbreviated witness list

Hiis testibus: domino Ricardo Sar(esburiensi) episcopo et aliis iusticiariis prenominatis, Henrico de Scaccario,[e] Galfrido Gibwin', Johanne[f] de Bakepuz, Roberto Achard, Jordano forest(ario), Alano de Englefeld, Roberto de Burgefeld, Nicolao de Chauseia, Roberto fratre eius, Roberto de Huffintun', Hugone filio Raimundi, Gilleberto supra pontem, Thoma de Henleg', Andrea Ruffo, Osberto camberlano, et multis aliis.

^a *A has* Marmium   ^b Turevill' *B,C*
^c Stoke *B,C*   ^d *B ends with* T', *C ends*
^e *Boarstall Cartulary omits following witnesses*
^f *A has* Joh'es

During the Berkshire eyre of 1219 (Clanchy, *Berks. Eyre of 1248*, xciii). Cf. nos. 503–4, made at the same time and also concerned with the water of the Thames.

780 Record of the proving of the age of Henry son of Adam of Cholsey (*Chaus'*), heir of Nicholas son of William son of Peter of Cholsey, taken on Monday 6 March, 35 Edward I, in the presence of Abbot N(icholas) [of Whaplode] of Reading, his chamberlains and others. Walter *Miles* of Cholsey, sworn and examined, says that he was 22 years old on the feast of St Martin last [11 Nov.], and this he knows because in the first year of Abbot William [of Sutton],[1] Abbot N(icholas's) predecessor, who lived for 14 years and more, in the presence of Thomas of Goring (*Garyng'*), then chamberlain, and J(ohn) Vachell (*Fachel*), steward, in the court of the view of Cholsey, Henry's mother presented him as the next heir of the said Nicholas son of William son of Peter in all his lands and tenements in the vill of Cholsey, he being 7 years old; an inquest was then held in the said court and it was found to be as presented; the abbot took seisin of and held the lands and tenements of the said inheritance and the said heir in his hands as his right and that of Reading Abbey. He also says that Henry was born (*ortum traxit*) in the parish of St Mary Major in Wallingford (*Wallyngford'*)^a and that he is the legitimate son of the aforesaid by Margery, his mother above-named. Richard *Watmot'*, Richard *Philipp'*,^b William *Absolon* and John Smith (*Faber*) of Cholsey, sworn and examined, agree in all respects with Walter. Roger *Maiscent*,^c sworn and examined, says that he knows Henry to be of full age in that in the time of Abbot Robert [of Burgate],[2] predecessor of Abbot William aforesaid, for part of whose time he was hundred bailiff (*hundredarius*), he knew Henry's mother and then Henry himself as an infant walking about in his mother's house and legitimately born, and after the lapse of such a time he would now be of full age. This proof was made (*hec facta sunt*) at the suit of Henry, in witness whereof both Henry and Walter, Richard, Richard, William, John and Roger have affixed their seals at Reading.   6 Mar. 1307

B f226v; C f138r

^a Walyngford' *C*   ^b Ph'm *C*
^c Maisent' *C*

781 Agreement, indented, dated Saturday after the feast of St John at the Latin Gate [6 May], 1 Edward II, at Blewbury (*Bleb(eria)*),[a] between Abbot Nicholas [of Whaplode] of Reading and Geva, widow of Richard *Watmot* of Cholsey (*Chels(eia)*). The abbot has granted and sold to Geva the wardship and marriage of Walter, son and heir of the said Richard, for 10 marks sterling, of which Geva will pay at Pentecost next 6 marks, on the feast of St James [25 July] following 2 marks and at Michaelmas following 2 marks, which wardship and marriage the abbot had by reason of the tenement which the said Richard held of him in Cholsey. The wardship and marriage are to be held by Geva until the full age of Walter by rendering annually to the abbot and his successors the due and customary rents and services from the said tenement. If Walter dies before full age, the abbot grants that Geva shall have the wardship and marriage of the other heirs of Richard, one after another, until the full age of one of them. Sealing by both parties *alternatim*   11 May 1308

B f 73r; C f 38r–v

[a] Bleobir' C

COMPTON

782 Notification and confirmation by [a]the dean and[a] the master of the school of St Edward of Shaftesbury (*Seftebyr'*),[1] judges-delegate of Pope Gregory IX, quoting the papal commission,[2] of the settlement before them in the church of St Nicholas at Wilton (*Wilton'*) [Wilts.] of the dispute between Simon, rector of the church of Compton (*Cumton'*) belonging to the abbess of Wherwell (*Werewell'*) [Hants.], and Reading Abbey over the tithes which the abbey receives within the parish of Compton and which Simon claims belong by common right to his church.[3] The abbey, appearing by R. its sacrist,[4] has ceded the tithes to the said church and rector and his successors in perpetuity, in return for an annual payment of 8s to the sacrist at Reading within the octave of Easter. Both parties have bound themselves by a corporal oath to observe this settlement, submitting themselves to the jurisdiction and coercion of the archdeacon of Berkshire and the [rural] dean of Newbury (*Neubir'*) in this regard. The abbey may resume possession of the tithes if the payment is not made by the stated term. Done in the year of grace 1234   [before 17 Aug.] 1234

B f 195r–v; C ff 114v–115r

a-a Interlined in B

Before the confirmation by the biship of Salisbury (no. 783).

1. The abbey of St Mary and St Edward the Martyr, Shaftesbury (Dorset).
2. This refers to a complaint by Simon, rector of Compton, that Reading Abbey, the prior of *Leghis* and others of the dioceses of Salisbury, Winchester and Lincoln have wronged him over tithes, possessions and other things.
3. For the tithes in question, see no. 783.
4. Ralph was sacrist in 1226 (see no. 54); Robert was sacrist in 1262 (*Cal. Pat. R. 1258–66*, 207).

783 Confirmation by Robert [Bingham], bishop of Salisbury, of the same settlement, specifying the tithes in question as certain tithes of William *Gernun* and of the prioress of Kington [St Michael] (*Kingtone*)*a* [Wilts.]. Sealing   17 Aug. 1234

B ff 195v–196r; C f 115r; BL Egerton 2104 (Wherwell Cartulary) ff 97v–98r

Hiis testibus: *b*[magistris Rad(ulfo) de Gnoshal', Clemente de Melcheborn', canonicis Sar', magistro Stephano de Manacettr,*c* Petro de Combe senescallo nostro, Ricardo de Middelton' capellano, Galfr(edo) de Otteford et Galfr(edo) de Bedeford clericis nostris, et aliis].*b* Dat' *d*[apud Potern(am) per manus Walteri de la Wil' capellani nostri, xvi. kal' Septembris]*d* pontificatus nostri anno vi.

a Kingone in B,C; Kington' in Wherwell Cartulary
b-b Om. in B,C; supplied from Wherwell Cartulary
c Reading doubtful; Ms apparently has Manacell'r
d-d As b–b

William Gernon and the prioress of Kington St Michael held parts of the manor of Compton originally given by Henry II to Gilbert Crispin (*VCH Berks.*, iv. 16). The same bishop confirmed to Reading Abbey 8s in the church of Compton in 1240 (see no. 212), and in 1291 the abbey had a pension of 8s 5¼d in the vicarage of Compton (*Taxatio*, 188), but the origins of its claim to tithes in the parish remain obscure. In 1328 a dispute with the then vicar of Compton was settled leaving Reading in possession of the pension (BL Add. Ch. 19640), which, moreover, continued to be received by the sacrist (see the account of Gilbert London, sacrist, in 1443—BL Add. Roll 19652).

EAST GINGE (in West Hendred)

784 *Notification by Richard, abbot of Waltham, and the priors of Waltham and Cathale, judges-delegate of Pope Honorius III, of the settlement before them* *of the dispute between the prior and monks of Wallingford, on one side, and Robert, rector of Thatcham [Berks.], on the other, concerning the demesne tithes of East Ginge, the abbot and convent of Reading asserting their own right in the same. Wallingford Priory renounces [its right in] the tithes, but will hold them at perpetual farm of Reading Abbey for an annual payment of 25s, of which two-thirds will be passed on to the rector of Thatcham* [1216 × 27]

Bf193r–v; Cf113r
Pd. Barfield, *Thatcham*, ii. 57–8

Universis sancte matris ecclesie filiis ad quos presens scriptum pervenerit R(icardus) dei gratia abbas de Waltham' et de Waltham' et de Cathale priores, eternam in domino salutem. Mandatum domini pape suscepimus in hec verba.

Honorius episcopus servus servorum dei dilectis filiis abbati de Waltham, de Waltham et de Cathale prioribus, Lond(oniensis) et Linc(olniensis) diocesum, salutem et apostolicam benedictionem. Ex parte prioris *et conventus* de Walingford(ia) nobis est oblata querela quod abbas et conventus de Becco et quidam alii Linc(olniensis) et Sar(esburiensis) diocesum super decimis, possessionibus, redditibus et rebus aliis iniuriantur eisdem. Ideoque discretioni vestre per apostolica scripta mandamus, et cetera.

Cum igitur auctoritate istarum litterarum mota esset controversia [*f193v*] inter priorem et monachos de Walingf(ordia) ex una parte et R(obertum)*b* rectorem ecclesie de Tacham ex altera super decimis de dominico de Esthange, abbate et conventu de*c* Rading(ia) coram nobis appellantibus pro iure suo et ius suum in predictis decimis protestantibus, post multas altercationes et allegationes ex utraque parte propositas, lis tandem hoc fine coram nobis*d* conquievit. Videlicet prior et monachi de Walingf(ordia), renuntiantes impetratis et impetrandis quo ad dictas decimas, tenebunt dictas decimas petitas ad perpetuam firmam de ecclesia de Rading(ia) solvendo annuatim ecclesie de*c* Rading(ia) apud Rading(iam) .xxv. solidos sterlingorum ad duos terminos anni, scilicet ad festum sancti Michaelis .xii. solidos et .vi. denarios et ad Annuntiationem beate Marie .xii. solidos et .vi. denarios. Ita quod rector ecclesie de Tacham*e* percipiat duas partes dictorum .xxv. solidorum annuatim de ecclesia de*c* Rading(ia) ad predictos terminos. Si vero dicti*f* prior et monachi aliquo predictorum terminorum cessaverint a solutione firme dicte,*g* dabunt dicte ecclesie de Rading(ia) preter debitum canonem illius termini dimidiam marcam argenti nomine pene coercione iurisdictionis ordinarie solvendam. Et si forte cessaverint a solutione per triennium, liceat abbati et conventui de Rading(ia) dictas decimas resumere et in manu sua tenere, omni appellatione et cavillatione remotis et postpositis, donec ipsis tam de pena quam de firma fuerit satisfactum. Hanc autem compositionem sub predicta forma fideliter et inviolabiliter sine aliqua fraude tenendam partes prestito iuramento confirmaverunt. Et ut hec conventio firma et inconcussa in perpetuum permaneat, nos eam presentis scripti nostri auctoritate et sigillorum nostrorum appositione communire curavimus. Hiis testibus, et cetera.

a-a Interlined in B
c Om. in C
e Tacheham C
g predicte C

b For expansion, see no. 785
d Both texts repeat hoc fine here
f predicti C

The dating limits are those of Honorius III's pontificate. Reading Abbey's claim to tithes in East Ginge derived from its possession of Thatcham church, for which see nos. 1108–9. Wallingford Priory's interest arose from its possession of West Hendred church, in whose parish East Ginge was alleged to lie (*VCH Berks.*, iv. 303, 307; J.G. Milne, 'Muniments of Holy Trinity Priory, Wallingford', *Oxoniensia*, v (1940), 52–6). For a discussion of this case, see B.R. Kemp, 'The mother church of Thatcham', *Berks. Arch. Journ.*, lxiii (1967–8), 18.

785 *Notification by Prior Thomas and the convent of Wallingford of the same settlement, and obligation of the priory to pay annually to Reading Abbey 25s sterling* [1216 × 27]

Original charter: BL Add. Ch. 19623
B ff 193v–194r; C f 113r–v
Pd. Barfield, *Thatcham*, ii. 58; (cal.) Hurry, *Reading Abbey*, 175

[U]niversis*a* sancte matris ecclesie filiis *b*presens scriptum visuris*b* T(homas) prior de Walingeford*c* et eiusdem loci conventus unanimis *d*eternam in domino*d* salutem. Ad notitiam vestram volumus pervenire quod cum per literas*e* venerabilis patris Honorii summi pontificis movissemus litem Roberto de Taccheham*f* qui gerebat se pro rectore ecclesie de Taccheaham*f* super decimis de dominico de Estgeyng'*g* que site sunt infra limites parrochie ecclesie*h* nostre de Henred,*i* et abbas et conventus de Rading(ia) opposuissent se nobis adversarios eo quod tam ipsi quam ecclesia sua de Taccheham*f* fuissent in pacifica possessione dictarum decimarum per longissimum tempus etiam per tantum tempus cuius non extat memoria, lis demum de consensu abbatis et conventus de Sancto Albano hoc fine conquievit coram abbate de Waltham et de Walth(am) et de Cathale prioribus iudicibus a domino papa delegatis. Videlicet quod dicti abbas et conventus de Rading(ia) consensu dicti Roberti concesserunt nobis dictas decimas petitas tenendas ad perpetuam firmam reddendo inde annuatim ecclesie de Rading(ia) nomine firme viginti quinque solidos sterlingorum ad duos terminos anni, scilicet ad festum sancti Michaelis duodecim solidos et sex denarios, et ad Annunt[iationem]*a* beate Marie duodecim solidos et sex denarios. Nos quidem obligavimus nos quod fideliter et sine dolo solvemus perpetuo d[ictos vi]ginti*a* quinque solidos dictis abbati et conventui de Rading(ia) ad terminos statutos apud Rading-(iam) sub pena dimidie marce [ei]s*a* solvende ad˙quemlibet termi-num, si forte ad aliquem terminum cessaverimus a solutione dicte pecunie. Et si per triennium cessaverimus a solutione dicte firme, concessimus quod liceat abbati et conventui de Rading(ia) libere et sine omni contradictione ingredi possessionem dictarum decimarum et ipsas in manus suas*j* retinere donec predictis abbati et monachis tam de pena quam de pecunia satisfecerimus. Ut autem suprascripta maiorem firmitatem obtineant,*k* sigilla abbatis de Sancto Albano et conventus de Walingeford*c* huic scripto sunt apposita.

Endorsed: Obligacio monachorum de Walingf' de solutione firme [*13th cent.*] de decimis de Estheng' [*13th cent., different hand*]
Size: 150 × 130 mm
Seal: tags for two seals

> *a Original charter slightly damaged in places; letters in square brackets supplied*
> *b-b Om. in B,C*   'Walingf' *B*, Walingford' *C*
> *d-d Om. in B,C*   'litteras *B*
> *j Tacham B,C*   *g Estheng' B,C*
> *h Om. in B,C*   *i Hanrede B,C*
> *j Accusative case sic in all texts*   *k optineant B,C*

For the date and further comment, see no. 784 n.

EAST HENDRED

786 *Agreement between the abbeys of Bec and Reading whereby the latter will hold of the former the tithes of the demesne of [East] Hendred and of the tenants of the same for an annual payment of 20s*   [*c.* 1160 × 1193]

Original charter: Hendred House (Oxon.), Muniments, No. 2¹
A f47v; B ff 194v–195r; C f 114r; Windsor, St George's Chapel, xi.G.11, no. 33 (Ogbourne Roll) (not collated)
Pd. *Select Documents of the English Lands of the Abbey of Bec*, ed. M. Chibnall, Camden 3rd Series, lxxiii (1951), 18 (from Ogbourne Roll)

Hec est conventio inter abbatem Bechci*a* et abbatem Rading' et utriusque loci conventum. Abbas et conventus Rading' tenebunt de abbate et conventu Bechci*a* decimationes de dominio*b* de Henrede*c* et decimationes hominum tenentium de eodem dominio pro .xx. solidis annuatim solvendis ad festum sancti Michaelis. Si quis autem ven-dicare voluerit predictas decimationes, abbas et conventus Bechci*a* tanquam principales possessores pro eisdem decimationibus defen-sionis onus suscipient. Hiis testibus:*d* Willelmo clerico de Stivent(ona),*e* Sansone et Willelmo filio ipsius de Wanet(ing), Clemente de Sti-

vent(ona),[e] Ricardo serviente de Wanet(ing), Gaufrido de Bixa, Petro
clerico de Rading(ia), Radulfo dispensatore Rading(ie).

CYROGRAPHVM

Endorsed: Abbatis et conventus de Becco super decimationibus de
    Henreda [*13th cent.*]; *also early 19th-cent. endorsement recording production
    of this deed as evidence in a suit in the Exchequer, 11 May 1812*
Size: 152 × 88 mm
Seal: oval of green wax, damaged, on plaited leather thong; frontal
    standing ecclesiastic in chasuble holding book in raised right hand
    and cross in raised left hand; legend: SIGILLVM . . .

[a] Becci *B,C*	[b] dominico *B,C*
[c] Hendreda *A*	[d] *B ends, C ends with* et cetera
[e] 'Stivint' *A*	

Geoffrey of Bix occurs in several Reading deeds of 1173 × 1213, Peter the clerk in
several of 1158 × 86, and Ralph the steward in several of 1165 × 95 (see below, index
sub nominibus); since the agreement was entered in the original section of A, it dates not
later than 1193. The origin of Bec's title to these tithes is obscure, since the church of
East Hendred was held by the priory of Noion (*VCH Berks.*, iv. 302), but it may perhaps
have arisen in connection with Reading's obligation to pay annually to Bec the £5
which Reading originally owed King Stephen for its manor in East Hendred (*Select
Documents of Bec*, 16, 24; above, no. 8).

    1. I am greatly indebted to the kindness of Mr T.M. Eyston for permission to inspect
and print this charter.

787 Perpetual lease by Abbot Henry and the convent of Bec (*de
Becco*) to Reading Abbey of the tithes of the latter's demesne of East
Hendred (*Esthenred*') and of the tenants of the same, with the addition
of 1 acre sown with wheat (*et cum augmento unius acre frumenti bladate*),
for 2 marks of silver to be paid annually within the octave of
Michaelmas at Bec's manor of Wantage (*Wanneting*).[a] For this Reading
has satisfied on Bec's behalf the rector of East Hendred[b] regarding 25
marks of silver which Bec owed him by a composition made between
them concerning the same tithes. If Reading defaults in payment of
the 2 marks at the established term, Bec may take the tithes into its
hands and do with them what it will. Sealing with the abbot's and
convent's seals. Done in A.D. 1230   1230

    Original charter: Hendred House (Oxon.), Muniments, no. 3[1]
    A f 77v; B f 194v; C f 114r

Endorsed: Henr' abb' de Becco de decimis de Astanred' [*13th cent.*];
    R/S Middelton' [*late medieval*]; Decime de Esthenred' [*16th cent.*];
    also early 19th-cent. endorsement as on no. 786
Size: 188 × 152 mm
Seal: parchment tags for 2 seals, one missing, the other partially lost:

circular of green wax, obverse showing Virgin holding a lily in right hand with Child on her lap; legend: SIG. BECC ...; counterseal, small, circular, showing frontal head and shoulders of ? an abbot with head of pastoral staff to his left

^a Waneting *A*, Waneting' *B*, Wanetyng' *C*
^b Esthenrede *A*, Esthenreth' *C*

B notes another charter concerning the same in almost the same words. The dean and chapter of Salisbury's confirmation of the composition between Bec and Philip, rector of East Hendred, is at Hendred House (Muniments, no. 4). It refers to the greater and lesser tithes of Reading Abbey's demesne and the tithes of small tenements held by others named, and it reserves to the rector and his church 'the crop of 1 acre of wheat of the demesne of the abbot and convent of Reading'. The rector was Philip of Beauvais, appointed in 1228 (*Sarum Charters and Documents*, 198–9).

1. This charter was made available by the kindness of Mr T.M. Eyston.

788 Inspeximus and confirmation of the same by Robert [Bingham], bishop of Salisbury. Sealing   27 May 1230 × 26 May 1231

A ff 77v–78r; B f 195r; C f 114r–v

Dat' ^aapud Hort(onam)^a ^b[pontificatus nostri anno ii. Hiis testibus].^b

^{a-a} *Om. in B,C*
^{b-b} *Om. in A, supplied from B,C*

The dating clause is clearly incomplete. The bishop was consecrated 27 May 1229. The text in A quotes the whole of no. 787, those in B and C include about half of it.

789 Final concord in the king's court at Westminster in the quindene of Michaelmas, 26 Henry III, before Walter [de Gray] archbishop of York and primate of England, Walter [Mauclerc] bishop of Carlisle, William Cantilupe (*de Cantilupo*), William of York provost of Beverley, Robert *Passelewe* and others, between Abbot Richard [I] of Reading, plaintiff, and John de Turberville (*Turbervill'*) concerning pasture of the abbot in [East] Hendred (*Henrede*),^a *unde idem abbas questus fuit quod predictus Johannes vi et armis ingressus fuit terram ipsius abbatis in eadem villa et pavit pasturam suam que vocatur Aldefeld' et arbores suas excidit et extirpavit contra pacem domini regis.* In settlement, John recognized the said pasture *cum spinis in ea crescentibus* to be the right of the abbot and abbey of Reading, and for this the abbot granted to John and his heirs in perpetuity pasture in the same for 125 sheep throughout the year, 25 draught-animals (*averia*), of which up to 5 shall be draught-horses (*affri*) if John or his heirs wish, each year from the end of the octave of St Philip and St James [i.e. 8 May], or earlier if the abbot or his successors put their own draught-animals there earlier, and 30 pigs each year when there is acorn-mast (*pessona cenellarum*) there from the end of the quindene of Michaelmas [i.e. 13 Oct.] to the end of the quindene of Martinmas [25 Nov.], provided that John or his heirs or any of his men do not pull down the fruits of the thorn-bushes. The abbot or his successors may not over-burden the pasture so that there is insufficient for the animals of John and his heirs.   13 Oct. 1242

A ff 84v–85r; B ff 168v–169r; C f 99r–v

a Hanrede *B,C*

The foot of this fine is PRO CP 25(1)/7/14/20. John de Turberville was lord of the manor of Arches in the parish of East Hendred (*VCH Berks.*, iv. 297). *Aldefeld*[a] is now Aldfield Farm (*Berks. Place-Names*, ii. 480). In 1158 × 65 Abbot Roger granted to an earlier John de Turberville that he might become a monk of Reading *ad succurrendum* (Hendred House, Muniments, MTD/1/1a and 1b).

790 *Record of the action brought by Thomas Ferling against the abbot of Reading, before the king's justices at Westminster, as to whether he holds 40 acres of land of the abbot in [East] Hendred by villein services or by an annual payment only. The jury find that he held by a greater rent than he claimed and by doing villein services*   3 Feb. 1254

A f 103r–v; B f 144r–v; C f 84v

Anno regni regis Henrici quarti[a] filii Johannis regis xxxviii. Thomas Ferling[b] de Henred' tulit breve domini regis super abbatem de Rading(ia) sub hac forma.

Rex vicecomiti Berk(esire), salutem. Precipimus tibi quod venire facias corum justic(iariis) nostris apud Westm(onasterium) in crastino Purificationis beate Marie .xii. juratores de consensu partium electos ad recognoscendum super sacramentum suum si Th(omas) Ferling teneat .xl. acras terre cum pertinentiis in Hanred' in vilenagio de abbate de Rading(ia), ita quod idem Th(omas) semper solebat reddere eidem abbati et predecessoribus suis pro predicta terra .xxxv. solidos per annum, scilicet medietatem ad festum sancti Michaelis et alteram medietatem ad Pascha, et similiter invenire eidem abbati totam familiam suam excepta uxore sua ad tres bedripas[c] in autumpno ad cibum abbatis, et similiter invenire eidem abbati duos homines triturantes blada ipsius abbatis per duos dies ad custum suum proprium, et similiter dare merchettum[d] pro filiabus et sororibus suis maritandis, et facere eidem abbati auxilium pro voluntate ipsius abbatis, sicut idem abbas dicit; vel si idem Th(omas) teneat predictas .xl. acras terre de predicto abbate libere per servitium .xl. denariorum per annum absque omni villano servitio inde faciendo, sicut idem Th(omas) dicit; quia tam predictus Th(omas) quam predictus abbas inter quos inde contentio est posuerunt se inde in inquisitionem illam.

Postea ad diem illum venerunt iurati qui dicunt super sacramentum

quod predictus Th(omas) toto tempore suo tenuit predictas .xl. acras
terre simul cum aliis terris de predicto abbate et predecessoribus^e suis
per servitium reddendi ei .xxxv. solidos per annum, scilicet ad duos
terminos prenominatos [$f\,103v$] et postea facere solebat predicto abbati
et successoribus suis omnes alias villanas consuetudines sicut predictus
abbas ab eo exigit. Ideo consideratum est quod de cetero faciat
predicto abbati predictum annuum redditum et predictas villanas
consuetudines, et sit in misericordia pro falso clamore.

^{a} *Sic in all texts, rectius* tertii ^{b} Ferthyng' *C*
^{c} bedrippas *C* ^{d} merechettum *B,C*
^{e} *In C, written above* successoribus *marked for deletion*

This case was referred to in 1261, when Thomas's son Henry *Ferthing'* attempted to
recover the 40 acres from the abbot of Reading (PRO JUST 1/40, m. 13). A deed by
Abbot William I shows the family to have been tenants of the abbey as early as
1165 × 73 (Hendred House, Muniments, MTD/1/1c).

791 *Record of the action brought by the abbot of Reading against John de
Turberville for wrongfully seizing into the king's hand 40 acres of the abbot's
land in* [*East*] *Hendred*   [Nov. 1255 × May 1259]

A f 103v

[Johannes de Turbervill']^a attachiatus fuit ad respondendum abbati
Rading' de placito qua ratione cepit in manum^b domini regis .xl.
acras terre cum pertinentiis in Hanred' et fecit intelligere Johanni
Walerando esch(aetori) domini regis quod terra illa fuit eschaeta
domini regis, eo quod predictus abbas dicit in curia domini regis quod
predictus Johannes de Turb(ervill') fraudulenter et per odium cepit
in manum domini regis terram illam et quod terra illa est villenagium
ipsius abbatis de dono predecessorum domini regis regum Angl(ie).
Et unde predictus abbas querit quod, cum ipse in curia domini
regis coram justic(iariis) suis apud Westm(onasterium) per iudicium
eiusdem curie recuperasset seisinam suam de predicta terra cum pertinentiis et de villenagio suo et inde fuit in seisina pacifica, idem
Johannes fraudulenter et per odium fecit intelligere predicto Johanni
Walerando, et cetera, quod terra illa fuit eschaeta domini regis, unde
dampnum habet ad valentiam .xl. librarum. Et Johannes venit et
dicit quod quicquid fecit de predicta eschaeta fecit per predictum
Johannem Walerandum qui fuit capitalis esch(aetor) domini regis, et
de hoc vocat inde ad war(antum). Et supervenit predictus Johannes
Walerandus et, requisitus si per ipsum vel per preceptum eius predictus Johannes de Turb(ervill') fecit inquisitionem quam fecit, dicit
quod non. Et quia predictus Johannes de Turb(ervill') deadvocatus
est, ideo in misericordia. Et inde abbas sine die et remaneat in seisina
sua quam prius habuit et habere debet.

Rubric: Johannes de Turbervill' in misericordia pro pluribus def(altis)

ᵃ Ms has Idem, *referring to preceding rubric*
ᵇ Corrected from Ms manu

John Walerand was appointed escheator south of Trent 3 Nov. 1255, his successor being appointed 2 June 1259 (*Cal. Pat. R. 1247–58*, 446; *ibid. 1258–66*, 27). John de Turberville was made sub-escheator in Berkshire in 1251 and was still in office in 1261 (*Close Rolls 1247–51*, 515; *ibid. 1259–61*, 363); he was sheriff of Berkshire and Oxfordshire for part of 1254 (*List of Sheriffs*, 107). This case and no. 789 reveal bad blood between him and Reading Abbey. Since the 40 acres concerned here are probably those which Thomas Ferling held and about which he was in dispute with the abbey as to services in 1254 (no. 790), John de Turberville's animosity towards the abbey may have involved Thomas Ferling as well. The plea roll containing this case is lost.

792   Agreement, in chirograph form, dated 50 Henry III, between Abbot Richard [II, Bannister] and the convent of Reading, on one side, and John son of Thomas *Ferthing*,ᵃ on the other, whereby the abbot and convent, at the instance of Richard [of Hendred], abbot of Abingdon (*Abendon'*), have given to John for his homage and service the land which his father held of them in East Hendred (*Esthanreth'*) along with 40 acres of land which an inquest said were in Steventon (*Stivinton'*). To be held with house, mill, meadows [etc.] by John and his heirs or assigns, excluding a place of religion, freely by hereditary right in perpetuity by rendering annually to the abbot and convent 40s and 20d sterling, viz., 20s 10d each at Michaelmas and Easter, and by doing two suits only in the year, at the two views of frankpledge of the abbot and convent, with their free men at their court of Blewbury (*Blebur'*)ᵇ or [East] Hendred (*Hanreth'*) by reasonable summons, saving also to the abbot and convent wardships, reliefs, escheats and marriages when they arise. Warranty, except to a place of religion. For this John has given the abbot and convent £10 of silver. Sealing by both parties   28 Oct. 1265 × 27 Oct. 1266

B ff 143v–144r; C f 84r–v

Hiis testibus: domino Nicholao de Sivrewastᶜ tunc vicecomite Oxon' et Berk', Waltero de la Rivere, Henrico de Peseia, Nicholao de Hanreth', militibus, Willelmo de Spersolte tunc sen(escallo) Abendon', Willelmo de Blebur',ᵇ Willelmo de Witele, Nicholao de Middilton', Martino le Rus de Hanneia, Johanne le porter, Thoma de la Sale de Stivinton', Johanne clerico, et aliis.

ᵃ Om. in C   *ᵇ* Bleobur' *C*
ᶜ Siverewast *C*

Nicholas de Sifrewast was sheriff 19 Sept. 1265–23 Nov. 1267 (*List of Sheriffs*, 107). In 1286 the abbey sold the wardship of John's son to his widow, Matilda (BL Add. Ch. 19634).

793 Quitclaim by Henry son of Thomas *Ferthing^a* to Abbot Richard [II] and the convent of Reading of all his right in all the lands and tenements which his father sometime held of them in East Hendred (*Esthanreth'*) and elsewhere. Sealing [*c.* 1265 × 66]

B f143v; C f84r

Hiis testibus: domino Nicholao de Hanreth', Willelmo de Spersolte, Willelmo de Blebur',^b Nicholao de Middilton',^c Willelmo de Witel(e), Johanne le porter, Johanne clerico, et aliis.

^a Ferthyng' *C*   ^b Bleobury *C*
^c Middeltone *C*

Of approximately the same date as no. 792, since all the witnesses also appear in that deed. Cf. No. 790 n.

794 Gift by Sarah daughter of Robert Franklin (*le Frankelein*) of East Hendred (*Esthenred'*) to Reading Abbey of whatever falls (*accidere*), or could at any time fall, to her by hereditary right in all the land of her father in East Hendred. Warranty. For this the abbey has granted her provision of food and clothing for life, as is contained in the charter which she has from the abbot and convent. Sealing. Witnesses^a [omitted] [13th cent.; not later than 1258]

B f73v; C f38v

^a *Om. in C*

Dating very uncertain. The deed was not entered in A and appears in the original section of B. A Robert Franklin occurs in 1248 (Clanchy, *Berks. Eyre of 1248*, 386, 466), but whether he is the same as Sarah's father is not clear.

ENGLEFIELD

795 *Confirmation by Jocelin [de Bohun], bishop of Salisbury, of the gift by William of Englefield of the church of Englefield to Reading Abbey* [*c.* 1180 × 1184]

A f52r; B f190r; C f110r–v

Omnibus Christi fidelibus ad quos presens carta pervenerit Iocelinus dei gratia Sar(esburiensis) episcopus, salutem in domino. Noverit universitas vestra nos ratam et firmam habere donationem ecclesie de Englef(eld) factam per manum Willelmi eiusdem ecclesie advocati dilectis filiis nostris abbati et conventui Rading'. Quod ut perpetua gaudeat firmitate, carte presentis attestatione et sigilli nostri munimine roboramus. His^a testibus:^b Bald(ewino) cancellario Sar(esburiensi), Roberto de Geld', magistro Nicolao de Hid', et magistro Hamone de Waltham.

a Hiis *B,C*   *b* *B,C* end with et cetera

Before the bishop's death in 1184 and probably a few years before the revision of William of Englefield's gift in 1183 × 84 (nos. 797–8); William became lord of Englefield after 1166 (*VCH Berks.*, iii. 406). Baldwin does not certainly occur as chancellor of Salisbury before the early 1180s (D. Greenway, 'The false *Institutio* of St Osmund', *Tradition and Change: Essays in honour of Marjorie Chibnall*, ed. D. Greenway, C. Holdsworth and J. Sayers (Cambridge, 1985), 85) and was still in office in 1197 × 1205 (BL Egerton 3316 (Bath Cartulary), f69v). A Master Hamo of Waltham witnessed a charter concerning White Waltham (Berks.) in 1184 × *c.* 1197 (BL Cotton Tib. C ix (Waltham cartulary), f139r—I owe this reference to the kindness of Dr Rosalind Ransford) and a Hamo of Waltham witnessed a deed concerning Whitley in 1186 × 99 (below, no. 1211). For the text of William of Englefield's gift, of which the present act is a confirmation, see no. 799.

796 *Admission by Jocelin [de Bohun], bishop of Salisbury, at the presentation of Reading Abbey, of Walter clerk of Englefield as perpetual vicar of Englefield, paying annually 1 mark of silver to the abbey*   [*c.* 1180 × 1184]

A f52r; B f190r–v; C f110v

Omnibus Christi fidelibus *a*ad quos presens carta pervenerit Iocelinus dei gratia Sar(esburiensis) episcopus, salutem in domino.*a* Ad universitatis vestre notitiam volumus pervenire nos, ad presentationem dilectorum filiorum nostrorum abbatis et monachorum Rading-(ensium), recepisse Walt(eru)m clericum de Englefeld in perpetuum vicarium ecclesie de Englefeld, ita quidem ut ipse eandem ecclesiam cum omnibus pertinentiis suis integre habeat et possideat, solvendo exinde annuatim unam marcam argenti ecclesie *b*de Rading(ia).*b* Quod ut inconvulsum in posterum perseveret, presentis carte sigillo nostro munite testimonio confirmamus.*c* His*d* testibus:*e* B(aldewino) cancellario Sar(esburiensi), Roberto de Geld', magistro Nicholao de Hid', et magistro Hamone de Waltham, et multis aliis.

a–a et cetera *B,C*   *b–b* Radingensi *B,C*
c *C ends*   *d* Hiis *B*
e *B ends with* et cetera

Of the same date as no. 795, since the witnesses are identical. Walter's perpetual vicarage was of the pension-paying type, for which see C.R. Cheney, *From Becket to Langton* (Manchester, 1956), 133; B.R. Kemp, 'Monastic possession of parish churches …', *JEH*, xxxi (1980), 150–3. By 1201 the incumbent was called a parson (see no. 211).

797 *Notification by William of Englefield that, after his earlier gift of the church of Englefield to Reading Abbey, and because he was displeased to have no right left in the church, Abbot Joseph and the convent of Reading have conceded to him and his heirs that, after the death of the vicar of Englefield, they shall present to the abbey a suitable clerk whom the abbey will present to the* *bishop of Salisbury as perpetual vicar, paying an annual pension of 1 mark to the abbey* [1183 × 84]

Af39v; Bf199v; Cf118r

Sciant presentes et futuri quod ecclesia de Englefeld a pristinis temporibus de iure fuit monasterii Rading(ensis) et ei pensionalis. Sed, quia cautele abundantia*ᵃ* parit securitatem, ego Willelmus dominus de Englefeld eandem ecclesiam pro salute anime mee et meorum prefato monasterio donavi ipsamque donationem carte mee confirmatione roboravi. Verum, quoniam postea moleste tuli ego et amici mei quod nichil iuris in eadem ecclesia mihi et heredibus meis esset relictum, Ioseph abbas Rading(ensis) et conventus pro bono pacis concesserunt mihi et heredibus meis ut, decedente vicario de Englefeld, ego Willelmus et heredes mei presentemus eis idoneum clericum quem ipsi episcopo Sar(esburiensi) in perpetuum vicarium presentabunt. Ipse tamen vicarius prius in capitulo Rading(ensi) de fide monachis servanda et annua pensione*ᵇ* unius marce solvenda iuratoriam prestabit cautionem. Quod ut perpetua gaudeat firmitate, presenti scripto et sigilli mei appositione roboravi.*ᶜ* His Testibus: Azone archidiacono Sar(esburiensi), Ricardo vicearchidiacono Berkesc(ire), magistro Alexandro medico, Daniele de Ponte, Roberto filio Ursonis, et multis aliis.

ᵃ habundantia *B,C*
ᵇ *A has* impensione *with first two letters marked for deletion*
ᶜ *B ends with* T', *C ends*

Before the death of Jocelin, bishop of Salisbury, who confirmed the new arrangement (no. 798), and while Walter was prior of Wallingford (see no. 799 n.). An almost identical document, but in the name of Abbot Joseph and the convent of Reading, is PRO E210/3128 (Anc. Deed D 3128). It states that the abbey's concession was made in the presence of Jocelin, bishop of Salisbury, and it has the following witness list: Azone archidiacono Salesb', Ricardo vicearchidiacono Berrucsire, magistro Alexandro medico, Daniele de Ponte, Rodberto filio Ursonis, magistro Rodberto de Gildeford, canonicis Salesb', Waltero capellano, Nicholao de Heliun, Mauricio clerico, Rodberto de Mara, Willelmo de Mara, Gillone de Pincheni, Rodberto de Lideneia, militibus, Iohanne Amis. It seems likely that all or most of these also witnessed William of Englefield's deed.

798 *Confirmation in chirograph form by Jocelin* [de Bohun], *bishop of Salisbury, of the arrangement made in his presence between William of Englefield and Reading Abbey concerning the advowson of the vicarage of Englefield*
[1183 × 84]

Original charter (damaged): PRO E210/3439 (Ancient Deed D 3439)
Af52v; Bf190v; Cf110v

CYROGRAPHVM

Omnibus ^aad quos presens scriptum pervenerit Iocelinus dei gratia
Sar(esburiensis) episcopus, eternam in domino salutem.^a Ex subiectis
vobis innotescat quod ecclesia de Englefeld' a pristinis temporibus de
iure fuit monasterii Rading(ensis) et ei pensionalis. Sed quia cautele
habundantia^b parit securitatem, Willelmus de Englefeld' eandem ecclesiam [pro salute anime sue et]^c antecessorum suorum prefato monasterio donavit ipsamque donationem [sue carte confirmatione
roboravit]. Verum quoniam postea tulit moleste Willelmus et eius
amici quod nichil iu[ris in eadem ecclesia sibi et heredibus s]uis esset
relictum, monachi Rad(ingenses) pro bono pacis in nostra presentia
e[is concesserunt ut dec]edente vicario Willelmus vel eius heredes
idoneum clericum eis presentent. Ipsi vero eundem mihi vel successoribus meis in perpetuum vicarium presentabunt. Ipse tamen
vicarius prius in capitulo Rad(ingensi) de fide monachis servanda
et de annua pensione unius marce solvenda iuratoriam prestabit
cautionem. Quod ut perpetua gaudeat firmitate, presenti scripto cum^d
sigilli mei appositione duxi roborandum.^e Testibus hiis: Azone archidiacono Sar(esburiensi), Ricardo vicearchidiacono Berch(esire),^f
magistro Alexandro medico,^g Daniele de Ponte, magistro Roberto filio
Ursonis, et magistro Roberto de Guldef(ord), canonicis Sar', Galterio
capellano, Nicholao de Eliun, et Mauricio clerico, Willelmo de Mara,
Gillone de Pincheni, et Roberto de Lideneia, militibus, et magistro
Willelmo Cumin.

Endorsed: Ecclesia^h de Englef' [*16th cent.*]
Size: 162 × 143 mm
Seal: missing; tag through slit in fold at bottom

^{a-a} et cetera *B,C*   ^b abundantia *A*
^c *Original damaged, this and other passages in square brackets being supplied from A*
^d et *B,C*   ^e *B ends with* Hiis t', *C ends*
^f Sar' *A* (*in error*)   ^g *A ends with* et multis aliis
^h *Reading uncertain*

Contemporary with no. 797. The absence of a normal Reading Abbey endorsement
on the PRO original shows this to have been William of Englefield's part of the
chirograph.

799 *Notification by Walter, prior of Wallingford, that he has received in
custody the charter by which William of Englefield confirmed his gift of the
church of Englefield to Reading Abbey. The charter will be released to neither
party without the consent of the other, unless to the abbey if William withdraws
from the second agreement made between them*   [1183 × 84]

Original charter: PRO E210/3127 (Ancient Deed D 3127)
Af40r; Bf199r; Cf118r

Sciant ad quos presens cartha*a* pervenerit quod ego Walt(erius) prior
de Walengef(ordia)*b* recepi in custodia per consensum ecclesie Rad-
ing(ensis) et Willelmi de Englefeld cartham*a* euisdem Willelmi in
qua confirmavit donationem suam de ecclesia de Englefeld ecclesie
Rading(ensi), cuius iste est tenor.

Universitati fidelium Willelmus de Englefeld, salutem. In publicam
veniat notitiam quod ecclesia de Englefeld ab antecessorum meorum
temporibus iuris fuit ecclesie Rading(ensis). Inde est quod Sexi et
Walt(erius),*c* quorum alter post alterum in eadem ecclesia monachorum Rading(ensium) nomine ministravit, annuam .iiii. denariorum pensionem*d* eisdem monachis longo tempore persolverunt.
Quia vero modernis temporibus contra fraudes exquisitas abundans*e*
cautela non nocet, ego Willelmus prefatis monachis predictam ecclesiam donavi cum omnibus pertinentiis suis et hanc meam donationem
presentis carthe*a* attestatione cum sigilli mei impressione communivi.*f*
His testibus:*g* Willelmo capellano, Gauf(redo) de Bixe, Iohanne Amis.

[*c. 1180 × 1184*]

Debet autem predicta cartha*a h* ita custodiri ut neutri parti sine
assensu alterius reddatur, nisi forte ecclesie Rading(ensi) si predictus
Willelmus resiliverit a pactione secunda que confirmata est inter illum
et ecclesiam Rading(ensem) et sigillis utriusque*i* confirmata.

Endorsed: Carte*j* de Walingeford' [*14th cent.*] in qua confirmavit don-
acionem de ecclesia de Englefeld' ecclesie de Radynge [*16th cent.*]
Size: 245 × 67 mm
Seal: large fragment in white wax on tag; no features recognisable

a carta, *or appropriate case, A,B,C*
b Waling' *A*, Walingford' *B*, Walyngford' *C*
c Walteri *C*
d impensionem *A, with first two letters marked for deletion*
e habundans *B,C*   *f C ends*
g B has Hiis t' *and ends*   *h Insert* mea *A (in error)*
i Insert partis *A*   *j Sic*

Walter's predecessor as prior of Wallingford became abbot of Malmesbury in 1183
(*Heads of Relig. Houses*, 97). This document no doubt formed part of the arrangements
for the revision of William of Englefield's gift of Englefield church (nos. 797–8), since
Prior Walter has received in custody the original charter of gift, which Bishop Jocelin
had confirmed (no. 795). The new arrangement was also confirmed by Jocelin, who
died in 1184 (no. 798). It is notable that William's original gift (quoted here) specified
an annual pension of 4d, but that Bishop Jocelin allowed a pension of 1 mark when
admitting a perpetual vicar on the abbey's presentation (no. 796). The form of the
endorsement suggests that the PRO original was made for William of Englefield.

800 Notification, in chirograph form, by Giles, archdeacon of Berkshire, and W(illiam)[a] rector of Basildon (*Bestlesdene*), his official, that, whereas a suit was brought before them by Reading Abbey against T., rector of Englefield (*Englefeld*) concerning an annual pension of 1 mark; and Sir William of Englefield, knight, son of Alan of Englefield, patron of the church, seeing his own interest at issue since the case involved the advowson, joined the defence; after various letters had been obtained from the legate Otto, all suits concerning the pension were settled, saving the jurisdiction of the diocesan and of the archdeacon of Berkshire to compel observance of the settlement. Namely, that Reading Abbey has conceded in perpetuity that, when rectors of Englefield die, William and his heirs shall, as patrons of the church, present their clerks for the rectory directly to the bishop of Salisbury, notwithstanding any deeds (*instrumenta*) made by William's predecessors or others concerning the said pension; and William, for himself and his heirs, *quantum in eo est*, and T., rector of Englefield, for himself and his church and successors, have conceded that the rector and his successors shall pay to Reading Abbey in perpetuity an annual pension of 1 mark, which from of old the abbey has been accustomed to receive from the church *nomine pensionis*, viz., half each at Michaelmas and Easter. Neither the payment of the pension nor previous deeds concerning it shall prejudice the right of direct presentation of William and his heirs, nor the rectory of the rectors. Done at Reading, Friday before the Nativity of St John Baptist, A.D. 1239. Sealing *alternatim*   17 June 1239

Original charter: PRO E210/81 (Ancient Deed D 81)
B ff 198v–199r; C ff 117v–118r
Pd. (cal.) *Cat. Anc. Deeds*, iii. 412–13

Hiis testibus:[b] dominis Rad(ulfo) de Mortuomar(i), Rogero de Hyda, Rich(ero) Neirenut, P. de Gadingeld', Gaufr(edo) Martel, Roberto de Uffint(ona), Johanne de la Huse, W. tunc decano de Rading(ia), magistris Jacobo et W(illelmo)[a] de Rading(ia), et dominis Henrico de la Stan', Rad(ulfo) de Englef(eld), Ricardo de Hechelhamt', Alano de Englef(eld), et multis aliis.

Endorsed: Compositio indentat' inter rectorem de Englefyld' et abbat' et convent' Rading' pro solutione unius marce annuatim [?] recipiend' Radyng' 23 H. 3 [*16th × 17th cent.*]
Size: 264 × 210 mm (to points of indentation 236 mm)
Seal: tags for 5 seals, of which 3 remain: (i) oval of white wax, nearly complete; worn impression of standing ecclesiastic; part of legend remains but illegible; (ii) fragment of large oval of white wax (abbot's seal); obverse, standing abbot with book in left hand and pastoral staff in right, legend missing; on reverse complete counterseal, hand of St James between two scallops, legend: ORA

PRO NOB. SANCTE IACOBE (see above, no. 229); (iii) large fragment of oval of white wax; obverse, fragment of Virgin and Child (i.e., Reading Abbey seal); reverse, part of counterseal with hand of St James, as above; legend illegible

a For expansion, see below, no. 1202
b B,C end

Since the original bears no medieval endorsement, it may not be the abbey's copy. The abbey's right in the advowson appears already to have lapsed by 1232, when a new parson was instituted at the presentation of William of Englefield (BL Add. Ch. 20252).

801 Confirmation of the same by Robert [Bingham], bishop of Salisbury. Sealing   1 Oct. 1239

Original charter: PRO E210/82 (Ancient Deed D 82)
Bf190v; Cf110v
Pd. (cal.) *Cat. Anc. Deeds.* iii. 413

Data*a* apud Wodeford per manum Walteri de la Wyle cappellani et canonici nostri, kl' Octobris pontificatus nostri anno xi.

Endorsed: none
Size: 184 × 48 mm
Seal: small fragment in green wax on tag

a B,C end with et cetera

802 Record of the action brought by Reading Abbey against Ralph, rector of Englefield (*Englefeld*), before Giles archdeacon of Berkshire, *auctoritate ordinaria cognoscente*, in the church of St Laurence, Reading, on Wednesday after the octave of Easter, A.D. 1249, concerning the annual pension of 1 mark from the church of Englefield, which has not been paid for 3 years. The abbey appeared by its proctor, but Ralph, though lawfully and peremptorily cited, did not appear. The abbey sought that it be restored to possession of the annual pension in accordance with the synodal constitution regarding pensions due to men of religion and wrongfully detained.[1] After consultation with the [ruridecanal] chapter (*habito capituli consilio*), and following the said constitution, the archdeacon awarded possession of the pension to the abbey and ordered Ralph to pay the arrears of 3 marks for the previous 3 years. Execution of the sentence was committed to the [rural] dean, who was to compel Ralph to pay the 3 marks and to pay the pension in future on pain of suspension and excommunication and, if necessary, sequestration and disposal of his goods.

14 Apr. 1249

B f 199v; C f 118r–v

Rubric: Quod rector ecclesie de Englef' compellendus est per decanum loci ad solutionem pensionis

1. Presumably referring to no. 49 of Bishop Bingham's synodal statutes, dating 1238 × 44 (*Councils and Synods*, ii, part I, ed. F.M. Powicke and C.R. Cheney (Oxford, 1964), 385).

FRILSHAM

803 Gift in free alms by Matilda Peche (*Peche*), lady of Frilsham (*Fridlesham*), widow, for the health of her soul and for the souls of Sir Nicholas Peche her father, Alice Peche her mother, Sir Oliver *Deyncort* and Sir Walter *de Rideware* her husbands deceased, Sir Ralph Peche, Hawise his wife, Nicholas and John the donor's sons, Alice her daughter, Roger *de Rideware* and Alice his wife, Richard *le Wales*, and all her ancestors [etc.], to Reading Abbey of all the land which she had in the vill of Frilsham called *La Hide*, which she bought from Nicholas Butler (*le Boteler*) of Reading and Juliana his wife and John *Flawel* of Chichester (*Cicestr'*), which they had bought from Roger *Willard*; saving to herself a parcel [of land] which she bought from Margery, widow of Walter *Wilard*, for the term of Margery's life. To be held with all appurtenances and the homage and service of Robert Black (*Niger*) and whatever belonged to her from the said Robert or his heirs, by rendering annually to her and her heirs a root of ginger and a rose at the nativity of St John Baptist for all service, suits of court, secular exaction and demand, saving hidage, scutage and all other foreign service which is due from the said land. Warranty. For this the monks have received Matilda, her ancestors, successors and children in all benefits of the conventual church of Reading in perpetuity. Sealing   [1270]

B ff 211v–212r; C ff 127v–128r

Hiis testibus: dominis Waltero de Ripar(io), *ª*Willelmo de Brutenoll',*ª* Bartholomeo de ʒatingeden',*ᵇ* Nicholao de Henred, Willelmo Huscarle, Roberto de Bergefeud,*ᶜ* militibus, Waltero de Riddeware filio meo, Willelmo de Blebur',*ᵈ* *ᵉ*Nicholao de la Haʒe,*ᵉ* Adam de Burchildebur',*ᶠ* Willelmo de la Weye, Rogero le Waleys, *ᵍ*Thoma Butun,*ᵍ* Thoma de*ʰ* Morton' clerico, et aliis.

ª⁻ª Om. in C   *ᵇ ʒatingden' C*
ᶜ Burgfeld' C   *ᵈ Bleobir' C*

The cartulary rubrics say that there were two copies (*et hec duplicata*). The date is derived from the complementary act by Abbot Robert of Reading, dated 28 July 1270, establishing a chantry in the abbey for those named in Matilda's deed ('The Rydeware Chartulary', ed. I.H. Jeayes and G. Wrottesley, William Salt Arch. Soc., *Coll. Hist. Staffs.*, xvi (1896), 283; I am indebted to Miss J.M. Boorman for this reference). Matilda was the only daughter and heir of Sir Nicholas Peche, lord of Frilsham. She married firstly Walter de Rideware, who occurs as tenant of Frilsham in 1235–6, and secondly Oliver de Aincourt, who held the manor in 1242–3 and died in 1246, after which Matilda continued to hold the manor until as late as 1275–6 (*VCH Berks.*, iv. 71; for Oliver's death, see Sanders, *English Baronies*, 15–16). The deeds by which she acquired the land, here given to Reading, from Nicholas and Juliana Butler and John Flavel are printed in 'The Rydeware Chartulary', 281–2; they probably date from shortly before 1267, since in April of that year she paid Nicholas and Juliana the final instalment of the price for their part (*ibid.*, 293). To judge from a *precipe* of 1270, the property consisted of a messuage, 3 virgates of land, 4 acres of wood and 5s rent (*ibid.*).

804 Grant and quitclaim in free alms by Matilda Peche (*Pecche*),[a] lady of Frilsham (*Fridlesham*), widow, for the health of her soul and for the souls [etc., as in no. 803], to Reading Abbey of pasture for 12 oxen, 2 horses, 200 sheep and 20 pigs on the pasture of *Brunnigemere*,[b] which pasture she bought from Sir Nicholas *de Sifrewast*. To be held of the said Nicholas and his heirs or assigns freely, by rendering annually to them 2s sterling, viz., 12d each on the vigil of St Michael and on the vigil of the Annunciation, for all service, custom, suits of court of the said Nicholas and all suits, and for all secular exaction and demand. For this the monks have received Matilda, her ancestors, successors and children in all benefits of the conventual church of Reading in perpetuity. Sealing [prob. 1270]

B f212r–v; C f128r–v

Hiis testibus: dominis Waltero de Ripar(io), 'Willelmo de Brutenoll',[c] Bartholomeo de ӡatingedene,[d] Nicholao de Henred, Willelmo Huscarle, Roberto de Bergefeud,[e] militibus, Waltero de Riddeware filio meo, Willelmo de Blebur',[f] [g]Nicholao de la Haӡe,[g] Adam de Burchildebur',[h] Willelmo de la Wey, Rogero le Waleys, Thoma Butun, Thoma de Morton' clerico, et aliis.

ᵃ Peche C
ᶜ⁻ᶜ Om. in C
ᵉ Burghfeld' C
ᵍ⁻ᵍ Om. in C

ᵇ Brunnyngemer' C
ᵈ ӡatingden' C
ʲ Bleobur' C
ʰ Burghilb'i C

Probably of the same date as no. 803.

805 Gift by Nicholas *de Sifrewast*,[a] knight, to Lady Matilda Peche (*Peche*) and her heirs or assigns who shall hold the land called *la Hid(e)* in the vil of Frilsham (*Fridlesham*), of pasture for 12 oxen, 2 horses, 200 sheep and 20 pigs on the whole of his pasture of *Brunnigemere*.[b] To be held freely, with free entry and exit at all times of the year and in all places appurtenant to the pasture of *Brunnigemere*,[c] whether they have their own oxen [etc.], or ones belonging to others, by rendering annually to him, his heirs or assigns 2s sterling, viz., 12d each on the vigil of St Michael and on the vigil of the Annunciation, for all service, custom, suits of his court and all suits, and for all secular exaction and demand. For this Matilda has given him 100s sterling. Warranty and sealing   [*?c.* 1267]

B f212v; C f128v; BL Egerton 3041 (Rydeware Cartulary) f34r (not collated)
Pd. 'The Rydeware Chartulary', ed. I.H. Jeayes and G. Wrottesley, *Coll. Hist. Staffs.*, xvi (1896), 282 (from Egerton 3041)

Hiis testibus: domino Petro de Ʒatingeden',[d] domino Waltero de Ripario, domino Willelmo de Brutenoll', militibus, Bartholemeo de Ʒatingeden',[d] Willelmo de la Wey,[e] Rogero le Waleys, [f]Nicholao de la HaƷe, Willelmo de Everingtune,[f] Gaufrido de la Wile, Andrea Buchnel, Petro a la Grave de Ʒatingeden',[d] et aliis.

[a] Syffrewast *C*   [b] Brunnyngemer' *C*
[c] Brunnyngmer' *C*   [d] Ʒatyngden' *C*
[e] Weye *C*   [ff] *Om. in C*

The date is derived from the fact that at Michaelmas 1267 Matilda paid Nicholas de Sifrewast all the money she owed him, presumably in respect of this acquisition ('The Rydeware Chartulary', 293).

806 Acknowledgement by Richard *atte Well'* of Hampstead [Norris] (*Hampsted'*) of his obligation to pay annually to Reading Abbey 10s sterling at Michaelmas for the whole tenement which sometime belonged to Matilda Peche (*Peche*) and which he holds of Reading Abbey in Frilsham (*Frideleshame*); and concession that, if he and his heirs default in payment, the abbot's bailiffs may distrain them in the said tenement on all their movable and immovable goods and retain the distresses, without gage and pledge, at the abbot's court in Bucklebury (*Burghildebury*) until full satisfaction of the rent has been made. In [witness] whereof, etc. [*text incomplete*]
                                            [late 13th × early 14th cent.]

B f68v; (noted) B f70v; C f36r[1]

This deed is later than no. 803. It was noted in B in a hand of the late 13th or early 14th century before C was copied from B, but, after that copy had been made, the nearly complete text was entered in B in a 14th-century hand.

1. Carta Ricardi de Fonte obligatoria de decem solidis reddendis pro terra de la Hyde in Fridlesham (*C has* Fridelsham)

HARTLEY (in Shinfield)

807 Gift in free alms by Amis *de Peletoth'*[a] to Reading Abbey of 14d rent which William *de la Schete*[b] used to pay him in Hartley (*Hurtleg'*),[c] to be received from William and his heirs at two terms of the year, viz., at Michaelmas 8d and on the feast of St Thomas the apostle 6d. Warranty and sealing[d]   [*c.* 1220 × June 1248]

B ff 58v–59r; C f 26r–v; C f 219r

Hiis testibus:[e] [Willelmo de Engelfeld, Rogero de Hyda, Roberto de Uffyntone, Johanne de la Huse, Rogero de Whytcherche, Gilberto de Mora, Radulpho de Mora, et multis aliis].

[a] Peletot' *C f 26r–v*, Pelytot *C f 219r*   [b] Syethe *C f 219r*
[c] 'Hurtlegh' *C f 26r–v*, Hurtle *C f 219r*   [d] *C f 26r–v ends*
[e] *B ends, the remainder being supplied from C f 219r*

In the early years of Henry III's reign Amis held one hide in Hartley, in Shinfield, perhaps the estate later known as Hartley Amys (*VCH Berks.*, iii. 263). Roger of Whitchurch, among the witnesses, was dead by June 1248 (Clanchy, *Berks. Eyre of 1248*, 175).

808 Gift by Amis *de Peletot* to Reading Abbey of 21d rent in Hartley (*Hurtleg'*),[a] viz., from Aldwin *Kibesoth* 7d, from Alward *Kibesoth* 9d and from Laurence *de Lomwode* 5d. To be held freely by rendering to Amis and his heirs ½d at Michaelmas for all service, exaction and demand. For this the abbey has given him 20s sterling. Warranty and sealing. Witnesses [omitted]   [*c.* 1220 × 1258]

B f 59r; C f 26v

[a] Hurtlegh' *C*

Entered in the original section of B and, therefore, not later than 1258. Amis was dead by Feb. 1261 (see no. 708 n.). In another deed, dated 1239–40, he gave to the almonry of Reading an annual rent of 20d from Walter Vachell (*Fachel*) in Hartley, for which Robert the almoner paid him 16s (D f 22r–v).

809 Gift in free alms by Richard *Toky* of Hartley (*Hertl(eg')*)[a] to Reading Abbey of 12d rent to be received annually from his whole tenement in Hartley (*Hortleg'*)[a] which he held of Richard of Dummer (*Dummere*) by his or his heirs' hands, viz., 6d each at Michaelmas and

the Purification [2 Feb.]. Warranty and sealing. Witnesses [omitted]
[? *c.* 1225 × 1258]

B f59r; C f26v

a Hertlegh' *C*

The donor occurs in 1248 (Clanchy, *Berks. Eyre of 1248,* 172). Richard of Dummer was
lord of the manor of Hartley Dummer, in Shinfield, in which this tenement presumably
lay, and occurs between 1226 × 38 and 1249 (*VCH Berks.,* iii. 262; below, no. 1098;
Fees, ii. 849; Clanchy, *ibid.,* 184–5). This deed was entered in the original section of B.

HINTON (in Hurst) and SHEEPBRIDGE (in Swallowfield)

810   Gift in free alms by William Longespee (*Lunghespeie*)*a* to Reading
Abbey of 40s annual rent at Hinton (*Henton'*) and Sheepbridge (*Scheperige*)*b* to be received on the morrow of St Martin [11 Nov.], viz., from
Sir Thomas *le Blond* *c* and his heirs 1 mark, from Sir Henry *de Mara*
and his heirs 1 mark and from Richard *del Hech* *d* and his heirs 1 mark.
To be held freely, saving to the donor and his heirs the homage and
any other services of the said Thomas, Henry and Richard and their
heirs. Warranty. Grant of power to the abbey to distrain the said men
and their heirs if they shall default in payment, and to take the
distresses to Whitley (*Witele*), as the men's charters testify. The donor
binds himself in respect of any kind of security concerning the said
40s which the king's justices or other discreet men shall require to be
made (*providerint faciendam*). Sealing   [*c.* 1238 × 1250]

Original charter: BL Add. Ch. 19622
A f86v; B ff 55v–56r; C f24r; C f150r
Pd. *Arch. Journ.,* xxii. 159; (cal.) Hurry, *Reading Abbey,* 177–8

Hiis testibus:*e* dominis Philippo Basset, Henrico de Mara, Willelmo
de Englefeld,*f* Everardo le Tyeis, Rogero de la Hide, Roberto de
Uffinton', militibus, Henrico del Estane, Ricardo del Hek', Johanne
Pipard, et aliis.

Endorsed: Carta Willelmi de Lungespeie [*13th cent.*] de xl. sol' annui
redditus apud Hentone et Scipruge [*13th cent., similar hand, different
ink*]
Size: 250 × 148 mm
Seal: circular (*c.* 42 mm diameter), nearly perfect, in green wax on tag;
obverse a shield charged with six lioncels, legend: + SIGILLVM.
WILL..... GESPEIE; on reverse complete counterseal, circular
(*c.* 26 mm diameter), long sword and baldrick, legend:

+ SECRETVM. WILLELM. LVGGESPE; with part of velvet
and silk bag

a Lungespeye *B, Cf24r*
b Scheperuge *A,B*, Shepruge *Cf24r*, Scheperigge *Cf150r*
c Blund *A*   *d* Hec *B,Cf24r*, Bech (*sic*) *Cf150r*
e *A,B,Cf24r* end   *f* *Cf150r* ends *with* et aliis

Hinton and Sheepbridge were held by Ela, countess of Salisbury, in 1236 (*VCH Berks.*,
iii. 271) and it seems likely that she retained them until she resigned the earldom in
1238. Her son, the present donor, died in 1250. See also *Bracton's Note Book*, iii. 286–8.

811 Acknowledgement by Henry *de la Mare* of his obligation to
pay to Reading Abbey, by assignment of Sir William Longespee
(*Lungesp(eie)*),*a* the annual rent of 1 mark at Hinton (*Hentone*) on the
morrow of St Martin, which he used to pay the same William, saving
to the latter and his heirs all other services from the said tenement. If
he or his heirs default in payment, the abbey may distrain them at
Diddenham (*Dideham*)[1] and take the distresses into its fee at Whitley
(*Witele*)*b* and impound them there. Sealing. Witnesses [omitted]
                                                    [*c.* 1238 × 1250]

A f87r; B f55v; C f24r; C f150r

a Lungespeye *B,Cf24r*, Longesp' *Cf150r*   *b* Whitele *Cf150r*

Probably contemporary with no. 810. William Longespee had given his lands in
Sheepbridge, Diddenham, Farley [Hill] and Hinton with their tenants to Henry de
Mara (*Bracton's Note Book*, iii. 286–7).

   1. Later Diddenham Farm, now in Shinfield parish (*Berks. Place-Names*, i. 104), but
originally in Sheepbridge in Swallowfield.

812 Acknowledgment by Richard *del Heck'* of his obligation to pay
to Reading Abbey, by assignment of Sir William Longespee (*Lun-
gesp(eie)*),*a* the annual rent of 1 mark at Hinton (*Hentone*) on the
morrow of St Martin, which he used to pay the same William, saving
to the latter and his heirs all other services from the said tenement. If
he or his heirs default in payment, the abbey may distrain them at
Hinton and take the distresses into its fee at Whitley (*Witele*)*b* and
impound them there. Sealing. Witnesses [omitted] [*c.* 1238 × 1250]

A f87r; C f150r; (noted) B f55v; C f24r

a Longesp' *Cf150r*   *b* Whytele *Cf150r*

Probably contemporary with no. 810.

813 Acknowledgement by Thomas *le Blund*[a] of his obligation to
pay to Reading Abbey, by assignment of Sir William Longespee

(*Lungesp(eie)*),[b] the annual rent of 1 mark at Sheepbridge (*Scheperugge*)[c] on the morrow of St Martin, saving to the same William and his heirs all other services from the said tenement. If he or his heirs default in payment, the abbey may distrain them at Sheepbridge[d] and take the distresses into its fee at Whitley (*Witele*) and impound them there. Sealing   [*c.* 1238 × 1250]

A f87r; C f150r; (noted) B f55v; C f24r

Hiis testibus:[e] [dominis Ph(ilipp)o Basset, Henrico de Mara, et aliis].

[a] Blond *C f150r*   [b] Longespeie *C f150r*
[c] Scheperug' *C f150r*   [d] Scheperig' *C f150r*
[e] *A ends, the remainder being supplied from C f150r*

Probably contemporary with no. 810. Thomas Blund was a tenant of William Longespee, who retained his service when he gave Sheepbridge and other lands to Henry de Mara (*Bracton's Note Book*, iii. 286).

MIDGHAM

814 *Gift in free alms by Ghilo de Pinkeny to Reading Abbey of the cotland which Peter son of Jordan held of him in Midgham*
                                      [? late 12th × early 13th cent.]

A f84r; A f106v; B f69r; C ff34v–35r

Sciant presentes et futuri quod ego Gilo[a] de Pinkeni, de consensu[b] et voluntate domini Roberti heredis mei, pro salute anime mee et omnium antecessorum et successorum meorum, dedi et concessi et hac presenti carta mea confirmavi deo et beate Marie de Radinges et monachis ibidem deo servientibus in puram liberam et perpetuam elemosinam illam cotcetlam[c] terre quam Petrus filius Iurdani[d] tenuit de me in Micheam[e] que iacet iuxta molendinum de blado et Rademore. Ita tamen quod predictus Petrus et heredes sui predictam terram tenebunt de abbate Radingie et eiusdem loci conventu, reddendo inde annuatim ecclesie Rading(ie) dimidiam marcam argenti pro omni servitio ad duos terminos, scilicet ad Annuntiationem beate Marie quadraginta denarios et ad festum sancti Michaelis .xl. denarios, salvo tamen servitio domini regis de quo respondebunt predictus Petrus et heredes sui. Ut autem hec mea donatio rata et inconcussa permaneat, [f][eam tam][f] sigillo meo quam sigillo filii mei duxi roborandam.[g] Hiis testibus.

[a] Giloi *B,C*   [b] concessu *A f106v*
[c] cotcehtlam *A f106v*, cotsethlam *B,C*   [d] Iordani *A f106v*

ᵉ Migeham B, Migham C   *ᶠ⁻ᶠ Om. in A f 84r, supplied from all other texts*
ᵍ B ends with T', *C ends*

This deed is difficult to date, since the donor was not one of the holders of the Pinkeny barony (*Complete Peerage*, x. 521–4; Sanders, *English Baronies*, 94), of which Midgham formed a part (*VCH Berks.*, iii. 320). He seems to have been a junior member of the family with a holding in the place but not lord of the manor (*ibid.*, 320 n. 52). He occurs as a witness to charters of 1154 × 73, 1183 × 4 and 1197 × 8 (see nos. 1076, 798; *Ancient Charters*, 106). The deed is not in the original section of A, perhaps indicating a date after 1193, but the text on A f 106v appears among early 13th-century deeds written in one hand immediately before entries in another hand dating 1220 and before 1220 (nos. 542, 892).

NEWBURY

815 *Notification and confirmation by the abbot of Waverley and the priors of Waverley and [Monk] Sherborne, judges-delegate of Pope Honorius III, of the settlement before them of the action between Reading Abbey, on one side, and the abbot and convent of Préaux [Eure, Normandy] and Gervase clerk of Newbury, on the other, concerning the church of Newbury, which Reading Abbey claimed was a chapel within the parish of Thatcham. The church of Thatcham shall continue to receive 2s annually from the church of Newbury, as before, and the abbot and convent of Préaux shall pay 4s 8d annually to the abbot and convent of Reading, who shall indemnify them in respect of themselves and the clerks holding the other portions of Thatcham church* [1216 × 24]

B f 193r; C f 112v
Pd. Barfield, *Thatcham*, ii. 56

Universis Christi fidelibus ad quos presens scriptum pervenerit abbas de Waverleg'ᵃ et eiusdem loci et de Syreburn' priores, salutem. Noveritis nos mandatum domini pape in hec verba suscepisse.

Honorius episcopus servus servorum dei dilectis filiis abbati et priori de Waverl(eg'),ᵃ Cisterciensis ordinis, et priori de Syreburn', Winton(iensis) diocesis, salutem et apostolicam benedictionem. Dilecti filii abbas et conventus de Rading(ia) nobis conquerendo monstrarunt quod abbas et conventus de Pratellis et G(ervasius)ᵇ clericus Sar(esburiensis) diocesis super capella Neubir(ie) et rebus aliis iniuriantur eisdem. Ideoque discretioni vestre per apostolica scripta mandamus quatinus partibus convocatis audiatis causam et appellatione remota fine debito terminetis, facientes quod decreveritis per censuram ecclesiasticam firmiter observari. Testes autem qui fuerint, et cetera.

Huius igitur auctoritate mandati, partibus in presentia nostra in maiori ecclesia de Winton(ia) per procuratores idoneos constitutis tam ad litigandum quam ad componendum destinatos, necnon et

G(ervasio)^b clerico de Neubir(ia) personaliter comparente, lis tandem inter eos mota super ecclesia de Neubir(ia), quam iidem monachi de Rading(ia) asserebant infra limites parrochie de Tacham^c sitam esse et ob hoc ad ecclesiam de Tacham^c pertinere, ac per hoc tam ipsos abbatem et conventum de Pratellis necnon et G(ervasium)^b clericum amovendos, in hunc modum quievit. Videlicet quod ecclesia de Tacham^c percipiet singulis annis .ii. solidos de ecclesia de Neubir(ia) sicut antea percipere consuevit. Preterea abbas et conventus de Pratellis singulis annis de bonis suis pro bono pacis .iiii. solidos et .viii. denarios persolvent infra oct(avas) sancti Michaelis abbati et conventui de Rading(ia). Predicti etiam abbas et conventus ^dde Rading(ia)^d [ipsos]^e tam de se quam adversus clericos residuas portiones possidentes si quas possederint^f in ecclesia de Tacham^c conservabunt indempnes sub forma predicta. Et ut hec perpetua compositio stabilis et firma permaneat, de consensu ac instantia partium huic scripto sigilla nostra apposuimus et eam quantum ad nos pertinet confirmavimus.

^a Waverlegh' C   ^b For expansion, see no. 816
^c Tacheham C   ^d ^d Om. in C
^e Not in either text, but supplied to make the sense (cf. no. 816)
^f possiderint C

During the pontificate of Honorius III and while Geoffrey was archdeacon of Berkshire (see no. 816). For a discussion of this case, see B.R. Kemp, 'The mother church of Thatcham', Berks. Arch. Journ., lxiii (1967–8), 17–18, and cf. above, nos. 784–5.

816 *Notification by Abbot Simon and the convent of Reading of the same settlement*   [1216 × 24]

B f 197r–v; C f 116r–v; D f 21r–v; Evreux, Archives départementales de l'Eure, H 711 (Préaux cartulary) ff 55r–56r (not fully collated)
Pd. Barfield, *Thatcham*, 57

Omnibus sancte matris ecclesie filiis presens scriptum inspecturis Symon dei gratia abbas Rading(ensis) et euisdem loci conventus, salutem. Noverit universitas vestra controversiam motam inter nos ex una parte et abbatem et conventum de Pratellis et G(ervasium)^a de Newebir(ia)^b clericum ex altera super ecclesia de Newebir(ia),^b abbati et priori de Waverleg'^c et de Syreburn' priori iudicibus a domino papa delegatis commissam, auctoritate eorundem iudicum de consensu partium et consilio iurisperitorum sub hac forma pacis quievisse. Videlicet quod, cum abbas et conventus de Pratellis in iudicium tracti per litteras domini pape per procuratores tam ad litigandum quam ad componendum constitutos in maiori ecclesia de Winton(ia) in iudicio coram predictis iudicibus comparuissent et G(ervasius)^a pro se [f 197v] personaliter compareret, et idem^d convenirentur auctoritate litterarum domini pape super ecclesia de Newbir(ia),^b quam sitam esse dicebamus infra limites parrochie de Tacheham et ob hoc ad ecclesiam de Tacham' pertinere, unde tam ipsos abbatem et conventum de Pratellis quam G(ervasium)[a] clericum ab ecclesia de Neubir(ia) intendebamus amovere, tandem post multas allegationes et exceptiones hinc inde propositas communi assensu coram iudicibus nostris et iurisperitis eis assidentibus amicabiliter provisum est, iuramento ab utraque parte interposito ad formam pacis fideliter observandam, quod ecclesia de Tacham' percipiet singulis annis duos solidos de ecclesia de Neubir(ia) sicut antea percipere consuevit. Abbas preterea et conventus de Pratellis singulis annis de bonis suis pro bono pacis persolvent .iiii. solidos et octo denarios abbati et conventui de Rading(ia) infra oct(abas)[f] sancti Michaelis sine aliqua difficultate vel cavillatione que possit provenire de solucione vel termino solucionis predictorum denariorum sub obligatione eiusdem iuramenti. Nos autem ipsos tam de nobis quam adversus clericos residuas portiones possidentes si quas possederint[g] in ecclesia de Tacham' conservabimus indempnes sub forma predicta. Et ut hec compositio perpetua et stabilis permaneat in posterum, eam sigillorum nostrorum appositione roboramus. Hiis testibus:[h] [Gaufr(edo) archidiacono Berkesir', magistro Roberto de Bingh(am), Roberto de Tacheham clerico, Thoma[i] de Henleg', Johanne filio Hugonis, et multis aliis].

[a] *Name given in full in D and in Préaux cart.*
[b] Neubir' *(or minor variant) C,D, Préaux cart.*
[c] Waverlegh' *C*   [d] iidem *D*
[e] Tacheh' *or* Tacheham *D and Préaux cart.*
[f] octabas *D and Préaux cart.*   [g] possiderint *C*
[h] *B,C,D end, the remainder being supplied from Préaux cart.*
[i] Thomas *in Ms*

During the pontificate of Honorius III (see no. 815) and before Geoffrey ceased to be archdeacon of Berkshire, i.e. before 28 June 1224, when William of Merton was archdeacon (*Sarum Charters and Documents*, 166). The rubrics of B and C describe this act as a chirograph.

PADWORTH

817 *Gift in free alms by Sewale English [or the Englishman] to Reading Abbey of 2s [? rent] from the land of Padworth* [*c.* 1150 × 75]

A f40r; B f71r; C f36r

Notum sit omnibus tam presentis quam futuri temporis Christi fidelibus quod ego Sewale Anglicus do et concedo ecclesie sancte Marie de Rading(ia) in perpetuam elemosinam duos solidos de terra de

Pedewrde.[a] Et ut hec donatio rata sit,[b] appositione sigilli mei confirmo, pro anima mea et uxoris mee et omnium predecessorum et successorum meorum.[c] His testibus: Willelmo Stalon, Ernaldo Springard, Georgio presbitero de Weregrava, Simone dapifero, Walt(erio) coc(o).

[a] Pedewrþe B, Padewrþe C   [b] Insert et stabilis C
[c] B ends with T', C ends

Dating uncertain. Simon the steward witnessed abbatial deeds in Reading and Tilehurst in 1165 × 73 (nos. 825–7, 1136); Walter the cook witnessed abbatial deeds in East Hendred, Reading, Tilehurst and Whitley in the years 1158 × 86 (Hendred House, Muniments, MTD/1/1b; below, nos. 825, 827, 831, 1138, 1208). The deed was entered in the original section of A and its unsophisticated diplomatic would suggest a fairly early date, although the donor had his own seal. Precisely what he gave is not clear, for while the rubric of A refers to two *solidati terre*, those of B and C have two *solid' redd'*. The gift cannot be traced later, probably because it was administered as part of the abbey's adjacent manor of Beenham, as seems clear from the rubrics of B and C, which read: ... *de terra de Pedewrþe [Padewrþe C] apud Bienham*. The donor, who seems otherwise unrecorded, may have been a successor to one of the two important sub-tenants of Padworth in 1086 (*VCH Berks.*, i. 367; see also *ibid.*, iii. 413).

PANGBOURNE

818   Licence by King Edward III to John son of William of Blewbury (*Blebury*) to alienate in mortmain to Reading Abbey one messuage, 70 acres and 1 rood of land, 1½ acres of wood and 11s 3d rent in Pangbourne (*Pangeburne*), which are not held of the king in chief and which are worth annually 23s 6¾d as appears by the inquest held by Robert *Selyman*, escheator in Hants., Wilts., Oxon., Berks., Beds. and Bucks.; to be held by the abbey in perpetuity at the value of 37s 11d in part satisfaction of the £10 worth of land and rent which the abbey has the king's licence to acquire. Licence also to the abbot and convent to receive and hold the same   1 Feb. 1333

C f 224r
Pd. (cal.) *Cal. Pat. R. 1330–34*, 399 (from Patent Roll)

Teste me ipso apud Eborac(um) primo die Februarii, anno regni nostri septimo.

The mortmain licence for £10 worth of land and rent is *Cal. Pat. R. 1327–30*, 61.

PURLEY

819   *Gift in free alms by Isabel de Sifrewast to Reading Abbey, for the souls of among others Robert de Sifrewast her father, Emma her mother, and her husbands buried at Reading, of half a virgate of land in Purley*
                            [1194 × early 13th cent.]

A f 81v; B f 63r; C f 30r

Sciant presentes et futuri quod ego Ysabella de Siffrawast[a] dedi et[b] concessi et[c] presenti carta mea confirmavi deo et sancte Marie de Rading(ia) et monachis ibidem deo servientibus, pro salute anime mee et pro anima[d] Roberti de Siffrawast[a] patris mei et Emme matris mee et pro animabus maritorum meorum qui apud Rading(iam) sepeliuntur, et pro animabus omnium antecessorum meorum[e] et successorum meorum, dimidiam virgatam terre in Purleya quam tenet in vilenagio Osbertus[f] filius Godwini[g] piscatoris, cum omnibus pertinentiis suis, in perpetuam et puram elemosinam liberam et quietam ab omni consuetudine et exactione et demanda, et immunem ab omni servitio seculari; et ut abbas et conventus Rading(enses) transmutent predictum Osbertum[f] et progeniem suam ad voluntatem et dispositionem ipsorum [h]sive ad opus vilenagii sive ad censum annuum.[h] Ego autem et heredes mei respondebimus pro servitio forinseco, siquid forte ab eis aliquando exactum fuerit. Quod ut ratum in perpetuum permaneat, sigilli mei appositione confirmavi.[i] Hiis testibus:[j] [Iohanne capellano, Thoma Sorel, et multis aliis].

[a] Syfrewast *B*, Syffrewast *C*   [b] *Om. in C*
[c] *Insert* hac *B,C*   [d] *A has* anime
[e] *Om. in B,C*   [f] Oseb' *C*
[g] Godwin *C*
[h-h] sive ad censum annuum sive ad opus vilenagii *B,C*
[i] *B ends with* T', *C ends*
[j] *A ends, the remainder being supplied from following* inspeximus

This charter was clearly given in Isabel's widowhood and can therefore be dated not earlier than 1194, since she had been married to Michael de Baseville (see no. 498), with whom as 'Isabel his wife' she brought an action in 1194 against Richard de Sifrewast in Dorset concerning the dower given her by her (former) husband, Simon son of Robert (*Rot. Cur. Reg.*, i. 81–2); her husbands buried at Reading were presumably therefore Simon son of Robert and Michael de Baseville. The charter was inspected and confirmed by William de Sifrewast not earlier than 1217 (see no. 820). The virgate in question was in the Sifrewast manor of Purley Parva (*VCH Berks.*, iii. 420), but the relationship of Isabel's father, Robert, to the known holders of the manor is unclear. This charter is discussed and partially translated by D.M. Stenton, *English Society in the Early Middle Ages*, 4th edn. (1965), 145–6.

820 *Inspeximus and confirmation by William de Sifrewast of the same gift of land made by his aunt, Isabel, which, since it was given to her as a marriage portion, might otherwise be thought to revert to the donors and their heirs*

[1217 × 44; ? 1217 × c. 1230]

A ff81v–82r; B f63r; C f30r

Omnibus presentem cartam inspecturis vel audituris Willelmus de Siffrawast,[a] salutem in domino. Noverit universitas vestra me inspexisse cartam Ysabel amite mee in hec verba.

[b]Sciant presentes et futuri ...[etc., as in no. *819*, reading in line *13* of

that text sive ad censum annuum sive ad opus vilenagii]. Hiis testibus: Johanne capellano, Thoma Sorel, et multis aliis.[b]

[*f82r*][c] Licet itaque videretur quod dicta terra ad ipsos donatores qui eandem terram eidem Ysabel donaverunt in maritagium et ad eorum heredes merito reverti deberet, ego tamen pro me et pro heredibus meis et pro anima eiusdem Ysabel et omnium antecessorum et successorum meorum, dictam donationem et concessionem predicte Ysabel ratam habens totam et integram predictam terram cum pertinentiis abbati et monachis Rading' presenti carta mea et sigilli mei appositione confirmavi. Et ego Willelmus et heredes mei dictam terram cum pertinentiis secundum tenorem carte predicte Ysabel de omni servitio acquietabimus et eam dictis abbati et monachis contra omnes gentes warantizabimus.[d] Hiis testibus.

[a] Syfrewast *B*, Syffrewast *C*
[b-b] Sciant presentes quod ego Isabella de Syfr', et cetera ut supra *B,C*
[c] *The printed text resumes in line 9 of f 82r*
[d] *B ends with* T', *C ends*

William de Sifrewast here clearly acts as lord of the manor and is therefore to be identified with the William who succeeded his father Halnoth in 1217 and died in 1244 (*VCH Berks.*, iii. 420; above, nos. 660–1 notes). This inspeximus was entered in A in a hand which copied other deeds dating down to *c.* 1230. William's reference to Isabel as his aunt makes it likely that her father, Robert, was also the father of his own father, Halnoth, although the *VCH* (loc. cit.) suggests that Halnoth may have been the son of William de Sifrewast, who is presumed to have held the manor in the 1160s (*Red Bk. Exch.*, i. 308; *PR 14 Henry II*, 203). The references to Isabel in this charter imply that she was already dead. The sentence immediately following the text of her deed contains an unusual reference to a woman's limited rights in her marriage portion.

READING

In this section nos. 821–1041 appear mainly in the order in which they occur in C, ff 168r–218v, 224v and 228r–230v, except that the abbatial deeds of the 12th and early 13th centuries, which are entered on ff 193v–198r, are given first in approximate chronological order. No. 1042 is concerned with the Reading market regulations and is followed by deeds relating to *Burnemede*, Coley, 'Herewardsley' and Caversham (nos. 1043–64).

821 *Lease for life by Abbot Anscher of Reading to Tomus of a house in Reading, with the custom called* heusir', *and two corner plots, one of meadow and one of marsh*   [1130 × 35]

C f 197v

Sciant presentes et futuri quod ego Anscherius abbas Radyng(ensis), consilio et consensu*a* fratrum nostrorum, concessi huic Tomo domum quandam in burgo Radyng(ie) in vita sua tenendam pro servitio suo ita quietam et liberam ne alicui inde respondeat nisi decano, quod si contigerit ipsum Tomum aliquando ab servitio nostro cessare de domo illa predicta reddet decano singulis annis .xviii. d'. Concessimus ei quamdam consuetudinem in eadem domo habere que dicitur heusir', duos quoque angulos contiguos domui sue apud villam, unum de prato et alterum de mora, *b*illi concessimus.*b* Isti vero anguli et domus*c* predicta post obitum ipsius Tomi in dominium nostrum redibunt. Huius rei testes sunt Hugo testab(u)l(arius), Rad(ulfu)s prepositus, Gaufr(edus) dapifer,*d* Rad(ulfu)s eius socius, Simon famulus.

a concensu *in Ms*
c *Ms repeats* et domus
b b *Interlined*
d *Ms has* dapif'o

The dating limits are those of Anscher's abbacy. The custom called *heusir'*, which occurs in various spellings in a number of 12th-century deeds in Reading and its neighbourhood, is nowhere defined, but the same word, with the meaning of an ancient rent, occurs also on manors of Ramsey Abbey (see Slade, 'Whitley Deeds', 239–40; N. Neilson, 'Customary Rents' in *Oxford Studies in Social and Legal History*, ii (Oxford 1910), 84–5).

822 *Grant by Abbot Anscher of Reading to Ralph Gray of the custom called* heuescyri *in his house in front of the abbey gate and in the other houses which were in his possession when Anscher became abbot* [1130 × 35]

C f 197v

Sciant presentes et futuri quod ego Anscherius abbas Radyng(ensis), consilio fratrum nostrorum, concedo Rad(ulf)o Graio liberam et quietam consuetudinem que vocatur heuescyri que fiet in domo sua in qua ipse habitat et in aliis domibus de quibus inveni eum seisitum quando in abbatiam receptus sum. Hec est videlicet illa [in]*a* qua ipse manet ante portam nostram, altera quam tenet Iohannes homo eius iuxta domum predictam, et sopa una et terra illa quam ultra pontem [habet]*a* pro scambio terre illius quam prius habuerat in vico ante abbatiam et terra*b* quam Geroldus tenet de eo. Ipsum quoque Rad-(ulfu)m retineo in manu nostra ut nulli alii respondeat pro forisfactura quam*c* ipse faciet nisi michi vel cui iussero fratri.

a *Supplied*
c *Ms has* qua
b *Ms has* terram

For the date and the custom called *heuescyri*, see no. 821 n.

823 *Gift by Abbot Roger of Reading to Warin son of Ralph of Wycombe of the land in Reading which belonged to Osbern Driebried, which has come into the abbot's hands through forfeiture of Osbern's heirs*   [1158 × 65]

C ff 196v–197r

Sciant presentes et futuri sancte ecclesie filii quod ego Rog(erius) abbas Radyng(ensis) concessi et dedi, assensu et consilio capituli nostri, Warino filio Rad(ulf)i de Wycumba et heredibus suis illam terram in burgo Radyng(ie) que fuit Osberni Driebried ad tenendam bene et honorifice in feodo et in hereditate pro .xvi. denariis annuatim reddendis ad festum sancti Michaelis. Sciendum est autem quod ipsa terra per magnum forisfactum heredum Osberni eis adiudicata*a* fuit et ablata et in manus nostras venit per iudicium sicut proprium dominium nostrum ad faciendum inde beneplacitum nostrum. Nos autem eandem terram concessimus et dedimus Warino et heredibus suis perpetuo tenendam ut supradictum est, partim pro amore et fideli servitio, partim propter heredes eius, qui sunt de progenie Osberni, partim propter pecuniam quam ab eo pro ista concessione accepimus, scilicet .ii. marcas argenti. Hiis testibus: Hamone de Cotesbroc, Godwyno de Thaccham, [*f 197r*] Petro clerico, Herewardo de Medenhacche, Petro et Willelmo fratre eius, Willelmo Cailli, Roberto Olie(n)t',*b* Edmundo de Tyghelhurst', Edmundo et Edwardo fratre eius, Gilberto presbitero de Tyghelhurst', Waltero filio Lyulfi de Stokes.

  a Sic   *b Reading uncertain*

The dating limits are those of Roger's abbacy. The mixture of first person singular and plural is notable.

824 *Lease by Abbot Roger and the convent of Reading to Geoffrey the clerk and his heirs of the land in Reading by the River Kennet which Richard son of Raulin held in the time of war and was afterwards adjudged to the same Richard's heirs in the court of St Mary and that of the abbot and convent; to be held with the liberties and customs which a burgess has in the borough of Reading. Geoffrey has remitted all actions against the abbey concerning the lands and chattels of his ancestors and has quitclaimed the land which he formerly held*
[1158 × 65]

Cf 197r

Rogerus abbas et conventus servorum sancte Marie Radyng' omnibus hominibus et fidelibus suis, salutem perpetuam. Sciatis nos concessisse et presenti carta confirmasse Gaufr(ed)o clerico tenendam de nobis

iure hereditario pro .xii. d' annuatim reddendis ecclesie nostre ad
festum sancti Michaelis illam terram in villa Radyng(ie) iuxta aquam
Canete, quam terram Ricardus filius Raulini tenuit tempore guerre
et que postea adiudicata fuit heredibus eiusdem Ricardi in curia
sancte Marie et nostra. Et volumus ut predictus Gaufr(edu)s et heredes
sui post eum illam terram habeant et teneant libere, honorifice, cum
illis libertatibus et iustis consuetudinibus quas habet in burgo nostro
Radyng(ie) unus illorum burgensium nostrorum qui melius et liberius
et iustius tenent in quantum lex et dignitas burgagii ville nostre iuste
potest et debet exigere. Ipse vero Gaufr(edu)s remisit ex toto omnes
querelas quas adversus domum nostram habeat, sive de terris sive de
domibus sive de catallis antecessorum suorum, et aliam quandam
terram quam prius tenebat quietam nobis clamavit *in perpetuum.*
Actum est hoc hiis testibus: Roberto dapifero, Hamone de Sotesbrok',
Warino de Ponte, Radulpho Bilhog, Rain(aldo) Agno.

a-a *Ms has* imperpetuum

The dating limits are those of Roger's abbacy.

825 *Gift by Abbot William [I] of Reading to Walter the marshal of a*
messuage in the borough of Reading   [1165 × 73]
   Cf 196v

Sciant presentes et futuri quod ego Willelmus abbas ecclesie*a* Rad-
yng(ensis), voluntate et consilio conventus, dedi Waltero marescallo et
heredibus sius in burgo de Radyng(ia) mansuram illam que est inter
mansuram Gilberti de Tacham et inter mansuram Wlfrici filii Crupelli pro .xii. d' annuatim ecclesie Radyng(ensi) persolvendis*b* ad
festum sancti Michaelis.*c* Hiis testibus: Simone dapifero, Rad(ulf)o de
Radyng(ia), Reginaldo pincerna, Ph(ilipp)o, Roberto camberlano,
Waltero coco, Rad(ulfo) canonico, Petro clerico, Gaufr(ed)o preposito, Alfwino fratre Walteri coci.

a *Ms has* et conventus, *but this will not fit with* dedi; *cf. nos. 826–7*
b,c *These words have over them respectively the letters* a *and* b, *perhaps indicating that* persolvendis *should be moved to the end of the sentence*

The dating limits are those of William I's abbacy.

826 *Grant by Abbot William [I] of Reading to Osbert of Rotherwick and*
his heirs of the liberty called heusira *in the borough of Reading*

                                                      [1165 × 73]

Cf196v

Sciant presentes et futuri quod ego Willelmus abbas ecclesie Rad-
yng(ensis), voluntate et consilio conventus, dedi [et]*a* concessi Osberto
de Rerdewica et heredibus eius in burgo Radyng(ie) illam libertatem
que dicitur heusira.*b* Volumusque ut eam bene quiete et libere habeat
sicut ceteri liberi homines nostri qui eandem libertatem melius et
liberius et quietius habent. Hiis testibus: Roberto de Waltham,
Rad(ulf)o de Bulehuda, Willelmo de Waltham, Simone dapifero,
Rad(ulf)o dapifero, Petro clerico, Roberto camberlano, Roberto de
Walleng(efordia), Warino preposito, Galfr(ed)o preposito.

a Supplied   *bMs apparently has* hensira

The dating limits are those of William I's abbacy. For the liberty called *heusira*, see
no. 821 n.

827   *Lease by Abbot William [I] of Reading to Geoffrey the clerk and his
heirs of three messuages in Reading, viz., the one in which he lives and two
which he bought from the chamberlain, Edward*   [1165 × 73]

Cf197r

Sciant presentes et futuri quod ego Willelmus abbas ecclesie Rad-
yng(ensis), voluntate et consilio conventus, concessi Gaufredo clerico
et heredibus suis in burgo de Radyng(ia) tres mansuras tenendas ea
libertate qua qui melius et liberius et quietius tenet in burgo; illam
videlicet iuxta pontem in qua habitat pro qua .xii. d' annuatim solvet
et duas alias quas emit a camerario Edwardo, unam videlicet in
veteri vico quam camerarius emit de Iohanne clerico, pro qua solvet
annuatim duos solidos, et aliam in novo vico quam camerarius emit
de Roberto filio Hugonis de Bonavilla, pro qua reddet annuatim .xx.
d'. Hec quoque donatio rata erit et stabilis quamdiu predictum censum bene reddiderit. *a*[Hiis testibus]:*a* magistro Gilberto, Rannulpho
de Bulehuda, Simone dapifero, Rad(ulfo) dapifero, Roberto camberlano, Reginaldo Lamb, Warino preposito, Waltero de Oxeneford,
Gilberto super pontem, Willelmo Bevyn, Daniele clerico, Rad(ulf)o
Cepernail,*b* Walt(ero) coquo, Waltero filio Aldewini Wille.

a-a Supplied   *b Sic*

The dating limits are those of William I's abbacy.

828   *Lease by Abbot William [I] of Reading to Rannulf son of Tomus and
his heirs of the tenement which his father held*   [1165 × 73]

Cf 197r–v

Sciant presentes et futuri quod ego Willelmus abbas Radyng(ensis), consilio*a* et voluntate conventus, concessi Ranulfo filio Tomi et heredibus eius pro .vi. s' annuatim ecclesie Radyng(ensi) persolvendis tenementum quod Tomus pater eius tenuit pro sex [solidis].*b* Volo itaque ut libere et quiete teneat pro sex solidis et easdem libertates et consuetudines quas pater [*f 197v*] suus habuit pro predicta censa habeat iste pro sua. Hec quoque donatio rata erit et stabilis quamdiu predictam*c* censam bene reddiderit et fidelis nobis extiterit. Hiis testibus.

a Ms has concilio   *b Supplied*
c Ms has predictarum

The dating limits are those of William I's abbacy. The Tomus named here may be the same as the Tomus who received a lease from Abbot Anscher in 1130 × 35 (see no. 821).

829 *Grant by Abbot Joseph and the convent of Reading to master William of Lincoln of the perpetual vicarage of St Mary's in Reading, as master Gilbert held it for 60s annually* [1173 × 86]

Cf 193v

Sciant presentes et futuri quod [ego]*a* I(oseph) abbas Radyng(ensis) et totus eiusdem loci conventus concessimus et presenti carta confirmavimus magistro Willelmo de Lincoln(ia) perpetuam vicariam sancte Marie de Radyng(ia) libere et quiete de nobis tenendam sicut magister Gilbertus eam tenuit pro .lx. solidis annuatim solvendis quatuor terminis, ad Pascha .xv., ad festum sancti Iohannis .xv., ad festum sancti Michaelis .xv., ad Natale domini .xv. Hec autem conventio rata erit et stabilis quamdiu prefatus magister Willelmus fidelis nobis extiterit et predictam pensionem nobis plenarie solverit. Hiis testibus.

a Supplied

The dating limits are those of Joseph's abbacy.

830 *Lease by Abbot Joseph and the convent of Reading to Adam the clerk of* Essend(ene)[1] *and his heirs of a messuage in Reading* [1173 × 86]

Cf 195v

Sciant presentes et futuri quod ego Ioseph abbas Radyng(ensis) eiusdemque loci conventus concessimus Ade clerico de Essend(ene) et heredibus suis tenere de nobis mesuagium quoddam in villa Radyng(ie) per duos solidos annuatim nobis infra oct(avas) sancti Michaelis reddendos. Tenebunt autem et heredes eius hoc*a* mesuagium ita libere et quiete per predictos duos solidos sicut melius et quietius et liberius aliquis tenet in villa Radyng(ie). Hec carta rata erit et stabilis quamdiu prefatus Adam et heredes sui nobis fideles extiterint et predictam pensionem bene et plene reddiderint. Testibus: Herveo presbitero, Petro clerico, Gaufr(ed)o preposito, Willelmo Bevyn, Willelmo dispensatore, Petro pincerna, Henrico filio Walteri, Iohanne nepote Ade, et cetera.

a *Ms has here* hom *deleted*

The dating limits are those of Joseph's abbacy.

1. Possibly either Essendon (Herts.) or Easington (Oxon.).

831   *Lease by Abbot Joseph of Reading to William son of Robert of Reading and his heirs of the land near the marshes which Godwin, monk of Reading, gave to the abbey when he became a monk*   [1173 × 86]

C f 195v

Sciant presentes et futuri quod ego Ioseph abbas Rad(ingensis), consilio et consensu totius conventus, concessi Willelmo filio Roberti de Radyng(ia) et heredibus suis terram que est iuxta paludes, quam Godwinus frater noster secum dedit ecclesie nostre, pro tribus solidis annuatim solvendis, dimidia parte in festo sancti Michaelis persolvenda et dimidia in Pascha. Hec conventio rata erit et stabilis quamdiu ipse vel heredes sui nobis fideles extiterint et predictum censum bene reddiderint. Hiis testibus: Fulcredo vinitore, Rad(ulfo) dapifero, Osberto de Maidenhacche, Rad(ulf)o de Stanford, magistro W., Warino Wafree, Rogero pictore, Waltero coco, Hugone nepote Lamberti camerarii,*a* Huberto nepote Hugonis de Sulham, Gilberto latore, Warino preposito, Ham(one) scriptore, et cetera.

a *Ms repeats* camerarii

The dating limits are those of Joseph's abbacy.

832   *Gift by Abbot Joseph of Reading to Durand of the king's chapel, at the request of Walter Marshal, of the messuage which belonged to the latter in Reading*   [1173 × 86]

C f 195v

Sciant presentes et futuri quod ego I(oseph) abbas Rad(ingensis), voluntate et consensu totius conventus et prece Walt(eri) Marescalli, dedi Durando de capella regis et heredibus suis in burgo de Rad(ingia) mansuram illam que fuit Walteri Marescalli, que est inter mansuram Gilberti de Techam et mansuram Wlfrici Crupelli, pro .xii. d' annuatim ecclesie Radyng(ensi) ad festum sancti Michaelis persolvendis. Hec conventio rata erit et stabilis quamdiu predictus Durandus et heredes sui nobis fideles extiterint et predictum censum nobis fideliter reddiderint. Hiis testibus: Gaufr(ed)o clerico de Bixe, Rad(ulf)o seniscallo, Adam de Benham, Willelmo Bevin, Galfr(ed)o clerico de Rad(ingia), Remundo filio Rogeri, Waltero de Oxeneford(ia), Waltero Furmage, W(illelmo)*ᵃ* Furmage, Pagano Fachel, Rad(ulfo) Purcel, Willelmo Boistard'.

ᵃ For expansion, see witnesses to no. 833

The dating limits are those of Joseph's abbacy. For Abbot William I's gift of this messuage to Walter the marshal, see no. 825.

833 *Lease by Abbot Joseph of Reading to Durand of the chapel and his heirs of a messuage beyond the new bridge of Reading* [1173 × 86]

Cf196r

Sciant presentes et futuri quod ego Ioseph abbas Radyng(ensis), consilio et consensu totius conventus, concessi et presenti carta confirmavi Duranno de capella et heredibus eius mesuagium unum ultra novum pontem Radyng(ie) inter viam molendini et stagnum eiusdem molendini, libere et quiete tenendum pro .x. denariis annuatim solvendis ad festum sancti Michaelis pro omni servitio. Hec autem concessio rata erit et stabilis quamdiu predictus Durannus et heredes ipsius *ᵃ*[nobis fideles extiterint]*ᵃ* et predictum censum fideliter et plenarie nobis reddiderint. Hiis testibus: Gaufredo de Bixe, Osberto de Maidenhacche, Rad(ulf)o de Chauresham, Alexandro de Blebury, Waltero de Essindine, Huberto de Clere, Rad(ulfo) Purcel, et Badwi(no)*ᵇ* armigero eius, Waltero de Constanc', Nicholao capellano, Ricardo Boistard, Herberto Furmache, Waltero Furmache, Willelmo fratre eius, Willelmo Boistard, Waltero de Oxeneford, Willelmo Bevin', Rad(ulf)o de Oxeneford, Nicholao filio eius, Hamone de Radyng(ia).

ᵃ⁻ᵃ Om. in Ms, supplied from other deeds of Abbot Joseph to complete the sense
ᵇ Reading uncertain

The dating limits are those of Joseph's abbacy.

834 *Lease by Abbot Joseph of Reading to Ralph Purcel and his heirs of all the land on the eastern side of the road between the new ditch and the [River] Kennet* [1173 × 86]

Cf196r

Sciant presentes et futuri quod ego I(oseph) abbas Radyng(ensis), consensu conventus, concessi Rad(ulfo) Purcel et heredibus sius totam terram ex orientali parte vie que est inter novum fossatum et Kanetam, pro .ii. solidis et .iiii. denariis annuatim solvendis ecclesie nostre ad festum sancti Michaelis, cum omnibus libertatibus et liberis consuetudinibus liberioris hominis de tenemento nostro Radyng(ie). Hoc autem erit ratum et stabile quamdiu nobis ipse vel heredes sui fideles extiterint et predictum censum fideliter reddiderint. Hiis testibus: Edwardo priore, Gaufr(ed)o precentore, Roberto P(ar)tes,[1] Gaufr(ed)o de Bixe, Rad(ulfo) dapifero, et Remundo filio eius, Reinaldo de Suleham, Ricardo de Accle, Huberto de Clere, Gaufrido pincerna.

The dating limits are those of Joseph's abbacy.

1. A monk of Reading and a writer of poems, some of which are contained in BL Egerton 2951 (see *British Museum Catalogue of Additions 1916–20*, 297–302; W. H. Cornog, 'The poems of Robert Partes', *Speculum*, xii (1937), 215–50). This deed and no. 835 provide important additional corroboration that Robert Partes was a Reading monk.

835 *Lease by Abbot Joseph of Reading to Ralph Purcel and his heirs of a messuage in Reading beyond the bridge* [1173 × 86]

Cf 196r

Sciant presentes et futuri quod ego I(oseph) abbas Radyng(ensis), consensu conventus, concessi Rad(ulf)o Purcel et heredibus suis in Radyng(ia) unam mansionem ultra pontem, habentem .iiii. perticas in fronte anteriori*a* et .xxiiii. perticas et .viii. pedes in longitudine et a posteriori*b* parte .vi. perticas et dimidiam, pro .xii. d' annuatim solvendis [ecclesie]*c* nostre ad festum sancti Michaelis, cum omnibus libertatibus et liberis consuetudinibus liberioris hominis de tenemento nostro Radyng(ie). Hoc autem erit ratum et stabile quamdiu nobis ipse vel heredes sui fideles extiterint et predictum censum fideliter reddiderint. Hiis testibus: Edwardo priore, G(aufredo) precentore, R(oberto) P(ar)tes, Gaufr(edo) de Bixe, Rad(ulfo) dapifero, Remundo filio eius, Reinaldo de Sulham, Ricardo de Acle, Huberto de Clere, G(aufredo) pincerna.

a Ms has anteriore	*b* posterior' *Ms*
c Supplied

Of the same date as no. 834, since the witnesses are identical.

836 *Lease by Abbot Joseph and the convent of Reading to Adam of Earley and his heirs of a messuage in Reading beyond the two bridges*

[1173 × 86]

Cf196r

Sciant presentes et futuri quod ego Ioseph abbas Radyng(ensis) et
conventus concessimus Ade de Erlea et heredibus eius post ipsum pro
servitio suo tenere de nobis unum mesuagium in Radyng(ia) ultra
duos pontes, reddendo annuatim ecclesie nostre .xii. d' ad festum
sancti Michaelis. Hoc autem mesuagium tenebit Adam et heredes eius
post eum per istos .xii. d' ita libere et quiete, bene et in pace, sicut
aliquis in villa Radyng(ie) liberius [et]*a* quietius aliquod burgagium
tenet. Hec autem conventio rata erit et stabilis quamdiu predictus
Adam vel heredes sui nobis fideles extiterint et predictum censum
bene et plene reddiderint. Hiis testibus: Iohanne de la Rivera, Geroldo
filio eius, Azone de Sunnyngges, Ricardo privigno eius, Hugone de
Dunesdene, Ricardo filio eius, Roberto de Waltham, Willelmo filio
eius, Remundo mercatore.

a Supplied

The dating limits are those of Joseph's abbacy.

837   *Lease by Abbot Joseph and the convent of Reading to Adam of Earley
and his heirs of three messuages in Reading, viz., one between the two bridges
and two beyond the bridge*   [1173 × 86]

Cf196v

Sciant presentes et futuri quod ego I(oseph) abbas Radyng(ensis)
eiusdemque loci conventus concessimus Ade de Erleia et heredibus
eius post ipsum pro servitio suo tenere de nobis tria mesuagia in
Radyngia, unum inter duos pontes et duo ultra pontem, reddendo
annuatim ecclesie nostre quatuor solidos in festo sancti Michaelis. Hec
autem mesuagia tenebit Adam et heredes eius post eum per istos .iiii.
solidos ita libere et quiete, bene*a* et in pace, sicut aliquis in villa
Radyn(gie) melius et liberius et quietius aliqua*b* burgagia tenet. Hec
autem conventio rata erit et stabilis quamdiu predictus Adam vel
heredes sui nobis fideles extiterint et predictum censum bene et plene
reddiderint. Hiis testibus: Iohanne de Larmere, Geroldo filio eius,
Azone [de]*c* Sunningges, Ricardo privigno eius, Hugone de Dunes-
dena, Ricardo filio eius, Roberto de Waltham, Willelmo filio eius,
Remundo mercatore.

a Ms has in bene   *b Sic*
c Supplied

Of the same date as no. 836, since the witnesses are identical.

838   *Restoration by Abbot Hugh [II] and the convent of Reading to Sir Peter Blund and his heirs of a messuage which his father held in Reading before the abbey gate, to make a lodging-house there, provided that it be not to the harm or scandal of the abbey or the neighbours*   [1186 × 99]

Cf 197v

Sciant presentes et futuri quod ego Hugo abbas Radyng(ensis) eiusdemque loci conventus reddidimus domino Petro Blundo intuitu honestatis servitii ipsius unum mesuagium quod pater eius tenuit in Radyng(ia) ante portam abbatie, reddendo annuatim .xii. d' ad festum sancti Michaelis. Hanc autem terram prefatus [Petrus]*a* hospitabit quo melius et commodius poterit ad suam voluntatem et nostram vicinorumque indempnitatem, nec in mesuagio illo scienter receptabit vel illud locabit personis per quas scandalum nobis vel vicinis possit orriri vel honestatis opinio obfuscari. Libere itaque et honorifice, bene quiete et plene hoc tenementum tenebit prefatus Petrus et heredes eius post eum per prefatum servitium sicut pater eius illud melius et liberius tenuit vel tenere debuit. Hec carta rata erit et stabilis quamdiu prefatus Petrus et heredes sui nobis fideles extiterint et prefatum censum bene et plene reddiderint. Testibus: W(illelmo) comite Saresb(urie), Adam de Port, Rog(ero) de Sancto Iohanne, Walt(ero) de Oxonia, Ramundo mercatore, Reginaldo Agno, Alexandro pincerna, et multis aliis.

a Supplied

The dating limits are those of Hugh II's abbacy. The earl of Salisbury is either William fitzPatrick (d. 1196) or William Longespee (styled 1197). Peter Blund was given lands in Shinfield and Trunkwell (Berks.) by Waleran, earl of Warwick, in 1190 × 91 (BL Harley Ch. 83 A. 4; pd. *Pal. Soc. Facs.*, 2nd ser., pl. 80).

839   *Gift in free alms by Abbot H. and the convent of Reading to Benedict of York of the vicarage of the church of St Mary in Reading, for the ancient pension of 60s annually*   [1186 × 1213]

Cf 193v

Omnibus Christi fidelibus ad quos presens scriptum pervenerit H. divina miseratione Radyng(ensis) monasterii minister humilis et totus eiusdem loci conventus, salutem in domino. Noverit universitas vestra nos divini amoris intuitu concessisse*a* et dedisse Benedicto de Eboraco in puram et perpetuam elimosinam*b* vicariam ecclesie sancte Marie de Radyng(ia) cum omnibus pertinentiis suis, exceptis decimis de blado, de pisis et fabis et agnis, salva etiam nobis debita et antiqua

pensione sexaginta solidorum ad hos terminos solvendorum, scilicet
ad festum sancti Michaelis .xv. solidos, ad Natale domini .xv. solidos,
ad Pascha domini .xv. solidos, ad Nativitatem sancti Iohannis Baptiste
.xv. solidos. Et ut hec nostra concessio ac ʿ[donatio rata sit et stabilis
nec]ʿ posterius aliquando possit in dubium revocari, presentem paginam sigillorum nostrorum appositione confirmavimus. Hiis testibus:
domino Adam priore Radyng(ensi), et Symone subpriore, et magistro
Daniel, et Hugone de Mortemeri, Willelmo capellano de Colleia,
Daniele Scoto, et multis aliis.

ᵃ *Ms has* concesse   ᵇ *Sic*
ᶜ⁻ᶜ *Supplied to make sense of the sentence, which clearly has some such omission here*

The abbot is either Hugh II (1186–99) or Elias (1200–13), the latter of whom appears
in the Reading cartularies with the spelling *Helias*. Unlike Abbot Joseph's grant of the
vicarage to William of Lincoln for the same pension (no. 829), this act specifically
excludes the tithes of corn, peas, beans and lambs; the same tithes were confirmed to
the abbey in the general diocesan confirmation by Herbert Poore in 1201 (no. 211).

840 *Gift by Abbot H. of Reading to master R. carpenter of a messuage outside
the gate in front of St Laurence's church, to be held by him for life for 12d
annually, and by his heirs for 3s annually*   [1186 × 1213]

Cf 194r

Sciant presentes et futuri quod ego H. abbas Radyng(ensis) ex communi consensu capituli dedi et concessi magistro R. carpentario pro
servitio suo unum mesuagium extra portam coram ecclesia sancti
Laurentii, tenendum de nobis omni tempore quo vixerit libere et
quiete, pacifice et honorifice secundum communem legem et liberam
consuetudinem aliorum burgensium Rad(ingie) qui liberius tenent,
persolvendo nobis annuatim pro omni servitio .xii. d' ad festum sancti
Michaelis. Ita videlicet quod heredes prefati R. eandem terram cum
supradictis libertatibus teneant,ᵃ reddendo annuatim ad tres terminos
tres solidos, videlicet ad festum sancti Michaelis .xii. denarios,ᵇ ad
Purificationem beate Marie .xii. d', ad festum sancti Iohannis Baptiste
in estate .xii. d'. Hec conventio rata erit et stabilis [. . . .].ᶜ Testibus:
Waltero de Oxeneford, Waltero de Bollyngeshull', Raimundo, Alano
fratre eius, Rad(ulfo)ᵈ Wille, et Iordano fratre eius, Hugone Meisent,
Rogero de Collee, Pagano Fachel, Roberto sellario, et multis aliis.

ᵃ *Interlined*   ᵇ *Ms has* d' denar'
ᶜ *The sentence is clearly incomplete and no doubt continued as in no. 837*
ᵈ *Ms has* Bad', *but cf. nos. 841, 843–4*

Date as for no. 839.

841 *Lease by Abbot H. and the convent of Reading to Alan the merchant of
Reading and his heirs of land between the house of Payn Vachell and that which*

belonged to Robert the vintner, which land was adjudged to the abbey in the
portmoot as its escheat. Alan has given to the abbey 20s and to Christina, who
had held the land for some years, 16s by the abbey's order in compensation for
her expenditure on the land   [1186 × 1213]

Cf194r

Sciant presentes et futuri quod ego H. abbas Radyng(ensis) eiusdemque loci conventus concessimus Alano mercatori de Radyng(ia)
et heredibus suis tenere de nobis reddendo annuatim .iii. solidos ad
festum sancti Michaelis illam terram que est inter domum Pagani
Fachel et domum que fuit Roberti vinitoris, que nobis in portimoto
per iuramentum ville adiudicata est tamquam escheeta nostra. Huius
concessionis gratia dedit prefatus Alanus nobis .xx. solidos et per
nostrum preceptum .xvi. solidos Christine que terram illam aliquot
annis tenuerat, tamen ut acommodatam sine redditu et aliquando
reddendo .vi. denarios. Istos autem prefatos .xvi. solidos accepit prefata Christina in portimoto intuitu pietatis ut, si quid in hac terra
tempore quo eam tenuerat expendisset, in hoc illi recompensentur.
Hec concessio rata erit et stabilis quamdiu predictus A(lanus) fidelis
nobis extiterit et predictum censum bene nobis reddiderit.[a] Hiis
testibus: Remundo mercatore, Ricardo Wille, Waltero Wille,
Rad(ulfo) Wille, Iordano Wille, Raerio, Willelmo infante, Willelmo
de Elimosinaria.

[a]*Ms has* reddidit

Date as for no. 839.

842   *Lease by Abbot H. and the convent of Reading to Nicholas son of Henry*
the goldsmith and his heirs of the messuage which Nicholas his grandfather held
of the abbey in New Street, Reading   [1186 × 1213]

Cf194r

Sciant presentes et futuri quod ego H. abbas Radyng(ensis) et eiusdem
loci conventus concessimus Nicholao filio Henrici aurificis et heredibus
suis mesuagium illud quod Nicholaus avus eius de nobis tenuit in novo
vico Radyng(ie), tenendum de nobis iure hereditario pro quinque
solidis annuatim nobis reddendis ad festum sancti Michaelis. Et pro
hac concessione dedit prefatus Nicholaus centum solidos. Hec concessio rata erit et stabilis quamdiu ipse et heredes sui nobis fideles
extiterint et predictum censum bene et plene reddiderint. Hiis testibus:
Gautero clerico, Reginaldo senesch(allo), Willelmo camberlano,
Osmundo de Acleia, Willelmo pincerna, Remundo et Alano fratre
suo, Gilberto de supra pontem, Gilberto filio suo, Waltero de Stokes,
et multis.

Date as for no. 839.

843 *Gift by Abbot H. and the convent of Reading to William Chamberlain of two messuages in New Street and land behind the cemetery of St Giles' church*
[1186 × 1213]

Cf 194r–v

Sciant presentes et futuri quod ego H. abbas Radyng(ensis) et eiusdem loci conventus dedimus Willelmo Camberlano et heredibus suis duo mesuagia in novo vico in quo*a* [*f 194v*] Gilbertus super pontem mansit, scilicet illa que sunt inter domum G(alfredi)*b* de Bixe et domum que fuit Ramundi mercatoris, tenenda de nobis sibi et heredibus suis libere et quiete, pacifice et honorifice*c* sicut alii liberi et honorifici burgenses de Radyng(ia) tenent, reddendo nobis annuatim duos solidos ad festum sancti Michaelis pro omni servitio. Dedimus etiam predicto W(illelmo) et heredibus suis terram retro cimiterium sancti Egidii quam Bodwynus filius Wiant tenuit de Petro de Cosham preter duo mesuagia que Alardus presbiter et Willelmus Luffe tenent de eadem terra, tenendam*d* de nobis per prefatam libertatem, reddendo sex denarios per annum ad predictum terminum. Hiis testibus: Willelmo de Waltham, Ernaldo maresc(allo), Rahero, Willelmo pincerna, Willelmo dispensatore, Rogero de Waltham, Lamberto coco, Achelmanno coco, Ramundo mercatore, et Alano fratre suo, Waltero de Oxonia, et Waltero genero suo, Gilberto super pontem, Galfrido clerico, et Turgiso genero suo, Edwardo Gentil, Rad(ulfo) Wille, Simone stabulario, Waltero Peg', et aliis multis.

a Sic, possibly error for quibus   *b For expansion, see nos. 832-5*
c Ms has honororifice   *d Ms has* tenenda

Date as for no. 839.

844 *Sale and lease by Abbot H. and the convent of Reading to William Chamberlain and his heirs of a messuage in New Street, and lease to the same of three stalls next to the abbey wall and a stall in the middle of the market of Reading*
[1186 × 1213]

Cf 194v

Sciant presentes et futuri quod ego H.*a* abbas Radyng(ensis) et eiusdem loci conventus vendidimus Willelmo Camberlano pro .iiii. marcis unum mesuagium in novo vico versus Lond(oniam) quod emimus a Galfr(ed)o de Bixe pro tribus marcis et concessimus eidem et heredibus suis tenere idem mesuagium de nobis pro duobus solidis nobis ad festum sancti Michaelis annuatim reddendis. Concessimus etiam eidem W(illelmo) et heredibus suis tres seldas iuxta murum curie nostre, scilicet illas que sunt inter seldam Lamberti coci et seldam Gaufridi super pontem, ita quidem ut murum curie nostre habeat in parte orientali in predictarum seldarum parietem et ante seldas decem pedum spatium infra postes et seldas, ut liberum sit iter euntium et redeuntium infra postes illos, reddendo nobis annuatim ad predictum festum sancti Michaelis .iiii. solidos; cum vicine selde reddere nobis soleant per annum singule .xii. d', pro muro curie nostre et .x. pedum spatio ante seldas illas augmentavit redditum suum predictus Willelmus de .xii. d' per annum. Concessimus etiam eidem Willelmo et heredibus suis unam seldam in medio foro de Radyng(ia), scilicet illam que est inter murum et seldam Walteri de Oxeneford, pro quinque solidis annuatim nobis reddendis ad predictum festum sancti Michaelis. Tenebit autem predictus Willelmus et heredes sui omnes predictas terras bene et in pace, libere et quiete, pacifice et honorifice, reddendo nobis predictum censum ad prefatum terminum pro omni servitio. Hiis testibus: Gautero clerico, Reginaldo Camberlano, Willelmo pincerna, Lamberto coco, Archenbaudo, Osmundo de Oclee, Simone stabulario, Willelmo Crawe, Alemanno coco, Iohanne coco, Gilberto filio suo, Waltero de Oxon(ia), et Hamone filio suo, Waltero de Stokes, et Waltero filio suo, Ramundo mercatore, et Gilberto, Martino et Hugone filiis suis, Alano fratre Ramundi, Rad(ulfo) Wylle, Gilberto Conpernays, Iordano Wille, Iordano Conpernays, Iohanne de Catain',[b] et Rog(ero) de Camera, et cetera.

[a] *Ms has* Henricus, *clearly in error for* Hugo *or* Helias
[b] *Doubtful reading, but cf. nos.* 617, 1069

Date as for no. 839. It is interesting to note the scribe's error in writing *Henricus abbas*, since he may well have been copying this deed in the abbacy of Henry of Appleford, who became abbot in Feb./Mar. 1342 (see vol. I, p. 12).

845   *Lease by Abbot H. and the convent of Reading to Godfrey of Binfield and his heirs of a messuage in Reading between the two courses of the [River] Kennet next to the land which belonged to Adam of Earley*   [1186 × 1213]

C f 195r

Sciant presentes et futuri quod ego H. abbas Radyng(ensis) et eiusdem loci conventus concessimus et hoc presenti scripto confirmavimus Godefrido de Benetfeld' et heredibus eius post eum unum mesuagium in Radyng(ia) inter duos rivos aquarum de Keneta iuxta terram que fuit Ade de Hurle, reddendo nobis annuatim .xii. d' ad festum sancti Michaelis pro omni pensionali et annuali servitio. Hoc mesuagium tenebit prefatus G(odefridus) et heredes sui libere, quiete, plene et honorifice secundum legem burgensium honorabilium in villa de Radyng(ia) commorantium. Hec conventio rata erit et stabilis quamdiu prefatus G(odefridus) et heredes sui nobis fideles extiterint et predictum censum reddiderint. Hiis testibus: Willelmo Camberlano, Ramundo mercatore, et Alano fratre suo, Waltero de Oxonia, et Waltero genere suo, Turgiso, Edwardo Gentil, et Simone stabulario, et multis aliis, et cetera.

Date as for no. 839.

846 *Lease by Abbot H. and the convent of Reading to Osbert of Waltham and his heirs of all the land between the [River] Kennet and the messuage which Adam of Earley held of the abbey in Reading, except the quay and its appurtenances which shall be 30 feet by 16 feet; and of a quay to the east of his house to be made and repaired from his own resources, the profits of which shall be divided between Osbert and his heirs and the abbey* [1186 × 1213]

Cf195r–v; Cf149v

Sciant presentes et futuri quod ego H. abbas Rad(ingensis) et eiusdem loci conventus concessimus Osberto de Waltham et heredibus suis tenere de ecclesia nostra totam terram que est inter Kenetam et mesuagium*a* quod Adam de Erle*b* de nobis tenuit in Radyng(ia), excepto kaio et eius pertinentiis quod erit .xxx. pedum in longitudine et .xvi.*c* in latitudine, reddendo annuatim .ii. solidos ad festum sancti Michaelis pro omni alio*d* servitio ad nos pertinente. Kaium etiam ita ei concessimus in orientali parte domus sue ut illud de suo faciat et quotiens opus fuerit reficiat et heredes eius post eum et custodiat et procuret ita quod nec pro aquarum inundatione in yeme*e* vel alio tempore nec pro siccitate in estate naves ibidem*f* applicare inpediantur. Ante kaium autem tam amplum plenum et planum procurabit spatium et*g* per mediam curiam suam viam ad kaium illud ne naves vel quadrige hinc inde advenientes in cartando vel decartando aliquatenus prepediri possint. Emolumentorum autem kaii illius pro hac custodia et procuratione concessimus*h* undecumque provenerint medietatem predicto O(sberto) et heredibus suis*i* post eum, medietatem alteram nobis retinentes. Volumus igitur ut predictus O(sbertus) et heredes eius predictum tenementum teneant libere et quiete, pacifice et honorifice, sicut alii liberi et honorabiles burgenses de Radyng(ia)*j* tenent. [*f195v*] Hec autem concessio rata erit et stabilis quamdiu predictus O(sbertus) et heredes sui nobis fideles extiterint*k* et predictum censum bene et plene reddiderint. Hiis testibus:*l* Willelmo de Waltham et magistro Hamone fratribus eius, Meuselmo*m* de Bulehud' et Nicholao fratre suo, Hugone de Sotebroc et Roberto fratre suo, Wyce de Shotebrok', Gautero clerico de Leomenstria, Willelmo camberl(ano), Willelmo dispensatore, Radul(f)o ianitore, Lamberto coco, Ernaldo Rufo, Ramundo mercatore et Alano fratre suo, Rad(ulf)o

Wille, Waltero Wille, Waltero de Oxonia, Willelmo vinitore, Hugone filio Meisent, Daniele clerico, Hugone mercatore.

a masagium *Cf 149v*
c *Insert* pedum *Cf 149v*
e hieme *Cf 149v*
g ut *Cf 149v*
i eius *Cf 149v*
k *Cf 195r–v has* constiterint
m *Reading uncertain*

b Erlee *Cf 149v*
d annuali *Cf 149v*
f ibi *Cf 149v*
h *Om. in* *Cf 149v*
j Redyng' *Cf 149v*
l *Cf 149v ends with* et cetera

Date as for no. 839. The copy on Cf 149v is in a rapid late 14th-century hand.

847   *Letter of confraternity by Abbot H. and the convent of Reading to Walter of Oxford, who has given to the abbey himself and all his land in Reading, except the capital messuage, which land he has received for his life for an annual rent of 50s; he has also given 40 marks of silver, and at his death will give 30 marks or half his chattels, whichever the abbey wishes*   [1186 × 1213]

Cf 198r

Universis Christi fidelibus ad quos presens scriptum pervenerit frater H. Radyng(ensis) ecclesie minister humilis et totus eiusdem loci conventus, eternam in domino salutem. Noverit universitas vestra quod nos suscepimus Gauterum de Oxonia in fratrem et participem omnium bonorum que sunt in ecclesia nostra tam in vita quam in morte; qui *a* per salutem *a* anime sue dedit deo et ecclesie nostre se et totam terram suam quam habet in Radyng(ia), excepto capitali mesuagio quod ei remanebit et heredibus suis, salvo redditu eiusdem mesuagii; ita videlicet quod, postquam in manus domini abbatis predictam terram resignavit, eam ipsius auctoritate suscepit *b* quoad vixerit persolvendo inde nobis singulis annis .l. solidos, ad festum videlicet sancti Michaelis .xxv. solidos, ad festum sancti Petri quod *c* dicitur Advincula .xxv. solidos. Dedit preterea ecclesie nostre .xl. marcas argenti et in obitu suo dabit nobis .xxx. marcas argenti vel medietatem totius catalli sui, et in arbitrio domini abbatis erit et monachorum utrum e duobus velint accipere. Concessit preterea servitium suum domui nostre, ut patet in indentura, et cetera.

a–a *Sic, but perhaps in error for* pro salute
b *Ms has* susceptam; *however,* susceptam *may be correct and* tenebit *or the like may have been omitted*
c *Ms has* que

Date as for no. 839.

848   *Grant by Abbot Elias and the convent of Reading to John the chaplain, their clerk, of the perpetual vicarage in the church of St Laurence [Reading], with details of the provisions, lodging and revenues assigned to him*   [1200 × 1213]

Cf 193v

Sciant presentes et futuri quod ego Hel(ias) dei gratia abbas Rad-
yng(ensis) et eiusdem loci conventus concessimus Iohanni capellano
clerico nostro, unanimi consensu et voluntate, perpetuam vicariam
ᵃin ecclesiaᵃ sancti Laurentii toto tempore vite sue possidendam. Ita
quidem quod prefatus Iohannes percipiet per manum elimosinarii
nostri viginti solidos annuatim ad indumenta sua et panem et potum
sicut unus monachorum nostrorum, cum septem denariis per
unamquamque ebdomadamᵇ pro companagio, et hospitium honestum
et legata sua usque ad sex denarios et infra; supra autem quod excre-
verit cum elimosinario dimidiabit. Oblationes etiam suas percipiet,
scilicet sex denarios ad Natale domini et sex denarios ad Purificationem beate Marie et sex denarios ad Pascha et sex denarios ad
festum sancti Laurentii. Et cum vocatus fuerit ad sinodum pro statutis
ecclesie audiendis semel in anno elimosinarius providebit ei equumᶜ
idoneum. Ut autem hec nostra concessio rata et inconcussa
permaneat, sigilli nostri appositione eam duximus corroborandam.

ᵃ⁻ᵃ Interlined   ᵇ Ms has ebdomodam
ᶜ Ms has equm

The dating limits are those of Elias's abbacy.

849   *Lease and gift by Abbot Elias and the convent of Reading to Agatha
daughter of Gilbert* de Felda *and her heirs of half the land lying between the
two courses of the* [River] *Kennet which her father held. Agatha and her husband
and heirs have renounced their right in the rest of the land which her father had
held and which he freely recognized in the abbey's court to be villein tenure*

[1200 × 1213]

Cf 195r

Sciant presentes et futuri quod ego Hel(ias) dei gratia abbas Radyng-
(ensis) et eiusdem loci conventus concessimus et dedimus Agathe filie
Gilberti de Felda et heredibus suis medietatem totius terre iacentis
inter duas aquas Kenete tam in moris quam pratis et pascuis quam
tenuit pater suus Gilbertus, tenendam de nobis sibi et heredibus suis
libere et quiete et pacifice, reddendo nobis annuatim triginta denarios
pro omni servitio ad festum sancti Michaelis. Pro hac autem nostra
concessione et donatione prefata Agatha cum sponso suo et heredes
sui abiuraverunt super textum sancti ewangelii in plena curia nostra
siquidᵃ iuris habere potuerunt in reliqua terra quam Gilbertus pater
suus tenuerat quam ipse G(ilbertus) recognovit spontanee in curia

nostra operariam de vilenagio fuisse. Hiis testibus:[b] [Oddone de Berg-efeld et Gileberto filio eius, Willelmo de Uffinton', Reimundo de Rad-ing(ia), et Alano fratre eius, Gervasio Puncun, Roberto Puncun, Gile-berto Pincun, Willelmo de Colle, et Tom(o) filio eius, Ricardo de Colle, Hugone de Herewaldesleg', et toto hundredo de Rading(ia)].

[a] *Sic, probably a miscopying of* quicquid, *as in no. 849a*
[b] *Ms ends here with* et cetera, *the remainder being supplied from the original of no. 849a*

The dating limits are those of Elias's abbacy. The other half of Gilbert de Felda's land between the two courses of the Kennet was leased and given to Agatha's sister Eva and her heirs (see no. 849a).

849a Note of the same indenture made word for word to Eva, sister of the said Agatha   [1200 × 1213]

C f 195r

The original survives as an un-numbered item in PRO C109/68, part 2 (Chancery Masters' Exhibits, Master Humphrey's Box). The text is *mutatis mutandis* virtually identical to no. 849, and both deeds were no doubt given on the same date. The PRO deed is indented and bears two fragmentary seals, viz. of the abbey and of Abbot Elias.

850 Gift by Ralph *le Buch'* of Shinfield (*Sunnyngefeld*) to Gerard Stabler (*Stabularius*) of Reading, for his homage and service, of a messuage in London Street (*in vico London'*), Reading, between that which belonged to William Miller (*Molitor*) and that which belonged to Matilda *le Bruthere*. To be held freely by rendering annually to Ralph and his heirs 5s at Michaelmas for all service, secular exaction and demand. For this Gerard has given him 20s as entry-fine. War-ranty and sealing   [? *c.* 1220 × 50]

C f 168r

Hiis testibus: Hugone le Bolur, Willelmo le Bolur, Gilberto Cissore, Alano Janitore, Thoma de Hanleia, Nicholao filio presbiteri, Johanne vinitore, Johanne Tinctore, Osberto de la Garstone, Ricardo filio Johannis de Swalefeld', Roberto de la Garston(e), Bartholomeo Chan-terel, et multis aliis in portesmot.

Dating uncertain. Hugh le Bolur witnesses deeds in 1219 (see nos. 1271, 1273), occurs as a clothier in Reading in 1241 (PRO JUST 1/37, mm. 25B d, 26, 35d) and may have been dead by June 1248 (Clanchy, *Berks. Eyre of 1248*, 181). Thomas of Henley witnesses in 1216 × 24, 1219 and 1249 (nos. 816, 779, 1223–4). A John dyer, of whom there may have been more than one, was a juror for Reading in 1241 and 1248 (PRO JUST 1/37, M. 27d; Clanchy, *ibid.*, 296).

851 Gift by Walter Gerard (*Gerard*) of Reading to Giles *de Mees*, for his service and a certain sum of money, of 3s annual rent in Reading, viz., 18d each at Michaelmas and Easter, from three tenements in London Street which formerly belonged to Walter Messenger (*le Messenger*), Thomas *le Bout* and Robert of Shottesbrooke (*Sottesbrok'*) and which are situated between the tenement of John *Pecamundus* on the north and that of Philip of Newbury (*Neuburi*) on the south. To be held of the chief lords of the fee freely. Warranty and sealing

[1290 × c. 1310]

Cf168r

Hiis testibus: Johanne Fachel, Johanne le Acatur, Radul(f)o de Alta Ripa, Matheo de Cicestria, Gilberto de Ponte, Ricardo de Thaccham, Radul(f)o clerico, et multis aliis.

The fact that the donees are to hold of the chief lords of the fee dates this deed to the period after *Quia emptores* (1290) – see *Fitznells Cartulary*, ed. C. A. F. Meekings and P. Shearman, Surrey Rec. Soc., xxvi (1968), cxlv. By *c.* 1310 the majority of deeds made in Reading seem to have been dated. The donor occurs between ?1290 and 1311 (see nos. 1241–2, 963) and was mayor of Reading in 1301–2, the first whose name is known (*VCH Berks.*, iii. 346). The witnesses are of little assistance in dating, since there was more than one John Vachell and more than one John le Acatur in Reading in the later 13th and earlier 14th centuries, but a Matthew of Chichester occurs there in 1284 and 1297 (PRO JUST 1/43, m. 12; *Berks. Arch. Journ.*, lx (1962), 105).

852 Gift by Giles *de Mees* to John *le Acatour*, for his service and a certain sum of money, of the same 3s annual rent in Reading [detailed exactly as in no. 851 and to be paid in the same instalments]. To be held of the chief lords of the fee freely. Warranty and sealing

[1290 × c. 1310]

Cf168v

Hiis testibus: Johanne Vachel, Rad(ulf)o de Alta Ripa, Thoma le Tanner', Matheo de Cicestria, Gilberto de Ponte, Ricardo de Thaccham, Rogero clerico, et multis aliis.

Date as for no. 851. The text is *mutatis mutandis* the same as that of no. 851 and many of the witnesses are the same.

853 Quitclaim by John son of John *le Acat(ur)* of Reading to Abbot John [I, of Appleford] and the convent of Reading of all his right in 3s annual rent from tenements in London Street, Reading, which formerly belonged to Walter Messenger (*le Messinger*), Thomas *le Bout'* and John of Shottesbrooke (*Shotesbrok'*), and which Walter Gerard of Reading lately held. Warranty. For this the abbot and convent have given him a certain sum of money. Sealing   18 Feb. 1336

Cf168v

Dat' apud [?]*a* die dominica proxima post festum sancti Valentini [14 Feb.], anno regni regis Edwardi tercii a Conquestu decimo.

a Place omitted, probably Reading

The tenements concerned here are the same as those in nos. 851–2.

854 Gift in free alms by John the vintner, son of Robert the vintner, to Reading Abbey of 17d rent in the Old Market [of Reading]*a* which master Walter the cook used to owe him annually for a house which he held of him and his ancestors. For this the abbot and convent have remitted 10s of silver which John owed them. Warranty

[? *c.* 1220 × 50]

Bf 48r; Cf19v; Cf169r

Hiis testibus:*b* [Alano Janitore, Alano Nigro vinitario, tunc prepositis, Gilberto cissore, Hugone le Bolur, Willelmo filio suo, Roberto Wille, Gilberto supra pontem, Willelmo Bascat, et aliis].

a Supplied from rubrics in B,Cf19v
b B,Cf19v end, the remainder being supplied from Cf169r

Not later than 1258, since it was entered in the original section of B. Although a Walter the cook occurs in 1158 × 86 (see no. 817 n.), the witnesses favour a 13th-century date. For Hugh le Bolur, who may have been dead in 1248, see no. 850 n. For Robert Wille, see no. 855 n. A William Baskat was a juror for Reading borough in 1241 (PRO JUST 1/37, m. 27d).

855 Gift by Robert *Wille* to Robert of Preston (*Preston'*) and Joan his wife, for their service, of a meadow within the Seven Bridges of Reading, between the meadow sometime belonging to John Dyer (*Tinctor*) and that sometime belonging to John Bishop (*Bisshop*), and of 16d annual rent at Michaelmas from a pasture within the Seven Bridges between the messuage of William of Hoo (*Ho*) and that which belonged to John Dyer, with free entry and exit through the middle of the said pasture and through its middle gate. To be held freely by rendering annually to Reading Abbey 2s at Michaelmas, and to the donor and his heirs 1 clove at Michaelmas, for all secular service, exaction and demand. Warranty and sealing   [*c.* 1260 × 90]

Cf169r

Hiis testibus: Willelmo de Blebury, Willelmo de Whitele, Willelmo de Mussendene, Thoma de Bunetfeld, Willelmo Tilly, Johanne vinitario, Thoma le Acatur, et aliis.

Before *Quia emptores* (1290). William of Blewbury, steward of the abbey in 1267, 1285 and 1303 (BL Add. Ch. 19627; below, nos. 1240, 1045), occurs from 1265×6 (see no. 792). The identity of the donor is uncertain, since there were clearly at least two of that name in Reading. One occurs as a draper in 1241, 1248 and 1261 (PRO JUST 1/37, m. 35d; Clanchy, *Berks. Eyre of 1248*, 396; JUST 1/40, m. 29d), and was elector and juror for Reading borough in 1241 (JUST 1/37, m. 27d) and coroner of Reading in 1248 (Clanchy, *ibid.*, 391). He may have been the same as either the Robert Wille who witnesses in Reading in 1204×20 (no. 892) or he who witnesses in Whitley in 1317 (no. 1261).

856   Gift in free alms by Henry Bannister (*Banastre*) of Reading to Reading Abbey of a plot (*placea*) of land, 7 perches by 3 perches, in the parish of St Giles, Reading, between the lane called Mill Lane (*Mullelane*) and the curtilage of Gilbert *de Ponte*; one of its ends (*capud*) abuts on Henry's tenement on the east and the other on that of Adam, called Cook (*Cocus*), chaplain, on the west. Warranty and sealing

[? *c.* 1300]

C f 169v

Hiis testibus: Willelmo de Bleobury, Gilberto Pinson, Johanne Vachel, Thoma de Leicestre, Waltero Gerard, Gilberto de Ponte, Willelmo Bonafannt, Willelmo de Whitele, Johanne Fyngod, Thoma Syward, et multis aliis.

The donor occurs in Reading in 1297, as do Thomas of Leicester, Walter Gerard, Gilbert de Ponte, William Bonafannt and Thomas Syward (*Berks. Arch. Journ.*, lx (1962), 101–3, 106). Walter Gerard was mayor of Reading in 1301–2 (*VCH Berks.*, iii. 346) and Thomas of Leicester mayor some time before 15 Apr. 1304 (see no. 947). William of Blewbury occurs 1265/6–1303 (see no. 855 n.). John Fyngod is not known to witness in Reading before 1301 (no. 949).

857   *Gift by Gilbert Pincent to Reading Abbey of a messuage at Battle* [*in Reading*], *in return for remission by the abbot and convent of 74s which Gilbert owed them*   [13th cent.; ? before *c.* 1230]

A f 81r; B f 49r; C f 20r; C f 169v

Sciant presentes et futuri quod ego Gilebertus*ᵃ* Pinzun*ᵇ* dedi, concessi et hac presenti carta mea confirmavi abbati et conventui *ᶜ*de Rading(ia)*ᶜ* unum mesuagium apud Bellum cum pertinentiis, videlicet illud quod Ricardus porcarius tenuit de me pro tribus solidis annuis, tenendum et habendum dictum mesuagium in perpetuum libere, quiete,*ᵈ* bene et in bona pace absque ullo retenemento*ᵉ* ad me vel ad heredes meos contingente.*ᶠ* Pro hac autem donatione, concessione et carte mee confirmatione, remiserunt mihi*ᵍ* prefati abbas et conventus *ʰ*sexaginta et quatuordecim*ʰ* solidos in quibus tenebar dictis abbati et conventui. Predictum vero mesuagium cum pertinentiis ego Gilebertus*ⁱ* et heredes mei warantizabimus dictis abbati et conventui versus omnes homines.

Et ut hec mea donatio,[j] concessio et carte mee confirmatio rata et
stabilis perseveret, presens scriptum sigillli mei appositione roboravi.
Hiis testibus:[k] [Willelmo de Engelfeud', Nicholao Pincerna, Ricardo
de Collea, Roberto Bienshief[l] de Kenthe, Radulpho Saraguze, Gilberto Frankeleyn, Hugone[m] de Kenetwode, et multis aliis].

[a]Gilbertus C f 169v   [b]Pinson C f 169v
[c-c]Rading' B, Radyng' C f 20r and f 169v
[d]Om. in C f 169v   [e]retinemento B, C f 20r
[f]pertinente B, C f 20r   [g]michi C f 169v
[h-h].lxxiiii. B, C f 20r   [i]Gilb' C f 20r, Gilbertus C f 169v
[j]Insert et C f 20r
[k]A, B, C f 20r end, the remainder being supplied from C f 169v
[l]Ms has Bienshiel   [m]Ms has Hugo

Not in the original section of A but among 13th-century additions of deeds dating
mostly from before c. 1230. A Gilbert Pincent occurs in 1200 × 13, 1226 × 38 and 1248
(no. 849; PRO C109/68, part 2, no. 336; Clanchy, *Berks. Eyre of 1248*, 186). Nicholas
Butler occurs between 1197 × 8 and 1241, when he was coroner of the abbot's liberty
(*Ancient Charters*, 107; PRO JUST 1/37, m. 34); Robert Beansheaf in 1226 × 38 and 1249
(C109/68, part 2, no. 336; below, no. 1223); and both Gilbert Franklin and Hugh of
Kentwood in 1248, when the latter was a juror for Reading hundred (Clanchy, *ibid.*,
172, 182, 295). The precise date of this deed is thus uncertain, and the first witness,
William of Englefield, is of little help (see *VCH Berks.*, iii. 406), but on the whole a date
later rather than earlier in the suggested range seems the more likely. The messuage
concerned was in the manor of Battle, which lay in the parishes of St Mary and St
Laurence in Reading (*ibid.*, 366). The rubric of C f 20r describes the messuage as *in
Radyng' apud le Bateyll' iuxta fratres minores*, i.e. near the house of the Grey Friars at the
western end of what is now Friar Street, Reading.

858 Quitclaim by Peter *de Eston'* to Reading Abbey of all his right
in a plot (*placea*) of land lying between the two water courses of the
mill which is beyond the bridge in the vill of Reading, abutting on
the mill on the west and on the tenement of William of Whitley
(*Whitele*) on the east, which plot formerly belonged to Nicholas the
clerk. Sealing   [c. 1260 × 1300]

C f 170r

Hiis testibus: Willelmo de Bleobury senesc(allo), Johanne le Lomb,
Willelmo de Mussendene, Ricardo de Whitele, Matheo de Cicestr(ia),
Johanne Fachel, Johanne Aurifabro, Stephano le Grom, Willelmo le
Chamberlenc, et aliis.

Peter de Estone was a juror for Reading vill in 1269 and occurs there in 1284 (PRO
JUST 1/42, m. 19; 1/44, m. 15d); he witnessed below no. 960. For William of Blewbury,
steward, see no. 855 n. John Lamb occurs in 1284 (PRO JUST 1/43, m. 9); Matthew
of Chichester in 1284 and 1297 (see no. 851 n.); and Stephen Groom in 1269 × 87
(no. 881). Nicholas the clerk was dead by Feb. 1261 (PRO JUST 1/40, m. 29d).

859 Remission by Luke the hospitaller, master of Brimpton (*Brom-*

ton'),[a] in the name of the prior and brethren of the Hospital of Jerusalem in England, to Reading Abbey and all its servants, of all causes, disputes and plaints (*cause, questiones et querele*) occasioned by a certain messuage in Reading, since all have been settled by an amicable composition between the parties on Tuesday after the feast of the Translation of St Benedict [11 July] in the year of grace 1254. Sealing 14 July 1254

A f35r; B f5or; C f21r; C f17or

[a]Brimton' *B,C f21r*; Brymtona *C f17or*

860 Notification by Luke the hospitaller, keeper of the manor of Brimpton (*Brimton'*),[a] in the name of the prior and brethren of the Hospital of Jerusalem in England, that he has received from the abbot and convent of Reading 25 marks of silver by the hand of Roger, their chamberlain, by virtue of the peace made between them concerning all disputes and pleas in courts Christian and secular occasioned by a certain messuage in Reading, and release of the messuage to the abbot and convent. Sealing 29 Sept. 1254

B f5or; C f21r; C f17or

Dat' apud Brimton'[a] anno gratie M.CC.liiii, die sancti Michaelis.[b] Valete.

[a]Brintona *C f17or*
[b]*C f17or ends with* Valeat universitas vestra in domino

861 Gift by William *Gurnard*, with the consent of Emma his wife, to Thomas *Wille*, son of Robert *Wille*,[a] for his service, of a stall in the Corn Market of Reading (*in foro Radyng' ubi bladum venditur*) between the stall of Alan the vintner and that which formerly belonged to William Battle (*Bataille*). To be held freely by rendering annually to the lord of the fee 3s at Michaelmas, and to William and his heirs 1d as increment at the same term, for all secular service, exaction and demand. For this Thomas has given him 4 marks of silver as entry-fine. Warranty. If Emma shall outlive her husband and presume to implead Thomas and his heirs or assigns regarding the said stall, it is agreed between Thomas and Emma before good and trustworthy men called for this purpose that she shall pay him and his heirs or assigns 100s as penalty for promoting a plea (*si ... querelam inde suscitaverit*). Sealing [13th cent.; not later than 1258]

Cf170v; (noted) Bf49v; Cf20v

Hiis testibus: Henrico Wille, Alano vinit(ario), Adam clerico, Johanne Wille, Willelmo de Mussenden', Thoma de Henl(eia), Johanne Tinctore, Nicholao clerico, Thoma cissore, Jacobo clerico, et multis aliis.

a Ms repeats filio Roberti Wille

Not later than 1258, since it was noted in the original section of B. Henry Wille was a steward of the Reading gild in 1254 (see no. 69). Alan vintner and John dyer were borough jurors in 1241 and 1248 (PRO JUST 1/37, m. 27d; Clanchy, *Berks. Eyre of 1248*, 296). Adam clerk and Nicholas clerk, coroners of the borough of Reading, were both dead by Feb. 1261 and both served as borough jurors in 1241 (JUST 1/40, m. 29d; 1/37, m. 27d). For Thomas of Henley, see no. 850 n. For a similar deed, see no. 969.

862 Gift by Robert *Wille* to John *Wille* his son, for his service, of the whole messuage in London Street, Reading, between that of Roger Brown (*Broun*) and that of Adam *le Hunte*. To be held freely by rendering annually to Reading Abbey 2s at Michaelmas, and to Robert and his heirs or assigns 1 clove, for all secular service, exaction and demand. Warranty and sealing

[not later than 1258; ? mid-13th cent.]

Cff170v–171r; (noted) Bf49v; Cf20v

Hiis testibus: Henrico Wille, Daniele*a* Wlveseie, Nicholao clerico, Ada clerico, Johanne Wille, Willelmo de Mussenden', Gilberto super pontem, Gilberto Scot, Johanne Tinctore, et multis aliis.

a Ms has Danie

Not later than 1258, since it was noted in the original section of B; in view of the placing of Henry Wille and Daniel Wolvesey at the head of the witness-list, perhaps of the time when they were stewards of the Reading gild, which they certainly were in 1254 (no. 69). Daniel was dead by Feb. 1261 (PRO JUST 1/40, m. 12). For the donor, see no. 855 n. There were clearly two men called John *Wille* at this time, for in the present deed one is the donee and another witnesses (cf. no. 864).

863 Gift in free alms by John son of Robert *Wille* of Reading to Reading Abbey of 2 marks annual rent in Reading to be received at Michaelmas, viz., from a messuage which Ralph of Leicester (*Leic'*)*a* holds in London Street between the messuage of Adam *le Hunte* and that formerly belonging to Roger Brown (*Brun*) 10s, from a messuage which Hugh *Blacsalt*ᵇ holds in the same street next to the messuage of G(ilbert)ᶜ the merchant and that formerly belonging to Ralph the baker (*pistor*) 7s 4d, from a messuage between that of Walter Wisdom (*Wisdom*) and that formerly belonging to Laurence *Katayne*ᵈ in Great

Street (*in magno vico*) 7s, and from a shop which Walter the tailor (*le taillur*) holds in the Lormery (*Lormeria*) between the stall which belonged to William Battle (*Bataille*) and that of John the vintner 3s 6d. Warranty and sealing   [13th cent.; not later than 1258]

B f50r–v; C f21r–v; C f171r

Hiis testibus:[*e*] [domino Roberto de Mapeldorham, Stephano de la Wyle, Willelmo de Whiteley, Daniele Wlvesey, Ada clerico, Nicholao clerico, Johanne Tinctore, Thoma de Kaversham, David fabro, Stephano de Sancto Albano clerico, et multis aliis cum toto portesmot' Radyng(ie)].

[*a*]Leicestr' *C f171r*   [*b*]Blaksalt *C f171r*
[*c*]Expansion from *C f171r*   [*d*]Kateyne *C f171r*
[*e*]B,C f21r–v end, the remainder being supplied from *C f171r*

Entered in the original section of B. Sir Robert of Mapledurham was sheriff of Berkshire in 1232–3 and 1234, was steward of Reading Abbey some time between *c.* 1240 and 1258, and was prominent in the Berkshire eyre of 1248 (*List of Sheriffs*, 6; below, no. 926; Clanchy, *Berks. Eyre*, 157, etc.) For Daniel Wolvesey, see no. 862 n. For Adam clerk, Nicholas clerk and John dyer, see no. 861 n. For Great Street, see no. 867 n. 1. The first messuage and the shop named in the present deed are those of, respectively, nos. 862 and 861; the second messuage named is presumably that in no. 864, and the third is that in no. 868.

864 Gift by William the chaplain, son of Ralph Baker (*le Baker'*), baker, to John son of Robert *Wille*, for his service, of a half messuage in London Street, Reading, next to the messuage of Gilbert the merchant to the north. To be held freely by rendering annually to Reading Abbey 8d at Michaelmas, to Ralph Baker (*Pistor*) and his heirs 1d, and to the donor and his heirs ½d as increment at the same term, for all secular service, exaction and demand. For this John has given him 2 marks of silver as entry-fine. Warranty and sealing
[not later than 1258; ? mid-13th cent.]

C f171v; (noted) B f49v; C f20v[1]

Hiis testibus: Henrico Wille, Daniele Wlveseye, Johanne Wille, Adam de Kyneware, Alano vinit(ario), Willelmo de Mussenden', Nicholao clerico, Johanne Tinctore, Jacobo clerico, et multis aliis.

Date in general as for no. 862.

1. In these notes the donor is called William *pistor capellanus*.

865 Lease, in chirograph form, by Petronilla, wife of Robert *Wille*, with the assent of Thomas her son, to Walter Parker (*P(ar)ker*) of a shop in the great market (*in magno mercato*) of Reading, between the shop of John the vintner and that of Ralph *le celer*, which shop

Petronilla bought for the use of the said Thomas. To be held by Walter and his heirs legitimately born of him from Michaelmas in the [?]*a* year of Henry III until the death of Petronilla, freely by rendering annually to her 6s 6d for all service. She enjoins Thomas, as he wishes to have her blessing, to hold the shop after her death according to the said agreement, unless he shall have married or entered religion, but, if after her death he does not wish to keep the agreement, he shall pay Walter the costs and expenses which by the view of lawful men he shall have laid out on the said shop. If Walter dies and his heir legitimately born of him does not maintain the shop in the condition in which Walter received it in accordance with the said agreement, Petronilla or Thomas her son shall take it back (*recipere*). Sealing *alternatim*   [before 1261; ? mid-13th cent.]

Cff 171v–172r

Hiis testibus: Henrico Wille, Daniele Wlveseye, Willelmo de Whitele, Johanne aurifabro, Reginaldo Dibel, Roberto de Shotesbrok', Radulpho le celier, et multis aliis.

a Numeral om.

Daniel Wolvesey was dead by Feb. 1261 (see no. 862 n.). In view of the placing of Henry Wille and Daniel at the head of the witness-list, the lease may date from the time when they were stewards of the Reading gild, which they certainly were in 1254 (see no. 69). Robert of Shottesbrooke witnesses in 1255 (no. 875) and was a juror for Reading vill in 1269 (PRO JUST 1/42, m. 19). Robert Wille was not dead at the time of this lease, since he occurs as a draper in Reading in 1241, 1248 and 1261 (see no. 855 n.).

866 Quitclaim by Geoffrey *Waukelyn* to Richard of London (*London'*), carpenter, of 6d of the 2s which he used to render to him annually from the land in High Street (*in alto vico*), Reading, between the messuage which belonged to William *Bussel* and that which belonged to Gilbert Tailor (*Cissor*), so that Richard and his heirs or assigns shall render annually at Michaelmas 18d for all secular service and demand. For this Richard has given him 5s sterling as entry-fine. Warranty and sealing   [? *c.* 1220 × 50]

Cf 172r

Hiis testibus: Hugone le Bolur, Alano Janitore, Alano vinitario, Thoma de Henleia, Nicholao supra pontem, Henrico Wille, Daniele Wlveseye, Johanne vinitore, Willelmo Deeuliait, et multis aliis.

Dating uncertain, but in general as for no. 850. A William *Deulyet* was a juror for Reading borough in 1241 (PRO JUST 1/37, m. 27d).

867 Gift by Richard of London, the Carpenter (*le Charpenter*), to

Thomas *Wille*, son of Robert *Wille*, for his service, of a messuage in Great Street (*in magno vico*),[1] Reading, between the messuage formerly belonging to William *Busshel* and that formerly belonging to Gilbert Tailor (*Cissor*). To be held freely by rendering annually to the heirs of Geoffrey *Waukelyn* 18d at Michaelmas and to the donor's heirs[a] 1 clove as increment at the same term, for all secular service, exaction and demand. For this Thomas has given him 4 marks of silver as entry-fine. Warranty and sealing [*c.* 1220 × 1261; ? mid-13th cent.]

Cf172r–v

Hiis testibus: Henrico Wille, Daniele Wlveseye, Willelmo de Mussenden', Alano vinitore, Adam Mobone, Thoma de Henle, Johanne Tinctore, Thoma cissore, Nicholao clerico, et multis aliis.

[a] *Sic, but perhaps a miscopying of* 'to Richard and his heirs'

After no. 866 and before Feb. 1261, when Daniel Wolvesey and Nicholas clerk were dead (see nos. 861 n. and 862 n.); perhaps of the time when Henry Wille and Daniel were stewards of the Reading gild (see no. 865 n.).

1. The messuage concerned here is clearly the same as that in no. 866, where the location is given as High Street. High Street is well known as a medieval street-name in Reading (Slade, 'Reading', 5), but it clearly had the alternative name of Great Street. Cf. no. 889 n.

868 Quitclaim by Alice, widow of Richard of London, to Thomas son of Robert *Wille* of all her right in a messuage in High Street (*in alto vico*), Reading, between the messuage of Walter *Wysdom* and that formerly belonging to Laurence *Catayn*. For this Thomas has given her 3s sterling. Sealing [*c.* 1220 × 1261; ? mid-13th cent.]

Cf172v

Hiis testibus: Henrico Wille, Daniele Wlveseye, Stephano de la Wyle, Thoma Cordewanar', Ada clerico, Alano vinitore, Johanne Wylle, Thoma mercatore, Thoma de Kaversham, Stephano de Sancto Albano, et multis aliis.

Date as for no. 867, although the present deed is later than it. It may be also not later than 1258, since John Wille gave rent from this messuage to Reading Abbey not later than 1258 (see no. 863), in which case Richard of London was dead by then and no. 867 should be dated accordingly.

869 Gift in free alms by Richard *de la Watere* to Reading Abbey of 6d annual rent at Michaelmas from a tenement in Reading in the lane leading from Old Street (*a veteri vico*) to the fulling mill in the parish of St Giles, between the tenement of William Dyer (*Tinctor*) and the said mill. Warranty and sealing [? *c.* 1260 × 90]

Cf172v

Hiis testibus: Willelmo de Whiteley, Willelmo le Teynturer, Willelmo de Mussenden', Henrico Ballivo, et aliis.

Dating very uncertain. The deed was not entered in B, which possibly suggests that the gift had not been made by 1258, while the fact that the abbey is to hold in free alms of the donor and his heirs, and not of the chief lords of the fee, suggests a date before *Quia emptores* (1290). The only witness who helps in dating is William Dyer, who occurs in 1261 and was a borough juror in 1284 (PRO JUST 1/40, m. 14; 1/44, m. 21d).

870 Gift in free alms by Nicholas *supra pontem* to Reading Abbey of 40s rent [in Reading],*ᵃ* viz., from the houses which Adam *de Kineware* held of him in fee 11s, from the stall which belonged to the widow of Turgis 4s, from the stall which belonged to Jordan of Coley (*Colle*) 4s, from a shop in All Saints Street 2s 6d, from a house which Nicholas's mother held 4s, from a shop which Adam *de Popler'* held 3s 7d, from a house which belonged to Ralph of Whitsbury (*Wichebur(ia)*)*ᵇ* 17d, from a house which John *de Heya* held 2s, from vacant land (*vacua terra*) which Henry *Wille* held 6d, and from 9 acres of arable land in the fields of Whitley (*Witeleya*)*ᶜ* 7s. To be held freely by rendering annually to Nicholas and his heirs 1d at Michaelmas for all service, exaction and demand. Warranty and sealing

[13th cent.; before Oct. 1241]

Bf47r–v; Cf18v; Cf173r
Pd. (in part) *New Pal. Soc. Facs.*, 1st ser., pl. 87 (with facsimile) (from Bf47r only)

Hiis testibus:*ᵈ* [Willelmo de Englefeld', Roberto de Auvers, Rogero de Hyda, Gilberto Ruffo, Hugone le Bolur, Roberto Wylle, Henrico Wille, Alano le Port(er), Daniele Wlveseye, Thoma de Henl(eia), Alano vinitario, Gervasio Galun, Adam de Kyneware, et multis aliis].

ᵃ Supplied from B, Cf18v rubrics   *ᵇ Whicchebury Cf173r*
ᶜ Whiteleia Cf173r
ᵈ B ends, Cf18v ends with et cetera, *the remainder being supplied from Cf173r*

Gilbert Ruffus was dead by Oct. 1241, being survived by his widow Agatha (PRO JUST 1/37, m. 35d); he occurs in Tilehurst in 1225 (JUST 1/36, m. 2) and is called 'of Reading' in 1228 (*Close Rolls 1227–31*, 70). Gervase Galun was a Reading borough juror in 1241 (1/37, m. 27d). For Henry Wille and Alan vintner, see no. 861 n.; for Daniel Wolvesey, see no. 862 n.

871 Quitclaim by William *Tripel*, nephew of Nicholas *Tripel*, to Reading Abbey of all his right in the capital messuage which belonged to Nicholas *Tripel* his uncle and in a workshop (*fabrica*) and stall which belonged to the said Nicholas in St Mary's parish, Reading. For this the abbey has given him 2 marks of silver and remitted to him 31s 4d. Sealing [? *c.* 1220 × 50]

B f48r; Cf19v; Cf173r

Hiis testibus:[a] [Hugone Bulatore, Henrico Wille, Roberto Wille, Nicholao supra pontem, Alano vinit(ario), Thoma de Henlea, et multis aliis].

[a] *B,Cf19v end, the remainder being supplied from Cf173r*

Date in general as for no. 850, q.v. for Hugh Bulator and Thomas of Henley, although the position of Henry Wille in the witness-list may suggest a date later rather than earlier in the range (see no. 861 n.). The deed was entered in the original section of B.

872 Gift by Alice T., widow of Thomas the merchant, to Henry Draper (*Draperius*), for his service, of a half messuage in High Street (*in alto vico*), Reading, next to the messuage which formerly belonged to Alexander of Coley (*Colley*). To be held freely by rendering to the chief lords of the fee the annual customary rent. Also quitclaim to the same of all her right in the same. For this Henry has given her 20s sterling as entry-fine, and will pay the debt of 15s which Thomas the merchant owed to John Butler (*le Butiller*). Warranty and sealing

[*c.* 1250 × 70]

Cf173v

Hiis testibus: Johanne Tinctore, Johanne de Oxonia, Mauricio Scot, Waltero Payn, Rad(ulf)o Pygaz, Johanne le Brid, Waltero Wisdom, Simone le Petit, Herberto Wundorclut, et Willelmo Bataille, et multis aliis.

The donor's husband was still alive in 1249 (see no. 1223). John Dyer was alive in 1261, but dead by Oct. 1284 (PRO JUST 1/40, m. 13d; 1/43, m. 8d). Alexander of Coley was a juror for Reading vill in 1248 (Clanchy, *Berks. Eyre of 1248*, 296). Walter Wisdom and William Battle do not certainly occur after 1261 (see nos. 861, 863, 868, 876). For Walter Payn, see no. 921.

873 Gift in free alms by Richard *Gerland* and Matilda, his wife, to Reading Abbey of a messuage in New Street which belonged to Nicholas the cook (*cocus*). To be held after the donors' deaths freely. Sealing [not later than 1258; ? mid-13th cent.]

B f49v; Cf21r; Cf173v

Hiis testibus:[a] [Henrico Wille, Daniele Wlveseye, Adam clerico et Johanne le Muleth tunc prepositis, Willelmo de Mussenden', Thoma de Henlea, Alano vinitario, Johanne Tinctore, Alexandro de Collea, Waltero de grangia, et multis aliis].

ª B,C f 21r end, the remainder being supplied from C f 173v

Entered in the original section of B and perhaps of the time when Henry Wille and Daniel Wolvesey were stewards of the Reading gild (see nos. 69, 862 n.). A John *Mulech'* and Alexander of Coley were jurors for Reading in 1248 (Clanchy, *Berks. Eyre of 1248*, 296).

874   Gift by Peter of Woking (*Wokynges*) to Hervey the goldsmith of the 2s annual rent which he used to receive at Michaelmas from the message which Peter *Chito(n)* held of him in Reading in Great Street (*in magno vico*). To be held freely and quit of all service and secular demand. For this Hervey has given him 20s. Warranty and sealing
[? *c.* 1220 × 50]

C f 174r; (noted) B f 49v; C f 20v

Hiis testibus: Hugone le Bolur, Henrico Wille, Roberto Wille, Alano vinit(ario), Alano Janitore, Thoma cissore, Nicholao clerico, Ada clerico, et multis aliis.

Date in general as for no. 850, q.v. for Hugh le Bolur, although the high position of Henry Wille in the witness-list suggests a date later rather than earlier in the range. Hervey the goldsmith was a juror for Reading in 1248 (Clanchy, *Berks. Eyre of 1248*, 296), as was Thomas the tailor in 1241 and 1248 (PRO JUST 1/37, m. 27d; Clanchy, *ibid.*, 296). Nicholas clerk and Adam clerk were dead by Feb. 1261 (see no. 861 n.). The deed was noted in the original section of B.

875   Lease, in chirograph form, by Walter, son of Gilbert the merchant, to William *Bordel*ª of a stall on the north side of the market of Reading between the house which belonged to Gilbert, Walter's father, and the stall of Roger son of Samson Spicer (*le Spic(er)*). To be held by William and his heirs or assigns for 4 years from Michaelmas, 39 Henry III, by rendering annually to Walter and his heirs or assigns 5s, viz., 2s 6d each at Michaelmas and Easter, for all service. For this William has given him 2s. Sealing by both parties
[*c.* 29 Sept. 1255]

C f 174r; (noted) B f 49v; C f 20v

Hiis testibus: Willelmo vinitario, Willelmo Osmund, Roberto de Sotesbrok', Willelmo aurifabro, Hugone Hayne, Petro cissore, et aliis.

ªBurdel in notes in B,C f 20v

The date must be approximately that from which the lease was to run.

876   Quitclaim and surrender in the full court of Reading by William son of Roger to Walter of Humber (*Humbre*), then granger (*gernetarius*) [of Reading Abbey], of all the land which his father Roger sometime held in the street called *Lundemersshelane* in Reading. For this the granger has given him 4s sterling and a tunic, and has remitted 18s arrears of rent. Sealing [before 1261; ? mid-13th cent.]

Cf174r–v

Hiis testibus: Roberto Wille, Daniele Wlveseye, Henrico Wille, Alano vinitore, Willelmo de Mussenden', Thoma le Taillour, Ada clerico, Thoma de Henle, Willelmo Bataille, Gilberto Scot', et multis aliis.

Daniel Wolvesey and Adam clerk were dead by Feb. 1261 (see nos. 861 n., 862 n.). For Robert Wille and Thomas tailor, see respectively nos. 855 n., 874 n. Henry Wille occurs as a vintner in Reading between 1241 and 1261 (PRO JUST 1/37, m. 35d; 1/40, m. 29d) and was a steward of Reading gild in 1254 (see no. 69). Gilbert Scot was a juror for Reading in 1241 and 1248 (JUST 1/37, m. 27d; Clanchy, *Berks. Eyre of 1248*, 296). The granger probably came from Humber, near the abbey's priory of Leominster (Herefs.).

877   Gift by Roger *Banstr'*,[a] tailor, to Alan *atte Knolle*, for his service and a certain sum of money, of 16d annual rent which he used to receive at Easter and Michaelmas in equal portions from a messuage in Old Street, Reading, between the tenement of Richard Tailor (*le Taillour*) and that of Robert *Hendy*. To be held freely of the chief lords of the fee by the due and customary services. Warranty and sealing

5 Jan. 1317

Cf174v

Hiis testibus: Rad(ulf)o de Bello, Thoma Syward, Johanne le Acatur, Henrico de Greywell', Rad(ulf)o le Foughel, Rogero Cosyn, Johanne de Pangebourne, Willelmo de Foulrithe, Rad(ulf)o Monncy, et aliis. Dat' die mercurii proxima in vigilia Epiphanie domini, anno regni regis Edwardi filii regis Edwardi decimo.

[a] *Sic, ? rectius* Banastr'

878   *Gift by Hamo of Oxford, clerk, to Reading Abbey of ½ mark's worth of rent to be received from his stalls in the Drapery of Reading at the end of the 5 years during which the abbey has all his rents in Reading, saving to the abbey 24s 6d annually which he owes from his rents in Reading*

[late 12th × early 13th cent.]

Af99v; Bf48r; Cf19r; Cff174v–175r

Sciant tam[a] presentes quam[b] futuri quod ego Hamo de Oxeneford[c] clericus, pro animabus patris[d] et matris mee et mea et predecessorum meorum, dedi et concessi ecclesie Rading(ensi)[e] et abbati et monachis ibidem deo servientibus dimidiam marcatam redditus in Rading(ia),

salvis eisdem[j]quolibet anno[f] viginti quatuor solidis[g] et sex denariis
quos eis per annum de redditibus meis in Rading(ia) reddere debeo,
assignandam super seldas meas in Draperia[h] in fine illorum quinque
annorum per quos habent omnes redditus meos de[i] Rading(ia). Ita
quod quicumque seldas illas tenuerint de predicta dimidia marca
quolibet anno dictis abbati et monachis satisfacient. Et ut hec mea
donatio et concessio rata et inconcussa permaneat, presens scriptum
sigilli mei appositione[j] roboravi. Hiis testibus:[k] Hugone Maisant,[l]
Rogero vinetario[m] et Turgiso [n][tunc prepositis, Hugone filio Remundi,
Gilberto fratre eius, Roberto de Walingford, Gilberto Fachel,][n] et
multis aliis.

[a] Om. in B and both texts in C
[c] 'Oxon' B,Cf19r
[e] Radyngie Cff174v–175r
[g] A has solidos
[i] in Cff174v–175r
[k] B,Cf19r end
[m] vinitario Cff174v–175r
[n-n] Om. in A, supplied from Cff174v–175r

[b] et B, both C texts
[d] Insert mei Cff174v–175r
[ff] Om. in Cff174v–175r
[h] draparia Cff174v–175r
[j] apposiscione Cff174v–175r
[l] Maysent Cff174v–175r

This deed was entered among 13th-century additions in A. The donor is presumably
the Hamo son of Walter of Oxford who witnesses in Reading in 1186 × 1213 (no. 844).
Hugh *Maisant* and Turgis witness in the same period (nos. 840, 845); Hugh son of
Raymond witnesses in 1204 × 15 and 1219 (nos. 392, 779) and Robert of Wallingford
in 1165 × 73 and 1189 × 93 (no. 826, Appendix B, no. 1).

879   Quitclaim by John son of John Goldsmith (*le Goldsmyth*) of
Reading to Abbot Nicholas [of Whaplode] and the convent of Reading of all his right in a shop which formerly belonged to his father in
the Lormery[1] (*lormeria*), Reading, between the tenements of Edmund
Barber (*le Barbur*) on each side. Sealing   [1305 × 28]

Cf175r

Hiis testibus: Radul(f)o de la Bataille, Thoma Syward, Johanne Lacatur, Rad(ulf)o de Helme, Gilberto de Copenhull', et multis aliis.

The dating limits are those of Nicholas of Whaplode's abbacy.

  1. *Alias* Lorimer Lane, called in modern times Hosier Street (Slade, 'Reading', 5).

880   Gift by William *le Poer* of Stoke Basset[1] (*Stok' Basset*) to Robert
Fulconis of Reading, for his service and 40s sterling, of 6s annual rent
which he used to receive in Reading, viz., from the messuage which
Walter the smith (*faber*) held of him in Minster Street (*la Munstrestret*)
between the messuage of William *Tilli* and that of Richard *Pig* 4s,
and from the messuage which Scholastica of Maidenhatch (*Maden-
hacche*) held of him in the street leading to the house of John Franklin
(*le Frannkelayn*) 2s. To be held freely by rendering annually to the

donor and his heirs 1 clove at Easter for all secular service, exaction and demand. Warranty and sealing [*c.* 1260 × 1284]

C f 175r–v

Hiis testibus: Willelmo de Bleobury, Willelmo de Whitele, Willelmo Tilly, Willelmo de Mussendene, Johanne le Grom, Galfr(ed)o Gomme, Bartholomeo de Wlveseye, Nicholao le Butiller, Radul(f)o de Heghfeld, et aliis.

The donee served as a royal justice-in-eyre between 1280 and May 1287 (Crook, *General Eyre*, 160–8) and was dead by 8 Sept. 1287 (*Cal. Fine R. 1272–1307*, 240). William of Blewbury occurs from 1265 × 6 (see no. 855 n.) and Bartholomew Wolvesey was dead by Oct. 1284 (PRO JUST 1/43, m. 9). Geoffrey Gomme was an elector and juror for Reading in 1269 (JUST 1/42, m. 19) and occurs in *c.* 1273 and 1284 (see no. 998; JUST 1/44, m. 15d). Ralph of Heckfield was a juror for Reading in 1248 and 1269 (Clanchy, *Berks. Eyre of 1248*, 296; JUST 1/42, m. 19) and a bailiff of the borough in 1261 (JUST 1/40, m. 14d), and occurs with his wife Joan in 1286 (*Cal. Close R. 1279–88*, 435).

1. I.e. North Stoke, Oxon. (M. Gelling, *The Place-Names of Oxfordshire*, part I, English Place-Name Soc., xxiii (1953), 49).

881 Gift and quitclaim by Robert *Fulcon'* to Abbot Robert [of Burg-ate] and the convent of Reading of 5s [annual]*ª* rent in Reading, of which 4s come from a messuage house (*de quadam mesuag' domo*) which Richard *le Pig* holds next to Tothill (*Tothull'*), and 12d from a mes-suage which Henry Cooper (*le Coupere*) sometime held and now John of Romsey (*Romeseye*) holds. For this the abbot and convent have given him in exchange a messuage which formerly belonged to Alexander Millward (*le Muluard*) next to the messuage which formerly belonged to Oliver of Haseley (*Haselegh'*) in Old Street, and another messuage which formerly belonged to Robert *Agath'* in the same town. Warranty and sealing [1269 × 87]

C f 175v

ᵇ[Hiis testibus:]*ᵇ* domino Rolando de Erle, domino Bartholomeo de Erle, Willelmo de Blebury, Roberto de Preston', Gilberto Pynson, Nicholao le Butiller, Johanne Vachel, Stephano le Grom, Radul(f)o de Agmodesham, et aliis.

ª Supplied   *ᵇ⁻ᵇ Supplied*

After Robert of Burgate became abbot and before the death of Robert Fulconis (see no. 880 n.).

882 Gift by Geoffrey the smith (*faber*) and Petronilla his wife to Sir Robert *Fulcon'* of 12d annual rent at Michaelmas from a messuage in Old Street, Reading, within the Seven Bridges opposite the messuage of Thomas Tanner (*le Tannur*). To be held freely by rendering annu-

ally to the donors and their heirs a rose on the feast of the Nativity of
St John [Baptist]*a* for all secular service, exaction and demand. For
this Sir Robert has given them 1 mark of silver. Warranty and sealing
with the donors' seals   [*c.* 1270 × 1287]

C ff 175v–176r

Hiis testibus: Gilberto Pynsun, Gilberto de Molesham, Radul(f)o de
la Bataille, Willelmo de Mussenden', Nicholao le Butiller, Willelmo
le Chamberlayn, Johanne Aurifabro, Elia mercatore, Johanne clerico,
et aliis.

a Supplied

Before the death of Robert Fulconis (see no. 880 n.). Gilbert Pincent (different from
the Gilbert of no. 857) was a juror for Reading hundred in 1269 and occurs as late as
1303 (PRO JUST 1/42, m. 19; below, no. 975). Gilbert of Moulsham occurs in 1275
and 1278 (nos. 764, 512) and Ralph of Battle witnesses Reading deeds down to 1317
(no. 977).

883 Gift in free alms by Robert *Fulcon'* to Reading Abbey of 22s 9d
annual and quit rent in Reading, which he acquired from the executors of John *Lyl*, his late partner (*socius*), of which 13s 6d rent come
from the capital messuage which formerly belonged to Reginald *le
fourbour*[1] in London Street, and 2s 3d from a messuage which Robert
Rufus sometime held of the said John and now Robert Tailor (*le
Taillour*) holds in the same street. Warranty and sealing
                                         [*c.* 1270 × 1287; ? 1278 × 87]

C f 176r

Hiis testibus: domino Rolando de Erle, Bartholomeo de Erle, miltibus,
Roberto de Preston', Nicholao le Botiller, Willelmo le Chamberlayn,
Johanne Vachel, Ricardo de Grenham, Radul(f)o de Hecfeud, Wil-
lelmo le Clerk', et multis aliis.

Before the donor's death (see no. 880 n.); if John *Lyl* is the same as John *Lill'* in no. 512,
after Oct. 1278. Robert of Preston was involved in cases in Reading and Earley in 1284
and occurs as a witness between 1278 and 1290 (PRO JUST 1/43, mm 9d, 12; see nos.
512, 1245). William Chamberlain was an elector and juror for Reading borough in
1284 and occurs down to 1297 (JUST 1/44, m. 21d; below, no. 952; *Berks. Arch. Journ.*,
lx (1962), 104). Richard of Greenham occurs in Reading in 1284 (JUST 1/43, m. 9).
The rents specified fall short of the total given by 7s.

    1. ? the furbisher.

884 *Gift by Robert of Woking to Roger Gold of Oxford of his land with a
messuage in the northern part of Great Street, Reading. If, after the donor's
death, his wife Alice or her heirs shall claim any right in the land so that Roger
or his heirs shall suffer damages or lose it, they shall compensate them for their
expenses on the same*   [*c.* early 13th cent.]

Cf176v; (noted) Bf49v; Cf20v

Sciant presentes et futuri quod ego Robertus de Wokynge, consensu et bono favore Alicie uxoris mee et heredum meorum, dedi et concessi et hac presenti carta mea confirmavi Rogero Golde*a* de Oxonia pro homagio suo et servitio suo terram meam cum quodam mesuagio*b* et omnibus pertinentiis suis in Radyng(ia) in boriali parte magni vici ex opposito domus venalis que vocatur Bredhous, quam adquisivi de proprio questu meo proximam inter domum Rad(ulf)i de Wogh-enerse*l* et terram quam cepi in liberum maritagium cum uxore mea Alicia predicta. Tenend(am) et habend(am) de me et heredibus meis sibi et heredibus suis iure et hereditarie, bene et in pace, libere et quiete ab omni servitio et ab omni consuetudine et omni demanda, reddendo annuatim michi et heredibus meis decem solidos ad quatuor terminos anni quocumque casu*c* vel taillag(io) contingente, scilicet ad festum sancti Michaelis triginta denarios et ad Natale domini triginta denarios et ad festum sancte Marie in Marcio triginta denarios et ad Nativitatem sancti Iohannis Baptiste triginta denarios. Et si contingat quod Alicia predicta, mulier prefati Roberti, fraude vel ingenio vel aliqua suggestione post decessum viri sui Roberti predicti ius aliquod in *d*terra predicta*d* clamaverit unde nocumentum emergat predicto Rogero vel heredibus suis, vel perdere debeant predictam terram, Alicia illa predicta recompensabit totum custum predicti Rogeri de predicto tenemento rationabiliter et plenarie, vel heredes si idem clamare voluerint, per visum fidelium virorum qui melius veritatem sciant. Pro hac autem donatione et concessione dedit mihi predictus Rogerus unam marcam argenti in introitu et de recognitione. Et ego et heredes mei warantizabimus predictam terram predicto Rogero et heredibus suis contra omnes [homines]*e* et omnes feminas. Ut hoc sit [ratum]*f* et stabile *g*in perpetuum,*g* sigilli mei appositione corroboravi. Hiis testibus: Hugone Maycent, Ricardo Bullok', Rogero vinit(ario), Turgis, Thoma de Henl(eia), Herberto mercatore, Rogero Brutun, Osberto Wlveseye, Gilberto Fachel, et multis aliis.

a Ms has Bolde, *but the more carefully written* Golde *in the notes in B and Cf 20v seems preferable*
b Ms has domo *marked for deletion,* mes' *interlined*
c *Reading uncertain; Ms has* caū
d-d Ms has terram predictam   *e Supplied*
f Interlined   *g g Ms has* imperpetuum

Hugh Maycent, Roger vintner, Turgis and Gilbert Vachell also witness no. 878 (q.v.). For Richard *Bullok*', see no. 618 n. For Thomas of Henley, see no. 850 n. The suggested date is also supported by the interesting and somewhat archaic diplomatic of the deed. For Great Street, see no. 867 n. 1.

1. Possibly Winnersh (Berks.).

885 Quitclaim by Abbot Richard [of Appletree] and the convent of
Osney to Abbot Richard [I, of Chichester] and the convent of Reading
of an annual rent of 38d which the abbot and convent of Osney used
to receive by assignment and bequest of Peter son of Robert *Bodyn* of
Oxford from the tenements which sometime belonged to Geoffrey son
of Baldwin in Great Street (*in magno vico*), Reading. Sealing with the
chapter seal   22 Feb. 1260

> C ff 176v–177r; BL Cott. Vitell. E xv (Osney cartulary) f 20v
> Pd. *Cartl. Oseney*, vi. 164–5 (from Osney cartulary)

Facta fuit hec scriptura apud Osen(eiam) in Cathedra sancti Petri
apostoli, anno [regni]*ᵃ* regis Henrici filii regis Johannis quadragesimo
quarto. Valete.

> *ᵃ Supplied from Osney cartulary*

Reading Abbey paid Osney 40s for this quitclaim (*Cartl. Oseney*, vi. 164).

886 Quitclaim by Sarah, widow of Andrew Palmer (*Palm(er)*), and
Walter, son of Andrew Palmer, to Robert *Bodyn* and his heirs or assigns
of the whole tenement in Reading which belonged to Geoffrey son of
Baldwin, Sarah's father, from which the abbot of Reading used to
render 18d annually to Sarah and Walter, and of the whole tenement
which belonged to the same Geoffrey in the same town, from which
Ralph Palmer (*Palmer'*) used to render them 20d annually; saving
that the said abbot and the said Ralph shall hold in inheritance of
the said Robert as they held of Sarah and Walter. For this Robert
has given them 2 marks of silver as entry-fine. Sealing with the seals
of Sarah and Walter   [*c.* 1220]

> C f 177r; BL Cott. Vitell. E xv (Osney cartulary) f 20v
> Pd. *Cartl. Oseney*, vi. 164

Hiis testibus: Thoma filio Edwini*ᵃ* tunc maiore Oxon(ie), Turaldo
Cordewan(ario), Thoma filio Wid(onis), Petro filio Turaldi, Gal-
fr(edo) de Stowell', Willelmo Tannur, Willelmo filio eius, Rad(ulfo)
Palm(er) de Radyng(ia), Alano de Radyng(ia), Johanne Laudias, et
aliis.

> *ᵃ C has* Edwardi, *corrected reading from Osney cartulary; the latter text ends at this point with*
> et cetera

The date is that suggested by Salter in *Cartl. Oseney*. Thomas fitz Edwin occurs several
times as mayor of Oxford—see, e.g., *A Cartulary of the Hospital of St John the Baptist*, ed.
H. E. Salter, 3 vols. (Oxford Historical Soc., 1914–16), i. 20, 207, etc.; ii. 71, 112, etc.
The first mayor of Oxford by name occurs at the beginning of the 13th century, and
the early mayors seem to have held office for life (*VCH Oxon.*, iv. 58).

887 Gift by Agnes, daughter of the late William *Galopyn*, to Thomas the merchant, for his service, of a messuage which she had in Great Street (*in magno vico*), Reading, between the messuage which formerly belonged to Alexander of Coley (*Colleya*) and that which formerly belonged to Richard [*Pucius*],[a] and of 29d annual rent at Michaelmas, viz., from a messuage which formerly belonged to Herbert the merchant in High Street (*in alto vico*), Reading, next to the messuage of John *le War*(*e*)[b] on the east 16d, and from a messuage which formerly belonged to Robert Glover (*le Glover'*) in Great Street (*in magno vico*), Reading, next to that which formerly belonged to Stephen of St Albans on the west, 13d. To be held freely by rendering annually to Reading Abbey 9d, to Robert *de Auvers* and his heirs 12d, to Ralph the goldsmith and his heirs 9d, and to the donor and her heirs ½d as increment at Michaelmas, for all secular service, exaction and demand. For this Thomas has given her 40s sterling as entry-fine. Warranty and sealing   [before 1261; ? mid-13th cent.]

Cf 177r–v

Hiis testibus: Henrico Wille, Daniele Wlveseie, Alano vinit(ario), Adam clerico, Nicholao clerico, Thoma de Henl(eia), Johanne Tinctore, Adam Mobone, Willelmo le Paum(er), et multis aliis.

[a] *Om. in Ms, supplied from no. 889*
[b] *For expansion, see no. 889*

Daniel Wolvesey, Adam clerk and Nicholas clerk were dead by Feb. 1261 (see nos. 861 n., 862 n.). The position of Henry Wille and Daniel Wolvesey in the witness-list suggests the time when they were stewards of the Reading gild (see no. 862 n.). This deed appears to differentiate between Great Street and High Street, but they were in fact the same (see no. 889 n. and above no. 867 n. 1).

888 Gift by Agnes, daughter of the late William *Galopyn*, to Thomas the merchant of Reading, for his service, of half a messuage in High Street (*in alto vico*), Reading, next to the messuage which formerly belonged to Alexander of Coley (*Colle*) on the east, and of 8d annual rent appurtenant to that half from a messuage which formerly belonged to Herbert the merchant in High Street (*in alto vico*), Reading, and of 6½d annual rent appurtenant to the same half from a messuage which formerly belonged to Robert Glover (*Glovar'*) in the same street, next to the messuage of the said Herbert on the east. To be held freely by rendering annually to Reading Abbey 4d for all secular service, exaction and demand, and to the chief lords of the fee the customary annual rent, viz., to Robert *Dauvers* 6d and to Ralph of Wallingford (*Walingford'*) the goldsmith 4½d, and to the donor and her heirs 1 clove, all at Michaelmas, for all service and demand. For this Thomas has given her 20s of silver as entry-fine. Warranty and sealing   [before 1261; ? mid-13th cent.]

C ff 177v–178r

Hiis testibus: Daniele Wlveseye, Thoma le*a* Cordewaner, Ada de le
Popeler, tunc prepositis, Johanne Wille, Johanne Tinctore, Willelmo
Palmar(io), Willelmo Osmund, Stephano de Celar(io), Stephano de
Sancto Albano, et multis aliis.

a Ms repeats le

Daniel Wolvesey was dead by Feb. 1261 (see no. 862 n.). For John Dyer, see no. 850 n.
Adam de Popeler occurs in Reading in 1248 (Clanchy, *Berks. Eyre of 1248*, 397) and
William Osmund witnesses in 1255 (no. 875). This deed apparently concerns half the
property given in no. 887 and cannot be much different in date, although here the rent
is said to be in High Street (see no. 889 n.). For the half messuage alone, see no. 872.

889 Quitclaim by Agnes, daughter of the late William *Galoppyn*, to
Thomas the merchant of Reading of all her right in 29d annual rent
appurtenant to a messuage in High Street (*in alto vico*), Reading,*a*
between the messuage formerly belonging to Alexander of Coley
(*Collee*) and that formerly belonging to Richard *Pucius*, which rent
Agnes used to receive from the said Thomas from two messuages in
High Street (*in alto vico*), Reading, viz., from that formerly belonging
to Herbert the merchant to the east of the house of John *le Ware* 16d,
and from that formerly belonging to Robert Glover (*Glovar'*) next to
the messuage which formerly belonged to Stephen of St Albans on
the west 13d, at Michaelmas. *b*[To be held]*b* by rendering annually
to Reading Abbey 9d of the said 29d, and to Sir Robert *Dauvers* 12d,
both at Michaelmas, and to Ralph of Wallingford (*Walingford*) the
goldsmith 9d. For this Thomas has given her 4s sterling. Warranty
and sealing   [before 1261; ? mid-13th cent.]

C f 178r

Hiis testibus: Daniele Wlveseye, et multis aliis.

*a Ms has here the later passage concerning Herbert merchant's messuage, copied in error at this
point and marked for deletion*
b-b Supplied

Before Daniel Wolvesey's death (see no. 862 n.). This deed quitclaims the same rents
given in no. 887 and stipulates payment of the same dues there specified, except for the
½d payable to Agnes and her heirs. The date is probably similar. Unlike no. 887, this
deed locates the main messuage and the messuages from which the appurtenant rents
are due all in High Street, thereby confirming that Great Street and High Street were
the same (see also no. 867 n. 1).

890 Quitclaim by Elena *de la Cumbe* to John Butler (*le Butiller*) of all
her right in the whole tenement which formerly belonged to William

Galopyn in High Street (*in alto vico*), Reading, between the tenement of Ralph *le Lummer* and that of Daniel Wolvesey (*Wlveseye*). For this John has given her 2s of silver as entry-fine. Sealing

[before 1261; ? mid-13th cent.]

Cf178v

Hiis testibus: Stephano de la Wyle, et multis aliis.

Daniel Wolvesey, who appears to be still alive, died before Feb. 1261 (see no. 862 n.). Stephen de la Wyle witnesses several Reading deeds of before 1261 and one in Whitley of ?1249 (no. 1224), and occurs in 1248 and 1261 (Clanchy, *Berks. Eyre of 1248*, 182; PRO JUST 1/40, m. 29d). It is uncertain whether John Butler can be connected with the John Butler of Bradfield who was a juror for Theale hundred in 1269 and 1284 (PRO JUST 1/42, m. 19; 1/44, m. 21d).

891 *Gift by John son of John to his lord, William Achard, of two islands at Reading, viz., a large one nearest the Gild Hall and a small one next to the island where the tenter-yard was, and also the place opposite the large island for access, all in exchange for certain land which William has given him in Sparsholt* [*Berks.*] [1204 × 15]

Cf178v; (noted) Bf49r; Cf20r

Sciant presentes et futuri quod ego Iohannes filius Iohannis dedi et concessi Willelmo Achard domino meo duas insulas apud Radyng-(iam), scilicet magnam insulam proximam de Gildhalle et parvam insulam iuxta insulam ubi tentorium fuit, et preterea totam placeam coram magna insula versus vicum per quam habebit introitum suum in magnam insulam, tenend(as) sibi et cui voluerit de me et heredibus meis *a*in perpetuum.*a* Et sciendum est quod ego et heredes mei debemus acquietare predictas insulas cum predicta placea versus abbatem de Radyng(ia) *b*in omnibus*b* pro escambio cuiusdam terre quod predictus Willelmus mihi fecit in Spersolt'. Et ego et heredes mei debemus warantizare predicta tenementa predicto Willelmo et cui voluerit *a*in perpetuum.*a* Et ut hec donatio et concessio rata et stabilis permaneant, presentis scripti testimonio et sigilli mei appositione confirmavi. Hiis testibus: Iohanne de Wokenholt' tunc vic(ecomite), et multis aliis.

a-a Ms has imperpetuum   *b-b Interlined*

John de Wickenholt was sheriff of Berkshire 1204–15 (*List of Sheriffs*, 6). A marginal note in Cf178v reads: *Redyng' iuxta Gyldhallam.* This deed contains the earliest known reference to the Reading Gild Hall (cf. *VCH Berks.*, iii. 344) and an early indication of cloth-making in Reading.

892 *Quitclaim by William Achard to Reading Abbey of the whole tenement which he sometime had from John of Sparsholt in Reading, viz., the same two islands and place; for this the abbey has given him 22 marks of silver in his* *great need for the ransom of his body*   [1204 × 20]

A f 108r; B ff 48v–49r; C f 2or; C ff 178v–179r

Sciant presentes et futuri quod ego Willelmus Achard, pro maximo
comodo meo, dimisi et resignavi et quietum clamavi abbati et conventui de Rading(ia) totum tenementum quod aliquando habui de
Iohanne de Spersolte in villa de[a] Rading(ia), videlicet duas insulas,
magnam scilicet insulam que est iuxta Gildhalle ultra aquam et
parvam insulam que est iuxta insulam ubi tentorium fuit, cum placia[b]
que est coram magna insula versus vicum et cum omnibus que super
tenementum illud fuerint[c] vel ad dictum tenementum pertinuerint;
habend(um) et tenend(um) [d]predictis abbati[d] et conventui in dominico suo vel sicut eis placuerit iure perpetuo absolute et quiete absque
aliquo retinemento[e] vel aliqua vexatione vel demanda que eis unquam
fieri possit a me [f]vel ab[f] heredibus meis vel ab aliquo ex meis aliquo
tempore. Quod ut firmum et stabile sit in perpetuum, presenti scripto
sigillum meum apposui et coram villata de Rading(ia) in plena potestate mea[g] sponte me et omnes meos de predicto tenemento in perpetuum dimisi et predictos abbatem et conventum inde plenarie
saisivi.[h] Et propter[i] hanc donationem, resignationem et quietam clamationem de toto iure quod ego vel heredes mei habuimus vel habere
potuimus in predicto tenemento, dederunt mihi predictus[j] abbas et
conventus viginti duas marchas[k] argenti in magna[l] necessitate mea
pro redemptione corporis mei. Hiis testibus:[m] G(alfredo) archidiacono
Berkesir(e),[n] magistro Nicholao Martel, Henrico de Kamel, Thoma
de Erleia, Gilone Revel, Rogero fratre suo, Roberto Painel, Gervasio
Puncon, Hugone filio Maisent, Alano vinitore, Rad(ulfo) Wille, Reginaldo senescallo, Roberto Wille, Turgisio, Roberto de Sideham, Petro
de Ruðerwika, Giliberto Ruffo, Fulcone fratre suo, et multis aliis.

[a] *Om. in* C f 2or
[c] fuerunt C f 2or
[e] *Insert* mei C ff 178v–179r
[g] *Insert* et C ff 178v–179r
[i] per C ff 178v–179r
[k] marcas *in all other texts*
[m] B,C f 2or end
[n] de Berk', *followed by* et multis aliis C ff 178v–179r

[b] placea C f 2or
[d-d] A *has* predicti abbatis
[f-f] et C f 2or
[h] seisivi C ff 178v–179r
[j] predicti *in all other texts*
[l] maxima *in all other texts*

After no. 891 and before William Achard's death, which had occurred by 1220 (K. J.
Stringer, 'Some documents concerning a Berkshire family and Monk Sherborne Priory,
Hampshire', *Berks. Arch. Journ.*, lxiii (1967–8), 34). The rubrics of B and C f 2or read:
Carta Willelmi Achard de duabus insulis et quadam placia in Rading', to which C adds in a
later hand: *iuxta Gyldhallam*. C f 178v has in the margin: *Redyng' iuxta Gyldhallam*.

893   *Gift by Ralph Purcel to Reading Abbey, for 10 marks, of the land which
the abbey gave him in Reading for his service*   [1173 × early 13th cent.]

B f48r–v; C f19v; C f179r

Universis sancte matris ecclesie filiis ad quos presens scriptum pervenerit Rad(ulfus) Purcel,[a] salutem in domino. Noverit universitas vestra me [f48v] dedisse et concessisse, pro amore dei et intuitu caritatis et pro decem marcis quas mihi pre manibus dederunt, abbati et monachis de Rading(ia) terram illam quam mihi pro servitio meo dederunt in Rading(ia), scilicet illam[b] que est ex orientali parte vie que est inter novum fossatum et Kanetam et modo edificata est. Ut autem hec mea donatio rata et inconcussa in perpetuum permaneat, eam presenti scripto et sigilli mei munimine duxi confirmare.

[a] Porcel *C f179r* [b] *Om. in C f179r*

Not earlier than 1173, since this is the land leased to Ralph Purcel and his heirs by Abbot Joseph (no. 834); Ralph received another deed from that abbot and witnessed two further deeds by him (nos. 835, 832–3). Perhaps of about the same date as no. 894, q.v.

894 *Release, quitclaim and gift in free alms by Ralph Purcel to Reading Abbey of all the land which he held of it in Reading, viz., that which William Scot held of him and that which Alan the vintner held of him*

[late 12th × early 13th cent.]

B f48v; C ff 19v–20r; C f179r

Sciant presentes et futuri quod ego Rad(ulfus) Purcell', pro salute anime mee et omnium meorum, reddidi et quiet(am)clamavi,[a] dedi, concessi et hac presenti carta mea confirmavi deo et beate Marie et abbati et conventui de Rading(ia) totam terram quam de eis tenui in villa de Rading(ia) cum omnibus pertinentiis suis, videlicet terram cum domibus et edificiis[b] quam de me tenuit W(illelmus)[c] Scot et terram cum domibus et edificiis[b] et omnibus pertinentiis quam de me tenuit Alanus vinitor. Habendam et tenendam in liberam puram et perpetuam elemosinam quietam et absolutam ab omni demanda et calumpnia que eis unquam[d] fieri possit de me vel de heredibus meis in perpetuum. Et ne eis aliqua vexatio unquam[d] de predicta terra in posterum fieri possit, illam et quicquid iuris in ea[e] habui vel habere potui pro me et pro heredibus meis abiuravi et coram multis viris eis reddidi et presenti scripto et sigilli mei appositione[f] predictam resignationem et quiet(am)clam(ationem),[g] donationem et concessionem fideliter roboravi.[h] [Hiis testibus: Willelmo Basset, et multis aliis.]

[a] quietumclamavi *C ff 19v–20r*, quietam clamavi *C f179r*
[b] edeficiis *C ff 19v–20r* [c] *Expansion from C f179r*
[d] umquam *C f179r* [e] eam *C f179r (in error)*
[f] apposiscione *C f179r*

ᵍquietamclam' *C.ff 19v–20r*, quietam clamationem *C f 179r*
ʰ*B,C ff 19v–20r* end with 'T', *the remainder being supplied from C f 179r*

Ralph Purcel occurs from the time of Abbot Joseph, 1173–86 (see no. 893n.). The later dating limit is suggested by the reference to Alan vintner; whether he is the same as the Alan vintner who was a borough juror in 1241 and 1248 (see no. 861 n.) is uncertain, but he can be identified with 'Alan of Reading, vintner,' and 'Alan vintner of Reading' who occurs between 1215 and 1224 (*Rot. Lit. Claus.*, i. 242, 330; *Cur. Reg. R.*, xi. 469) and with the Alan vintner who witnessed a gift to Reading Abbey in Sawbridgeworth in 1204 × 15 and a deed to the abbey in Reading in 1204 × 20 (nos. 392, 892); see also nos. 854, 909.

895   Gift by Ralph Baker (*Pistor*) to Roger of Stanford (*Stanford*), for his service, of 1d annual rent at Michaelmas which Nicholas the clerk used to pay him for a messuage and a half messuage which he held of him in London Street, Reading, viz., from the half messuage next to the messuage of Robert *Wille* on the south ½d, and from the messuage between that of Robert *Wille* and that of Roger Carpenter (*Carpenter*) ½d. To be held freely and quit of all secular service, exaction and demand. For this Roger has given him 12d sterling as entry-fine. Warranty and sealing   [not later than 1258; ? mid-13th cent.]

C f 179v; (noted) B f 49v; C f 20v

Hiis testibus: Henrico Wille, Daniele Wlveseye, et aliis.

Noted in the original section of B and perhaps of the time when Henry Wille and Daniel Wolvesey were stewards of the Reading gild (see no. 862 n.).

896   Gift by the same to the same, for his service, of 1d annual rent at Michaelmas which John *Rufus* used to pay him for a half messuage which he held of him in London Street, Reading, next to the messuage of the said John on the north. To be held freely and quit of all secular service, exaction and demand. For this Roger has given him 12d as entry-fine. Warranty and sealing
[not later than 1258; ? mid-13th cent.]

C f 179v; (noted) B f 49v; C f 20v

Hiis testibus: Henrico Wylle, Daniele Wlveseye, et aliis.

Date as for no. 895.

897   Gift by John of Malmesbury (*Malmesbury*) to William of Stanford (*Stannford*), citizen and merchant of London, for his service, of a messuage in New Street, Reading, between the messuage of Richard *Fregant* and that of William *Channtrel*, as defined by the boundaries on all sides. To be held freely by William, his heirs or assigns or by anyone to whom he may wish to give, sell, bequeath or assign it, by rendering annually to Reading Abbey 10d at Michaelmas, to Robert of Preston (*Preston'*) and his heirs 6s, viz., 3s each at Easter and Michaelmas, and to the donor and his heirs 1 clove at Michaelmas, for all secular service, custom, exaction and demand. Warranty. For this William has given him 100s as entry-fine. Sealing   [*c.* 1270 × 90]

Cf 180r

Hiis testibus: Willelmo le Chamberleyn, et aliis.

Before *Quia emptores* (1290). For Robert of Preston between 1278 and 1290, and William Chamberlain between 1284 and 1297, see no. 883 n.

898 Gift by Hugh *le Norreys* to John of Malmesbury (*Malmesbury*), for his service, of a messuage in New Street, Reading, between the messuage of Richard *Fregant* and that of William *Channtrel*. To be held freely by rendering annually to Reading Abbey 10d at Michaelmas, to Robert of Preston (*Preston'*) and his heirs 6s, viz., 3s each at Easter and Michaelmas, and to the donor and his heirs 1 clove at Michaelmas, for all secular service, exaction and demand. Warranty and sealing   [*c.* 1270 × 90]

Cf 180r

Hiis testibus: Willelmo le Chamberlayn, et aliis.

Date as for no. 897, although this clearly pre-dates that deed, however short the interval between them may have been. A comparison of the rents payable in each deed shows that in no. 897 John of Malmesbury simply stepped into Hugh le Norreys's position, the latter dropping out of the chain.

899 Gift by William of Stanford (*Stannford'*) to William Carter (*le Careter*) and Matilda his wife and their heirs or assigns, for their service and $4\frac{1}{2}$ marks of silver, of a messuage in New Street, Reading, which sometime belonged to Hugh *le Norreys* between the messuage of Richard *Fregaunt* and that of William *Chauntrel*. To be held freely by rendering annually to Reading Abbey 10d at Michaelmas, to Robert of Preston (*Preston'*) and his heirs 6s, viz., 3s each at Easter and Michaelmas, and to the donor and his heirs 1 clove at Michaelmas, for all secular service, exaction and demand. Warranty and sealing   [*c.* 1270 × 90]

Cf 180v

Hiis testibus: Willelmo le Chamberlayn, et aliis.

Date as for no. 897, although this is later than it, however short the interval between them may have been. Again, as in no. 897, the donor here steps into the position of the previous recipient of the clove rent.

900 Quitclaim by Robert of Preston (*Preston'*) to William Carter (*le Charetter*) and Matilda, his wife, of all his right in the 6s annual rent which he used to receive from them in equal portions at Michaelmas and Easter from a tenement in New Street, Reading, between the messuage of Richard *Fregannt* and that of William *Chauntrel*. Sealing
[? late 13th cent.]

C f 180v

Hiis testibus: Willelmo de Bleobur' tunc senescallo, et aliis.

After no. 899. For Robert of Preston, see no. 883 n. William of Blewbury occurs as steward of Reading Abbey between 1267 and 1303 (see no. 855 n.).

901 Gift by Joan, widow of the late William *de Porta* of Reading, to John of Long Sutton (*Longgesuthtone*), perpetual vicar of St Laurence's church, Reading, of a tenement in New Street, Reading, between the tenement of Ralph of Battle (*de Bello*) and that of Philip the merchant. To be held freely of the chief lords of the fee by the services due. Warranty and sealing　　　　　　　　　　　　　　　5 Nov. 1304

C ff 180v–181r

Dat' Radyng' die jovis proxima post festum Omnium Sanctorum, anno [regni]*ᵃ* regis Edwardi tricesimo secundo. Hiis testibus: Johanne le Acatur, et multis aliis.

ᵃ Supplied

902 Gift by John of Long Sutton (*Longgesuthton'*), vicar of St Laurence's church, Reading, to Nicholas *de Lucy*, for a certain sum of money, of a tenement which John had by demise (*dimissio*) of Joan, widow of William *de Porta*, in New Street, Reading, between the tenement of Ralph of Battle (*de Bello*) and that of Philip the merchant. To be held freely of the chief lords of the fee by the due and customary service. Warranty and sealing　　　　　　　　　　2 Aug. 1305

C f 181r

Hiis testibus, et cetera. Dat' Radyng' secundo die Augusti, anno regni regis Edwardi filii regis Henrici tricesimo tercio.

903 Gift by Nicholas *de Lucy* to John of Pangbourne (*Pangebourne*), son of Thomas of Binfield (*Benetfeld*), for his service and a certain sum of money, of a plot (*placea*) of land which Nicholas had by demise of John of Long Sutton (*Longesutthone*), formerly vicar of St Laurence's church, Reading, in New Street, Reading [specified as in nos. 901–

2]. To be held freely of the chief lords of the fee by the due and customary service. Warranty and sealing   27 May 1312

Cf181r–v

Hiis testibus, et cetera. Dat' die sabbati proxima post festum sancti Augustini [26 May], anno [regni]*a* regis Edwardi filii regis Edwardi quinto.

a Supplied

The St Augustine of the dating clause must be Augustine of Canterbury, since in 5 Edward II the feast of St Augustine of Hippo (28 Aug.) fell itself on a Saturday.

904 Quitclaim by Matilda daughter of Walter *Serich*, with the assent of Alice her daughter, to the almonry of Reading of 14d annual rent [in Reading]*a* which she used to receive by the hand of the almoner from the land of Edward *Galun* near St Mary's church on the eastern side, and of 4d which she used to receive annually from Alexander Lorimer (*Lorimarius*) and his heirs from a tenement neighbouring the said Edward's land. Also gift to the almonry of 2d annual rent which Edward *Galun* used to pay her for a certain portion of land lying between the said two lands. The said 20d to be held freely. For this Richard*b* the almoner has given her 10s sterling in her great need, apart from many other goods (*bona*) which he has often conveyed to her and hers. Sealing   [? 1231 × 40]

Bf142v; Cf83r; Cf181v; Df22v

Hiis testibus:*c* [Hugone Bulur, et multis aliis].

a Supplied from rubrics in B,C f 83r
b Om. in C f 181v
c All texts end except C f 181v, from which the remainder is supplied

The suggested dating depends on the reference to Richard the almoner, for whom see above, no. 712 n. For Hugh *Bulur*, see no. 850 n. In B this deed appears in the section devoted to the Almoner's charters.

905 Quitclaim by Ralph Miller (*Molendinarius*) to the almonry of Reading of all his right in the messuage between that which belonged to Gilbert *Lil* and that which belonged to Edward *Galun* in Reading, opposite the church of St Mary towards the east. *a*[To be held]*a* by rendering annually to Gilbert *le Bunt* or his heirs or assigns 1 clove at Michaelmas for all secular service, custom and demand. For this Alan of Andover (*Andevere*) the almoner has given him ½ mark of silver. Sealing. Witnesses [omitted]   [1256 × 97]

Cff 181v–182r

Alan of Andover was almoner of Reading at some date between Robert of Oxford in 1256 and Henry of Gloucester in 1297 (D f 58r, f 36v). Gilbert Lil witnessed a deed by almoner Robert of Oxford in Burghfield in 1256 (D f 58r).

906　Gift by Gilbert *le Bunt* to Ralph Miller (*Molendinarius*) of a messuage in Reading, opposite St Mary's church, between the messuage which belonged to Gilbert *Lil* and that which belonged to Edward *Galoun*. To be held freely by rendering annually to the almoner of Reading 5s, viz., 2s 6d each at Easter and Michaelmas, and to the donor and his heirs 1 clove as increment at Michaelmas, for all secular service, exaction and demand. For this Ralph has given him 20s sterling as entry-fine. Warranty and sealing　[? 1240 × 70]

C f 182r

Hiis testibus: Stephano de la Wyle, et aliis.

Dating very uncertain. The deed is clearly earlier than no. 905, which is concerned with the same messuage. For dated references to Stephen de la Wyle, see no. 890 n.

907　Gift by Roger son of Robert *Hode* to the almonry of Reading of two messuages in Reading, of which one is in Castle Street (*Castelstrat*)*a* between the land of Matilda *Blunda* and the land of William *le poter*,*b* and the other is in Lorimer Lane (*Lurtemerelane*)*c* between the land of Roger Cook (*Cok*)*d* and that of Richard *Repye*;*e* the two messuages abut on one another. To be held freely by rendering anually to the chamberlain of Reading [Abbey] 28d at Michaelmas, and to the parish church of St Mary, Reading, 12d, viz., 6d each at Michaelmas and Easter, for all services, customs and demands. Warranty and sealing*f*　　　　　　　　　　　　　　　　　　[? 1240 × 1258]

B f 143r; C f 83v; C f 182r–v

Hiis testibus:*g* [Willelmo de Whitele, et multis aliis].

a Castelstret *C f 182r–v*
b Sic in B, but perhaps error for Porter, *as in both C texts*
c Lortemerelane *C f 182r–v*　　　　　　*d* Cok' *C f 182r–v*
e Ripye *C f 182r–v*　　　　　　　　　　*f* C f 83v ends
g B ends, the remainder being supplied from C f 182r–v

Not later than 1258, since it was entered in the original section of B. William of Whitley occurs in 1248 and 1261 (Clanchy, *Berks. Eyre of 1248*, 395–6; PRO JUST 1/40, m. 14) and witnessed as bailiff two deeds in Reading of ? mid-13th century (see nos. 956–7); he also witnessed an agreement in East Hendred in 1265 × 6 (no. 792) and was first witness to the abbey's gift of its Oxford property to Walter de Merton in 1266 (*Merton*

Muniments, ed. P. S. Allen and H. W. Garrod (Oxford, 1928), 18), and may also be the William of Whitley who witnessed in 1273 (no. 999), although another of that name was active in the late 13th century (see no. 952). In B this deed was entered in the section devoted to the almoner's charters. Lorimer Lane was in modern times called Hosier Street (see no. 879 n. 1).

908   Gift by Peter *Bred(e)*[a] of Reading to the almonry of Reading of 2s free rent which he used to receive at Michaelmas from a stall which Henry *Page* held of him by inheritance in Butcher Row (*in macekaria*) between the stall of Walter *Surbred*[b] and that of Edward *Galun*. To be held freely by rendering to the donor and his heirs or assigns $\frac{1}{2}$d annually at Easter. For this Robert the almoner has given him 20s sterling. Warranty and sealing   [? *c.* 1240 × 1258]

   B f 142r; C f 82v; C f 182v; D ff 22v–23r

Hiis testibus:[b] [Henrico Wille, et multis aliis].

   [a] *Expansion from C f 182v*
   [b] *All texts end except C f 182v, from which the remainder is supplied*

Not later than 1258, since it was entered in the original section of B; it is also in the original section of D. A Robert the almoner occurs in 1239/40 and a Robert of Oxford, almoner, in 1256 (see nos. 727 n., 905 n.). For Henry Wille, see no. 876 n. Butcher Row existed at the eastern end of Broad Street, Reading, until the 19th century (Slade, 'Reading', 5).

909   *Gift in free alms by Walter Olaf to the almonry of Reading, for the support of the poor living there, of all his lands and rents in Reading, both those which he has now and those which may come to him in the future. Made in the portmoot*   [prob. early 13th cent.]

   B f 142r; C f 82r–v; C ff 182v–183r; D f 23r–v

Sciant presentes et futuri quod ego Walt(erus) Olaf dedi, concessi et hac presenti carta mea confirmavi deo et beate Marie et elemosinarie[a] de Rading(ia), ad sustentationem pauperum ibidem degentium, pro salute anime mee et omnium antecessorum et successorum meorum, omnes terras meas cum pertinentiis suis in villa[b] Rading(ie) et redditus meos, quas scilicet terras et redditus ad presens habeo, et omnes terras et redditus que in posterum aliquo [iure][c] mihi accidere possunt[d] in eadem villa. Habend' et tenend' et 'in eternum[e] possidend' dicte elemosinarie[a] libere et quiete, bene et in bona pace in liberam puram et perpetuam elemosinam,[f] reddendo inde [annuatim][c] domino camerario et ceteris dominis feodorum predictorum redditum de predictis feodis illis debitum, sicut ego eis reddere consueveram, et reddendo inde insuper annuatim heredibus meis .iiii. d' ad festum sancti Michaelis pro omni servitio et seculari exactione. Et ego W(alterus) et heredes mei warantizabimus et defendemus predicte elemosinarie[a] predictas terras et redditus predictos contra omnes gentes in perpetuum. Ut autem hec mea donatio, concessio, confirmatio, warantia perpetua gaudeat firmitate, eam sigilli mei appositione roboravi, et ad maiorem securitatem plenariam saisinam dicte ele-mosinarie[a] feci in portesmoth et me omnino dimisi. Hiis testibus:[g] [Alano vinitore, et aliis].

[a] elimosinarie C ff 182v–183r   [b] Insert de D
[c] Supplied from C ff 182v–183r and D
[d] possint C ff 182v–183r and D
[e] 'e imperpetuum C ff 182v–183r   [f] elimosinam C ff 182v–183r
[g] All texts end except C ff 182v–183r, from which the remainder is supplied

The suggested dating depends on the witness, who seems likely to be the Alan vintner who was prominent in Reading in the early decades of the 13th century (see no. 894 n.), particularly since the somewhat primitive diplomatic of parts of this deed suggests a fairly early date. It is clearly after the foundation of the hospital at the abbey gate (see no. 224). In B this is the first deed entered in the section devoted to the almoner's charters.

910   Quitclaim by Agilia, widow of Gilbert *Stutt'*,[a] to Alfred,[b] almoner of Reading, of all her right in the whole land which formerly belonged to her husband in Reading. To be held freely without contradiction or claim from her. For this the almoner has given her in her great need ½ quarter of wheat, ½ quarter of barley, a tunic and a cloak, and to her son a tunic. Witnesses [omitted]   [? c. 1250]

B f 143r–v; C ff 83v–84r; C f 183r

[a] Sturt' C f 183r   [b] C f 183r has 'Andrew'

Agilia widow of Gilbert *Stut'* was accused with others of larceny in Reading in 1248 (Clanchy, *Berks. Eyre of 1248*, 396). Although she and the others were acquitted, her poverty evident in the present deed perhaps suggests a similar date.

911   Gift in free alms by Petronilla, widow of John *le Akatur*[a] of Reading, to the almonry of Reading of 1d annual rent to be received at Michaelmas from the stall which William *Amfrey*[b] sometime held of her marriage-portion in Shoemakers' Row (*in suweria*[c]), Reading. Sealing   [not later than 1258; ? mid-13th cent.]

B ff 142v–143r; C f 83r; C f 183r

Hiis testibus:[d] [Daniele Wlveseye, et multis aliis].

[a] Acator C f 183r   [b] Anfrey C f 183r
[c] sueria C f 183r
[d] B ends, C f 83r ends with et cetera, the remainder being supplied from C f 183r

Not later than 1258 since it was entered in the original section of B, among the almoner's charters. Daniel Wolvesey occurs as a clothier in Reading in 1241, was a steward of the Reading gild in 1254 and was dead by Feb. 1261 (PRO JUST 1/37, m. 35d; above, no. 862 n.); his position as first witness suggests a mid-13th-century date. The rubrics of B and Cf83r describe Petronilla as relict of John le Acatur. Shoemakers' Row was on the east side of the Market Place, backing on to the west wall of the abbey's precinct (Slade, 'Reading', 5).

912 Gift by Warin *Walkelin* to Reading Abbey of the rent of 6d which G(eoffrey)[a] *Walkelin* used to pay him for a messuage which he held of him in Reading, so that G(eoffrey) and his heirs shall pay the 6d to the almonry of Reading annually at Michaelmas. Warranty. For this the abbey has given him 6s of silver as entry-fine. Sealing[b]

[*c.* 1220 × 1241]

Bf142v; Cf83r; Cf183r; Df23r

Hiis testibus:[c] [Hugone le Bolur, et aliis].

[a] *Expansion from Cf183r and D*   [b] *Cf83r ends*
[c] *B,D end, the remainder being supplied from Cf183r*

Warin Walkelin was dead by Oct. 1241, being survived by his widow Eva (PRO JUST 1/37, m. 26). For Hugh le Bolur, see no. 850 n. The deed was entered in the original section of B among the almoner's charters, and in the original section of D.

913 Gift by John of the Cemetery (*de Cimiterio*) to God and St Mary and the chapel of the Holy Ghost at Caversham Bridge (*capella Sancti Spiritus de Kaversham Sancti Spiritus ad pontem*) of a stall in the Drapery (*draperia*) of Reading, to maintain a lamp there in perpetuity. To be held freely, saving the rent of 2s due to the abbot of Reading at Michaelmas for all service pertaining to him or his heirs. Warranty and sealing

[? *c.* 1240 × 70]

Cf183v

Hiis testibus: Henrico Wille, et multis aliis.

Dating uncertain and depending on the dates of Henry Wille, for whom see no. 876 n. For a 15th-century reference to the chapel, see *VCH Berks.*, ii. 248; *Berks. Arch. Journ.*, lxi (1963–4), 51.

914 Gift in free alms by William, son of Alan the vintner, to Reading Abbey, for the use of the infirmary (*ad opus fratrum infirmorum*), of two stalls in the great market (*in magno mercato*) of Reading, between the cellar and the solar which belonged to John the vintner, William's brother. To be held freely by rendering annually to the chamberlain of the abbey 5d at Michaelmas for all secular service, exaction and demand. Warranty and sealing

[? 1240 × 70]

Cf184r

Hiis testibus: Stephano de la Wyle, et aliis.

Dating uncertain. William vintner occurs in 1248, 1255 and (if the same person) 1284 and 1296 (Clanchy, *Berks. Eyre of 1248*, 296, 396; above, no. 875; PRO JUST 1/44, m. 21d; below, no. 1007). He was presumably the son of the Alan vintner who occurs from the early 13th century (see no. 894 n.). The dates of John vintner are uncertain, since, although one of that name was a juror for Reading in 1269 and occurs in 1284 (JUST 1/42, m. 19; 1/43, m. 8d), there was another John vintner, son of Robert vintner, who occurs rather earlier (see, e.g., no. 916). For Stephen de la Wyle, see no. 890 n.

915   Gift by Luke *Maysent*, son of Hugh *Maysent*, to Reading Abbey, for the use of the infirmary (*ad opus fratrum infirmorum*), of 2s annual rent to be received by the infirmarer from a messuage which William *Maysent*, chaplain, his late brother, held of him next to St Giles's church. To be held freely by rendering annually to the donor and his heirs 1d at Michaelmas for all service, secular exaction and demand. Warranty. For this the abbey has given him 20s of silver as entry-fine by the hand of Roger *de Walebi*,[a] infirmarer (*custos infirmarie*). Sealing
[? *c.* 1240 × 1258]

Bf49r; Cf20r–v; Cf184r

Hiis testibus:[b] [Henrico Wille, et multis aliis].

[a] Walesby *Cf184r*
[b] *B,Cf20r–v end, the remainder being supplied from Cf184r*

Not later than 1258, since it was entered in the original section of B. For Henry Wille, see no. 876 n.

916   Gift by John, son of Robert the vintner, to Ralph of the Infirmary (*de Infirmaria*[a]), for his homage and service, of a messuage in Reading next to the house which belonged to Jordan *Reiner* to the north. To be held freely by rendering annually to the donor and his heirs 2s 6d, viz., 15d each at Michaelmas and Easter, for all secular service. For this Ralph has given him 2 marks of silver as entry-fine. Warranty and sealing   [earlier 13th cent.; ? *c.* 1220 × 30]

Cf184v; (noted) Bf49r; Cf20v

Hiis testibus: Hugone filio Remundi, et multis aliis.

[a] *Ms has* Infirmario

Hugh son of Raymond witnesses in 1204 × 15 and 1219 (nos. 392, 779) and occurs as a person of some importance in a Tilehurst context in 1225 (PRO JUST 1/36, m. 2). The form of this deed favours a later rather than an earlier date. See also no. 917 and, for another deed by John vintner, no. 854.

917 Sale and quitclaim by John the vintner, son of Robert the vintner, to Ralph of the Infirmary (*de Infirmaria*) and his heirs or assigns, of 16d of the 18d rent which Ralph used to pay him annually at two terms of the year, Michaelmas and Easter, from the whole messuage in Reading between that which belonged to Jordan *Reiner* and that of Ralph himself which he holds of Gilbert *Rufus*, so that John or his heirs will not demand more than 2d annually, viz., 1d each at Michaelmas and Easter. For this Ralph has given him 14s 6d sterling. Warranty and sealing   [? *c.* 1220 × 30]

Cf184v; (noted) Bf49r; Cf20v

Hiis testibus: Hugone filio Remundi, et multis aliis.

Date in general as for no. 916. although this is later than no. 916. It is certainly earlier than Oct. 1241, when Gilbert Rufus was dead (see no. 870 n.).

918 Lease, in chirograph form, for 20 years by John the vintner to Thomas of Sherborne (*Shirebourn'*), infirmarer of Reading Abbey, of a cellar with a solar above, not including the two stalls in between, in High Street (*in alto vico*), Reading, opposite the house of John *Monncy* where the same John lives, and between the cellar of Gilbert *conversus* and the tenement of *Sucr'*[a] daughter of Matthew. To be held by Thomas and his successors as keepers of the infirmary for 20 years from Michaelmas, 53 Henry III, by rendering annually to Reading Abbey 14d at Michaelmas, and to Richard son of Matthew and his heirs 5s 6d at Michaelmas by the view of the said John and his heirs or assigns. For this the said Thomas has given him 10 marks sterling. Warranty. Thomas and his successors as infirmarers shall adequately maintain the cellar and solar from their own resources during the said term, except in the case of fire. If John and his heirs shall wish to demise or give in fee the said cellar and solar within the said term, the said Thomas and his successors as keepers of the infirmary shall have first refusal (*in illa empcione erunt propinquiores*). Sealing *alternatim*
                                                                    [*c.* 29 Sept. 1269]

Cf185r

Hiis testibus: Willelmo de Bleobury, et multis aliis.

[a] *Reading doubtful*

The date must be close to that from which the lease was to run. William of Blewbury probably witnessed as steward of the abbey (see no. 855 n.). The cellar, solar and two stalls in between are presumably those referred to in no. 914.

919 Gift in free alms by master John of the Mill (*de Molendino*) to Reading Abbey, for the use of the monks,[a] of 4s 6d annual rent in

equal portions at Michaelmas and Easter *b*[from a tenement]*b* which
Walter Messenger (*le Messag(er)*) inhabits and which sometime
belonged to Richard *Wendepeny* and afterwards to William, the donor's
father. Warranty and sealing   [13th cent.; before 1261]

Cf 185r–v

Hiis testibus: Nicholao clerico, et aliis.

a Sic, ? rectius 'infirm' (*see note*)
b–b Om. at this point, supplied from habendum *clause*

Nicholas clerk was a Reading borough juror in 1241, coroner of Reading vill in 1248
and was dead by Feb. 1261 (PRO JUST 1/37, m. 27d; Clanchy, *Berks. Eyre of 1248*,
391; JUST 1/40, m. 29d). Since this gift was entered among the infirmarer's deeds, it
seems likely that it was for the infirmary.

920   Gift in free alms by Gilbert *Galun*, called Chaplain (*dictus Capellanus*), of Reading to Reading Abbey, for the use of the infirmary (*ad
opus infirmorum*), of the 3s 6d annual rent which Juliana, widow of
Roger of Burghfield (*Burchefeld'*), used to pay him from a stall in
Butcher Row (*in Mascekaria*), Reading, between the stall which
belonged to Henry Cook (*Cok'*) and that which formerly belonged to
Peter the chaplain. Warranty and sealing   [? *c.* 1240 × 70]

Cf 185v

Hiis testibus: Henrico Wille, et aliis.

Date as for no. 913. For Butcher Row, see no. 908 n.

921   Gift by Walter *Payn* to master James, parson*a* of St Giles,
Reading, for his service, of 6s 6d annual rent at Michaelmas, viz.,
from the messuage which Gilbert *de la Stane* holds in Great Street (*in
magno vico*), Reading, next to the messuage which belonged to Philip
Cook (*Cok'*) on the west, 42d; from the messuage which Robert, son
of Ralph Baker (*Pistor*), holds in New Street, Reading, next to the
messuage which belonged to Arnold Baker (*Pistor*) on the west, 12d;
and from the messuage which Richard son of William *le Torchur* holds
in New Street next to that of William *Mascy* on the east, 2s. To be
held freely by rendering annually to Reading Abbey 12d and to
Robert of Ufton (*Offinton'*) and his heirs 4d at Michaelmas for all
secular service, exaction, custom and demand. For this James has
given him 3½ marks of silver as entry-fine. Warranty and sealing
          [*c.* 1226 × 1242]

Cff185v–186r; (noted) Bf49r; Cf20v

Hiis testibus: Henrico Wille, et aliis.

a Sic, but see note

James was vicar of St Giles's church, Reading, which had been appropriated to the abbey since at least 1201 (see no. 211). He occurs as such in 1226 × 38 (below, Appendix B, no. 2) and as master James of St Giles in 1241 (no. 1202). He had ceased to be vicar by 29 Nov. 1242, when a master Giles was 'parson' (BL Add. Ch. 20372), and was certainly dead by Feb. 1261 (PRO JUST 1/40, m. 11).

922 Gift by William, son of the late Robert *le Blound*, to Agatha his sister, for her service, of 20d annual rent at Michaelmas from the messuage which Eva *la Winpelire*[1] holds in New Street, Reading, next to that of Stephen *Hogeman* on the west. To be held freely by rendering annually to Reading Abbey 8d at Michaelmas for all secular service, exaction and demand. For this Agatha has given him 5s sterling as entry-fine. Warranty and sealing   [? *c.* 1240 × 70]

Cf186r

Hiis testibus: Henrico Wille, et multis aliis.

Date as for no. 913. A Robert *Blundus* was dead by Jan. 1240 (*Close Rolls 1237–42*, 165). The Robert *Blundus* accused of breach of the peace and robbery in Blewbury hundred in 1248 (Clanchy, *Berks. Eyre of 1248*, 358) was probably not connected with this family. Stephen *Hoggeman* occurs in New Street in 1248 (*ibid.*, 397).

1. ? the Wimple-maker.

923 Gift by John *Gont(er)*[a] of Reading to John Warner (*le Warener*) of the whole stall in Shoemakers' Row (*in sutoria*), Reading, between the tenement of William *Doubleday* to the south and that formerly belonging to John *le Cave* to the north. To be held freely by rendering annually to the donor and his heirs or assigns 1 clove at Easter, and to Nicholas Butler (*le Butiller*) and his heirs 4s, viz., 2s each at Easter and Michaelmas, for all services, suits, exactions, customs and secular demands. Warranty. For this John has given him 4 marks of silver as entry-fine. Sealing   [*c.* 1270 × 90]

Cf186r–v

Hiis testibus: Gilberto Pynson, Johanne Vachel, et multis aliis.

a Expansion uncertain, but probably variant of Gunter (*cf. nos. 985–6*)

Before *Quia emptores* (1290). John Warner witnessed a Reading deed in 1296 (no. 1007). Nicholas Butler (different from the Nicholas of no. 857 n.) witnessed Reading deeds of 1273 and 1287 (nos. 999, 996) and was an elector and juror for Reading in 1284 (PRO JUST 1/44, m. 21d). Gilbert Pincent was a juror for Reading hundred in 1269 and occurs as late as 1303 (see no. 882 n.). A John Vachell witnesses in Reading from 1285 (*Cartl. Hospital of St John Baptist* (see no. 886 n.), ii. 45). For Shoemakers' Row, see no. 911 n.

924   Gift in free alms by John called Warner (*le Warener*), burgess of Reading, to Reading Abbey, at the instance of Richard of Northampton (*Norhampton'*), infirmarer (*custos infirmorum*), of the stall which he had from John *Gont(er)*[a] in Shoemakers' Row (*in sutoria*), Reading [as in no. 923]. To be held of the donor, his heirs and assigns freely, saving to Nicholas Butler (*le Butiller*) and his heirs 4s annually, viz., 2s each at Easter and Michaelmas, for all services, suits, exactions, customs and secular demands. Warranty and sealing

[*c.* 1270 × 90]

C f 186v

Hiis testibus: Willelmo de Blebury senescallo, et aliis.

[a] *See no. 923*

Date in general as for no. 923, but after it.

925   Gift by Matilda, daughter of Thomas of London (*London'*), to Ralph of the Infirmary (*de Infirmaria*), for his homage and service, of half the messuage between the same Ralph's messuage and that of the donor, which she held of William of Cholsey (*Chelseia*), viz., the half next to Ralph's messuage. To be held freely by rendering annually to her and her heirs 9d of fixed rent (*redditus assisus*) and 1d as increment at Michaelmas for all service, secular exaction and demand pertaining to her or her heirs. For this Ralph has given her 20s sterling as entryfine. Warranty and sealing   [earlier 13th cent.; ? *c.* 1220 × 30]

C f 187r; (noted) B f 49r; C f 20v

Hiis testibus: Hugone[a] filio Remundi, Willelmo filio eius, et multis aliis.

[a] *Ms has* Hugo

Date as for no. 916.

926   Gift in free alms by William of Missenden (*Messendene*),[a] burgess of Reading, to Reading Abbey of 14s annual rent which William the tailor (*le taillur*[b]) used to pay him from the messuage which the donor had between the two bridges in London Street, Reading, between the messuage of Henry *Wille* and that formerly belonging to Ralph of the infirmary (*de infirmaria*), saving to Gilbert *Scot* and his heirs 5s annually at Michaelmas for all secular service, exaction and demand; also of 6s annual rent which Hugh *le Hunte* used to pay him from the messuage between that of Gregory of Houghton (*Hoctun'*)[c] in Minster Street (*Munstrestrete*)[d] and that of Luke of Streatley (*Stretlee*),[e] saving to the almoner of Reading 12d annually at Michaelmas for all secular service, exaction and demand. Warranty and sealing

[*c.* 1240 × 1258]

Bf50v; Cf21v; Cf187r–v

Hiis testibus:[f] [domino Roberto de Mapeldorham tunc senescallo, et multis aliis in portesmot'].

[a] Mussenden' *Cf187r–v*   [b] Taillour *Cf187r–v*
[c] Hoctune *Cf187r–v*   [d] Munstrestret *Cf187r–v*
[e] Strettle *Cf187r–v*
[f] B,Cf21v end, the remainder being supplied from Cf187r–v

After no. 928 and not later than 1258, since it was entered in the original section of B. The donor was a juror for Reading in 1241 and 1248, and acting coroner of Reading in 1261 (PRO JUST 1/37, m. 27d; Clanchy, *Berks. Eyre of 1248*, 296; JUST 1/40, m. 29d); he was dead by Oct. 1284, being survived by his widow Agnes and his son, also called William (JUST 1/43, m. 12). For Sir Robert of Mapledurham, see no. 863 n.

927 Gift in free alms by Walter Tailor (*Cissor*) *de parco* to Reading Abbey, at the instance of Robert of Abingdon (*Abyndon'*), infirmarer of Reading, of 12d annual rent to maintain a lamp burning before the cross in the infirmary, to be received at Michaelmas from a tenement in New Street, Reading, between the tenement[a] of William of Blewbury (*Bleobury*) and that which sometime belonged to Stephen *Hogeman*. Warranty and sealing   [? *c.* 1260 × 80]

Cf187v

Hiis testibus: Willelmo de Whitele, et aliis.

[a] Ms has here the later passage concerning Stephen Hogeman's messuage, copied in error at this point and marked for deletion

Dating very uncertain. For William of Whitley, see no. 907 n. For William of Blewbury, whose earliest dated occurrence is in 1265 × 6, see no. 855 n. Stephen Hogeman, who may here be dead, was alive in 1248 (see no. 922 n.).

928 Gift by Gilbert *le*[a] *Scot* to William of Missenden (*Mussendene*), for his service, of a messuage in London Street, Reading, between the two bridges, between the messuage formerly belonging to Ralph *Wille* and that formerly belonging to Ralph of the Infirmary. To be held freely by rendering annually to the donor and his heirs 5s at Michaelmas for all secular service, exaction and demand. Warranty and sealing   [? *c.* 1240 × 1258]

C ff 187v–188r; (noted) B f50v; C f21v

Hiis testibus: Henrico Wille, et multis aliis.

a Interlined

Noted in the original section of B. Before no. 926 and in the period when Henry Wille was most prominent in Reading (see no. 876 n.). For Gilbert Scot in 1241 and 1248, see *ibid*. This messuage is the first of those given to the abbey by William of Missenden in no. 926, and a comparison between the two deeds suggests that Henry Wille may have been the son of Ralph Wille (cf. PRO JUST 1/40, m. 13). The note in B has alongside it: *Infirmar'*.

929 Gift by Robert son of *Reiner*, brother and heir of Jordan *Reiner*, to Henry the merchant of Reading of the entire messuage between the house which belonged to Ralph *Wille* and that which belonged to Ralph of the Infirmary. To be held freely by rendering annually to the donor and his heirs 1d at Michaelmas for all service, secular exaction and demand. For this Henry has given him 10s sterling and a tunic of russet as entry-fine. Warranty and sealing [*c.* 1220 × 50]

C f188r; (noted) B f50v; C f21v

Hiis testibus: Hugone le Bolur, et multis aliis.

After nos. 916–7, which mention the neighbouring messuages of Jordan Reiner and Ralph of the Infirmary, and certainly not later than 1258, since it was noted in the original section of B; but also of the time when Hugh le Bolur was prominent in Reading (see no. 850 n.).

930 Gift by Robert of Ufton (*Uffynton'*) to master James of St Giles, Reading, for his service, of 4d annual rent at Michaelmas from the messuages which Robert, son of Ralph Baker (*Pistor*), holds in New Street, Reading, next to that which belonged to Arnold (*Ernald*) Baker on the west. To be held freely and quit of all secular service, exaction and demand. For this master James has given him 4s sterling as entry-fine. Warranty and sealing   [*c.* 1226 × 1242]

C f188r–v; (noted) B f49r; C f20v

Hiis testibus: Henrico Wille, et multis aliis.

After no. 921 and while master James was vicar of St Giles's church (see no. 921 n.). The present deed releases James from the rent payable to Robert of Ufton in the earlier deed.

931 Gift in free alms by Gilbert *supra pontem* of Reading to Reading Abbey, for the use of the infirmary (*ad opus infirmorum*), of 5s annual rent which John the goldsmith used to pay him at Michaelmas from a stall in the Lormery (*Lormeria*), Reading, between the stall of Agatha *Ruffa* and that of Daniel Wolvesey (*Wolvesegh'*).[a] Warranty and sealing[b]

[c. 1240 × 1258]

B ff 50v–51r; Cf 22r; Cf 188v

'[Hiis testibus: Stephano de la Wyle, et multis aliis.][c]

[a] Wlveseye *Cf 188v*
[b] *B ends with* T', *Cf 22r ends*
[c-c] *Supplied from Cf 188v*

Not later than 1258, since it was entered in the original section of B. Stephen de la Wyle occurs between 1249 and 1261 (see no. 890 n.). Agatha Ruffa was the widow of Gilbert Ruffus, who was dead by Oct. 1241 (see no. 870 n.); she occurs as a vintner in Reading in 1241, 1248 and, with the name Agatha of Reading, 1255 (PRO JUST 1/37, m. 35d; Clanchy, *Berks. Eyre of 1248*, 396; *Close Rolls 1254–56*, 90–1).

932 Confirmation by Gilbert *Scot* to Henry the merchant of Reading of the gift and sale which Robert son of *Rener*, heir of Jordan son of *Rener*, made to him of the messuage in Reading between the house which belonged to Ralph *Wille* and that of Ralph of the Infirmary. To be held freely, as Robert's charter to him witnesses. For this Henry has given him 1 gold coin (*bisantium*). Sealing   [c. 1220 × 50]

Cf 188v; (noted) B f 50v; Cf 21v

Hiis testibus: Hugone le Bolur, et aliis.

Probably of the same date as no. 929. The note in B has alongside it: *Infirmar'*.

933   *Gift in free alms by John of the Chamber to the almonry of Reading, for the maintenance of the poor of Christ, of 2s annual rent from a messuage in the alley opposite St Mary's church, Reading*   [? earlier 13th. cent.]

B f 142r–v; Cf 82v; Cf 189r

Sciant presentes et futuri quod ego Johannes de Camera dedi, concessi et hac presenti carta mea confirmavi deo et beate Marie et beato Jacobo et elemosinarie Rading', pro salute anime mee et pro animabus omnium antecessorum et successorum meorum, in liberam puram et perpetuam elemosinam illas .ii. solidatas annui redditus[a] in perpetuum percipiendas de Johanne Ring[b] et Alicia uxore sua et de heredibus ipsius Alicie, videlicet sororis mee, ad sustentationem pauperum Christi per manus elemosinarii[c] abbatie[d] Rading';[e] quos quidem .ii. solidos dicti J(ohannes)[f] et A(licia) uxor eius mihi aliquando reddere solebant, videlicet ad Annuntiationem[g] .xii. d' et ad festum sancti Michaelis .xii. d', de uno mesuagio in Rading(ia) [h]cum pertinentiis[h] in viculo qui est ex opposito[i] beate Marie in parte occidentali versus Lortemere quod iacet inter terram Thome de Hanl(eia)*ʲ* et terram Danielis Wlvesege.*ᵏ* Et ad huius rei perpetuam securitatem presentem cartam sigilli mei appositione roboravi.*ˡ* Hiis testibus:*ᵐ* [Hugone de Ivinton' tunc camerario Radyng', et aliis].

ᵃ Insert singulis annis *Cf189r*
ᶜ elimosinarii *Cf189r*
ᵉ Radyngie *Cf82v*
ᵍ Insert beate Marie *Cf189r*
ʰ⁻ʰ Cf189r has these words after mesuagio
ⁱ Insert ecclesie *Cf189r*
ᵏ Wlveseye *Cf189r*
ᵐ B ends, the remainder being supplied from Cf189r

ᵇ Kyng' *Cf189r*
ᵈ abbathie *both C texts*
ᶠ Insert Kyng' *Cf189r*

ʲ Hanle *Cf189r*
ˡ Cf82v ends

Dating uncertain. Thomas of Henley occurs between 1216 × 24 and 1249 (see no. 850 n.) and Daniel Wolvesey died between 1254 and 1261 (see no. 862 n.). The names of several chamberlains of Reading in the 13th century are known, but it has not been possible to establish their sequence. However, the somewhat primitive tone of this deed and the absence of a warranty clause appear to suggest a fairly early date. The deed was entered in the original section of B, among the almoner's charters. The margin of Cf189r has: *Iuxta ecclesiam S. Marie.*

934 *Testament of Alan of Banbury* 4 Nov. 1311

Cf189r–v

In dei nomine amen. Ego Alanus de Bannebury condo testamentum meum die jovis proxima post festum Omnium Sanctorum, anno domini M.CCC.xi. In primis lego animam meam deo omnipotenti, beate Marie et omnibus sanctis et corpus meum ad sepeliendum in cimiterio Sancti Laurentii Radyng(ie). Item lego fabrice Sar(esburie) .vi. d'. Item hospitali de Crowemersch' .vi. d'. Item in pane ad distribuendum pauperibus die sepulture mee .x. s'. Item lego ad exequies faciend(as) .xii. s'. Item in cervisia emenda et danda nocte vigilant(ibus) circa corpus meum .xii. d'. Item operi fratrum minorum Rad(yngie) .v. s'. Item duobus pueris Elie fratris mei .ii. s'. Item Alicie filie ux(oris) Alani predicti .xii. d'. Item Johanne*ᵃ* uxori Roberti de Hampton' .xii. d'. Item Roberto de Hampton' .xii. d'. Item Ricardo de Asschebourn' .ii. s'. Item Johanni le Cave .ii. s'. Item vicario Sancti Laurentii .ii. s'. Item cuilibet altari in ecclesia sancti Laurentii .iii. d'. Item altari beate Marie in ecclesia sancti Laurentii .xii. d'. Item lego Christine uxori mee quinque solidatas annui redditus in vico London' percipiendas ad duos anni terminos de quodam tenemento quod quidem tenementum Thomas Hubert' quondam tenuit de dicto Alano. Item Johanni le Cave de Bleobury capellam meam integram scitam apud Totehull' *ᵇ*in perpetuum.*ᵇ* Item lego Christine uxori mee et Margar(ie) filie mee omnia bona mea existencia in predicta capella die quo moriar. Item lego Margerie filie mee .iii. s' .iiii. d' annui redditus quos solebam recipere de Ricardo de Stratfeld ad terminum

sancti Michaelis in alto vico Radyng(ie). [*f189v*] Item lego Margerie
predicte .iiii. acras terre arrabilis in campo qui dicitur Northfeld quas
quidem .iiii. acras terre cepi cum matre sua in maritagium nomine
pecunie. Item lego integre tenementum meum in quo sedeo cum
pertinentiis Christine uxori mee omnibus diebus vite sue; defuncta
autem dicta Christina volo quod dictum tenementum cum pertinentiis
suis integre revertatur Margerie filie mee. Item lego medietatem eris
mei Christine uxori mee et aliam medietatem Margerie filie mee.
Siquid autem bonorum meorum residuum fuerit non legatum, volo et
concedo quod remaneat integre Christine uxori mee et Margerie filie
mee. Huius autem testamenti ad hanc execucionem fideliter et indilate
faciendam constituo et ordino Ricardum de Assheburn' et Johannem
le Cave de Bleobury executores meos prout melius viderint anime mee
expedire. Item lego Agneti famule*c* mee .xii. d'. Item volo et concedo
quod dictus Johannes de Bleobury habeat et custodiat Margeriam
filiam meam cum omnibus catallis suis post diem meum tam cum
omnibus redditibus sibi*d* iure hereditario et ex legacione Alani patris
sui accidentibus quam cum aliis bonis suis sibi*d* pertinentibus,
quousque pervenerit ad annos nubiles, et postea maritetur per consilium et auxilium dicti Johannis cum propriis catallis suis quamcicius
dictus Johannes viderit dicte Margerie expedire. In cuius rei testimonium hoc presens testamentum meum sigilli mei impressione
roboravi die et anno supradictis. Item lego Christine uxori mee Robertum servientem nostrum cum suo servicio quousque termini inter
ipsum et me statuti perseverant.

a Ms has Joh'i   *b b Ms has* imperpetuum
c Ms has famulie   *d Interlined*

935 Lease, indented, for lives in survivorship, made Wednesday after
the feast of St Laurence the martyr [10 Aug.], 8 Edward II, by
Nicholas [of Whaplode], abbot of Reading, to John son of Thomas *le
Cave* of Blewbury (*Bleobury*) of the corner stall (*selda angularis*) opposite
Tothill (*Tothulle*) in the Drapery (*draperia*) of Reading which Alan of
Banbury (*Bannebury*) formerly held. To be held by John and Edith his
wife for the term of their lives by rendering annually to the abbot and
his successors 5s 1d at Michaelmas. John and Edith shall keep and
maintain the stall in the condition in which they received it, or better,
and shall not demise it to any one out of their hands. If these conditions
are not observed, the abbot and his successors may immediately
resume possession of the stall and dispose of it according to their will.
After the deaths of John and Edith the stall shall revert fully to the
abbot and his successors. Warranty and sealing *alternatim*. Given at
Reading on the date aforesaid   14 Aug. 1314

C ff 189v–190r

Hiis testibus: Radulfo de Helme, et aliis.

936 Notification by Margery, daughter and heir of the late Alan of Banbury (*Bannebury*) merchant of Reading, that she has received from John *le Cave* all the goods and chattels which remained in his custody and which ought by right to come to her after the death of Alan, her late father. Also remission and quitclaim of all actions and demands which she had against him for any transgression (*delictum*) existing between them from the beginning of the world to the date of these presents. Sealing   9 Jan. 1318

C f 190r

Dat' Radyng' die lune proxima post festum Epiphanie domini, anno regni regis E(dwardi) filii regis Edwardi undecimo. Hiis testibus: Johanne le Acatur, et aliis.

937 Gift by Emma, daughter of the late Gervase Tanner (*Tannator*), to Robert *Agathe,*[a] for his service, of a messuage in St Giles's Street, Reading, next to the messuage which formerly belonged to Hamo of Oxford (*Oxonia*) on the south. To be held freely by rendering annually to the lords of the fee the due and customary service, to Roland son of Robert son of the priest (*sacerdos*) and his heirs 1d at Michaelmas, and to Emma and her heirs 1 clove as increment at the same term, for all secular service, exaction and demand. For this Robert has given her 2 marks of silver as entry-fine. Warranty and sealing
[? *c.* 1240 × 70]

C f 190r

Hiis testibus: Henrico Wille, et aliis.

[a] *Ms has* Achete *deleted,* Agathe *interlined*

Date as for no. 913. If this messuage is the same as that in no. 938, the two deeds would probably be of similar date.

938 Quitclaim by John Burgess (*Burgeys*) to Robert *Agathe* and his heirs or assigns of all his right in a messuage in Old Street, Reading, which Gervase, John's father, gave to the said Robert with Emma his daughter in free marriage-portion. For this Robert has given him 5s sterling. Sealing   [before 1261]

Cf 190r–v

Hiis testibus: Ada clerico, et multis aliis.

Adam clerk was a borough juror in 1241 and served as a coroner of Reading before his death, which had occurred by Feb. 1261 (see no. 861 n.). If this messuage is the same as that in no. 937, Old Street and St Giles's Street were the same.

939 Notification by Thomas of Sandleford (*Sandelford*) that he has received from John of Woburn (*Woburn'*), Nicholas of Cowfold (*Cofaud*) and Joan le Bryk', executors of the testament of John le Bryk', deceased, 1 mark of silver of the portion of Roger, son of the deceased, which belonged to him from his father's goods, for faithful custody until Roger shall come of age; and obligation of himself and his heirs to pay to Roger 1 mark of silver when he shall come of age or to his assigns bearing these letters. Also grant that, to ensure payment, the sheriff of Berkshire and his bailiffs may distrain on all the goods of Thomas and his heirs or executors wherever they be found; and promise to give the sheriff or his bailiffs 2s for any such distraint. Thomas's executors shall not have administration of his goods until the mark of silver has been paid in full to Roger, with any damages and expenses incurred by Roger through its non-payment. Thomas also submits himself to the jurisdiction of the ordinary for excommunication until payment has been made. Sealing   25 June 1288

Cf 190v

Hiis testibus: Rogero Luvekyn', et multis aliis. Dat' apud Neubury die veneris proxima post festum Nativitatis sancti Johannis Baptiste, anno regni regis Edwardi xvi.

Although this deed is entered among Reading deeds, its connection with Reading is unclear.

940 Gift by Laurence Dubber (*le Dubbar'*)[1] of Reading to Richard of Acton (*Actone*), for a certain sum of money, of the whole curtilage appurtenant to Laurence's capital messuage in Old Street, Reading, between the tenement of Sir John Sifrewast (*Cyfrewast*), knight, on the south and that of John Vachell (*Vachel*) on the north, the curtilage being 14 perches 10 feet in length and 36 feet in width, with sufficient way and free entry and exit through the middle of Laurence's tenement for Richard and his heirs or assigns. To be held freely of the chief lords of the fee by the due and customary services. Warranty and sealing   21 Dec. 1339

Cff 190v–191r

Hiis testibus: Johanne le Goldsmyth *a*tunc maiore Rad(yng')*a*, et aliis. Dat' apud Radyng' die martis in festo sancti Thome apostoli, anno regni regis Edwardi tercii a Conquestu terciodecimo.

a–a Interlined

1. A dubber was a beater of leather.

941 Quitclaim by John *le Blake* of [?]Cornwall (*Cornwayle*) to Laurence Dubber (*le Dobbar'*) of Reading and his heirs, for a certain sum of money, of all his right in a plot (*placea*) of land with a cellar and the whole solar built above, which he had by gift and enfeoffment of the said Laurence for the term of his life, in Old Street, Reading, between the tenement of Sir John Sifrewast (*Cyfrewast*), knight, on the south and that of the said Laurence Dubber (*le Dubbare*) on the north. Sealing   18 June 1340

Cf 191r

Hiis testibus: Johanne le Goldsmyth tunc maiore Radyng', et aliis. Dat' Radyng' die dominica proxima post festum sancti Butulphi abbatis [17 June], anno regni regis Edwardi tercii a Conquestu quartodecimo.

942 Quitclaim by the same to Richard of Acton (*Actone*), burgess of Reading, for a certain sum of money, of all his right in a cellar with the whole solar built above, which he had for the term of his life by gift of Laurence Dubber (*le Dubbar'*) in Old Street, Reading [specified as in no. 941, reading (*Syfrewast*)]. Sealing   26 June 1340

Cf 191r–v

Hiis testibus: Johanne le Goldsmyth tunc maiore Radyng', et aliis. Dat' Radyng' die lune proxima post festum sancti Johannis Baptiste, anno regni regis E(dwardi) tercii a Conquestu quartodecimo.

943 Gift by Laurence Dubber (*le Dubbar'*) of Reading to Richard of Acton (*Actone*), burgess of Reading, for a certain sum of money, of a cellar with the whole solar built above and a parcel (*particula*) of land adjacent to it, being 15 feet long west to east and 10 feet wide, in Old Street, Reading, between the tenement of Sir John Sifrewast (*Syfrewast*), knight, on the south and Laurence's tenement on the north, and between the said Richard's curtilage on the west and the main road (*via regia*) from Reading to Winchester (*Wynton'*) on the east. To be held freely of the chief lords of the fee by the pertinent services. Warranty and sealing   9 July 1340

Cf 191v

Hiis testibus: Johanne le Goldsmyth' tunc maiore Radyng', Waltero
le Hert, Johanne de Buccynggebury, Johanne le Rowe, Roberto
Channtrel, Ph(ilipp)o Holepouk', Willelmo le Maist(er), Gilberto
clerico, et aliis. Dat' apud Radyng' die dominica proxima post festum
translationis*sancti Thome martiris [7 July], anno regni regis Edwardi
tercii a Conquestu quartodecimo.

ᵃ *Interlined*

944 Lease [?indented]ᵃ for lives in survivorship, made Sunday the
feast of St David the bishop, 6 Edward III, by Abbot John [I, of
Appleford] and the convent of Reading to John Brewer (*le Brasiare*)
and Alice, his wife, of the corner tenement which Edith *atte Crouch*
formerly held in London Street, Reading, opposite Fair Cross (*bella
crux*), between the tenement of Richard of Whitley (*Whytelegh*) on the
north and the street called Bread Lane (*le Brendelane*) on the south.
To be held for their lives by rendering annually to the abbey 13s 4d at
Michaelmas and Easter in equal portions, the said tenement reverting
entirely to the abbey after their deaths. For this John and Alice have
undertaken to improve the building(s)ᵇ of the tenement within 10
years out of their own resources (*bona*) to the value of 20 marks, and
to maintain it in a good state throughout their lives at their own cost.
Sealingᵃ   1 Mar. 1332

Cf 192r

Hiis testibus: Waltero le Hert maiore, et cetera.

ᵃ *Text abbreviated at end*
ᵇ *Ms has edific'*

This and no. 945 are written in hands different from the main hand of this part of the
cartulary, which resumes on f 193v after the blank ff 192v–193r.

945 Lease, indented, made 22 March, 10 Edward II, by Abbot
Nicholas [of Whaplode] and the convent of Reading to Thomas
Cooper (*le Coupere*) of Streatley (*Stretlegh*) and the legitimate heirs of
his body of a messuage with a garden in London Street, Reading,
between the tenement of Matilda Gold (*Golde*) and a small stream
running down from the mill of the abbot and convent. To be held
freely and by hereditary right in perpetuity by rendering annually to
the granger (*granetarius*) [of Reading Abbey] 12s at the Annunciation
and Michaelmas in equal portions. If legitimate heirs of the body fail
in any generation, the messuage and garden shall revert fully to the

abbot and convent. If Thomas or his heirs shall make waste in the messuage and garden, or not maintain them adequately, or cut down the trees, or fail in the payment of the rent for one year, the abbot and convent and their successors may immediately enter and recover them in fee. Warranty and sealing *alternatim*   22 Mar. 1317

Cf192r

Hiis testibus: T(homa) Syward, et aliis, et cetera. Dat' Rad(yng') die et anno supradictis.

See note to no. 944.

946   Gift in free alms by Agnes of Denmead (*Denemed'*), widow, to Reading Abbey of the tenement which she had by gift and demise of Walter[a] *le Reynny* in a lane in Reading called Holy Water Lane (*Halewatereslane*),[1] except for a certain part of this tenement which she previously sold to Laurence Chapman (*le Chapman*);[2] and of 5s annual rent from a tenement in London Street, Reading, which Robert *Toth* [holds],[b] viz., 2s 6d each at Michaelmas and Easter; and of a shop in Shoemakers' Row (*in suteria*), Reading, which she had by demise of Lucy formerly wife of Thomas *Grym*,[3] between the shop formerly belonging to John *Grym* on the south and that formerly belonging to Ralph of Heckfield (*Heghfeld'*) on the north. Warranty and sealing
27 July 1308

Cf198v

Hiis testibus: Johanne le Acatour, Rad(ulf)o de Bello, Thoma Syward, Thoma Leicestre, Rad(ulf)o de Helme, Elia de Bannebury, Willelmo Bonenfannt, et aliis. Dat' Radyng' die sabbati proxima post festum sancti Jacobi apostoli [25 July], anno regni regis Edwardi filii regis Edwardi secundo.

   [a] *Sic, but called* 'William' *in no. 949*
   [b] *Supplied conjecturally*

The donor was the widow of John of Denmead (see no. 948). Holy Water Lane was off New Street, now Friar Street (Slade, 'Reading', 5 n. 51).

   1. See no. 949.
   2. See no. 1040.
   3. See no. 948.

947   Gift by Nicholas of Stanstead (*Stanstede*) to Thomas *Grym*, for 5 marks of silver, of a messuage in Shop Row (*la Shoppereuwe*), Reading, between the shop formerly belonging to Ralph of Heckfield (*Heughfeld'*) and that formerly belonging to Gilbert *de la More*. To be held of the chief lords of the fee freely by rendering annually the due and customary service, and to the donor and his heirs 1 clove at Michaelmas for all secular service, exaction and demand. Warranty and sealing   [1290 × 15 Apr. 1304]

C ff 198v–199r

Hiis testibus: Thoma de Leicestr(e) tunc maiore Radyng', Gilberto Pinzonn, Johanne Fachel, Thoma Syward, Johanne le Acatur, Rad(ulf)o de Bello, Nicholao le Butiller, Roberto Hardy, et aliis.

After *Quia emptores*, and before no. 948. The date of Thomas of Leicester's mayoralty is unknown (cf. below, no. 1020 n.). A comparison between this deed and nos. 946 and 948 suggests that Shop Row and Shoemakers' Row were identical.

948 Gift by Lucy, widow of Thomas *Grym*, to John of Denmead (*Denemed'*) and Agnes his wife, for their service and a certain sum of money, of a shop in Shoemakers' Row (*in Suteria*), Reading, between the shop of John *Grym* on the south and that formerly belonging to Ralph of Heckfield (*Heghfeld'*) on the north, which shop Thomas, her late husband, bequeathed to her in his last will. To be held freely of the chief lords of the fee by rendering annually the due and customary service. Warranty and sealing   15 Apr. 1304

C f 199r

Hiis testibus: Johanne le Acatour, Rad(ulf)o de Bello, Rad(ulf)o de Helme, Adam le Puleter, Waltero Gerard', Willelmo Bonafannt, Ricardo de Asshburne, Willelmo le Enngher, Gilberto de Heghfeld clerico, et aliis. Dat' Radyng' quintodecimo die Aprilis, anno regni regis Edwardi filii regis Henrici tricesimo secundo.

949 Gift by William*ª* de Reny to John of Denmead (*Denemed'*) and Agnes, his wife, of the tenement which he had by demise of William *la Cave* in Holy Water Lane (*la Haliwatereslane*), Reading; and of 7s annual rent from the tenement in which Walter *de Kymelon* lives in London Street, Reading, on the north of the tenement *le Rede*. To be held freely [no lord(s) specified] by rendering annually to the donor during his lifetime 4d at Michaelmas, and to his heirs or assigns after his death 1 grain of wheat (*unum granum frumenti*) at the same term, for all services, secular exactions and demands. Warranty and sealing   6 Feb. 1301

C f 199r

Hiis testibus: Johanne Vachel, Gilberto Pynsun, Johanne le Acatour, Petro Aurifabro, Elia de Bannebury, Waltero Gerard, Johanne Fyngod, et multis aliis. Dat' Radyng' die lune proxima post festum

Purificacionis beate Marie virginis, anno regni regis Edwardi vicesimo nono.

ª Sic, but called 'Walter' in no. 946

This deed seems little affected by *Quia emptores.*

950 Gift by Mary, widow of the late David Marshal (*Marescallus*), to John *le Waleys* and Alice of Stratfield Mortimer (*Stratfeld' Mortimer*), his wife, for their service, of a messuage in Old Market (*in veteri foro*), Reading, between the messuage which formerly belonged to Stephen *Baufiz* and that of Robert de Mortimer (*de Mortuo Mari*). To be held freely by rendering annually to Reading Abbey 26d, to Richard of Lyford (*Lifford*) and his heirs 1d, and to the donor and her heirs 21d as increment, all at Michaelmas, for all secular service, exaction and demand. For this John and Alice have given her 10s sterling as entry-fine. Warranty and sealing   [*c.* 1240 × 1261]

Cf 199v

Hiis testibus: Henrico Wille, Willelmo de Whitele, Daniele Wolves-ithe, Adam clerico, Nicholao clerico, Thoma le Cordewaner, Waltero de la Mare, Johanne filio Ph(ilipp)i drapar', Hugone Knebbe, Willelmo Weresly, et multis aliis.

Daniel Wolvesey, Adam clerk and Nicholas clerk were all dead by Feb. 1261 (see nos. 861 n., 862 n.). Henry Wille occurs prominently from *c.* 1240 (see no. 876 n.).

951 Gift by Alice *le Geres* of Reading, widow, to Gunnilda, daughter of the late Walter *de la Hethe* of Stratfield Mortimer (*Stratfeld' Morteo-mar'*), for her service and a certain sum of money, of a messuage with curtilage in Old Street, Reading, between the tenement formerly belonging to Robert of Shottesbrooke (*Sottesbrok'*) to the north and that formerly belonging to Robert Mortimer (*le Mortem(er)*) to the south. To be held of the chief lords of the fee freely by doing annually the due and customary service. Warranty and sealing

11 Sept. 1295

Cff 199v–200r

Dat' apud Radyng' die dominica proxima post festum Nativitatis beate Marie virginis [8 Sept.], anno regni regis Edwardi filii regis Henrici vicesimo tercio. Hiis testibus: Johanne Fachel, Gilberto Pinson, Radul(f)o de la Bataille, Johanne le Acatour, Roberto le Taillour, Ricardo de Mapeldorham, Waltero de Shirebourn' clerico, et aliis.

952 Gift by Gunnilda, daughter of the late Walter *de la Hethe* of

Stratfield Mortimer (*Stratfeld' Mortimer*), to William of Whitley junior (*iuvenis de Whitele*) and Alice his wife, for a certain sum of money, of a messuage in Old Street, Reading, between the messuage formerly belonging to Robert of Shottesbrooke (*Sottesbrok'*) on the north and that formerly belonging to Robert Mortimer (*Mortimer*) on the south. To be held of the chief lords of the fee freely by rendering annually the due and customary service. Sealing   25 Apr. 1297

C f 200r

Dat' Radyng' die sancti Marci ewangeliste, anno regni regis Edwardi vicesimo quinto. Hiis testibus: Elia de Bannebury, Willelmo le Chamberlayn, Andrea de la More, Galfr(ed)o le Engleys, Petro Loffeneye, Roberto Cissore, Willelmo le ȝunghyne,[1] et multis aliis.

1. Cf. below, no. 1040.

953 Quitclaim by Gilbert Pincent (*Pinzon*) to William *Pycot* of 1d annual rent from the said William's tenement in which he lives in Wood Street (*Wodestret*), Reading, which rent Gilbert had by demise of William David (*David*). Sealing   30 Sept. 1294[1]

C f 200r

Dat' apud Radyng' die[a] proxima post festum sancti Michaelis, anno regni regis Edwardi vicesimo secundo. Hiis testibus· Johanne Fachel, Johanne le Acathur, Rad(ulf)o de la Bataille, Willelmo Pinzon, Rogero de Cokenhull',[b] Nicholao le Cotiller, Reginaldo Samuel, et aliis.

[a] *Probably the day of the week om., since the normal formula for the day after a feast is* in crastino
[b] *Sic, but prob. error for* Copenhull' (*cf. no. 1019*)
1. This is the date strictly required by the text, but see textual note *a*.

954 Gift by Richard *Coppe* to Reginald *le Fourbour*,[1] for his service, of a stall in Shoemakers' Row (*in suteria*), Reading, between the stall of William *Ratele* and that of William Cooper (*le Copere*). To be held freely by rendering annually to the donor and his heirs 3s 2d at Easter, and to the chamberlains of Reading [Abbey] 3s 10d at the same term, for all secular service, exaction and demand. For this Reginald has given him 10s sterling as entry-fine. Warranty and sealing
[*c.* 1260 × 1284]

C f 200r–v

Hiis testibus: Elia de Bannebury, Stephano le Grom, Johanne Fachel, Nicholao le Botiller,[a] Galfr(edo) Gomme, Rad(ulf)o de Heghfeld', Roberto Hardi, Stephano Aurifabro, Osberto le Bevour, Willelmo Ratele, et multis aliis.

a Ms Botille

Richard Coppe occurs in Reading in 1248, was a bailiff of the borough in 1261 and a
borough juror in 1284 (Clanchy, *Berks. Eyre of 1248*, 395; PRO JUST 1/40, m. 14d;
1/44, m. 21d). Stephen Goldsmith was dead by Oct. 1284 (JUST 1/43, m. 11). Elias
of Banbury witnessed as late as 1312 and was an assessor of the ninth in Reading in
1297 (see no. 1041; *Berks. Arch. Journ.*, lx (1962), 101). For Ralph of Heckfield between
1248 and 1286, see no. 880 n.

   1. ? Furbisher (cf. no. 883).

955 Acknowledgement by Ralph Cooper (*le Coupere*) of Reading of
his and his heirs' obligation to pay annually to Abbot Nicholas [of
Whaplode] and the convent of Reading and their successors 3s annual
rent in perpetuity, at Michaelmas and Easter [in equal]*a* portions,
from his shop in Shoemakers' Row (*in suteria*) next to the wall of
Reading Abbey, between the shop which Richard of Ashbourne (*Assheburn'*) holds and that which Ralph holds for a term of years by
lease (*tradicio*) of William Cooper. The abbot and convent, through
themselves or their officers (*ministri*) or officer appointed for this
purpose, may distrain on the shop whenever the rent is not forthcoming in whole or in part, and retain the distresses until it is paid in
full. Sealing   14 Feb. 1313

  C f 200v

Dat' Radyng' die mercurii proxima post festum beate Scolastice vir-
ginis [10 Feb.], anno regni regis Edwardi filii regis Edwardi sexto.
Hiis testibus: Radul(f)o de Helme, Henrico de Greywell', Waltero
Watshod, Gilberto de Copenhull', Rogero le Hurt', Edmundo le
Barbour, Adam le Horner', et aliis.

  a Supplied

956 Gift by Robert son of Sewal of Reading to William son of Sewal,
his brother, of 6s annual rent, viz., 3s each at Michaelmas and Easter,
which Ralph of Faringdon (*Pharindone*) used to pay him from a stall
in High Street (*in alto vico*), Reading, on the side of Butcher Row
(*mascecraria*) on the west, between the messuage of Christina *Puk'*
and the round house called Bread House (*Bredhuse*). To be held by
rendering annually to the donor and his heirs or assigns 1 root of
ginger for all exaction and demand. For this William has given him
5 marks of silver as entry-fine. Warranty and sealing
                 [before 1261; ? mid-13th cent.]

Cff200v–201r

Hiis testibus: Henrico Wille, Daniele Wlvesege, Willelmo de Whitele tunc ballivo, Gilberto super pontem, Nicholao clerico, Ad(a) clerico, Rolanndo clerico, Petro le Taillour, Fulcone Remund, Rad(ulf)o de Pharendon', Roberto de Henle, et multis aliis.

Daniel Wolvesey, Nicholas clerk and Adam clerk were all dead by Feb. 1261 (see nos. 861 n., 862 n.); in view of the position of Henry Wille and Daniel Wolvesey at the head of the witness-list, perhaps of the time when they were stewards of the Reading gild (see no. 862 n.).

957 Gift in free alms by William son of Sewal to Reading Abbey of 6s annual rent, viz., 3s each at Michaelmas and Easter, which Ralph of Faringdon (*Farendon'*) used to pay to Robert, William's brother, from a stall in High Street (*in alto vico*), Reading, which formerly belonged to his father, Sewal, on the west side of Butcher Row (*macerria*) between the messuage of Christina *Poke* and the round house called Bread House (*Bredhous*). Warranty and sealing

[before 1261; ? mid-13th cent.]

Cf201r

Hiis testibus: Henrico Wille, Daniele Wlvesee, Stephano de la Wyle, Willelmo de Whitele tunc ballivo, Gilberto super pontem, Nicholao clerico, Johanne clerico, Ad(a) de Kyneware, Gilberto de Benham, Fulcone Remund, et multis aliis.

Date as for no. 956. Since the deed was not entered in B, it may possibly be not earlier than 1258.

958 Gift in free alms by Peter of Rotherwick (*Rotherwik*)[a] to Reading Abbey, with his body, of the following annual rents at Michaelmas in Reading to provide an annual pittance on the day of his anniversary: viz., from the messuage which Adam the cooper (*cuvarius*) held of him 10d; from that which Eva and Roesia[b] of Battle (*de Bello*) held of him 20d; from that which Thomas *Chizci*[c] and Matilda his wife held of him 2s; from that which Richard Earl (*Comes*) held of him 15d; from that which Hugh *de Breusa*[d] held of him 3s 4d; from the messuage in Potters' Lane (*Pottereslane*)[e] which William *Chanterel*[f] held of him 5s; from the stall which William the cordwainer (*cordubanarius*) held of him in Cordwainers' Street (*in vico coriversorum*) 5s. Also gift in free alms of the plot (*placia*)[g] of land extending from the front of the main road (*a fronte regalis itineris*) leading to Pangbourne (*Pangeburn'*)[h] as far as the messuage which belonged to Robert *But.*[i] To be held freely after the death of Mabel, Peter's wife, by rendering annually at Michaelmas to the chamberlain of Reading [Abbey] 4s 2d, and to Eustace, son of Alexander the parmenter (*parmentarius*), 8d, and, to provide a lamp over the altar of the Blessed Virgin where *Salve sancta parens* is sung 11d, for all service, secular exaction and demand. Sealing[j]

[*c.* 1220 × 1241]

Bf47r; Cf18v; Cf201v
Pd. *New Pal. Soc. Facs.*, 1st ser., pl. 87 (with facsimile)

Hiis testibus:[k] [Hugone le Bolur, Willelmo le Bulur, Gilberto Rufo, Alano Janitore, Henrico Wille, Roberto Wille, Daniele Wlveseye, Willelmo Bascat, Thoma de Hanleya, Roberto de Mortuo Mar(i), Johanne vinitore, Bartholomeo Channterel, et multis aliis].

[a] Rotherwich *Cf201v*
[c] Chizoi *Cf201v*
[e] Poctereslane *Cf18v*
[g] placea *Cf201v*
[h] Pangebourne *Cf18v*, Pangebourn' *Cf201v*
[i] Butt *Cf201v*
[b] Roseia *Cf18v*
[d] Bruesa *Cf201v*
[f] Chanteler *Cf201v*
[j] *Cf18v ends*
[k] *B ends, the remainder being suupplied from Cf201v*

Peter of Rotherwick, who is clearly near to death here, witnessed a Reading deed before 1220 (no. 892) and two Windsor deeds in 1219 (nos. 1271, 1273). Gilbert Rufus was dead by Oct. 1241 (no. 870 n.). For Hugh le Bolur, see no. 850 n.

959 Quitclaim by Richard *de la Hyde* to Reading Abbey of all his right in the tenement which James Forester (*le Forester*) sometime held in the parish of St Giles, Reading, near the fulling mill (*molendinum fuleret*). For this the abbey has remitted (*relaxaverunt*) the 70s arrears of rent which Richard owed the abbey from a fulling mill in Pangbourne (*Pangebourne*). Sealing   [*c.* 1270 × 85; ? *c.* 1270 × 81]

Cff201v–202r

Hiis testibus: dominis Rolando de Erleya, Johanne de Thetmers, militibus, Willelmo de Blebury, Thoma Huscarl, Gilberto Pinzon, Nicholao le Butiler, Willelmo Tylly, Jacobo Bukkehorn, Willelmo de Waketon', Johanne le Grom, Johanne Aurifabro, Thoma de Mortone clerico, et aliis.

Roland of Earley occurs as a knight from 1270 and was dead in 1305 (see no. 749 n.). John of Tidmarsh occurs as a knight from 1275 and was sheriff of Berks. and Oxon. May 1281–June 1285 (see no. 764; *List of Sheriffs*, 107). Thomas Huscarl was a juror for Theale hundred in 1284 (PRO JUST 1/44, m. 21d) and was certainly a knight in Apr. 1285 (see no. 1240), in which case, since John of Tidmarsh appears second among the witnesses and is not called sheriff, the deed may be not later than May 1281. For Nicholas Butler, see no. 923 n.

960 Gift by Thomas of Binfield (*Benefeud*) and Joan, his wife, to

Robert of Preston (*Preston'*) of 6s 6d annual rent, [viz.] from William of Missenden (*Mussenden'*) 4s from a tenement which he holds of them in Shop Row (*Shoprewe*), Reading, next to the messuage which belonged to Stephen Tailor (*le Taillour*); from the heirs of William *Reinild'* 2s from the tenement which they hold of them in London Street, Reading; and from Geoffrey *le Fenere* 6d from a tenement which he holds of them in the field of Earley (*Erle*). To be held freely by rendering annually to the donors and their heirs 1 clove at Easter for all secular services, customs, exactions and demands. Warranty and sealing with the donors' seals   [*c.* 1265 × 90]

Cf 202r

Hiis testibus: Willelmo de Blebur' senescallo Radyng', Gilberto Pinzon, Willelmo de Mussendene, Galfr(ed)o Gomme, Petro de Aston', Roberto Hardi, Matheo de Cicestr', Willelmo le Diere, Roberto Bygod, Benedicto de la Bruere, Simone de Buham, et aliis.

The donor was bailiff of the two hundreds of Reading and Theale in 1269 and made a gift to Reading Abbey in Burghfield in 1272 (PRO JUST 1/42, m. 19; Df46v). William of Blewbury occurs as steward of the abbey between 1267 and 1303 (see no. 855 n.). Gilbert Pincent was a juror for Reading hundred in 1269, and Geoffrey Gomme and Peter de Aston' jurors for Reading vill (PRO JUST 1/42, m. 19). Geoffrey Gomme, Matthew of Chichester, Robert Bygod and Robert of Preston were all involved in cases in the eyre of 1284 (JUST 1/44, m. 15d; 1/43, m. 12), and John Dyer was a Reading juror in the same (1/44, m. 21d).

961 Acknowledgement by Philip Chapman (*le Chapman*) of Reading of his and his heirs' obligation to pay to Abbot Nicholas [of Whaplode] and the convent of Reading and their successors 2s annual rent in perpetuity, at Michaelmas and Easter in equal portions, from his shop in the Lormery (*in Lormeria*), Reading, between the shop of Thomas *Huberd* and that which Robert Saddler (*le Sadelar'*) holds. The abbot and convent, through themselves or their officer (*minister*) or officers appointed for this purpose, may distrain on the shop whenever the rent is not forthcoming in whole or in part, and retain the distresses until it is paid in full. Sealing   4 Jan. 1313

Cf 202r–v

Dat' Radyng' die jovis proxima post festum Circumcisionis domini [1 Jan.], anno regni regis Edwardi filii regis Edwardi sexto. Hiis testibus: Rad(ulf)o de Helme, Henrico Greiwell', Waltero Watshod, Gilberto Copenhull', Rogero le Hurt', Edmundo le Barbour, Adam le Hornere, et multis aliis.

Cf. no. 955. For the Lormery, alias Lorimer Lane, see no. 879 n. 1.

962 Gift and quitclaim by Adam *le Polet(er)* of Reading to Abbot Nicholas [of Whaplode] and the convent of Reading of 21s annual rent which he used to receive at Easter and Michaelmas in equal portions in Reading, viz., from a corner tenement which formerly belonged to Nicholas Cutler (*le Coteler*) next to the Corn Market (*forum ubi blada venduntur*) 11s; from a tenement of Thomas Wise (*le Wyse*) in the Lormery (*lormeria*), Reading, opposite the said market, 3s; from a tenement of Geoffrey *Dodewale* in the lane called Gutter Lane[1] (*Guttereslane*) 4s; and from a corner house in Gutter Lane towards High Street (*versus altum vicum*) which sometime belonged to Nicholas *Laward* 3s, which last rent Adam had from Henry Bannister (*Banastre*). Sealing   3 Feb. 1316

Cf202v

Hiis testibus: Rad(ulf)o de Helme, Thoma Syward, Rad(ulf)o de Bello, Johanne le Acatour, Gilberto de Copenhull', Thoma de Leicestre, et Johanne de Pangebourn', et aliis. Dat' Radyng' die martis in crastino Purificacionis beate Marie virginis, anno regni regis Edwardi filii regis Edwardi nono.

1. Gutter Lane is represented by the modern Cross Street (Slade, 'Reading', 5).

963 Gift by Matilda, daughter and heir of Ralph of Whitley (*Whitele*), to Peter of Waltham (*Waltham*), for his service and a certain sum of money, of three messuages in Sivier Street[1] (*le Sivekarestret*), Reading, between the tenement of Adam Tyler (*le Tywelur*), clerk, on the north and that which formerly belonged to Alexander of the Foudry (*Fulrithe*) on the south. To be held freely of the chief lords of the fee by rendering annually the due and customary services. Warranty and sealing   5 Mar. 1311

Cf202v

Hiis testibus: Waltero Gerard, Willelmo Bonafannt, Johanne Fyngod, Willelmo le Fulur, Johanne Golde, Ricardo de Whitele, Ricardo de Sunnyngges, Gilberto de Heghfeld', et aliis. Dat' Radyng' quinto die mensis Marcii, anno regni regis Edwardi filii regis Edwardi quarto.

1. Also known as Synkar Street, now Silver Street (Slade, 'Reading', 5).

964 Gift by Peter of Waltham to John of Whaplode (*Quappelade*), clerk, of three messuages in Reading which he had by gift of Matilda, daughter and heir of Ralph of Whitley (*Whitele*), in Sivier Street (*le Syvekarestret*) between the tenement of John Dancer (*le Danncere*) on the north and that which belonged to Alexander of the Foudry (*Fulrithe*) on the south. To be held freely of the chief lords of the fee by the due and customary services. Warranty. For this John has given him 40s of silver. Sealing 27 July 1326

Cf203r

Hiis testibus: Thoma Syward maiore burgi Radyng', Johanne Fyngod, Hugone Danyel, Ricardo de Whitele, Ricardo le Tyghelere, Waltero le Tyghelere, Johanne de Warneford, et aliis. Dat' apud Radyng' die dominica proxima post festum sancti Jacobi apostoli [25 July], anno regni regis Edwardi filii regis Edwardi vicesimo.

965 Gift by Henry of Culham (*Culnham*) to Geoffrey *de Grava* of a messuage in Old Market (*in veteri mercato*), Reading, next to the tenement of John *Alhurthe* and extending up to the stile (*scalarium*) of St Mary's church to the south. To be held of the chief lords of the fee freely by rendering annually the due and customary rent pertaining to such a messuage. Warranty and sealing 4 Feb. 1298

Cf203r

Hiis testibus: Thoma Syward, Rad(ulf)o de Bello, Rogero Cosyn, Nicholao atte Beche, Roberto le Taillour, Rad(ulf)o le Foghel, Johanne Meycent, et aliis. Dat' Radyng' die martis proxima post festum Purificacionis beate Marie, anno regni regis Edwardi vicesimo sexto.

966 Gift by Roger, son and heir of Geoffrey *atte Grove* of Reading, to Martin *atte Frithe*, miller, of a messuage in Old Market, Reading, next to the tenement formerly belonging to John *Alhurte* and extending up to the stile of the graveyard of St Mary's [church].[a] To be held freely of the chief lords of the fee by the due and customary services. Warranty. For this Martin has given him 20s of silver. Sealing 24 Mar. 1331

Cf203v

Hiis testibus: Waltero le Hurt tunc maiore Radyng', Thoma Syward, Johanne le Foghel, Johanne de Bisshopestone, Johanne Abbod, Thoma le Hurt, Stephano le Dubbare, Willelmo Baude, et aliis. Dat' apud Radyng' die dominica in festo Ramispalmarum, anno regni regis Edwardi tercii a Conquestu quinto.

[a] *Supplied*

967 Quitclaim by Alice, widow of Geoffrey *atte Grove* of Reading, to Martin *atte Frithe*, miller, and his heirs of all her right in a messuage [etc., as in n. 966], which formerly belonged to Geoffrey, her late husband, and which Martin had by gift and enfeoffment of Roger, son of Geoffrey. Sealing   25 Mar. 1331

C f 203v

Hiis testibus: Waltero le Hurt tunc maiore Radyng', Thoma Syward, Johanne le Foughel, Johanne de Bisshopestone, Johanne Abbod, Thoma le Hurt, Stephano le Dubbar(e), Willelmo Baude, et aliis. Dat' apud Radyng' die lune in crastino dominice in festo Ramispalmarum, anno regni regis Edwardi tercii a Conquestu quinto.

968 Gift by Martin *atte Frithe* to Thomas *Bernard* of a messuage in Old Market, Reading [etc., as in no. 966]. To be held freely of the chief lords of the fee by the due and customary services. Warranty. For this Thomas has given him 20s of silver. Sealing

14 Apr. 1337

C f 204r

Hiis testibus: Johanne Aurifabro maiore ville Radyng', Henrico Foliot', Johanne de Aldermanston', Ricardo Turnepeny, Roberto Channtrel, et aliis. Dat' Radyng' die lune in crastino dominice in [festo]*ᵃ* Ramispalmarum, anno regni regis Edwardi tercii a Conquestu undecimo.

ᵃ Supplied

This deed is followed by a gap before no. 969, which begins at the foot of the folio.

969 Gift by John *Blancbulli*, with the consent of Alice his wife, to Gilbert Long (*Longus*), merchant, for his service, of two stalls which Nicholas Hill (*Hulle*) sometime held of him in Reading, between the stall of Thomas Tailor (*Cissor*) and that of Samson the spicer (*speciarius*), and of certain land lying behind the said stalls and between the messuage of Samson the spicer and that of Ralph *le Wayte*,[1] viz., in the Corn Market (*in foro ubi bladum venditur*). To be held freely by rendering annually to the donor and his heirs 1 mark of silver, viz., $\frac{1}{2}$ mark each at Michaelmas and Easter, for all secular service, exaction and demand. Warranty. If Alice, John's wife, shall outlive him and presume to implead Gilbert or his heirs on account of the said stalls and land, it is agreed between Gilbert and Alice before trustworthy men called for this purpose that she shall pay Gilbert or his heirs 10 marks of silver as a penalty for promoting a plea (*si . . . aliquam querelam inde suscitaverit*). Sealing with the seals of John and Alice

[*c.* 1220 × 1248]

Cf204r–v; (noted) Bf49v; Cf20v

Hiis testibus: Hugone le Bolor, Roberto Wille, Henrico Wille, Alano Janitore, Alano vinit(ario), Daniele Wlveseye, Thoma cissore, Sansone speciario, Thoma Budde, Jacobo clerico, et multis aliis.

The donor was still alive in 1241, but was dead by June 1248 (PRO JUST 1/37, mm 26, 35d; Clanchy, *Berks. Eyre of 1248*, 169–70). Hugh le Bolur occurs from 1219 and may have been dead in 1248 (see no. 850 n.). For Henry Wille, who occurs prominently from 1241, see no. 876 n. For a similar deed, see no. 861.

1. Called *le Gayte* in no. 974. The meaning is probably Porter.

970 Gift in free alms by Alan, son and heir of John *le Achatur*, to Reading Abbey of a messuage in New Street, Reading, in the parish of St Laurence, between the house which belonged to William of Sherborne (*Syreburne*) and that which belonged to William *Buche*. Sealing. Witnesses [omitted] [not later than 1258; ? *c.* 1240 × 1258]

Bf49v; Cf21r

Not later than 1258, since it was entered in the original section of B. For some reason it was not copied in the second main part of C, as was the case for all other Reading town deeds entered in B. It is inserted at this point, since another deed by the same Alan follows, q.v. for dating in general. William Buche occurs in Reading in 1248 (Clanchy, *Berks. Eyre of 1248*, 185) and himself made a gift to the abbey (below, no. 1011).

971 Gift by Alan son of John *le Achatour*[1] to John *Pykard*, for his service, of 6s annual rent in Reading to be received at Michaelmas, viz., from the messuage which Stephen of St Albans, clerk, holds of him in New Street next to the messuage of Ingelasia Small (*Yngelasia la Smale*) on the west 5s, and from the two messuages which Stephen of the Cellar (*de Celar(io)*) holds in New Street next to the messuage formerly belonging to Gervase *Galun* on the east 12d. To be held freely by rendering annually to the donor and his heirs 1 clove at Easter for all secular service, exaction and demand. For this John has given him 4 marks of silver as entry-fine. Warranty and sealing
[not later than 1258; ? mid-13th cent.]

Cff204v–205r; (noted) Bf49v; Cf20v

Hiis testibus: Henrico Wille, Daniele Wlveseye, Alano vinit(ario), Ad(a) clerico, Thoma le Cordewan(er), Johanne filio Ph(ilipp)i Drapario, Thoma de Henle, Johanne Tinctore, Willelmo de Mussenden', Nicholao, Gilberto Scot, Thoma mercatore, et multis aliis.

Noted in the original section of B. John Pykard occurs as a vintner in Reading in 1255 (*Close Rolls 1254–56*, 90–1) and is called the abbot of Reading's butler in no. 974. The deed perhaps dates from the time when Henry Wille and Daniel Wolvesey were stewards of the Reading gild (see no. 862 n.). Although there was a later John le Acatur (see, e.g., no. 975), the father of the present donor was dead by 1258, being survived by his widow Petronilla (see no. 911).

1. The marginal rubric (contemporary with the text) calls him Alan *Chatour*.

972   Gift by Henry *le Bruton* to John *Pycard*, for his service, of 12d annual rent to be received at Michaelmas from the messuage which Peter of Englefield (*Englefeld'*) holds in Reading in Old Market (*in veteri foro*), between the messuage of Richard the smith (*faber*) and the little lane leading from the Old Market to the graveyard of St Mary's [church].*ᵃ* To be held freely by rendering annually to the donor and his heirs 1 clove at Michaelmas for all secular service, exaction, custom and demand. For this John has given him 6s sterling as entry-fine. Warranty and sealing   [not later than 1258; ? mid-13th cent.]

C f 205r; (noted) B f 49v; C f 20v

Hiis testibus: Henrico Wille, Stephano de la Wyle, Daniele Wlvesey, Willelmo de Whiteleya, Adam Clerico, Willelmo de Mussinden', Nicholao clerico, Rogero de Camera, Gilberto super pontem, Thoma*ᵇ* de Benetfeld'*ᶜ* clerico, et multis aliis.

ᵃ Supplied   *ᵇ Ms has Thomas*
ᶜ Perhaps another name omitted (see note)

Date as for no. 971, although Daniel Wolvesey appears third in the witness-list. For Stephen de la Wyle, see no. 890 n. Thomas of Binfield is not otherwise described as a clerk and, from other references (nos. 903, 960; D f 47r), was clearly married.

973   Gift by Richard *Hecmar* to John *Pykard*, for his service, of a messuage in Old Street, Reading, between the messuage of master Robert of London (*Lond'*) and that of Gilbert *le Norays*. To be held freely by rendering annually to Reading Abbey 12d at Michaelmas, and to the donor and his heirs 1 clove as increment at the same term, for all secular service, exaction and demand. For this John has given him 20s sterling as entry-fine. Warranty and sealing
[not later than 1258; ? mid-13th cent.]

C f 205r-v; (noted) B f 49v; C f 20v

Hiis testibus: Henrico Wille, Daniele Wlveseye, Alano vinit(ario), Thoma de Henl(e), Willelmo de Mussenden', Nicholao clerico, Thoma le Corwaner, Johanne Tinctore, Willelmo Grosso vinit(ario), Rogero de Camera, et multis aliis.

Date as for no. 971. Cf. no. 983.

974 Gift by Walter, son of Gilbert Long (*Longus*) the merchant of Reading, to John *Pykard*, known as Butler of the abbot of Reading (*Pincerna dictu(s) abb(atis) Radyng'*),[a] for his service, of two stalls in Reading between the stall of Robert *Wille* and that which sometime belonged to Samson Spicer (*le Spic(er)*), and of a messuage behind the said stalls between the messuage which sometime belonged to the said Samson Spicer and that which sometime belonged to Ralph *le Gayte*,[1] viz., in the Corn Market. To be held freely by rendering annually to the donor and his heirs or assigns 1 clove at Michaelmas, and to the lord of the fee 1 mark of silver, viz., $\frac{1}{2}$ mark each at Michaelmas and Easter, for all secular service, exaction and demand. Warranty. For this John has given him 6 marks of silver. Sealing

[? *c.* 1240 × 1258]

C f 205v; (noted) B f 49v; C f 20v

Hiis testibus: Willelmo de Whitele, Stephano de la Wyle, Daniele Wolveseye, Henrico Wylle, Nicholao clerico, Ad(a) Kynewar, et aliis.

[a] *Latin seems possibly corrupt here, and the English rendering may be in doubt*

Noted in the original section of B. After no. 969, q.v., and perhaps some years before Henry Wille and Daniel Wolvesey were stewards of the Reading gild (see no. 862 n.). For William of Whitley, see no. 907 n. For another deed by the donor, see no. 875.

1. Called *le Wayte* in no. 969.

975 Gift by Edmund *Bullok'*[a] of Oakley (*Okle*) to John *le Acatour* and Alice, his wife, and the heirs or assigns of John *le Acatour*, of a messuage called the Bread House (*le Bredhous*) in the Fish Market (*in foro le Vyschepyng'*) in High Street (*in alto vico*), Reading. To be held of the chief lords of the fee by rendering annually the due and customary services. Warranty and sealing   3 Dec. 1303

C ff 205v–206r

Hiis testibus: Gilberto Pynson, Rad(ulf)o de la Bataille, Waltero Gerard, Willelmo Bonenfannt, Rad(ulf)o de Helme, Petro de Hayle, Johanne Fyngod, Andrea clerico, et aliis. Dat' Radyng' die martis proxima ante festum sancti Nicholai [6 Dec.], anno [regni][b] regis Edwardi tricesimo secundo.

[a] *Interlined*   [b] *Supplied*

976 Gift by John *le Foughel* of Reading to master Hubert Constable (*le Conestable*), clerk, of a house called Bread House (*Bredhous*) in High Street (*in alto vico*), Reading, which John had by gift and enfeoffment of John *le Acatour* of Reading. To be held freely of the chief lords of the fee by the due and customary services. Sealing   27 June 1327

Cf206r

Hiis testibus: Johanne Aurifabro maiore burgi Radyng', Thoma Syward, Henrico Foliot, Roberto Sauc(er), Willelmo Gynfull', Johanne clerico, et aliis. Dat' apud Radyng' die sabbati proxima ante festum apostolorum Petri et Pauli [29 June], anno regni regis Edwardi tercii a Conquestu primo.

This may be the messuage in Reading which master Hubert Constable obtained a mortmain licence in 1335 to alienate to Reading Abbey (see no. 106), especially since in nos. 975 and 977 it is described as a messuage.

977   Gift by John *le Acatour* and Alice, his wife, to John *le Foughel* of Reading of the messuage called Bread House (*Bredhous*) in High Street (*in alto vico*), Reading, in the Fish Market (*in foro vocato Vyschepyng'*). To be held of the chief lords of the fee freely by doing annually the due and customary services. Warranty and sealing with the donors' seals   21 Feb. 1317

Cf206r

Hiis testibus: Thoma Syward, Rad(ulf)o de la Bataille, Rad(ulf)o de Helme, Henrico de Greiwell', Henrico Banastr(e), Gilberto de Copenhulle, Waltero Watshod, Rogero le Hurt, Edmundo le Barbour, Johanne de Stoke, Adam le Hornere, Johanne de Pangebourn', et multis aliis. Dat' Radyng' vicesimo primo die mensis Februarii, anno regni regis Edwardi filii regis Edwardi decimo.

The historical sequence of deeds concerning this messuage was nos. 975, 977, 976.

978   Gift by Walter Petworth (*Petteworthe*) to John Goldsmith (*Aurifaber*) of a tenement in New Street, Reading, between the tenement of Hugh Marshal (*Marescallus*) and that of John Petworth. To be held freely by rendering annually to Reading Abbey 2s at Michaelmas, and to the donor and his heirs 1 clove at the same term, for all secular service, exaction and demand. For this John has given him 4 marks of silver as entry-fine. Warranty and sealing   [? *c.* 1240 × 1261]

Cf206v

[Hiis testibus] domino Stephano de la Wyle, Willelmo de Whitele, Daniele Wlveseye, Ada Kynewar', Gilberto Convers, Willelmo Marescallo, Johanne le Grom, Johanne le Cave, Ricardo le Celar', Johanne Crouwe clerico, et multis aliis.

a a Supplied

Daniel Wolvesey was dead by Feb. 1261 (see no. 862 n.). For Stephen de la Wyle and William of Whitley, who both occur from the 1240s, see nos. 890 n., 907 n. Gilbert Convers was a vintner in Reading in 1261 and a tenant there in 1269, and was dead by Oct. 1284 (PRO JUST 1/40, m. 29d; above no. 918; JUST 1/48, m. 8). John Groom and John le Cave witness in 1273 (see nos. 998–9). John of Petworth occurs in 1248 and 1261 (Clanchy, *Berks. Eyre of 1248*, 397; PRO JUST 1/40, m. 11).

979 Gift by Hugh*a* Marshal (*Marescallus*), son of Richard Marshal, to John Goldsmith (*Aurifaber*) and Christina, his wife, of a messuage in New Street, Reading, between the messuage formerly belonging to John Petworth (*Petteworthe*) and *la Medgate*. To be held freely by rendering annually to Reading Abbey 6d at Michaelmas, and to the donor and his heirs 4s, viz., 2s each at Michaelmas and Easter, for all secular service, exaction and demand. For this John and Christina have given him 4 marks of silver. Warranty and sealing

[? *c.* 1250 × 1284]

Cf206v

Hiis testibus: Willelmo de Whitele, Willelmo de Mussenden', Johanne le Cave, Gilberto Converso, Johanne le Grom, Waltero le Taillour, Willelmo le Barbour, et multis aliis.

a Interlined

Before Oct. 1284, when Gilbert Convers was dead (see no. 978 n.). John Goldsmith was a juror for Reading vill in 1269 (PRO JUST 1/42, m. 19). The witnesses include none who were prominent only before *c.* 1260. For John le Cave and John Groom, see no. 978 n.

980 Gift in free alms by John Goldsmith (*Aurifaber*) of Reading to Reading Abbey of a messuage in New Street, Reading, between the gate of East Mead (*Estmed*) on the east and the messuage of Elias of Banbury (*Bannebury*) on the west; and of a plot (*placea*) in High Street (*in alto vico*), Reading, between the messuage of Ralph of Cholsey (*Chaus'*) on the east and the lane leading to St Mary's church on the west. To be held for the almonry of Reading [Abbey]. Warranty and sealing

[*c.* 1270 × 1300]

Cf207r

Hiis testibus: domino Rolando de Erle, domino Thoma Danvers, domino Rogero de Burfeld, militibus, Willelmo de Bleburi, Gilberto Pinzon, Johanne Fache,*a* Waltero Gerard', Elia de Bannabury, Ricardo de Whitele, et multis aliis.

a ? rectius Fachel

Roland of Earley was a knight by 1270 and was dead by 1305 (see no. 749 n.). Thomas Danvers was lord of Wokefield (Berks.) and sheriff of Berks. and Oxon. 1286–9 (*VCH Berks.*, iii. 424). Roger of Burghfield, lord of one manor in Burghfield, occurs from 1279 (*Cal. Misc. Inq.*, i. 350) until his death in 1327 (*VCH Berks.*, iii. 400); he was a juror for Theale hundred in 1284 (PRO JUST 1/44, m. 21d) and gave up the coronership of the Liberty of Reading to enter the king's service in 1297 (see no. 100). For William of Blewbury, see no. 855 n.

981   Confirmation in free alms by John, son of John Goldsmith (*Aurifaber*) of Reading, to Reading Abbey of his father's gift of the whole messuage in New Street, Reading, between the gate of East Mead (*Estmed*) on the east and the tenement of Elias of Banbury (*Bannebury*) on the west, and extending from the said street to the ditch of Vastern[1] (*Fasterne*). Warranty and sealing

[prob. late 13th cent.]

C f 207r

Hiis testibus: Elia de Banneburi, Willelmo le Chamberlayn, Willelmo le Charett(er), Willelmo de Bracino, Johanne Bordel, Nicholao clerico, et aliis.

After no. 980. The deed is apparently undated, suggesting a date before or shortly after 1300. William Chamberlain occurs down to 1297 (see no. 883 n.). John Bordel was a borough juror in 1284 and witnessed in 1287 (PRO JUST 1/44, m. 21d; below no. 996). Nicholas the clerk is clearly different from the prominent Reading figure earlier in the century who died before Feb. 1261 (see no. 861 n.).

1. The name given to the area of meadow north of the town in the Middle Ages, and preserved today in the street name, Vastern Road.

982   Quitclaim in free alms by John, son of John Goldsmith (*Aurifaber*) of Reading, to Reading Abbey of all his right in a tenement with a plot (*placea*) of land; the tenement is between the gate of East Mead (*Estmed*) on the east and the tenement of Elias of Banbury (*Bannebury*) on the west, and the plot of land lies ᵃ[between the messuage]ᵃ of Ralph of Cholsey (*Chuls'*) and the lane leading to St Mary's church. Sealing   [prob. late 13th cent.]

C f 207r–v

Hiis testibus: Elia de Banneburi, Willelmo le Chaumberlayn, Willelmo le Charett(er), Willelmo de Bracino, Johanne Bordel, Nicholao clerico, et aliis, et cetera.

ᵃ ᵃ *Om. in Ms, supplied from no. 980*

The witness-list is identical with that of no. 981, and both deeds were probably made on the same day.

983 Quitclaim by William of Shottesbrooke (*Sottesbrok'*) and Matilda *Hicmar*, his wife, to Richard *Hicmar* and his heirs or assigns of all their right in name of dower in the whole messuage which formerly belonged to Nicholas *Hicmar* in Old Street, Reading, between the messuage of master Robert of London (*Lond'*) and that of Gilbert *le Norays*. For this Richard has given them 10s sterling. Sealing with their seals   [not later than 1258; ? mid-13th cent.]

  C f 207v; (noted) B f 49v; C f 20v

Hiis testibus: Henrico Wille, Daniele Wlveseye, Alano vinit(ario), Ad(a) clerico, Thoma de Henl(e), Thoma le Cordewan(er), Willelmo de Mussendene, Nicholao clerico, Johanne Tinctore, Rogero de Camera, Gilberto supra pontem, Johanne aurifabro, et multis aliis.

Date as for no. 862. This messuage is the same as that in no. 973, which belongs to the same dating range.

984 Gift in free alms by John Goldsmith (*Aurifaber*) of Reading to Reading Abbey of 3s annual rent from his stall in the Lormery (*Lorimaria*), Reading, between the tenement of William Barber (*le Barbur*) and the same William's stall in the same street. Warranty and sealing   [*c.* 1270 × Sept. 1287]

  C f 207v

Hiis testibus: domino Roberto Fulcon(is), domino Rolando*ª* de Erle, milit', Roberto de Preston', Nicholao le Butiller, Willelmo le Chamberlayn, Johanne Fachel, Ricardo de Grenham, et multis aliis.

  ª Ms has Roberto (*in error*)

Roland of Earley occurs as a knight from 1270 (see no. 749 n.). Robert Fulconis, a justice-in-eyre in the 1280s, was dead by 8 Sept. 1287 (see no. 880 n.).

985 Gift in free alms by Godhalda, widow of Thomas *de Estley*, to Reading Abbey of a messuage with garden beyond the water (*ultra aquam*) in Reading, which messuage formerly belonged to Hugh *le Bolur* and is between the messuage of Henry *Channtrel* and that formerly belonging to Roger *Harm*. To be held by rendering annually to John of Woodcote (*Wodecot'*) and Juliana, his wife, 1d at Easter for all secular service, exaction and demand. Sealing   [? *c.* 1250 × 70]

C f 208r

Hiis testibus: Stephano de la Wyle, Willelmo de Whiteley, Henrico Wille, Willelmo de Mussenden', Gilberto supra pontem, Johanne tinctore, Johanne vinitore, Thoma le Cordewaner, Ricardo Gunt(er), Rad(ulf)o de Heghfeld', Nicholao de Walyngford, Johanne filio Ph(ilipp)i, Johanne Aurifabro, Stephano de Sancto Albano clerico, et multis aliis.

Dating uncertain, but after no. 986. Stephen de la Wyle and Henry Wille do not definitely occur after 1261 (see nos. 890 n., 876 n.). For William of Whitley, see no. 907 n. John dyer was a Reading juror in 1241 and 1248 (see no. 861 n.) and was dead by Oct. 1284 (PRO JUST 1/43, m. 8d). Richard Gunter was one of the bailiffs of the borough of Reading in 1261 and an elector and juror in 1269 (JUST 1/40, m. 14d; 1/42, m. 19). For Ralph of Heckfield between 1248 and 1286, see no. 880 n.

986 Gift by John of Woodcote (*Wodecot'*) and Juliana, his wife, to Godhalda, widow of Thomas *de Estley*, of a messuage in Reading which was formerly the capital messuage of Hugh *le Bolur*, between the messuage which formerly belonged to Henry *Channtrel* and that which formerly belonged to Roger *Harm*. To be held freely by rendering annually to the chamberlain of Reading [Abbey] 14d from the garden and 3d from the bridge beyond the great water (*de ponte ultra magnam aquam*) at Michaelmas, and to Matilda Palmer (*la Paumer'*) 1d, and to the cellarer of Reading [Abbey] 1 mark, viz., ½ mark each at Michaelmas and Easter, and to the donors and their heirs 1d as increment at Michaelmas, for all secular service, exaction and demand. For this Godhalda has given them 11 marks of silver as entry-fine. Warranty and sealing with their seals   [1241 × 61]

C f 208r

Hiis testibus: Willelmo de Whiteley, Johanne clerico, Henrico Wille, Daniele Wlveseye, Nicholao clerico, Ad(a) clerico, Johanne tinctore, Gilberto sur le pond, Ricardo Gunt(er), Thoma le Cordewaner, Stephano clerico, et aliis.

Since the messuage was formerly the capital messuage of Hugh le Bolur, he had presumably died by the time of this deed; he was still alive in 1241, but may have been dead by June 1248 (see no. 850 n.). Daniel Wolvesey, Nicholas clerk and Adam clerk were all dead by Feb. 1261 (see nos. 861 n., 862 n.). The donors were impleaded in 1248 over a messuage in Reading, possibly the present messuage (Clanchy, *Berks. Eyre of 1248*, 181).

987 Gift by Robert *le Blund* to John Goldsmith (*Aurifaber*), for his service, of a messuage in New Street, Reading, next to the messuage of Griffin Mason (*Cementarius*) on the west. To be held freely by rendering annually to Reading Abbey 12d at Michaelmas, and to the donor and his heirs ½d as increment at the same term, for all secular service, exaction and demand. For this John has given him 1 mark of silver as entry-fine. Warranty and sealing [? *c.* 1230 × 40]

Cf208v

Hiis testibus: Henrico Wille, Willelmo de Wyteley, Stephano de la Wyle, Johanne clerico, Ad(a) clerico, Daniele Wlveseyche, Nicholao clerico, Gilberto supra pontem, Griffino le Mazonn, Stephano Hogeman, et multis aliis.

A Robert *Blundus* was dead by Jan. 1240 (see no. 922 n.). Adam clerk, Daniel Wolvesey and Nicholas clerk were all dead by Feb. 1261 (see nos. 861 n., 862 n.). Henry Wille occurs down to 1261 (see no. 876 n.). John clerk occurs in Reading in 1241 (PRO JUST 1/37, m. 25B d). For William of Whitley and Stephen de la Wyle, see nos. 907 n., 890 n.

988 Gift by John Goldsmith (*Aurifaber*) and Christina, his wife, to Peter *de la Broke* of Burghfield (*Burghfeld*), for 18s sterling, of a messuage in New Street, Reading, between the messuage which sometime belonged to Gilbert Cook (*Cocus*) on the west and their own messuage on the east, which messuage they had by gift of Robert White (*le White*).[1] To be held freely by rendering annually to Reading Abbey 12d at Michaelmas, and to the donors and their heirs 1 clove at Michaelmas, for all secular service, exaction and demand. Warranty and sealing (*sigillum meum apposui*) [? *c.* 1260 × 90]

Cf208v

Hiis testibus: Willelmo le Chamberlayn, Ricardo de Whitele, Stephano le Grom, Elia mercatore, Johanne Fachel, Ricardo de Grenham, Rad(ulf)o de Heucfeud, Ricardo Coppe, Osberto le Bevor, Henrico Lupo, Thoma le Acatur, Waltero Coco, Nicholao clerico, et aliis.

Before *Quia emptores*. William Chamberlain occurs from the 1280s (see no. 883 n.). Stephen Groom witnesses in 1269 × 87 (no. 881). Richard of Greenham occurs in 1284 (PRO JUST 1/43, m. 9). For Ralph of Heckfield between 1248 and 1286, see no. 880 n. For Richard Coppe between 1248 and 1284, see no. 954 n.

1. *Alias* le Blund (see no. 987).

989 Gift by Peter *de la Broke* of Burghfield (*Burghfeld'*) to Henry *Thurebern* of Wokingham (*Wokyngham*), carpenter, for a certain sum of money, of a messuage in New Street, Reading, between the messuage of Philip the merchant on the east and that formerly belonging to Gilbert Cook (*Cocus*) on the west. To be held freely by rendering annually to Reading Abbey 12d at Michaelmas, and to the donor and his heirs 1 rose on the feast of the Nativity of St John Baptist, for all secular service, exaction and demand. Warranty and sealing

[? *c.* 1280 × 90]

Cf209r

Hiis testibus: Elia mercatore, Willelmo le Chamberlayn, Willelmo le Charett(er), Willelmo Braciatore, Henrico de Greywell', Johanne Bordel, Willelmo de Molesford, et aliis.

Before *Quia emptores*. None of the witnesses definitely occurs earlier than 1280. For William Chamberlain, see no. 883 n. Henry of Greywell occurs from 1297 to 1317 (*Berks. Arch. Journ.*, lx (1962), 105; above, no. 977). For John Bordel in 1284 and 1287, see no. 981 n.

990 Quitclaim by Richard son of William *le Blonnt* to Peter *de la Broke*, for a certain sum of money, of all his right in a messuage and in ½d annual rent to be received from it, which messuage Peter formerly bought from John Goldsmith (*Aurifaber*), on the north side of New Street, Reading. Sealing   [? *c.* 1260 × 90]

Cf209r

Hiis testibus: Gilberto Pynchun, Johanne Fachel, Ricardo de Grenham, Willelmo le Chamberleng', Elia mercatore, Johanne Bordel, Thoma de Maynhull', et aliis.

This dates after no. 988 and before no. 989. It releases Peter de la Broke from the rent retained to the *Blund* or *Blonnt* family in the gift of this messuage to John Goldsmith (no. 987).

991 Gift in free alms by Agnes *Orry*, widow of Henry *Thurbern*, carpenter, to the almonry of Reading Abbey of a messuage in New Street, Reading, between the tenement of Philip the merchant on the east and that formerly belonging to Gilbert Cook (*Cocus*) on the west, which messuage Henry, her late husband, bequeathed to her in his last will. To be held freely of the chief lords of the fee by the due and customary service, rendering annually to the chamberlain of the said abbey 12d at Michaelmas for all secular service, exaction and demand. Warranty and sealing   [1290 × *c.* 1310]

Cf209r–v

Hiis testibus: Elia de*a* Bannebury, Willelmo le Chamberleng', Willelmo le Charett(er), Willelmo de Bracino, Henrico Greywell', Gilberto de Copenhull', Johanne Bordel, Gilberto clerico, et aliis.

a *Ms repeats* de

After *Quia emptores* and probably before 1310, by which date Reading deeds seem generally to have been dated.

992 Gift by John Gold (*Golde*) to Robert *Person* and Edith, his wife, of 6d annual rent which he used to receive at Michaelmas from the tenement of William Corker (*le Cork(er)*) in London Street, Reading, next to the tenement of Adam *Pecamondus*, and of 1d rent which he used to receive at the same term from the stall of John *Perseval* in Shoemakers' Row (*in suteria*), Reading, next to the stall of Richard of Ashbourne (*Asshebourn'*). For this Robert has given him a certain sum of money. Warranty and sealing   30 Dec. 1315

C f 209v

Hiis testibus: Thoma Syward, Rad(ulf)o de Bello, Johanne le Acatur, Johanne Fyngod, Henrico de Greiwell', Willelmo le White, Gilberto de ponte, et aliis. Dat' Radyng', die martis in crastino sancti Thoma martiris [29 Dec.], anno regni regis Edwardi filii regis Edwardi nono incipiente.

It is notable that, although this deed is after *Quia emptores*, there is no provision for the donees to hold of the chief lords of the fee, or indeed of any one.

993 Gift by Robert *le Blund* to John Goldsmith (*Aurifaber*), for his service and in place of the 10 marks of silver which Robert had promised John with Clemencia his daughter, whom John has married, of a messuage in New Street, Reading, between the messuage of Stephen *Hogeman* and that of Robert *de gardino*. To be held freely by rendering annually to Reading Abbey 8d, to Matilda of Oakley (*Hocly*) and her heirs 2s, to Richard of Southcote (*Southcote*) and his heirs 1d, to Simon Brian (*Brian*) and his heirs 1d, and to the donor and his heirs ½d as increment, all at Michaelmas, for all secular service, exaction and demand. Warranty and sealing   [? *c.* 1230 × 40]

C ff 209v–210r

Hiis testibus: Henrico Wille, Willelmo de Whiteley, Stephano de la Wyle, Daniele Wlveseye, Ad(a) clerico, Nicholao clerico, Willelmo de Mussinden', Stephano Hogeman, Griffino Cementario, et multis aliis.

Date as for no. 987, q.v. Matilda of Oakley was the wife (or perhaps the widow) of Richard *Bulluc* of Oakley (see no. 618 n.).

994 Gift by John Goldsmith (*Aurifaber*) to William of Blewbury

(*Blebury*), for his service, of a messuage in New Street, Reading, between the messuage of Stephen *Hogeman* and that formerly belonging to Robert *de Gardino*. To be held freely by rendering annually to Reading Abbey 9d, to Adam of Oakley (*Hokle*) and his heirs 2s, to the heirs of Robert *le Blont* ½d, and to the donor and his heirs 1 clove, all at Michaelmas, for all secular service, exaction and demand. For this William has given him 8 marks sterling. Warranty and sealing
[*c.* 1260 × 1284]

Cf210r

Hiis testibus: Willelmo de Whitele, Rogero Fachel, Gilberto Converso, Johanne le Grom, Willelmo le Porter, Bartholomeo Wlveseye, Petro le Tayllur, Willelmo de Mussinden', et aliis.

Before Oct. 1284, when Gilbert Convers and Bartholomew Wolvesey were dead (see nos. 978 n., 880 n.). William of Blewbury occurs from the 1260s to the early 14th century (see no. 855 n.). Roger Vachell and William Porter were Reading jurors in 1269 (JUST 1/42, m. 19). Peter Tailor witnessed in 1255 and 1273 (nos. 875, 999). Adam of Oakley was the son of Richard and Matilda of Oakley (Df61r).

995 Gift by John Goldsmith (*Aurifaber*) to William of Blewbury (*Bleburi*), for his service, of a messuage in New Street, Reading, between the messuage which sometime belonged to Stephen *Hogeman* and that of William Tiler (*Tegulator*), and of 16d annual rent which the donor used to receive from the messuage of the said William Tiler. To be held freely by rendering annually to Reading Abbey 9d, to Adam of Oakley (*Hocle*) and his heirs 2s, to the heirs of Robert *le Blont* ½d, all at Michaelmas, and to the donor and his heirs 1 clove at Easter, for all secular service, exaction and demand. For this William has given him 9 marks sterling. Warranty and sealing [*c.* 1260 × 1284]

Cf210r–v

Hiis testibus: Willelmo de Whitele, Rogero Fachel, Willelmo Tylly, Johanne le Grom, Willelmo de Mussinden', Nicholao le Butiller, Bartholomeo Wlveseye, Thoma de Morton' clerico, Johanne clerico, et aliis.

After no. 994, since William Tiler now holds the messuage formerly belonging to Robert de Gardino, and before the death of Bartholomew Wolvesey (see no. 994 n.).

996 Quitclaim by Richard *ᵃson of Williamᵃ le Blonnt'* of Reading to William of Blewbury (*Blebury*) and his heirs and assigns of all his right in a messuage which belonged to Robert, Richard's grandfather, on the south side of New Street, Reading, and in the rent arising from the said house. Sealing   9 Nov. 1287

Cf210v

Hiis testibus: Gilberto Pinzon, Johanne Fachel, Galfr(edo) le Engleys, Johanne Bordel, Elya de Bannebury, Nicholao le Butiller, Nicholao le Cotiller, Thoma clerico, et aliis. Dat' die dominica proxima ante festum sancti Martini [11 Nov.], anno regni regis Edwardi quinto-decimo.

a–a Ms has filius Gulemini (*cf. no. 990*)

Richard's grandfather, Robert, was the donor in nos. 987, 993.

997   Gift by William *Lovekyn* to William of Blewbury (*Blebury*), for his service, of a messuage with a curtilage measuring 127 feet in length and 17 feet in width in New Street, Reading, between the said William of Blewbury's messuage and that of John *Burdel*. To be held freely by rendering annually to Sir Roland of Earley (*Erlegh'*) and his heirs 2s, and to the donor and his heirs 1 clove, at Michaelmas for all secular service, exaction and demand. For this William has given him 20s sterling. Warranty and sealing   [*c.* 1270 × 90]

Cf211r

Hiis testibus: Willelmo de Wyteley, Nicholao le Butiller, Willelmo de Mussenden', Galfr(ed)o Gomme, Johanne le Grom, Willelmo,*a* Johanne aurifabro, et aliis.

a Surname probably om.

Before *Quia emptores* and after *c.* 1270, from which time Roland of Earley occurs as a knight (see no. 749 n.).

998   Gift by Walter *Poperich* to William of Blewbury (*Blebury*), for his service, of the entire messuage in New Street, Reading, between the messuage of Agatha of Battle (*de Bello*) and the tenement of John Goldsmith (*Aurifaber*). To be held freely by rendering annually to Reading Abbey 8d at Michaelmas for all secular service, exaction and demand. For this William has given him 7s sterling. Sealing

[? 1273, before 1 May]

Cf211r

Hiis testibus: [Willelmo]*a* de Wyteley, Nicholao le Butiller, Willelmo Tylly, Galfr(ed)o Gomme, Johanne le Grom, Johanne Aurifabro, Thoma de Morton', Johanne clerico, et aliis.

a Supplied from contemporary deeds, e.g. no. 999

The date cannot be far different from that of no. 999.

999 Gift by the same to the same, for his service, of the same messuage [details exactly as in no. 998]. To be held of Reading Abbey freely by rendering annually to the abbey 8d at Michaelmas for all secular service, exaction and demand. For this William has given him ½ mark of silver. Sealing   1 May 1273

Cf211v

Hiis testibus: Willelmo de Whitele, Nicholao le Butiller, Willelmo de Mussenden', Johanne le Kave, Gilberto Pinzon, Willelmo de Camera, Petro Cissore, et aliis. Dat' apud Radyng' ex concessione et assensu Walteri de Forncestr', tunc camerarii Radyng', die apostolorum Ph(ilipp)i et Jacobi, anno regni regis Edwardi filii regis Henrici primo.

In no. 998 William and his heirs were to hold of the donor and his heirs, but in this deed they are to hold of the abbot and convent of Reading. As steward of the abbey, it probably suited William to hold in this way (see no. 855 n.).

1000 Gift by William *de Bydeford*[1] to Thomas *de Morton'*, clerk, for his service, of a messuage in New Street, Reading, between the tenement of William of Blewbury (*Blebury*) and that of John Goldsmith (*Aurifaber*). To be held freely by rendering annually to the said John Goldsmith and his heirs 2s, viz., 12d each at Michaelmas and Easter, and to the donor and his heirs 1 rose on the feast of the Nativity of St John Baptist. For this Thomas has given him 60s sterling. Warranty and sealing   [*c.* 1270 × 90]

Cf211v

Hiis testibus: Willelmo de Whitele, Willelmo de Mussenden', Nicholao le Butiller, Willelmo Tilly, Johanne le Grom, Johanne Aurifabro, Radul(f)o[a] Gomme, Thoma Kute,[b] Johanne clerico, et aliis.

[a] *Sic, possibly error for* Galfredo (*cf. nos. 987–8*)
[b] *Reading uncertain*

Before *Quia emptores*. For William of Whitley, see no. 907 n. Nicholas Butler occurs from 1273 (see no. 923 n.). A William Tilli was a vintner in Reading in 1261 and, if the same person, witnessed as late as 1311 (PRO JUST 1/40, m. 29d; below, no. 1008). Geoffrey Gomme (if that is the correct reading in the witness-list) occurs between 1269 and 1284 (see no. 880 n.).

1. Possibly either Bideford (Devon) or Bidford (Warks.).

1001 Gift by Walter *le Walays* of Reading to [William[a] of Blewbury[b]] and Hawisia, his wife, for their service, of 8s annual rent, viz., 4s each at Easter and Michaelmas, from a stall in Reading, situated on the corner opposite Shoemakers' Row (*suteria*), which sometime belonged to John *Gille*. To be held freely by rendering annually to Reading Abbey 28d, and to the donor and his heirs 1 clove, at Michaelmas for all secular service, exaction and demand. For this William and Hawisia have given him 3 marks of silver as entry-fine. Warranty and sealing [*c.* 1260 × 70]

Cf212r

Hiis testibus: Nicholao de Middeltone, Willelmo de Wytele, Willelmo de Mussenden', Gilberto converso, Rogero Fachel, Radul(f)o le Lomb, Willelmo le Port(er), Ricardo Gunt(er), Gerardo de Granng', et aliis.

ᵃ Om. at this point, supplied from later in text
ᵇ Om. in Ms, supplied from no. 1018

Nicholas of Middleton occurs as a witness in East Hendred in 1265 × 6 (see no. 792). For Gilbert Conversus in 1261 and 1269, see no. 978 n. Roger Vachell, William Porter and Richard Gunter were Reading jurors in 1269 (PRO JUST 1/42, m. 19). Ralph Lamb occurs in 1255 and 1261 (PRO CP 25(1)/8/21/31; JUST 1/40, m. 29d). Gerard of the Grange is presumably the Gerard the Granger who occurs in Reading in 1261 (JUST 1/40, m. 14).

1002 Gift by William Goldsmith (*Aurifaber*) and Gunnilda, his wife, to Simon of Wakerley (*Wakerle*), for his service, of a vacant plot (*area*) in High Street (*in alto vico*) between the stall of Walter *Surbred* on the east and that formerly belonging to Nicholas of Wallingford (*Walyngford*). To be held freely by rendering annually to Reading Abbey 2s, and to the donors and their heirs or assigns 4s, at Michaelmas for all secular exaction and demand. For this Simon has given them 18d sterling as entry-fine. Warranty and sealing with the donors' seals [? *c.* 1240 × 60]

Cf212r

Hiis testibus: Waltero Fachel, Rogero Kotᵃ filio suo, Waltero coquo, Johanne de Oxon(ia), Ricardo Samwell', Roberto de Walyngford', Gilberto Franckillano, et multis aliis.

ᵃ Reading uncertain, possibly deleted

Dating uncertain. The donors occur in a case in Reading in 1248 (Clanchy, *Berks. Eyre of 1248*, 173). Simon of Wakerley occurs in 1254 (PRO CP 25(1)/8/21/17). Walter Vachell and Nicholas of Wallingford were jurors for Reading in 1248 (Clanchy, 296) and Gilbert Franklin occurs in 1248 and 1249 (see no., 857 n.). A Walter cook and a Robert of Wallingford occur in the later 12th century (see nos. 817 n., 878 n.), but these are most probably not the same as the witnesses to the present deed.

1003 Gift by William of Earley (*Erlye*), son of Roland of Earley (*Erleye*) knight, to John Warner (*le Warener*) son of Simon Warner of Reading, for his service and 40s of silver, of 4s annual rent which the donor used to receive at Michaelmas from the said Simon from a shop in Butcher Row (*maceria*), Reading, between the shop which sometime belonged to Walter *Surbred* and that formerly belonging to Richard of Henley (*Henley*). To be held freely by rendering annually to the donor and his heirs 1 clove at Christmas for all manner of secular services and demands. Warranty and sealing   [? *c.* 1280 × 90]

Cf212v

Hiis testibus: Johanne Fachel, Adam Fachel,[a] Ricardo de Grenham, Willelmo de Alremaston', Willelmo le vinit(er), Ricardo de Mapeldorham, Rad(ulf)o de Chauseye, Willelmo le White, Gilberto de Hecfeud' clerico, et aliis.

[a] *Ms repeats this man's name*

Before *Quia emptores*. John Vachell occurs several times in Reading from the 1280s and was a steward of Reading Abbey in 1291 (see no. 780). John Warner witnessed in 1296 (no. 1007). Richard of Greenham occurs in 1284, in which year William Vintner and William White were Reading borough jurors (PRO JUST 1/43, m. 9; 1/44, m. 21d). William of Aldermaston occurs in 1297 (*Berks. Archaeol. Journ.*, lx (1962), 102) and Richard of Mapledurham in 1295 (see no. 951).

1004 Gift by William Warner (*le Warner*), son of the late Simon Warner (*le Warener*) of Reading, to William of Rotherfield (*Rutherfeld'*), for his service and 4 marks sterling, of a messuage which he had by gift and enfeoffment of Henry of Fawley (*Falleye*) and Alice, his wife, in High Street (*in alto vico*), Reading, opposite Butcher Row (*mascecreria*), between the tenement of the granger of Reading Abbey on the east and that which formerly belonged to the said Simon Warner (*le Warner*) on the west. To be held freely of the chief lords of the fee by rendering annually the due and customary services. Warranty and sealing   12 Nov. 1301

Cf212v

Hiis testibus: Radul(f)o de la Bataille, Johanne le Acatur, Rad(ulf)o de Helme, Johanne de Denemed, Adam de Maydenhacche, Henrico Banast(re), Johanne Ughtrad, Gilberto de Hecfeld', et aliis. Dat' Radyng' die dominica in crastino sancti Martini episcopi [11 Nov.], anno regni regis Edwardi filii regis Henrici vicesimo nono.

1005 Quitclaim by Ralph *Monncy* to William of Rotherfield (*Rutherfeld'*) and his heirs or assigns, for a certain sum of money, of all his right in 6s annual rent which he used to receive at Easter and

Michaelmas in equal portions from a messuage which the said William has by his gift and enfeoffment in High Street (*in alto vico*), Reading, opposite Butcher Row (*macecr(eria)*), between the tenement which the same William holds of him for life on the west and a tenement which he holds of him in fee on the east. Sealing   9 Mar. 1306

Cf213r

Dat' Radyng' die mercurii proxima ante festum sancti Gregorii pape [12 Mar.], anno regni regis Edwardi filii regis Henrici tricesimo quarto. Hiis testibus: Adam le Polet(er) tunc maiore de Radyng', Rad(ulf)o de Bello, Thoma Syward, Johanne le Acatur, Rad(ulf)o de Helme, Henrico Banastr(e), Radul(f)o de Lovelane, Adam de Maidenhacch', Gilberto de Hecfeud, et aliis.

1006 Quitclaim by Ralph *Monncy* to William of Rotherfield (*Rutherfeld'*) and Alice, his wife, and their heirs or assigns, for a certain sum of money, of all his right in the messuage which they previously held of him by indenture for life in High Street (*in alto vico*), Reading, opposite Butcher Row (*macecrer(ia)*), between the tenement of the said William on the east and that which Ralph *de Lovelane* and Edulina his wife have by his enfeoffment on the west. Sealing   9 June 1306

Cf213r

Hiis testibus: Rad(ulf)o de Bello, Thoma Syward, Johanne le Acatur, Rad(ulf)o de Helme, Henrico Banastr(e), Rad(ulf)o de Love Lane, Adam de Maidenhacch', Gilberto clerico, et aliis. Dat' Radyng' die jovis proxima ante festum sancti Barnabe apostoli [11 June], anno regni regis Edwardi filii regis Henrici tricesimo quarto.

1007 Quitclaim by Henry of Fawley (*Falley*) to Alice Warner (*le Warner*), his wife, of all his right in messuage or in rent which he had in Reading by reason of the said Alice, so that she and her heirs or assigns may sell, alienate or assign the same wherever and whenever they wish. Sealing   7 July 1296

Cf213v

Dat' Radyng' die sabbati in festo translacionis sancti Thome martiris, anno regni regis Edwardi filii regis Henrici vicesimo quarto. Hiis testibus: Johanne atte March', Willelmo vinitario, Stephano Pellipario, Stephano le Dubbar', Johanne le Warner, et multis aliis.

1008 Quitclaim by Alice, daughter of the late Simon Warner (*le Warner*) of Reading and widow of Henry Carter (*le Charett(er)*),[1] to

William of Rotherfield (*Rutherfeld'*) and his heirs and assigns, for his service and a certain sum of money, of all her right in a messuage in High Street (*in alto vico*), Reading, which she had by gift of the said Simon, between the tenement formerly belonging to the said Simon on the west and that of Reading Abbey on the east. To be held of the chief lords of the fee freely by due and customary services. Sealing

1 July 1311

Cf213v

Hiis testibus: [Johanne]*a* lacatur, Adam le Polet(er), Willelmo Bukke, Henrico le Banastr(e), Rad(ulf)o de Helme, Waltero Watshod, Willelmo Tilly, Thoma de Morton', et aliis. Dat' London' die jovis proxima post festum Petri et Pauli [29 June], anno regni regis Edwardi filii regis Edwardi quarto.

a Om. in Ms, supplied from contemporary deeds

The messuage concerned is presumably that in no. 1004.

1. *Alias* Henry of Fawley (see no. 1007).

1009 Quitclaim by Richard *le Blonnd'* son of William *le Blonnd'* of Reading to Abbot Nicholas [of Whaplode] and the convent of Reading of all his right in three messuages in Reading which sometime belonged to Robert *le Blund'*, his grandfather. Sealing

16 Dec. 1311

Cf214r

Hiis testibus: Rad(ulf)o de la Bataille, Rad(ulf)o de Helme, Henrico de Greiwelle, Elia de Banneburi, Ricardo de Asshebourne, Rogero le Hurt, Gilberto de Copen'hulle, et aliis. Dat' Radyng' die jovis proxima post festum beate Lucie virginis [13 Dec.], anno regni regis Edwardi filii regis Edwardi quinto.

The remainder of Cf214r is left blank.

1010 Gift by James Dawtrey (*de Alta Ripa*), chaplain, to Reading Abbey, for the support of the works of the abbey, of a messuage in New Street, Reading, which he formerly bought from the lord William of Tubney (*Tubeneye*), then keeper of the works (*custos operum*), next to the messuage of Gilbert *de Hacslade* on the west. To be held freely by rendering [annually]*a* to Reading Abbey 6d at Michaelmas for all secular service, exaction and demand. For this Maurice, keeper of the works, has given him 10s sterling as entry-fine. Sealing

[? c. 1260 × 70]

Cf214v

Hiis testibus: Willelmo de Bleobury, Willelmo de Whitele, Willelmo de Mussenden', Johanne Tinctore, Johanne vinitario, Rad(ulf)o de Heghfeld', Ricardo Guntt(er), Gilberto le Scot, et aliis.

ª Supplied

The dates of Maurice as keeper of the works are unknown, but he certainly held office before 1261 (see, e.g., no. 1012) and had been preceded at an unknown date by William of Tubney, named in this deed, and by Andrew, who occurs in 1226 (*Sarum Charters and Documents*, 171). The position of William of Blewbury in the witness-list suggests that he may already be steward of the abbey, which he certainly was in 1267 (see no. 855 n.); he is not known to occur earlier than 1260. William of Whitley was a bailiff of Reading in ? the mid-13th century (see nos. 956–7). For Richard Gunter in 1261 and 1269, see no. 985 n. Gilbert Scot was a borough juror in 1241 and 1248 (PRO JUST 1/37, m. 27d; Clanchy, *Berks. Eyre of 1248*, 296).

1011 Gift in free alms by William *Buche* and Margery, his wife, to Reading Abbey, for the support of the works, of a messuage in New Street, Reading, between the house which belonged to Osbert Weaver (*Telarius*) and the house of Edward Hurry (*Hurry*). To be held freely, saving to the chamberlains*ª* of Reading [Abbey] 8d, and *ᵇ*[to the donors and]*ᵇ* their heirs 1d, which the keeper of the works shall pay annually at Michaelmas. For this Maurice, keeper of the works, has given them 1 mark of silver as entry-fine and 1 load of wheat (*summa frumenti*). Warranty and sealing with their seal [? c. 1240 × 60]

Cf214v

Hiis testibus: Gregorio Sementario, Sewalo de Southcot', Waltero coco, Waltero Nuncio, Ricardo Gerlannd', Roberto Wille, Henrico Wille, Thoma de Hanlegh', Waltero Porcario, Roberto forestario, et multis aliis.

ª Sic
ᵇ⁻ᵇ Om. in Ms, supplied as almost certainly in original

Dating very uncertain. The donors occur in Reading in 1248 (Clanchy, *Berks. Eyre of 1248*,185). Gregory Mason occurs there in 1241 (PRO JUST 1/37, m. 26). For Robert Wille and Henry Wille, see nos. 855 n., 876 n. For Thomas of Henley between 1216 × 24 and 1249, see no. 850 n. Robert forester may be the Robert le Forester who was appointed an attorney of the abbot of Reading in 1257–8 (*Close Rolls 1256–9*, 329).

1012 Gift in free alms by John Vintner (*le Vanur*) to Reading Abbey, for the support of the works, of a messuage in New Street, Reading, between the messuage formerly belonging to Ralph Baker (*le Pestur*) and that which belonged to William Lion (*le Lionn*). To be held freely by rendering annually to the chamberlain of Reading [Abbey] 4d; and for a lamp above the altar of St Mary in the church of St

Laurence, Reading, 6d; and to Adam of Woking (*Wokynge*) 1d; and to the donor and his heirs 1 clove, all of which the keeper of the works shall pay at Michaelmas for all secular service, exaction and demand. For this Maurice, keeper of the works, has given him 18s of silver as entry-fine and 1 quarter of wheat. Warranty and sealing

[? *c.* 1240 × 1261]

Cf215r

Hiis testibus: Daniele Wlveseye, Stephano de la Wyle, Willelmo de Mussenden', Willelmo de Whiteleye, Johanne aurifabro, Rad(ulf)o le Pestur, Willelmo le Lyonn, Roberto Janitore, et multis aliis.

Daniel Wolvesey was dead by Feb. 1261 and his position in the witness-list suggests the period of his prominence in Reading in the 1240s and 1250s (see nos. 862 n., 911 n.). For Stephen de la Wyle and William of Whitley, both of whom occur from 1248, see nos. 890 n., 907 n.

1013 Gift in free alms by Hugh of the Sartry (*de Sart(er)ia*) to Reading Abbey, for the support of the works, of a messuage in Old Street, Reading, between the house of Richard Ring (*Ryng'*) and that of Richard *de Grava*. To be held freely by rendering annually to the chamberlain of Reading [Abbey] 8d, and to the donor and his heirs 1d, which the keeper of the works shall pay at Michaelmas for all service and secular exaction. For this Maurice, keeper of the works, has given him 18s of silver as entry-fine and 1 quarter of wheat. Warranty and sealing   [? *c.* 1240 × 1261]

Cf215r

Hiis testibus: Daniele Wlveseye, Stephano de la Wyle, Willelmo de Mussendene, Willelmo de Whitele, Roberto Wille, Henrico Wille, Johanne aurifabro, Roberto forestario, Ricardo Ryng', Ricardo de Grava, et multis aliis.

Dating in general as for no. 1012.

1014 Gift in free alms by Jocelin of Caversham (*Kaversham*) and Alice, his wife, to Reading Abbey, for the support of the works of the abbey, of a messuage in New Street, Reading, between the messuage of John the porter (*portarius*) and that of widow *Breus*. To be held freely by rendering annually to the donors and their heirs or assigns 1d, and to the chamberlain of Reading [Abbey] 8d, at Michaelmas for all secular service, custom, exaction and demand. Warranty. For this Maurice, keeper of the works, has given them 1 mark of silver and 1 quarter of wheat. Sealing with the donors' seals

[? *c.* 1240 × 60]

Cf215v

Hiis testibus: Thoma de Hanl(e), Joesepho, Thoma le Cordewan(er), Johanne Tinctore, Stephano Hogeman, Mauricio Scot', Thoma de Leom(inistria), Johanne Sherewynd, et aliis.

Thomas of Henley witnesses between 1216 × 24 and 1249 (see no. 850 n.) and his position in the witness-list suggests his prominence in the town. Thomas Cordwainer does not certainly occur after *c.* 1260. John Dyer was a Reading juror in 1241 and 1248 (see no. 850 n.) and occurs there in 1261 (PRO JUST 1/40, m. 13d). Stephen Hogeman occurs there in 1248 (see no. 922 n.).

1015 Gift in free alms by John, called 'dispenser' (*dictus dispensator*), of Reading and Isabel his wife to Reading Abbey, for the support of the works of the abbey, of a messuage in Old Street, Reading, between the messuage of Roland son of Agnes *de la Lane* and that of Nicholas the cook (*cocus*). To be held freely by rendering annually to the donors and their heirs or assigns 1d at Michaelmas, and to the chamber (*Camera*) of Reading [Abbey] 20d, for all secular service, custom, exaction and demand. Warranty. For this Maurice, keeper of the works, has given them 1 mark of silver and 1 quarter of wheat. Sealing with the donors' seals [? *c.* 1260 × 70]

Cf215v

Hiis testibus: Willelmo de Bleobury, Willelmo de Whitele, Thoma de Benetfeld', Gilberto de ponte, Gilberto Scoto, Johanne Tinctore, Radul(f)o de Hecfeld', et multis aliis.

The date is probably similar to that of no. 1010, which has several witnesses in common with this deed. For Thomas of Binfield, see nos. 960 n., 972. This is the last deed to be entered in the original hand of the second main part of this cartulary (see vol. I, p. 11).

1016 Gift by Walter of Bec (*de Becco*) of Abingdon (*Abbendon'*)[a] to Reading Abbey of 11s 2d of rents in Reading, viz., from a messuage which Gilbert *le Blik* holds in All Saints Street towards the north between Reginald the priest (*presbiter*) and Richard *Colhoppe*[b] 18d, from a messuage which Hugh of Cholsey (*Chaus(eia)*)[c] holds in the same street towards the south between Walter[d] *de la Mere* and Alice *Billog'* 3s, from a messuage which Reginald the chaplain holds in the same street between Ralph *le Samchepare*[1] and Gilbert *le Blik* 12d, from a messuage which Richard *Colehoppe*[e] holds in the same street between G(ilbert) *le Blik* and Matilda of Calcot (*Caldecot'*)[f] 20d, from a messuage which John son of Philip the draper (*le draper*) holds in the Forbury (*in Forbyr'*) opposite Reginald the priest 12d, from a messuage which Edith widow Black (*Blak*) holds in High Street (*in* *alto vico*) between John the dyer (*tinctor*) and Matilda of Oakley (*Oclye*) 20d, from a cellar which Agatha *Rufa*[g] holds on the corner opposite Helen *la gentille* 8d, and from a stall which Peter the tailor (*cissor*) holds in the Drapery (*in draperia*) on the corner towards Daniel Wolvesey (*Wlves*(*eie*))[h] 8d; saving to Reading Abbey the ancient customary rent of 4s 2d, in which G(ilbert) *le Blik*, Reginald the priest and Richard *Colehoppe*[i] shall satisfy the abbey annually for 18d, 12d and 20d respectively.[2] To be held freely by rendering annually to the donor and his heirs 1 clove on the feast of St James [25 July] for all secular service, exaction and demand. For this the abbey has given him 100s sterling as entry-fine. Warranty and sealing

[not later than 1258; ? *c.* 1240 × 1258]

B ff 47v–48r; C f 19r; C f 216r

Hiis testibus:[j] [domino N(icholao) de Henrede tunc senescallo domini abbatis, Daniele Wulveheg', et aliis].

[a] Abyndon' *C f 216r*	[b] Colehoppe *C f 216r*
[c] Chausei *C f 216r*	[d] 'William' *C f 216r*
[e] Colhoppe *C f 19r*	[f] Kaldecote *C f 216r*
[g] Ruffa *C f 216r*	[h] Wulvesheg *C f 216r*
[i] Colhoppe *C f 19r*, Kolehoppe *C f 216r*	
[j] B, *C f 19r* end, the remainder being supplied from *C f 216r*	

Not later than 1258, since it was entered in the original section of B. The dates of Sir Nicholas of Hendred's stewardship are unknown, but he was already a knight in 1248 (Clanchy, *Berks. Eyre of 1248*, 155) and was sheriff of Berkshire 1250–9 (*List of Sheriffs*, 107); he was still alive in Apr. 1273 (*Cal. Inq. P.M.*, ii. 29). Agatha *Rufa*, or *Ruffa*, was the widow of Gilbert Rufus; he was alive in 1228, but dead by Oct. 1241 (see no. 870 n.). The entry on C f 216r is in a hand which is different from the original hand of the second main part of the cartulary (see vol. I, pp. 11–12) and which continues for nos. 1017–23. The word *supprior'* is written at the top of C f 216r.

1. ? Samite-seller.
2. These are the rents specified from these individuals earlier in the deed.

1016a Note of another charter by the same concerning the same in almost the same words, but sealed with another seal

[not later than 1258; ? *c.* 1240 × 1258]

B f 48r

Date as for no. 1016.

1017 Quitclaim by Thomas Cordwainer (*le Cordewaner*) of Reading to Reading Abbey of all his right in a stall in Shoemakers' Row (*in suteria*), Reading, between the stall of William *Dubbeltay* and that of Simon *Gilo*. Sealing

[? *c.* 1260 × 70]

Cf216r

Hiis testibus: Willelmo de Witel(e), Rad(ulf)o de Hecfeud', Johanne le Vyneter, Willelmo Lylli,^a Ricardo le Gunter, Ph(ilipp)o le stabler, et aliis.

^a *Sic, but almost certainly error for* Tylli (*cf. no. 1000*)

Dating uncertain. William of Whitley occurs from 1248 (see no. 907 n.). Ralph of Heckfield occurs between 1248 and 1286 (see no. 880 n.). John Vintner may be the one who occurs between 1269 and 1284 (see no. 914 n.). William Tilly occurs from 1261 (see no. 1000 n.). Richard Gunter occurs in 1261 and 1269 (see no. 985 n.).

1018 Gift in free alms by William of Blewbury (*Blebur'*) to his beloved lords the abbot and monks of Reading, for the health of his soul and that of Hawisia, his wife, of 5s 8d annual rent in Reading, to be received half at Easter and half at Michaelmas from a stall on the corner opposite Shoemakers' Row (*suteria*), which stall sometime belonged to Walter *le Waleys*. Warranty and sealing [*c.* 1260 × 70]

Cf216r

Hiis testibus: Rolando de Erley, Willelmo de Wytele, Johanne de Colle, et aliis.

After no. 1001 and before May 1270, by which time Roland of Earley was a knight (see no. 759). The reference to the donor's 'beloved lords' suggests that he may already have become steward of the abbey, which he certainly had by 1267 (see no. 855 n.). It is interesting to note that Walter *le Walays* gave William of Blewbury 8s rent from the stall, charged with an annual payment of 28d to Reading Abbey (no. 1001), and that now William gives the abbey the difference of 5s 8d.

1019 Gift by John *Muncy* to Roger *de Copenhulle* and Matilda, his wife, for their service and 1 mark of silver, of a barn (*grangia*) in Lorimer Lane (*Lortemerelane*), Reading, which John *Seman* used sometime to hold, between the tenement of Gilbert *le Fowel* and that of Richard *Lanval*. To be held freely by rendering annually to the donor and his heirs 18d, viz., 9d each at Michaelmas and Easter, for all service, exaction and demand. Warranty and sealing [*c.* 1270 × 90]

Cf216r–v

Hiis testibus: Willelmo le Chaumberleyn, et aliis.

Before *Quia emptores.* John Muncy, vintner, occurs between 1261 and 1284 (PRO JUST 1/40, m. 29d; 1/44, m. 15). Roger *de Cepenhull'* occurs in 1297 (*Berks. Arch. Journ.*, lx (1962), 103) and probably in 1294 (above, no. 953). Gilbert *le Fowel* (alias *le Foghel* and *le Fouel*) was a juror for Reading in 1269 and 1284 (JUST 1/42, m. 19; 1/44, m. 21d). For William Chamberlain between 1284 and 1297, see above, no. 883 n.

1020 Quitclaim by Ralph *Mounci*, for himself and his heirs, executors or assigns, to Reading Abbey, for a certain sum of money, of all his right in a plot of a certain tenement (*in quadam placea cuiusdam tenementi*) in Lorimer Lane (*Lortemerelane*), Reading, between the tenement formerly belonging to Gilbert *le Foghel* and that of Richard *Lanval*. This quitclaim he recognized in the full court of the abbot and convent to have been made by him to them and their successors. Sealing

[early 14th cent.; after Mar. 1307]

Cf216v

Hiis testibus: Johanne de la Lude tunc sen(escallo) Rad(yng'), Thoma de Leicestre tunc maiore, et aliis.

After no. 1019. William of Blewbury was still steward of Reading Abbey in Feb. 1303 (see no. 1045) and John de la Lude had become steward by 1308 × 16 (no. 1048), but Nicholas of Woodmancote came between them, occurring as steward in 1303 × 8 and in Mar. 1307 (nos. 1046, 666). Thomas of Leicester was mayor of Reading at some date before 15 Apr. 1304 (see no. 947), but he clearly became mayor again later; there are considerable gaps in the list of Reading mayors for the early 14th century (C. F. Slade, *Mayors of Reading* (Reading Public Libraries, 1969), no page nos.).

1021 Gift by John *atte Mulle de Aston'* to Roger of the Infirmary (*de infirmitorio*) of Reading and Gunnilda, his wife, for their service and 7 marks of silver, of a messuage in High Street (*in alto vico*), Reading, between the larger and the smaller waters of the [River] Kennet, between the tenement of Nicholas Butler (*le Boteler*) on the north and that of Geoffrey *Gomme* on the south. To be held by them and the heirs or assigns of Roger of the abbot of Reading freely by rendering annually to the same 2s, and to the subprior ½ mark, and to Stephen *le Convers* 3s, and to the church of St Laurence 14d, all at Michaelmas, and to the subprior ½ mark at Easter, for all secular service, exaction and demand. Warranty and sealing   [? *c.* 1290 × 1300]

Cf216v

Hiis testibus: Johanne Vachel, Gilberto Pynzon, et aliis.

Presumbly after *Quia emptores*, since the donees are to hold of the abbot of Reading and not of the donor. The date cannot be much, if at all, after 1300, since the Nicholas Butler named here is probably the one who occurs in the later 13th century (see no. 923 n.) and Geoffrey Gomme occurs between 1269 and 1284 (see no. 880 n.).

1022 Gift by Adam *le Poleter* of Reading to Abbot Nicholas [of Whaplode] and the convent of Reading of a messuage in New Street, Reading, on the north side between the tenement of Robert *Person* on the west and that of John Vintner (*le Vannare*) on the east, which messuage formerly belonged to Philip of Greywell (*Grewelle*). ᵃFrom this tenement the subprior shall receive the whole rent except for 10d due to the chamberlain.[a] Warranty and sealing   27 Sept. 1316

Cf216v

Hiis testibus, et cetera. Dat' apud Radyng' die lune proxima post festum sancti Mathei apostoli [21 Sept.], anno regni regis E(dwardi) filii regis E(dwardi) decimo.

[a] [a] *Interlined*

1023 Gift by John of Southwood (*Southwode*) to Reading Abbey of 10s annual rent from his messuage in Minster Street (*Mensterestrete*), Reading, between the messuage of William of Wittenham (*Wyttenham*) and Joan his wife on the east and that of Henry *Foliot* on the west, to be received by the subprior, half at the Annunciation and half at Michaelmas, for spices (*species*) of the convent. John obliges himself and his heirs to pay the said rent faithfully at the said terms. If the rent is in arrears in whole or part, the abbot and convent may distrain on the said messuage, to whomsoever it shall have come, and retain the distresses until full satisfaction of the arrears with damages and expenses has been made. Sealing   3 Mar. 1332

Cf217r

Hiis testibus: N. de Southwode filio et herede meo, et aliis. Dat' apud [?][a] tercio die Marcii, anno regni regis E(dwardi) tercii a Conquestu sexto.

[a] *Place omitted*

This deed concludes the group of deeds written in the same hand and headed by the word *supprior*' (see no. 1016 n.).

1024 *Notification, in the form of a chirograph, by Abbot Adam [of Lathbury] and the convent of Reading that they have charitably accommodated the Friars Minor in the vill of Reading in the Vastern towards Caversham Bridge, where they may build and live so long as they are without property. The friars have conceded that, if they acquire property or break any of the specified conditions to which they have agreed, the abbey may expel them from its land. The abbot and convent have conceded that, if they seek to expel the friars for reasons other than those stated, the king and his heirs may accommodate them there so that they shall have by his grace what they previously had by the abbey's grace*
14 July 1233

Cf217v

Pd. Coates, *Hist. of Reading*, App. II; Thomas of Eccleston, *De Adventu Fratrum Minorum in Angliam*, ed. A. G. Little (*Collection d'études et de documents sur l'histoire religieuse et littéraire du moyen age*, VII, Paris 1909), App. 171–2; (cal.) *Cal. Chart. R.*, i. 187 (the last two from Charter Roll)

Sciant presentes et futuri quod ego Adam dei gratia abbas Radyng'
et eiusdem loci conventus unanimis[a] hospitavimus caritative fratres
minores in villa nostra de Redyng' in loco quodam in cultura de
Vasterna secus viam regiam versus pontem de Kaversam continente[b]
triginta tres perticas in longitudine et viginti tres perticas in latitudine,
ex gratia nostra eis concedentes quod ibidem possint edificare et
inhabitare quamdiu fuerint sine proprietate. Si vero aliquo tempore
quocumque casu vel qualicumque modo contigerit fratres minores
proprietatem habere vel proprium, concesserunt pro se et successoribus suis in perpetuum quod liceat nobis et successoribus nostris
auctoritate propria ipsos expellere a tota terra nostra, sublato cuiuslibet contradiccionis et appellacionis obstaculo. Concesserunt eciam
pro se et successoribus suis quod nusquam in terra nostra aliam
querent habitacionem et, si forte terminos quos eis constituimus alicubi
prorogari vel dilatari procuraverint, liceat nobis omni contradiccione
et appellacione remota a tota terra nostra ipsos expellere. Concesserunt eciam pro se et successoribus suis quod, si aliquam exhi-
bicionem a nobis aliquando quesierint nisi in hiis que gratis et spontanea voluntate eis concedere voluerimus, liceat nobis ipsos, sicut
supradictum est, expellere. Concesserunt eciam pro se et successoribus
suis quod numquam reponentur in cymiterio suo apud Redyng'
corpora mortuorum nisi tantum corpora fratrum minorum sine licencia nostra speciali, cum pene predicte adieccione. Concesserunt eciam
pro se et successoribus suis quod, si aliquo tempore perceperint oblaciones vel decimas vel legata ecclesie nostre debita, liceat nobis ipsos
expellere, sicut superius dictum est. Nos autem pro nobis et successoribus nostris concessimus quod, si nos aliquo tempore fratres
minores a predicta habitacione ob alias causas a supradictis velimus
expellere, dominus rex et heredes sui omni appellacione et contradiccione remota possit eos ibidem libere et quiete inhospitare, ita
quod ex gratia sua habeant quod prius ex gratia nostra habuerunt.
Si vero contigerit aliquando fratres minores a dicta inhabitacione
spontanea voluntate recedere, ipsum solum[c] cum omnibus edificiis
tanquam proprium abbati et conventui remaneat. Ut autem omnia
supradicta perpetuum firmitatis robur optineant, huic scripto in
modum cirographi confecto, quod penes dominum regem remanet,[d]
sigilla nostra sunt apposita. Actum est hoc anno gracie millesimo
ducentesimo tricesimo tercio apud Radyngiam quartodecimo die
Julii.

[a] Sic
[b] Ms has continentem
[c] Sic, perhaps referring to locum
[d] Sic, perhaps error for remaneat

The Charter Roll states that the part of the chirograph remaining with the abbot and
convent was sealed with the common seal of the Franciscans in England and the seals
of the king, the archbishop of York and the bishops of Winchester, Coventry and

Worcester. The clause restraining the abbey from expelling the friars at will was contrary to St Francis's precepts and was probably included to overcome hostility from the abbey to the friars' settlement in Reading (*Ann. Mon.*, iii. 134). Albert of Pisa, minister-general of the Franciscans in England 1236-8, fervently returned the charter to the monks and offered to remove the friars if they wished, but he could do little in the face of Henry III's strenuous patronage of the Reading friars—see Thomas of Eccleston, *De Adventu Fratrum Minorum in Angliam*, ed. A.G. Little (Manchester, 1917), 8; R.B. Brooke, *Early Franciscan Government* (Cambridge, 1959), 188-9. [The reference to this incident in D. Knowles, *The Religious Orders in England*, i (Cambridge, 1948), 192, is misleading.] In any case, the offending clause re-appeared in the new settlement of 1285 (no. 1025).

1025 *Notification, in the form of a chirograph, by Abbot Robert [of Burgate] and the convent of Reading that they have charitably received the Friars Minor in the vill of Reading in a plot at the end of New Street, of which they have hitherto had the use by the abbey's grace. They may build and live there so long as they are without property and observe their profession of highest poverty. The friars have promised to observe specified conditions and have conceded that, if they contravene any of them, the abbey may expel them from the plot. If the abbot and convent seek to expel the friars for other reasons, the king and his heirs shall have power to accommodate them there so that they shall have by his grace the use which they previously had by the abbey's grace*   26 May 1285

Cf 217r–v

Pd. Coates, *Hist. of Reading*, App. IV; (cal.) *Cal. Close R. 1279–88*, 428–9 (from Close Roll)

Sciant presentes et futuri quod nos R(obertus)[a] dei gratia abbas Radyng' et eiusdem loci conventus unanimes hospitando caritative recepimus ex gratia speciali secundum modum inferius subiungendum fratres minores in villa nostra Radyngie in area quadam sita inter domum domini Stephani capellani tunc temporis rectoris ecclesie de Sulham versus orientem ex parte una et fossatum sabulosum versus occidentem ex altera, et extenditur a vico communi qui dicitur Vicus Novus usque ad finem aree, cuius usum hactenus fratres predicti habuerunt de nostra gratia speciali et habent et sunt [b]in posterum[b] habituri, salvis condicionibus inferius adiungendis, que quidem area continet sedecim perticas in latitudine et sedecim et dimidiam in longitudine. Ita quod liceat dictis fratribus in dicta area edificare et habitare pro libito quam diu sine proprietate fuerint et iuxta professionem suam observatores altissime paupertatis. Promiserunt insuper nobis et concesserunt fideliter dicti fratres pro se et successoribus suis [c]in perpetuum[c] quod nunquam et nusquam in terra nostra habitacionem aliam sibi querent nec per se predictos terminos dilatabunt nec procurabunt per alios dilatare, et quod a nobis nunquam petent elemosinam ex debito set tantum ex misericordia et gratia speciali. Promiserunt insuper quod, quantacumque libertate

gaudeant sepulture vel sint *b*in posterum*b* gavisuri, nunquam recipient
in suo cimiterio vel ecclesia vel alibi tumulanda corpora defunctorum
parochianorum monasterii nostri vel ecclesiarum nobis appro-
priatarum in villa Radyng' vel extra sine nostra licencia speciali; et
quod in hoc a nostro et nostrorum preiudicio penitus abstinebunt; et
quod nunquam insuper recipient decimas vel oblaciones vel legata ex
certa sciencia que ecclesie nostre de iure vel consuetudine debeantur.
Concesserunt eciam dicti fratres quod, si in aliquo predictorum artic-
ulorum ex certa sciencia defecerint seu contravenire presumpserint,
liceat nobis auctoritate nostra propria, sublato cuiuslibet appellacionis
seu contradiccionis obstaculo, ipsos fratres expellere ab area
memorata. Quod, si nos aliquo tempore dictos fratres a predicte aree
inhabitacione ob alias causas a supradictis [*f 217v*] velimus expellere,
extunc dominus rex et heredes sui eosdem fratres omni appellacione
et contradiccione remota inhospitandi ibidem liberam habeant pote-
statem, ita quod usum ex gratia sua habeant quem prius ex nostra
gratia habuerunt. Ut autem omnia supradicta *'*in perpetuum*'* robur
firmitatis obtineant, huic scripto in modum cyrographi confecto tam
sigilla nostra ex parte una quam sigilla ministrorum generalis et
provincialis ex parte altera, una cum sigillo illustris regis Angl(ie) et
venerabilis patris nostri domini Cant(uariensis) archiepiscopi, sunt
appensa. Dat' Radyng' vii. kln. Junii, anno domini millesimo CC.
lxxx. quinto.

a Ms has A. *interlined, but* R. *is correct*
b-b Ms has imposterum   *c-c Ms has* imperpetuum

It is interesting that, while the first agreement with the Franciscans (no. 1024) was
enrolled on the Charter Roll, this one was entered on the Close Roll. It represents a
transfer of the friars from the low-lying outskirts of Reading into the town itself, the
only other Franciscan community to which this is known to have happened being at
Northampton (A. G. Little, *Studies in English Franciscan History* (Manchester, 1917), 11).
The reason for the move at Reading was the inconvenience of the original site, which,
being near the Thames, was too open and liable to flooding in winter, as is clear from
a request to the abbey in 1282 from John Pecham, archbishop of Canterbury, himself
a Franciscan, to provide the friars with a better site (*Registrum Epistolarum Johannis
Peckham*, ed. C. T. Martin (RS, 1882–5), ii. 414–16). In asking the minister-general of
the Franciscans to confirm the move in Nov. 1285, the archbishop elaborated on the
inconveniences of the original settlement (*ibid.*, iii. 911–12).

1026   Gift by Margery, widow of Laurence Dubber (*le Dubbare*) of
Reading, to Richard of Acton (*Actone*) called *Cotes*, burgess of Reading,
of a tenement which she had in St Giles's Street, Reading, between
the tenement of the said Richard *Cotes* on the south and that formerly
belonging to John Vachell (*Vachel*) on the north. To be held of the
chief lords of the fee by the due and customary services in perpetuity.
Warranty and sealing   20 May 1343

Cf218r

Hiis testibus: Waltero de Stannton' tunc maiore Rad(yng'), Johanne
le Goldsmyth, et aliis. Dat' apud Rading' xx. die mensis Maii, anno
regni regis E(dwardi) tercii post Conquestum xvii.

Cf. nos. 940–3.

1027   Gift by Richard of Acton (*Acton'*) of Reading to Adam *atte
Aumerye*, chaplain, of Reading, of a messuage in St Giles's Street,
Reading, which he had by gift and enfeoffment of Laurence Dubber
(*le Dubbar'*) and Margery, his wife, between the tenement of Adam
Vicary (*le Vicari*), draper, on the south and that of Reading Abbey
which formerly belonged to J(ohn) Vachell (*Vachel*) on the north. To
be held of the chief lords of the fee by the pertinent services in
perpetuity. Warranty and sealing   23 Oct. 1343

Cf218r

Hiis testibus: Johanne Aurifabro tunc maiore, Adam le Vicari, et
multis aliis. Dat' Radyng' die jovis proxima post festum sancti Luce
evang(eliste) [18 Oct.], anno regni regis E(dwardi) tercii post Conquestum xvii.

This and no. 1026 occupy the upper third of f218r, after which there is a gap before
no. 1028, which is written in the same hand at the bottom.

1028   Gift by Joan, widow of Oliver of Haseley (*Hasele*), to John of
Haseley her son, for his service, of the entire tenement with messuage
and garden in Old Street in the parish of St Giles, between the
messuage of Stephen Dubber (*le Dubber'*) and that of Robert *Kyneware*.
To be held freely by rendering annually to John of Coley (*Colleie*) and
his heirs 6s 8d at Michaelmas, and to the donor during her lifetime
30s, viz., 15s each at Michaelmas and the feast of St John Baptist [24
June], for all secular service, exaction and demand. Warranty and
sealing. Witnesses [omitted]   [1270 × 87]

Cf218r

Oliver of Haseley was alive 27 May 1270 (see no. 759), but was dead by 10 Apr. 1278
(see no. 1175). This tenement passed into the hands of Sir Robert Fulconis (no. 1029),
who was dead by 8 Sept. 1287 (see no. 880 n.). This deed and nos. 1029–30 are grouped
together in the same hand at the bottom of f218r and the upper half of f218v, the
remainder of the latter being blank.

1029   Gift and quitclaim by John, son of Oliver of Haseley (*Hasele*),
to Sir Robert *Fulcon(is)*, his kinsman (*consanguineus*), of the entire

messuage with garden which formerly belonged to Oliver his father and Joan his mother, of her inheritance, in the parish of St Giles, Reading, next to the house of Stephen Dubber (*le Dubbere*). To be held freely by rendering annually to the chief lords of the fee the due and customary services, and to the donor during his lifetime ½d at Michaelmas for all service and secular demand. Warranty. for this Robert has given him 70 marks. Sealing. Witnesses [omitted]

[1270 × 87]

Cf218r–v

After no. 1028 and before the donee's death (see no. 880 n.).

1030 Notification by Roland of Earley (*Erle*), Robert of Preston (*Preston'*), Walter Vachell (*Fachel*), Thomas *Syward* and Ralph of Barford (*Bereford*) that, whereas Sir Robert *Fulcon(is)*, lately deceased, in the testament of his last will appointed them his executors and bequeathed all his tenements in Reading to be sold by them and the money so received to be distributed for his soul by their discretion, they have accordingly sold to John Vachell of Reading for 60 marks of silver a tenement between the tenement formerly belonging to William Dyer (*tinctor*) on the north and that sometime belonging to Stephen Dubber (*le Dubbare*) on the south. To be held by John and his heirs or assigns of the chief lords of the fee freely in perpetuity by rendering annually the due and customary service. Sealing with the seals of the executors, the seal of the official of Berkshire, and the seal of the community of the burgesses of Reading (*sigillum communitatis burgensium Rad'*)   16 Nov. 1288

Cf218v

Hiis testibus: Willelmo de Bleburi, et cetera. Dat' Rad(yng') die martis in festo sancti Edmundi Cantuar(iensis) archiepiscopi, anno domini M.CC.lxxxviii.

It is interesting that, although this deed pre-dates *Quia emptores* (1290), its terms anticipate the provisions of that enactment.

1031 Licence by King Edward III to John son of John Bannister (*Banastr(e)*) to alienate in mortmain to Reading Abbey seven messuages and four shops in Reading, which are held of the abbey and are worth 14s annually, as appears by the inquest held by William Trussel, escheator this side of the Trent, to be held by the abbey at the value of 20s in part satisfaction of the £10 worth of land and rent which the abbey has the king's licence to acquire. Licence also to the abbot and convent to receive and hold the same   27 Apr. 1338

Cf224v
Pd. (cal.) *Cal. Pat. R. 1338–40*, 51 (from Patent Roll)

Teste me ipso apud Westm(onasterium) xxvii. die Aprilis, anno regni nostri xii.

The licence for £10 worth of lands and rent was granted 23 Mar. 1327 (*Cal. Pat. R. 1327–30*, 61).

1032 Licence by King Edward III to Walter *atte More,* baker (*bakere*), and Adam *atte Aumerye,* chaplain, to alienate in mortmain to Reading Abbey, respectively, one messuage in Reading and 3½ [acres]*a* of land in Whitley (*Whitele*), which are not held of the king in chief and are worth 6s 3d annually, as appears by the inquest held by Robert fitz Elys, escheator in Oxfordshire and Berkshire, to be held by the abbey at the vale of 7s 1d in full satisfaction of the £10 worth of land and rent which the abbey has the king's licence to acquire. Licence also to the abbot and convent to receive and hold the same

24 July 1342

Cf224v
Pd. (cal.) *Cal. Pat. R. 1340–43*, 499 (from Patent Roll)

Teste me ipso apud Westm(onasterium) xxiiii. die Julii, anno regni nostri Anglie xvi, regni vero nostri Francie tercio.

a Supplied from Patent Roll

The Patent Roll adds: by a fine of 1 mark at the instance of Queen Philippa. For the £10 licence, see no. 1031 n.

1032a Note of a charter concerning a tenement acquired from Hawis(ia) of Newbury (*Neubury*) in the corner tenement in London Street [Reading] on the eastern side, and of 3½ acres next to *la Lynche* in Katesgrove (*Cadelesgrove*) acquired from Gilbert of Heckfield (*Heghfeld'*) 24 July, 16 Edward III   24 July 1342

Cf225v

This appears among notes mostly of royal licences of mortmain. It seems likely, therefore, that it is related to the preceding mortmain licence of the same date, since Katesgrove was in Whitley (cf. below, no. 1264).

1033 Licence by King Edward III to John son of John Vachell (*Vachel*) of Tilehurst (*Tighelhurst*), by a fine which he has made with the king,[1] to alienate in mortmain to Reading Abbey the reversion of one messuage and 15 acres of land in Reading and Whitley (*Whitele*), which Alice, widow of John Vachell, holds in dower of the inheritance

of the said John son of John and which ought to revert to him and
his heirs after her death, to find two wax candles to burn daily at the
altar of St Mary in the conventual church of Reading while mass is
celebrated there for the souls of John son of John's ancestors and for
his own after his death in perpetuity. Licence also to the abbot and
convent to enter and hold the same after Alice's death

24 July 1342

C ff 224v–225r
Pd. (cal.) *Cal. Pat. R. 1340–43*, 493 (from Patent Roll)

Teste me ipso apud Westm(onasterium) xxiiii. die Julii, anno regni
nostri Anglie xvi, regni vero nostri Francie tercio.

1. The Patent Roll adds that the fine was 20s.

1034 Gift by Robert Butler (*le Boteler*) of Reading to Abbot Henry
[of Appleford] and the convent of Reading of a plot (*placea*) of land
between the said Robert's curtilage next to Great Bridge[1] (*magnus
pons*), Reading, on the south and the curtilage of Henry of Kersey
(*Kersy*) on the west, the head of which plot extends to the abbot's
tenement on the north, and the plot comes down to the bank of the
[River] Kennet. It measures 76 feet in length and 15 feet in width
along the bank of the Kennet in the south. To be held freely. Warranty
and sealing   31 Jan. 1345

C f 228r–v

Hiis testibus: Johanne de Aldermanston' tunc maiore Radyng',
Johanne le Goldsmyth', Willelmo Bedwynde, Henrico Danvers, Waltero Hobescut', et aliis. Dat' apud Redyng' die lune proxima ante
festum Purificacionis beate Marie virginis, anno regni regis Edwardi
tercii a Conquestu decimo nono, et cetera.

This is the second of a group of entries made in a separate hand on C ff 228r–229v.
They begin with a London deed (above, no. 480) and comprise also nos. 1035–8.

1. Probably an alternative name for High Bridge (Slade, 'Reading', 5).

1035 Gift by Robert son of Robert Butler (*le Boteler*) to Robert
Butler, his father, of two cottages (*cotagia*) with adjacent curtilages in
High Street (*in alto vico*), Reading, between the two bridges, between
the tenement of the abbot of Reading on the north and that of the
said Robert his father on the south. To be held of the chief lords of
the fee by the due and customary services in perpetuity. Warranty
and sealing   16 Apr. 1348

C f 228v

Hiis testibus: Thoma de ȝevynton' tunc maiore Radyng', Henrico de Grenham, Georg(io) le Marescal', et cetera, et aliis. Dat' apud Redyng' die mercurii proxima post festum in ramis palmarum, anno regni regis Edwardi tercii a Conquestu xxii.

1036   Gift by Robert Butler (*le Boteler*) of Reading, senior, to Adam *de Aumerye*, chaplain, of his whole capital messuage with all messuages and adjacent curtilages which he had in High Street (*in alto vico*), Reading, between the two bridges, viz., between the bank of the [River] Kennet on the south and the messuage of the abbot of Reading on the north. To be held of the chief lords of the fee by the due and customary services. Warranty and sealing   5 May 1348

C ff 228v–229r

Hiis testibus: Thoma de ȝevyndon' tunc maiore Radyng', Waltero de Staunton', Waltero le*a* Hurt', et aliis. Dat' apud Redyng' die lune proxima post festum Invencionis sancte crucis [3 May], anno regni regis Edwardi tercii a Conquestu vicesimo secundo.

ᵃ Ms has de

1037   Quitclaim by Henry, son of Robert Butler (*le Boteler*) of Reading senior, to Adam *atte Aumery*, chaplain, of all his right in the whole capital messuage and in all other messuages with adjacent curtilages which Robert Butler, his father, had in High Street (*in alto vico*), Reading, between [etc., as in no. 1036]. Warranty by all the lands and tenements which Henry has in Reading and Earley (*Erle*), and sealing   7 May 1348

C f 229r–v

Hiis testibus: Thoma de ȝevyndon' maiore Radyng', Waltero de Staunton', Rogero de Stanstede, et aliis. Dat' apud Redyng' die mercurii proxima post festum Invencionis sancte crucis, anno regni regis*a* Edwardi [tercii]*b* a Conquestu vicesimo secundo.

ᵃ Ms has here H. *deleted*   *ᵇ Supplied*

1038   Quitclaim by Henry, son and heir of Robert Butler (*Boteler*) senior, to Abbot Henry [of Appleford] and the convent [of Reading]*a* of all his right in two plots (*placete*) of land which Robert his father and Robert his brother gave to the abbot and convent in perpetuity out of (*de*) their curtilage in High Street (*in alto vico*), Reading, between the two bridges, on the western side, as appears by the bounds in the

charters of the said Robert and Robert to the abbot and convent.
Warranty and sealing   14 Mar. 1345

Cf229v

Hiis testibus: Johanne de Ardermanston tunc maiore, Johanne
Goldsmyth', Willelmo de Bedwynde. Dat' apud Redyng' die lune
proxima post festum sancti Gregorii pape [12 Mar.], anno regni regis
Edwardi [tercii a Conquestu]*a* decimo nono, et cetera.

a Supplied

The charter by Robert Butler senior is no. 1034.

1039 Memorandum that the abbey had copies of the two following
charters from the charters of William *Bartram*, cook of the abbot of
Reading. The land lies between High Street (*altus vicus*) on the south
and New Street on the north, viz., between the tenements of Laurence
Chapman (*Chapman*) and Adam *Pultur* on the north and that of John
Denmead (*Denemede*) on the south. The rent is divided between the
said Laurence and Adam, as is recorded in the rental of 7 Edward II.
[after 1313–14]

Cf229v

This refers to nos. 1040–1, which with no. 1039 are entered in a hand similar, and
perhaps identical, to that of nos. 1034–8. The memorandum must date after 7 Edward
II, but how much later is uncertain, since, although it was entered after the preceding
Butler deeds, the latest of which (no. 1037) is dated 7 May 1348, it may have been
composed earlier.

1040 Gift by Agnes *de la Holilonde*, widow of John of Denmead
(*Denemede*) of Reading, to Laurence Chapman (*le Chapman*) of Reading
and Alice his wife, for a certain sum of money, of a house in New
Street, Reading, in the lane called Holy Water Lane (*Holiwaterleslane*)
between her own house on the south and the said Laurence's house
on the north. To be held, as defined by the boundaries and enclosed
by walls, by Laurence and Alice and the legitimate heirs of their
bodies or their assigns freely of the chief lords of the fee by the due
and customary services, and by rendering annually to her and her
heirs or assigns 1 clove at Michaelmas for all other services. Warranty
of the house with its enclosing walls, and sealing   20 Nov. 1307

Cf230r

Dat' Radyng' in festo sancti Edmundi regis, anno regni regis Edwardi
filii regis Edwardi primo. Hiis testibus: Ricardo Asseburne, Gilberto
Copenhulle, Roberto Person, Gilberto Modi, Willelmo Yongshine,
Ricardo Hattere, Ricardo Shrintone, et aliis.

As Agnes of Denmead, the donor referred to this deed in her gift to Reading Abbey in 1308 (no. 946).

1041 Gift by John Chamberlain (*le Chamberlayn*) to Adam *le Puletyer*,[a] for his service and a certain payment of money (*firma pecunie*), of the whole tenement which he had in Reading in the lane called Holy Water Lane (*la Holiwaterleslane*), which tenement formerly belonged to John Denmead (*Denemede*). To be held freely of the chief lords of the fee by rendering annually to them 2s 4d at Michaelmas for all secular service, exaction and demand. Warranty and sealing

? 22 July 1312

Cf230r–v

His testibus: Radulpho de Bello, Johanne le Acatur, Radulpho de Helme, Elia de Bannesbury, Ricardo de Assheburne, Gilberto de Copenhulle, Laurencio Mercatore, Gilberto clerico, et aliis. Dat' Radyng' [? in festo][b] sancte Marie Magdalene, anno regni regis Edwardi filii [regis][c] Edwardi sexto.

[a] *Preceded by* Pulter *marked for deletion*
[b] *Supplied, but original may have read a certain day before or after the feast day*
[c] *Supplied*

For uncertainty regarding the exact date, see textual note *b*.

1042 Market regulations in the town of Reading [in French], headed *Puncta gilde*   [14th cent.]

Bff162v–163v; Ff123r–v
Pd. Coates, *Hist. of Reading*, Further Additions (no page nos.)

Both copies are in 14th-century hands.

1043 Gift in free alms by William Bastard (*Bastard*), with the consent of John his son and heir, to Reading Abbey of the whole portion which he had in the meadow called *Burnemed*[a] [in Reading].[1] To be held freely by rendering annually to him and his heirs for all service 2d at Michaelmas, to be paid by the almoner of Reading, to whose department (*bailliva*)[b] the said meadow is assigned. Warranty. For this Jordan (*Jurd(anus)*)[c] the almoner, in whose time this transaction (*negocium*) was procured, has given to him 5½ marks of silver, and to John his heir 6d to buy spurs. Sealing. Witnesses [omitted]

[13th cent., ? before 1230]

Bf143r; Cf83v; Df22r

[a] Burnemede *C*   [b] balliva *C*
[c] 'Jurdan' *D*

Dating uncertain, but not later than 1258, since it was entered in the original section of B (and also of D). A William Bastard occurs in 1241 and 1251 in Whitley (PRO JUST 1/37, m. 25A; below, no. 1226) and was an elector and juror for Charlton hundred in 1248 (Clanchy, *Berks. Eyre of 1248*, 296), but a rather earlier date is suggested by the reference to Jordan the almoner, who is not otherwise recorded and who possibly held office before 1230 at the latest, by which time a series of known almoners starting with Walter begins to occur (see nos. 710, 712 n., 716 n., 731 n.).

1. The deed was entered in B and C among those concerning the almoner's possessions in Reading. *Burnemede* was presumably therefore in the manor of Reading, although in view of no. 1213 it may have been in or near Whitley.

COLEY (in Reading)

1044 Gift by Beatrice, widow of William of Coley (*Colle*), to Nicholas of Whitley (*Whitele*), clerk, of *Oxemore Mede* in the vill of Coley, as it is enclosed on all sides by hedges and ditches. The said meadow to be held for the whole of her life by Nicholas and his heirs or assigns freely of the chief lords of the fee by the due and customary services pertaining to such a tenement. For this Nicholas has given her 10 marks sterling. Warranty for her life and sealing   27 Nov. 1298

C f 160r

Hiis testibus: Willelmo de Blebury, Gilberto Pynson, Elia de Bannebury, Michaele Belet, Henrico de Greywell', et multis aliis. Dat' apud Collee die jovis proxima ante festum sancti Andree apostoli [30 Nov.], anno regni regis Edwardi vicesimo septimo.

Marginal note: modo Fachel tenet ex dimissione abbatis pro la Grovelond

1045 Quitclaim by Hugh called *de Stokes* and Alice, his wife, to Nicholas of Whitley (*Whitele*), clerk, of all their right in perpetuity in a plot (*placea*) of meadow called *Oxemoremed* in Coley (*Colle*) next to Reading, enclosed by a ditch on all sides, which meadow Beatrice, widow of William of Coley, held in dower and demised to the said Nicholas for the term of her life, and which ought to revert to the said Alice after the death of Beatrice, as her right and inheritance. To be held by Nicholas and his heirs of the chief lords of the fee by the due and customary services. Warranty by Hugh and Alice and the heirs of Alice, and sealing with their seals   26 Feb. 1303

C f 160r

Hiis testibus: Willelmo de Bleobury tunc senescallo abbatis, Gilberto Pinson, Rad(ulf)o de la Bataille, Johanne filio Ricardi de Benham, Henrico*a*, Willelmo Clerico, et aliis. Dat' Radyng' die martis proxima post festum sancti Mathie apostoli [24 Feb.], anno regni regis Edwardi tricesimo primo.

^a Surname possibly om. here

1046 Quitclaim by Alice, widow of Hugh called *Stoke*, to Nicholas of Whitley (*Whitele*), clerk, of all her right in a plot (*placea*) of meadow called *Oxenemoremede* in Coley (*Collee*) next to Reading, enclosed by a ditch on all sides, which meadow Nicholas had by gift of Beatrice, formerly wife of William of Coley (*Colle*). To be held [etc., as in no. 1045], with free entry and exit. Warranty and sealing

[1303 × 1308]

C f 160v

Hiis testibus: domino Rogero de Burghfeld' milite, Nicholao de Wodemancote tunc senescallo Radyng', Willelmo Bailloil, Willelmo de Offinton, Matheo Barthelmeu, Nicholao de Colle, Johanne de Benham, et multis aliis.

After no. 1045 and before no. 1047.

1047 Demise in duplicate (*scriptum bipartitum*) for 45 years by Nicholas of Whitley (*Whitele*), vicar of St Mary's church, Reading, to Reading Abbey of a meadow called *Oxemoremed'*, enclosed by a ditch on all sides, in Coley (*Colleye*) next to Reading, which meadow formerly belonged to William of Coley (*Colle*). To be held of Nicholas and his heirs for the use of the sacristy freely for 45 years from the feast of St Dunstan the bishop [19 May], 1 Edward II, by doing to the chief lords of the fee all due and customary services. For this the abbey has remitted and quitclaimed to him £13 10s which he owed as arrears of the pension of the said church. Warranty, and sealing by both parties *alternatim*

[c. 19 May 1308]

C f 160v

Hiis testibus: Thoma Syward, Rad(ulf)o de Bello, Johanne le Acatur, Thoma de Leicestre, Nicholao de Colleye, Johanne le Foghel, Henrico de Greywelle, Gilberto clerico, et aliis.

Marginal note: [modo]^a Henricus Fachel tenet per escambium pro Grovelond

^a Ms damaged

The date is presumably close to that from which the lease was to run.

1048 Gift in free alms by Nicholas of Whitley (*Whitele*), vicar of St Mary's church, Reading, to Reading Abbey of the same meadow called *Oxonemoremede* in the vill of Coley (*Colle*), between the abbey's

meadow called Fobney (*Vobeneye*) and the meadow of Thomas *Syward*.
To be held freely for the use (*officina*) of the sacristy. Warranty and
sealing   [1308 × 16]

C f 161r

Hiis testibus: Johanne de la Lhude senescallo, Rad(ulph)o de Bello,
Johanne le Acatour, Thoma Syward, Thoma Leicestria, Willelmo
Bonafannt', Radulpho de Helme, et multis aliis.

Marginal note: modo Fachel tenet per escambium pro Grovelond

After no. 1047 and before 5 May 1316, when Richard of Puriton was presented to the
vicarage (*The Registers of Roger Martival, Bishop of Salisbury*, ed. K. Edwards *et al.* (Cant.
and York Soc., 1959–75), i. 26). This deed converted the previous lease for 45 years
into a perpetual gift in free alms. It is interesting that, despite its being after *Quia
emptores*, the abbey was to hold of the donor and his heirs or assigns.

'HEREWARDSLEY' (in Reading)

1049 *Gift in free alms by Robert of 'Herewardsley' to Reading Abbey of 7
acres of land in the field next to Reading on the west, and the meadow in
'Langney' which his father had in exchange for pasture in Calcot*
                                                            [late 12th cent. × 1213]

A ff 80v–81r; A f 91r; B f 61r; C f 28r

Sciant presentes et futuri quod ego Robertus de Herwardesl(e)*ᵃ* dedi
et presenti carta mea*ᵇ* confirmavi deo et conventui de*ᶜ* Rading(ia),
pro salute anime mee et omnium antecessorum et successorum
meorum, .vii. acras terre*ᶜ* de terra mea que iacent in campo proximo
de Rading(ia) in occidentali parte, quas Robertus cognomento Rex
aliquando de patre meo *ᵈ*in vadium*ᵈ* tenuit; insuper [*f 81r*] et totum
pratum in Langeneya*ᵉ* quod pater meus habuit in escambium pasture
sue de Caldecote, in liberam et perpetuam elemosinam.*ᶠ* Hiis testibus:*ᵍ*
[Willelmo de Colleia, Gilleberto de Felde, Waltero de Oxenef(ordia),
Rogero de Colleia, Andrea de Waling(efordia), Simone de Wal-
ing(efordia), et multis aliis].

ᵃ Herewardesl' *A f 91r, B*; Herewardesleg' *C*   *ᵇ Om. in A f 91r, B*
ᶜ Om. in A f 91r, B,C   *ᵈ ᵈ Om. in A f 91r*
ᵉ Langneya *C*   *ᶠ B ends with* T', *C ends*
ᵍ A ff 80v–81r ends; A f 91r has Testibus *and supplies the remainder*

The deed was not entered in the original section of A, suggesting a date after 1193.
Gilbert de Felde was dead by 1213 at the latest (see no. 849). The place-name
Herwardesle and its variants is now lost, the form 'Herewardsley' being here offered as
a convenient modern version, and its exact location is unknown, although it was in the

lordship of Reading to the west of the town; it has been suggested that the name is an earlier form of Hadsey (*Berks. Place-Names*, i. 180). It may possibly derive from the Hereward of Coley, who occurs in the period 1158 x 86 (see nos. 1135, 1208–9). This deed is entered in B and C among charters certainly relating to 'Herewardsley', but the precise location of 'Langney', whose name has similarly not survived, is uncertain (cf. nos. 1152, 1170; *Berks. Place-Names*, i. 183).

1050 *Gift in free alms by Alan of Englefield to Abbot Simon and the monks of Reading of all the land in 'Herewardsley' which he had of Thomas of 'Herewardsley'*
[1213 x 26]

A f 80r–v; B f 6ov; C f 27v

Sciant presentes *ᵃet futuriᵃ* quod ego Alanus de Englefeld in ligia potestate mea dedi concessi et hac presenti carta mea confirmavi deo et *ᵇ*beate Marie et ecclesie*ᵇ* de Rading(ia) et Symoni abbati et monachis ibidem deo servientibus, pro salute anime patris mei et anime matris mee et omnium antecessorum et successorum meorum, in liberam puram et perpetuam elemosinam totam et integram illam terram cum pertinenciis in Herward(esle)*ᶜ* quam aliquando habui de [*f 8ov*] Thoma de Herward(esle).*ᵈ* Habendam et tenendam eidem abbati et successoribus suis et ecclesie de Rading(ia) in perpetuum sicut meam liberam puram et perpetuam elemosinam, quietam ab omni *ᵉservicio seculari,ᵉ* exactione et consuetudine et omnibus rebus ad me vel ad heredes meos pertinentibus. Ut autem hec mea donacio, concessio et carte mee confirmacio rata et stabilis in perpetuum permaneat, presentem cartam meam*ᶠ* sigilli mei testimonio roboravi.*ᵍ* Hiis testibus.

ᵃ ᵃ Interlined in A   *ᵇ ᵇ* ecclesie beate Marie *B, C*
ᶜ Herewardesl' B,C   *ᵈ* Herewardesl' *B*, Herewardeslegh' *C*
ᵉ 'seculari servitio *B,C*   *ᶠ Om. in B,C*
ᵍ C ends

The dating limits are those of Simon's abbacy. See also no. 1051.

1051 *Agreement, in the form of a chirograph, between Abbot Simon of Reading and Alan of Engelfield, by which Alan quitclaimed to the abbey the land which he had of Thomas of 'Herewardsley' in 'Herewardsley' in return for a remission to him for life of 3s 4d of the annual rent which he owed the abbey for burgages in Reading, which he held of Osbert Wolvesey and Emma of Wallingford. Alan will pay 4d rent [only] for the burgages during his life, but after his death his heirs will pay the full rent of 3s 8d*
[1213 x 26]

A f 80v; B f 6ov; C ff 27v–28r

Hec est convencio facta inter Symonem abbatem de Rading(ia) ex una parte et Alanum de Engelfeld ex altera. Videlicet quod idem Alanus remisit et *ᵃ*quietum clamavit*ᵃ* de se et heredibus suis in perpetuum dicto abbati et successoribus suis et ecclesie de Rading(ia)

A ff 79v–8or; B f 61r; C f 28r–v

ª Herewardesl' *B*, Herewardesleg' *C*   *ᵇ Om. in C*

Dating very uncertain, but before June 1248, by which time Thomas was dead (see no. 1052 n.).

1054 Quitclaim by William of Coley (*Colleya*)*ª* to Reading Abbey of the whole land which he sometime claimed against Thomas of 'Herewardsley' (*Herwardesleg*')*ᵇ* by the king's writ and which the same Thomas in full court recognized to be his right and inheritance. For this the abbey has given him 8 acres of land and 2 acres of meadow in Coley.*ᶜ* Warranty of the said land of 'Herewardsley' (*Herewardesleg*');*ᵈ* if he or his heirs shall be unable to warrant it, they will return (*restituere*) the said 8 acres of land and 2 acres of meadow to the abbey. Witnesses*ᵉ* [omitted]   [13th cent., before 1248]

A f 8or; B f 61v; C f 28v

ª Colleg' *B,C*   *ᵇ* Herewardesl' *B*, Herewardesleg' *C*
ᶜ Colley *B,C*   *ᵈ* Hereward' *B*
ᵉ Om. in C

Before 1248, since it was confirmed by Thomas of 'Herewardsley' in no. 1055. Cf. the claim by Thomas's heir against the abbot of Reading, involving reference to William of Coley, in 1248 (Clanchy, 183). The identity of the present William of Coley is uncertain, since there were at least two of that name in the 12th and 13th centuries. One occurs as early as 1165 × 73 (no. 1136) and may be he who was an assessor and collector of the thirtieth in Reading Abbey's lands outside Herefordshire in 1237 (*Close Rolls 1234–7*, 557). It was presumably another who was coroner of the Liberty of Reading in 1261 and of Reading hundred in 1284 (PRO JUST 1/40, m. 28d; 1/44, m. 15d) and who was dead by Nov. 1298 (above, no. 1044). One of these was a juror for Reading hundred in 1248 (Clanchy, 295). Yet another William of Coley occurs in the 14th century (e.g., below, nos. 1148, 1158, 1178).

1055 Quitclaim by Thomas of 'Herewardsley' (*Herwardesleg*')*ª* to Reading Abbey of all his right in the land which he sometime held in 'Herewardsley',*ᵇ* and confirmation to the abbey of the gift by William of Coley (*Colleya*) of all the said land, which William recovered against him in the court of Reading by the king's writ as his right and inheritance. Witnesses*ᶜ* [omitted]   [13th cent., before 1248]

A f 79v; B f 61v; C f 28v

ª Herewardesl' *B*, Herewardesleg' *C*   *ᵇ* Hereward' *B*, Herewardesleg' *C*
ᶜ Om in C

Date as for no. 1053.

1055a Notes of the following:
(i) charter by the same Thomas[1] against Nicholas Butler (*le Butiller*) concerning 2 acres of meadow in 'Herewardsley' (*Herewardesl'*)
(ii) another by the same against the same
(iii) charter by the same Thomas against Thomas son of Simon
(iv) charter by the same against William of Coley (*Colley*)[a] concerning a quitclaim of certain land in 'Herewardsley'[b]
(v) another by the same against the same concerning the same

[13th cent., before 1248]

B f 61r; C f 28v

[a] Colleye *C*　　　　　　　　[b] Herewardesleg' *C*

Date as for no. 1053. Items (iv) and (v) relate to the land in nos. 1054–5.

1. In the cartularies these notes follow no. 1053.

WHITLEY (in Reading)
See below, pp. 311–39

CAVERSHAM (in Reading)
(formerly in Oxfordshire)

1056 *Gift in free alms by Isabel, countess of Pembroke* [*widow of William Marshal the elder, earl of Pembroke*], *with the assent of her son William Marshal, earl of Pembroke, to Reading Abbey of two named purprestures, 8s rent and an island called* Horseiat [*in Caversham*]

[prob. mid × late May 1219]

A f 100r; B f 87r–v; C ff 44v–45r

Sciant presentes et futuri quod ego Ysabel[a] comitissa [b]de Penbroc',[b] assensu et consilio Willelmi Marescalli filii mei primogeniti, pro anima nobilis viri domini mei Willelmi Marescalli comitis Penbroc'[c] et pro salute anime mee et Willelmi filii mei comitis Penbroc'[c] et aliorum liberorum meorum et pro salvacione omnium antecessorum meorum[d] et successorum, dedi et concessi et hac presenti carta mea confirmavi deo et beate Marie et beatis apostolis Johanni et Jacobo et abbati et conventui de Rading(ia) in liberam puram et perpetuam elemosinam totam purpresturam quam dominus meus[e] fecit purprestare in Fuelmaresfeld[f] cum pastura que est in eadem purprestura, et illam purpresturam que apellatur^g Crockerescrundele ex utraque parte vie que tendit versus Hanleiam et sicut alia via que extendit versus Roderesfeld^h et fossata undique predictam purpresturam includunt; habendam et tenendam cum omnibus ⁱpertinenciis et libertatibusⁱ suis in perpetuum. Dedi etiam et concessi eisdem octo solidatos redditus quos Rog(erus) Venator solebat reddere domino meo annuatim^j ad duos terminos, scilicet ad festum sancti Michaelis quatuor solidos et ad Pascha quatuor solidos, de terra quam idem Rog(erus) de domino meo tenuit; habendos et recipiendos^k predictis abbati et conventui a predicto Rog(ero) vel ab eo qui terram predictam tenuerit in perpetuum. Concessi etiam quod, si predictus Rog(erus) vel aliquis successorum suorum qui terram predictam tenuerit dictos octo solidos ad terminos statutos non reddiderit, liceat^l abbati et conventui predictum Rogerum vel^m suos successores namia sua capiendo ad solucionem distringere. Preterea dedi et concessi eisdem abbati et conventui insulam que vocatur Horseiat cum omnibus pertinenciis et libertatibus suis. Habenda et tenenda omnia predicta libere et quiete, integre et plenarie,ⁿ in liberam puram et perpetuam elemosinam absque omni retenemento^o et absque omni exactione et demanda que eis ab aliquo mortali inde fieri possit.^p Hiis testibus: Ricardo Marescallo, Henrico filio Geroldi, Johanne de Herlega, Johanne filio eiusdem, Willelmo de Leg', domino Ph(ilippo) clerico, et multis aliis.

^a Ysabell' *B,C*
^c Pembrok' *B,C*
^e *Insert* W. *B,C*
^g appellatur *B,C*
^{i i} libertatibus et pertinenciis *B,C*
^k percipiendos *C*
^m et *B,C*
^o retinemento *B,C*

^{b b} Pembrok' *B,C*
^d *Placed after* successorum *B,C*
^f Fuelmar'feld *B*, Fulemar'feld' *C*
^h Roperesfeld *B,C*
^j *Om. in B,C*
^l licebat *C (in error)*
ⁿ plene *C*
^p *B ends with* T', *C ends*

William Marshal, earl of Pembroke, died at his house in Caversham on 14 May 1219. His body was brought first to Reading Abbey and placed in a rich chapel of his own foundation while mass was celebrated for him, after which it was taken to Westminster Abbey and thence to the Temple Church in London for burial (S. Painter, *William Marshal* (Baltimore, 1933), 289, citing *Histoire de Guillaume le Maréchal* (see below); another version states that at Reading the body was placed in the choir—continuation of William of Newburgh's *Historia Rerum Anglicarum* in *Chronicles of . . . Stephen, Henry II and Richard I*, ed. R. Howlett, ii (RS 1885), 526). The last rites had been administered to the earl at Caversham by the abbots of Reading and Notley (the latter having a cell there) and, while the body rested at Reading, the countess and her son gave the abbey 100s of rent for his soul (*L'Histoire de Guillaume le Maréchal*, ed. P. Meyer (Société de l'histoire de France, 1891–1901), ii. ll. 18963–5, 18997–19000). The present charter no doubt recorded this gift and may have been given either at the time of the obsequies or soon afterwards, particularly since Henry FitzGerold and John of Earley were among the earl's most trusted followers who were present at his death (Painter, 285–8). The countess died in 1220 (*Complete Peerage*, x. 364). Caversham was in Oxfordshire until incorporated into Reading in 1911.

1057 Gift in free alms by William Marshal (*Marescallus*) [junior], earl of Pembroke (*Pembrok'*),[a] to Reading Abbey, for the 10 marks worth of land which he was obliged to give to the abbey for the damage and destruction caused by him and his men during the war,[1] of 72 acres of land in his wood of Caversham (*Cavereham*),[b] viz., all the land with trees (*cum vestitura bosci*) within the following bounds: from *Haselmere* north by the circuit of *Haselmereden(e)*, from the latter eastward to the croft of William the smith (*faber*), thence to the croft of Jordan son of *Ireveus*, thence by *Grimeshole* to *Oselakemere*, and thence by his wood back to *Haselmere*, as the land was measured and assigned to the abbey by Alan of Hyde (*Hyda*), the donor's steward, and by good men of the neighbourhood, and as it is enclosed by boundaries. Warranty and sealing[c]   [1219 × 31; ?1219 × 20]

Original charter: BL Add. Ch. 19616
A ff 85v–86r; B f 87r; C f 44v
Pd. *Arch. Journ.*, xxii, 158; *Pal. Soc. Facs.*, 1st ser., pl. 217 (with facsimile); (cal.) Hurry, *Reading Abbey*, 174–5

Hiis testibus:[d] Johanne Marescallo, Willelmo Crasso primogenito, Hamone Crasso, Henrico de Braibou', Waltero Foliot, Henrico de Scaccario, Alano de Englef(eld), Roberto de Bergef(eld), Alano de Hyda, magistro Deodato, magistro Roberto de Chinun, magistro Jacobo de Cicestr', Nicholao de Chaus', Nicholao pincerna, Waltero de Bachamton', Rogero de Cundicot', Johanne Bulluc, et multis aliis.

Endorsed: Carta Willelmi M(are)scalli de terra in bosco de Caveresham [*13th cent.*]
Size: 194 × 123 mm
Seal: missing; plaited red and white cord through three holes in fold at bottom (short length only remaining, seal cut off)

[a] Penbrok' *A*
[b] Kaverresham *A*, Kaveresham *B*, Kaversham *C*
[c] B ends with T', C ends   [d] *A ends*

No. 1058 proves that the donor was William Marshal junior, earl of Pembroke, who, unlike his father, joined the rebels against King John (Painter, *William Marshal*, 185–6; *Complete Peerage*, x. 365–6). The dating limits are those of his earldom, but, since the gift compensated for damage caused in the recent war, the charter may date from shortly after he became earl. B adds a note of another charter by the same concerning the same.

1. Between the Crown and the rebellious barons.

1058 Quitclaim by Roger of Condicote (*Cundicot'*) to Reading Abbey of the whole land which he held of it in Caversham (*Kaversham*), viz., that which William Marshal (*Marescallus*) the Younger, earl of Pembroke (*Penbroc*), gave to the abbey, and of the whole half-hide of land in Caversham (*Kaveresham*) which sometime belonged to Roger the Huntsman (*Venator*) and which similarly he held of the abbey. To be held freely with homages, reliefs, suits, perquisites (*purcacia*), pleas, escheats and all rents, easements and liberties belonging to the said lands. For this the abbey has granted to him and to Cecily, his wife, corrodies and clothing (*warniamenta*) for life, as is contained in the charter which they have from the abbey. Sealing. Witnesses [omitted]

[1219 × 44; ?*c.* 1240 × 1244]

A f 86r

After no. 1057 and before no. 1062. The grant of corrodies to the donor and his wife suggests a date towards the end of his life; he was still alive in 1241 × 44 (see no. 1061).

1059 Quitclaim by the same to the same of the whole land which he held of the abbey in Caversham (*Caveresham*),*a* viz., that which William Marshal (*Marescallus*) the Younger, earl of Pembroke (*Penbroch*),*b* gave to it; and gift in free alms of all his right in the half-hide of land in Caversham which sometime belonged to Roger the Huntsman (*Venator*). To be held [etc., as in no. 1058]. For this [etc., as in no. 1058]. Sealing. Witnesses*c* [omitted]

[1219 × 44; ?*c.* 1240 × 1244]

A f 86r; B f 88r; C f 45v

a Kaveresham *B*, Kaversham *C*   *b* Pembrok *B,C*
c Om. in *C*

Date as for no. 1058. The two deeds are very similar, except that here the land formerly belonging to Roger the Huntsman is not quitclaimed, but all right in it is given in free alms. This deed may have superseded no. 1058, which was accordingly not copied into B and C.

1060 Gift in free alms by Roger of Condicote (*Cundic(ote)*) to Reading Abbey of the whole half-hide of land which Roger the Huntsman sometime held in Caversham (*Kaveresham*)*a* and gave to the donor. Warranty and sealing. Witnesses*b* [omitted]

[1219 × 44; ?*c.* 1240 × 1244]

B f 88v; C f 46r

a Kaversham *C*   *b* Om. in *C*

Probably contemporary with or after no. 1059, since here Roger the Huntsman's former land is given in free alms.

1060a Notes of the following:

(i) charter by Roger the huntsman to Roger of Condicote (*Cundic(ote)*) concerning the same land   [1219 × 44]

(ii) charter by William Marshal (*Marescallus*) to Roger the hunts-
      man concerning the same land   [?1189 × 99]
      B f 88v

(i) dates after no. 1056, when Roger the huntsman was still in possession, and before
the latest possible date for nos. 1058–60.
(ii) dates not earlier than 1189, when William Marshal senior acquired Caversham
by marriage (Sanders, *English Baronies*, 62; Painter, *William Marshal*, 78), and probably
not later than 1199 since he is not styled earl, which he became in May of that year.
No. 1056 shows that Roger the huntsman originally held of this William Marshal.

1061 Gift in free alms by Roger of Condicote (*Cundic(ote)*) to Reading
Abbey of the whole croft called *la Breche* in Caversham (*Kaveresham*).[a]
To be held freely by rendering annually to Walter Marshal, earl
of Pembroke (*Pembrok'*), and his heirs 2s 8d, viz., 16d each at the
Annunciation and Michaelmas, and to the donor and his heirs $\frac{1}{2}$d at
Michaelmas, for all custom, exaction, demand, suit of court and
secular service. Warranty and sealing. Witnesses[b] [omitted]
                                        [27 Oct. 1241 × 17 Nov. 1244]
      B f 88r–v; C ff 45v–46r

[a] Kaversham C   [b] *Om. in C*

After Walter Marshal became earl of Pembroke, and before the latest date for no. 1062.

1062 Confirmation by Margery,[a] countess of Pembroke (*Penbroc*)[b]
and sister of the king of Scotland, in her widowhood, to Reading
Abbey of the gift in free alms by William Marshal [junior],[c] earl of
Pembroke, and Isabel countess of Pembroke, his mother, of lands,
rents, tenements and tenants in Caversham (*Kaveresham*)[d] [nos. 1056–
7]; and of the half-hide of land in Caversham which belonged to
Roger the Huntsman and which Roger of Condicote (*Cundecote*) gave
to the abbey in free alms [No. 1060] with the croft called *la Breche*
[no. 1061], the abbey rendering to her annually for the croft 2s 8d,
viz., 16d each at the Annunciation and Michaelmas, for all custom,
exaction, demand, suit of court and secular service. Sealing. Given
A.D. 1244   25 Mar. × 17 Nov. 1244
      A f 86v; B f 87v; C f 45r

[a] *A has* 'Margaret'   [b] Pembrok' B,C
[c] *Supplied from B,C*   [d] Kaversham C

Margery was the daughter of William I of Scotland and sister of Alexander II, who
reigned 1214–49. She married Gilbert Marshal, earl of Pembroke, who died in 1241,
and died herself on 17 Nov. 1244 (*Complete Peerage*, x. 374). The date given here assumes
that the year began on 25 March.

1063   Confirmation by Richard de Clare, earl of Gloucester and Hertford, to Reading Abbey of the same gifts by William Marshal junior, earl of Pembroke (*Pembrok'*), and Isabel countess of Pembroke, his mother, and by Roger of Condicote (*Cundecote*) in Caversham (*Kaversham*);[a] and gift in free alms to the abbey of the annual rent of 32d due from the abbey to him and his heirs for the croft called *la Breche*. Warranty of the rent and sealing. Witnesses[b] [omitted]

[*c.* early 1247]

B ff 87v–88r; C f 45r–v

[a] Kaversham *C*   [b] *Om. in C*

Richard de Clare was earl of Gloucester and Hertford 1243–62. Through his mother, one of the five daughters of William Marshal I, earl of Pembroke, he secured a fifth of the Marshal lands, including Caversham, following the extinction of the male line in 1245 (*Complete Peerage*, v. 696, x. 377; *Cal. Pat. R. 1364–67*, 274). In 1238 he married Maud de Lacy, daughter of John de Lacy, earl of Lincoln. The date of this deed is probably not long before no. 1064.

1064   Ratification by Margaret[a] de Lacy, countess of Lincoln and Pembroke, of the remission by Richard de Clare, earl of Gloucester and Hertford, her son, to Reading Abbey of 32d of annual rent and suit of court from the tenements which the abbey has in Caversham (*Kaversham*).[b] The abbey shall hold the said tenements freely in accordance with the charter which it has from the earl. Letters patent

3 Mar. 1247

B f 88r; C f 45v
Pd. Kennett, *Parochial Antiquities*, i. 359

Dat' tercia die Marcii, anno regni regis H(enrici) filii regis Johannis xxxi.

[a] *Both texts have* 'Margery'   [b] Kaversham *C*

The lady was Margaret de Quincy, heiress of the earldom of Lincoln, who married (i) John de Lacy, created earl of Lincoln (d. 1240), whose daughter Maud married Richard de Clare, earl of Gloucester and Hertford (see no. 1063), and (ii) Walter Marshal, earl of Pembroke (d. 1245) (*Complete Peerage*, vii. 679–80). She thus had not only a direct interest in the Marshal lands through her second husband, but also a further link with part of them through her daughter. This deed describes Richard de Clare as her son, but he was strictly her son-in-law.

STANFORD-IN-THE-VALE

1065   *Gift in free alms by William, Earl Ferrers [earl of Derby] to Reading Abbey of 20 acres of arable land and 5 acres of meadow in his manor of Stanford [-in-the-Vale]*   [*c.* 1168 × 1189]

A f 40v; B f 70v; C f 36r

Sciant presentes et futuri quod ego Willelmus comes de Ferr(es)*ᵃ* dedi
deo et ecclesie de Rading(ia) in liberam et perpetuam elemosinam
.xx. acras de terra arabili in manerio meo Stanford(ie) iuxta ecclesiam
apud occidentalem partem et .v. acras prati, scilicet .iiii. acras quas
Samson pro duobus solidis tenuit et quintam quam Gilebertus de
Wicha*ᵇ* tenuit. Hanc terram tenebunt prefate ecclesie monachi, in
expectationem melioris et prestantioris doni mei, libere et quiete ab
omni consuetudine et exactione seculari, pro salute anime mee et
Sibille comitisse uxoris mee et omnium filiorum meorum et pro anima
patris mei et matris mee et omnium antecessorum et successorum
meorum.*ᶜ* Testibus:*ᵈ* Nicholao filio Pagani dapifero meo, Rog(erio)
de Fifhida, Roberto de Bachepuz, Iohanne filio eius, Henrico de
Kinchest(una), Walt(erio) de Stokes, Iohanne Chatin', et multis aliis.

*ᵃ Expansion from no. 1066, which precedes this in all cartularies; B,C rubrics for no. 1066
have* Ferrariis
ᵇ Wiche *B,C*　　　　　　　　　　　*ᶜ C ends*
ᵈ B ends

The donor was William de Ferrers, 3rd Earl Ferrers or earl of Derby (1161/2–1190),
who married Sibyl, daughter of William de Braose (*Complete Peerage*, iv. 193). Nicholas
fitz Payn became his steward after *c.* 1168 (*Sir Christopher Hatton's Book of Seals*, 104),
and the gift was included in Richard I's general confirmation to the abbey in Sept.
1189 (see no. 34). The manor was part of the Honour of Tutbury (*VCH Berks.*, iv.
479).

1066　*Gift in free alms by William, Earl Ferrers [earl of Derby], to Reading
Abbey of a messuage in Stanford[-in-the-Vale], with the land and meadow
previously given by him*　　　　　　　　　　　　　*[c. 1168 × 1189]*

A f 40v; B f 70v; C f 36r

Willelmus comes de Ferres*ᵃ* omnibus hominibus suis et amicis presentibus et futuris, salutem. Sciatis omnes me dedisse deo et sancte
Marie et monachis deo servientibus de Rading(ia) unum masagium*ᵇ*
in Stanfordia propinquius de ecclesia, scilicet inter domum Willelmi
clerici et ecclesiam, in puram et perpetuam elemosinam, liberum et
quietum in omni actione, cum terra et cum prato quam eis prius dedi
et carta mea confirmavi, pro anima mea et uxoris mee et liberorum
meorum et antecessorum meorum et successorum.*ᶜ* His testibus:
Roberto de Ferres fratre comitis, Luciano de Seila, Hugone de Toren-
duna, Willelmo de Stant' clerico comitis de Ferr(es), R. filio Hugonis,
et multis aliis.

ᵃ Ferr' *B,C*　　　　　　　　　　　*ᵇ* mesuagium *B,C*
ᶜ B ends with T', *C ends*

Date as for no. 1065.

1066a Note of a charter by W. of Stanford (*Stanford'*) to [?] Reginald (*Regin'*) concerning the land of G. *de la Waye* [not later than 1258]

B f 70v

In the original section of B.

STRATFIELD MORTIMER

1067 *Gift by Hugh de Mortimer to Hugh, his son, of [Mortimer] Worthy [Hants.] and Stratfield [Mortimer] in England and of St Riquier with appurtenances in Normandy* [*c.* 1170 × 73]

A f 36v; (noted) B f 56v

Hugo de Mortuomari omnibus hominibus et fidelibus suis citra mare et ultra, salutem. Sciatis me dedisse et hac carta mea confirmasse Hugoni filio meo, pro homagio et servitio suo, in Anglia Wordiam et Estratfeld, sibi et heredibus suis tenend(as) de me et heredibus meis cum omnibus pertinentiis suis in feudo et hereditate per servitium dimidii militis, et in Normannia Sanctum Richerum cum pertinentiis suis, scilicet Dancurt et Prusevilla, per servitium dimidii militis. Quare volo et concedo ut predictus filius meus predictas terras habeat et teneat et heredes sui post eum cum omnibus pertinentiis suis, in bosco et plano, in pratis et pasturis, in aquis et molendinis, in viis et semitis et in omnibus aliis locis et aliis rebus ad easdem pertinentibus, bene et in pace, libere et quiete et plenarie et honorifice per predictum servitium. His testibus: W(illelmo) comite de Aubemara, Reginaldo de Warenna, Hugone de Creissi, Rogero de Clera, Willelmo Pecc(at)o, Reginaldo de Wassumvilla, Willelmo de Spineto, Radulfo filio Modberti, Olivero Costard, Roberto de Portmort.

The suggested date is that of Henry II's confirmation (no. 1068). The donor was Hugh de Mortimer of Wigmore, who died in 1180 × 1 (*Complete Peerage*, ix. 272). Mortimer Worthy is in the parish of Headbourne Worthy, Hants.

1068 *Confirmation of the same by King Henry II* [1170 × 73]

A f 23r; (noted) B f 27v

Henricus rex Anglie et dux Normannie et Aquitanie et comes Andegavie archiepiscopis, episcopis, comitibus et baronibus, iustic(iariis) et vicecomitibus et omnibus ministris et fidelibus suis Anglie et Normannie, salutem. Sciatis me concessisse et presenti carta confirmasse Hugoni filio Hugonis de Mortuo Mari Wordiam et Estratfeld' cum

pertinentiis suis, que sunt in Anglia, et Sanctum Richerum cum
pertinentiis suis, scilicet Dancurt et Prusevilla, que sunt in Normannia,
quas terras Hugo de Mortuo Mari dedit eidem Hugoni filio suo pro
homagio et servitio suo sibi et heredibus suis tenend(as) de eo et
heredibus suis in feodo et hereditate per servitium determinatum in
carta patris sui. Quare volo et firmiter precipio quod predictus filius
Hugonis de Mortuo Mari et heredes sui post eum habeant et teneant
prenominatas terras cum omnibus pertinentiis suis in bosco et plano,
in pratis et pasturis, in aquis et molendinis, in viis et semitis et in
omnibus aliis locis et aliis rebus ad easdem pertinentibus, ita bene et
in pace et libere et quiete et plenarie et honorifice sicut Hugo de
Mortuo Mari pater suus ei dedit et carta sua confirmavit. Testibus:
G(alfredo) archidiacono Cant(uariensi), Ricardo archidiacono Pic-
tav(ensi), comite W(illelmo) de Aubemara, comite W(illelmo) de
Mand(evilla), Ricardo de Luci, Ricardo de Hum(eto) const(a-
bulario), Reginaldo de Curtenai, Willelmo de Albineio, Reginaldo de
Pavilli, Hugone de Creissi, Roberto de Mortuo M(ari), Waltero de
Dunst(anvilla). Apud Gloec(estriam).

William de Mandeville succeeded to the earldom of Essex in Oct. 1166; Geoffrey Ridel,
archdeacon of Canterbury, and Richard of Ilchester, archdeacon of Poitiers, were
elected bishops of Ely and Winchester respectively in late Apr. 1173. Between Mar.
1166 and Mar. 1170 Henry II was out of England (Eyton, 92, 135). The absence of
dei gratia from the royal style (on which this cartulary is generally scrupulous) confirms
a date not later than 1173.

1069 *Gift in free alms, with his body, by Hugh de Mortimer [junior] to
Reading Abbey of lands in Stratfield [Mortimer], his part of the mill of Worthy
[Hants.] and his whole rent in Winchester*   [*c.* 1170 × 1181]

A f 36v

Sciant presentes et futuri quod ego Hugo de Mortuo Mari dedi et
concessi deo et sancte Marie de Radinges et abbati et monachis ibidem
deo servientibus, in perpetuam elemosinam liberam et quietam ab
omni servitio terreno, cum corpore meo, pro salute anime mee et
anime patris mei et omnium predecessorum meorum et successorum
meorum, totam terram Godwini de la Torne quam de me tenuit in
Stratfeld, et totam terram Ricardi de la Torne in Stratfeld, et totam
terram Turstani de la Scete et totam terram Alfrici de la Scete in
Stratfeld, et totam terram Iohannis Eilaf in Stratfeld. Omnes istas
terras dedi et concessi prefate ecclesie cum omnibus pertinentiis suis
in bosco, in plano, in pratis et pascuis et aliis pertinentiis. Dedi etiam
et concessi prefate ecclesie omnia prata mea de la Redmed in Stratfeld
et totum boscum meum de la Torne, et totam partem meam in
molendino de Wordia, et totum redditum meum de Wintonia infra

burgum. Ut autem hec donatio mea firma in perpetuum perseveret, eandem sigilli mei munimine confirmavi. His testibus: Rogero capellano de Stratfeld, Simone de Sancto Laurentio, Radulfo de Vilers, Reginaldo Camberlano, Roberto de Nene, Amis de Peletot, Iohanne de Catainne, Iohanne de Cellario, Helia de Mora.

The donor died without offspring in the lifetime of his father, the donor of no. 1067, who himself died in 1180 × 1 (*Complete Peerage*, ix. 272). The deed dates after no. 1067 and before the latter's death. For a deed by the present donor in Winchester, see no. 322. *La Redmed* is Red Meade (*Berks. Place-Names*, i. 219).

1070 Final concord in the king's court at Westminster in 1 month from Easter, 9 Henry III, before Martin of Pattishall (*Pateshill'*),[a] Thomas of Moulton (*Muleton'*), Thomas *de Heyden'*, Robert of Lexington (*Lexint'*),[b] Geoffrey Savage (*le Sauvage*), justices, and others, between Hugh de Mortimer (*de Mort(uo)m(ari)*),[c] seeking by Tristram *de Ribbeford'* as attorney, and Abbot Simon of Reading, holding by Henry *Aubin* as attorney, concerning 5½ virgates of land and a meadow called Red Meade (*Redemed'*) with appurtenances in Stratfield [Mortimer] (*Stratfeld'*). The abbot recognized the said land and meadow to be the right of Hugh and quitclaimed them for himself and his successors to Hugh and his heirs in perpetuity. For this Hugh gave in free alms to the abbot and his successors and the abbey of Reading 4 virgates of land with the tenants and their progeny (*sequela*) and a wood called *le þorn* in Stratfield [Mortimer], viz., 1 virgate held by Gilbert *Aylaf*, ½ virgate by Gilbert *le Wyne*, ½ virgate by Robert *Tompe*, ½ virgate by Goda the widow, 1 virgate by Geoffrey *Wiking*[d] and ½ virgate by Richard *de[e] la Legh'*.   27 Apr. 1225

B f 170v; C ff 100v–101r

[a] Pateshull' *C*	[b] Lexinton' *C*
[c] Mortim(er) *C*	[d] Wyking' *C*
[e] *Om. in C*	

The foot of this fine is PRO CP 25 (1)/7/8/24. This Hugh de Mortimer was the son of Roger, son of the Hugh de Mortimer who made the enfeoffment in no. 1067.

1071 Gift in free alms by Hugh de Mortimer (*de Mortuomari*), son of Roger de Mortimer, for the souls of among others Roger his father and Isabel his mother, to Abbot Simon and the convent of Reading of 4 virgates of land in his manor of Stratfield [Mortimer] (*Stratfeld*) with the tenants and their progeny (*sequela*), viz., 1 virgate held by Gilbert *Ayllaf*, ½ virgate by Richard *de la Legh'*, ½ virgate by Gilbert *le Wyne*, ½ virgate by Robert *Tompe*, ½ virgate by Goda the widow and 1 virgate by Geoffrey *Wiking*,[a] and of a wood called *Thorn* which the abbey previously held in his said manor of Stratfield [Mortimer]. Also grant that all men of the abbot and his successors living on the said land shall have common pasture in woods and moors and wherever else they had common when the land was in his hand, with free entry and exit. Warranty and sealing [late Apr. × May 1225]

B f 56v; C f 24r–v

a Wikyng' C

This charter records the gift to which Hugh agreed in the final concord (no. 1070). A note at the bottom of B f 56v points out that the fine was made before nos. 1071–2.

1072 Gift in free alms by Hugh de Mortimer (*de Mortuomar'*)*a* to Reading Abbey of all the land in Stratfield [Mortimer] (*Stretfeld'*)*b* which he recovered by concord from Simon, late abbot of Reading,[1] viz., $\frac{1}{2}$ virgate which Edith *de la Thorne* held, 1 virgate which *Bondi* held, 1 virgate which Adam *de la Schete* held, $\frac{1}{2}$ virgate which Hugh *Alfricus* held, and the whole meadow called Red Meade (*La Redmede*); with his heart and viscera for burial in the abbey.[2] Warranty and sealing [13 Feb, 1226 × 10 Nov. 1227]

Original charter: BL Add. Ch. 19628
A f 82r; B ff 56v–57r; C f 24v
Pd. *Arch. Journ.*, xxii. 156; (cal.) Hurry, *Reading Abbey*, 175–6

Hiis testibus:*c* Nicholao capellano de Stratfeld', Philippo de Mortuo Mari, Rogero de Burewardeleg', Willelmo de Neumeinill', Ada Costard', et multis aliis.

Endorsed: Carta Hugonis junioris*d* de Mortuomar' de terra de Stretfeld [*13th cent.*] scilicet .iii. virgatis terre et prato de Redmed [*13th cent., diff. hand*]

Size: 194 × 92 mm
Seal: missing; tag through slit in fold at bottom

a Mortuomari A,C   *b* Stratfeld B,C
c A,B,C end   *d* Interlined

After Abbot Simon's death and before that of Hugh de Mortimer (*Complete Peerage*, ix. 275).

1. See no. 1070.
2. A marginal note in a 14th-century hand in A reads: Nota de corde Hugonis Mortemer sepulto inter tumbas ante altare beate Marie.

STREATLEY

1073 *Concession in free alms by William de Mandeville, earl of Essex, to Reading Abbey of the land which Alfric son of Croc of Kiddington held in his manor of Streatley* [prob. 1175]

A ff 40v–41r; B f 73r; B f 145r; C f 38r; C f 85r; D ff 21v–22r

Sciant presentes et futuri quod ego Willelmus de Mandevill(a)[a] comes Essexie concessi et presenti carta[b] confirmavi deo et ecclesie sancte Marie de Rading(ia) et monachis ibidem deo servientibus totam terram quam tenuit Aluricus filius Croc de Katend(ena)[c] in manerio meo de Stratleia,[d] reddentem .xxvi. solidos et .iiii. d', in perpetuam elemosinam cum omnibus pertinentiis suis in bosco et plano, in pratis et pasturis, in viis et[e] semitis, cum omnibus libertatibus et liberis consuetudinibus suis quas Aluricus filius[f] Croc vel aliquis successorum eius unquam melius habuit in manerio meo de Stratl(eia). Tenebunt autem predicti monachi et perpetuo possidebunt prenominatam terram reddentem sibi .xxvi. solidos et .iiii. d' pro omni servitio, libere et quiete et absque omni terreno servitio, salvo tamen servitio domini regis quod eadem terra facere solebat. Cum autem contigerit quod relevari[g] debeat prefata terra, relevabunt[h] eam hii qui eam hereditarie possessuri[i] sunt solvendo .x. solidos predictis monachis de Rading(ia). Si vero forisfecerint, satisfacient pro forisfacto monachis Ra[f 41r]ding'[j] sicut dominis suis per iudicium curie ipsorum monachorum. His[k] testibus:[l] Rog(ero) Bigot,[m] Gileberto[n] de Veir, Hugone Talebot,[o] [Willelmo filio Rog(eri), Sawalo de Osevil', Iohanne de Rochell', Waltero cubiculario, Waltero filio Bernardi, et Waltero filio eius, Willelmo capellano de Pangeb(urna), Haimone de Rading(ia)].

[a] Mandewill' *B f 73r, C f 38r*   [b] *Insert* mea *C f 85r*
[c] Ceten'd'ne *B f 73r, C f 38r*; Cettend'ne *B f 145r, D*; Cetend'ne *C f 85r*
[d] Stratleg' *D*   [e] *Insert* in *B f 73r, C f 38r*
[f] *Om. in B f 73r, C f 38r*   [g] revelari *B f 73r, C f 38r*
[h] revelabunt *B f 73r, C f 38r*
[i] *Altered from* possuturi *B f 73r*; possuturi *C f 38r*
[j] de Radyng' *C f 38r*   [k] Hiis *B f 145r, both C,D*
[l] *B f 145r, C f 85r end*   [m] Big'od *B f 73r, C f 38r*
[n] Gilleberto *B f 73r*
[o] *A ends with* et multis aliis, *D ends with* et cetera, *the remainder being supplied from B f 73r, C f 38r*

The date is probably similar to that of Henry II's confirmation (no. 1074). Cf. no. 389. In B the entry on f 145r was part of the original composition, and that on f 73r was added soon afterwards.

1074 *Confirmation of the same by King Henry II*
[prob. Oct. × Dec. 1175]

A f 24r–v; B f 27v; B f 145r; C f 85r; D f 22r

Henricus dei gratia rex Anglie [a]et[b] dux Normann(ie) et Aquit(anie) et^c comes Andeg(avie)^a archiepiscopis, episcopis, abbatibus, comitibus, baronibus, iustic(iariis), vicecomitibus et omnibus ministris et fidelibus suis [*f 24v*] Anglie, salutem. Sciatis me concessisse et presenti carta confirmasse ecclesie sancte Marie de^d Rading(ia) et monachis ibidem deo servientibus totam terram quam tenuit Alwricus^e filius Croc de Katendena^f quam comes Willelmus de Mandevilla^g eis dedit in perpetuam elemosinam, que est in manerio suo de Stratleia.^{h} Quare volo et firmiter precipio quod predicta ecclesia et monachi habeant et teneant terram illam cum omnibus pertinentiis suis in bosco et plano, in pratis et pasturis, in viis et semitis et in omnibus aliis locis et aliis rebus ad eandem terram pertinentibus, bene et in pace, libere et quiete, integre et honorifice, cum omnibus libertatibus et liberis consuetudinibus suis, sicut carta ipsius comitis quam inde habent testatur.^{i} Testibus:^{j} Radulfo thesaurario Sancti Hil(arii) Pictav(ensis)^d, Ricardo de Canvilla, Gisleberto^k Malet, Seihero de Quinci, Roberto filio Bernardi, Roberto de Stutevilla, Ricardo Giff(ard),^{l} Rogero filio Reinfridi, Gerardo de Canvilla.^{m} Apud Windesor(es).^{n}

^{a} ^{a}et cetera *B f 145r, C*
^{b} *Om. in B f 27v, D*
^{c} *Om. in D*
^{d} *Om. in B f 27v*
^{e} Aleoricus *B f 27v*, Aluricus *B f 145r, C,D*
^{f} Kentedena *B f 27v*, Ketendena *B f 145r, C,D*
^{g} Mandewilla *B f 27v*
^{h} Stratleg' *D*
^{i} *C ends*
^{j} *B f 145r, D end*
^{k} Gileberto *B f 27v*
^{l} Viff' *B f 27v*
^{m} Camvilla *B f 27v*
^{n} Windelesor' *B f 27v*

Certainly after Oct. 1166, when William de Mandeville succeeded as earl of Essex, and probably not earlier than 1173 in view of the inclusion of *dei gratia* in the royal style. The Richard de Camville who appears first among the lay witnesses is probably the one who died in 1176 rather than his son Richard (see no. 495 n.). Ralph, treasurer of St Hilary of Poitiers, was with Henry II at Reading, possibly in Apr. 1177 (Eyton, 212), and may have accompanied the king on his crossing to England in May 1175. William de Mandeville was in attendance on the king at Windsor in Oct. 1175. The probable date for this charter, and also of the earl's gift, is therefore some time in the last three months of 1175, in all three of which the king spent some time at Windsor (*ibid.*, 197). The entries on B f 145r and C f 85r are among the almoner's charters, while the rubric of B f 27v reads: Carta eiusdem de terra in Stratle quam W. de Mandevill' dedit elemosinarie. In B the entry on f 145r was part of the original composition, that on f 27v being a later addition.

SULHAMSTEAD ABBOTS

1075 *Settlement between Reading Abbey and Elias of Englefield over the mill of* Russiford[1] *[in Sulhamstead Abbots], with the assent of King Henry II and*

Willelmo de la Mare, Gilone de Pignei, Widone filio Ascolfi, Walterio clerico, Girardo clerico, Henrico de Pignei, Gaufr(edo), Gisleberto; et ex parte monachorum, Petro clerico, Luwino ianitore, Reimundo, Hamone, et Hamone filio Willelmi, Roberto stabulario.

a Elyas *C*	*b* Russiford' *B*, Russeford *C*
c *Supplied from other copies*	*d* marcha/marcham *A ff 82v–83r*
e hiis *B,C*	*f* Verumptamen *B,C*
g *Om. in A ff 82v–83r*	*h* michi *C*
i itaque *B,C*	*j* quandocunque *A ff 82v–83r*
k aut *A ff 82v–83r*, vel *B,C*	*l* Hiis *A ff 82v–83r, B,C*
m *All other texts end*	

Dating as for no. 1075, since the rubric of no. 1075 on A f 39v shows that it concerned the same 'gift'. The rubrics of the present deed in B and C describe it as a chirograph. The last sentence before the witness-list is in the third person, suggesting that it may have been a hastily added afterthought though part of the original text.

1077 *Gift by Gervase Pincent to Reading Abbey of his whole land of* Shaies [*in Sulhamstead Abbots*] *and of all rents and lands acquired by him during his life; and recognition of the abbey's lordship in the lands of* la Wlfhulle *and* Benewell', *which he holds of the abbey for life and which the abbey has agreed shall be held by Ragenilda his wife at annual rents for life if he dies or becomes a monk at Reading before her death, and recognition of the abbey's rights at will in the other tenements which he holds of it* [late 12th × early 13th cent.]

A f 106v; B f 67v; C ff 33v–34r

Sciant presentes et futuri quod ego Gervasius Punchun*a* dedi et concessi et*b* presenti carta mea confirmavi deo et sancte*c* Marie et ecclesie de Radinges et abbati et conventui eiusdem loci, pro salute mea et omnium amicorum*d* meorum, totam*d* terram meam de Shaies cum pertinentiis suis quam tenui de Hereberto le Mul et de Matilde*e* uxore sua per servitium quadraginta denariorum per annum. Dedi etiam et concessi predicte ecclesie omnes redditus ac terras meas quas adquisivi vel adquirere potero tota vita mea, per idem servitium quod facere debeo dominis meis. Terra vero quam de predictis abbate et conventu de Rading(es) teneo de la Wlfhulle*f* et de Benewell' cum omnibus pertinentiis suis post decessum meum integre et plenarie ad eandem ecclesiam revertetur, quia illam non habui nisi tantummodo in vita mea. De aliis etiam tenementis que de ipsis teneo nichil habeo nec habere debeo nisi ad voluntatem ipsorum, quoniam poterunt illa revocare ad se quando voluerint. Si vero monachatum in domo Rading(ensi) in vita mea accepero, sicut carta mea quam de eis habeo testatur, similiter tunc predicta terra ad ipsos statim revertetur. Predicti tamen abbas et monachi concesserunt Ragenilde uxori mee quod, si me supervixerit vel postquam vitam meam*d* mutavero in seculo fuerit, teneat predictam terram de eis tantum in vita sua, pro dimidia marca de Wlfele^g et viginti septem denariis de Benewell' annuatim reddendis, ita quod post decessum suum sine omni calumpnia tota predicta terra integre ad predictam ecclesiam revertatur.^{h} Hiis testibus.

^{a} Punzun *B,C*	^{b} *Insert* hac *C*
^{c} beate *C*	^{d} *Om. in B,C*
^{e} Matill' *B,C*	^{f} Wlshull' *B,C (in error)*
^{g} Wlfhull' *B,C*	^{h} *B ends with* T', *C ends*

The rubrics of B and C describe *Shaies* as in Sulhamstead. The donor was a member of the Pincent family of Sulhamstead Abbots, which may have derived its name from a Pincent of Sulhamstead who occurs in 1173 × 86 and in the later 12th century after 1186 (see no. 1209; BL Add. Ch. 7202). Gervase was a brother of Robert Pincent (see no. 1141), who made several deeds to the abbey in the late 12th or early 13th century (nos. 1078–85). Gervase occurs as a witness in 1200 × 1213 and 1204 × 1220 (see nos. 849, 1141, 892). Since the present deed is not entered in the original section of A, it may be not earlier than 1193.

1078 *Release and quitclaim by Robert Pincent to his lords the abbot and convent of Reading of the meadow which he held of them called* Stodham *and of 1 acre in the same meadow in* Midelmestedole, *on account of which they have given him 5 marks and remitted 6d of his annual rent*

[late 12th × early 13th cent.]

A f 73v; B f 63v; C f 30v

Sciant presentes et futuri quod ego Robertus Punchun^a reddidi et ^{b}quietum clamavi,^{b} dedi et concessi et presenti carta confirmavi dominis meis abbati et conventui de Rading(ia) pratum quod de eis tenui quod vocatur Stodham et unam acram in eodem prato in Midelmestedole. Habendum et tenendum iure perpetuo libere et quiete et absolute absque omni calumpnia^c vel demanda que inde eis unquam fieri possit de me vel^d heredibus meis. Ego enim et heredes mei totum predictum pratum adquietabimus^e cum alia terra nostra de omnibus rebus que ad predictum pratum pertinere vel evenire poterunt. Et propter hanc concessionem dederunt mihi predictus abbas et conventus quinque marcas argenti et remiserunt mihi^f sex denarios annuos de redditu meo.^{g} Hiis testibus.

^{a} Puncun *B*, Punzun *C*	$^{b-b}$quiet'clam' *B*, quietumclam' *C*
^{c} *Insert* vexatione *B,C*	^{d} *Insert* de *C*
^{e} acquietabimus *B,C*	^{f} michi *C*
^{g} *B ends with* T', *C ends*	

The deed was not entered in the original section of A and is perhaps similar in date to no. 1079. Robert Pincent was a brother of Gervase Pincent (see no. 1077 n.) and a tenant of Reading Abbey in Sulhamstead Abbots in the late 12th and early 13th centuries. He occurs as a witness between 1186 × 1213 and 1226 × 38 (BL Add. Ch. 7202; *Ancient Charters*, 107; above, no. 849; PRO E210/185 and /3527) and was certainly alive in 1231 x 2 (below, no. 1085). This deed is one of several which indicate Robert's financial difficulties. The rubrics of B and C locate the meadow in Sulhamstead.

1079   *Gift, as though in free alms, by Robert Pincent of Sulhamstead [Abbots] to Reading Abbey of his whole meadow of Stodham with 1 acre of meadow in Midemestedole. He and his heirs will still do full service for their land as before. The abbey has received him into confraternity and will give him the monastic habit at death, and at his death he [will] convey to the abbey with his body one third of his possessions including land*

[late 12th x early 13th cent.]

A f 100r; B ff 63v–64r; C f 30v

Sciant presentes et futuri quod ego Robertus Punchun*a* de Silhamstede dedi et concessi et hac presenti carta mea confirmavi deo et sancte Marie et abbati et conventui de Radinges totum pratum meum de Stodham cum una acra prati in Midemestedole. Habendum et tenendum quasi in*b* puram et perpetuam elemosinam, libere et quiete et absolute iure perpetuo absque ullo servitio et absque ulla demanda que uncquam*c* eis fieri possit a me vel aliquo ex meis. Ego autem et heredes mei nichilominus faciemus plenarie pro tota terra nostra totum servitium ecclesie Rading(ensi) quod facere consuevimus antequam dedissem illis*d* pratum istud.*e* Ipsi vero abbas et conventus*f* de Rading(es) intuitu dei receperunt me in fratrem domus sue et in communionem omnium bonorum que fiunt in ecclesia sua in perpetuum, ita quod ad obitum meum habitum monachalem*g* mihi dabunt et de cetero warantizabunt me tancquam*h* specialem fratrem domus sue pro posse suo. Ego vero totam tertiam pertem catalli mei et rerum mearum tam mobilium quam inmobilium et in blado, in terra et in omnibus aliis ad obitum meum domui Rading(ensi) confero cum corpore meo absque ulla contradictione meorum.*i* Hiis testibus: Iohanne filio Hugonis, Alano de Englefeld, magistro Willelmo de Linc(olnia), Henrico de Camel, et multis aliis.

a Punzun *B,C*	*b* Om. in *B,C*
c unquam *B,C*	*d* eis *B,C*
e illud *B,C*	*f* monachi *B,C*
g monachilem *B,C*	*h* tanquam *B,C*
i B ends with T', C ends	

For the donor, see no. 1078 n. John son of Hugh witnessed in Theale, in Tilehurst, in 1200 x 1213 (see no. 1141). Master William of Lincoln was appointed vicar of St Mary's church, Reading, in 1173 x 86 and had ceased to be vicar by 1213 at the latest (see nos. 829, 839).

1080   Gift by R(obert) Pincent (*Punzun*), with the consent and good will of Agnes his wife and of his heirs, to Reading Abbey of the whole part of meadow lying between the boundary (*fines*) of the meadow of Alan of Englefield (*Englef(eld)*),[a] which he holds of the donor next to Pincent's bridge (*pons predicti Punzun*), and the large willow; and of 1 acre of meadow, the first in the great meadow of Sulhamstead [Abbots] (*Silhamsted'*) towards the east, as allotted in the strip towards the grove by the custom in that strip (*quam sors dederit in cultura versus gravam sicut mos est ibidem in eadem cultura sortiri*). To be held freely and quit of all exaction and demand in perpetuity. For this the abbey has given him in his great need 1 mark of silver, to his wife 1 quarter of corn (*bladum*) and to his heir 5s and 1 quarter of corn. Witnesses [omitted]   [before 1231 × 32]

B f 64r; C f 31r

[a] Englefeld' *C*

Before no. 1085, by which Robert and his wife gave the abbey all their men and tenants with their lands in Sulhamstead and accepted in return a corrody of food and clothing for life. Agnes, Robert's wife, was the daughter of Tovus of Sulhamstead and had her own inheritance there (see nos. 1087–9).

1081 Gift by Robert Pincent (*Punzun*), with the assent of W(illiam) his son and heir, to Reading Abbey of the whole land in Sulhamstead [Abbots] (*Silhamsted'*) which Elisent (*Elisentus*) held. To be held freely, in demesne or by anyone to whom the abbey shall wish to demise it, by rendering annually to him and his heirs 1d at Michaelmas for all service. For this his lords, the monks of Reading (*domini mei de Rading'*), have remitted 23s and 10 loads of oats (*summe avene*) which he owed them in arrears of his rent. Warranty, with provision for reasonable exchange to the same value in the same vill, and sealing. Witnesses[a] [omitted]   [before 1231 × 32]

B f 64r; C ff 30v–31r

[a] Om. in *C*

Date as for no. 1080. Cf. no. 1093a.

1081a Note of a charter by the same against Robert, his son, concerning the same land   [before 1231 × 32]

B f 64r; C f 31r

Date as for no. 1080. The note is entered in the margin of B alongside no. 1081 and in the same original hand. It is in the same position in C. Cf. nos. 1093 n. and 1093a.

1082 Quitclaim by Robert Pincent (*Punzun*) to his lords, the abbot and convent of Reading, of 2 acres of his meadow in Widemead (*Widemede*) [in Sulhamstead Abbots], viz., 1 acre next to *Russeford* towards the west near the meadow of William Bannister (*Banastr'*), and 1 acre lying among the 10 acres which neighbours hold in the same meadow according as the lot each year assigns to them in the lower furlong towards the south (*prout sors singulis annis eis dederit in inferiori forlongo versus austr(um)*[a]). To be held in demesne (*in proprietate sua*) or as they shall please freely. Warranty. For this his said lords have given him and William his son and heir, who confirms this, 1 mark of silver in their great needs. Witnesses[b] [omitted]

[before 1231 × 32]

B f 64v; C f 31r–v

[a] australem *C*   [b] *Om. in C*

Date as for no. 1080. The rubrics describe the meadow as at Sulhamstead.

1083 Quitclaim by W(illiam) Pincent (*Punzun*) to his lords, the abbot and convent of Reading, of the same 2 acres [described as in no. 1082]. To be held [etc., as in no. 1082]. Warranty. For this his said lords have given to Robert his father, who confirms this, and to him 1 mark of silver in their great needs. Witnesses[a] [omitted]

[before 1231 × 32]

B f 65r–v; C f 32r

[a] *Om. in C*

This quitclaim is no doubt strictly contemporary with no. 1082, whose text *mutatis mutandis* it follows.

1084 *Deed by Robert Pincent, with the consent of William Pincent his heir, augmenting by 4s the rent of ½ mark which he owed annually to Reading Abbey from his patrimony in West Sulhamstead, for which the abbey has remitted to him and his wife and his heirs 100s which they jointly owed the abbey*

[before 1231 × 32]

B f 64r–v; C f 31r

Sciant presentes et futuri quod ego Robertus Punzun, consensu et voluntate Willelmi Punzun heredis mei, augmentavi annuum redditum de patrimonio meo in Westesilhamstede[a] de .iiii. solidis ultra dimidiam marcam quam dominis meis abbati et conventui Rading' [*f 64v*] singulis annis reddere debebam ad festum sancti Michaelis. Ita quod in perpetuum ego et heredes mei quolibet anno in festo sancti Michaelis .x. solidos et octo denarios de predicto patrimonio meo dominis meis abbati et conventui Rading' integre reddere debemus, excepto redditu hereditatis uxoris mee Agnetis in Silhamst(ede).[b] Pro incremento autem predictorum[c] solidorum de patrimonio meo, remiserunt mihi et uxori mee et heredibus meis centum solidos sterlingorum quos prefatis dominis meis abbati et conventui Rading' in solidum reddere debebamus.*d* Et si forte contigerit quod contra factum nostrum venire presumpserimus, dabimus dominis nostris abbati et conventui Rading' nomine pene centum solidos sterlingorum. Et in huius rei testimonium huic scripto sigillum meum apposui. T(estibus).*e*

a West Silhamsted' *C*   *b* Silhamsted' *C*
c Possibly .iiii. *om.*   *d* debeamus *C*
e Om. in *C*

Date as for no. 1080. It is possible that Robert's wife made a similar deed at the same time, but the only surviving text of a deed by her raising the rent from her patrimony by the same amount dates from her widowhood (no. 1087).

1085 Gift by Robert Pincent (*Punzun*) and Agnes his wife, with the assent and at the request of W(illiam) their son and heir, to Reading Abbey of all their men and tenants in Sulhamstead [Abbots] (*Silhamsted'*) with all their lands and progeny (*sequela*) and their services, viz., Simon *Merewine*, Alice *juxta silvam*, Alwin *de grava*, William the clerk, Hugh *de la burne*, Luke, Simon *Mage*, Serlo, Robert *Henteluve*, Richard the wheelwright (*rotarius*), Avice the widow, Adam the huntsman (*venator*), Thomas of Englefield (*Englef(eld)*), William of Englefield, Martin the chaplain, *a*Robert the chaplain,*a* William *Lece*, Adam Pincent, Walter of Alresford (*Alreford'*), Robert the tailor (*le taillur*b*), Stephen *Ode*, Hugh *Hereward* and John *a la grave*; and of 7d rent from the abbot and convent of Reading. Also gift of all the donors' rent in Sulhamstead [Abbots], beyond the 24s which they previously owed for their whole tenement there, which rent with 24s the said tenants ought and used to pay. To be held freely, saving to W(illiam), their son and heir, and his heirs the demesne, with 1 acre of meadow in Widemead (*Widemede*) and a plot (*placea*) of meadow next to Pincent bridge (*pons Punzun*) towards the south, which [demesne] was in their and his hands at the time of this gift, for which the said W(illiam) and his heirs shall pay annually to the abbey at Michaelmas 3s and 3 quarters of oats and 1 basket (*hop*) with the other customary services which the donors used to do previously. For this the abbey has granted to them, in their great and pressing need, food and clothing for life as the abbey's charter to them witnesses, and has remitted to them certain arrears of rent in money and oats to the value of 20s. Confirmation with an oath of faith, and sealing with the seals of the donors and of W(illiam) their son and heir. Witnesses [omitted]. Done in the year of grace 1231   25 Mar. 1231 × 24 Mar. 1232

B ff 64v–65r; C f 31v

ᵃ⁻ᵃ In C this name is placed after 'Adam Pincent'
ᵇ taylour C

The interpretation of the date assumes that the year began on 25 March.

1086   Inspeximus*ᵃ* and confirmation of the same by William Pincent (*Punzun*) [only the opening twelve words of no. 1085 quoted]. The confirmation clause reads: Ego autem Willelmus, videns paupertatem patris mei et matris mee et eis subvenire non valens, dictam donationem et concessionem ratam et gratam habeo et confirmo. Warranty and sealing. Witnesses*ᵇ* [omitted]   [1231 × 32]

B f 65r; C f 32r

ᵃ Inspexi in Mss   *ᵇ Om. in C*

Probably of about the same date as no. 1085.

1087   Deed by Agnes, widow of Robert Pincent (*Punzun*),¹ with the consent and good will of William Pincent her heir, augmenting by 4s the rent of 10s which she owed annually at Michaelmas to her lords, the abbot and convent of Reading, from her patrimony in East Sulhamstead (*Estsilhamsted'*),*ᵃ* so that she and her heirs in perpetuity ought to render annually 14s, apart from the rent for the inheritance of Robert, her late husband, in West Sulhamstead (*Westsilhamsted'*). For this the abbey has remitted to her and her heirs 100s sterling which they owed the abbey. If she or her heirs shall break this agreement, they will pay their said lords a penalty of 100s sterling. Sealing. Witnesses*ᵇ* [omitted]   [?c. 1231/2 × 40]

B f 66r; C f 32v

ᵃ Est Silhamsted' C (Est interlined)   *ᵇ Om. in C*

After no. 1085, when Robert Pincent was still alive, but probably not much later, especially since the text is *mutatis mutandis* very close to that of no. 1084.

    1. The rubrics call her Agnes of Sulhamstead. See also no. 1088 n.

1088   Gift in free alms by Agnes daughter of Tovus of Sulhamstead (*Silhamst(ede)*), widow, to Reading Abbey of whatever could come to her by hereditary right in the whole land of her said father in Sulhamstead [Abbots], except for certain lands written below which have remained in demesne to William her first-born son, viz., *Gancham* with messuage, apart from 1 acre which Serlo the miller holds; the whole of Wheathams (*Wetham*) apart from 2½ acres; 14 acres in *Wideham*; 4 acres in Pit Croft (*Putcroft*); a parcel of grove which Ailwin *de la* *grave* holds and another which Walter *Bobliseth* holds; and *la Formore*. Warranty. For this the abbey has granted her the necessaries of food and clothing for life as its charter to her witnesses. Sealing. Witnesses[a] [omitted] [?*c.* 1231/2 × 40]

B f 66r–v; C ff 32v–33r

[a] *Om. in C*

Date in general as for no. 1087. The donor was the widow of Robert Pincent. The land of Tovus, her father, was clearly her patrimony referred to in nos. 1087, 1089.

1088a Note of a quitclaim by the same concerning her dower
[?*c.* 1231/2 × 40]

B f 66v

Date as for no. 1087.

1089 Confirmation by W(illiam) Pincent (*Puncun*),[a] son and heir of Robert Pincent[a] and of Agnes his wife, to his lords, the abbot and convent of Reading, of the increase of 8s in the rent from the patrimonies of his father in West Sulhamstead (*Westsilhamsted'*) and of his mother in East Sulhamstead (*Estsilhamsted'*) which his father and mother made in return for the remission of 100s sterling which they owed the abbot and convent, so that he and his heirs in perpetuity ought to render annually at Michaelmas 24s 8d. Sealing. Witnesses[b] [omitted] [1231/2 × 58]

B f 65r; C f 32r

[a] *Punzun C*   [b] *Om. in C*

This confirms the increases in rent made in nos. 1084 and 1087, but it dates after the deaths of both Robert and Agnes since William and his heirs are now to pay the total rent of 24s 8d. The deed was entered in the original section of B. William Pincent occurs in 1248 in Whitley (Clanchy, *Berks. Eyre of 1248*, 181).

1090 Gift by William Pincent (*Punzun*) to Abbot A(dam)[a] and the convent of Reading of the whole land which Alfric *de la More* held [in Sulhamstead Abbots]. To be held freely by rendering annually to him and his heirs 1d at Michaelmas for all service. For this the abbot and convent have given him in his great needs 1 mark of silver as entry-fine. Warranty, with provision for exchange to the same value, and sealing. Witnesses[a] [omitted] [1226 × 38; ?*c.* 1231/2 × 1238]

B f 65v; C f 32r

a Om. in C

The outside dating limits are those of Adam of Lathbury's abbacy, but, if this gift was made after the death of William's father, it cannot be earlier than 1231/2 (see no. 1085). The rubrics locate the land in Sulhamstead.

1091 Gift by W(illiam) Pincent (*Punzun*), son and heir of Robert Pincent, to Reading Abbey of 3s annual rent in Sulhamstead [Abbots] (*Silhamst(ede)*),*a* viz., 33d which Walter of Alresford (*Alresford'*) used to pay him, 1d each which Richard the wheelwright (*rotarius*) and Hugh *Hereward* used to pay him, and 1d which Martin the chaplain used to pay him for a certain pasture. To be held freely. For this the abbey has remitted to him 2½ fardels (*furdelli*) of oats which he owed annually at mid-Lent. Sealing. Witnesses [omitted]   [1231/2 × 58]

   B f 65v; C f 32v

   a Silhamsted' C

Entered in the original section of B and, since the four named tenants were among those given to the abbey by William's father and mother in no. 1085, not earlier than 1231/2. Since they were all four still alive, the date may not be much later than 1231/2.

1092 Gift by W(illiam) Pincent (*Punzun*), son of Robert Pincent, to Reading Abbey of the 12d annual rent in Sulhamstead [Abbots] (*Silhamsted'*) which Ailwin *de la grave* used to render to him at Michaelmas for a certain grove which he held of him there. For this the abbey has given him 10s sterling. Warranty and sealing. Witnesses [omitted]   [1231/2 × 58]

   B ff 65v–66r; C f 32v

Date as for no. 1091. The tenant here is also named in no. 1085.

1093 Gift in free alms by Robert Pincent (*Punzun*), chaplain of Ufton (*Uffintun'*), for the soul of his father among others, to Reading Abbey of 8 acres of land in the field called *Suthfeld* in Sulhamstead [Abbots] (*Silhamst(ede)*),*a* which acres Robert his father gave him by charter. Warranty and sealing. Witnesses*b* [omitted]   [? 1231/2 × 58]

   B f 66v; C f 33r

   a Silhamsted' C   *b Om. in C*

Not later than 1258, since it was entered in the original section of B. If, as seems likely, the donor's father was already dead, the deed is after no. 1085. In view of no. 1093a, which immediately follows no. 1093 in B, and of no. 1081a above, the 8 acres may be the land of Elisent which Robert Pincent senior gave to the abbey earlier (no. 1081).

1093a Note of a charter between Agnes, wife of Robert Pincent
(*Punzun*), and Robert, her son, concerning the land of Elisent (*Elis-entus*)

B f 66v

Cf. nos. 1081–1081a, 1093.

1094 Remission by William of Englefield (*Englefeld*), knight, of all
plea and action which he had or could have against the abbot and
convent of Reading by reason of common of pasture or any other
nuisance (*nocumentum*) occasioned by the mill and pond made by them
in Sulhamstead [Abbots] (*Sylhamstude*)[a] on the [River] Kennet to the
west of Pincent bridge (*pons Punsun*[b]), and concession that they are to
hold the said pond and mill free of any interference and claim from
him or his heirs. For this the abbot and convent have given him 30s
sterling. Sealing. Witnesses [omitted]   [1226 × 58]

A f 89r; B f 67r–v; C f 33v

[a] Silhamsted' *B,C*   [b] Punzun *B,C*

This deed was entered among 13th-century additions in A in a hand which also copied
a deed of ?1249 (no. 1225). The William of Englefield concerned was therefore most
probably the one who held Englefield from shortly after 1226, when his father Alan
was still in possession (*VCH Berks.*, iii. 406). The deed is not later than 1258, since it
appears in the original section of B.

1094a Note of two charters by William Ellis (*Helys*) of Ufton Robert
(*Uffyntun' Roberd*) concerning a quitclaim of the mill and pond of
Sulhamstead (*Sylamsted'*)

B f 200r

Entered in a 14th-century hand at the foot of the folio. The identity of William Ellis
is unknown, but the mill and pond were presumably those of the abbey in Sulhamstead
Abbots.

1095 Gift in free alms by Philip of Hartridge (*Ertruge*)[a] to Reading
Abbey of ½ mark of annual rent which he used to receive from the
tenement which William *de Ponte* sometime held of him in Sulhamstead
Abbots (*Silhamstede Abbatis*), with wardships, reliefs, escheats, etc.,
which could arise from the said tenement; also of 3 acres of meadow
in a meadow called Widemead (*Wydemede*) in the same vill, annually
as the lot shall fall in perpetuity (*annuatim secundum quod sors ceciderit in
perpetuum*). Warranty and sealing   [c. 1260 × 1278]

B f 213r; C ff 128v–129r; (noted) B f 68v

Hiis testibus: dominis Willelmo de Englefeud,[b] Petro Achard, Petro de Codray, militibus, Olivero de Hasele, Willelmo de Colley,[c] Johanne de Benham,[d] Ricardo de Mora, Johanne de Colley,[e] Waltero de Madehach',[e] Willelmo Henri,[f] Thoma de Kenetwode,[g] Gilberto Pinsun,[h] et aliis.

[a] Ertrugge C; note on B f 68v has Hertrigge
[b] Englef' C
[d] Bienham C
[f] Henry C
[h] Pynzun C
[c] Colleye C
[e] Madehacch' C
[g] Kentwode C

The deed was neither noted nor entered in the original section of B, suggesting a date after 1258. The donor died in 1279 (VCH Berks., iv. 209), but Oliver of Haseley among the witnesses was dead by 10 Apr. 1278 (see no. 1175) and Peter Achard died before 11 Oct. 1278 (K.J. Stringer, 'Some documents concerning a Berkshire family ...', Berks. Arch. Journ., lxiii (1967–8), 24). William of Englefield may be either the one who died by Mar. 1271 (Cat. Anc. Deeds, iii. 441, D306) or his grandson who succeeded by 1277 (BL Add. Ch. 20253), but the former is more likely in view of his position in the witness-list.

1096 Gift in free alms by Gilbert Pincent (Pinzun)[a] of Sulhamstead [Abbots] (Silhamsted')[b] to the almonry of Reading of a fourth part in width of 1 acre of his land in his field called Stonicroft, extending in length from the land of Richard Serle on the north to the land called Heham on the south. To be held by rendering annually to him and his heirs ½d at Michaelmas for all services and exactions. For this Robert the almoner has given him ½ mark of silver as entry-fine. Warranty and sealing[c]   [?c. 1240]

B f 147v; C f 87r; D f 35r

[Hiis testibus: Roberto de Burfeld, Waltero Alard, Herveo Belet, Johanne Rumbald, Roberto Venatore, Thoma Turnegain, et multis aliis.]

[a] Pincun D   [b] Silanste D
[c] B ends with T', C ends, the witnesses being supplied from D

For the possible dates of Robert as almoner, see nos. 727 n., 729 n. The deed was entered in the original section of B, but not in that of D. There must be some doubt as to whether this land was in Sulhamstead Abbots and not in Burghfield, since the almoner had an estate in the latter rather than in the former, but, since it was adjacent to the land of the following deed, which is stated specifically to have been in Sulhamstead [Abbots], it is placed here; cf., however, no. 757.

1097 Gift in free alms by Richard Serle of Sulhamstead (Silhamst(ede))[a] to the almonry of Reading of his whole croft with ditch and hedge in Sulhamstead [Abbots] called *Ricardesdune Serle,*[b] lying in length east–west and in width north–south, and extending from the land of the almonry called *Ank(e)till(es)dune*[c] on the east as far as the moor of G(ilbert)[d] Pincent (*Pinzun*)[e] on the west, and from the donor's croft on the north to the land of G(ilbert)[d] Pincent called *Stonham* on the south. To be held by rendering annually to the donor and his heirs 2d at Michaelmas for all services, claims (*querele*) and secular exactions. For this Robert the almoner has given him 20s sterling as entry-fine. Warranty and sealing   [?*c.* 1240]

B f 147v–148r; C f 87r; D f 35r–v

Hiis testibus:[f] [Roberto de Burgefeld, Johanne Rumbald, Waltero Alard, Nicholao de Syreburne, Gileberto Pincun, Thoma Turnagayn, et multis aliis].

[a] Sylamstede *D*   [b–b] Ricardes dune Serle *D*
[c] Anchetilles dune *D*   [d] *Expansion from D*
[e] Pincun *D*
[f] *B ends, C ends with et cetera, the remainder being supplied from D*

Date as for no. 1096. Right of dower in this land, called *la Done, in villa de Cilhamstede abbatis*, was quitclaimed to Abbot Richard and the convent of Reading by Richard Serle's widow, Christina, in a deed which cannot be later than 11 July 1269 (D f 74r–v). This seems conclusive that the land was in Sulhamstead Abbots, but cf. no. 757.

GRAZELEY
(formerly detached part of Sulhamstead Abbots)

1098   Settlement, in chirograph form, of the dispute between Adam [of Lathbury], abbot of Reading, and Richard [of][a] Dummer (*Dummere*) concerning common of pasture of Grazeley (*Greysulle*).[b] The abbot has quitclaimed for himself and his successors to Richard and his heirs or assigns their entire plot (*placea*) lying between *Fulritham* and the road (*vicus*) leading from Trunkwell (*Truncwelle*) and whatever of right could come to the abbot or his successors from the said plot; to be held freely and in peace from all vexation or claim of the said abbot or his successors. For this Richard has quitclaimed for himself and his heirs to the abbot and his successors all purprestures which the abbot has made in the common of pasture of Grazeley[c] and all right and claim which he had or could have in the same. Sealing by both parties. Witnesses [omitted]   [1226 × 38]

A f 82v; B f 58r–v; C f 26r

[a] *Om. in A; supplied from B,C*   [b] Greyshull' *B,C*
[c] Greysull' *B*, Greyshull' *C*

The dating limits are those of Adam of Lathbury's abbacy. Richard of Dummer made another agreement with Abbot Richard I, quitclaiming common of pasture in Whitley and Grazeley (BL Add. Ms. 28870, f 21r–v).

1099 Remission and quitclaim*a* by John *Rembald'* of all action which he had or could have in the assarts and purprestures made in Grazeley (*Greyshull'*) by the abbot of Reading and his men. For this the abbot has conceded that he may make an enclosure to improve his land (*quod possim appruiare me*) in Burghfield (*Burgefeld*).*b* Sealing. Witnesses [omitted]   [*c.* 1240 × 1258]

B f 58v; C f 26r

a Described thus only in consideration clause   *b* Burgh'feld' *C*

The first element of John's second name occurs variously as *Rem-*, *Rim-*, *Rum-* and *Reyn-*. In addition to witnessing nos. 1096–7 above, he occurs in 1241, was a juror for Theale hundred in 1248 and 1269, and was dead by Oct. 1284 (PRO JUST 1/37, m. 25B; Clanchy, *Berks. Eyre of 1248*, 295; JUST 1/42, m. 19; JUST 1/43, m. 13). The deed is not later than 1258, since it was entered in the original section of B.

1100 Remission and quitclaim by Robert Butler (*le Butiller*) of Stratfield Saye (*Stratfeld Say*) of all action which he had or could have in the assarts and purprestures made in Grazeley (*Greyshull'*) by the abbot of Reading and his men. For this the abbot has given him $\frac{1}{2}$ mark of silver. Sealing. Witnesses [omitted]   [?*c.* mid-13th cent.]

B f 58v; C f 26r

Entered in the original section of B. Dating uncertain, but possibly of about the same date as no. 1099 since the two deeds are very similar.

1101 Agreement, dated the feast of St Andrew the apostle, 46 Henry III, between Sir Roger de Mortimer (*de Mortuo Mari*) and Reading Abbey, by which Roger has conceded and quitclaimed to the abbot and convent and their successors all purprestures made by them in Grazeley (*Greisull'*), Whitley (*Whitele*) and Sulhamstead [? Abbots] (*Silhampsted'*) and in the whole county of Berkshire up to the said date, such that the abbot and convent shall pay to Roger by the hand of the chamberlain of Reading 20s annual rent on the feast of St Peter and St Paul [29 June]. If they shall default in this payment, Roger or his heirs may distrain all their men living within the fee of Stratfield Mortimer (*Stratfeld Mortimer*) until full satisfaction of the rent has been made. Also the abbot and convent have conceded and quitclaimed to Roger and his heirs all purprestures made by him and his predecessors in Stratfield Mortimer [and]*a* Wokefield (*Wogh'feld'*) up to the said date.   30 Nov. 1261

B f 57r

a Supplied

This deed was entered in a 14th-century hand, but, since it is not in C, it must have been written after the contents of B were copied into C (see vol. I, pp. 10–11). The absence of a sealing clause may indicate that the text is incomplete.

SULHAMSTEAD BANNISTER

1102 *Gift by William Bannister son of John Bannister of Sulhamstead [Bannister] to Abbot Elias and the convent of Reading of 10 acres of meadow of his demesne in Widemead in Sulhamstead, lying between* Havekeresforde *and Middleham, for 2s annual rent. For this the abbey has given him 7 marks and a 3-year old colt from its stud*   [1200 × 1213]

A f 105r; B f 68r; C f 34v

Sciant presentes et futuri quod ego Willelmus Banastre filius Iohannis Banastre de Silhamstede dedi et*a* concessi et hac*a* presenti *b*mea carta*b* confirmavi deo et sancte Marie de Rading(ia) et beato Iacobo et Helie abbati Rading(ensi) eiusdemque loci conventui, pro salute anime mee et omnium predecessorum meorum*a* successorumque*c* meorum, decem acras prati de dominico meo in Widemeda*d* de Silhamstede, que iacet*e* inter Middelham et Havekeresforde, tenendas de me et heredibus meis in perpetuum, reddendo inde annuatim mihi et heredibus meis duos solidos ad festum sancti Egidii [1 Sept.] pro omni servitio et exactione seculari. Sciendum tamen quod pratum predictum solet singulis annis partiri per particas et distribui per sortes, sed quocumque modo fiat partitio seu per sortes distributio, quolibet anno remanebunt abbati Rading(ensi) et predicto conventui decem acre integre secundum quod per sortes eis*a* evenerit. Pro hac autem donatione et concessione et huius carte confirmatione dederunt mihi predictus abbas et conventus septem marcas argenti et unum pullum masculum trium annorum de haracio*f* suo. Ne autem hec donatio et concessio et confirmatio in posterum possit in irritum revocari, volui totum istud sigilli mei appositione communiri.*g* Hiis testibus.

a Om. in B,C	*b b carta mea B,C*
c et successorum B,C	*d Widemed' B, Widemede C*
e Sic in all texts	*f haratio B*
g B ends with T', C ends	

The dating limits are those of Elias's abbacy. In B and C the deed is entered after no. 1103 with a note in the rubrics that it should have been copied first (*Hec prescribi deberet*). The deed contains an interesting description of the methods for allocating meadow portions. The manor of Sulhamstead Bannister was held by the Bannister family of the Achard lords of Aldermaston (*VCH Berks.*, iii. 431). The parish runs

Dating uncertain, but William Bannister occurs in the late 12th and early 13th centuries (see no. 1103 n.) and the unusual form of the sealing clause suggests a fairly early date. The quitclaim appears to relate to the 12d rent retained in no. 1104, where however it is payable at Michaelmas, rather than to part of the 2s rent payable on the feast of St Giles in no. 1102, since this last was implicitly surrendered in no. 1103.

1105a Note of another charter concerning 4 acres of land in Sulhamstead (*Silhamstede*) in *la Hethfelde*

B f 68v

This is entered in a later hand after no. 1105, which concludes the Sulhamstead deeds in the original section of B, but whether the note concerns William Bannister is unclear. The same hand noted Philip of Hartridge's charter (above, no. 1095).

1106 Gift by John Bannister (*Banastr'*) of Sulhamstead [Bannister] (*Silhamst(ede)*)[a] to Abbot Richard [I] and the convent of Reading of 5s rent which he used to receive from them in Sulhamstead [Bannister], viz., from the land which sometime belonged to Philip of Cowley (*Covel(eye)*) in Sulhamstead. To be held freely by rendering annually to the donor and his heirs 1 pair of gloves, price 1d, at Easter for all secular service, exaction and demand, saving the foreign service pertaining to such a tenement according to the law of the land. For this the abbot and convent have given him 5 marks of silver. Warranty and sealing. Witnesses[b] [omitted]   [1238 × 51]

B f 67v; C f 34r

[a] Silhamsted' C   [b] Om. in C

After the election of Abbot Richard I of Reading received royal assent on 18 Apr. 1238, and probably of the same date as no. 752, which is not later than 1251 (see no. 752 n.). John Bannister was a juror for Theale hundred in 1241, 1248 and 1269 (PRO JUST 1/37, m. 27; Clanchy, *Berks. Eyre of 1248*, 295; JUST 1/42, m. 19).

1107 Licence by King Edward II to Edmund Pincent (*Pynson*), for a fine, to alienate in mortmain to Reading Abbey one messuage, 60 acres of land, 9 acres of meadow, 7 acres of moor and 7s rent in Sulhamstead Abbots (*Silhamstede Abbatis*) and Sulhamstead Bannister (*Silhamstede Banastre*), in exchange for 3 messuages, 3 virgates and 3½ acres of land, 10 acres of meadow and 12 acres of moor in Tilehurst (*Tyghelhurst'*), to be held by Edmund and the legitimate heirs of his body with reversion to the abbey in the event of failure of such heirs. Licence also to the abbot and convent to receive and hold the said messuage, 60 acres of land [etc.]   8 June 1317

C f 227r–v; (noted) C f 225v
Pd. (cal.) *Cal. Pat. R. 1313–17*, 662 (from Patent Roll)

Teste me ipso apud Westm(onasterium) viii. die Junii, anno regni nostri decimo.[a]

[a] *C adds:* scilicet E' filii regis E'

The Patent Roll adds that the fine was 2 marks, because he had already made fine of 1 mark for part of the lands contained in the charter. This clearly means the 1 mark fine paid for a licence to the abbey, dated 2 Dec. 1316, to convey to Edmund son of Gilbert Pincent of Tilehurst 3 bovates and $3\frac{1}{2}$ acres of land and 10 acres of meadow in Tilehurst (*ibid.*, 570).

THATCHAM

1108 Notification by Empress Matilda, daughter of King Henry, to the bishop of Salisbury and the archdeacon and all barons of Berkshire that she has given to Reading Abbey, for the health of her soul and that of King Henry her father and for the safety of the kingdom of England, the church of Thatcham, which is a manor of the monks, as well as Roger bishop of Salisbury held the church

[4 Dec. 1139 × 7 Apr. 1141]

A f 15v; B f 19r; D f 78v
Pd. *Regesta*, iii. 258 (no. 698); Barfield, *Thatcham*, ii. 50

[a]His[b] testibus: Mil(one) conestabulo,[c] et Unfr(edo)[d] de Buhun[e] dapifero, et Willelmo camerario de Pontearche.

[a] *B ends with* T'
[c] conastabulo *D*
[e] Buun *D*
[b] Hiis *D*
[d] Hunfr' *D*

After the death of Bishop Roger of Salisbury and before the Empress assumed the title Lady of the English. Miles the Constable became earl of Hereford 25 July 1141.

1109 Mandate by Henry, duke of Normandy, to Roger, archdeacon [of Berkshire],[1] not to presume[a] to alienate the church of Thatcham from the monks of Reading, to whom the Empress his mother and he have given it

[1150 × 7 Sept. 1151]

D f 57r; B f 24v
Pd. *Regesta*, iii. 260 (no. 705); Barfield, *Thatcham*, ii. 8

T(este)[b] Willelmo canc(ellario).[c] Apud Falesiam.

[a] *D has* presumas, *B* permittas (*in error*)   [b] *B ends*
[c] *D has* canic'

After Henry became duke of Normandy and before he became count of Anjou. The mandate is cited and partially quoted by van Caenegem, *Royal Writs*, 189 n. 1.

1. For this identification, see *Reg. St Osmund*, i. 218; *Cartl. Tutbury*, 29.

1110 Mandate by Henry, duke of Normandy and Aquitaine and count of Anjou, to all the men of Berkshire to go to the abbot of Reading's market of Thatcham as in the time of King Henry his grandfather and on the same day, on a forfeiture of £10

[Apr. 1153 × Apr. 1154]

A f 26v; B f 24v
Pd. *Regesta*, iii. 261 (no. 710); Barfield, *Thatcham*, ii. 8

T(este)*a* Reginaldo comite Cornubie. Apud Wiltonam.

B ends

Date as in *Regesta*: while Henry was duke of Aquitaine and in England.

1111 *Precept by King Henry II to the sheriff and his bailiffs of Berkshire that Reading Abbey shall have its market of Thatcham as in the time of King Henry his grandfather*   [1154 × 73]

B f 24v; (noted) A f 26v[1]
Pd. Barfield, *Thatcham*, ii. 8

H(enricus) rex Angl(orum) et cetera, vicecomiti et baillivis suis de Berk'sir', salutem. Precipio quod monachi mei de Rading(ia) habeant mercatum suum de Tacheham ita bene et in pace et libere et plen(arie) et iuste sicut melius et liberius habuerunt tempore Henrici regis avi mei et eo die quo tunc habuerunt. Et prohibeo ne super hoc aliquis eis iniuriam vel contumeliam faciat. T'.

The omission of *dei gratia* in the royal style suggests a date not later than 1173.

1. After its text of no. 1112 A has: *Item carta eiusdem de eodem. Item carta eiusdem de eodem.*

1112 *Precept by King Henry II to the same that Reading Abbey shall have its market at Thatcham on Sundays as in the time of King Henry his grandfather, and prohibition that the men of Newbury shall do no wrong to the abbey concerning the same*   [1173 × July 1188]

A f 26v; B f 24v
Pd. Barfield, *Thatcham*, ii. 8

Henricus dei gratia *a*rex Anglie et dux Norm(annie) et Aquit(anie) et comes Andeg(avie) vicecomiti de Berkesc(ira) et baillivis suis,*a* salutem. Precipio quod monachi de Rading(ia) habeant forum suum apud Tacheham diebus dominicis sicut tempore *b*H(enrici) regis*b* avi mei habere solebant. Et prohibeo ne homines de Niweb(er)ia*c* super hoc ullam inde eis iniuriam faciant de foro suo illa die. T(este) *d*Rann(ulfo) de Glanvill(a).*d* Apud Westm(onasterium).

a-a et cetera B   *b-b* regis H. B
c 'Niweber' B   *d-d* Om. in B

The inclusion of *dei gratia* in the king's style dates this not earlier than 1173. Henry left England for the last time on 10 July 1188 (Eyton, 288–9).

1112a Note of another [charter by the same] concerning the same and in the same words, given at Ludgershall (*Lotegar'h'*)

[?1173 × 88]

B f 24v; (noted) A f 26v[1]

The note in B is among Henry II's acts and follows no. 1112.

1. See no. 1111 n. 1.

1113 *Precept by King Richard I to the men of Berkshire to go to the abbot of Reading's market of Thatcham as in the time of King Henry I, on a forfeiture of £10*   12 Sept. [1189]

A f 28v; B f 33r; C f 8v
Pd. Barfield, *Thatcham*, ii. 10

Ricardus dei gratia *a*rex Anglie dux Normann(ie) Aquit(anie) comes Andeg(avie)*a* omnibus hominibus de Berkescire,*b* salutem. Precipimus vobis quod eatis ad forum abbatis *c*de Radingia*c* de Tacheham sicut solebatis tempore *d*regis Henrici*d* avi patris nostri, super forisfacturam .x. librarum, et eadem die qua tunc solebatis illud facere. Et nisi feceritis, iusticia nostra hoc fieri faciat. T(este)*e* comite Willelmo de Mandevilla. Apud Gaitintonam, xii. die Septembris.

a-a et cetera B,C   *b* Berk'sir' B,C
c-c Om. in B,C   *d-d* H. regis B,C
e B,C end

The abbey received a number of acts from Richard I at Geddington on 12 Sept. 1189 (see nos. 34–37). The text of this precept follows very closely that of Duke Henry's (no. 1110).

1114 *Confirmation by Herbert [Poore], bishop of Salisbury, to Reading Abbey, for the support of the house and the fostering of its hospitality, of 9 marks annually from the two portions of Thatcham church held by Robert, and before him by Nigel, as perpetual vicar, with half the lands, wood and meadows belonging to those portions, excluding the messuage and garden assigned to the vicarage; and of 34s 1d annually from the third portion of the church held by*

Hugh of Burgundy as perpetual vicar. Both vicars shall pay episcopal dues pertaining to their vicarages. For all burdens touching the church the vicars shall answer for their vicarages and the abbey for its parsonage like the vicars and parsons of neighbouring churches   18 Apr. 1201

A ff 95v–96r; B ff 191v–192r; C f 111v
Pd. Barfield, *Thatcham*, ii. 53–4

Omnibus Christi fidelibus ad quos presens scriptum pervenerit Herbertus dei gratia Sar(esburiensis) episcopus, salutem *[a]*in domino.*[a]* Cum fraterne dilectionis et pastoralis sollicitudinis toti gregi divina permissione nobis commisso simus debitores, illos tamen prerogativa cure et caritatis amplectimur quibus propter privilegium religionis specialius obligamur. Unde dilectis nobis filiis abbati et conventui Rading(ensibus), quorum publice fame testimonio viget et in hospitalitate caritas et in honestate religio, pio pastoris affectu providere et subvenire volentes, eisdem monachis ad domus sue sustentationem et hospitalitatis gratiam in ea fovendam *[b]*auctoritate pontificali*[b]* confirmamus in ecclesia de Thacham*[c]* de duabus portionibus quas nomine perpetue vicarie sue possidet Robertus clericus de Tacham et prius Nigellus predecessor eius possedit .ix. marcas argenti per manum perpetui vicarii a nobis vel successoribus nostris ad presentationem eorundem monachorum in predictis duabus*[d]* portionibus instituti annuatim percipiendas. Medietatem etiam terrarum et nemoris et pratorum ad predictas*[e]* portiones pertinentium, excepto masuagio*[f]* et orto specialiter ad ipsam vicariam deputato, prenominati monachi in perpetuum possidebunt. De tertia vero eiusdem ecclesie portione, quam Hugo Burgund(ie)*[g]* nomine vicarie sue possidet, eisdem monachis confirmamus *[h]*triginta et .iiii. solidos*[h]* et unum denarium per manum perpetui vicarii in eadem portione a nobis vel successoribus nostris ad presentationem eorundem monachorum instituti annuatim percipiendos. Duo autem vicarii quicumque pro tempore in eadem ecclesia predicto modo fuerint instituti omnia*[i]* episcopalia usitata et consueta quantum ad vicarias suas pertinet sustinebunt. In omnibus vero oneribus que ecclesiam illam variis de causis contingere possunt, sicut vicarii vicinarum ecclesiarum pro vicariis suis respondebunt. [*f* 96r] Abbas vero et conventus Rading(enses), sicut persone vicinarum ecclesiarum, plenarie respondebunt pro personatu. Quod ut ratum sit et firmum, presenti scripto et sigilli nostri munimine duximus confirmandum, salvis tamen in omnibus iure et*[j]* auctoritate*[k]* ecclesie nostre et nostra et successorum nostrorum. Dat'*[l]* apud Suning(es) per manum Willelmi Raimund' xiiii. kl' Maii, pontificatus nostri anno septimo. His testibus: magistris Hel(ia) de Chivel', Hugone de Gaherst, Rogero.

[a-a] *Om. in B,C*   *[b-b]* pontificali auctoritate *B,C*

^c Tacham *B,C*   ^d *Om. in B,C*
^e *Insert* duas *B,C*   ^f mesuagio *C*
^g *Om. in C*   ^{h-h}.xxxi. solidos *B,C*
ⁱ onera *B,C*   ^j *Om. in B*
^k *Insert* et dignitate *B,C*   ^l *B,C end with* et cetera

The only major variation between the cartulary texts is that B and C give 31s 1d as the payment due from Hugh of Burgundy's portion. This act is one of a number which refer to the fame of the abbey's hospitality (see vol. I, p. 13).

1115 *Mandate by Herbert [Poore], bishop of Salisbury, to the archdeacon of Berkshire to put the abbot of Reading in possession of the portion of Thatcham church which was Hugh of Burgundy's, since the bishop could not deny the abbot's right according to the charter of his predecessor*
[1201 × 1217; ?1206 × 1217]

B f 191v; C f 112r
Pd. Barfield, *Thatcham*, ii. 54

H(erbertus) dei gratia Sar(esburiensis) episcopus dilecto sibi in Christo filio archidiacono Berk(esire), salutem. Mandamus vobis quatinus mittatis dominum abbatem de Rading(ia) nomine ecclesie sue in possessionem plenam illius portionis ecclesie de Tacheham que fuit Hugonis Burgund(ie) cum omni iure suo et pertinentiis suis, quia nos de consilio capituli nostri secundum cartam predecessoris nostri id ei denegare non potuimus, sed ei plene et integre ius suum et Rading(ensis) ecclesie concessimus. Et ideo mandatum nostrum sine difficultate et dilatione exequamini. Bene^a valete.

^a *Om. in C*

After no. 1114, when Hugh of Burgundy was still in posession, and before the bishop's death in early Jan. 1217; however, since the mandate hints at conflict between the bishop and the abbey, it may date after the settlement of the dispute between them over the churches of Thatcham and Bucklebury, committed to judges-delegate by Innocent III in June 1206 (no. 161; see also no. 211 n.). The charter of the bishop's predecessor to which the present text refers is presumably Hubert Walter's licence to the abbey to appropriate the churches of Thatcham and Bucklebury when they become vacant (no. 205).

1116 *Ordination by Robert [Bingham], bishop of Salisbury, in the case between Gilbert de Biham, rector of Thatcham, and Reading Abbey over a third part of the lands, tithes [etc.] of Thatcham church and a pension of 9 marks, which case had been committed by papal authority to the archdeacon and [rural] dean of Oxford. The rector and his successors shall have the whole church and pay annually to the abbey 20 marks. The abbey shall contribute for its portion to any extraordinary burden imposed upon the church* 7 Feb. 1240

A f 112r; B f 192r–v; C f 112r; D f 20r–v
Pd. Barfield, *Thatcham*, ii. 59–60

Omnibus Christi fidelibus *a*ad quos presens scriptum pervenerit
Robertus miseratione divina Sar(esburiensis) ecclesie minister humilis,
salutem in domino.*a* Universitati vestre presentibus innotescat quod,
cum magister Gilebertus de Biham*b* rector ecclesie de Thacham*c*
dilectos filios abbatem et conventum*d* Rading' super tertia parte
omnium terrarum, decimarum, fructuum et proventuum eiusdem
ecclesie necnon et .ix. marcis*e* annuis eisdem monachis ad hospitalitatis
honera*f* subportanda*g* capituli nostri Sar(esburiensis) accedente assensu*h* in usus proprios et perpetuos de ecclesia supradicta concessis, et
rebus aliis ad dictam ecclesiam spectantibus, coram archidiacono et
decano Oxon' auctoritate domini pape traxisset in causam, partes in
nostra presentia constitute, litteris impetratis et impetrandis, ques-
tionibus motis et movendis et predictarum rerum concessionibus
sponte et absolute renuntiantes, ordinationi nostre sese penitus sub-
miserunt. Nos igitur, ut paci et tranquillitati partium et earum successorum futuris et perpetuis temporibus provideatur, habita deli-
beratione ordinationem super premissis ad ipsarum partium
instantiam in nos suscipientes, deum habendo pre oculis, de consilio
jurisperitorum, invocata spiritus sancti gratia taliter duximus ordi-
nandum. Videlicet quod dictus Gilebertus rector predicte ecclesie de
Thacham*i* et successores sui habeant et possideant totam ecclesiam de
Thacham*j* cum omnibus juribus suis, libertatibus et pertinentiis suis,*k*
libere quiete integre et pacifice in perpetuum sustinendo onera ordinaria spectantia ad ecclesiam supradictam. Ordinavimus etiam de
consensu dicti rectoris quod dicti abbas et conventus percipient*l* .xx.
marcas*m* annuas nomine perpetui beneficii a dicto rectore et *n*suis
successoribus*n* in perpetuum solvendas ad .iiii. anni terminos, videlicet
ad Natale domini .v. marcas, ad Pascha .v. marcas, ad festum Nativitatis sancti Johannis Baptiste .v. marcas et ad festum sancti Michaelis
.v. marcas. Ita tamen quod dicti abbas et conventus, cum aliquid
extraordinarium prefate ecclesie de Thacham*o* fuerit impositum, id
pro portione sua subeant et agnoscant. Nulli ergo hominum hanc
nostre ordinationis paginam audeant infringere vel ei ausu temerario
contraire. Si quis autem ausu temerario eam infringere temptaverit,
indignationem dei et beate virginis*p* et omnium sanctorum se noverit
incursurum. In huius rei testimonium presens scriptum sigillo nostro
duximus muniendum. Hiis testibus: *q*[E(gidio) archidiacono Berk'
tunc officiali nostro, Petro de Cumb(a), Waltero de la Wyle, Galfrido
de Bedef(ordia), canonicis Sar', Th(oma) de la Wyle senescallo nostro,
Roberto Foliot, Roberto de Wichamt(ona), Willelmo de Castellis,

clericis nostris, et aliis].^{q} Act(um) apud Ramebir(iam) vii. idus Februarii, anno gratie M.CC.xxxix.

$^{a-a}$ et cetera, Robertus Sar' episcopus salutem *B,C*
^{b} Byham *B,C*
^{d} *Insert* de *D*
^{f} onera *B,C,D*
^{h} consensu *D*
^{j} Tacham *B,C*, Tacheham *D*
^{l} percipiant *B,C*
$^{n-n}$ successoribus suis *B,C*
^{p} *Insert* Marie *D*

^{c} Tacheham *C,D*
^{e} marchis *D*
^{g} supportanda *B,C,D*
^{i} Tacham *C*, Tacheham *D*
^{k} *Om. in B,C*
^{m} marchas *D—later instances* marc'
^{o} Tacham *B,C*, Tachham *D*

$^{q-q}$ *Supplied from original inspeximus in no. 1117. After* Hiis testibus, *B has* et cetera. Act(um) anno gratie M.CC.xxxix. *C has the same without* et cetera

Comparison with the same bishop's act in no. 215, by which a third of Thatcham church and the 9 marks pension were appropriated to the abbey, shows that the date depends upon the year beginning on 25 March. On the process of ordination, sometimes resorted to in cases committed to judges-delegate, see J. E. Sayers, *Papal Judges Delegate in the Province of Canterbury 1198–1254* (Oxford, 1971), 107–8. In view of the interest of the process, this act has been printed in full. This is the latest dated entry in the original section of D.

1117 Inspeximus and confirmation of no. 1116 by Robert, the dean, and chapter of Salisbury   8 Feb. 1240

   Original charter: BL Add. Ch. 19620
   A f 112r–v; B f 192v; C f 112r–v; D ff 20v–21r
   Pd. Barfield, *Thatcham*, ii. 60; (cal.) Hurry, *Reading Abbey*, 176

Hiis testibus:^{a} dominis Roberto decano, Rogero precentore, Ada cancellario, Henrico thezaurario, E(gidio) archidiacono Berk', Th(oma) subdecano, magistris Elia de Derham, Radulfo de Eboraco, et aliis. Dat' Sar(esburie) per manus A(de) cancellarii nostri vi. idus Februarii, anno gratie M.CC.xxxix.

Endorsed: Confirmatio decani et capituli Sar' de .xx. marcis de ecclesia de Tacham [*13th cent.*]

Size: 221 × 204 mm

Seal: oval (*c.* 73 mm long) in red wax on brown and yellow plaited cord through two holes in fold; obverse Virgin and Child seated under trefoiled canopy, legend: +SIGILL'. SA...E. MAR.... ARESB'IENSIS; on reverse complete counterseal of the chancellor, oval (*c.* 45 mm long), showing him seated at a desk under trefoiled canopy, legend: SIGILL': ADE: CANCELLARII: SAR'

^{a} *A,B,C,D end*

The text in A quotes the bishop's act in full, but without the witness-list and dating clause. The text in D quotes it as far as *necnon et .ix. m' annuis*, while those in B and C quote only its three opening words.

1118   *Acknowledgment by Gilbert de Biham, rector of Thatcham, that, although by the ordination of Robert [Bingham], bishop of Salisbury, he is bound to pay Reading Abbey 20 marks annually and will do so in the first year, the abbey has remitted 5 marks annually to him personally, but not to his successors, so that after the first year he is obliged to pay 15 marks annually*

[*c*. Feb. 1240]

A f 112v; B ff 192v–193r; C f 112v; D f 21r
Pd. Barfield, *Thatcham*, ii. 60

Universis hoc scriptum inspecturis vel audituris innotescat quod, cum ego magister Gilebertus de Bih(am)*a* rector ecclesie de Thacham*b* tenear solvere viris venerabilibus abbati et conventui Rading' .xx. marcas*c* annuas secundum ordinationem venerabilis patris nostri Roberti Sar(esburiensis) [episcopi]*d* et eiusdem loci capituli confirmationem, quibus*e* ordinationi et confirmationi personaliter interfui et consensi, anno primo confectionis huius instrumenti solvam dictas .xx. marcas*c* plene ad hoc sponte obligatus ad terminos me petente concessos, videlicet ad Pascha .c. solidos, ad Nativitatem sancti Johannis Baptiste .c. solidos, ad festum sancti Michaelis .v. marcas,*c* nullo preiudicio generando ipsis ex mutatione terminorum solutionis in dictis ordinatione et confirmatione positorum quo ad successores meos. Dicti vero abbas et conventus sua liberalitate de dictis .xx. marcis mihi .v. remiserunt, et ego omni exceptioni et omni juris remedio sponte renuntians hac presenti carta me obligavi ad solvendum .xv. [marcas]*d* singulis annis post annum primum, scilicet .l. solidos ad Natale domini, .l. ad Pascha,*f* .l. ad Nativitatem beati*g* Johannis Baptiste,*f* .l. ad festum sancti Michaelis. Ita tamen quod successores mei nichil sibi possint credere remissum, cum specialiter mihi contemplatione persone mee*h* facta sit dicta remissio. In horum testimonium huic scripto signum meum apposui. Hiis testibus.

a Byh(am) *B,C*
c marchas *D*
e *Insert* scilicet *D*
g sancti *B,C,D*

b Tacham *B.C.D*
d *Om. in A, supplied from B.C.D*
f *Insert* et *D*
h *Om. in D*

Presumably of approximately the same date as nos. 1116–1117. This is the last entry on the last written folio of A.

1119   Grant by Pope Clement V to the abbot and convent of Reading of the Cluniac Order, Salisbury diocese, at the request of Isabella queen of England, whose petition referred to Henry I's foundation of the monastery and to his burial there at his choice, of the appropriation of the church of Thatcham (*Thaccham*), of which they are sole patrons and whose revenues according to the assessment for the tenth do not exceed 50 marks sterling annually, after the death or cession of the rector, saving the reservation of a suitable portion for a vicar, who shall be presented by the abbot and convent to the diocesan bishop

20 Sept. 1309

C f 223r–v
Pd. Barfield, *Thatcham*, ii. 65; (cal.) *Cal. Papal L.*, ii. 62 (both from Papal Register)

Dat' in prioratu de Grausello prope Malausanam, Vasionen(sis) diocesis, xii. kl' Octobris, pontificatus nostri anno quarto.

This and no. 1120 were given at Groseau in the diocese of Vaison.

1120 Mandate by Pope Clement V to the abbots of Chertsey (*Charteseya*) and Missenden (*Mussyndene*) and master [Gregory][a] *de Placentia*, archpriest of the people *de Monte Silice*, the pope's chaplain, of the dioceses of Winchester, Lincoln and Padua, or two or one of them, in pursuance of the same, to induct the abbot and convent of Reading or their proctor into corporal possession of the church of Thatcham (*Thacham*) after the death, cession or resignation of the rector

C f 223r   20 Sept. 1309

Pd. (Latin cal.) Barfield, *Thatcham*, ii, 65; (Eng. cal.) *Cal. Papal L.*, ii. 62 (both from Papal Register)

Dat' in prioratu de Grausello prope Malausanam, Vasionen(sis) diocesis, xii. kl' Octobris, pontificatus nostri anno quarto.

[a] *Supplied from cal. in Papal Register*

1121 Licence by King Edward II to the abbot and convent of Reading, for a fine of 40 marks made by the abbot, to appropriate in mortmain the church of Thatcham (*Thacham*), which is of their patronage   21 Mar. 1310

C f 227r; (noted) C f 225v
Pd. Barfield, *Thatcham*, ii. 64; (cal.) *Cal. Pat. R. 1307–13*, 220 (both from Patent Roll)

Teste me ipso apud Westm(onasterium) xxi. die Marcii, anno regni nostri tercio.[a]

[a] *C adds:* scilicet E' filii regis E'

There are two versions of this licence on the Patent Roll, one dated 1 Mar. 1310, without fine of 40 marks (Barfield, ii. 66; *Cal. Pat. R. 1307–13*, 225), and this one, with the fine, which has been crossed through and has a marginal note 'vacated because otherwise below without fine by the King's special grace' (PRO C66/133, m. 11). The note on C f 225v may refer to the licence without fine.

1122 Grant, in chirograph form, by Reading Abbey to the prior

and convent of Poughley (*Pochhele*) of [common of]*a* pasture pertaining
to the free tenement which they hold of the abbey in Thatcham
(*Tacham*), viz., 12 acres which they have by gift of Roger of Curridge
(*Cusserugg'*) lying within *Brodefeld'*; namely, that the canons shall have
in the common of Thatcham 6 cattle (*animalia*) and 80 sheep. Sealing
by both parties. Witnesses*b* [omitted]

[13th cent.; not later than 1258]

B f 69r; C f 35r
Pd. Barfield, *Thatcham*, ii. 9

a Supplied from rubrica   *b Om. in C*

Poughley Priory, in Chaddleworth parish, Berks., was founded in or after *c.* 1160 by
Ralph of Chaddleworth (*VCH Berks.*, ii. 85). In the 13th century it received from Roger
son of Roger of Curridge all his lands, etc., in Curridge, in Chieveley parish, Berks.,
which were confirmed by Henry III in 1248 (*ibid.*, iv. 59–60; *Mon. Ang.*, vi. 409). The
date of the present deed is uncertain, but, since it was entered in the original section
of B, it cannot be later than 1258.

1122a   Notes of the following:
   (i) chirograph between Abbot Hugh [II] and the convent of Reading
      and Thomas son of Eustace concerning Eustace's land in That-
      cham (*Tacham*)   [1186 × 99]
   (ii) charter by John son of Thomas son of Eustace to Felicia his sister
      concerning his tenement in Thatcham*a*   [not later than 1258]

B f 69r; C f 35r
Pd. Barfield, *Thatcham*, ii. 11

a Thacham C

The dating limits of (i) are those of Hugh II's abbacy. The date of (ii) cannot be later
than 1258, since both notes are in the original section of B. These notes belong in a
group with nos. 1123–1124a. Together they yield the following genealogy:

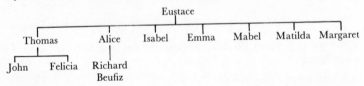

1123   Quitclaim by Richard *Beufiz* to Reading Abbey of all his right
in the land [in Thatcham]*a* which belonged to Eustace father of Alice,
his mother, and to Eustace's son Thomas, brother of his mother, and
afterwards to Thomas's son John, which land he sometime claimed
by a writ of King Henry III. For this the abbey has given him 1 mark
of silver. Witnesses*b* [omitted]   [1216 × 58]

B f 69r–v; C f 35r
Pd. Barfield, *Thatcham*, ii. 11

^{*a*} *Supplied from rubrics and by comparison with nos. 1124–5*
^{*b*} *Om. in C*

After the accession of Henry III and entered in the original section of B.

1124 Quitclaim by Isabel, daughter of Eustace of Thatcham
(*Tacham*), to Reading Abbey of all her right in the land in Thatcham
which belonged to Eustace her father, to his son Thomas her brother,
and afterwards to Thomas's son John, which land she sometime
claimed by a writ of King Henry III. For this the abbey has given
her 1 mark of silver. Witnesses^{*a*} [omitted]   [1216 × 58]

B f 69v; C f 35r–v
Pd. Barfield, *Thatcham*, ii. 11

^{*a*} *Om. in C*

Date as for no. 1123. The text is *mutatis mutandis* identical with no. 1123.

1124a Note of four charters by Emma, Mabel, Matilda and Margaret, daughters of Eustace, concerning the same land and in entirely
the same words   [1216 × 58]

B f 69v
Pd. Barfield, *Thatcham*, ii. 11

Date as for nos. 1123–4.

1125 Quitclaim by Jordan and Helewisa his wife to Reading Abbey
of all their right in the land in Thatcham (*Tacham*) which belonged
to Eustace, to his son Thomas, and afterwards to Thomas's son John,
which land they sometime claimed by a writ of King Henry III. For
this the abbey has given them 1 mark of silver. Witnesses^{*a*} [omitted]
                                                          [1216 × 58]

B f 69v; C f 35v
Pd. Barfield, *Thatcham*, ii. 11

^{*a*} *Om. in C*

Date as for no. 1123. This next is *mutatis mutandis* identical with those of nos. 1123–4,
but there is no indication of the relationship between Jordan and Helewisa and the
members of Eustace of Thatcham's family. However, Jordan's interest in the land may
have derived from an earlier marriage to Eustace's daughter Matilda (see no. 1125a
n.).

1125a Note of another [quitclaim] by the same Jordan and Matilda his wife, concerning the same land and in the same words

[1216 × 58]

B f 69v; C f 35v
Pd. Barfield, *Thatcham*, ii. 11

Date as for nos. 1123–5. Jordan clearly married twice. Matilda may have been one of Eustace of Thatcham's daughters (see nos. 1122a n., 1124a), in which case, since there is no evidence that Helewisa was connected with Eustace, Matilda would probably have been Jordan's first wife. Even so, if that was the case, it is odd that Jordan should make two quitclaims.

1126 Gift and quitclaim by John son of Thomas to Reading Abbey of his meadow of Thatcham (*Tacham*) called Tadslips (*Tadeslep*) with the land which William *Labbepone* held. To be held freely and quit of claim or demand from him or his heirs. For this the abbot and convent have remitted the 7 marks of silver for which he had mortgaged (*obligaveram*) his whole land to them. Sealing. Witnesses[a] [omitted]

[13th cent.; not later than 1258]

B f 70r; C ff 35v–36r
Pd. Barfield, *Thatcham*, ii. 13

[a] *Om. in C*

Not later than 1258, since it was entered in the original section of B. If, as seems likely, the donor was the same as John son of Thomas son of Eustace (see no. 1122a (ii)), the deed would perhaps be roughly contemporary with that of his cousin, Richard Beufiz (no. 1123).

1127 Gift in free alms by Peter fitz Herbert to Abbot Adam [of Lathbury] and the monks of Reading of a meadow in Thatcham (*Tacham*) which Walter *Lamere* sometime held, and 3 acres in Widmead (*Widemede*) in the place called Five Acres (*Fifacre*) next to the meadow of John *Kipping*, and 3 selions of arable land next to the king's way of Thatcham which the said Walter held. For this the abbot and convent have quitclaimed to him and his heirs all their right in a rent of 12s 1d and in the tenement from which it comes, as is contained in the charter which he has from them. Warranty with provision for reasonable exchange in the said meadow of Widmead to the value of 12s 1d rent. Witnesses [omitted]

[c. May 1226]

B ff 69v–70r; C f 35v
Pd. Barfield, *Thatcham*, ii. 12

The date is derived from that of the final concord by which the agreement was reached (no. 1129), which also reveals that Peter's tenement was in Crookham.

1128 Final concord in the king's court at Westminster in 1 month from Michaelmas, 41 Henry III, before Henry of Bath (*Bathon'*) and Robert *de Brywes*,[a] justices, and others, between Abbot Richard [I] of Reading, plaintiff by Godfrey *le Messager* as attorney, and Roger of the Chamber (*de la Chambre*) and Felicia his wife, defending, concerning $1\frac{1}{2}$ carucates of land in Thatcham (*Tacham*).[b] Plea of convention, by which the latter recognized the land to be the right of the abbot and abbey of Reading and quitclaimed it for themselves and the heirs of Felicia to the abbot and his successors and the abbey in perpetuity. The abbot received them and the heirs of Felicia into all benefits and prayers of the abbey in perpetuity.   27 Oct. 1257

B ff 170v–171r; C f 101r
Pd. Barfield, *Thatcham*, ii. 13, 236 (the latter from PRO foot: CP 25(1)/8/22/9)

[a] *Reading from PRO foot; B,C have* de Byxes *in error*
[b] Tacheham *C*

CROOKHAM (in Thatcham)

1129 Final concord in the king's court at Westminster in the quindene of Easter, 10 Henry III, before Martin of Pattishall (*Pat(es)hill'*), Thomas of Moulton (*Muleton'*), Thomas *de Heyden'*, Robert of Lexington (*Lexint'*), Geoffrey Savage (*le Sauvage*), Warin son of Joel,[a] justices, and others, between Simon abbot of Reading, plaintiff, and Peter fitz Herbert, holding—the concord being afterwards recorded and conceded in the same court before the same justices with Adam [of Lathbury], Simon's successor, he having lately died—concerning 12s 1d rent in Crookham (*Crocham*). The abbot quitclaimed for himself and his successors to Peter and his heirs all his right in the said rent and in the whole tenement from which it comes. For this Peter conceded in free alms to the abbot a meadow in Thatcham (*Thacheham*)[b], viz., that which Walter *Lammer* held, and 3 acres of meadow in Widmead (*Widemed'*) in the place called Five Acres (*Fifacr'*) next to the meadow of John *Kipping*, and 3 selions of arable land next to the king's way of Thatcham[b] which the said Walter *Lammer* held, all to be held by the abbot and his successors quit of all secular service and exaction. Warranty by Peter and his heirs with provision for reasonable exchange in the said meadow of Widmead to the value of 12s 1d rent   3 May 1226

B f 170r; C f 100v
Pd. Barfield, *Thatcham*, ii. 12–13

[a] 'John' *C*   [b] Tacheham *C*

The foot of this fine is PRO CP 25(1)/7/9/4. The main manor of Crookham appears to have been included in Henry I's gift of Thatcham to Reading Abbey (see no. 1) and was held of the abbey until the early 14th century by subtenants (*VCH Berks.*, iii. 314), of whom Peter fitz Herbert is the earliest known. This case began as an assize of novel disseisin in Michaelmas term 1225, and in Hilary term 1226 both parties gave $2\frac{1}{2}$ marks each for licence to concord (*Cur. Reg. R.*, xii. 196, 352). Abbot Simon died 13 Feb. 1226. In 1286 the manor was held of the abbot of Reading without service, save that the tenants were to do two suits annually at the abbot's view of frankpledge (*Cal. Inq. P.M.*, ii. 365). See also above, no. 1127.

1130 *Memorandum concerning a search made in the Book of Fees at the Exchequer at the request of Abbot William [II, of Sutton] of Reading regarding the manor of Crookham, the findings of that search, and the homage and fealty done to the abbot for the manor by John fitz Reginald, who paid a relief of 100s*
[Nov.–Dec. 1300]

B f 76r; B f 46v; C f 40r
Pd. Barfield, *Thatcham*, ii. 196 (from B f 46v, which is incomplete)

Memorandum quod anno regni regis Edwardi vicesimo viii. fecit dominus W(illelmus) dei gratia*ᵃ* abbas Rading' inquirere apud scaccarium domini regis et scrutari in libro Feodorum de manerio de Crokham, et certificabatur per custodem libri dictorum Feodorum sic.

Sancte religionis viro et amico *ᵇ*dilecto domino W(illelmo) dei gratia abbati Rading' suus Ph(illipu)s de Everdone munus*ᵇ* modicum semetipsum cum suo possibili ministerio profecturo. Scrutatus sum diligenti scrutinio ea que per vos litteratorie dicta sunt michi et letatus pro eo quod abbas Rading' manerium de Crokham cum aliis maneriis diversis in libro feodorum contentis tenet in puram et perpetuam elemosinam absque servicio seculari, set de domino Johanne*ᵃ* filio Reginaldi, de quo littera vestra cecinit nichil penitus reperitur, et ideo creditur quod de monasterio vestro possessor eiusdem manerii illud tenere debeat nisi per factum predicti monasterii vestri fuerit absolutus. Valete.*ᶜ*

Eodem anno die sabbati proxima ante festum sancti Andree apostoli [30 Nov.] venit dominus Johannes filius Reginaldi, dominus de Crokham, coram domino W(illelmo) dei gratia abbate predicto Rading' et coram consilio eiusdem et gratis fecit homagium suum dicto domino abbati pro manerio predicto tenendo de eo et de ecclesia Rading' predicta et facto homagio immediate fecit feodalitatem suam prout decet dicto domino pro manerio antedicto, et fecit finem pro relevio suo de centum solidis, presentibus subscriptis *ᵇ*qui predictis homagio et feodalitati factis interfuerunt,*ᵇ* videlicet fratribus R.¹ priore Rading' P. de Streng',*ᵈ* N(ichalao) de Quappelad', *ᵉ*Th(oma) de Garing',*ᵉ* *ᶠ*Johanne et Jordano de Suthton'*ᶠ* et aliis monachis multis,*ᵃ* item Willelmo de*ᵃ* Bleb(ury),*ᵍ* G(ilberto) Pynzon,*ʰ* J(ohanne) Fachel, *ⁱ*R. de Preston', R. de Guldeford', Ada de Schortecumbe, Petro de la Heose,

J. Bussard', R. de Burghildeb(ury), et aliis multis.[i]   28 Nov. 1300

Postea solvit idem dominus Johannes filius Reginaldi supradictos centum solidos pro fine relevii sui die et anno infradictis, de quibus centum solidis sic receptis conficiebatur talis littera indentata alternis sigillis consignata.

Die sabbati in vigilia Nativitatis domini, anno regni regis E(dwardi) xxix, dominus W(illelmus) permissione divina abbas Rading' recepit a domino Johanne filio Reginaldi centum solidos sterlingorum nomine relevii sui de manerio de Crokham quod idem dominus Johannes tenet de ecclesia Radingensi.[j] In cuius rei testimonium[k] tam dominus abbas predictus quam dictus dominus Johannes presentibus sigilla sua alternatim apposuerunt die et anno supradictis. Hiis testibus: magistro N. de Marisc', W(illelmo) de Bleb(ury),[g] W. de Baillol', G(ilberto) Pynzon, J(ohanne) Fachel, et aliis multis.   24 Dec. 1300

Et remanent predicte littere in thesaurar(ia) monasterii Rading'.

[a] *Om. in B f 46v*
[b-b] *Om. in B f 46v*
[c] *Om. in C*
[d] Straunsh' *B f 46v*
[e-e] T. Garyng *B f 46v*
[f-f] Jurdano Sutton' *B f 46v; C as text but reading* Suthon'
[g] Bleob' *C*
[h] Punson *B f 46v*
[i-i] et multis aliis *B f 46v*
[j] de Radyng' *B f 46v*
[k] *B f 46v ends with* et cetera

The overall date is derived from the dates of the documents quoted in the memorandum. The entry on B f 76r, from which C's text is copied, was made in a hand contemporary with the events recorded; that on B f 46v was made some decades later. The full text has been printed here on account of its unusual character and intrinsic interest. In 1242–3 the Book of Fees recorded the abbot and monks of Reading as holding inter alia Crookham in free alms (*Fees*, ii. 863). John fitz Reginald, grandson of the Peter fitz Herbert of no. 1129, succeeded to the manor on the death of his father in 1286 (*VCH Berks.*, iii. 314). Philip of Everdon was Lord Treasurer's remembrancer, 1295–1304 (D Crook, 'The early remembrancers of the Exchequer', *BIHR*, liii (1980), 23).

1. A Prior Robert occurs in 1305 and in 1328 (PRO C84/15/32; C84/22/2).

1131 Licence by King Edward III to William de Montague (*de Monte Acuto*), earl of Salisbury, to alienate in mortmain to Reading Abbey 10 acres of land in Crookham (*Crokham*), which are said to be held of the king in chief, to be held by the abbey in perpetuity in exchange for 7 acres of land, moor and alder-grove in the same vill, which are of the abbey's endowment, to be given and assigned to the earl and his heirs in perpetuity. The abbey shall hold the 10 acres as its endowment in the manner in which it previously held the 7 acres, and the earl and his heirs shall hold the 7 acres of the king and his heirs by the same services as he previously held the 10 acres.

1 Oct. 1337

C f 225r; (noted) C f 225v

Pd. Barfield, *Thatcham*, ii. 217–18; (cal.) *Cal. Pat. R. 1334–38*, 535 (both from Patent Roll)

Teste me ipso apud Westm(onasterium) primo die Octobris, anno regni nostri xi.

After a complicated history during the reign of Edward II the manor of Crookham was given by Edward III to William de Montague in 1331 (*VCH Berks.*, iii. 314). The latter was created earl of Salisbury on 16 Mar. 1337. The present exchange may have been connected with the earl's intention to empark part of Crookham, which he was empowered to do by Edward III on 10 Oct. 1337 (*Cal. Pat. R. 1334–38*, 539).

TILEHURST
(including Theale)

In this section nos. 1132–1187 appear mainly in the order in which they occur in C ff 155r–167v, except that the abbatial deeds of the 12th and early 13th centuries on ff 158v–159v are given first in approximate chronological order, two entries on f 156v concerning villeins in Tilehurst and elsewhere are given last, and documents from other parts of B or C are inserted as nos. 1142–4 and 1185a

1132 *Lease by Abbot Anscher of Reading to Ansculf of Englefield and his heir of the land which Oswy de Hathefelda held* [1130 × 35]

C f 159v

Ego frater Anscherius Radyng(ensis) abbas, consilio fratrum nostrorum, concessi Ansculfo de Englefelda et heredi eius terram illam quam tenuit Oswy de Hathefelda tenere de nobis ita videlicet ut reddat nobis pro ea .vii. solidos singulis annis ad festum sancti Michaelis.

The dating limits are those of Anscher's abbacy. From the position of this deed in C it is assumed that the land was in Tilehurst.

1133 *Notification by Abbot Anscher of Reading that Osward used to pay 12s annually and do the service called* radeniht *for all his land, but, since he has quitclaimed to the abbey the cultivated strip called* Wydham *which was proved to be of the demesne of Reading and which the abbot has resumed into demesne, the abbot has remitted 2s of his rent and the said custom of* radeniht, *so that he will pay 10s annually for his other land* [1130 × 35]

C f 159v

Sciant presentes et futuri quod Oswardus iste pro cultura quadam que vocatur Wydham, quam communem tenuerat cum quodam vicino suo Edwyno nomine, et pro reliqua sua terra reddere solebat annuatim .xii. solidos et servitium quoddam faciebat quod dicitur radeniht, set quoniam hec cultura predicta, scilicet Widham, mul-

torum testimonio de dominio Radyng(ie) fuisse probatur, ego Anscherius abbas Radyng(ensis) consilio nostrorum illam in dominium
nostrum resumpsi. Veruntamen, quoniam iste predictus Oswardus
culturam illam diu tenuerat, ut illam omnino nobis quietam clamaret
et sine calumpnia liberam dimitteret, consilio fratrum nostrorum
dimisimus ei de gabulo suo .ii. solidos et consuetudinem supradictam,
scilicet radeniht. De reliquo terre quod ei remanet reddet annuatim
.x. solidos. Hec concessimus illi et heredi suo iure perpetuo. Huius rei
testes sunt Ricardus prior, Rog(erius) decanus, Godwinus camerarius,
Rannulphus decanus, monachi; laici Rad(ulfus) prepositus, Robertus
Cheret, Rad(ulfus) Gray, Bristeordus, Paganus de Sunnyng',
Ricardus de Colleia, Ailwardus de Colleia, Gilbertus de Chanetwda.

Date as for no. 1132. For the custom called *radeniht*, a form of riding service, see F. M.
Stenton, *Anglo-Saxon England*, 3rd edn. (Oxford, 1971), 473, 475, 478 n. 2, the last
referring specifically to this deed.

1134   *Lease by Abbot Roger and the convent of Reading to Robert of Kent,
son of Ralph Picot, of the land which belonged to Osward, to be held by hereditary
right for an annual rent of $\frac{1}{2}$ mark and mowing, reaping and carrying services in
the autumn; and grant of the liberty of* inshir'   [1158 × 65]

C f 159v

Sciant presentes et futuri quod ego Rog(erius) abbas Radyng(ensis)
et fratrum conventus concessimus Roberto de Cantia filio Rad(ulf)i
Picot terram illam que fuit Oswardi, iure hereditario tenendam de
nobis pro dimidia marca annuatim reddenda ad festum sancti
Michaelis, et preter hoc in autumpno cum tempus fuerit inveniet
unius hominis operationem, una die ad prata nostra falcanda[a] et altera
ad segetes metendas, et per duos dies dimidium carrum sive unam
redam, una scilicet ad fenum et altera die ad bladum nostrum conportandum. Concessimus etiam ei quandam libertatem inshir'.[b] Hiis
testibus: Godwino fratre Alani,[c] Rad(ulf)o pincerna, Gilberto,
Rog(erio) dispensatore, Rad(ulf)o nepote domini Augustini, Waltero
mareschal(lo), Waltero filio Liulfi.[d]

[a] *Ms has* facand'
[b] *Sic in Ms, perhaps error for* iushir' (*see note*)
[c] *Ms has* Alano   [d] *Ms has* Liust', *but cf. no. 823*

The dating limits are those of Roger's abbacy. The liberty of *inshir'* is otherwise
unknown, but the 14th-century scribe may have misred *iushir'*, which could have been
a variant spelling for *heusire*, a customary right known to have existed in Reading in
the 12th century (see nos. 821–2, 826, 1205).

1135   *Lease by Abbot Roger and the convent of Reading to Edmund son of*

Edward of Tilehurst and his heirs of 1 virgate of land in Tilehurst which belonged to Audrey, his aunt, widow of Ailward Beadle, for an annual rent of ½ mark and mowing, reaping and carrying services [1158 × 65]

Cf159r–v

Sciant fideles sancte ecclesie quod ego Rog(erius) abbas Rad(ingensis) et conventus fratrum concessimus et presenti carta confirmavimus Edmundo filio Edwardi de Tyghelhersta tenendam de nobis et de ecclesia nostra iure hereditario illam virgatam terre in Tyghelherste que fuit Aldidere matertere sue uxoris quondam Ailwardi Bedelli. Pro hac terra autem reddet ecclesie nostre annuatim ad festum sancti Michaelis tam ipse quam heredes sui post eum dimidiam marcam argenti secundum antiquam consuetudinem liberiorum hominum nostrorum de territorio Radyng(ie) quam faciunt singuli pro quantitate tenure sue. Inveniet [*f159v*] unius hominis operationem, una die ad prata nostra falcanda et alia die ad segetes metendas, et per duos dies dimidium carrum sive unam redam, una scilicet die ad fenum et alia die ad bladum nostrum conportandum. Hiis testibus: Willemo presbitero Radyng(ie), magistro Gilberto de Colleia, et Rogero fratre eius, Hamone de Cotesbroc, Herewardo de Colleye, Simone et Edmundo et Ricardo fratribus, Roberto de Cantia, Roberto Biensief, Edmundo et Edwardo de Silhamsteda, Sewalo et Warino fratre eius, Roberto.

Date as for no. 1134, with which this deed has some passages in common.

1136 *Gift by Abbot William [I] of Reading to Simon of 'Herewardsley' of the hide and virgate of land which his ancestors sometime held in Theale, to be held, in addition to his patrimony, for 10s annually* [1165 × 73]

Cf159r

Sciant presentes et futuri quod ego Willelmus abbas Radyng(ensis) voluntate et consilio conventus dedi et concessi Simoni de Herewardeslegh' et heredibus eius post ipsum hidam illam et virgatam terre quam antecessores eius aliquando tenuerunt in Thele, tenend(as) de nobis preter patrimonium suum per .x. solidos annuatim ecclesie Radyng(ensi) ad festum sancti Michaelis persolvendos. Sic vero memoratam terram ei concessimus ut eam cui voluerit heredum libere possit concedere. Hec quoque donatio rata erit et stabilis quamdiu predictum censum bene reddiderint et nobis fideles extiterint. Hiis testibus: magistro Gilberto, Hamone, Simone dapifero, Willelmo Bevyn, Ricardo de Grava, Ailwardo de Felda, Roberto de Cantia, Edmundo de Tyghelhurst, Willelmo de Colleia, Hamone filio Turgodi.

The dating limits are those of William I's abbacy. Theale was until 1894 a tithing in the parish of Tilehurst (*VCH Berks.*, iii. 329).

1137   *Gift by Abbot William [I] of Reading to Edmund son of Ailward of the land which his brother Richard sometime held in arable and moors, for 7s annually*   [1165 × 73]

Cf159r

Sciant presentes et futuri quod ego Willelmus Radyng(ensis) ecclesie abbas assensu et voluntate eius conventus dedi [et]*a* concessi Edmundo filio Ailwardi et heredibus ipsius terram quam Ricardus frater ipsius aliquando tenuit in terra arrabili et in moris cum ceteris pertinentiis suis, tenend(am) de nobis pro .vii. solidis annuatim persolvendis ad festum sancti Michaelis. Hec quoque donatio rata erit et stabilis quamdiu predictum censum reddiderit et nobis fidelis extiterit. Hiis testibus: Herewardo fratre ipsius, et Iohanne nepote suo, Willelmo Bevyn, Tedbaldo Tochi*b* de Northcote, Osmundo carpentario.

a Supplied   *b Reading uncertain*

Date as for no. 1136.

1138   *Lease by Abbot Joseph of Reading to Geoffrey son of Bunde and his heirs of 1 virgate of land next to* Fildenac *which his father Bunde held, for an annual rent of 2s*   [1173 × 86]

Cf159r

Sciant presentes et futuri quod ego Ioseph abbas Radyng(ensis) consilio et consensu totius conventus concessi et presenti carta mea confirmavi Gaufr(ed)o filio Bunde et heredibus eius virgatam unam terre que est iuxta Fildenac quam Bunde pater eius tenuit libere et quiete pro duobus solidis annuatim solvendis pro omni servitio, quartam partem ad Annuntiationem dominicam, quartam ad festum sancti Iohannis Baptiste, quartam ad festum sancti Michaelis et quartam ad festum sancti Thome apostoli. Hec autem conventio rata erit et stabilis quamdiu predictus Gaufr(edus) et heredes eius fideles nobis extiterint et predictum censum nobis bene et fideliter solverint. Hiis testibus: Warino de Radyng(ia), Gaufr(edo) clerico, Roberto cementario, Rogero mercatore, Waltero quoquo,*a* Rad(ulfo) de Caversham, Frualdo*b* de Hurtrugge, Iohanne s(er)v(iente)*c* de Est', Ricardo filio Chan',*c* Waltero Heremit',*c* Gaufr(edo) filio Alani, Simone filio Gaufr(edi), Iohanne filio Gaufr(edi) mu'.*c*

a For coquo   *b Sic, possibly error for* Ernaldo
c Reading very uncertain

The dating limits are those of Joseph's abbacy.

1139 *Lease by Abbot Hugh [II] and the convent of Reading to Raymond the merchant and his heirs of 4 virgates of land [specified] and the land which was [? of] Huldehund, for an annual rent of 21s 6d. Raymond has given the abbey 10s*   [1186 × 99]

Cf158v

Sciant presentes et futuri quod ego Hugo abbas Radyng(ensis) et eiusdem loci conventus concessimus Raimundo mercatori et heredibus suis quatuor virgatas terre cum omnibus pertinentiis suis, scilicet unam que fuit Godwyni Wykyng et unam que fuit Aldwini de Luci et unam que fuit Sewini Rudde et unam que fuit Edmundi Warimund, et preterea terram que fuit Huldehund. Tenend(as) de nobis honorifice et pacifice, libere, quiete ab omni servitio et consuetudine pro viginti et uno solidis et sex denariis annuatim ad festum sancti Michaelis reddendis. Pro hac autem concessione dedit nobis prefatus R(aimundus) .x. solidos. Hec igitur conventio rata erit et stabilis quamdiu prescriptus R(aimundus) et heredes sui nobis fideles exstiterint et predictum censum bene et plene reddiderint. Hiis testibus: Alano fratre Raimundi, Rad(ulf)o Wille, Waltero de Oxonia, Waltero de Stoke, Gilberto de Ponte, Waltero senescallo, Willelmo pincerna, Willelmo dispens(atore), Waltero Peg, et aliis multis.

The dating limits are those of Hugh II's abbacy. Raymond the merchant occurs in several late 12th- and early 13th-century contexts (see, e.g., nos. 836–8, 841, 843–6) and the witnesses confirm the abbot as Hugh II.

1140 *Manumission from serfdom by Abbot Elias and the convent of Reading to Simon son of Aldwin of Theale, and gift of the land which his father held at Theale, for 20s annually, and of the pasture called Widmoor, for ½ mark annually and reaping service at harvest time*   [1200 × 1213]

Cf158v

Sciant presentes et futuri quod ego Hel(ias) abbas Radyng(ensis) et eiusdem loci conventus absoluimus Simonem filium Aldewini de Thela a servitute qua tenebatur ratione nativitatis. Dedimus etiam et concessimus ei totam terram quam Ailwinus pater eius tenuit apud Thelam cum pertinentiis suis in prato et alneto et pascuis et pasturis, tenend(am) de nobis iure hereditario reddendo annuatim viginti solidos ad festum sancti Michaelis pro omni servitio. Dedimus quoque eidem pasturam illam que vocatur Widemora cum pertinentiis, tenendam de nobis iure hereditario reddendo inde annuatim dimidiam marcam argenti ad Pascha, et in tempore messionis metet unam nedhalve[1] sicut ceteri homines solent metere. Hec autem duo tenementa tenebit ipse Simon et heredes sui post ipsum libere et quiete et honorifice per predictum servitium et censum quamdiu ipse et heredes sui nobis fideles extiterint et predictum censum ad terminos prenominatos plene et fideliter nobis reddiderint. Hiis testibus.

The dating limits are those of Elias's abbacy.

1. An unusual word meaning a 'boon half-acre' (cf. no. 686, p. 20).

1141 *Gift by Abbot Elias and the convent of Reading to Robert of Cholsey of the land which Simon the forester son of Aldwin of Thele held in Theale, for 20s annually, and of the pasture called Widmoor, for ½ mark annually and reaping service at harvest time* [1200 × 1213]

Cf158v

Sciant presentes et futuri quod ego Hel(ias) abbas Radyng(ensis) et eiusdem loci conventus*ᵃ* dedimus et presenti carta nostra confirmavimus*ᵇ* Roberto de Chelseia*ᶜ* totam terram quam Simon forestarius filius Aldewini de Thela tenuit in Thela cum pertinentiis suis in prato et alneto, in agris et pasturis, tenend(am) de nobis sibi et heredibus suis reddendo inde annuatim viginti solidos ad festum sancti Michaelis pro omni servitio. Dedimus etiam eidem R(oberto) pasturam illam que vocatur Wydemor*ᵈ* cum pertinentiis, tenend(am) de nobis iure hereditario reddendo nobis annuatim dimidiam marcam argenti ad Pascha, et in tempore messionis metet 'unam niedhalve'*ᵉ* sicut ceteri liberi homines solent metere.*ᶠ* Hec autem duo tenementa tenebit prefatus R(obertus) et heredes sui post ipsum qui de ipso exierint libere et quiete per predictum servitium et censum annuum quamdiu ipse et heredes sui nobis fideles extiterint et predictum censum nobis plene et fideliter reddiderint. Hiis testibus: Iohanne filio Hugonis, Roberto Puncun,*ᵍ* Gervasio fratre eius, Ricardo de Colle.*ʰ*

Marginal note: Carta de Morelond et Maupas¹ apud Thele

ᵃ *Ms has here* concessimus *marked for deletion*
ᵇ *Ms has* confirmavi
ᶜ *Ms has here interlined* postea Rob' atte More (*not in E210/1611—see note*)
ᵈ *Ms has here interlined* modo vocatur Maupas (*not in E210/1611*)
ᵉ⁻ᵉ *Ms has* una medhalve; *corrected reading from E210/1611*
ᶠ *Ms has* integre (*in error*)
ᵍ *Ms has* Pincerna; *corrected reading from E210/1611*
ʰ *The list probably continued as in E210/1611* (*see note*)

Date in general as for no. 1140, but this is clearly later than it. For *niedhalve*, see no. 1140 n.1.

PRO E210/1611 (Ancient Deed D 1611) is a pretended original deed by Abbot Elias and the convent of Reading to the same Robert of Cholsey giving the same land, but omitting the pasture and including a warranty clause. It is in fact a product of the 14th century, but was probably based upon a genuine original, since the witnesses, apart from the last, are the same as those for a genuine contemporary deed E210/6338 (see below). The witness-list of E210/1611 is as follows: Johanne filio Hugonis, Roberto Puncun et Gervasio fratre eius, Ricardo de Collei et Rowaldo [*rectius* Rolando *as in E210/6338*] fratre eius, Nicholao filio Everardi, Rogero filio Alize [*rectius* Ailwini *as in E210/6338*], Rogero armigero de Engelfeld, Gilberto Pincun, Daniele clerico de Rading', Ricardo de Turb'evile, Ricardo de Hendredo, Petro filio Ricardi de Chelseia, et multis aliis.

PRO E210/6338 (Ancient Deed D 6338) is a genuine original by Simon the forester giving to Azyra daughter of Roger of Coley all his land in Theale and a pasture called *La Wydemore*, for 1d annually, saving the services and rents due to the abbot of Reading, viz., 20s at Michaelmas, ½ mark at Easter and reaping *unam nidhalve* at harvest time.

1. I.e., Malpas.

1142 Final concord in the king's court at Reading on the morrow *[of All Souls],[a]* 26 Henry III, before William of York (*Ebor'*) provost of Beverley (*Beverl'*), John abbot of Abingdon (*Abbendon'*),[b] Roger of Thirkleby (*Turkeby*) and Gilbert of Preston (*Preston'*), justices-in-eyre, and others, between the abbot of Reading, seeking, and Geoffrey son of John, Adam son of Hervey and Juliana his wife, and Gunnora *de Bendenges,[c]* holding, concerning 3 acres of land in Theale (*Thele*). Geoffrey and the others recognized the land to be the right of the abbot and abbey of Reading. For this the abbot conceded the same to them, to be held by them and *[the heirs of Geoffrey, Juliana and Gunnora][d]* of the abbot and his successors and the abbey in perpetuity by rendering annually 12d at Michaelmas for all service and exaction.

3 Nov. 1241

B ff 166v–167r; C f 97v

a-a Supplied from PRO foot (see note)   *[b]* Abendon' C
[c] Bondenges B,C; PRO foot has ? Hendenges; *cf. Clanchy, Berks. Eyre of 1248, 154:* Bendeng'
d-d B,C have 'their heirs'; corrected reading from PRO foot

The foot of this fine is PRO CP 25(1)/7/14/6. The fine was made at the end of the Berkshire eyre of 1241 (Clanchy, *Berks. Eyre of 1248*, xciv). It is clear from a case in the 1248 eyre that Juliana was Geoffrey son of John's sister (*ibid.*, 154).

1143 Final concord in the king's court at Reading on the morrow of All Souls, 26 Henry III, before the same justices-in-eyre and others, between the abbot of Reading, seeking, and W (illiam) of Englefield (*Englef (eld'*)),[a] holding, concerning 7 acres of land in Theale (*Thele*). W (illiam) recognized the land to be the right of the abbot and abbey of Reading. For this the abbot conceded the same to him, to be held by him and his heirs of the abbot and his successors and the abbey in perpetuity by rendering annually 6d at Michaelmas for all service and exaction.

3 Nov. 1241

B f 167r; C f97v

^a Expansion from PRO foot (see note) and C

The foot of this fine is PRO CP 25(1)/7/14/7. In the Berkshire eyre of 1241 William of
Englefield paid ½ mark to concord with the abbot of Reading (PRO JUST 1/37,
m. 25B d; see also above, no. 124).

1144 Record of the agreement made before Robert *Fulcon(is)*, king's
justice assigned at Reading, dated Wednesday after St Bartholomew
[24 Aug.], 56 Henry III, between Abbot Robert [of Burgate] of
Reading and Margery, widow of William of Englefield (*Englefeud*),
by which the abbot granted to Margery common of pasture in *Pilhulle*
in the open season after the corn has been removed, and for this
Margery granted to the abbot and his men of servile condition of
Theale (*la Thele*) that they may plough and cultivate the lands and
tenements they now hold in *Pilehulle*, saving Margery's common in
the said manner   31 Aug. 1272

B f245v

1145 Gift, indented, by William *de la Grave* to John *Stouyng'* of
Reading, for his service and a certain sum of money, of a piece (*pecia*)
of arable land at The Grove (*la Grave*) between the donor's land on
both sides, viz., *la Breche* and *le Grofcroft* in the parish of Tilehurst
(*Tyghelhurst'*). To be held freely by rendering annually to the donor
and his heirs 1 grain of corn at Christmas for the first 24 years and
thereafter 20s annually at Easter for all service and demand. If John
and his heirs do not pay the said rent of 20s at Easter, the donor and
his heirs may resume and retain the said land in fee. Warranty and
sealing *alternatim*   11 Oct. 1320

C f155r

Hiis testibus: Johanne Vachel, et aliis. Dat' apud Tyghelhurst' die
sabbati proxima post festum sancte Fidis virginis [6 Oct.], anno regni
regis Edwardi filii regis Edwardi quartodecimo.

1146 Quitclaim by the same to the same John *Stounyng'* of Reading
and his heirs and assigns of the same piece (*pecea*) of land at The
Grove (*la Grave*) in the parish of Tilehurst (*Tyghelhurst'*) between the
donor's land on both sides, viz., the croft called *la Breche* on the north
and the croft called *la Grofcroft^a* on the south, which plot (*placea*) of
land he gave the said John by charter. Warranty and sealing
                                                        10 Jan. 1321

C f 155r–v

Testibus: Johanne de Pangebourne, et aliis. Dat' Radyng' die sabbati proxima post festum Epiphanie domini [6 Jan.], anno regni regis Edwardi filii regis Edwardi quartodecimo.

ᵃ Ms has Groscroft *(in error)*

1147   Gift by John *Stouyng*ᵃ of Reading to Richard of Greywell (*Greywelle*), for a certain sum of money, of a piece (*pecia*) of arable land containing 1½ acres which he had by enfeoffment of William *atte Grove*ᵇ of Tilehurst (*Tyghelhurst*) at The Grove (*la Grove*) between William's land on both sides, viz., *le Breche* and *le Grofcroft* in the parish of Tilehurst. To be held freely of the chief lords of the fee by the due and customary services. Warranty and sealing   21 June 1322

   Original charter: PRO E210/2934 (Ancient Deed D 2934)
   C f 155v

Hiis testibus: Johanne Lacator,ᶜ ᵈRad(ulf)o de Helme, Johanne de Pangeborne, Gilberto Wythened, Johanne le Bote, Hugone Etebred, Thoma Lock',ᵈ et aliis. Dat' Rading' die lune proxima ante festum Nativitatis sancti Johannis Baptiste, anno regni regis Edwardi filii regis Edwardi quintodecimo.

Endorsed: Carta Johannis Stouyng' de Radyng' de una crofta de ten'
    quondam Willelmi atte Grove, in Tylhurst' [*14th cent.*]
Size: 213 × 120 mm
Seal: missing; tag through slit in fold at bottom

   ᵃStounyng' *C*   ᵇ*Insert* de Grove *C*
   ᶜle Acat(ur) *C*   ᵈ⁻ᵈ*Om. in C*

1148   Gift by Richard son of Walter of Greywell (*Greywell'*) of Reading to John of Whaplode (*Quappelad'*), clerk, of a piece of arable land containing 1½ acres which he had by gift and enfeoffment of John *Stouyng'*ᵃ of Reading at The Grove (*la Grove*) in Tilehurst (*Tyghelhurst'*)ᵇ between the lands formerly of William *atte Grove* on both sides, viz., *le Breche* and *le Grofcroft'*. To be held freely of the chief lords of the fee by the due and customary services. Warranty and sealing
                                                                              5 Sept. 1328

   Original charter: PRO E210/11150 (Ancient Deed D 11150)
   C ff 155v–156r

Hiis testibus: Thoma Syward, ᶜJohanne Vachel, Thoma de Kentwod', Willelmo de Colle, Waltero de Aldermanston', Galfr(ed)o atte Grove,ᶜ et aliis. Dat' apud Tyghelhurst' die lune proxima ante festum

Nativitatis beate Marie virginis [8 Sept.], anno regni regis Edwardi tercii a Conquestu secundo.

Endorsed: Carta Ricardi de Grewelle de Rading' de una crofta de ten' quondam Willelmi atte Grove in Tylhurst' [*14th cent.*]
Size: 240 × 117 mm
Seal: missing; tag through slit in fold at bottom

*a*Stounyng' *C*   *b*Tylhurst *C*
c-c Om. in C

1149   Quitclaim by John of Whaplode (*Quappelad'*),*a* clerk, to Abbot John [I, of Appleford] and the convent of Reading of all his right in a piece of arable land containing 1½ acres which he had by gift and enfeoffment of Richard son of Walter of Greywell (*Greywell'*) of Reading in Tilehurst (*Tyghelhurst'*) at The Grove (*la Grove*) [specified as in no. 1148]. Sealing   29 Sept. 1328

> Original charter: PRO E210/1145 (Ancient Deed D 1145)
> C f 156r
> Pd. (cal.) *Cat. Anc. Deeds*, iii. 542

Hiis testibus: Thoma Syward', *b*Johanne Vachel, Willelmo de Colle, Thoma de Kentwod', Waltero de Aldermanston', Galfr(ed)o atte Grove,*b* et aliis. Dat' apud Tyghelhurst' die jovis in festo sancti Michaelis archangeli, anno regni regis Edwardi tercii a Conquestu secundo.

Endorsed: Quiet' clamant' Johannis de Quappelad' de una crofta de ten' Willelmi atte Grove in Tylhurst' [*14th cent.*]
Size: 242 × 105 mm
Seal: missing; tag through slit in fold at bottom

*a*Quappelade *C*   *b b Om. in C*

1150   Quitclaim by Richard son of Walter of Greywell (*Greywell'*) of Reading to the same Abbot John and convent of Reading of all his right in the same piece of arable land in Tilehurst (*Tyghelhurst'*) at The Grove (*la Grove*) [specified as in no. 1148]. Sealing
                                                                    8 Dec. 1328

> Original charter: PRO E210/1134 (Ancient Deed D 1134)
> C f 156r
> Pd. (cal.) *Cat. Anc. Deeds*, iii. 540

Hiis testibus: Thoma Syward', *a*Johanne Vachel, Willelmo de Colle, Thoma de Kentwod', Waltero de Aldermanston', Galfr(ed)o atte Grove,*a* et aliis. Dat' apud Tyghelhurst' die jovis in festo Concepcionis beate Marie, anno regni regis Edwardi tercii a Conquestu secundo.

Endorsed: Quiet' clamant' Ricardi Grewelle de Rading' de una crofta de ten' quondam Willelmi atte Grove in Tylhurst' [*14th cent.*]
Size: 240 × 95 mm
Seal: missing; tag through slit in fold at bottom

  a–a Om. in C

1151 Quitclaim, indented, by Thomas of Kentwood (*Kentwode*) to Abbot William [II, of Sutton] and the convent of Reading of all his right in common of pasture in the field called North Field (*Norhfeld*),*a* Reading, which the abbot and convent have caused to be enclosed with ditches and hedges. In exchange they have granted to him and his heirs common of pasture in *Schepcotefelde*,*b* Reading, viz., from the eastern acre of Walter Kent (*le Kent*) to *le Drovelane.* Sealing *alternatim*
[1290 × 1305]

  Original charter: PRO E210/8579 (Ancient Deed D 8579)
  C f 157r

Hiis testibus: Johanne Fachel,*c* Gilberto Pynzon,*d* *c*Johanne de Schaldeford, Matheo Grancurt, Thoma Syward, Willelmo Chamberlayn, Alano de Bannebir'*e* et multis aliis.

Endorsed: Quietaclam' Thome de Kentwd' de communia pasture in Northfeld' Rading'. Tihelhurst' [*14th cent., last word separate*]
Size: 210 × 73 mm
Seal: small oval in red wax on tag; sprig of foliage; legend: SIGILLV ... REDILECCIO

  a Northfeld *C*   *b* Shepecotefelde *C*
  c Vachel *C*   *d* Pynson *C*
  e–e Om. in C

The dating limits are those of William II's abbacy. Thomas of Kentwood was an elector and juror for Reading hundred in 1284 (PRO JUST 1/44, m. 21d) and witnessed as late as 1328 (see nos. 1148–50). Although North Field is here said to be in Reading, the endorsement of the original adds 'Tilehurst' and in no. 1153 the field is firmly described as in the vill of Tilehurst.

1152 Gift, indented, by Walter Kent (*le Kent*) to Reading Abbey of 4½ acres of arable land in the field of Reading called North Field (*Northfeld*), which the abbey has caused to be enclosed. To be held freely in perpetuity. Warranty. In exchange the abbey has given him 4 acres of arable land in the field called *Schepecotefeld'*a* between the abbey's land and his land, and 1 acre of meadow in the meadow called 'Langney' (*Langeneye*),[b] between the abbey's meadow and that of Robert Beansheaf (*Benschef*), for the same annual rent and customary services as he used to do for the 4½ acres in Northfield (*la Northfelde*). Also quitclaim by Walter to the abbey of all his right in the ground (*solum*) or common in the whole of North Field (*la Northfeld*[c]), as enclosed by ditches and hedges, in return for the abbey's grant to him and his heirs of common in the open season in *la Schypecotefeld*,[a] viz., from his eastern acre to *la Droflane*.[d] Sealing by both parties [*c.* 1290 × 1298]

Original charter: PRO E210/8578 (Ancient Deed D 8578)
Cf 157r

Hiis testibus: Johanne Fachel,[e] Gilberto Pynson, Rad(ulf)o de Bello, Nicholao de Colleye, [f]Willelmo de Colleye, Willelmo Chamberlano, Thoma de Kenetwode,[f] et aliis.

Endorsed: Carta [g]Walteri de Kent[g] de escambio .iiii. acrarum et dimidie terre in Northfeld' pro .iiii. acris terre in Schepcotefeld' et .i. acra prati. Tihelhurst [*14th cent.*]
Size: 228 × 150 mm
Seal: circular of red wax on tag, in perfect condition (22 mm diameter); crescent moon and star; legend: + S' WALTERI D' KENT

[a]Shepecotefeld *C*	[b]Langenheie *C*
[c]Northfelde *C*	[d]Drovelane *C*
[e]Vachel *C*	[f-f]et cetera *C*
[g-g]*Interlined*	

Probably of roughly the same date as no. 1151, in view of the reference to the enclosing of North Field, and before the death of William of Coley, which had occurred by 27 Nov. 1298 (see no. 1044).

1153 Gift in free alms by Bartholomew *de Thyngden*,[a] called *le Criur*,[b] to Reading Abbey of 2 acres of arable land in a field called North Field (*le Northfeld'*) in the vill of Tilehurst (*Tyghelhurst*), between the lands of the abbey on all sides. Warranty and sealing 31 July 1300

Original charter: PRO E210/8580 (Ancient Deed D 8580)
Cf 157r

Hiis testibus: Willelmo de Bleburi, [c]Gilberto Pynzon, Johanne Fachel, Ricardo de Benham, Michaele Belet, Thoma de Kenetwode, Roberto atte More, et multis aliis.[c] Dat' Rading' die dominica proxima ante festum sancti Petri ad Vincula [1 Aug.], anno regni regis Edwardi vicesimo octavo.

Endorsed: Carta Bartholomei de Thyngdene dicti le Criour, de .ii. acris terre in Northfeld' [*14th cent.*]

Size: 215 × 108 mm
Seal: small circular of white wax on tag; ? relief head in profile to
right; legend illegible

^aThyngdene *C*   ^bCriour *C*
^{c-c}et cetera *C*

1154   Lease for lives, [indented]^a and dated Thursday the feast of St
Laurence, 18 Edward I, by Abbot Robert [of Burgate] and the
convent of Reading to John of Tangley (*Tangeleye*) and Robert, his
first-born son, of 26 acres of arable land and 1 acre of meadow in the
vills of Reading and Tilehurst (*Tygh(elhurst)*), with the plot (*placea*)
and curtilage in which the houses of Robert *le Maister* were situated.
Of these, 1 acre lies behind the said curtilage, 7½ acres lie in *Uverwestham*
and *Netherwestham*, 9½ acres lie in North Field (*la Northfelde*), 5 acres
lie in the field between the sheepfold (*berkaria*) and the vill of Reading,
and 3 acres lie against the house of Henry *Lucas*, two of the last being
enclosed and the third unenclosed (*exclusa*) lying along (*desuper*) the
hedge on the western side of the other two. The acre of meadow lies
in 'Herewardsley' (*Herewardesle*). To be held freely for their lives by
rendering annually 13s 4d at Michaelmas and Easter in equal portions
for all secular service, exaction and demand, saving suit of court once
a year either in person or by attorney. John and Robert are not
permitted to sell or let the land at farm. Sealing by both parties^b

10 Aug. 1290

Cf158r

Hiis testibus: domino Rolando de Erle, et cetera.

^a *Assumed, although sealing clause incomplete*
^b *Sealing probably* alternatim, *but text abbreviated*

1155   Release (*reddidi concessi et tradidi*) by Robert son of John of
Tangley (*Tangele*) to Abbot John [I, of Appleford] and the convent
of Reading of all the lands and tenements which he held for his life
by demise of Abbot Robert [of Burgate], the said abbot's predecessor,
and the convent in Reading and Tilehurst (*Tygh(elhurst)*); and quitclaim of all his right in the same and in all other tenements of the fee
of the abbot and convent in the said vills. Sealing   3 Nov. 1330

Cf158r

Hiis testibus: Ed(mund)o Pynsun, et aliis. Dat' apud Radyng' die
sabbati in crastino Animarum [2 Nov.], anno regni regis E(dwardi)
tercii a Conquestu quarto.

1156 Lease for life, indented and dated Thursday after the Circumcision [1 Jan.], 4 Edward III, by Abbot John [I, of Appleford] and the convent of Reading to William of Wittenham (*Wyttenham*) of 34 acres of arable land and 1 acre of meadow in Reading and Tilehurst (*Tygh(elhurst)*), with the plot (*placea*) and curtilage in which the houses of Robert *le Maister* were situated. Of these, 1 acre lies [etc., as in no. 1154, reading *Uverewestham, Netherewestham, le Northfeld*, William *Lucas*, and continuing as follows], 2 acres lie in North Field (*le Northfeld*) between the land of Ed(mund) *de Copenhulle* and that of John *Ellond*, 1 acre lies in North Field between the land of Agnes widow of Robert Chandler (*le Chaundeler*) and that of Walter *le Hurt*, 2 acres lie in *le Worthe* between the land of William *Maisent* and that of Katherine Vachell (*Vachel*), 2½ acres lie in the field called *le Crondelfeld* towards the house of William *Lucas* next to the land of Mariota of Banbury (*Banneburi*), and ½ acre lies in the croft of John *de Stounyng'* in *Lortemere* called *le Poynt*. The acre of meadow lies in 'Herewardsley' (*Herewardesleie*). To be held for his life by rendering annually 13s 4d at Michaelmas and Easter in equal portions for all service, exaction and demand, saving suit of court once a year either in person or by attorney. William is not permitted to sell or let the said tenements at farm, on pain of resumption by the abbot and convent. Sealing *alternatim*.
3 Jan. 1331

Cf158r

Hiis testibus: Roberto Sauser, et aliis. Dat' apud Rad(yng') die et anno supradictis.

1156a Note that on Saturday the morrow of St James [25 July], 17 Edward III, the same W(illiam) conveyed (*tradidit*) the said lands and tenements to W. *Randolf* and John *le Wodereve* for the term of the life of the said W(illiam) with licence, etc.
26 July 1343

Cf158r

1157 Gift in exchange, in duplicate and dated Wednesday after St Mathias the apostle [24 Feb.], 30 Edward I, by Abbot William [II, of Sutton] and the convent of Reading to John Vachell (*Vachel*) of Reading of 3 acres of arable land in North Field (*la Northfeld'*) in the parish of Tilehurst (*Tyghelhurst'*) outside the abbot and convent's enclosure, which acres Geoffrey English (*le Engleys*) previously held of them for life; and 1 acre lies between the land of John *atte Mere* on the north and that of Nicholas of Coley (*Colle*), sometime held by Roger *atte Couwyk'*, on the south. For this gift John has given the abbot and convent 2 acres of land lying withing their enclosure in North Field, of which 1 acre he had by demise of Gilbert Franklin (*le Frankelayn*),

device resembling a spoked wheel; legend: +S' ROBERT[I] [BE]NSEIP[h]

[a]Bienshief C   [b]Kaversham C
[c]Tyghelhurst' C   [d]Berlegh' C
[e]Kenetwode C
[f]Sic, passage included ungrammatically in the text
[g-g]Om. in C
[h]Letters in square brackets partially missing and conjectural

Before Feb. 1261, by which time Daniel Wolvesey was dead (see no. 862n.). James of Caversham was alias James the Forester, who made a gift to the abbey probably not later than c. 1260 (no. 1162). Stephen de la Wile occurs in 1248 and 1261 (see no. 890n.). Gilbert Kent occurs as a witness in 1226 × 38 and 1241 (PRO C109/68, part 2, no. 336; above, no. 709). Gilbert Franklin occurs in 1248 (Clanchy, Berks. Eyre of 1248, 172).

1162 Gift in free alms by James the Forester (*Forestarius*) to Reading Abbey of 20s annual rent in the vill of Tilehurst (*Tichelhurste*),[a] viz., from Richard le Norais[b] 17d, from Thomas le Gos 3s 6d, from Godfrey Marshal (*le Marescal*[c]) 40d, from Marioth' 3s 6d, from Edith la Loveliche 16d, from Robert [?] Bailiff (*Baly*)[d] 3s 11d, and from Stoneham (*Stonham*) 3s, with all escheats, heriots, reliefs, wardships and fines of the said tenants for their tenements. Warranty and sealing[e]

[?c. 1240 × 60]

Original charter: PRO E210/7291 (Ancient Deed D 7291)
B f218r; C f132v; C f162v

Hiis testibus: Stephano de la Wyle, [f]Willelmo de Colle, Willelmo clerico de Bleburi, Roberto Benschef, magistro Ricardo de Benham, Johanne de Benham, Thoma de Bunetfeud, Johanne Crawe clerico,[f] et aliis.

Endorsed: Carta Jacobi Forestarii de .xx. sol' annui redditus in villa de Tilhyrste [*later 13th cent.*]
Size: 217 × 164 mm
Seal: oval (c. 30 mm long) in green wax on tag; foliated star-like device; legend: +S' JACOPVS D' CAV'

[a]Tyghelhurste B,C f132v, Tylehurst' C f162v
[b]Noreis B,C f132v, Norays C f162v
[c]Marescall' B,C f132v, Mareschal' C f162v
[d]Bali, B, Baili C f132v   [e]B ends with T', C f132v ends
[f-f]Om. in C f162v

The original is a handsome deed written in a hand of the mid-13th century. The entry in B, though in the original hand of that cartulary, lacks the standard decoration of the initial and occurs 14 folios after the end of the main compilation, suggesting that it was made shortly afterwards, perhaps 1258 × 60. Stephen de la Wyle occurs in 1248 and 1261 (see no. 890n.). If William clerk of Blewbury can be identified with the

William of Blewbury who was steward of the abbey in 1267 and still living in 1303 (see no. 855 n.), it is unlikely that this deed would date earlier than *c.* 1240; he was presumably married, however, since his son John occurs in 1333 (see no. 818).

1163   Gift by Robert son of John of Kentwood (*Kenetwde*)*ᵃ* to James of Caversham (*Kaversham*), for his service, of all messuages and lands which his tenants held of him in the vill of Tilehurst (*Tihelhurst*),*ᵇ* viz., the messuage and land which Richard *le Noreis*ᶜ held for 14d annually and other services, the messuage and land which Thomas *le Gos* held for 34d and a cock and hen annually and other services, the messuage and land which Henry *Marioth* held for 3s annually and other services, the house with curtilage which Edith *le Luveliche*ᵈ held for 12d annually and other services, and the messuage and land which Godfrey Tailor (*Scissor*)ᵉ held for 3s 4d annually, which land he will hold for the term of his life by the said service; and of the meadow which the donor had in Theale Meadow (*Le Thelemed*) called *Le Widemed,*ᶠ viz., that which he and Robert *Sarguz* have been accustomed to use alternately (*alternare*) each year. To be held freely by rendering annually to the donor and his heirs 1d at Michaelmas for all secular service, exaction, custom and demand. For this James has given him 28 marks sterling as entry-fine. Warranty and sealing   [?*c.* 1240 × 60]

   Original charter: PRO E210/7293 (Ancient Deed D 7293)
   C ff 162v–163r

Hiis testibus: domino Willelmo Hurscal*ᵍ* *ʰ*Roberto Bensef'. Willelmo de Collye, Thoma de Benetfeld, Gilberto Frankelano, Gilberto Blundel, Roberto Bensef iuniore, Thoma de Kenetwde, Gilberto Frankelano de Witelie, Nicholao Konsail, Ricardo de Grava, Godefrido de Colle,*ʰ* et multis aliis.

Endorsed: Carta Roberti de Kenetwode facta Jacobo Forestario de terris et mesuagiis in Tighelhurst [*13th cent.*]
Size: 259 × 205 mm
Seal: circular (*c.* 30 mm in diameter) in white wax on tag; eight-petalled flower; legend: + S' ROBERTI DE CV'ETWD'*ⁱ*

*ᵃ*Kenetwode *C*	*ᵇ*Tylehurst' *C*
*ᶜ*Noreys *C*	*ᵈ*Lovelich' *C*
*ᵉ*cissor *C*	*ᶠ*Wydemed *C*
*ᵍ*Huscarl *C*	*ʰ⁻ʰ*Om. in *C*
ⁱReading uncertain	

Perhaps within the same date range as no. 1161, but before no. 1162, by which James the Forester, alias James of Caversham, gave the rents from most of these tenants to the abbey. John of Kentwood, presumably the father of the donor, witnessed a deed by Abbot Adam of Reading, 1226–38 (PRO C109/68, part 2, no. 336). Nicholas *Konsail*, alias *Cunsail*, witnessed in 1249 and was a juror for Reading hundred in 1269 (below, no. 1223; PRO JUST 1/42, m. 19). The witness list shows that Gilbert Franklin was different from Gilbert Franklin of Whitley.

1164 Quitclaim by Alice, widow of Robert of Kentwood (*Kenet-wude*),[a] to Reading Abbey of all dower belonging to her (*que me contingit*) from the land and rent which Robert her late husband sold to James the Forester (*Forestarius*). For this the abbey has given her 10s sterling. Sealing   [?*c.* 1240 × 1278]

Original charter: PRO E210/7290 (Ancient Deed D 7290)
Cf 163r

Hiis testibus: Stephano,[b] Olivero de Hasel',[c] [d]Johanne de Colle, Willelmo de Wytel', Thoma de Ben'efeud, Willelmo de Weresle, Waltero de Madehach', Johanne de Benham,[d] et aliis.

Endorsed: Quietaclam' dotis Alitie relicte Roberti de Kenetwod' [*13th cent.*]
Size: 164 × 63 mm
Seal: oval (*c.* 34 mm long) in red wax on tag; upright foliated device; legend: + S' AL'CIE UXORIS ROB'TI

[a] Kenetwod' *C*
[b] *Possibly* de la Wyle *om.* (*cf. nos. 1161–2*)
[c] Hasele *C*   [d-d] *Om. in C*

Perhaps contemporary with no. 1162, since there is no record of Robert of Kentwood confirming that gift, but certainly before 10 Apr. 1278, by which time Oliver of Haseley was dead (see no. 1175).

1165 Gift by Gilbert Franklin (*le Frankelayn*) to John Vachell (*Fachel*), for his service and a certain sum of money, of 1 acre of arable land in the field called North Field (*Northfeld'*) between the land of William Gerard (*Gerard*) on the south and that of the abbot of Reading on the north. To be held of the chief lord of the fee freely by the due and customary service. Warranty and sealing   [1290 × Feb. 1302]

Cf 163v

Hiis testibus: Gilberto Pinzon, et multis aliis.

After *Quia emptores* and before no. 1157, by which John Vachell gave this acre to Reading Abbey.

1166 Gift by Elias of Banbury (*Bannebury*) to John Vachell (*Vachel*), for his service and a certain sum of money, of ½ acre of arable land in North Field (*la Northfeld*), Reading, within the enclosure of the abbot of Reading next to the land of William of Aldermaston (*Aldermaston'*).

To be held of the chief lords of the fee freely by the due and customary services. Warranty and sealing. Witnesses [omitted]

[1290 × Feb. 1302]

Cf163v

Date as for no. 1165.

1167 Gift, indented, by William of Aldermaston (*Aldermaston'*) to John Vachell (*Vachel*) of ½ acre of arable land in North Field (*la Northfeld'*), Reading, within the enclosure of the abbot of Reading next to the land of Elias of Banbury (*Bannebury*). To be held of the chief lords of the fee freely by the due and customary service. In exchange John has given William the 12d annual rent which he used to receive at Michaelmas from William's stall in Shoemakers' Row (*in suteria*), Reading. Warranty of the said ½ acre and sealing *alternatim*. Witnesses [omitted]   [1290 × Feb. 1302]

Cf163v

Date as for no. 1165.

1168 Quitclaim by Edmund son of Gilbert Pincent (*Pynson*) to John of Stonor (*Stonore*) and his heirs or assigns, of all his right in 12d annual rent which he used to receive from the tenement late of Thomas of Ockley (*Okle*) and sometime held by Robert Beansheaf (*Bienshief*) in Tilehurst (*Tyghelhurst*). Sealing. Witnesses [omitted]   20 Oct. 1319

Cf164r

Dat' Radyng' vicesimo die mensis Octobris, anno regni regis Edwardi filii regis Edwardi terciodecimo.

1169 Quitclaim by Thomas *atte Watere* of Theale (*la Thele*) to Abbot William [II, of Sutton] and the convent of Reading of all his right in a certain house in the vill of Theale in which the pleas of the foreign hundred of Reading are held (*in quadam domo cum pertinenciis in villa de la Thele in qua tenentur placita hundredi forinceci de Radyng'*). Sealing

[1290 × 1305]

Cf164r

Hiis testibus: domino Rolando de Erle, et aliis.

The presence of Sir Roland of Earley among the witnesses establishes the abbot as William II, whose abbacy provides the dating limits. Roland died before the abbot (see no. 1257), but the date of his death is unknown. This deed is of considerable interest, since it reveals why the name of the foreign hundred of Reading, i.e., the hundred of Theale, derived from a place within the in-hundred.

1170 *Agreement by which Stephen* Wynegod *and Stephen Bernard have*

*conveyed to Reading Abbey for 20 years their meadow in 'Langney' on the [River]
Kennet next to the abbot's meadow which belongs to Pangbourne, for a payment
of 1 mark and nothing further during the term*

[*either* 1216 *or* 25 Mar. 1216 × 24 Mar. 1217]

Cf164r

Hec est conventio facta inter abbatem et conventum de Radyng(ia),
ex una parte, et inter Stephanum Wynegod et Stephanum Bernard',
ex altera parte, scilicet quod ipsi tradiderunt abbati et conventui de
Radyng(ia) pratum suum quod iacet super Kenetam in Langeneia
iuxta pratum abbatis quod pertinet ad Pangebornam, ad habendum
et tenendum libere et quiete per .xx. annos, ita ut inde viginti vestituras
habeant. Et propter hoc abbas et conventus dederunt predictis Stephano Wynegod et Stephano unam marcam argenti, ita ut inde
amplius nichil possint requirere in toto termino viginti annorum.
Factum est autem hoc cirograffum anno quo mortuus est rex
Iohannes. Hiis testibus: Roberto de Offinton', et multis aliis.

The dating depends upon whether the year was at this time held to begin on 1 Jan.
or, as seems more likely in the light of slightly later practice at Reading, on 25 Mar.
The precise location of *Langeneia* is uncertain (cf. nos. 1049, 1152).

1171 Quitclaim by Robert *de Hyda*, in the name of himself and his
wife Reynilda, to Reading Abbey of the two parcels (*particule*) of
meadow which he had of the abbey in the vill of Tilehurst (*Tyelhurst'*),[a]
of which one parcel lies between the abbey's meadow and that of
Ralph of Speen (*Spina*) and the other lies between the same Ralph's
meadow and the moor of Calcot (*Caldecot'*). However, despite this
quitclaim, he and his heirs and assigns will pay entirely and in perpetuity the former customary rent, as is contained in the abbey's
charter which he has. He recognizes that he and his heirs and assigns
are bound faithfully to fulfil the same (*ad hec omnia . . . tenenda*). Sealing
24 Aug. 1300

Original charter: PRO E210/8445 (Ancient Deed D8445)
Cf164v

Hiis testibus: Willelmo Bayllol, [b]Willelmo de Blebur' senescallo
Radyng', Gilberto Pynzon, Johanne Fachel, Rad(ulf)o de Alta Ripa,
Thoma de Lamhuth', Johanne de Benham, et multis aliis.[b] Dat'
Radyng' die mercurii in festo sancti Bartholomei apostoli, anno regni
regis Edwardi vicesimo octavo.

Endorsed: Quietacl' Roberti de Hyda et Reynilde uxoris eius de .ii.
   particulis prati in Tighelhurst' [*14th cent.*]
Size: 207 × 116 mm
Seal: small circular in white wax on tag; details indecipherable

*a*Tylhurst' *C*   *b-b*et aliis *C*

1172 Gift by Richard Kent (*le Kent*), with the assent of Walter his son and heir, to Adam *Batte*, for his service, of 3 acres of land in the vill of Tilehurst (*Tihelhurst*)*a* in the field called Broomham (*Bromham*), the acres lying between the road (*cheminus*) called *Ieldestrete*b and the chaplain's acre and extending from *Hodeshulle* in the east to the donor's grove in the west. To be held freely by rendering annually to him and his heirs 7d, viz., at Michaelmas 6d and at [Holy] Innocents [28 Dec.] 1d, for all secular exaction and demand. For this Adam has given him 40s sterling as entry-fine. Warranty and sealing   [?*c.* 1240 × 70]

Original charter: PRO E210/3469 (Ancient Deed D 3469)
C ff 164v–165r

Hiis testibus: Ricardo*c* de Mora, *d*Gilberto Pinsun, Roberto Biensef, Thoma de Spina, Waltero de Axlade, Gilberto Frankelano, Roberto Sarguz, Willelmo de la Ellilond,*d* et multis aliis.

Endorsed: Carta unius crofte que vocatur Bromham *c*in Tyghelhurst*c* quam Adam Batte emit de Ricardo de Kent ex assensu et consensu Walteri Kent filii sui et heredis. Tylhyrst [*14th cent.; last word in different hand*]
Size: 270 × 86 mm
Seal: missing; tag through slit in fold at bottom

*a*Tylhurst *C*   *b*Yeldestrete *C*
*c*Rolando (*sic*) *C*   *d-d*Om. in *C*
*c-c*Interlined

Dating uncertain, but Walter *de Axlade* occurs in 1226 × 38 (see no. 1052 n.) and a Walter Kent, perhaps the present donor's son, as late as 1290 × 1305 (see no. 1151). The donor witnessed no. 1161, which is not later than 1261, and was certainly dead by Oct. 1284 (PRO JUST 1/48, m. 10).

1173 Quitclaim by Robert *Biz*, former tenant of Reading Abbey at Tilehurst (*Tylhurst*'), to Reading Abbey of all his right in the land of Calcot (*Caldecote*) which he had by demise of the chamberlains of the abbey, and of all action which he had or could have against the abbey for any reason from the beginning of the world to Pentecost, 14 Edward I. Letters patent   2 June 1286

C f 165r

Presentibus Willelmo de Bleobury, et aliis. Dat' Radyng' die Pent-(ecostes) anno supradicto.

1174 Gift in free alms by Joan, widow of Oliver of Haseley (*Hasele*) and daughter and heir of John *Blancbuli*, to Reading Abbey of 1d annual rent and the entire service of Nigel of Sanderville (*Sanndervilla*) and Alice his wife and their heirs, and whatever she used to receive from them for their tenement in Tilehurst (*Tylehurst*) or she or her heirs could in the future receive in service, homage, fealty, reliefs, wardships, heriots, escheats, summonses, distraints or other things. The said rent and service to be held in free alms quit of all custom, suit of court, exaction, demand and secular service. Warranty and sealing   [*c*. 10 Apr. 1278]

Cf165r–v

Hiis testibus: domino Rolando de Erle, et aliis.

Probably contemporary with no. 1175.

1175   Notification by Joan, widow of Oliver of Haseley (*Hasele*) and daughter and heir of John *Blannkbulli*, that she has deputed (*attornasse*) Nigel [of][a] Sanderville (*Sanndervill'*) and Alice his wife to hold of Reading Abbey the entire tenement which they held of her in Tilehurst (*Tylehurst*) and to pay the abbey the rent of 1d and all services due from the said tenement without reservation to herself or her heirs. Sealing   10 Apr. 1278

Cf165v

Dat' apud Radyng' die dominica post festum sancti Ambrosii [4 Apr.], anno regni regis Edwardi filii regis Henrici sexto.

[a] Supplied

1176   Gift by Joan *Blannkbulli*, widow of Oliver of Haseley (*Hasele*), to Roger son of Adam *Batte*, for his service, of 1 acre of land in the vill of Tilehurst (*Tilhurst*), as enclosed by hedge and ditch in the eastern part of Wide Field (*la Wydefeld'*), which acre Robert *de Fraxino* sometime held and which belonged to *la Wodehouse*, and which lies between the abbot of Reading's field called *Sandham* and the donor's land, and extends from *la Middelfeld* on the north to the king's road on the south. To be held freely, with free entry and exit, by rendering annually to the donor and her heirs 8d at Michaelmas for all secular services, exactions, wardships, reliefs, heriots, escheats, customs, suits of court and demands. For this Roger has given her 5s sterling. Warranty and sealing   [1270 × 90]

C f 165v

Hiis testibus: Nigello de Sanndervill', et aliis.

After 27 May 1270, when Oliver of Haseley was still living (see no. 759), and before *Quia emptores*.

1177   Gift by Joan, widow of Oliver of Haseley (*Hasele*), to Roger *Batte*, for his service, of 1 acre of land in the vill of Tilehurst (*Tygh-elhurst*), lying along the southern side of the hedge which is opposite the tenement of Walter Kent (*le Kent*) in *la Middelfeld'*, and extending towards *Wodefeld'* on the east and towards the tenement of Adam Granger (*le Grannger*) on the west. To be held freely by rendering annually to the donor and her heirs 12d at Michaelmas for all secular services, wardships, reliefs, heriots, escheats, customs, suits of court, exactions and demands. For this Roger has given her ½ mark of silver. Warranty and sealing   [1270 × 90]

C f 166r

Hiis testibus: Nigello Sanndervill', et aliis.

Date as for no. 1176.

1178   Bond[a] by William *atte Grove* of Tilehurst (*Tighelhurst*)[b] and Alice his wife to Abbot Nicholas [of Whaplode] and the convent of Reading in £20 sterling which they borrowed from them on Saturday after St Mathias the apostle [24 Feb.], 15 Edward II, to be repaid Sunday the feast of the Assumption of St Mary [15 Aug.] next following. As security William has demised his whole grove with ditches, hedges and other appurtenances, lying next to the abbot and convent's grove called *le Heygrof* in Tilehurst[c] on the north, until the debt has been paid in full. The abbot and convent may cut down the crop (*vestura*) of the said grove and carry it away while the grove is in their hands. Sealing with the seals of William and Alice   27 Feb. 1322

   Original charter: PRO E210/2192 (Ancient Deed D 2192)
   C f 166r–v

Dat' Radyng' die et anno supradictis. Hiis testibus: Thoma Syward, [d]Willelmo de Colle, Thoma de Kentwod', Galfr(ed)o atte Grove, Thoma Loc clerico,[d] et aliis.

Endorsed: Oblig(acio) W. atte Grove. Tygh' [*14th cent.*]
Size: 234 × 102 mm (measuring from the fold at the bottom, which is
   now opened out)[1]
Seal: seals missing; two tags through slits in fold at bottom

ª Original begins: Pateat universis per presentes; *C begins*: Sciant presentes et futuri
b Tyghelhurst' *C*   *c* Tyelhurst *C*
d-d Om. in C

The writing on the original is badly decayed through damp.

1. The size including the opened-out fold is 234 × 115 mm.

1179   Gift by William *atte Grove* of Tilehurst (*Tyghelhurst*)*ª* to Thomas
Lock (*Lock*) of Wittenham (*Wyttenham*),*b* clerk, for a certain sum of
money, of his grove containing 5 acres lying next to the abbot of
Reading's grove called *le Heygrof* on the north in the parish of Tilehurst.*c* To be held of the chief lords of the fee freely by the due and
customary services. Warranty and sealing   25 Mar. 1322

> Original charter: PRO E210/1115 (Ancient Deed D 1115)
> C f 166v
> Pd. (cal.) *Cat. Anc. Deeds*, iii. 538

Dat' apud Tyghelhurst die jovis in festo Anunciacionis*d* beate Marie
virginis, anno regni regis Edwardi filii regis Edwardi quintodecimo.
Hiis testibus: Thoma Syward, *'*Johanne Vachel, Edmundo Pynson,
Thoma de Kentwod', Willelmo de Colle, Michaele Belet, Rogero atte
Elilonde, Gilberto Everard,*c* et aliis.

Endorsed: Carta Willelmi atte Grove. Tyghelhurst' [*14th cent.*]
Size: 242 × 103 mm
Seal: missing; tag through slit in fold at bottom

ª Tylhurst' *C*   *b* Wittenham *C*
c Tyelhurst *C*   *d Sic*
e-e Om. in C

The writing on the original is badly decayed through damp and is in places only legible
under ultra-violet light.

1180   Quitclaim by Thomas Lock (*Lock*)*ª* of Wittenham (*Wyttenham*),
clerk, to Abbot Nicholas [of Whaplode] and the convent of Reading
of all his right in a grove containing 5 acres lying next to the abbot
and convent's grove in Tilehurst (*Tighelhurst*)*b* called *Heygrof* on the
north, which he had by demise and enfeoffment of William *atte Grove*
of Tilehurst.*b* Sealing   28 Mar. 1322

> Original charter: PRO E326/5172 (Ancient Deed B 5172)
> C f 166v

Hiis testibus: Johanne Vachel, *'*Thoma de Kentwod', Edmundo
Pynson, Thoma Syward, Johanne Lacatour, Johanne de Pangeborne,
Gilberto de Copenhulle,*c* et aliis. Dat' Radyng' die dominica proxima

post festum Annunciacionis beate Marie, anno regni regis Edwardi filii regis Edwardi quintodecimo.

Endorsed: Quiet'clam' Thome Lok de grava quondam W. atte Grove. Tygh' [*14th cent.*] Acquietl' Thome Lok' de grava quondam Willelmi atte Grove in Tygh' [*14th cent., different hand*]
Size: 247 × 101 mm
Seal: missing; tag through slit in fold at bottom

a Lock' C   *b* Tyghelhurst' C
c-c Om. in C

The original is dirty and difficult to read.

1181 Quitclaim by Alan son of William *atte Grove* of Tilehurst (*Tyghelhurst*')*a* to Abbot Nicholas [of Whaplode] and the convent of Reading of all his right in a grove containing 5 acres which formerly belonged to his father lying next to the abbot and convent's grove in Tilehurst called *Heyghegrof*'*b* on the north. Sealing   1 May 1322

Original charter: PRO E326/7093 (Ancient Deed B 7093)
C f 167r

Hiis testibus: Johanne*c* Vachel, *d* Thoma de Kenetwode, Edmundo Pynson, Roberto atte More, Willelmo de Colle,*d* et aliis. Dat' Radyng' in festo apostolorum Ph(ilipp)i et Jacobi, anno regni regis Edwardi filii regis Edwardi quintodecimo.

Endorsed: Quiet'clam' Alani atte Grove. Tygh' [*14th cent.*]
Size: 237 × 71 mm
Seal: missing; seal tongue

a Tylhurst C   *b* Heygrof C
c Om. in C   *d d* Om. in C

1182 Bond by William *atte Grove* of Tilehurst (*Tyghelhurst*')*a* and Alice his wife to Abbot Nicholas [of Whapode] and the convent of Reading in 100s sterling which they borrowed from them on Monday after Michaelmas, 16 Edward II, to be repaid at Christmas next following. As security William has handed over (*tradidi*) his croft containing 3 acres of land lying next to le *Heyghegrof*'*b* in Tilehurst on the east, until the debt has been paid in full. The abbot and convent may sow the said croft and have (*possidere*) the whole profit arising therefrom while the croft is in their hands. Sealing with the seals of William and Alice
4 Oct. 1322

Original charter: PRO E210/8006 (Ancient Deed D 8006)
Cf167r

Dat' Radyng' die et anno supradictis. Hiis testibus: Johanne Vachel, ^cThoma Syward, Willelmo de Colle, Edmundo Pynson, Thoma de Kenetwod',^c et aliis.

Endorsed: Oblig(acio) W. atte Grove et Alic' uxoris eius in Tygh' [*14th cent.*]
Size: 208 × 120 mm
Seal: seals missing; two tags through slits in bottom

^aTyghehurst *C*   ^bHeyegrof' *C*
^{c-c}*Om. in C*

1183   Gift by William *atte Grove* of Tilehurst (*Tyghelhurst'*) to Walter of Beenham (*Benham*), clerk, for a certain sum of money, of a croft containing 3 acres of land lying next to *le Heyghgrove^a* in Tilehurst on the east. To be held of the chief lords of the fee freely by the due and customary services. Warranty and sealing   16 Oct. 1322

Original charter: PRO E210/1884 (Ancient Deed D 1884)
Cf167r–v

Dat' apud Tylhurst' die sabbati proxima ante festum sancti Luce ewangeliste [18 Oct.], anno regni regis Edwardi filii regis Edwardi sextodecimo. Hiis testibus: Thoma Syward, ^bJohanne Vachel, Edmundo Pynson, Thoma de Kenetwode, Willelmo de Colle, Michaele Belet, Rogero atte Elilonde, Gilberto Everard,^b et aliis.

Endorsed: Carta Willelmi atte Grove de una crofta in Tygh' [*14th cent.*]
Size: 218 × 117 mm
Seal: missing; tag through slits at bottom

^aHeyegrove *C*   ^{b-b}*Om. in C*

The writing on the original is badly decayed through dirt and damp and is in places only legible under ultra-violet light.

1184   Quitclaim by Alan son of William *atte Grove* of Tilehurst (*Tyghelhurst'*)^a to Abbot Nicholas [of Whaplode] and the convent of Reading of all his right in a croft containing 3 acres of land which formerly belonged to his father lying next to ^b*le Heyghegrof'*^b in Tilehurst on the east. Sealing   11 Oct. 1322

Original charter: PRO E210/8881 (Ancient Deed D 8881)
Cf 167v

Dat' Radyng' die lune proxima post festum sancte Fidis virginis et martiris [6 Oct.], anno regni regis Edwardi ᶜfilii regis Edwardiᶜ sextodecimo. Hiis testibus: Thoma Syward, ᵈMichaele Belet, Thoma de Kenetwod', Willelmo de Colle, Rogero atte Elilond',ᵈ et aliis.

Endorsed: Acquiet' Alani atte Grove in Tygh' de .i. crofta in eadem [*14th cent.*]

Size: 188 × 110 mm

Seal: no sign of sealing, but possibly seal tongue cut off (cf. no. 1181)

ᵃTylhurst' C   ᵇ⁻ᵇHeygrove C
ᶜ⁻ᶜOm. in C   ᵈ⁻ᵈOm. in C

1185 Quitclaim by Walter of Beenham (*Benham*), clerk, to Abbot Nicholas [of Whaplode] and the convent of Reading of all his right in a croft containing 3 acres of land lying next to *le Heughgrove*ᵃ in Tilehurst (*Tyghelhurst*) on the east, which he had by gift and enfeoffment of William *atte Grove* of Tilehurst. Sealing   24 Oct. 1322

Original charter: PRO E210/3175 (Ancient Deed D 3175)
Cf 167v

Hiis testibus: Johanne Vachel', ᵇThoma de Kenetwode, Edmundo Punson, Thoma Syward', Johanne Lakator, Johanne de Pangebourne, Gilberto de Copenhulle,ᵇ et aliis. Dat' apud Rading' die dominica proxima post festum sancti Luce ewangeliste [18 Oct.], anno regni regis Edwardi filii regis Edwardi sextodecimo.

Endorsed: Quietacl' Walteri de Benham de .i. crofta in Tygh' quondam W. atte Grove [*14th cent.*]

Size: 190 × 92 mm

Seal: missing; tag through slit in fold at bottom

ᵃHeygrove C   ᵇ⁻ᵇOm. in C

A marginal note of the later 14th century in C adds: modo tenet Robertus Galopyn ad terminum vite sue.

1185a Note of a charter [probably a mortmain licence] concerning a tenement at The Grove (*la Grove*) in Tilehurst (*Tighelhurst*) acquired from master John of Coleshill (*Coleshulle*), clerk, and Walter of Speenhamland (*Spenhamlond*), and 5 messuages in Reading acquired from the said Walter alone   [prob. 22 Aug. 1354]

Cf225v

This appears among notes mostly of royal licences in mortmain and is almost certainly a reference to the licence granted on 22 Aug. 1354 to those named above for a messuage, carucate of land, 8 acres of meadow and 8 acres of pasture in Tilehurst, and to Walter alone for 5 messuages in Reading, to be alienated to Reading Abbey for a chaplain to celebrate daily in the abbey for the souls of the fathers and mothers of John and Walter (*Cal. Pat. R. 1354–8*, 98).

1186 *Recognition by a jury concerning the neifty of the progeny of named individuals in [? Tilehurst], Sulhamstead, Beenham, Grazeley and Whitley*   25 Jan. 1365 × 24 Jan. 1366

Cf156v

Nota de nativis anno regni regis Edwardi iii. xxxix

Duodecim juratores, videlicet Ricardus Stonyford, Adam Banastre, Symon le Fullere, Robertus Fachel, Johannes Stonyford, Ph(ilipp)us Summenour, Walterus Jurdan, Edmundus Kent', Robertus Blosme, Johannes Bochenel, Henricus Eylond et Gylbertus Taylour, dicunt super sacramentum suum quod tota progenies Willelmi Totebard est native condicionis, et tota progenies Johannis Horne, tota progenies Willelmi Doure, tota progenies de lez Copenhull' et tota progenies de lez Corteys sunt eiusdem condicionis. Item dicunt de Silhampstede quod tota progenies Johannis atte Schrobatte est native condicionis, et tota progenies Johannis Merwyne. De villata de Byenham ignorant. Item dicunt de Greysulle quod tota progenies de Rambaldus,[a] Petri le Cuper, Johannis Iacob, Petri le Taylour et Nicholai Lete sunt native condicionis. Item dicunt de Whytele quod tota progenies Roberti atte Hegge, Johannis Fryday, Ade Horne, Roberti atte Coumbe, Ricardi Bythewode, Henrici atte Wythege et Henrici Couherde sunt native condicionis.

[a] *Sic*

This and no. 1187 are written in a neat book hand with a minimum of abbreviation, quite distinct from the hands on surrounding folios. Since the entries were made in the part of the cartulary concerning Tilehurst deeds, and since no. 1187 refers to Tilehurst, it seems likely that the unlocated tenants in this list were in Tilehurst.

1187 *List of tenants in villeinage in Grazeley, Whitley, Beenham, Tilehurst, Sulhamstead and Pangbourne; and record of the jurors having elected named individuals to serve as reeve wherever it shall please the lord [? the abbot of Reading]*   25 Jan. 1365 × 24 Jan. 1366

Cf156v

Isti sunt qui tenent native, videlicet de Greysulle, Whytele, Byenham, Tyghelhurst', Sylhampstede et Pangebourne: Johannes Okky, Johannes Clerke, Hugo Okky, Thomas Everhard, Adam Hayward, Ricardus Cokunhulle, Willelmus Hoode, Mundi[a] Kent', Nicholaus Stretle, Nicholaus Caddok', Johannes le Reve, Robertus Consayle, Johannes atte Beche, Ricardus dorman, Thomas atte dene, Walterus le Smyth' et Ricardus Scure. Et postea iuratores elegerunt in periculum eorum ad officium prepositi faciendum ubicumque domino placuerit Ricardum Scur(e), Symonem[b] le Fuller, Robertum Bernard, Gylbertum atte Hyde, Robertum Blosme, Hugonem Okky, Johannem Clerke, Johannem Bochenel et Robertum Polhamptone. Acta sunt hec anno regni regis Edward tercii post conquestum xxxix.

[a] Sic   [b] Ms has Symonen

This is written in the same distinctive hand as no. 1186 and, though separated from it by a short gap, may be part of the same document. The events described clearly took place on the same occasion.

UFTON NERVET (in Ufton)

1188 Gift in free alms by Simon son of Nicholas and Isabel his wife to Reading Abbey of the whole land which Thomas son of Alan sometime gave them in the vill of Ufton [Nervet] (*Huffinton'*).[a] To be held freely by rendering annually to the said Thomas and his heirs 1d at Easter and to Richer *Neirnut*,[b] lord of the fee, and his heirs 7s sterling at Michaelmas for all custom, demand, suit and secular service, saving such foreign service as pertains to the said tenement, which the abbey will acquit. Warranty and sealing with their seals. Witnesses [omitted]   [13th cent.; before 1248]

Af85v; Bf62r; Cf29r
Pd. (transl.) A. M. Sharp, *The History of Ufton Court* (London, 1892), 7–8

[a] Uffintun' *B,C*   [b] Neirenut *B*

Not in the original section of A. The donors were both dead by June 1248, when this land was the subject of an assize of mort d'ancestor (Clanchy, *Berks. Eyre of 1248*, 178–9), but Isabel had outlived her husband (see no. 1190). Simon occurs in Bradfield, Berks., in 1225, was appointed one of four knights to collect the fortieth in Reading Abbey's lands outside Herefordshire in 1233, and a collector of the thirtieth in the same in 1237, and was a coroner of the abbey's Liberty in Berkshire in 1241 (PRO JUST 1/36, m. 2; *Close Rolls 1231–4*, 283, ibid. *1234–7*, 557; JUST 1/37, m. 34). The cartulary rubrics call this land *Marruge*, i.e. May Ridge (*Berks. Place-Names*, i. 225).

1188a Note of a charter by Thomas son of Alan of Bradfield (*Bra-*

defeld) to Simon son of Nicholas concerning land at Ufton [Nervet]
(*Uffintun'*) called May Ridge (*Marruge*)[a]   [before 1248]

B f62r; C f29r

[a] Marugge *C*

This concerned the land given to the abbey in no. 1188. The charter was proffered by
the abbot of Reading in the assize of 1248, in the account of which more details of its
terms are recorded (see no. 1188 n.).

1189   Confirmation by Richer *Neirenut* to Reading Abbey of the gift
by Simon son of Nicholas and Isabel his wife of the whole land
which sometime belonged to Thomas son of Alan in Ufton [Nervet]
(*Uffint(un')*).[a] To be held of Richer and his heirs freely by rendering
annually to them 7s at Michaelmas for all custom, demand and secular
service, saving to him and his heirs such foreign service as pertains to
the said land, which the abbey will acquit. Warranty. For this the
abbey has given him 2 marks of silver. Sealing. Witnesses[b] [omitted]
[13th cent.; before 1248]

B ff62v–63r; C f29v

[a] Uffintun' *C*   [b] *Om. in* C

Date as for no. 1188, which this confirms. Richer held the manor of Ufton Nervet
(*VCH Berks.*, iii. 441) and was one of four knights appointed to collect the fortieth in
the abbey's lands outside Herefordshire in 1233 and an elector and juror for Theale
hundred in 1241 (*Close Rolls 1231–4*, 283; PRO JUST 1/37, m. 27).

1190   Gift in free alms by Isabel of Rushall[1] (*Rushal(e)*),[a] widow of
Simon son of Nicholas, to Reading Abbey, for the health of the soul
of her late husband among others, of the whole land which Thomas
son of Alan sometime gave to Simon and to her in the vill of Ufton
[Nervet] (*Uffintun'*), as Thomas's charter to them witnesses. To be
held freely by rendering annually to the said Thomas and his heirs
1d at Easter and to Richer *Neirenut*, lord of the fee, and his heirs 7s
sterling at Michaelmas for all custom, demand, suit and secular
service, saving such foreign service as pertains to the said tenement,
which the abbey will acquit. Warranty and sealing. Witnesses [omit-
ted]   [Oct. 1241 x June 1248]

B f62v; C f29r–v

[a] Rushale *C*

After Oct. 1241, when Simon son of Nicholas was a coroner of Reading Abbey's liberty
in Berks., and before June 1248, when this charter was proffered by the abbot in the
assize of mort d'ancestor (see no. 1188 n.). This charter is *mutatis mutandis* largely a re-
issue of no. 1188.

1. In Bradfield, Berks. (*VCH Berks.*, iii. 397).

1191 Confirmation by the same of the gift which Simon and she sometime made to Reading Abbey of the whole land which Thomas son of Alan sometime gave to Simon and her in the vill of Ufton [Nervet] (*Uffint(un')*),*a* as is contained in the charter which Simon and she sometime made to the abbey. Sealing. Witnesses*b* [omitted]

[Oct. 1241 × June 1248]

Bf62v; Cf29v

a Uffintun' C   *b* Om. in C

Date as for no. 1190.

1192 *Settlement before [Giles of Bridport], archdeacon of Berkshire, of the dispute between John, rector of Ufton [Nervet], and Reading Abbey over the lesser tithes of May Ridge in that parish. The rector has renounced all right in the tithes, and the abbey has agreed to pay the rector by the hand of its chamberlain 2s annually for the same*   25 Mar. 1255 × 24 Mar. 1256

Bf200r; Cf118v

Memorandum quod, cum anno gratie M.CC.lv esset lis mota auctoritate ordinaria coram archidiacono Berk(esire) inter J(ohannem)*a* rectorem ecclesie de Uffinton' actorem, ex parte una, et religiosos abbatem et conventum Rading(enses), ex altera, super quibusdam decimis provenientibus de quadam terra et suis pertinentiis que vocatur Marruge*b* in parrochia predicta de Uffint(on'), quam dicti religiosi in propriam redegerunt culturam, et editum esset eisdem religiosis in hac forma:

Dicit*c* J(ohannes) rector ecclesie de Uffint(on') contra abbatem et conventum Rading(enses) quod dicti abbas et conventus iniuste detinent omnes minutas decimas provenientes ex tenemento quondam Symonis filii Nicholai de Bradef(eld') defuncti, videlicet lanam et*d* agnos et caseum et purcellos et denarium sancti Petri et alias minutas decimas quas predecessores sui plenarie perceperunt. Unde petit dictus J(ohannes) quod dicte ecclesie de Uffint(on') fiat restitutio et quod dicti abbas et conventus Rading(enses) ad condignam excessus et dampnificationis emendam et satisfactionem canonice compellantur. Hec dicit salvo sibi iuris beneficio addendi, et cetera;

licet iidem religiosi per litteras apostolicas et alia munimenta satis sint muniti ut a prestatione decimarum omnium terrarum quas propriis manibus aut sumptibus excolunt aut excoli faciunt liberi sint et absoluti,[1] pro bono tamen pacis realis inter partes predictas, auctoritate predicti archidiaconi interveniente, compositio intercessit. Videlicet quod predictus rector pro se et ecclesia sua et successoribus suis in perpetuum omni iuri et actioni sibi competenti ex quacumque causa quantum ad dictas decimas renuntiavit plenarie et absolute. Iidem vero religiosi, intuitu pietatis et ne in posterum aliquid question-is per aliquem pro tempore rectorem eiusdem ecclesie de Uffint(on') super premissis moveri possit, duos solidos sterlingorum annuatim eidem ecclesie suisque rectoribus, qui pro tempore fuerint, in festo sancti Michaelis per manus camerarii sui solvendos concesserunt, subicientes se cohertioni archidiaconi loci ut ipsos per censuram eccle-siasticam ad illius pecunie solutionem pro voluntatis sue arbitrio compellere possit, si in eius solutione cessaverint suo termino. In cuius rei testimonium presens scriptum in modum[e] cyrographi confectum, signis partium una cum signo archidiaconi signatum, penes partes hinc inde residet confectum.

[a] *For expansion see note*   [b] Maruge C
[c] Dictus C   [d] *Om. in* C
[e] *B repeats* in modum

The interpretation of the date assumes that the year began on 25 Mar. Giles of Bridport was elected bishop of Salisbury 13 Feb. x 15 Apr. 1256 and received the temporalities on 17 Aug. (*Handbook of Brit. Chron.*), but was still called archdeacon of Berkshire on *c.* 24 June (BL Add. Ms. 28870 (cartulary of Vaux College, Salisbury), f 18r). The rector concerned here occurs as 'John parson of Ufton' in 1248 and as 'John priest of Ufton Nervet' in 1261 (Clanchy, *Berks. Eyre of 1248*, 172; PRO JUST 1/40, m. 11). This document has been printed in full as an interesting example of a case involving Reading Abbey settled before an archdeacon with ordinary authority, and as an instance of the operation of the abbey's privilege of not paying tithes on land of its own cultivation.

1. This was specifically granted in Innocent III's general confirmation to Reading in 1207 (see no. 165).

1193 Gift by John *Neyrnut* to Reading Abbey of his manor of Ufton Nervet (*Offinton' Neyrnut*) with its appurtenances, to be held as freely as he ever held it, with homages, wardships, reliefs, heriots, amercements, suits, villeins and their progeny, escheats, etc., by doing to the chief lord of the fee the due and customary service, saving also such royal service as pertains to the said tenement. Warranty. For this the abbot and convent will find all his needs in food and clothing for life, in accordance with the chirograph made between them, and have received him into all benefits and prayers in the abbey in perpetuity. Sealing   [*c.* 13 June 1270]

B ff 210v-211r; C f 127r

Hiis testibus: dominis Nicholao de 3atingedene,[a] Petro Achard, Wal-tero de Ripariis, Nicholao de Henred, Bartholomeo de 3atingedene,[a] [b] Willelmo de Brutenoll',[b] Roberto de Burgefeud,[c] Willelmo Huscharl, militibus, Hervico[d] Belet, Roberto de Offinton', Willelmo de Bleburi,[c]

Nigello de Sandervilla, Waltero de Madehacch',^{f} Philippo de Herte-
rugge, Radul(f)o Banastr(e), Gileberto^g Pinzun, Thoma de Morton'^{h} clerico, et multis aliis.

^{a}3atingdene C	$^{b-b}$ Om. in C
^{c}Burgh'feld' C	^{d}Henrico C (in error)
^{e}Bleobury C	^{f}Madehach' C
^{g}Gilberto C	^{h}Mortone C

The date is approximately the same as that of no. 1194, since the witness-lists are
virtually identical.

1194 Confirmation in free alms by Henry de Pinkeny (*Pynkeney*),^{a}
knight, to Reading Abbey of the whole manor of Ufton Nervet (*Offinton' Neyrnut*), which is of his fee and which John *Neyrnut* has given to
the abbey. To be held as freely as it holds any alms, with homages,
wardships, marriages, reliefs, heriots, amercements, suits of court,
escheats, etc., so that neither he nor his heirs will be able to claim
anything in the said manor except 20s annually which are due from
that manor for castle-guard at Windsor (*Windesores*), which the abbey
will pay at three terms of the year, viz., $\frac{1}{2}$ mark each at the Nativity
of St John Baptist, Michaelmas and the Purification, and saving
foreign service when it falls due. For this the abbey has received Henry
as partaker in all benefits in the abbey in perpetuity. Sealing

13 June 1270

B f211r–v; C f127r–v

Hiis testibus: dominis Philippo Basset, Nicholao de 3atingedene,^{b} Petro
Aschard, Waltero de Ripariis, Nicholao de Henred, Bartholomeo
de 3atingeden(e),^{b} ^{c}Willelmo de Brutenoles,^{c} Roberto de Berfeud,^{d}
Willelmo Huschal,^{e} militibus, Hervico^f Belet, Roberto de Offinton',
Willelmo de Blebur',^{g} Nigello de Sandervill(a), Waltero de Mede-
hacch',^{h} Ph(ilipp)o de Hertrug',^{i} Radul(f)o Banastre, Gileberto^j
Pinsun,^{k} Thoma de Morton' clerico, et aliis. Dat' apud Windes(ores)
die veneris proxima post festum sancti Barnabe apostoli [11 June],
anno domini M.CC.lxx.

^{a}Pynkeneye C	^{b}3atingdene C
$^{c-c}$Om. in C	^{d}Burghfeld' C
^{e}Huscharl' C	^{f}Henrico C (in error)
^{g}Bleobur' C	^{h}Madehacch' C
^{i}Herterugge C	^{j}Gilberto C
^{k}Pinzun C	

The overlordship of Ufton Nervet was in the possession of the de Pinkeny family from
1086 to 1301 (*VCH Berks.*, iii. 441).

1195 Record of the action brought by Juliana widow of John

Rimbaud, Nicholas *de la Berton'*, Richard Long (*le Lung*) and Nicholas *Farun* against the abbot of Reading for recovery as their right of 1 messuage, 60 acres of land, 6 acres of meadow, 5 acres of wood and 16s rent in Ufton Nervet (*Offinton' Neyrnut*), in which the abbot has entry only by John *Neyrnut*, brother of the said Juliana and uncle of the said Nicholas, Richard [and Nicholas],[a] whose heirs they are, who demised the tenements when not of sound mind (*non compos mentis*). The abbot acknowledges that he has entry by John *Neirnut*, but says that he was of sound mind, since at the time and for two years afterwards he was coroner of the abbot's liberty; and for seven years after demising the tenements, and in return for the same, he received from the abbot annually the allowance (*liberacio*) of four monks, 10 marks and four garments, and always retained his senses. The jury, elected by consent of the parties, say that John was of sound mind when he demised the tenements to the abbot and was coroner for the five years following. Therefore the abbot *sine die* and the others in mercy for false claim   [3 × 12 Nov. 1284]

Bf231r

Marginal note: Inrotulatio de terra de Offintone

[a] *Supplied from plea rolls (see note)*

This case was heard during the Reading session of the Berkshire eyre of 1284 (Crook, *General Eyre*, 163), the account being a transcript from one of the plea rolls (e.g. PRO JUST 1/48, m. 15). In the same eyre it was reported that John *Neyrnut* had been coroner of Reading hundred since the last eyre, but was now dead (JUST 1/44, m. 15d). What was claimed by Juliana and the others probably constituted the manor of Ufton Nervet, since John made no other gift to the abbey.

1196   Lease [indented][a] for 60 years, dated Sunday after St Leonard [6 Nov.], 22 Edward III, by Abbot Henry [of Appleford] of Reading to Thomas son of Richard Paynel (*Paynel*) of a plot (*placea*) of land and moor, parcel of the manor of Ufton Nervet (*Offtone Neyrnut*) called *le Carpentereslond*, containing 9 acres of land lying next to the same Thomas's park in Ufton Robert (*Offtone Robert*), between the moor called *Clarissemor'* and the land called Heath Close (*Hethlond*); to be held for 60 years by rendering annually 3s, viz., 18d each at the Annunciation and Michaelmas. If the rent is in arrears, in part or in whole, for two months after any term, the abbot and his successors may re-enter and retain the plot in perpetuity without contradiction of Thomas or his heirs or any others to whom the manor [of Ufton Robert][b] shall come. Sealing *alternatim*   9 Nov. 1348

Bf74v

Hiis testibus: domino^c Ph(ilipp)o de Engelfeld', domino Michaele Beleth, militibus, Ricardo atte Mor(e), Johanne Banastr(e), Nicholao Kenetewode, et aliis. Dat' die et anno supradictis.

^{a} *Not so stated but implied by sealing clause*
^{b} *Supplied (see note)* ^{c} *Interlined*

The Paynels were lords of the manor of Ufton Robert for most of the 14th century. Thomas succeeded his father, Richard Paynel, who in 1338 had obtained from the Crown licence to enclose 300 acres of pasture and wood in Ufton to make a park (*VCH Berks.*, iii. 441).

UFTON ROBERT (in Ufton)

1197   *Gift in free alms by Ralph of Ufton to Reading Abbey of 1 virgate of land in Ufton [Robert]*   [before July 1182; ? not later than 1154]

Af44r; Af81v; Bf62r; Cf28v
Pd. (transl.) A. M. Sharp, *History of Ufton Court*, 27

Sciant omnes fideles quod ego Radulfus de Offintona^a dono et confirmo hac carta mea unam virgatam terre in Offentona^a pro salute anime mee et omnium parentum meorum in liberam et perpetuam elemosinam ecclesie de Rading(ia).^{b} His^c testibus:^{d} Helya de Englefeld, Edmundo de Benham, Turstano de Witeleia, Simone de Herwardesl', et multis aliis.

^{a} Uffentun' *Af81v*, Uffintun' *B,C* ^{b} Radinges *Af81v*
^{c} Hiis *Af81v, B,C* ^{d} *Af81v, B,C end*

Before 25 July 1182, when Thurstan of Whitley had been succeeded by his son Peter (see nos. 1213, 1214 n.), and, since the gift was included in Jocelin de Bohun's diocesan confirmation to Reading, possibly before the reign of Henry II (see no. 180). A fairly early date is also suggested by the simple diplomatic of the deed and by the fact that the donor's grandson confirmed the gift in 1191 (no. 1198). The donor was under-tenant of the manor of Ufton Robert (*VCH Berks.*, iii. 441).

1198   *Confirmation by William of Ufton of the gift by Ralph his grandfather to Reading Abbey of 1 virgate of land in Ufton [Robert] called* Wronkeshulle
[July 1191]

Af44r; Af81v; Bf62r; Cf29r
Pd. (transl.) A. M. Sharp, *History of Ufton Court*, 27

Sciant presentes et futuri quod ego Willelmus de Offinton(a)^a concedo et confirmo donationem quam Rad(ulfus) avus meus fecit monachis de Rading(ia) de quadam virgata terre in Offent(ona)^a cum per-

tinentiis suis omnibus, que vocatur Wronkeshulle, in liberam et perpetuam elemosinam et quietam ab omni servitio seculari. Si quis
autem aliquod servitium a prefatis monachis de predicta terra exiger-
it,[b] ego et heredes mei eos versus regem et versus omnes homines
acquietabimus. Dederuntque mihi predicti monachi pro ista donatione et confirmatione unam marcam argenti coram domino Iohanne
Marescallo et Oggero filio Oggeri[c] et magistro Siefrido[d] thesaurario
Cicestrensi et magistro Thoma de Husseburne, tunc iusticiariis domini
regis in Berscir'.[e] [f]His testibus: Stephano Martel, Baldewino de
Cuserugge, Iurdano Basset, et multis aliis.

[a]Uffentun' *Af8iv*, Uffintun' *B,C*   [b]exegerit *Af8iv, B*
[c]*Af8iv ends with* et multis aliis   [d]Syeffrido *B,C*
[e]'Berksyr' *B*, Berkesyr' *C*   [f]*B ends with* T', *C ends*

Seffrid was treasurer of Chichester from 1187/9 to 1196/7 (Mayr-Harting, *Acta of
Chichester*, 212). He and the other named justices were on eyre in Berkshire in July 1191
(*Pleas before the King or his Justices 1198–1202*, ed. D. M. Stenton, iii, Selden Soc., lxxxiii
(1966), lxxxix; John Marshal was also on eyre there in 1192, but none of the others
appear to have been (*ibid.*, xcii).

1199 Memorandum that Isabel, widow of William of Ufton (*Uffinton'*), holds a piece (*pecia*) of land in her garden without rent for life.
After her death her heirs will pay rent for the said land at the will of
the abbot.   [?1333 × 1348]

Bf210v; Cf127r

In B this is inserted in a 14th-century hand at the foot of the folio; in C it is in the
original section of the main part of the cartulary, copied from B in 1339 × 48 (see vol.
I, pp. 10–11). The later dating limit is thus 1348. The earlier is derived from the fact
that William of Ufton, Isabel's former husband, who held Ufton Robert in 1322 (*Cal.
Inq. P.M.*, vi. 256, 258), was still living in 1333 (Sharp, *History of Ufton Court*, 30).
However, according to *VCH Berks.*, iii. 441, William had a son William who died
without issue.

WALLINGFORD

1200 Gift by Richard son of Ralph (*Rand'i*), chaplain of Theale
(*la pele*),[a] to Reading Abbey of the whole land with rents and all
appurtenances which he had in the parish of St Mary in Wallingford
(*Walingford'*), viz., that lying between the messuage which belonged
to John *le Ferrun* and that which belonged to William *Orpedeman*. To
be held freely by rendering annually to him and his heirs 1d at
Michaelmas for all service, exaction and demand. Warranty and
sealing. Witnesses[b] [omitted]   [c. early Henry III]

Bf75v; Cf39v

ᵃla Thele C   ᵇOm. in C

Ralph, the donor's father, was almost certainly alias Ralph le Weymag', who was said to have held three stalls in Wallingford in King John's time (see no. 1201 n.). In view of the pleading by Nicholas de Stallis in 1251–2 (see ibid.) a date early in Henry III's reign seems likely for this gift.

1201   Quitclaim by Nicholas de Stall(is) of Wallingford (Walingeford)ᵃ to Reading Abbey of all his right in a stall which belonged to Richard, chaplain of Theale (la Theleᵇ), in the parish of St Mary in Wallingford,ᶜ lying between the messuage which belonged to John le Ferun and that which belonged to William Orpedeman, which stall Nicholas had by gift of Matilda, sister of the said Richard. Sealingᵈ

[prob. c. 1257 × 58]

Original charter: BM Add. Ch. 19619
Bf75v; Cff39v–40r
Pd. Arch. Journ., xxii. 161; (cal.) Hurry, Reading Abbey, 176

Hiis testibus: Alexandro Dublet tunc maiore de Walingeford, Symone Raven, Galfr(edo) de la Wik', Petro de Benham, Johanne le hine, Petro de la Wik', Johanne de Walingeford clerico, et aliis.

Endorsed: Quieta clam' Nicholai de Stall' de quadam selda in Walingeford [13th cent.]
Size: 195 × 130 mm
Seal: circular (c. 24 mm diameter) in dark green wax on tag; ? agnus dei, legend: + S' NICHOLAI. DE STALLIS

ᵃWalingford' B, Walyng'ford' C   ᵇpele B
ᶜWalingford' B, Walyngford' C   ᵈB ends with T', C ends

Alexander Dublet was mayor of Wallingford in c. 1245–6 and c. 1257–8 (N. M. Herbert, 'The Borough of Wallingford 1155–1400' (Reading University Ph.D. thesis, 1971), appendix iii, p. xii). In 1251–2 Nicholas de Stallis brought an action on a writ of right against the abbot of Reading in the court of Wallingford over three stalls in Wallingford which, he claimed, had been held by Ralph le Weymag' in King John's time, had then passed to Richard his son, and thence, via a number of others including Richard's sister Matilda, had come by descent to him (Berkshire Record Office, W/JBa 11; N. M. Herbert, 'The family of De Stallis at Wallingford in the thirteenth century', Berks. Arch. Journ., lxiv (1969), 22). If the stall in the present quitclaim was one of these stalls, as seems most likely, the quitclaim dates from Alexander Dublet's second mayoralty and probably represents part of the final settlement of the dispute.

1201a   Note of two charters concerning the tenement of Richard of Theale (la Thele) in Wallingford (Walingeford)

Bf71v

This is written in a later 13th-century hand after the note in the same hand of two charters relating to Winterbrook in Cholsey (no. 778a). Richard of Theale is perhaps the same as Richard, chaplain of Theale, in nos. 1200–1.

WARGRAVE

1202 Concession by William, perpetual vicar of the church of Wargrave (*Weregrave*),[a] to his lords the abbot and convent of Reading, of 1 acre of land belonging to the church of Wargrave,[b] viz., that on which their houses are situated, to be had freely in perpetuity. In recompense they have remitted to him and his successors 2s annually of the pension from the church. Sealing   [*c*. Mar. × 3 Apr. 1241]

Original charter: BL Add. Ch. 19625
Af84r; Bf54r; Cf22v
Pd. (cal.) Hurry, *Reading Abbey*, 176–7

Hiis testibus:[c] magistro Egidio archidiacono Berk' officiali domini episcopi Sar(esburiensis), magistro Willelmo de Bestlesden' officiali eiusdem, magistro Jacobo de Sancto Egidio, Petro capellano eiusdem, Ricardo vicario Sancti Laur(entii), Helia capellano de Weregrave, magistro Willelmo de Rading(ia), Henrico rectore ecclesie de Pangeburn', Johanne, Roberto, Thoma, servientibus de sacristeia Rading', et aliis.

Endorsed: Carta W. vicarii de Weregrave de acra de Weregrave [*13th cent.*]
Size: 153 × 104 mm
Seal: oval (*c*. 30 mm long) in green wax on tag; a hand with two fingers raised in blessing[1] between a moon and a star, legend: + DEXTERA DÑI EXALTAVIT ME

[a]Weregrava *B,C*   [b]Weregrava *C*
[c]*A,B,C end*

The date is probably near that of the episcopal confirmation (no. 1203). Reading Abbey acquired the church of Wargrave from Henry I, who had recovered it from the abbey of Mont St Michel (see nos. 3, 771). The annual pension had stood at 20s (see nos. 211–2).

1. Very similar to the Hand of St James on the abbey's counterseal (see nos. 229, 800).

1203 Confirmation by R(obert)[a] [Bingham], bishop of Salisbury, to Reading Abbey—*fervorem religionis quam in monasterio vestro florere novimus attendentes et ob hoc fructuosiori favore ipsum prosequi cupientes*—of the acre

on which the abbey's buildings are situated at Wargrave (*Weregrave*),
as the abbey justly and canonically possesses it. Sealing

3 Apr. 1241

Original charter: BL Add. Ch. 19621
A f84r; B f54r; C f22v
Pd. (cal.) Hurry, *Reading Abbey*, 177

Hiis testibus:[b] Petro de Cumb(a), Waltero de la Wile, Galfrido de
Bedeford, canonicis Sarr(esburiensibus), magistro Ricardo de
Binham, Petro de Wimborn', Willelmo de Castellis, et Roberto de
Wichampton', clericis, et aliis. Dat' apud Wudeford iii. non' Aprilis,
pontificatus nostri anno duodecimo.

Endorsed: De acra de Weregrave. Confirmacio R(oberti) episcopi Sar'
   [*13th cent.*]
Size: 164 × 70 mm
Seal[1]*:* oval (*c.* 68 mm long), imperfect, in green wax on tag; obverse,
   bishop standing frontally with pastoral staff in left hand and right
   hand raised in blessing, legend: ...OBERTVS...SAR....OPV...;
   reverse, counterseal oval (*c.* 48 mm long), Virgin and Child half-
   length under trefoiled canopy above half-length figure of bishop
   praying to right with pastoral staff and wearing mitre under trefoiled canopy, legend: +SALVE. SC̄A. PARENS. ENIX[A].
   PVERP'A. REGEM

   [a]C has 'Roger' (in error)   *[b]A,B,C end*

Robert Bingham was consecrated on 27 May 1229.

   1. See *B.M. Cat. Seals*, i. 341-2.

WHITLEY (in Reading)

1204   *Quitclaim, in chirograph form, by Abbot Roger and the convent of
Reading to William Pipard and his heirs of a serf called Richard son of Saric*
duole *and his heirs, at a price of 2 marks for their manumission*

[1158 × 65]

Original charter: BL Add. Ch. 19595
C f 139v
Pd. (cal.) Hurry, *Reading Abbey*, 167

Sciant fideles sancte ecclesie presentes et futuri quod Rogerus abbas
Rading(ensis) et conventus clamaverunt quietum Willelmo Pipardo
et heredibus suis quemdam hominem[a] nativum ecclesie Rading(ensis),
nomine Ricardum filium Sarici duole, et heredes suos. Et ut hec
quietantia firma et stabilis permaneat[a] sine omni deinceps calumpnia,

per istam cartam eam confirmaverunt abbas et conventus, accepto de manu Willelmi pretio redemptionis pro Ricardo et heredibus suis, scilicet duabus marcis argenti. Actum fuit hoc his[b] testibus: Amalrico[c] filio Radulfi, Willelmo de Duddevilla, Vicentio clerico, Hugone de bona villa, Godwino filio Nhott, et pluribus aliis.

CYROGRAPHVM

Endorsed: Contra Willelmum Pipardum [*12th cent.*]
Size: 87 × 91 (left) 101 (right) mm
Seal: no trace of sealing

  [a] Om. in C   [b] *hiis C*
  [c] Almarico C

The dating limits are those of Roger's abbacy. This does not certainly relate to Whitley, but it appears in the section of C concerning Whitley deeds.

1205 Lease, in chirograph form, by Abbot Roger and the convent of Reading to the heirs of Robert nephew of Albold of the half hide of land which the abbot's predecessors, Anscher and Edward, had leased to the said Robert, for the same service and with the same liberty, viz., by rendering 5s annually at Michaelmas; and gift of a dwelling-house (*mansura*) below Katesgrove (*Kadeles grava*) to be held for 12d with a certain part of that grove, in exchange for the dwelling-house which the said abbots had leased to Robert next to the abbey's vineyard, in which dwelling-house they are to have the liberty called *hyusira*   [1158 × 65]

  Original charter: BL Add. Ch. 19596
  C ff 139v–140r
  Pd. Slade, 'Whitley Deeds', 243–4 (no. 7), with facsimile, pl. XXI; (cal.) Hurry,
    Reading Abbey, 167

His[a] testibus: Edrico de Lond(onia), Turstano super pontem, Ricardo card', Gaufredo clerico, Rigero[b] filio Erlide, Herberto franco.

Endorsed: Contra heredes Roberti Chieret [*12th cent.*] Wythele [*14th cent.*] Wythele [*14th cent.*] transcript' est [*14th cent.*]
Size: 125 × 98 (left) 111 (right) mm
Seal: no trace of sealing

  [a] Hiis C   [b] *Rog' C*

The dating limits are those of Roger's abbacy. For the liberty of *hyusira*, see no. 821 n. The endorsement of the original shows that Robert nephew of Albold was also called Robert *Chieret* (cf. no. 1211).

1206 Grant by King Henry II to the abbot and monks of Reading that they may enclose a park in the place called *Cumba* for the benefit (*ad opus*) of the infirm monks and guests, and precept that they are to hold it as freely as they hold anything of the king's alms

[May 1165 × May 1172]

A f 23r; B f 24r
Pd. *Mon. Ang.*, iv. 42 (no. xii); Slade, 'Whitley Deeds', 241 (no. 1)

Testibus:[a] Willelmo filio Andel',[b] Alano de Nevilla, Rad(ulfo) filio Stephani camerarii. Apud Wodestoc(am).

[a] *B ends*   [b] *Sic; ? rectius* Audel'

Since it was Abbot William I who made the park (see no. 1208), this grant almost certainly dates from his time (after 20 Jan. 1165–Feb. 1173). During this period Henry was out of England until May 1165 and, after other visits, left England in May 1172 (Eyton, 79, 167). For the identification of *Cumba* with Whitley, see Slade, *ibid.*, 236.

1207 Notification, in chirograph form, by Abbot William [I] of Reading that he has received from the land of his man, Hamo son of Thurgod the mason (*cementarius*), 53 acres to make a park and, with the consent of the convent, he has given him in exchange 11 acres beside the road leading to the park, next to the cross on the west, beyond the ditch,[a] and 42 acres in front of the house of William of Earley. Hamo shall hold the exchange in the same manner and by the same service as he or his father held the land he has given up, so long as he does the due service and keeps the fealty he has promised.

[1165 × 73]

Original charter: BL Add. Ch. 19600
C f 140r
Pd. Slade, 'Whitley Deeds', 241–2 (no. 3); (cal.) Hurry, *Reading Abbey*, 168

Endorsed: [Co]ntra Hamonem filium Thurgodi [*12th cent.*] Wythelech'
    [*14th cent.*] transscript' est [*14th cent.*]
Size: 164 × 62 mm
Seal: no trace of sealing

[a] *Om. in C*

The dating limits are those of William I's abbacy.

1208 Release, in chirograph form, by Abbot William [I] of Reading to Oddo *Cunseil*[a] and his heirs of 3s of the rent of 5s which he used to pay, on account of the abbot's enclosure of land of his tenement in the park he has made at *Cumba*, so that he will pay 2s annually with the other customs which he used to do when he held the whole land

[1165 × 73]

Original charter: BL Add. Ch. 19599
C f 140r
Pd. Slade, 'Whitley Deeds', 241 (no. 2); (cal.) Hurry, *Reading Abbey*, 168

His*b* testibus: Petro clerico, Steffano*c* clerico, Waltero coquo, Ricardo Conseil, Oddone Waverai, Ricardo de Sart', Gilleberto, Adam filio Rad(ulfi), Nicolao*d* filio Sewaldi Bedelli, Herewardo de Coll(eia).*e*

Endorsed: Contra Oddonem Cunseil [*12th cent.*] Withele [*14th cent.*] script' est [*14th cent.*]

Size: 86 × 76 mm
Seal: no trace of sealing

Consail *C*   *b* Hiis *C*
c Stephano *C*   *d* Nicholao *C*
e Colle *C*

The dating limits are those of William I's abbacy.

1209   Lease, in chirograph form, by Abbot Joseph of Reading, with the assent of the convent, to William son of Thurgod and his heirs of all the tenement of his father in and outside the borough, except that land which is contained in the abbey's park, for which William has an exchange, for 20s annually at Michaelmas. And one day in autumn he will mow with one sickle in the abbey's meadow, one day with his cart he will bring in its hay, and one day its grain (*annona*), and one day he will reap ½ acre for a custom called *nedrip*.

[1173 × 86; ?July 1182]

Original charter: BL Add. Ch. 19601
C f 140r
Pd. Slade, 'Whitley Deeds', 242 (no. 4), with facsimile, pl. XX; (cal.) Hurry, *Reading Abbey*, 169

His*a* testibus: Rogerio filio Renfrei,*b* et Edwardo*c* fratre suo, Philippo Flameng, Adam de Herleia,*d* Osberto de Risford, Petro clerico, Hugone de Duna, et Adam fratre suo, Gaffredo nepote Reimundi,*e* Walterio*f* filio Bernardi, Willelmo de Essexa, Alexandro pincerna, Willelmo Beivin,*g* Gaffredo*h* clerico, Samuel aurifabro, Nicholao de Madenhecka,*i* Rogerio*j* de Colleia, Herewardo de Colleia, et Willelmo filio suo, Simone de Herewardesleia, Ponzon de Silamsteda.*k*

Endorsed: none
Size: 155 × 140 mm
Seal: no trace of sealing

a Hiis *C*   *b* Rienfrei *C*
c 'Filword' *C* (*in error*)   *d* Erleia *C*
e Remundi *C*   *f* Waltero *C*
g Beveyn *C*   *h* Galfr' *C*
i Maidenhecka *C*   *j* Rogero *C*
k Silhamsteda *C*

The outside dating limits are those of Joseph's abbacy, but, in view of the presence of Roger son of Reinfrey among the witnesses, the deed is perhaps contemporary with no. 1213. William son of Thurgod was the brother of Hamo son of Thurgod in no. 1207.

1210 Confirmation, in chirograph form, by Abbot J(oseph) of Reading, with the assent of the convent, to William son of Thurgod and his heirs of the land which Abbot William [I] gave to Hamo his brother in exchange for the 53 acres of land which the abbey has in its park, [namely] 11 acres beside the road leading to the park, next to the cross on the west, beyond the ditch, and 42 acres in front of the house of William of Earley (*Hereleie*).[a] William shall hold the exchange in the same manner and by the same service as his brother or father held the land given up for it. [1173 × 86]

Original charter: BL Add. Ch. 19602
C f 140v
Pd. Slade, 'Whitley Deeds', 242–3 (no. 5); (cal.) Hurry, *Reading Abbey*, 168

His[b] testibus: Adam de Herleie,[a] Galfrido de Bixe, Henrico fratre suo, Waltero filio Walteri, Warino preposito, Willelmo Beivin,[c] Waltero preposito, Stephano clerico.

Endorsed: Contra Willelmum filium Turg' [*12th cent.*] Wythele [*14th cent.*] transscript' est [*14th cent.*]

Size: c. 124 × 100 mm (torn at top right corner and slightly tapering there)

Seal: no trace of sealing

[a] Erleie C
[b] Hiis C
[c] Bevin C

The dating limits are those of Joseph's abbacy.

1211 Lease, in chirograph form, by Abbot Hugh [II] and the convent of Reading to Robert the mason, brother of Thurgod, and his heirs, in exchange for his land of *Widenham*, of 14 acres of land which belonged to Peter of Cosham, 6 acres of land which belonged to Walter *de Grava*, 2 acres of land which belonged to Ailric of Whitley, 8 acres of land which belonged to Robert *Cheret*, ½ acre of land which belonged to Godwin *Gubert*, the 'island' (*insula*) of meadow which E(dward)[a] *Burnegate*[b] held in exchange for arable land, 1 acre of unploughed land next to the said Robert's house and *ubham* and *infham* which he had previously held, 1 acre of meadow which Ralph Good (*Bonus*) held, and the fifth part of meadow of five men; for 5s to be paid to the abbey annually at Michaelmas for all service; and he will send into the abbey's meadow two men with sickles to mow for one day each year. This agreement will remain in force so long as Robert

and his heirs are faithful 'and render the aforesaid fully to the abbey.'
[1186 × 99]

Original charter: BL Add. Ch. 19608
C f 139v
Pd. Slade, 'Whitley Deeds', 243 (no. 6); (cal.) Hurry, *Reading Abbey*, 171

His*d* testibus: Waltero clerico, Raimundo* mercatore, et Alano fratre
eius, Willelmo camberlano, et Willelmo pincerna, Turgiso, Waltero
cementario, et Iordano*f* fratre eius, Archenbaldo et Hamonet*g* de
Waltham, Waltero Peg', et aliis multis.

Endorsed: Inquiratur si hec sit carta que tangit Willelmum [?] Cement'
et socios eius [*14th cent.*] Whytele [*14th cent.*] script' est [*14th cent.*]
Size: 108 × 114 mm
Seal: no trace of sealing

a For expansion, see no. 1212	*b Burnegat C*
c-c Om. in C	*d Hiis C*
e Ramundo C	*f Iurdano C*
g Hamone C	

The dating limits are those of Hugh II's abbacy. The rubric of C reads: *De terra Roberti
Veysy in Wytele.* For Robert *Cheret,* cf. the endorsement of no. 1205.

1212 Grant, in chirograph form, by Abbot H(ugh) [II] and the
convent of Reading to Aldeth, widow of Edward *Burnegate,a* of maintenance from the abbey, viz., *unum annuale*, and if this is not available
the chamberlains will provide for her sufficiently otherwise. The abbot
and convent will also provide her with a cow in their pasture from
which they will have the calves and she the milk, a house, a cartload
of firewood every 15 days and suitable clothing when necessary.
[1186 × 99]

Original charter: BL Add. Ch. 19607
C f 139v
Pd. Slade, 'Whitley Deeds', 244 (no. 8); (cal.) Hurry, *Reading Abbey*, 171

Testibus: Waltero de Oxon(ia), Raimundo,*b* Reinaldo Agno, Rahero,
Iurdano de infirmaria, Osmundo, et multis aliis.

Endorsed: [*one word, illegible, 14th cent.*]
Size: 205 × 29 mm
Seal: no trace of sealing

a Burnegat C	*b Ramundo C*

The dating limits are those of Hugh II's abbacy.

1213 Gift by Peter of Cosham to Philip the Fleming, for his homage
and service and for 9s, of 1 virgate and 10 acres of land of his demesne

in Whitley, which land Richard of Cosham held, and the whole meadow of *la Bournemed* and a tilery (*tegularia*). To be held in fee and inheritance by rendering annually to the donor 1 lb of cumin at Christmas for all service. Philip and his heirs will have their animals (*averia*) anywhere in pasture with the animals of the donor's court. Sealing   25 July 1182

C f 151r; (noted) A f 38r; B f 53r; C f 22r
Pd. Slade, 'Whitley Deeds', 245 (no. 10)

Facta est autem hec donatio ad festum sancti Iacobi proximum post decessum venerabilis viri domini Rogeri Eboracensis archiepiscopi. Teste*a* Rogero filio Reinf(ridi), et multis aliis.

a Sic

Roger of Pont l'Evêque, archbishop of York, died 26 Nov. 1181.

1214   Gift by Peter of Cosham to Walter *le Waleys*, for his service and because Peter's father Thurstan (*Turstinus*)*a* brought him up, of the croft called *Buriham*, the croft called *Walcroftam*, $2\frac{1}{2}$ acres in *Sutham* next to the land of Robert the mason (*Mazo*), 4 selions in *Waldesham*, 1 acre on the hill next to the acre of Oddo *Connseil*, and a meadow belonging to *Walcroftam*. To be held in fee and inheritance for 2s at Michaelmas, freely and quit of all other service, apart from royal service and one day's mowing with one man in the donor's meadow. He has made this gift for the soul of his father Thurstan (*Turstanus*).
                                                        [before Feb. 1184]

C f 151r-v; (noted) B f 53r; C f 22r
Pd. Slade, 'Whitley Deeds', 245 (no. 11)

Hiis testibus: Roberto de Ricford, et aliis.

a Interlined

Before the latest possible date for Henry II's confirmation of Peter of Cosham's gift to Reading Abbey of all his land in Whitley (see nos. 1216–7). The present deed is headed *Whyteleya*. Thurstan was called 'of Cosham' (see, e.g., no. 1218) and, since Peter of Cosham was also called 'of Whitley' (no. 1215), Thurstan is no doubt also the Thurstan of Whitley who occurs in no. 1197.

1215   Concession by Peter of Whitley to Robert brother of Gilbert of the land which he [Peter] had from Reading Abbey in exchange for 1 acre. To be held by him and his heirs of Peter and his heirs by hereditary right for 2s annually at Michaelmas, free and quit of all custom and other service, and as freely as any of his men holds land of him. For this Robert has given him 8s   [before Feb. 1184]

C f 151v
Pd. Slade, 'Whitley Deeds', 246 (no. 12)

Hiis testibus: Petro clerico, et aliis.

Date as for no. 1214. Peter of Whitley was alias Peter of Cosham.

1216   Gift in free alms by Peter of Cosham to Reading Abbey of his whole land of Whitley in and outside the borough. To be held freely for an entry-fine of £80 and an annual payment of 1 bezant to him and his heirs within the octave of St James [25 July] at Reading for all service and custom. Warranty   [25 July 1182 × Feb. 1184]

A ff 37v–38r; B f 53r; C f 22r; C f 151r
Pd. Slade, 'Whitley Deeds', 244–5 (no. 9)

Testibus:*a* Philippo de Duna,*b* Walterio de Oxoneford, Reimundo mercatore, multisque aliis testibus.

a B,C f 22r end
b C f 151r has Dune and ends with et multis aliis

After no. 1213, where Peter is still disposing of land in Whitley, and before no. 1217, Henry II's confirmation of the present gift. For discussion, see Slade, *ibid.*, 238.

1217   Confirmation by King Henry II of the agreement and fine made between Reading Abbey and Peter of Cosham and recorded in the king's court before his justices, concerning the land of Whitley which Peter has given to the abbey in free alms for an entry-fine of £80 and for 1 bezant to be paid to him and his heirs annually for all service and custom, with warranty, as the chirograph made between them and as Peter's charter witness   [3 July 1183 × 16 Feb. 1184]

A f 24v; B f 24r–v
Pd. Slade, 'Whitley Deeds', 246 (no. 13)

Testibus:*a* R(icardo) Cant(uariensi) archiepiscopo, W(altero) Linc-(olniensi), B(aldewino) Wigorn(iensi) episcopis, comite Willelmo de Mandevilla, Seherio de Quinci, Hugone de Creissi, Roberto de Stu-tevill(a), Hugone de Morwich dapifero, Hugone Bard(ulf) dapifero, Gaufr(edo) filio Petri, Gisleberto filio Reinfr(idi). Apud Ebroicas.

a B ends

After the consecration of Walter of Coutances as bishop of Lincoln and before the death of Richard of Dover, archbishop of Canterbury. For discussion, see Slade, *ibid.*, 238.

1218   *Gift by Christina, daughter of Thurstan of Cosham, to Hugh of Pagham,*

clerk, of her part of the land of Whitley, viz., a fourth part of the land of
Whitley held by her father at his death   [1198 × early 13th cent.]

C f 145r; (noted) B f 53r; C f 22r

Sciant presentes et futuri ad quos presens scriptum pervenerit quod
ego Cristina filia Thurstani de Cosham, per assensum et petitionem
Ricardi filii et heredis mei, dedi et concessi et presenti carta et sigillo
meo confirmavi Hugoni de Pageham clerico, pro servitio suo et homagio, totam partem terre de Whitele que me contingebat, scilicet totam
quartam partem totius terre de Whitele quam Thurstanus pater meus
tenuit die qua fuit vivus et mortuus. Tenend(am) sibi et heredibus
suis de me et heredibus meis libere quiete integre pacifice et honorifice
et plenarie *a*in bosco et*a* in plano, in viis et in semitis, in pascuis, aquis
et piscariis et vivariis et pratis, reddendo michi et heredibus meis pro
se et heredibus suis annuatim unum librum piperis ad festum sancti
Egidii [1 Sept.] *b*[pro omni servitio]*b* ad me vel heredes meos pertinent', salvo servitio regali. Hiis testibus, et cetera.

a–a Interlined
b–b Om. in Ms; suggested reading to complete the sense

Christina and her sister Alice (see no. 1219) were the two surviving sisters of Peter of
Cosham and, with the sons of two other predeceased sisters, were his coheirs at his
death (*The Cartulary of God's House, Southampton*, ed. J. M. Kaye (Southampton Records
Ser., 1976), i. 170 n. 20). Peter was alive in 1198, when he was preparing to set out for
the Holy Land (S. F. Hockey, *Quarr Abbey and its Lands* (Leicester, 1970), 52), but was
dead by 20 Nov. 1198, when Christina and Alice renounced to God's House their claim
in his land on the Isle of Wight (*Cartulary of God's House*, i. 177–8). The William of
Cosham mentioned in nos. 1219–20 was the son of a predeceased sister. From the
evidence of the Reading and God's House deeds the following genealogy can be drawn:

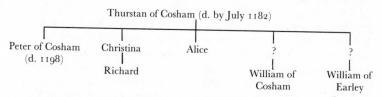

The order of birth of Thurstan's children is not known. Thurstan and Peter were
also called 'of Whitley' (see no. 1214 n.).

1219   *Confirmation by Alice, daughter of Thurstan of Cosham, of the gift to*
Hugh of Pagham, clerk, by William of Cosham her nephew of land at Cosham
[Hants.], and of the gift to the same Hugh by Christina her sister of her part
of the land of Cosham and of Whitley   [1198 × early 13th cent.]

C f 145r; (noted) B f 53r–v; C f 22v

Sciant presentes et futuri ad quos presens scriptum pervenerit quod ego Alicia filia Turstani de Cosham ratam habui et concessi et presenti carta et sigillo meo confirmavi totam donationem concessionem vel conventionem factam inter Hugonem de Pageham clericum et Willelmum de Cosham nepotem meum de terra de Cosham. Concessi etiam et hac carta et sigillo meo confirmavi omnem donationem seu venditionem vel conventionem factam inter prefatum Hugonem de Pageham et Cristinam sororem meam vel heredes suos de parte sua de terra de Cosham et de terra de Whiteleya sicut scriptum inter eos factum testatur. Tenend(as) sibi et heredibus suis de prefato Willelmo de Cosham vel Cristina et de heredibus eorum. Testibus: Guid(one) priore de Suþwic',ᵃ et cetera.

ᵃ *Ms has* Ouywic', *prob. a misreading of* Suþwic'

Date as for no. 1218. The dates of Guy's priorate of Southwick (Hants.) are uncertain, but he was prior by 1186 and was still in office in 1206; his predecessor occurs in 1177 and his next recorded successor died in 1227 (*Heads of Relig. Houses*, 184).

1220 *Confirmation by Christina, daughter of Thurstan of Cosham, of the gift to Hugh of Pagham, clerk, by William of Cosham her nephew of land at Cosham, and of the gift to the same Hugh by Alice [? his] wife, her sister, of Alice's part of the land of Cosham and of Whitley*

[1198 × early 13th cent.]

C f 145v; (noted) B f 53v; C f 22v

Sciant presentes et futuri ad quos presens scriptum pervenerit quod ego Christina filia Turstani de Cosham ratam habui et concessi et presenti carta et sigillo meo confirmavi totam donationem vel concessionem factam inter Hugonem de Pageham clericum et Willelmum de Cosham nepotem meum de terra de Cosham. Concessi etiam et hac carta mea confirmavi omnem donationem seu venditionem vel conventionem factam inter ipsum Hugonem de Pageham et Adelidem uxoremᵃ sororem meam vel heredes suos de parte sua de terra de Cosham et de terra de Whiteleia, sicut scriptum inter eos factum testatur. Tenend(as) sibi Hugoni et heredibus suis de prefatis Willelmo de Cosham et Adelide et de heredibus eorum. Test(ibus), et cetera.

ᵃ *? either* suam *or* eius, *or possibly another name,* om.

Date as for no. 1218. The deed between Hugh of Pagham and Alice to which this confirmation refers cannot be no. 1219, since that is a confirmation of other gifts to Hugh. It is far from certain that Alice was Hugh of Pagham's wife, but not impossible, since Hugh may not have been a clerk in orders. However, if they were married, the terms of this deed and of no. 1219 seem very odd, and it may be that *uxorem* here should be treated as an undeleted error.

1221 Final concord in the king's court at Winchester in the quindene of the Purification [2 Feb.], 33 Henry III, before Henry of Bath (*Bathon'*), Alan of Wassand (*Wasand*), William of Wilton (*Wilton'*), Reginald of Cobham (*Cobeham*) and William *le Breton'*, justices-in-eyre, and others, between Henry *Wille*, plaintiff, and John *de Solkeden'* and Ela his wife, defending, concerning a moiety of 174 acres of land and of 8s rent in Whitley (*Witteleg'*) and Reading. Plea of convention. John and Ela recognized the said moiety to be the right of Henry as that which he has by their gift, to be held by him and his heirs of them and the heirs of Ela in perpetuity by rendering annually 6d sterling at Michaelmas for all service, custom and exaction, and by doing to the chief lords of the fee all other pertinent services on behalf of John and Ela and the heirs of Ela. Warranty. For this Henry gave them 50s sterling. 16 Feb. 1249

A f 89v; (noted) B f 166v

The foot of this fine is PRO CP 25(1)/8/19/1.

1222 Final concord in the same court on the same date and before the same justices, between John Dyer (*le Teynturer*), plaintiff, and John *de Sulkeden'* and Ela his wife, defending, concerning a moiety of 174 acres of land and of 8s rent in Whitley (*Witel'*) and Reading. Plea of convention. John and Ela recognized the said moiety to be the right of John Dyer as that which [etc., as in no. 1221]. Warranty. For this John Dyer gave them 50s sterling. 16 Feb. 1249

A f 89v; (noted) B f 166v

The foot of this fine, which is *mutatis mutandis* identical with no. 1221, is PRO CP 25(1)/8/19/2.

1223 Gift by John *de Sulkedene* and Ela his wife to Henry *Wille* and John Dyer (*tinctor*) of Reading, of their whole land in Whitley (*Witele*),[a] viz., that which Thomas Bachelor (*le Bacheler*), John *Smud*[b] and Matilda the widow held of them in villeinage; and of all their right in the land which Hugh *Maysant*[c] held of them and in the land which Hugh *le Bulur*[d] had by gift of Hamo *de Hamme*; and of all lands, rents and possessions which they had in Reading. To be held freely, with homages, reliefs, rents, pleas, perquisites (*purgacia*), wardships, suits, heriots, escheats and all liberties, by rendering annually to Reading Abbey and due and customary service, and to the donors and their heirs 12d as increment at Michaelmas for all secular service, exaction, custom and demand. For this Henry and John have given them 100s of silver as entry-fine. Warranty and sealing with the donors' seals

[*c.* 16 Feb. 1249]

A ff 88v–89r; C f 146r; (noted) B f 53v; C f 22v

Hiis testibus: Daniele Wulveseye,^{ef}Roberto Wille, Thoma de Hannele, Nicholao clerico, Ada clerico, Johanne Wille, Jurdano Luvekin, Thoma cissore, Thoma mercatore, Roberto Benschef, Hugone de Kenethewod', Gileberto Franckelano de Witele, Nicholao Cunsail, Stephano clerico,^{f} et multis aliis.

<table>
<tr><td>^{a}Whitele C</td><td>^{b}Reading uncertain; Sund C (Cf. no. 1235)</td></tr>
<tr><td>^{c}Maisent C</td><td>^{d}Bolur C</td></tr>
<tr><td>^{e}Wlveseye C</td><td>$^{f-f}$Om. in C</td></tr>
</table>

Contemporary with the final concords, nos. 1221–2.

1224 Quitclaim by Henry *Wille* to Reading Abbey of all his right in a moiety of 174 acres of land and of 8s rent in Whitley (*Witeleye*)^a and Reading, which he had by gift of John *de Sulkedene*^{b} and Ela his wife, and concerning which a final concord was made between them in the king's court at Winchester in the quindene of the Purification, 33 Henry III, before Henry of Bath (*Bathon'*) and his fellow justices-in-eyre. To be held freely in perpetuity by rendering annually, on behalf of Henry and his heirs, to the said John and Ela and the heirs of Ela 6d sterling at Michaelmas for all service, custom and exaction. For this the abbey has given him 6½ marks of silver. Sealing

[? 1249]

A f 88v; B f 53v; C f 22v; C f 152r

Hiis testibus:^{c} Daniele Wlveseg',^{d} Roberto Wille, Thoma le Tayllur, Nicholao clerico, Willelmo de Musselden', Thoma de Hanl(e), Henrico de Lastane, Stephano de La Wile, Roberto Bensyeph, Hugone de Kenetwde, Willelmo Le Poer, et multis aliis.

<table>
<tr><td>^{a}Whitele C f 152r</td><td>^{b}Sukkedene C f 152r</td></tr>
<tr><td colspan="2">^{c}B,C f 22v end</td></tr>
<tr><td colspan="2">^{d}C f 152r has Wlveseye and ends with et aliis</td></tr>
</table>

It seems likely that this and no. 1225, which together conveyed to the abbey the two moieties which Henry Wille and John Dyer had obtained from John *de Sulkedene* and his wife in nos. 1221–3, passed on the same date. Since seven of the present witnesses also witnessed no. 1223, the date is possibly not long after that of the final concords.

1225 Quitclaim by John Dyer (*le Teynturer*) of Reading to Reading Abbey of all his right in a moiety of 174 acres of land and of 8s rent in Whitley (*Witeleye*)^a and Reading, which he had [etc., as in no. 1224]. To be held freely in perpetuity by rendering annually, on behalf of John and his heirs, to John *de Sulkedene* and Ela and the heirs of Ela 6d sterling at Michaelmas [etc.]. For this the abbey has given him 6½ marks of silver. Sealing [? 1249]

A f 89r; C f 152r; (noted) B f 53v

His[b] testibus:[c] [Daniele Wlvesegh', et aliis].

[a] Whiteley C   [b] Hiis C
[c] A ends, the remainder being supplied from C

Probably contemporary with no. 1224.

1226 Remission by William *Bastard*[a] of all action which he had or could have in the assarts and purprestures made in Whitley (*Witel'*)[b] by the abbot of Reading and his men up to the feast of St Simon and St Jude, 36 Henry III. Sealing[c] [c. 28 Oct. 1251]

B f 53r; C f 22r; C f 144r

Hiis testibus:[d] [Rogero de Hyda, et aliis].

[a] le Bastard C f 144r   [b] Whitele C f 144r
[c] C f 22r ends
[d] B ends, the remainder being supplied from C f 144r

The date is probably close to the *terminus* stated in the deed.

1227 Remission and quitclaim by Alan *Lysewis*[a] of Hartley (*Horthleg'*)[b] of all action which he had or could have in the assarts and purprestures made in Whitley (*Witeleya*)[c] by the abbot of Reading and his men. For this the abbot has given him ½ mark of silver. Sealing [c. mid-13th cent.]

B f 53r; C ff 22v–23r; C f 145r

Hiis testibus:[d] [domino Willelmo de Engelfeld', et aliis].

[a] Lesewys C f 145r
[b] Horthlegh' C ff 22v–23r, Hurthleghe C f 145r
[c] Whitelegh' C f 145r
[d] B,C ff 22v–23r end, the remainder being supplied from C f 145r

Possibly of similar date to no. 1226 and certainly not later than 1258, since it was entered in the original section of B. Alan *de Lisewys* of Shinfield occurs in 1248 (Clanchy, *Berks. Eyre of 1248*, 483).

1228 Quitclaim by Henry of Earley (*Erlegh'*), knight, to Reading Abbey of all his right in a path (*semita*) in the field called *Berefeld'*, which path is between the vill of Reading and Earley (*Erleya*), so that neither he nor his heirs will be able to demand or claim any right in the path while the said field is under crop (*seminatus*). Sealing

[1231 × 72; ? 1258 × 72]

C f 147r

Hiis testibus: domino Waltero de Ripariis, et aliis.

A Henry of Earley succeeded his brother John as lord of the manor of Earley White-knights in 1231, was living in 1251 and died in 1272 (*VCH Berks.*, iii. 214). The suggested dating from 1258 is based on the very inconclusive evidence that the deed was neither entered nor noted in B.

1229 Gift by Walter *de la Wyke* and Emma his wife to John *Monncy*, for his service, of two crofts of land enclosed by hedge and ditch on all sides in Whitley (*Whitele*), extending south–north and at their southern end lying between Walter's messuage and the king's road under the park of Reading Abbey, viz., along either side of the road leading to the court (*curia*) of Sir Henry of Earley (*Erle*). To be held freely by rendering annually to the donors and their heirs or assigns 3d, viz., 1½d each at Michaelmas and Easter, for all secular services, exactions [etc.]. For this John has given them 6 marks of silver as entry-fine. Warranty and sealing with the donors' seals

[? *c.* 1250 × 1272]

C f 147r

Hiis testibus: domino Waltero de Ripariis, et aliis.

Before the death of Henry of Earley (see no. 1228 n.). Walter de la Wyke occurs in 1248 and 1261 (Clanchy, *Berks. Eyre of 1248*, 397; PRO JUST 1/40, m. 13). John *Muncy* occurs as a vintner in Reading in 1261 and 1284 and was a juror for Reading vill in 1269 (JUST 1/40, m. 29d, 1/44, m. 15, 1/42, m. 19).

1230 Gift by Walter *de la Wyke* to John *Monncy*, for his service, of 1 acre of land in the vill of Whitley (*Whitele*) in a croft opposite Walter's messuage and lying between Walter's land on each side and extending northwards from the road leading to the court of Henry of Earley at its southern end (*et extendit se in parte australi a chemino que* [sic] *ducit apud curiam Henrici de Erle versus aquilonem*). To be held freely by rendering annually to the donor and his heirs 1d at Michaelmas for all services, exactions, customs, suits of court and all manner of secular demands. For this John has given him 14s sterling as entry-fine. Warranty and sealing   [? *c.* 1250 × 1272]

C f 147v

Hiis testibus: Rolando de Erle, et multis aliis.

Date as for no. 1229. Roland had become a knight by May 1270 (see no. 759), but the omission of *domino* in the witness-list is not certainly reliable; Roland was dead by June 1305 (see no. 1257).

1231 Gift by Walter *de la Wyke* to John *Monncy*, for his service, of a croft of land enclosed by hedge and ditch on all sides in the vill of Whitley (*Whitele*), lying between the king's road and the road leading to the court of Sir Henry of Earley (*Erle*), and extending from north to south as far as the land of Robert the forester (*forestarius*). To be held freely by rendering annually to the donor and his heirs or assigns 2d, viz., 1d each at the Nativity of St John Baptist and Michaelmas, for all services [etc., as in no. 1230]. For this John has given him 2 marks of silver as entry-fine. Warranty and sealing

[? *c.* 1250 × 1272]

C ff 147v-148r

Hiis testibus: Rolando de Erle, et multis aliis.

Date as for no. 1229; see also no. 1230 n.

1232 Gift by Emma, daughter of Walter *de la Wyke*,[a] to John *Monncy*, for his service, of a croft of land enclosed by hedge and ditch on all sides in the vill of Whitley (*Whitele*) lying between the king's road [etc., as in no. 1231]. To be held freely by rendering annually to the donor and her heirs or assigns 2d, viz., 1d each at the Nativity of St John Baptist and Michaelmas, for all services [etc., as in no. 1230]. For this John has given her 2 marks of silver as entry-fine. Warranty and sealing [1261 × 72]

C f 148r–v

Hiis testibus: Rolando de Erle, et multis aliis.

[a] *Ms has* Wyle

The text is *mutatis mutandis* the same as that of no. 1231. It appears to be a confirmation given after her father's death and dates between 1261, when he was still living, and 1272, when Henry of Earley died (see no. 1229 n.).

1233 Gift by Emma, daughter of Walter *de la Wyke*, to John *Monncy*, for his service, of 1 acre of land in Whitley (*Whiteleya*) in a croft opposite Emma's messuage and lying between Emma's land on each side and extending northwards from the road leading to the court of Henry of Earley (*Erle*) at its southern end. To be held freely by rendering annually to the donor and her heirs 1d at Michaelmas for all services [etc., as in no. 1230]. For this John has given her 14s sterling as entry-fine. Warranty and sealing [1261 × 72]

C f 148v

Hiis testibus: Rolando de Erle, Rogero de Erle, et multis aliis.

The text is *mutatis mutandis* the same as that of no. 1230. Date as for no. 1232.

1234 Gift by Bartholomew Wolvesey (*Wlveseye*) to John *Monncy*, for his service, of $\frac{1}{2}$ acre of land with ditch lying next to Katesgrove (*Cadelesgrave*) between the lane (*viculus*) leading to Katesgrove and the land of Geoffrey the smith (*faber*). To be held freely by rendering annually to the donor and his heirs 5d at Michaelmas for all service, custom, suit of court, secular exaction and demand. For this John has given him 1 mark of silver as entry-fine. Warranty and sealing

[*c.* 1260 × 1284]

C f 148r

Hiis testibus: Willelmo de Colley, et multis aliis.

The donor was the son and heir of Daniel Wolvesey, who was living in 1254 but dead by Feb. 1261 (see no. 69; PRO JUST 1/40, m. 12). The donor was dead by Oct. 1284 (JUST 1/43, m. 9). For John Monncy, see no. 1229 n. William of Coley was coroner of the Liberty of Reading in 1261 and of Reading hundred in 1284 (see no. 1054 n.).

1235 *Concession and remission by John Sund to Simon Lovel of half the land and tenement in Whitley which he, John, shall be able to recover as his inheritance before the king's justices, so that Simon shall aid him in the recovery. If John breaks this agreement, the sheriff of Berkshire shall distrain him, taking 20s for each distraint and levying 1 mark for the fabric of Westminster Abbey*

15 June 1268

C f 146v

Omnibus Christi fidelibus ad quos presens scriptum pervenerit Johannes Sund, salutem in domino. Noverit universitas vestra me concessisse et remisisse Simoni Lovel et heredibus suis vel suis assignatis medietatem totius terre et tenementi cum omnibus pertinentiis quam coram justic(iariis) domini regis in villa de Whitele occasione hereditatis mee potero recuperare, ita quod dictus Simon michi sit in auxilio dicte terre perquirende. Et si vero contingat me vel aliquo[a] alio nomine contra convencionem resistere vel venire, concedo quod vicecomes Berk' qui pro tempore fuerit me distringat per omnia bona mea mobilia et inmobilia ubicumque fuerint inventa ad dictam convencionem retinere, et quod pro qualibet districtione facienda de bonis meis propriis habeat viginti solidos, et quod levat fabrice ecclesie Westm(onasterii) unam marcam. Et quod hoc firmum sit et stabile, huic scripto sigillum meum apposui. Hiis testibus: Willelmo Colleg', et aliis. Dat' die veneris proxima post festum sancti Barnabe apostoli [11 June], anno regni regis Henrici filii regis Johannis quinquagesimo secundo.

^a *Possibly in error for* aliquem

This deed was made during the Berkshire eyre of 1268, which was in session in Reading 4–27 June (Clanchy, *Berks. Eyre of 1248*, xcvii). It has been printed in full on account of its very interesting provisions.

1236 Quitclaim by Joan, widow of Simon Lovel (*Lovel*), to Reading Abbey of all her right in name of dower in a third part of the tenement which belonged to the said Simon her husband in the vill of Whitley (*Whiteleya*). For this the abbot has given her 1 mark of silver. She agrees (*volo et concedo*) to have her boys in her custody until they come of age without demanding anything from the abbey or from any tenement in Whitley for their maintenance or cost. Sealing

[1268 × c. 1280]

C f 146r–v

Hiis testibus: Hervico Belet, et multis aliis.

After no. 1235, where Simon Lovel is alive. Hervey Belet held the manor of Southcote in 1242/3 and occurs as late as 1275 (*Fees*, ii. 863; above, no. 764).

1237 Concession by Roger de Mortimer (*de Mortuo mari*) that the abbot and convent of Reading and their men may have and hold peacefully all purprestures so far made by the abbot and convent and their men, in woods and in other places, on the eastern side of the road from Winchester (*Wynton'*) to Reading in the vill of Whitley (*Whitele*), and cultivate and enclose them without impediment of him or his heirs or their bailiffs or ministers. Sealing   18 Apr. 1273

C f 144r

Dat' apud Stratfeld' die martis quintodecimo kalend' Maii, anno domini millesimo ducentesimo septuagesimo tercio. Hiis testibus: domino Roberto Fokes tunc justic(iario), et aliis.

In 1273 the 15th kalend of May, i.e. 17 Apr., fell on a Monday. I have assumed that Tuesday 18 Apr. is intended. Sir Robert Fokes is to be identified with the royal justice, Sir Robert Fulconis, who had local interests (see nos. 880–3, 1029–30) and was dead by 8 Sept. 1287 (see no. 880 n.). Whether he witnessed here in a judicial capacity is unknown.

1238 Agreement, in duplicate (*scriptum bipartitum*), between Reading Abbey and John *de Monasterio* of Shinfield (*Shinngfeud*) by which John has quitclaimed to the abbot and convent and their successors all purprestures made in the vill of Whitley (*Whitele*) by the abbot or by anyone else from the beginning of the world to the feast of the Nativity of St John Baptist, 2 Edward I, for which the abbey was quitclaimed to John and his heirs or assigns in perpetuity a purpresture in the vill of Whitley between the purpresture of Nicholas of Diddenham (*Didenham*) and Whitley Wood (*boscus de Whitele*) for 3s 6d to the abbey annually at the Annunciation for all secular service, exaction and demand. Sealing by both parties   [*c.* 24 June 1274]

C f 144r–v

Hiis testibus: domino Rolando de Erle, milite, et aliis.

The date is probably close to the *terminus* stated in the deed.

1239 Lease for life, in chirograph form, by Abbot Robert [of Burgate] and the convent of Reading to Robert of Preston (*Preston'*) of the messuage and whole land which belonged to Eborald *Crapalt'* in the vill of Whitley (*Whiteleye*). Robert will provide the said Eborald with his needs for as long as he shall live, as may be agreed between them, and render annually to the abbot and convent 1d at Michaelmas for all secular service, exaction and demand. Robert will not burden the abbey's pasture more than belongs to the said tenement, and after his death it will revert to the abbey in the same state as it was before he received it. Warranty for his life and sealing with their seals

12 Nov. 1284

C f 141r

Dat' in capitulo nostro Radyng' in crastino sancti Martini [11 Nov.], anno domini M.CC. octogesimo quarto.

1240 Agreement, in chirograph form, dated Tuesday after the quindene of Easter, 13 Edward I, between Abbot Robert [of Burgate] and the convent of Reading, on one side, and Sir John son of Roger de St John, lord of Swallowfield (*Swalefeld*), on the other, in a dispute concerning certain woodland (*solum et boscus*) lying between the abbey's land of Whitley (*Wytel'*)[a] and that of the said John at Shinfield (*Shinigefeld*),[b] beginning at *Collane* and extending, along the ditch of the tenants of John at Shinfield[c] and the old boundary sometime made with the abbey's side in Whitley,[a] as far as the cultivated strip (*cultura*) of the said John called *Cock(es)muome*.[d] The woodland is to be equally divided by consent of the parties, the half nearer to the abbot and convent remaining to them in fee and inheritance and belonging to their liberty of Reading, the other half nearer to John remaining to him and his heirs freely and by hereditary right, neither side being able to demand or claim any right or claim in the other's part, except for pasture on a mutual basis there as in times past. Sealing *alternatim*

10 Apr. 1285

B f 171v; C f 102r; C f 144v

Hiis testibus' et presentibus; dominis Ricardo de Coleshull', Rolando de Erle, Thoma Huscarl', Bartholomeo de Erl(e), militibus, Willelmo de Blebir'ˢ senescallo Rading', Waltero Dragu(n), Johanne de Flore, Johanne de Sottesbroc, Willelmo de la Hou, Gilberto Pyncun, Johanne de Shaldeford,ᵍ Roberto de Wautham, et aliis. Dat' et act' die et anno quibus supra.

ᵃ Whitele *C both*
ᵇ Shingfeld' *C f 102r*, Shenyngfeld' *C f 144v*
ᶜ Shenyngfeld' *C f 144v*
ᵈ Cockmuome *C f 102r*, Cockesmuome *C f 144v*
ᵉ *C f 144v ends with* et cetera   ᶠ Bleobir' *C f 102r*
ᵍ Shaldeforde *C f 102r*

Sir John St John was lord of the manor of Shinfield, which seems normally to have been regarded as part of his manor of Swallowfield (*VCH Berks.*, iii. 262, 268).

1241 Gift by Abbot William [II] and the convent of Reading to Walter *Gerard* of Reading of a piece (*pecia*) of land formerly belonging to William *Bournegat'* in the vill of Whitley (*Whitele*) in the field of *Twelfacres* between the land of William *de la Welde* on the east and that of Nicholas *Connsail* on the west. To be held freely by rendering annually to the donors and their successors 12d, viz., 6d each at Michaelmas and Easter, for all secular service, exaction and demand. In exchange for this Walter has given the abbot and convent a piece of land in *la Wynerchfeld'* between the abbot's land on one side and that formerly belonging to William of Missenden (*Mussindene*) on the other. Warranty and sealing   [1290 × 1305; ? Dec. 1290]

C f 140v

Hiis testibus: dominis Rolando de Erle, Rogero de Burghfeld', Bartholomeo de Erle, militibus, Roberto de Prestone, Willelmo de Blebury, Gilberto Pinzon, Johanne Vachel, Rad(ulf)o de Bello, Willelmo le Chamberlayn, Johanne le Acatour, Thomaᵃ Syward', et multis aliis.

ᵃ *Ms has* Thomas

The outside dating limits are those of William II's abbacy, but comparison with the witness-list of no. 1245 suggests that this may be of similar date.

1242 Gift and quitclaim in free alms by Walterᵃ *Gerard* of Reading

correct, he was acting as abbot before diocesan confirmation and therefore also before doing fealty to the Crown and receiving the temporalities from the prior and convent (see *Cal. Close R. 1288–96*, 154–5). The date is possibly incorrect, however, since the unusual form 'on the day of St Nicholas' suggests the omission of a particular day of the week 'next following the feast of St Nicholas', which would be a more normal method of dating and might take the date beyond that of the diocesan confirmation.

1247 Gift in free alms by William *Maysent* to Reading Abbey of the meadow which he had in the vill of Whitley (*Whiteley*) called *Suthammesmed*, and of 5s annual rent in the same vill which he used to receive from Richard son of William of Whitley from a croft called *Hutham*. Warranty and sealing   [? before Dec. 1290]

C f 153r–v

Hiis testibus: domino Rolando de Erley, et multis aliis.

Certainly before 24 June 1305, by which date Abbot William II had died, since Roland of Earley predeceased the abbot (see no. 1257). This makes it probable that the donor is the same as that of nos. 1243–5, who made over to the abbey his whole tenement in Whitley in Dec. 1290 (nos. 1245–6).

1248 Release and quitclaim by Peter son of Walter Parker (*le Parker*) to Reading Abbey of the whole tenement which sometime belonged to the said Walter his father in Whitley (*Whitele*).[a] Sealing[b]
19 Mar. 1291

C f 146v; B f 155r; C f 94r

'Dat' Radyng' die lune proxima ante festum Annunciacionis beate Marie, anno regni regis Edwardi decimo nono.[c] Hiis testibus:[d] magistro Stephano de Wycumbe, et multis aliis.

[a] Wytteleye *B*	[b] *B,C f 94r omit most of sealing clause*
[c-c] *Om. in B,C f 94r*	[d] *B ends, C f 94r ends with* et cetera

The reading of C f 146v is preferred, since, although B is an earlier copy (later copied on C f 94r), it severely abbreviates the sealing clause, omits the dating clause and gives no witnesses. The rubrics of B and C f 94r describe the tenement as the land of Walter *de Parco*.

1249 Gift and release in free alms, indented, by William de Monterville (*de Monte Revell(i)*[a]), knight,[b] to Reading Abbey of 12 acres of arable land lying behind the leper hospital and formerly belonging to John of Woodcote (*Wodecote*), to be held quit of all secular service. In exchange for this the abbot and convent have given him the whole tenement which, at the time this deed was made, they had by demise of William *Maysent* in the vill of Whitley (*Whiteleye*),[c] to be held by him and his heirs by rendering annually to the abbey, both for the

lands and tenements which belonged to John of Woodcote and for
the lands and tenements which belonged to William *Maisannt*,[d] 5s at
Michaelmas for all service. He will not be allowed to have common
[of pasture] in the abbot's demesnes by reason of the said tenement
other than in the fields of *Foxle*, *Twelfacres* and *Clerkenewellefeld*. Mutual
warranty and sealing *alternatim*   1 Apr. 1291

    C f 142r; C f 149r

Dat'[e] Radyng' die dominica proxima post festum Annunciacionis[f]
beate Marie,[g] anno regni regis Edwardi [h]filii regis Henrici[h] decimo
nono. Hiis testibus:[i] Rolando de Erley,[j] Bartholomeo de Erle,
militibus, Gilberto Pinson, Willelmo de Bleobury, Johanne Fachel,
Willelmo de Baylollo, Willelmo de Colleye, Thoma de Kenetwode, et
aliis.

  [a] Rivelli *C f 149r*   [b] *Om. in C f 149r*
  [c] Whiteley *C f 149r*   [d] Maysent *C f 149r*
  [e] *Insert* apud *C f 149r*   [f] *C f 142r has* Anuciacionis
  [g] *Insert* virginis *C f 149r*   [h-h] *Om. in C f 149r*
  [i] *Insert* dominis *C f 149r*
  [j] *C f 149r has* Erle *and ends with* et cetera

It is clear from a note after C f 149r that the two texts in the cartulary were two
separate charters *sub eisdem verbis*. The text on C f 142r is in the original hand of the
second main part of the cartulary, that on f 149r is in a different 14th-century hand.

1250 Recognition by William de Monterville (*de Monte Revelli*) that,
although the whole tenement which belonged to William *Maysent* of
Whitley (*Wyteleye*) is contained in the enfeoffment made to him by
the abbot and convent of Reading, neither he nor his heirs will be
able to claim any right or claim, by reason of the said enfeoffment, in
the messuage, curtilage and garden in which William *Maysent* used to
live, which are to remain to the abbot and convent and their successors
in perpetuity. Sealing   1 Apr. 1291

    C f 149r

Dat' apud Radyng' die dominica proxima post festum Annunciacionis
beate Marie virginis, anno regni regis E(dwardi) xix. Hiis testibus:
dominis Rolando de Erle, Bartholomeo de Erle, Johanne de Thede-
merssh, Johanne de Chause, militibus, Willelmo de Bleburi, Johanne
Vachel, Willelmo de Colle, Thoma de Kentwode, et aliis.

1251 Lease for life, indented, by Abbot William [II] and the convent
of Reading to Sir William de Monterville (*de Monte Rivelli*), for his
past and future laudable service, of the whole tenement which Richard
of Whitley (*Wytele*) held of them for life called *Dwoleslond* in the vill

of Whitley (*Whitele*); to be held for life freely without any payment of rent. Warranty for life. Reversion to the abbey after his death. For this William concedes and has sworn a corporal oath that in the future he will to his power assist, maintain and promote all the affairs of the abbey (*omnia negocia ecclesiam Rading' contingentia*) and defend them wheresoever (*penes quoscumque*) and will procure their defence and protection whenever and as often as he shall be asked by the abbot and convent or their proctor. He further concedes never to seek, demand or procure anything of the abbey's demesne lands, pastures, tenements or rents to the prejudice or loss of the abbey or against its will, nor to retain anything gained in this way, nor to attempt anything himself or through his [men] to the injury of the abbey or to permit any such attempt. Sealing by both parties   1 Apr. 1291

C f 149r

Dat' Rading' die dominica proxima post festum Annunciacionis beate Marie virginis, anno regni regis Edwardi xix. Hiis testibus: domino Rolando de Erle, Bartholomeo de Erle, et multis aliis, et cetera.

1252   Quitclaim by William de Monterville (*de Monte Revelli*), knight, to Abbot William [II] and the convent of Reading of all his right in the messuage and curtilage formerly belonging to William *Maisent* in Whitley (*Whytelee*), and in any action whatsoever which he could have against them in respect of the same. Sealing   2 Apr. 1291

C f 149r–v

Dat' die lune proxima post oct(avas) Annunciacionis beate Marie, anno regni regis E(dwardi) xix.

1253   Gift, release and quitclaim in free alms by Clemencia, widow of Richard of Whitley (*Whitele*), and Richard *"of Whitley,"* her son, to Abbot William [II] and the convent of Reading of a piece (*pecia*) of land in Whitley in the field called *Wynerdfeld* between the land formerly belonging to John of Woodcote (*Wodecote*) and that formerly belonging to William of Missenden (*Mussenden'*). Warranty. In exchange for this the abbot and convent have given them a piece of land, as is contained in their charter of enfeoffment.*ᵇ* Sealing with the donors' seals   [1290 × 1305]

C f 142v

Hiis testibus: dominis Rolando de Erle, et multis aliis.

ᵃ⁻ᵃ Interlined   *ᵇ Sentence incomplete*

The dating limits are those of William II's abbacy, but Roland of Earley predeceased the abbot (see no. 1257).

1254 Gift and quitclaim in free alms by William, son and heir of the late Richard of Whitley (*Whitele*), to Abbot William [II] and the convent of Reading of a plot (*placea*) of land in London Street lying in length between the curtilage of Walter *Gerard*, formerly belonging to Walter Messenger (*le Messager*), and the street leading from Fair Cross (*Bella Crux*) towards London, and in width between the heads of the curtilages of Philip of Newbury (*Neubury*), Simon Tiler (*Tegulator*) and Plasancia *Simon* on one side and the ditch of *la Wynerdfeld'* on the other. Warranty and sealing [1290 × 1305]

C ff 142v–143r

Hiis testibus: dominis Rolando de Erle, et aliis.

Date as for no. 1253. The deed is entered in the Whitley section of the cartulary, but the plot of land must have been very near the boundary of the town of Reading.

1255 Gift, release and quitclaim in free alms by Matilda, widow of Richard of Whitley (*Whitele*), to Abbot William [II] and the convent of Reading of a plot (*placea*) of land in London Street lying [etc., as in no. 1254, omitting 'Simon' from 'Simon Tiler' and reading Plasencia *Snow*]. Warranty and sealing [1290 × 1305]

C f 143r

Hiis testibus: domino Rolando de Erle, et aliis.

Date as for no. 1253. It is clear from nos. 1253–5 that there were two men called Richard of Whitley, both of whom were dead at the latest by June 1305. One was survived by a widow Clemencia and a son Richard, the other by a widow Matilda and a son and heir William. Richard of Whitley, presumably the son of the first, witnessed a deed by William, the son of the second, in 1317 (no. 1261) and witnessed other deeds in 1311 and 1326 (nos. 963–4).

1256 Gift, release and quitclaim by Roland of Earley (*Erle*) to Reading Abbey of a part of his land in the vill of Whitley (*Whitele*) called *Bastardescroft*, lying between the abbey's land on every side. To be held freely without any reservation of him or his heirs. Warranty and sealing [before June 1305]

C f 145v

Hiis testibus: domino Bartholomeo de Erle, et aliis.

Before the death of Abbot William II, which had occurred by 24 June 1305, since Roland of Earley predeceased the abbot (see no. 1257).

1257   Quitclaim by Margery, widow of Sir Roland of Earley (*Erle*), knight, to Abbot William [II] and the convent of Reading of all her right, in name of dower ot otherwise, in all the lands and tenements which the abbot and convent held in the vill of Whitley (*Whitele*) on the day this deed was made (*die confectionis presencium*). Sealing

[1297 × 1305]

C f 145v

Hiis testibus: Willelmo de Blebury, et aliis.

After June 1297, when Roland of Earley was still alive (*Parliamentary Writs and Writs of Military Summons*, ed. F. Palgrave (Rec. Comm., 1827–34), i. 290), and before 24 June 1305, by which date Abbot William II had died.

1258   Quitclaim by Isabel, widow of G. *de la Strode*, to Abbot W(illiam) [II] and the convent of Reading of all her right in all the lands and tenements which her late husband held at Cowick (*la Couwyk'*) in the vill of Whitley (*Whitele*). Sealing   [1290 × 1305]

C f 148v

Hiis testibus: Willelmo de Bleobury, G(ilberto) Pynson, et aliis.

William of Blewbury among the witnesses establishes the abbot as William II, whose abbacy provides the dating limits.

1259   Quitclaim by Roger *Meycent* of Reading to Reading Abbey of all his right in a meadow in the vill of Whitley (*Whitele*) between Katesgrove (*Cadelesgrove*) and the [River] Kennet. Warranty of the said meadow by him and his heirs in perpetuity. Sealing. Witnesses [omitted]   3 June 1304

C f 153r

Dat' Radyng' die mercurii proxima post festum beate Petronille virginis [31 May], anno regni regis Edwardi filii regis Henrici tricesimo secundo.

1260   Release (*tradidi et reddidi*) by John *le Acatour* of Reading to Abbot Nicholas [of Whaplode] and the convent of Reading of all the lands

and tenements which he held for life in Whitley (*Whitele*) by demise
of William [II], late abbot of Reading and predecessor of Abbot
Nicholas, and which John *Dwole* sometime held. Sealing

2 Feb. 1313

C f 152r–v

Hiis testibus: Thoma Syward, et aliis. Dat' Radyng' die veneris in
festo Pur(ificacionis) beate Marie virginis, anno regni regis Edwardi*[a]*
sexto.

[a] filii regis Edwardi *probably om.* (*see note*)

The naming of Abbot Nicholas establishes that the king of the dating clause is Edward
II, although as it stands the text suggests Edward I. Regarding John *Dwole*, cf.
Dwoleslond in no. 1251.

1261   Quitclaim by William son of Richard of Whitley (*Whitele*) to
Abbot Nicholas [of Whaplode] and the convent of Reading of all his
right in 6s rent which they will receive in Whitley from the tenement
which William of Kimble (*Kenebell'*) holds and Nicholas *atte More*
sometime held. Sealing   22 Mar. 1317

C f 142r–v

Hiis testibus: Thoma Syward, Johanne le Acatur, Rad(ulf)o de
Helme, Henrico de Greiwell', Henrico Banastr(e), Waltero Watshod,
Johanne de Stoke, Roberto Wylle, Johanne Fyngod, Ricardo de
Whitel(e), Edmundo le Barbour, Rogero le Hurt', et aliis. Dat'
Radyng' vicesimo secundo die mensis Marcii, anno regni regis
Edwardi filii regis Edwardi decimo.

1262   Quitclaim by John, son and heir of William of Earley (*Erle*),
to Abbot Nicholas [of Whaplode] and the convent of Reading of all
his right in 2s annual rent which he used to receive from them at
Michaelmas in Whitley (*Whitele*). Sealing   10 July 1323[1]

C f 143v

Hiis testibus: Thoma Syward, Johanne le Acatur, Rad(ulf)o de
Helme, Ada le Hornere, Johanne Vachel, et aliis. Dat' Radyng' die
dominica proxima post festum Translacionis sancti Thome archiepiscopi et martiris [7 July], anno regni regis Edwardi filii regis
Edwardi sextodecimo.

William of Earley and his son John were sub-tenants within the manor of Earley
Whiteknights (see *VCH Berks.*, iii. 217–8).

1. The regnal years of Edward II ended on 7 July, i.e. the feast of the Translation
of St Thomas Becket. This interpretation of the dating clause depends strictly on the

fact that the feast in 16 Edward II fell in 1323. However, it is possible that, since any day after that feast was actually in the following regnal year, the date was calculated accordingly and should therefore be read as 11 July 1322.

1263   Gift, release and quitclaim in free alms by Walter, son of the late John Franklin (*le Frannkelayn*) of Whitley (*Whitele*), to Reading Abbey of a plot (*placea*) of his land called *Cadelesgroveslynch'* within the boundary of the manor of Reading (*infra proscinctum manerii Radyng'*), between the land of Gilbert of Heckfield (*Heghfeld'*) on the east and the bank of the [River] Kennet on the west, and [between] the garden of John Vachell (*Vachel*) on the north and the wood of the abbot on the south. Warranty and sealing   [late 13th × early 14th cent.]

C f 152v

Hiis testibus: Johanne Vachel, et multis aliis.

Rubric: Carta de le lynche apud Catusgrove

There were two John Vachells, father and son, in the later 13th and earlier 14th centuries (see no. 1158). The elder was a steward of Reading Abbey in 1291 (see no. 780) and does not certainly occur before 1280. Gilbert of Heckfield witnessed Reading deeds between 1285 and 1311 (*Cartl. Hospital of St John Baptist* (see no. 886 n.), ii. 45; above, no. 963) and had a son also called Gilbert (see no. 1264).

1264   Quitclaim by Gilbert, son and heir of Gilbert of Heckfield (*Hegtfeld'*),[a] to Abbot John [I] of Reading and his successors of all his right in a plot (*placea*) of land at *la Lynche* next to Katesgrove (*Cadelesgrove*) in the vill of Whitley (*Wytele*),[b] between Gilbert's own land on the east and the said abbot's quarry (*quarrera*) on the west, as defined by the boundary between him and the abbot on all sides. Warranty and sealing   21 Sept. 1335

B f 155r; C f 94r; C ff 152v–153r[1]

Dat' apud Rading' die jovis proxima post festum Exaltacionis Sancte Crucis [14 Sept.], anno regni regis E(dwardi) tercii post Conquestum nono.

[a] Hegfeld' *C f 94r*, Heghfeld' *C ff 152v–153r*
[b] Whiteleye *C f 94r*, Whitele *C ff 152v–153r*

1. An entirely blank folio, un-numbered in the current foliation, separates the two parts of this copy.

1265   Writ of novel disseisin by King Edward III to the sheriff of Berkshire in a plea by the abbot of Reading against Claricia *atte Churche*, William *Folk'* of Hartley (*Hertleigh'*) and William *Hodeman* concerning the abbot's free tenement in Whitley (*Whitele*), to be heard

before William of Shareshill (*Shareshull'*), John of Stowford (*Stouford'*)
and Richard of Burton (*Birton'*) on a day and at a place to be notified
by them   25 Jan. 1352

B f 89r

Teste me ipso apud Westm(onasterium) xxv. die Januarii, anno regni
nostri Anglie xxvi, regni vero nostri Francie xiii.

1266 Assize of novel disseisin to recognize whether Claricia *atte
Churche*, William *Folk* of Hartley (*Hertleigh'*) and William *Hodeman*
unjustly disseised the abbot of Reading of his free tenement in Whitley
(*Whitele*). The abbot complains that they disseised him of a messuage
and 15 acres of land with appurtenances, etc. The defendants appear
by John *atte dale* as their bailiff. The bailiffs of the abbot of Reading
come and claim his liberty in this case, viz., to have cognizance of the
plea before him and delivery to him of the original writ with the list
of jurors (*panellum*). Since liberty of this kind has on other occasions
(*alias*) been allowed to them [the bailiffs] by royal writ, they are to
have their liberty in this plea, and have appointed a day for the parties
at Reading on Thursday in a week of Easter (*in septimana Pasche*).
They are told that full and swift justice is to be shown to the parties,
and the original writ of the assize with the list of jurors is delivered to
the bailiffs here in court.   20 Feb. 1352

B f 89r

Rubric: Placita assise nove disseisine apud Walyngford coram Johanne
de Stouford' et Ricardo de Birton' justic(iariis), et cetera, die lune
proxima ante festum sancti Petri in Cathedra [22 Feb.], anno regni
regis E(dwardi) tercii a Conquestu xxvi.

This case illustrates the abbot's liberty of return of writs in operation (cf. no. 683). The
liberty was expressly confirmed to the abbey in Edward III's general confirmation of
1338 (see no. 109).

WINDSOR

1267 *Testimony by Abbot Walter [de Lucy] and the convent of Battle to
Abbot R. and the convent of Reading that, when they held [Windsor] Underoure,
it was always in their demesne and no one held it of them*   [1154 × 65]

A f 47r

Venerabili R. abbati de Rading(ia) domino et amico suo totique
eiusdem loci conventui frater Walt(erius) humilis minister ecclesie
sancti Martini de Bello et humilis eiusdem loci conventus, civitatis

illius cives fieri de qua psalmista cecinit dicens, 'Gloriosa dicta sunt de te, civitas dei'.[1] Sicut iam pridem paternitati vestre intimavimus, ita adhuc viva voce testamur quod terra de Underorora quondam nostra semper in dominio nostro fuit, nec aliquis illam de nobis tenuit, sed monachi nostri, qui etiam adhuc supersunt, illam in dominio nostro tenuerunt. Hoc dicimus, hoc affirmamus, et his litteris ecclesie vestre de illa terra huiusmodi testes sumus. Valeat paternitas vestra in domino, dilectissime pater et fratres.

Walter de Lucy was abbot of Battle 1139–71 (*Heads of Relig. Houses*, 29). The abbot of Reading was either Reginald (1154–58) or Roger (1158–65). This appears to be the only evidence that Battle ever held Underoure, a now lost place-name in Windsor (*Berks. Place-Names*, i. 29; *VCH Berks.*, iii. 66). Battle's testimony was probably called for in the difficulties Reading Abbey was experiencing in recovering Underoure from William Martel (see no. 1268; cf. no. 12).

1. Ps. 86: 3.

1268 *Restoration by William Martel to Reading Abbey of its whole hide of land in [Windsor] Underoure, which he long held of the abbey at farm against its will*   [1139 × 66; prob. 1154 × 66]

A f 41r–v; B f 54v; C f 23r

Willelmus Martel omnibus hominibus suis et amicis Francis et Anglis, salutem. Sciatis me, concessione uxoris mee et filiorum meorum, pro devitando animarum nostrarum periculo [*f 41v*] reddidisse monachis Rading(ensibus) terram suam de Underhore*a* totam integre hidam quam ipsis invitis aliquandiu*b* de eis ad firmam tenebam, ut inde tanquam de iure suo faciant amodo quod voluerint. Neque enim in terra illa ego vel heredes mei ius aliquod hereditarie clamamus vel clamare in perpetuum pertemptabimus. Ego Galfridus Martel hanc raditionem*c* concedo et confirmo. Huius rei sunt testes:*d* Willelmus capellanus, Rogerius Martel, Alanus dapifer, Willelmus Belez, et multi alii.

a Underora B,C	*b* aliquamdiu B,C
c redditionem B,C	*d* B,C end with et cetera

Certainly after no. 11 (q.v.) and before 1166, by which time William Martel was dead, since his son Geoffrey sent in his *carta* to Henry II (*Red Bk. Exch.*, i. 217); probably, in the light of no. 1267, not earlier than 1154. The deed was possibly a death-bed restoration. Roger Martel was William's younger son (Round, *Cal. Docs. France*, 356).

1269 *Quitclaim by Geoffrey Martel to Reading Abbey of the whole hide of [Windsor] Underoure which his father held of the abbey and has restored to it. His mother has quitclaimed the same for herself and her heirs*

[1139 × 66; prob. 1154 × 66]

A f 41v; B f 54v; C f 23r

Sciant presentes et futuri quod ego Gaufr(edus) Martel clamo quietam monachis de Rading(ia) totam ex integro hidam de Underhora[a] quam pater meus aliquandiu[b] de illis tenuit, sed pro devitando anime sue periculo eam reddidit ipsis monachis. Et mater mea ʿtotam hidam illam clamavit[c] quietam de se et de omnibus heredibus suis. Hanc redditionem ego concedo et confirmo, nec aliquid iuris hereditarii in illa terra in perpetuum clamabo nec heredes mei post me.[d] Huius rei testes sunt: Rog(erius) Martel, Alanus dapifer, Willelmus Belet, et multi alii.

[a] Underora B,C
[b] aliquamdiu B,C
[cc] clamavit totam illam hidam B,C
[d] B ends with T', C ends

Contemporary with no. 1268, since the witness-lists are similar and Geoffrey Martel was associated with his father's restoration of the land.

1270 Final concord in the court of Simon, abbot of Reading, 3 Henry III on the feast of St Milburga the virgin, *coram Waltero Foliot, Johanne de Wikenholt',[a] justic(iariis) itinerantibus missis ad curiam dicti abbatis a domino Ricardo Sar(esburiensi) episcopo, Matheo filio Hereberti,[b] Rad(ulfo) Hareng, Waltero Foliot, Jacobo de Poterna, Waltero de Rip(ariis), Mauricio de Turevill', Johanne de Wikenholt', just(iciariis) itinerantibus in comitatu Berk' ut audirent et viderent quod curia illa unicuique exhiberet iustitiam quam per cartas regum Angl(ie) quas idem abbas porrexit et per libertates ecclesie Rading(ensis), quibus idem abbas et monachi tempore precedenti semper[c] usi sunt, quas etiam abbas Rading(ensis) per iudicium curie domini regis Johannis et per iudicium baronum de Scaccario aliquando disrationavit, et ideo per iudicium militum de comitatu Berk' et aliis comitatibus ibidem tunc presentium coram eisdem justic(iariis) adiudicata fuit curia predicto abbati*, between the abbot and convent of Reading, seeking, and Walter of Hurley (*Hurleg'*),[d] holding, concerning half a mill, $3\frac{1}{2}$ acres of land and 42d rent in Windsor (*Windlesor'*). Plea of warranty of charter. Walter recognized the same to be the right of the‚abbot and convent and remitted all his right in the same to them for himself and his heirs in perpetuity, to be held in free alms, as his charter to them\witnesses.

23 Feb. 1219

B ff 169v–170r; C f 100r

[a] Wikenholte C
[b] Herb' C
[c] Om. in C
[d] Hurle C

For discussion of the sending of two of the itinerant justices to the abbot's court, see no. 675 n. Cf. also nos. 678, 1272. It is interesting in the case of the present fine and no. 1272 that no parallel fine is recorded in the king's court before the full panel of itinerant justices.

1271   Surrender (*resignavi*) and gift in free alms by Walter of Hurley (*Hurleg'*) to Abbot Simon and the monks of Reading of half the mill of Windsor Underoure (*Windelesor' Underhore*),[a] which half was sometime in his possession and belonged to him by hereditary right, and of the whole other tenement which he held of them in the same vill, viz., 3½ acres of land, which he had in demesne, and 42d rent, of which John the draper (*le draper*) paid him 18d annually, John *Hagemund* 12d and Osbert *Beaufiz* 12d. However, the abbot and convent, having obtained possession of this tenement, have leased the said land to him for life for 2s annually at Easter, so that after his death all the aforesaid will revert to them free of all claim of him or his; and in his great need the abbot and convent have given him as their brother (*sicut fratri suo*) 8 marks of silver. Sealing[b]   [*c.* 23 Feb. 1219]

A ff 98v–99r; B f 55r–v; C f 23v

Hiis testibus: Waltero Foliot, Johanne filio Hugonis, Henrico de Scaccario, Galfrido Gibbewine, Roberto Achard, Alano de Englefeld, Thoma Huscarl, Matheo de Burgefeld, Osmundo de Ocleg', Roberto pincerna, Petro de Rutherwic', Rogero vinetario, Hugone le bulur, Willelmo filio camberlani, Johanne le draper, Roberto filio Ivonis, Galfrido Est, et multis aliis.

[a] Windles' Underore *B*, Wyndlesore Underore *C*
[b] *B,C end with* T'

The date is approximately that of the final concord (no. 1270), since the first witness was one of the eyre justices sent to the abbot's court. However, since the witness-lists of this and no. 1273 are identical, both may have been given on the same day, although the fine relating to the latter was made on 25 Feb.

1272   Agreement and final concord in the court of Simon, abbot of Reading, 3 Henry III on the morrow of St Mathias the apostle [24 Feb.], *coram Waltero Foliot* [etc., as in no. 1270, reading *per iudicium domini regis Johannis* and inserting *de* before *aliis comitatibus*], between the abbot and convent of Reading, seeking, and William *Barberel* and Matilda his wife, holding, concerning half a mill, 7½ acres of land and ½ mark and 1d rent in Windsor (*Windlesor'*). Plea of warranty of charter. William and Matilda recognized the same to be the right of the abbot and convent and remitted all their right in the same, with all improvements they have made in the same, to the abbot and convent for themselves and their heirs in perpetuity, to be held in free alms. For this the abbot and convent have conceded that William and Matilda may hold of them the whole said mill and 7½ acres of land with the said rent at farm for their lives in survivorship by the service of 40s annually, viz., 20s each at Michaelmas and Easter, for all service. Reversion to the abbot and convent after their deaths. It is agreed between the parties that, if anyone moves a plea against either the abbot and convent or William and Matilda, neither party will settle (*pacem facere*) without the other nor seek to defraud this agreement. 25 Feb. 1219

B f 169r–v; C ff 99v–100r

For discussion, see nos. 675 n., 1270 n.

1273 Surrender (*resignavimus*) and gift in free alms by William *Barberel* and Matilda his wife to Abbot Simon and the monks of Reading of half the mill of Windsor Underoure (*Windelesore Underhore*),[a] which belonged to Matilda by hereditary right, with all improvements made by them, and of the whole other tenement which they held of them in the same vill, viz., 7½ acres of land, which were in their demesne, and the whole rent which they had from their tenants of the fee of the abbot of Reading, viz., from William *Coupun* 18d, from William *Fardel* 3s, from Geoffrey the baker (*pistor*) 12d, from Osbert *Beaufiz* 12d and from Girard some of Girard *Coterel* 3d. If the abbot and convent should convey the said mill with the said land to William and Matilda at farm for their lives, they will pay them annually 3 marks of silver, viz., 20s each at Michaelmas and Easter; and, if they did not pay the said farm at the said terms, the abbot and convent might seize the said mill into their hand and take its profits until they received the farm and its arrears. After their deaths the whole mill, land and rent shall revert to the abbot and convent. Sealing with their seals

[*c.* 25 Feb. 1219]

A f 99r; B ff 54v–55r; C f 23r–v

Hiis testibus:[b] Waltero Foliot, Johanne filio Hugonis, Henrico de Scaccario, Galfrido Gibbewine, Roberto Achard, Alano de Englefeld, Thoma Huscarl', Matheo de Burchefeld, Osmundo de Ocleg', Roberto pincerna, Petro de Rutherwike, Rogero vinetario, Hugone Bulur, Willelmo filio camberlani, Johanne le draper, Roberto filio Yvonis, Galfrido Est, et multis aliis.

[a] Windesore Underore *B*, Wyndlesore Underore *C*
[b] *B,C end*

The date is approximately that of the final concord (no. 1272), but see no. 1271 n.

1274 Surrender (*resignavi*) and quitclaim by Matilda of Boveney (*Buveneye*), widow, to Reading Abbey of 7½ acres of arable land which belonged to the mill of [Windsor] Underoure (*Underore*) and 6s 9d of assised rent, viz., from Geoffrey the baker (*pistor*) and his heirs 12d, from John *de la Dene* and his heirs 18d, from William *Fardel* and his heirs 3s, from Osbert *Beaufiz* and his heirs 12d and from Girard *Coterel* and his heirs 3d. Nevertheless, she will [still] pay annually to the abbey the full 40s for the mill of Underoure. For this the abbey has given her in her great need 6 marks of silver. Sealing. Witnesses [omitted]   [1219 × *c.* 1230]

B f 55r; C f 23v

Matilda was clearly the widow of William Barberel, who was alive in Feb. 1219 (see nos. 1272–3). This deed is probably not a great deal later than 1219, since only one of the rent-paying tenants in no. 1273, William *Coupon*, has been replaced by another, John *de la Dene*.

1275 *Gift and quitclaim by William of Boveney to Reading Abbey of his serfs Gerold of Windsor and William his brother with their progeny, for which the abbey has given him 8s*   [? earlier 13th cent.]

A f 107r; B f 55v; C f 23v

Sciant presentes et futuri quod ego Willelmus de Buveneia,*a* pro salute anime mee et pro anima patris mei et matris mee et omnium antecessorum et successorum meorum, dedi deo et beate Marie de Rading(ia) et *b*quietos clamavi*b* in eternum Geroldum de Windelsore*c* et Willelmum fratrem suum nativos meos cum omni sequela et posteritate eorum. Et dederunt mihi pro ista quieta clamacione*d* abbas et monachi Rading(enses) octo solidos.*e* Hiis testibus.

a Buveneye *B,C*   *b b* quiet'clamavi *B,C*
c Windlesor' *B*, Wyndlesor' *C*   *d* Insert mea *B,C*
e *B,C* end with T'

Dating very uncertain. It appears among 13th-century additions in A, but was entered in the original section of B and is therefore not later than 1258. The primitive diplomatic suggests, however, a rather earlier date. A William of Boveney occurs in 1202 and 1214 and was dead by July 1218 (*Bucks. Feet of Fines*, 22, 37 bis), but he was succeeded by a son, William of Boveney, who occurs in 1224 and 1232 (*ibid.*, 49, 63). On balance, the elder of these seems the more likely. The donor may have been related to Matilda of Boveney, wife and then widow of William Barberel (see nos. 1272–4), especially since the rubrics of B and C locate the serfs in Windsor.

SCOTTISH CHARTERS

The arrangement of the charters in this section is mainly chronological and not according to place. The royal charters are given first, followed by a small group of comital or abbatial charters.

1276 Notification by King David I of Scotland to Abbot E(dward), Brian [fitz Count] and the convent of Reading, of his gift in free alms to Reading Abbey of the vill of Rhynd (*Rindalgros*) [Perthshire], as perambulated by the king, William Giffard, Herbert the Chamberlain and others. If the king or his heirs should add to the gift so that a convent could be maintained, the abbey shall send a convent there.

[1141 × 51]

A f 36r; B f 19r
Pd. *Mon. Ang.*, iv. 60–1 (no. i); Stuart, *Records of May*, 1–2 (no. 1); Lawrie, *Early Scottish Charters*, 123–4 (no. 161) (all from Edward I's 1307 inspeximus)[1]

Presentibus testibus:[a] fratre Willelmo Giffardo, Gaufrido abbate de Dunfermelin, Edwardo cancellario, Waltero de Bidun, Nicolao clerico, Dunecano comite, Hugone de Morevill', Herberto camerario, Waltero de Lindesie, Leod' de Brechin. Apud Dunfermelin.

[a] *B ends with* et cetera

Edward was David I's chancellor from not earlier than 1141 and became bishop of Aberdeen in 1147 × 51. The inclusion of Brian fitz Count in the address suggests a time after King Stephen's capture at the Battle of Lincoln, 2 Feb. 1141, since Brian was a staunch Angevin supporter who appears to have assumed a close, quasi-patronal relationship with Reading Abbey in the 1140s (G.W.S. Barrow, *The Kingdom of the Scots* (1973), 185–6; see also nos. 667–8). A cell was established at Rhynd by 1147 × 53 (see nos. 1285–6), but was abandoned in *c.* 1160 in favour of a priory on the Isle of May established by 1151 (see no. 1279 and Duncan, 'Documents of May', 55–7).

1. PRO C53/93, no. 31 (Charter Roll 35 Edward I). This is an inspeximus for the abbot of Reading, dated 4 Mar. 1307 at Kirkcambeck, of 20 charters by kings of Scotland to Reading Abbey or its cell of May—pd. Stuart, *Records of May*, 1–13; brief notice in *Cal. Chart. R.*, iii. 84.

1277 Gift in free alms by King David I of Scotland to the monks of May, of Pittenweem (*Pednewem*) and St Monance (*Inverin que fuit Averin*) [Fife]

[1141 × 51]

A f 60v
Pd. Stuart, *Records of May*, 3 (no. 4); Lawrie, *Early Scottish Charters*, 120 (no. 155) (both from 1307 inspeximus)

Testibus: abbate Gaufrido de Dunfermelin, et comite Dunec(ano), et

Hugone de Morevill',[a] [et Edwardo cancellario, et Alfwino MacAr-
chil, et Macbet MacTorfin. Apud Edeneburgum.]

> [a] *A ends with* et multis aliis, *the remainder being supplied from the printed texts*

Date as for no. 1276.

1278   Grant by King David I of Scotland to the monks [? of May]
and their men of the liberty of selling fish in their port as in a burgh;
and precept that they be not impleaded for trading any more than
for buying in the king's demesne burgh   [1141 × 51]

> A f 60v
> Pd. Lawrie, *Early Scottish Charters*, 131 (no. 166); Duncan, 'Documents of May', 70
> (no. 43)

Testibus: Gaufr(edo) abbate de Dunfermelin, Edwardo cancellario,
et multis aliis.

> Date as for no. 1276. Proximity to the sea suggests that the monks were of May rather
> than of Rhynd.

1279   Notification by King David I of Scotland, addressed generally
and to Gilleserf of Clackmannan, of his gift in free alms to Prior
[Achard][a] and the monks of May of common in the wood of Clackmannan   [1141 × 51]

> A ff 60v–61r
> Pd. Stuart, *Records of May*, 3–4 (no. 5); Lawrie, *Early Scottish Charters*, 120–1 (no.
> 156) (both from 1307 inspeximus)

Testibus: Gaufredo abbate de Dunfermelin, et Edwardo cancellario,
et Herberto camerario. Apud Dunfermelin.

> [a] *Om. in A, supplied from printed texts*

> Date as for no. 1276. For Gilleserf, see Duncan, 'Documents of May', 52 n. 5.

1280   Precept by King David I of Scotland to all good men of his
land that, wherever a ship of the monks of May shall berth in his
land, it shall be quit of can, toll and all custom
                                        [1141 × 53; ? × *c.* 1144]

> A f 61r
> Pd. Lawrie, *Early Scottish Charters*, 131 (no. 167); Duncan, 'Documents of May',
> 70–1 (no. 44)

Testibus: Gaufrido abbate de Dunfermelin, et Edwardo cunesta-
bulario. Apud Edeneburh.

After no. 1276, since the existence of a cell at May followed the gift of Rhynd (Duncan, 55), and before the king's death. Professor Barrow implies, however, that Edward the constable would probably not have occurred much after *c.* 1144 (*Regesta Regum Scottorum*, i. 34).

1281 Gift in free alms by King David I of Scotland to the monks of May of half of *Balegallin*,[1] as perambulated by Gillecolm mac Imbethin (*mac Chimbethin*), Macbeth mac Torphin and Malmure thane of Kellie (*Chellin*), so long as there shall be a convent of monks in May; and grant of common of pasture without payment in the 'shires'[2] of Kellie and Crail (*Cherel*) [Fife] and throughout his land

[*c.* 1146 × 1153]

A f 6ov

Pd. *Mon. Ang.*, iv. 62 (no. ii); Stuart, *Records of May*, 2–3 (no. 3); Lawrie, *Early Scottish Charters*, 166–7 (no. 207) (all from 1307 inspeximus)

Testibus: G(regorio) episcopo de Dunichelden, et Andrea episcopo de Cateneis,[a] [et Willelmo Giffard, et Dunecano comite, et Alwino filio Archil. Apud Dunfermelin.]

[a] *A ends with* et multis aliis, *the remainder being supplied from the printed texts*

Andrew is unlikely to have become bishop of Caithness much before 1146 (*Regesta Regum Scottorum*, i. 158 n. 2); the king died in 1153.

1. Not certainly identified, but possibly Baglillie or Boglily (in Kinghorn), Fife (see *ibid.*, index *sub* Balegallin).

2. For these subordinate shires within the county of Fife, see *ibid.*, 41–2.

1282 Gift in free alms by King David I of Scotland to the monks of May of a toft in his burgh of Haddington [E. Lothian]

[*c.* 1146 × 1153]

A f 6ov

Pd. Lawrie, *Early Scottish Charters*, 186–7 (no. 231); Duncan, 'Documents of May', 70 (no. 42)

Testibus: Andrea episcopo de Cateneis, et Gaufredo abbate de Dunfermelin, et multis aliis.

Date as for no. 1281.

1283 Gift in free alms by Kind David I of Scotland to the prior and monks of May of a toft in Berwick; and precept that they are to hold it as freely as any abbots or priors of his land hold their alms, and that the men living therein shall be free of all service and exaction

[1147 × 53]

A f 6ov

Pd. *Mon. Ang.*, iv. 62 (no. i); Stuart, *Records of May*, 2 (no. 2); Lawrie, *Early Scottish Charters*, 148 (no. 184) (all from 1307 inspeximus)

Testibus: Ernaldo abbate de Calchoh, Osberto priore de Jedewort,[a] [Waltero cancellario, Hugone de Morvilla, Waltero filio Alani, Gilleberto de Umframvilla, Waltero de Bolebec. Apud Kyngor.]

[a] *A ends with* et multis aliis, *the remainder being supplied from the printed texts*

Arnold became abbot of Kelso in 1147 and Walter de Bidun became chancellor between 1147 and 1151 (*Regesta Regum Scottorum*, i. 14, 28); the king died in 1153.

1284 Precept by King David I of Scotland to the sheriffs, provosts, ministers and all men of his land that the prior and monks of May and the dependants (*clientes*) of the house of May are to be quit of can and toll throughout the king's land and to have licence to sell their own goods (*res*) and buy necessaries for the house   [1147 × 53]

A f 6ov

Pd. Stuart, *Records of May*, 4 (no. 6); Lawrie, *Early Scottish Charters*, 163 (no. 201) (both from 1307 inspeximus)

Testibus:[a] [Herberto episcopo de Glascu, et Andrea episcopo de Cateneis, et Ernaldo abbate de Chegho.[b] Apud Strivelin.]

[a] *A ends, the remainder being supplied from the printed texts*
[b] *Possibly early 14th-century transcribal error for* Calchoh

After 24 Aug. 1147, when Herbert was consecrated bishop of Glasgow, and before the king's death. The precept was not included in the original section of A, but added in an early 13th-century hand at the foot of the folio.

1285 Precept by King David I of Scotland to all men of Perthshire to give to the monks of Rhynd (*Rendelgros*) their tithes in corn, cheese and all things in which tithes are owed   [1147 × 53]

A f 61r

Pd. *Mon. Ang.*, iv. 61 (no. ii); Stuart, *Records of May*, 4 (no. 7); Lawrie, *Early Scottish Charters*, 163 (no. 202) (all from 1307 inspeximus)

Testibus: Dunecano comite, et Waltero cancellario. Apud Scone.

After Walter de Bidun became chancellor (see no. 1283 n.) and before the king's death.

1286 Gift and confirmation by King Malcolm IV of Scotland to the monks of Rhynd (*Rindelgros*) of all tithe belonging to the church of that vill both in fishings in the waters of the Tay and the Earn and in lambs, cheeses and all things in which tithes are owed

[1153 × 59]

A f 61v

Pd. Stuart, *Records of May*, 5 (no. 8) (from 1307 inspeximus); *Regesta Regum Scottorum*, i. 198 (no. 137)

Testibus his: Waltero cancellario, Hugone de Morvill', Nicholao clerico. Apud Berewic.

After the king's accession and before Nicholas the clerk became chamberlain (*ibid.*, 11).

1287 Confirmation by King Malcolm IV of Scotland to the prior and monks of May of the gift and grant made to them by his grand-father King David; and precept that no one shall do them injury nor demand more from them than in his grandfather's time

A f 61r   [1153 × 62]

Pd. Stuart, *Records of May*, 6 (no. 10); *Regesta Regum Scottorum*, i. 211 (no. 161) (both from 1307 inspeximus)

His presentibus testibus: Waltero cancellario, comite Cospatrico, Hugone de Morvill',*a* [Willelmo de Sumervill. Apud Linlitch(u).]

a A ends with et multis aliis, *the remainder being supplied from Regesta text*

After the king's accession and before Walter de Bidun ceased to be chancellor (*ibid.*, 28). This charter probably confirms David I's gift of May, which has not survived (Duncan, 'Documents of May', 55).

1288 Precept by King Malcolm IV of Scotland to all good men and fishermen fishing round the Isle of May to pay their tithes to the monks *a*[of May]*a* as they had them in the time of his grandfather King David   [1153 × 62]

A f 61r

Pd. Stuart, *Records of May*, 6 (no. 11); *Regesta Regum Scottorum*, i. 212 (no. 162) (both from 1307 inspeximus)

Testibus: Waltero cancellario, Walt(ero) filio Alani dapifero, *a*[Wal-tero de Lindesia]*a*. Apud Dunferm(elin).

a a Om. in A, supplied from printed texts

Date as for no. 1287. For tithes, or teinds, in general, see *ibid.*, 65–6, 272–3.

1289 Notification by King Malcolm IV of Scotland to all good men of his land that he has received the monks of May in his firm peace; and prohibition that no one shall fish in their waters nor construct buildings on their islands except by their permission, nor dig or take grass on the Isle of May   [1153 × 62]

A f 61v

Pd. Duncan, 'Documents of May', 71 (no. 46); *Regesta Regum Scottorum*, i. 215 (no. 169)

Testibus: Waltero cancellario, Roberto Avenel, Waltero de Lindes'. Apud Berew(ic).

Date as for no. 1287.

1290 Confirmation by King Malcolm IV of Scotland to the saints of May, of Pittenweem (*Pennewem*) and St Monance (*Inverin que fuit Averin*) [Fife], as perambulated by Matthew archdeacon [of St Andrews], Gillepatrick mac Torphin and others; and gift of common of pasture in the 'shire' of Ardross (*Erdros*) as they have in the 'shire' of Kellie (*Callin*) [1153 × 62]

A f 61v

Pd. Stuart, *Records of May*, 5 (no. 9) (from 1307 inspeximus); *Regesta Regum Scottorum*, i. 215 (no. 168)

T(este) Hugone de Morvill'. Apud Edeneburg.

After the king's accession and before the death of Hugh de Morville, the constable, in 1162 (*ibid.*, 29 n. 7).

1291 Gift in free alms by King Malcolm IV of Scotland to the monks of May, who are of Reading, of 5 marks annually to be paid by the king's provosts of Perth from the first can of ships coming to Perth, in exchange for the chapel and tithes of Perth which they have had for several years by gift of his grandfather King David. The monks of Dumfermline used to receive these 5 marks from the king's provosts and ministers of Perth by gift of the said king his grandfather, and he has therefore given them to the monks of May at the wish and counsel of Dunfermline Abbey. [1157 × 60]

A f 61r

Pd. Duncan, 'Documents of May', 71 (no. 45); *Regesta Regum Scottorum*, i. 210 (no. 158)

Testibus his: Willelmo episcopo de Morav(ia), Gregorio episcopo de Duncheld', et multis aliis. Apud Edeneburh.

This charter is probably of the same date as the king's gift of the church of Perth to Dunfermline Abbey (*ibid.*, 209, no. 157), which is witnessed by, among others, Malcolm mac Heth, who was released from imprisonment after 23 years in 1157 (*ibid.*, n. 2), and Arnold abbot of Kelso, who became bishop of St Andrews in 1160.

1292 Precept by King William I of Scotland to the sheriffs, provosts, ministers and all men of his land that the prior and monks of May and the dependants of the house of May are to be quit of can and toll throughout the king's land and to have licence to sell their own goods and buy necessaries for their house, as the charter of King David his grandfather witnesses   [1165 × 71]

A f 62r
Pd. Duncan, 'Documents of May', 72 (no. 48); *Regesta Regum Scottorum*, ii. 126 (no. 6)

Testibus: Nicholao cancellario,ᵃ Ricardo de Morvill', et multis allis. Apud Pert.

ᵃ *Ms has* ancell'

After the king's accession and before the death of Nicholas the chancellor in 1171 (*ibid.*, 6). This is a re-issue of no. 1284.

1293 Precept by King William I of Scotland to all fishermen fishing round May to render their tithes, customs and dues (*rectitudines*) to the prior and monks of May which they had in the time of King Malcolm his brother, as his charter witnesses, and as they had before the time of Prior William   [1165 × 71]

A f 62r
Pd. Stuart, *Records of May*, 11–12 (no. 18); *Regesta Regum Scottorum*, ii. 186 (no. 93) (both from 1307 inspeximus)

Testibus: Nicholao cancellario, Ricardo de Morvill' constab(ulario), Walt(ero) ᵃ[filio Alani]ᵃ dapifero. Apud Eneburg.

ᵃ⁻ᵃ *Om. in A, supplied from printed texts*

Date as for no. 1292. This is partly a re-issue of no. 1288.

1294 Grant in free alms by King William I of Scotland to the prior and monks of May of common of the wood of Clackmannan, as the charter of King David his grandfather witnesses   [1165 × 71]

A f 62r
Pd. Duncan, 'Documents of May', 73 (no. 49); *Regesta Regum Scottorum*, ii. 126 (no. 7)

Testibus: Nicholao cancellario, Ricardo de Morvill' const(abulario), Waltero filio Alani, et multis aliis. Apud Pert.

Date as for no. 1292. This is a re-issue of no. 1279.

1295 Precept by King William I of Scotland to all good men of Scotland that the monks of May shall hold their lands in Scotland[1] freely and quit of all services, and that especially they shall be quit of aids and labour services during the time that Prior W(illiam) is in charge of the house of May [1165 × 71]

A f 62v
Pd. Duncan, 'Documents of May', 73 (no. 50); *Regesta Regum Scottorum*, ii. 186 (no. 92).

Testibus: Eng(elramo) episcopo de Glascu, Nic(holao) cancellario, et multis aliis. Apud Eneburg.

Date as for no. 1292.

1. According to G.W.S. Barrow, north of the Forth (*ibid.*, 44–5).

1296 Gift in free alms by King William I of Scotland to the prior and monks of May , of *Balegallin*[1] provided that the prior of May be not removed except for manifest fault previously made known before the king or his successors and the bishop of St Andrews, and that henceforth there will be at May a convent of 13 monks of the Cluniac order; and precept that the monks shall hold *Balegallin* with all the lands which King David his grandfather and King Malcolm his brother gave them as freely as any abbey holds its alms in his kingdom [1166 × 71]

A f 62r
Pd. Duncan, 'Documents of May', 72 (no. 47); *Regesta Regum Scottorum*, ii. 195 (no. 109)

Testibus: David fratre meo, Nicholao cancellario, comite Walð(evo), comite Dunec(ano), et multis aliis. Apud Sanctum Andream.

Waltheof became earl of Dunbar in 1166; Nicholas the chancellor died in 1171 (see no. 1292 n.). The effect of this charter was to give the monks the whole of *Balegallin*, half of which they had received from David I (see no. 1281). For discussion of the clauses concerning the prior and convent, see Duncan, *ibid.*, 60.

1. See no. 1281 n. 1.

1297 Confirmation in free alms by King William I of Scotland to Prior [William][a] and the monks of May, observing the Cluniac order, of the gifts made to them by King David his grandfather and King Malcolm his brother; viz., from the former, Pittenweem and St Monance (*Inverin que fuit Averin*), half of *Balgallin* since the king has given the other half himself,[1] common of pasture in the 'shires' of Kellie and Crail, and a toft in Berwick; from the latter, 5 marks annually from the can of ships coming to Perth. Also precept that all who fish round the Isle of May shall pay their right tithes to the priory, and prohibition that no one shall fish in their waters, construct buildings on the Isle of May, dig the land of May or take grass there without their permission. Also confirmation of a house (*mansura*) with toft in Dunbar and a berth for one ship to carry necessaries for the priory, given by Earl Gospatrick and confirmed by King Malcolm. All to be held freely, provided that there shall always be at May a convent of 13 monks of the Cluniac order, and that the prior shall not be removed except for manifest fault previously made known to the king and the bishop of St Andrews [1166 × 71]

A ff 61v–62r
Pd. Stuart, *Records of May*, 7–8 (no. 12); *Regesta Regum Scottorum*, ii. 127 (no. 8) (both from 1307 inspeximus); cf. *Mon Ang*., iv. 62 (no. iii)

Testibus: David fratre meo, Nicholao cancellario, *b*[Matheo archidiacono Sancti Andree, comite Wald(evo), comite Dunec(ano), Ricardo de Morevilla constabul(ario), Waltero filio Alani dapifero, D(avid) Olif(ard), Nesio filio Willelmi, Hugone Ridel, Galfrido de Malevilla].*b* Apud Pert.

a Om. in A, supplied from printed texts
b-b et multis aliis A, the remaining witnesses being supplied from Regesta text

Date as for no. 1296.

1. See no. 1296 and n.

1298 Gift in free alms by Gospatrick, earl of Dunbar, to St Ethernan and the monks of May, of a toft next to his port of *Bele*[1] quit of all custom [1141 × 58]

A f 62v
Pd. Duncan, 'Documents of May', 74 (no. 53)

His testibus: filio comitis Walðef, et comitissa Derd', et multis aliis. Apud Dunbar.

After no. 1276, since the creation of a cell at May followed the gift of Rhynd to Reading (Duncan, 55), and before the latest possible date of Pope Adrian IV's general confirmation to Reading (above, no. 145), which includes 'a house in a port by gift of Earl Gospatrick'. On the reference to St Ethernan, see Duncan, 55, 75; G.W.S. Barrow, *The Kingdom of the Scots* (1973), 186 and n.

1. Presumably Belhaven, beside Dunbar (Duncan, 75).

1299 Grant by Abbot G(eoffrey) and the convent of Dunfermline to the prior and monks of May of the tithes of *Balgallin*, to be held of them in perpetuity by rendering annually 10s, half at Michaelmas and half at Easter. *Valete* [1141 × 78]

A f 63r

Pd. *Liber Cartarum Prioratus Sancti Andree in Scotia*, ed. T. Thomson (Bannatyne Club, 1841), 392–3; Stuart, *Records of May*, 29 (no. 37)—both from a cartulary of St Andrews formerly belonging to Lord Panmure and now missing (G.R.C. Davis, *Medieval Cartularies of Great Britain* (1958), 136)

After no. 1276 and before the death of Abbot Geoffrey II of Dunfermline on 14 Oct. 1178 (G.W.S. Barrow, 'A Scottish collection at Canterbury', *Scottish Historical Review*, xxxi (1952), 27 n. 10).

1300   Grant in free alms by Edward, son of Gospatrick earl [of Dunbar], to the monks of the Isle of May of a chalder of flour (*cheldra farine*) from his mill of Belton[1] annually on the feast of St Cuthbert for the soul among others of his wife Sibyl, and with the assent and confirmation of his son and heir Waltheof   [1147 × 93]

A f 62v
Pd. Duncan, 'Documents of May', 75 (no. 54)

. . . hos adhibeo testes: Paganum canonicum de Alnewic, et Herveum canonicum socium eius, Adam de Dunbar, Waldevum filium meum, Stephanum de Hant', et multos alios.

After the foundation of the Premonstratensian abbey of Alnwick, 1147 × 8, and, since the charter was entered in the original section of A, not later than 1193. Edward was still living in 1180 (Duncan, 75).

    1. Probably Belton, near Dunbar (*ibid.*).

1301   Confirmation by Duncan, earl of Fife, to the prior of May and his men of his whole land, of quittance of army and expedition, as King M(alcolm) confirms to the prior by his charter
                 [1153 × 93; prob. 1153 × 78]

A f 62v
Pd. Duncan, 'Documents of May', 74 (no. 52)

His testibus: Reginaldo de Warenna, et Michaele clerico, et multis aliis.

After the accession of Malcolm IV and, since it was entered in the original section of A, not later than 1193; however, since the earl does not refer to William I's charter (see below), probably not later than 1178. The earl is either Duncan I, who died in 1154, or Duncan II, 1159–1204. The dating makes it probable that Reginald de Warenne was the first of the Warennes of Wormegay (Norfolk), who became a monk in 1178 × 9 (*EYC*, viii. 27), *pace* Duncan, 74. The charter of Malcolm IV has not survived, but a similar charter by William I is *Regesta Regum Scottorum*, ii. no. 158, dating 1173 × 78, prob. 1176 × 77.

1302 Notification by Ada, countess [of Northumberland] and mother of the king of Scotland, to her men of Crail and elsewhere and her bailiffs of Crail that she has taken into her protection the prior of May with all possessions of the monks of May in her fief of Crail; and mandate that they aid the monks in their affairs and protect their possessions (*res*), to be held as freely as the charter of King William of Scotland her son witnesses and confirms [1165 × 78]

A f 62v

Pd. Duncan, 'Documents of May', 73 (no. 51)

Testibus: Alexandro de Sancto Martino, Hugone de Mailol, et multis aliis.

After the accession of William I and before Ada's death in 1178 (*Early Sources of Scottish History 500 to 1286*, ed. A.O. Anderson (Edinburgh, 1922), ii. 299). The daughter of William de Warenne II earl of Surrey, she married Henry of Scotland earl of Northumberland and Huntingdon (d. 1152) and was mother of Malcolm IV and William I of Scotland.

MISCELLANEOUS DOCUMENTS

1303 Extracts from Domesday Book   [1086]

(i) The king's manor of Blewbury [Berkshire]

B f 39v; C f 13r
Pd. see *Domesday Book, seu Liber Censualis Willelmi Primi Regis Angliae* ... [ed. A. Farley, Rec. Comm.] (1783), i. f 56v

(ii) The king's manor of Cholsey [Berkshire]

B f 39v; C f 13r–v
Pd see *Domesday Book*, i. ff 56v–57r

(iii) The king's manor of Bucklebury, Berkshire

B f 39v; C f 13v
Pd. see *Domesday Book*, i. f 57r

(iv) The bishop of Bayeux's manor of Aston, Hertfordshire

B f 40r; C f 13v
Pd. see *Domesday Book*, i. f 134r

(v) Hugh de Grandmesnil's manor of Rowington [Warwickshire]

B f 40r; C f 13v
Pd. see *Domesday Book*, i. f 242r

In B, (i) and (ii) are entered in a hand of *c.* 1270–80, the rest in a different late 13th-century hand; in C all are in the original hand of the main part of the cartulary. The five manors came into the abbey's possession, but why the Domesday entries for other Reading manors were not copied is unclear. It is possible that the Blewbury entry was copied in connection with the abbey's dispute with the men of Blewbury over services in 1279–84 (see nos. 683–6).

1304 Magna Carta, 1225, as confirmed by King Henry III [in 1265]

1225/[14 Mar. 1265]

B ff 7r–9v
Pd. (1225 text only) see *Statutes of the Realm*, i, Charters of Liberties, 22–5

*a*Hiis testibus: venerabilibus patribus H(enrico) London(iensi), W(altero) Wygorn(iensi), J(ohanne) *b*Wynton(iensi), R(oberto) Dunelm(ensi), H(ugone) Elyensi, R(ogero) Coventr(ensi), R(icardo) Linch(olniensi), S(tephano) Cycestr(ensi), W(altero) Bathon(iensi) et Well(ensi), et W(illelmo) Landavensi episcopis, Simone de Monteforti comite Leycestr(ie), Hugone le Despens(er) justic(iario) Anglie, Thoma de Clare, Johanne de Burgo, Johanne filio Johannis, Petro de Monteforti, Rad(ulfo) de Cames, Adam de Novo Mercato, Egidio de Argente(o)m, Rogero de Sancto Johanne, Nicholao de Seigrave, Willelmo de Monte Canys(io), J(ohanne) de Vescy, Willelmo de Marmyon, Waltero de Crepping', Roberto de Insula, Rad(ulfo) de Sancwico, et aliis. Dat' et cetera.

a This is the witness-list of the confirmation
b Ms has here Wygorn' *marked for deletion*

The confirmation dates after 24 Sept. 1262, when Stephen Bersted was consecrated bishop of Chichester, and before 4 Aug. 1265, when Simon de Montfort and Hugh le Despenser were killed at Evesham. Despenser was in these years justiciar only July–Oct. 1263 and after 14 May 1264. The see of Bath and Wells was vacant 3 Apr. 1264–4 Jan. 1265. These facts enable the confirmation to be identified as that of 14 Mar. 1265 (see *Statutes of the Realm*, i, Charters of Liberties, 31–2).

1305 The Charter of the Forest, 1225, as confirmed by King Henry III [in 1265]   1225/[14 Mar. 1265]

B ff 9v–10v
Pd. (1225 text only) see *Statutes of the Realm*, i, Charters of Liberties, 26–7

This lacks the witness-list given in no. 1304 and even breaks off at the beginning of the witness-list of the 1225 text with the words: *Hiis testibus, et cetera sicut in Magna Carta libertatum aliarum positis invenire, et dat' die eodem sicut in eadem carta continetur.* However, since it is written in the same hand as no. 1304. which it follows immediately in the cartulary, it is almost certainly the confirmation of the same date.

1306 Charter by King Henry III concerning disafforestation in Berkshire   10 May 1227

A f 35v; B f 37v; C f 12r
Pd. (cal.) *Cal. Chart. R.*, i. 39[1] (from Charter Roll)

*a*Hiis testibus: venerabilibus patribus J(ocelino) Bathon(iensi), R(icardo) Sarr(esburiensi), W(altero) Carleol(ensi) episcopis, H(uberto) de Burgo comite Kanc(ie) justic(iario) nostro, R(annulfo) comite Cestr(ie) et Lincoln(ie), G(ilberto)*b* comite Glouc(estrie) et Hertford(ie), Willelmo Marescallo comite Penbrok', Henrico de Aldi-thel', Rad(ulf)o filio Nicholai, Ricardo de Argent(eom), Godefrido de Craucumb' senescallis nostris, Henrico de Capella, et aliis. Dat' per manum venerabilis patris Radulphi Cicestr(ensis)*c* episcopi, can-cellarii nostri, apud Wyndlesor(es) decimo die Maii, anno regni nostri undecimo.

a B,C end with T'   *b A has* T'
c A has Cistr'

The copy in A is of the 14th century and is written in the second main hand of C (see vol. I, p. 4); the copies in B and C are in the original hands of those cartularies.

1. The gaps for place-names in this calendar can be supplied from the Reading texts as: *Aleburn'* and *Batele*. The calendar also omits the witnesses and dating clause.

1307   Assize of Bread and Ale   [?temp. Henry III]

B f 245r
Pd. cf. *Statutes of the Realm*, i, Statutes, 199–200

The Reading text is similar to that in *Statutes of the Realm*, but it has several differences
of detail, takes the price of wheat only to 12s per quarter, and omits the last two
paragraphs on p. 200; it also includes two short sentences not in the printed version.
The Assize in this form is traditionally assigned to 51 Henry III (*ibid.*, 199 n.), but its
original date and status are far from certain; it was exemplified by Richard II in 1379
(*Cal. Pat. R. 1377–81*, 335). The text in B is in a late 13th-century hand.

1308   Statute of Marlborough   18 Nov. 1267

B ff 234r–237v
Pd. see *Statutes of the Realm*, i, Statutes, 19–25

1309   Statute of Gloucester   [1278]

B ff 224r–226r; C ff 137v–138r (item [I] below only)
Pd. see *Statutes of the Realm*, i, Statutes, 45–50

[I] Latin version of the preamble to the Statute, dealing with *Quo
warranto* enquiries [the version in *Statutes*, 45–6, being in French],
preceded by the text of a writ to the sheriff of York to allow the prior
of Christ Church, Canterbury, as others of the county, to enjoy the
liberties he claims in that county until the arrival there of the king or
his itinerant justices for common pleas to examine and judge them,
or until the king shall order otherwise; and including the text of
another model writ and notice of a third

For the relationship between the French and Latin versions of the preamble, and the
difficulty of establishing definitive texts, see D.W. Sutherland, *Quo Warranto Proceedings
in the Reign of Edward I, 1278–1294* (Oxford, 1963), 190; a fuller version of the Latin text
is printed *ibid.*, 190–3, but its writ concerning enjoyment of liberties before trial is in
general terms. The Latin version in *Registrum Malmesburiense*, ed. J.S. Brewer (RS 1879-
80), i. 238–40, is closer to the Reading text and shares its specific reference, in that
writ, to the sheriff of York and the prior of Canterbury.

[II] The legal measures of the Statute [In French]

The Reading text differs from that printed in *Statutes of the Realm* in that many of the
sections are re-arranged into a different sequence and, apart from several minor
variants, the last paragraph on p. 50 is omitted.

1310   Inspeximus and confirmation by Otto, cardinal deacon of St
Nicholas in Carcere Tulliano and papal legate, at the instance of the
chamberlain of Lewes, of a privilege by Pope Honorius III to the
abbot and convent of Cluny, dated at the Lateran, 12 Jan. 1222, that
they and their brethren, wheresoever they be, shall not be sued by
papal letters unless mention is made of the Cluniac order

                                                  4 Mar. 1239

Af 79r–v

Dat' London' iiii. no. Martii, pontificatus domini Gregorii pape noni*a* anno duodecimo.

Marginal note (in different hand): Nota bene istud privilegium.

a Ms has nono

1311 Inhibition by Pope Innocent IV in favour of the abbots and convents of the Cistercian order in the provinces of Canterbury and York. They have informed him that, although they have an indult from the apostolic see that no tithes are to be exacted from their gardens, copses (*virgulta*), meadows, pastures, woods, salt-pans, mills and fisheries acquired before and after the Council, and from the food of their animals (*animalium nutrimenta*),[1] nevertheless many prelates of churches and clerks of those provinces harass them in this, declaring that the indult does not extend to acquisitions made after it. The pope therefore, believing the indult to extend to acquisitions made afterwards, inhibits anyone from harrassing them on this account.

9 Feb. [1244]

Cf 154v
Pd. (cal.) *Cal. Papal L.*, i. 205

Dat' Lateran' v. idus Februarii, pontificatus nostri anno.*a*

a Sic

The year-date is supplied from the papal register. In the later Middle Ages Cistercian exemption from tithes on lands acquired after the 4th Lateran Council (1215) extended only to lands on which tithes had not previously been paid (see G. Constable, *Monastic Tithes from their origins to the Twelfth Century* (Cambridge, 1964), 306). The present bull is entered in C in a later 14th-century hand immediately following the settlement of 1195 × 1213 with the Cistercian nuns of Pinley, Warks. (no. 625), which is in the same hand. The bull was of interest to Reading in the 14th century, since it bore directly on the abbey's tithe dispute with Pinley priory in 1348 and may well have been the special papal privilege for all Cistercians which the nuns produced in support of their case (see no. 637).

1. For uncertainty as to the meaning of this phrase, see Constable, *op. cit.*, 236–7.

1312 Constitutions *Pro zelo fidei*[a] of Pope Gregory X announcing the decision of the [Second] Council of Lyons to mount a Crusade for the relief of the Holy Land and the imposition of a tenth on ecclesiastical incomes for six years from the Nativity of St John Baptist following, with instructions for the encouragement of contributions from the laity, the banning of various activities inimical to the Crusade on pain of excommunication, and the grant of a plenary indulgence to those serving in person or contributing to the expenses according to their ability, and lesser indulgences to those giving aid and counsel

[18 May 1274]

B ff 238r–239v
Pd. see H. Finke, *Konzilienstudien zur Geschichte des 13. Jahrhunderts* (Münster, 1891),
113–16 (from a manuscript in the Osnabrück Rathsgymnasium—several minor
variant readings)

ª The text begins [Z]elus fidei

The pope is identified by the conclusion of no. 1313, which immediately follows these
Constitutions in the cartulary. The Constitutions were issued in the second session of
the Council, held on 18 May 1274 (Potthast, ii. 1678). They were not included in
Gregory X's register and copies are rare (W.E. Lunt, 'Papal taxation in England in
the reign of Edward I', *EHR*, xxx (1915), 401 n. 24). They probably owe their
preservation at Reading to the fact that, owing to a complication arising from care-
lessness, the abbey had difficulty in proving that its contribution to the tenth had been
paid (see nos. 230–2). For a full discussion of the Constitutions, see P.A. Throop,
Criticism of the Crusade (Amsterdam, 1940), 236–54.

1313   *Licence by Pope Gregory X to leave the [Second] Council of Lyons before
its end, to the non-mitred abbots and priors and other abbots and priors who had
not been summoned by name, and to provosts, deans, archdeacons and other
prelates of churches, and to the proctors of prelates, chapters and other convents,
provided that they leave proctors behind at the Council, viz., a specified number
for each kingdom or region*   [May × July, ?18 May, 1274]

B f 239v
Pd. see H. Finke, *ibid.*, 116–17 (from the same Osnabrück manuscript—several
variant readings, some significant)

[N]on nobis set domino damus gloriam et honorem et ipsi gratiam
reddimus quod ad tam sacrum concilium patriarcharum, primatum,
archiepiscoporum, episcoporum, abbatum, priorum, decanorum,
archidiaconorum et aliorum ecclesiarum prelatorum tam per se quam
per procuratores, necnon capitulorum, collegiorum et conventuum
procuratorum*ª* *ᵇ*[copiosa multitudo]*ᵇ* ad vocacionem nostram
convenit. Sane licet pro felici prosecucione tanti negocii eorum esset
consilium oportunum et in ipsorum tanquam dilectorum filiorum
presencia delectemur et quidem spirituali gaudio affluamus, circa
nonnullos tamen eorum, propter varia incommoda*ᶜ* que ipsorum
copiositas ingerit, ne pre turba nimia se diucius mutuo conprimant
[et]*ᵈ* eorum absencia ipsis et ipsorum ecclesiis posset esse dampnosa,
provida pietate commoti de fratrum nostrorum consilio super hoc
salubriter providere decrevimus, ut sic ipsorum gravaminibus occur-
ratur quod prosecucione huius negocii, quod ferventi spiritu et sol-
licitudine indefessa prosequimur, nullatenus derogetur. Omnes igitur
patriarchas, primates, archiepiscopos, episcopos, abbates et priores
*ᵉ*mitratos, necnon et alios abbates et priores*ᵉ* per nos nominatim et
specialiter evocatos, sic remanere decrevimus ut ante diffinitum concilium absque nostra speciali licencia non discedant. Ceteris vero

abbatibus et prioribus non mitratis et abbatibus aliis et prioribus qui per nos non fuerint[f] nominatim et specialiter evocati, necnon prepositis, decanis, archidiaconis et aliis ecclesiarum prelatis ac quorumcumque prelatorum, capitulorum et conventuum procuratoribus, recedendi cum dei et nostra benediccione clementer licenciam inpartimur, mandantes ut omnes taliter recedentes primitus prout infra scribitur sufficientes procuratores dimittant, ad suscipienda nostra mandata et ea que in presenti concilio ordinata sunt et in futuro domino autore contigerit ordinari. Omnes scilicet de regno Francie taliter recedentes quatuor, de regno Alemannie quatuor, de regno Hispanniarum .iiii., de regno Anglie .iiii., de regno Scocie unum, [g]de Lumbardia duos, de Tuscia unum, [h]de regno Dascie[h] unum, de regno Cilicie .ii., de terris [.....],[i] de regno Norweye unum, de regno Suevie unum, de regno Hung(ar)ie unum,[g] de regno Dacie unum, de regno Boemie unum, de ducatu Polonie unum, procuratores sufficientes dimittant.

[j]Expliciunt statuta Gregorii pape X in Concilio Lugdun(ensi).[j]

[a] B has procuratores	[b-b] Om. in B, supplied from Finke
[c] B has incomoda	[d] Om. in B, supplied from Finke
[e-e] Om. in Finke	[f] Sic in B, fuerant in Finke
[g-g] Om. in Finke	[h-h] Under-dashed in B, perhaps for deletion
[i] Blank space in B	[j-j] Om. in Finke

The Council lasted from 7 May to 17 July 1274 (Potthast, ii. 1677, 1681), but, since this licence immediately follows no. 1312 in the cartulary and no other proceedings of the Council were copied, it is possibly of the same date. Only the major variants between this and Finke's text have been noted.

1314 Bull *Cum pro negotio* by Pope Gregory X to master Raymond de Nogaret, papal chaplain and nuncio in England, and friar John of Darlington O.P., collectors in England of the tenth recently assigned at the [Second] Council of Lyons for the relief of the Holy Land, containing detailed instructions for the collection of the same

5 Nov. 1274

B ff 240r-242r

Dat' Lugdun' non' Novembris, pontificatus nostri anno tercio.

For copies of this bull in other English cartularies, see W.E. Lunt, *EHR*, xxx (1915), 404 n. 47. There the bull is said to be dated 23 Oct., which is different from the date of the Reading text. The instructions were re-issued with slight modifications by Nicholas IV in 1291 for the sexennial tenth imposed in England (*ibid.*; *Cal. Papal L.*, i. 553-4). For the two collectors, see W.E. Lunt, *Financial Relations of the Papacy with England to 1327* (Cambridge, Mass., 1939), 618.

Endorsed: Inter nos et Barth(olomeum) de ecclesia de Burghildebir'
[*late 12th cent.*] Cirografum inter abbatem de Rading' et Bartholomeum de Burkildebir' [*14th cent.*]
Size: 138 × 90 mm
Seal: fragment in green wax on tongue; very worn Virgin and Child

   ª For expansion, see no. 211 n. 2   *ᵇ Original has* oventionibus

Date as for nos. 694–6.

2   *Grant by Abbot Adam [of Lathbury] and the convent of Reading to Geoffrey
Martel of divine service to be provided on specified days in his chapel [of
Marlston] in the parish of Bucklebury by the vicar of Bucklebury or his assign;
on three days in the year Geoffrey and his household and tenants are to come to
the mother church of Bucklebury. Geoffrey has given in free alms 9 acres of his
land in Bucklebury, and Richard of Stanford 1 acre of the free tenement he holds
of Geoffrey in the same, to support a chaplain in the said chapel. Geoffrey has
also granted to the church of Bucklebury the tithes of mills, fisheries, gardens
and all other lesser tithes which he did not give previously, and to the church and
vicar of Bucklebury 1 quarter of wheat and 1 quarter of maslin annually to
support the chaplain*   [1226 × 38]

   Copy dated 1675, Marlston church vestry
   Pd. (transl.) Humphreys, *Bucklebury*, 354–5 (see note)

Omnibus Christi fidelibus ad quos presens scriptum pervenerit Adam
dei gratia abbas Radingensisª eiusdemqueᵇ loci conventus, eternam in
domino salutem. Noverit universitas vestra nos divine pietatis intuitu
ad instantiam Galfridi Martell militis concessisse dicto Galfrido et
heredibus suis in perpetuum celebrationem divinorum in capella dicti
Galfridi que constructa est in feodo suo quod est in parochia de
Burghulburyᶜ faciendam per vicarium nostrum de Burghulbury vel
per alium assignatum suum sub hac forma, videlicet quod dictus
vicarius vel eius assignatus celebrabit divina in dicta capella qualibet
die dominica [et]ᵈ omni quarta et sexta feria; et si dies feriandus
generaliter contigerit in aliis diebus in ebdomada et maluerit Galfridus
Martell vel heredes sui in illo die feriato divina sibi celebrari quam in
quarta vel sexta feria, pro quarta vel sexta feria computabitur; sin
due festivitates feriande in una ebdomada evenerint, tunc preterᵉ tres
dies consuetos vicarius noster vel ejus atturnatus in una earum ibidem
divina celebrabit. Preterea concedimus quod vicarius noster vel ejus
assignatus in dicta capella plenarium servitium in nocte et die
Omnium Sanctorum faciat et in nocte et in die Natalis domini,
Purificationis beate Marie et Pasce. Debet autem dictus Galfridus et
heredes sui si ibi fuerint et familia sua et tenentes sui venire ad
matricem ecclesiam de Burghulbury per tres dies solemnes in anno,

scilicet in die dedicationis ecclesie, in die Pentecostes et in die Assumptionis beate Marie. Dedit autem dictus Galfridus miles in liberam puram et perpetuam elemosinam[f] ecclesie de Burghulbury ad sustentationem capellani deservientis in dicta capella novem acras in terra sua in Burghulbury que vocatur Labreche Kine Wardelhach. Et Ricardus[g] de Stanford similiter dedit unam acram de libero tenemento suo quod tenet de predicto Galfrido per chartam in eadem cultura. Concessit etiam dictus Galfridus miles dicte ecclesie de Burghulbury decimalitatem molendinorum, piscariorum, gardinorum et omnes alias minutas decimas quas antea non dedit. Concessit etiam dictus Galfridus in perpetuum ecclesie de Burghulbury et vicario nostro ibidem deservienti annuatim unum quarterium de frumento et unum quarterium de mestillone de grangia sua de Burghulbury solvend(a) ad festum sancti Andree contra Natale ad sustentationem capellani deservientis in capella sua.[h] Et ut hec concessio nostra stabiliat[i] et perpetuam habeat firmitatem, eam presentis scripti testimonio et sigillorum nostrorum appositione roboravimus. His testibus: Roberto rectore ecclesie de Thacham, Jacabo vicario ecclesie sancti Egidii Radingensis,[a] Ricardo[j] vicario ecclesie beati Laurentii, Martino capellano ecclesie beate Marie Radingensis,[a] Willelmo[k] clerico nostro, Willelmo[k] de Englefeld,[l] Rogero de Hyda, Roberto de Cunerl,[m] Roberto de Burgfeld', Roberto de Uffintone, Johanne de Hola, Rogero de Whitechurch, Simone[n] de Waya, Roberto filio Adam[o] de Thacham, et multis aliis, etc.

[a] *Ms has* Reading   [b] *Ms has* eiusdem
[c] *Spelling throughout Ms, but probably not so in original*
[d] *Supplied*   [e] *Suggested reading; Ms has* preces
[f] *Ms has* eleemosynam   [g] *Ms has* Richardus
[h] *Suggested reading; Ms damaged, but ancient transl. has* our *(see note)*
[i] *Sic; ? error*   [j] *Ms has* Richardo
[k] *Ms has* Willielmo   [l] *Ms has* Englefeild
[m] *Sic in Ms, but ancient transl. has* Bradfeild
[n] *Ms has* Simon   [o] *Sic*

In this text the classical diphthong *ae*, where it occurs in the 1675 copy, has been rendered as *e*. The dating limits are those of Adam of Lathbury's abbacy. The sole surviving copy of this deed, dated 1675, is very faded. It is accompanied by a copy of a translation headed 'Englished anciently' (this being the version printed by Humphreys), and the whole is endorsed: 'A Copie of the Composition for Marlestone Chappell taken & Examind in August 1675 by me John Hearne'. The identity of the latter is uncertain, but he clearly had access to the original, or an earlier copy, with an earlier translation, both apparently now lost. I am grateful to the churchwardens of St Mary's, Marlston, for permission to print this deed.

INDEX OF PERSONS AND PLACES

References in this index are to volume and page numbers. County locations for English, Welsh and Scottish place-names are in accordance with the pre-1974 boundaries. Abbots, bishops, earls, etc., are detailed under their names (or surnames, if known), with cross-references from their abbeys, bishoprics, etc. Personal names consisting of a forename and a calling or profession are given under the latter, except for simple designations of 'chaplain', 'clerk' and 'priest'. The following abbreviations are used: doc.=document; K.=King; kt.=knight; Mr.=Master; Q.=Queen. The abbreviation 'n.' refers only to numbered notes or footnotes.

A., prior of Reading, **I,** 188–9
—, sub-prior of Reading, **I,** 188
Aalidis, *see* Adeliza
Abbas, Geoffrey, **I,** 350
Abbedonia, etc., *see* Abingdon
Abbod, John, **II,** 181–2
Abbot, Abboth, Richard, **II,** 41–2; daughter of, *see* Mary; granddaughter of, *see* Isabel
Aberdeen, bishop of, *see* Edward, chancellor
Abergavenny, Henry of, bishop of Llandaff, **I,** 178
Abingdon, Berks. (Abbedonia, Abbendon', Abendonia, Abyndon', Habyndon'), abbey of, abbot of, *see* Hendred, Richard of; Hugh; Ingulf; John; steward of, *see* Sparsholt
—, dean of, *see* Hugh
—, Richard of, **II,** 38; *another*, Mr., **I,** 367 *bis*
—, Robert of, **I,** 367
—, —, infirmarer of Reading, **II,** 163
—, *and see* Bec
Abraham, chaplain, **I,** 169
Abricatensis, Abrincis, etc., *see* Avranches
Absolon, William, **II,** 78
Acatur (Acathur, Acator, Acatour, Achatour, Achatur, Akatur, Chatour, Lacator, Lacatour, Lacatur, Lakator):
—, Alan le, **II,** 183 *bis*, 184n.
—, John le, of Reading, father of Alan, **II,** 184; widow of, *see* Petronilla
—, —, *another*, **II,** 127 *ter*, 130, 139–40, 152, 168, 172–5, 180, 185–6, 193, 198–200, 217, 219–20, 280, 296,

299, 329, 331, 336–7; wife of, Alice, **II,** 185–6
—, —, son of preceding, **II,** 127
—, Thomas le, **II,** 128, 191
Accle, *see* Oakley
Ach, Achis, Akes, Alac, Herefs. (unidentified), 'parish' of, **I,** 289; spirituality of, **I,** 287; tithes of, **I,** 288
Achard, prior of May, **II,** 346
Achard (Aschard), family, lords of Aldermaston, **I,** 120; **II,** 253
—, Peter, kt., **I,** 119–20; **II,** 250, 304–5
—, Robert (12th cent.), **I,** 120
—, — (13th cent.), **II,** 77, 342–3
—, William, **II,** 147–8
Achatour, etc., *see* Acatur
Acheals, Azceals, Echeles, Echles, Warks. (? Eccles, in Rowington), **I,** 431–2, 434–5
Achi, **I,** 432
Achonry, Sligo (Achadensis), bishop of, *see* O Maicin; O Ruadhan
Acle, Aclee, Acleia, *see* Oakley
Acton, Richard (Cotes) of, burgess of Reading, **II,** 169–70, 210–11
Ada, countess of Northumberland, mother of William I of Scotland, **II,** 355
Adaleis, *see* Adeliza
Adam, **II,** 38
—, abbot of Reading, *see* Lathbury
—, canon of Waltham, **I,** 301
— the clerk, **II,** 132–3, 135, 138–9, 145, 169, 174, 177, 183–4, 189–91, 193, 322; as coroner of Reading, **II,** 132; as reeve [of Reading], **II,** 137
—, clerk, of Essend', **II,** 113–14

—, Richard the, **II,** 38
—, Samuel the, **II,** 314
—, Stephen the, **II,** 175
—, William the, **II,** 138, 197; wife of, Gunnilda, **II,** 197
—, *and see* Wallingford, Ralph of
Gomel, John, **II,** 17-18
Gomme, Geoffrey, **II,** 141, 175, 179, 195-6, 206
—, Ralph, **II,** 196 (? error for Geoffrey)
Gonter, *see* Gunter
Good (Bonus), Ralph, **II,** 315
Good Christian (Bonus Christianus), Stephen, **I,** 215 *bis*
Goring, Oxon. (Garing', Garyng'), Thomas of, monk of Reading, **II,** 270; as chamberlain, **II,** 78
Gorron, Robert de, abbot of St Albans, **II,** 27, 29-30
Gos, Gurbert son of, **I,** 335
—, Thomas le, **II,** 288-9
Gosepett', Edward de, heirs of, **I,** 332-3; sons of, Henry and John, and John their brother, **I,** 333
Gospatrick II, earl of Dunbar (d. 1138), son of, *see* Edward
— III, earl of Dunbar (d. 1166), **I,** 131; **II,** 349, 353; son of, *see* Waltheof; wife of, *see* Derdere
Gozo, constable of Q. Adeliza, **I,** 302; cf. Godescalcus
Grain, Kent (Grean, Gren, Grene), **I,** 333
—, Thomas of, **I,** 348
—, William of, son of John, **I,** 325, 333
Granator's Brook, Granger's Brook, *see* Holy Brook
Grandcourt (Grancurt, Grantcurt), Matthew de, **II,** 22, 282
Grandmesnil, Hugh de, **I,** 349, 448; **II,** 356
Grandson, Gerard de, bishop of Verdun, papal collector, **I,** 188-91
Grange, Gerard of the (Gerard the Granger), **II,** 197
—, Walter of the, **II,** 137
Granger, Adam, **II,** 295
Grant, Richard, archbishop of Canterbury, **I,** 176? and n.
Gratian, papal sub-deacon and notary, **I,** 134
Grausellum, *see* Groseau
Grava, Grave, *see* Grove
Graveley, Herts. (Gravele), Robert of, **I,** 307-8

—, Walter of, rector of Aston, **I,** 307-8
—, —, son of William of (? *same*), **I,** 307-9
—, William of, **I,** 308
Gravesend, Richard, bishop of Lincoln, **II,** 356
Gray, Grey (Graius, Grei), Henry de, **I,** 344-6
—, John de, archdeacon of Cleveland, **I,** 72; as bishop of Norwich, **I,** 166?, 174, 324
—, —, *another*, father of Walter, **I,** 465-6
—, —, *another*, son of Richard, **I,** 344, 346
—, Ralph, **II,** 109, 273
—, Richard de, **I,** 346; *another*, **I,** 346
—, Walter de, bishop of Worcester, **I,** 465-8; as archbishop of York, **I,** 176, 468 *ter*; as justice, **II,** 85; as regent, **I,** 94
—, William, **II,** 53-5, 57
Grazeley, Berks. (Greisull', Greyshulle, Greysulle), **II,** 40, 251-2, 300
—, Luke of, **II,** 40
—, William of, **I,** 249-50
Grean, *see* Grain
Great Malvern, Worcs. (Maior Malvern'), prior of, **I,** 299
Great Munden, Herts., *see* Munden
Great Tew, Oxon., *see* Tew
Green (la grene), William on the, **I,** 123
Greenford, John of, bishop of Chichester, as judge-delegate, **I,** 234-40; clerks of, *see* Edmund; London, Philip of
Greenham, Berks. (Grenham), Henry of, **II,** 215
—, Richard of, **II,** 142, 189, 191-2, 198
Greenway, Dr Diana, **II,** 36
Greenwich, Kent, **I,** 30
Gregory, bishop of Dunkeld, **II,** 347, 350
—, canon of Salisbury, **I,** 159
—, chaplain, **I,** 206
—, chaplain and clerk (of Bishop Mapenore of Hereford), **I,** 267, 294
— IX, pope, **II,** 79
— X, pope, **I,** 8; acts by, **II,** 359-61
Greinwile, Gilbert de, **I,** 207
Greisull', *see* Grazeley
Gren, Grene, *see* Grain
Grendon Underwood, Bucks. (Grendon'), **I,** 140, 208; **II,** 362
—, Robert of, clerk, **I,** 208
Grenham, *see* Greenham
Grewelle, *see* Greywell
Grey, *see* Gray
Greyshulle, Greysulle, *see* Grazeley

Scot (le Scot, Scotus), Adam (or Andrew), **I**, 121n., 421
—, Daniel, **II**, 119
—, Gilbert, **II**, 132, 139, 162–3, 165, 183, 201, 203
—, Maurice, **II**, 137, 203
—, William, **II**, 149
Scotland, kingdom of, **II**, 361; chamberlain of, *see* Herbert; chancellors of, *see* Bidun; Edward; Nicholas the clerk; constables of, *see* Edward; Moreville
Scraveleia, Screvele, *see* Shrewley
Scribe (scriptor), Hamo the, **II**, 114
Scrope, Geoffrey le, chief justice, **I**, 126
Scufeld, *see* Sheffield
Scure, Richard, **II**, 301
Scures, John de, commissioner of array, etc., **I**, 103
Seagrave (Segrava, Segrave, Seigrave), Gilbert of, **I**, 86
—, Nicholas of, **II**, 357
—, Stephen of, justice, **I**, 363, 372, 472
Seaton (Seyton'), Roger of, Mr., justice, **I**, 344
Sebernus, **I**, 206
Sebricteswrthe, etc., *see* Sawbridgeworth
Seething, Norfolk, cf. Sahinges
Séez, Orne (Sagiensis), abbot of, *see* Gilbert
Sefeld, Sefeud, *see* Sheffield
Seffrid I, bishop of Chichester, **I**, 35–6, 38, 44
— II, dean of Chichester, **I**, 239
—, treasurer of Chichester, as justice, **II**, 308
Seftebyr', *see* Shaftesbury
Segar, Seger, Richard, widow of, *see* Matilda
Segrava, etc., *see* Seagrave
Seila, Lucian de, **II**, 231
Sellarius, *see* Saddler
Selton', *see* Shelton
Selyman, Robert, escheator in Hants., etc., **II**, 106
Seman, John, **II**, 205
Sementarius, *see* Mason
Sene, William, **II**, 15, 17, 20
Senliz, *see* St Liz
Sepehale, *see* Shephall
Serich, Nicholas, **II**, 48
—, Walter, daughter of, *see* Matilda
Serle, Ansketil, son of Robert, **II**, 62 *bis*, 64–5
—, John, of Burghfield, **II**, 47–8

—, Richard, of Sulhamstead, **II**, 250; widow of, Christina, **II**, 251
—, William, **II**, 47; *another*, **II**, 64–5
Serlo, **II**, 245; ? = Miller, Serlo the, q.v.
—, Mr., **I**, 226–7, 303, 404, 416, 483; as clerk of Q. Adeliza, **I**, 225, 301
—, priest of Kinnersley, **I**, 277
Sernesfelda, *see*, Sarnesfield
Servant (famulus), Simon the, **II**, 109
Sessun, Riulf de, **II**, 6
Sevar, Ralph son of, **I**, 483
Sevewella, etc., *see* Showell
Sewal (Sewald), **I**, 59; **II**, 71
—, ? *another*, and Warin his brother, **II**, 274
—, ? *another*, **II**, 177
—, —, Robert son of, **II**, 176–7
—, —, William son of, brother of Robert, **II**, 176–7
Sewell', *see* Showell
Sewine, Ralph, **II**, 15
Sexi, Sexy, clerk (incumbent) of Englefield, **II**, 93
—, Nicholas (son of Sexus), miller of Burghfield, **II**, 42, 51–2
Seyant, Gervase son of, **I**, 429
Seyton', *see* Seaton
Shaftesbury, Dorset (Seftebyr'), abbey of, **II**, 80n.; dean and master of school of, as judges-delegate, **II**, 79
Shaies, *see* Sulhamstead Abbots
Shalford (? in Brimpton, Berks.) (Schaldeford, Shaldeford), John of, **II**, 282, 329
Shardlow, Derbs. (Sherdelawe), Robert of, Mr., justice, **I**, 372
Shareshill, Staffs. (Shareshull'), William of, justice, **II**, 339
Sharnford, Leics. (Scharneford', Sharneford'), **I**, 349; *and see* Rannulf, Walter son of; Thomas, John son of
Sheepbridge, in Swallowfield, Berks. (Scheperige, Scheperigge, Scheperuge, Scheperugge, Scipruge, Shepruge), **II**, 100–2; *and see* Diddenham
Sheffield, in Burghfield, Berks. (Scefeld', Scefeud, Schefeld, Schofeld, Scufeld, Sefeld, Sefeud, Shefeld', Sofeld, Suffeld), **I**, 140, 170n., 379; **II**, 60–71; manor of, **II**, 61, 63–5; mills in (corn and fulling), **II**, 67–70
—, places in:
—, —, Anchetillesdune, Anketillesdune (Dune), **II**, 62–3, 251